HOSTELLING
INTERNATIONAL

Americas, Africa, Asia & the Pacific 99

Photographs on this page by Lonely Planet

Welcome, Bienvenue
Willkommen, Bienvenido

Hostelling International is the brand name of the International Youth Hostel Federation, the organization that represents Youth Hostel Associations, worldwide.

For budget accommodation you can trust look for the blue triangle symbol.

The information in this Guide has been supplied by the Youth Hostel Associations of each country represented. Every effort has been made to ensure that it is correct and Hostelling International can accept no responsibility for any inaccuracies or for changes subsequent to publication.

© Hostelling International 1998.

Hostelling International is also a registered trade mark in many countries.

ISBN 0 901 496 537

How to use this Guide

Welcome to the world of Hostelling International – a unique network of accommodation centres where you can enjoy a good night's sleep in friendly surroundings at an affordable price.

This guide provides details on the facilities available at Youth Hostels that are registered with the

INTERNATIONAL YOUTH HOSTEL FEDERATION

You will find these details listed **alphabetically by country and city.**

In this introductory section we provide some general information about Hostelling International, its services for guests, its membership benefits and its commitment to a level of assured standards which all hostels must work to achieve.

If you require any information about hostels worldwide you can

either:

Contact your local Youth Hostel Association (YHA) prior to departure

or:

Visit our Internet home page at **http://www.iyhf.org**

An Introduction to Hostelling International

The youth hostel movement was founded in Germany in the early years of this century, and spread rapidly between the Wars, especially in Europe.

Today, Hostelling International offers you a choice of nearly 4,500 accommodation centres in more than 60 countries worldwide.

At Youth Hostels in Europe, Asia, Africa, the Americas and the Pacific we hope to offer you a consistently high service – a good night's sleep in friendly surroundings at an affordable price.

This guide provides details of the hostels that you can choose from. Today it is possible to book a bed up to 6 months in advance using the International Booking Network (IBN) system – you can find details about IBN within this guide.

NO AGE LIMIT

Despite their name, Youth Hostels are open to people of all ages in virtually every country where they are located.

A small number of German hostels have a maximum age restriction, which is a requirement of local legislation.

Guests under 14 years of age should be accompanied by an adult, and many hostels now offer family rooms.

Most hostels accept group bookings and the majority now offer a variety of accommodation options – you can find single, double and dormitory rooms in most major hostels.

PRIVILEGES OF MEMBERSHIP

To stay at a Youth Hostel you must become a member of your National Youth Hostel Association (YHA). Additional to your membership you will receive certain special services and benefits.

This guide gives you details of the major international benefits, but you will find many more discounts and concessions in the country you are visiting.

To get details of these you should contact the YHA of the country you are visiting. Most provide detailed guides of their country which includes information about special services that exist for members.

If you do not have a national YHA in your country, you can purchase a Hostelling International Card or a 'welcome stamp' when you arrive at your chosen hostel.

Assured Standards

Hostelling International recognizes that consistent quality and service are important to budget travellers. That is why we have introduced our Assured Standards Scheme, to ensure that you can rely on a consistent level of services and facilities wherever you stay in our hostels.

What do Assured Standards at hostels mean to you?

WELCOME

Hostels are open to everyone, irrespective of age, sex, culture, race or religion. If you do not already have membership, you will be able to take out full or short-term membership at the hostel you stay at.

You will be able to reserve a bed in advance, by fax, email, post or through the IBN system. **You are normally able to check-in (or out) between 0700 hrs and 1000 hrs and 1700 hrs and 2230 hrs at most hostels.**

If the hostel closes for a period during the day, you will have access to shelter and storage for your luggage.

Above all, welcoming you will be the priority for the hostel staff and they will be committed to providing the support and information that you need to get the most out of your stay.

COMFORT

You can expect a good, comfortable night's sleep, sufficient showers, WCs and washing facilities, plus a good supply of hot water. Where it is not included in the overnight charge, freshly laundered linen will be available for hire if you require it.

Although meals are generally available, where only self-catering is provided you will normally be able to buy basic food supplies in the hostel or close by. Hostels provide food storage, preparation and cooking and washing up areas for you to use.

CLEANLINESS

Wherever you travel you can expect the highest standards of cleanliness and hygiene from Hostelling International.

SECURITY

Hostel staff will make every endeavour to ensure your personal security, and the security of your possessions during your stay. Lockers will be available to store your own luggage and valuables.

PRIVACY

Although you may find yourself sharing a room with other hostellers of the same sex (unless you have reserved a private family room) the Assured Standards Scheme promises privacy when you need it – especially in showers, washing areas and toilets.

A Commitment to our Environment

ENVIRONMENTAL CHARTER

In addition to these Assured Standards, hostels will also adhere to the IYHF Environmental Charter which lays down the criteria for the consumption and conservation of resources, waste disposal and recycling, nature conservation and the provision of environmental education.

For many people the essence of simple hostels is that they are found in remote, unusual locations and are often very special buildings.

We must admit though, that it is hard to apply the same standards across all locations – in the middle of a rain forest or in a remote shepherd's hut.

Because of these variations we do make some exceptions to standards for small hostels and those with simple facilities where you may find limited staffing and shorter opening hours. This type of hostel is clearly indicated as a **simple hostel.**

Standards will be monitored by Hostelling International and by you, the user. There are comment forms within this guide to help you contact us.

The International Booking Network (IBN)

BOOK AHEAD THROUGH IBN

Our computerized booking system offers you a simple and cheap advance booking option for more than 300 key hostels worldwide.

Wherever you see this IBN symbol in the guide, it means that you can book a bed up to 6 months in advance of your stay (depending on availability).

These hostels and other IBN booking centres listed within each of the country sections offer a service which is unique in the budget accommodation sector.

- You can pay for reservations in the local currency from where you are making the booking, before your departure.
- You can make reservations during your travels from any IBN hostel or local booking centre.
- In many cases you can pay by credit card.
- In many countries you can call a single Central Reservations Office to book a series of overnight stays in several hostels in advance.

OTHER BOOKING INFORMATION

You can arrive at a hostel without a reservation, but in busy times we advise strongly that you reserve ahead of time to avoid disappointment.

- Family rooms are soon occupied and groups should also book ahead of time.
- You can book hostel beds by sending a fax or letter to the hostel of your choice.
- If you book by letter, be sure to enclose an international postal reply coupon (available at most post offices) and a self-addressed envelope.
- If you make an advance booking without paying a deposit you will usually be required to arrive at the hostel by 1800 hours, unless a different time is agreed.

We know you will enjoy the hostel experience. You will certainly be able to afford it. We look forward to meeting you.

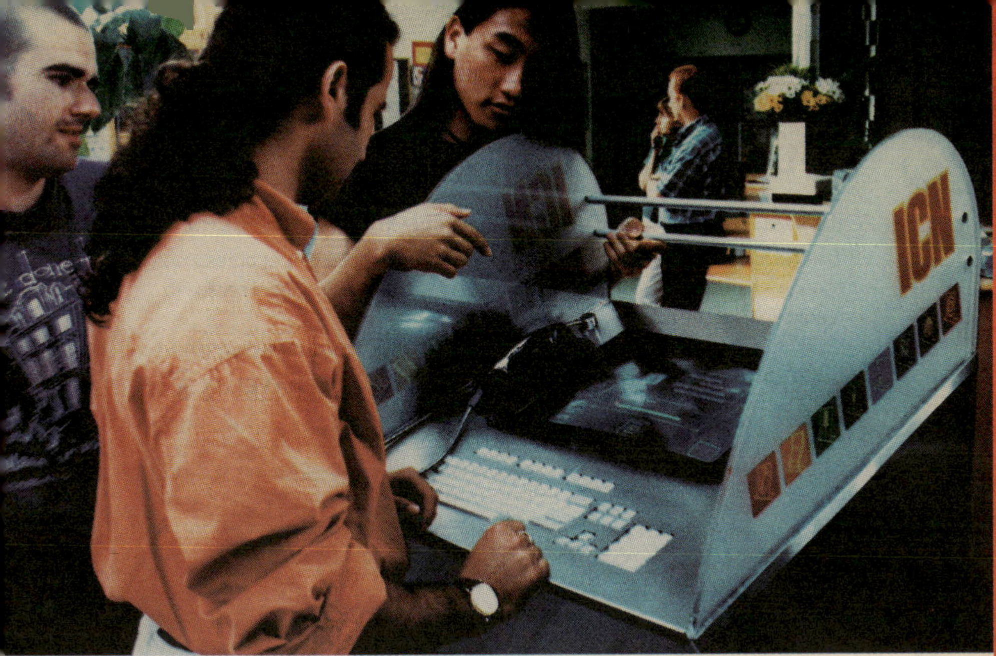

The International Communications Network (ICN)

ICN is a comprehensive, low cost communications service which has been specially designed for independent travellers. 

Where you see the ICN symbol you will be able to purchase an ICN communication card. With this card you are able to use a variety of services at very low prices.

- As a simple calling card from any telephone.
- To send and receive e-mails from any ICN kiosks located at key hostels.
- To send faxes to family and friends.
- To find out local travel information.
- To set up your own e-mail box to receive e-mail whilst you are travelling.
- To check the availability of beds at other hostels – *(this service will come into operation at a later stage)*

With ICN you can keep in touch with family and friends wherever you happen to be. ICN is a major advance in guaranteeing that hostel users can travel with security, and that your family at home can be safe in the knowledge that they can always contact you in an emergency situation.

ICN is exclusively available to members of Hostelling International.

Commission Free Currency Exchange

A SPECIAL OFFER FOR HOSTELLING INTENATIONAL MEMBERS

TRAVELEX – the world's largest airport and passenger terminal bureau de change – has offered Hostelling International members a very special service to reduce the cost of international travel.

By showing your membership card you can enjoy Commission Free Currency Exchange at any of the Travelex offices listed below.

TRAVELEX

NORTH AMERICA

Canada - airports
Edmonton
Halifax
Winnipeg
Vancouver

USA - airports
Atlanta
Baltimore
Boston
Cleveland
Columbus
Detroit
Fort Lauderdale
Indianapolis
JFK (all terminals)
Kansas
La Guardia
Las Vegas
Los Angeles (all terminals)
Memphis
Minneapolis
New Orleans
Newark (all terminals)
Norfolk, Virginia
Omaha
Ontario, California
Palm Springs
Pittsburgh
Portland (Oregon)
Raleigh Durham
San Diego
San Francisco
Tampa

PACIFIC

Australia - airports
Brisbane International
Cairns International
Ansett Sydney
Ansett Melbourne
Ansett Brisbane
Ansett Coolangatta
Qantas Sydney
Qantas Melbourne
Qantas Brisbane
Qantas Adelaide
Qantas Perth
Qantas Coolangatta
Alice Springs
Cairns
Canberra
Hamilton Island

New Zealand - airports
Auckland
Christchurch
Queenstown
Rotorua

This fabulous service will save you a significant amount, especially when you are planning to visit more than one country.

Exclusive Travelex Buy Back Plus: For a nominal fee, we will buy back any unused currency at exactly the same rate that you bought it, commission free!

Comment vous servir de ce Guide

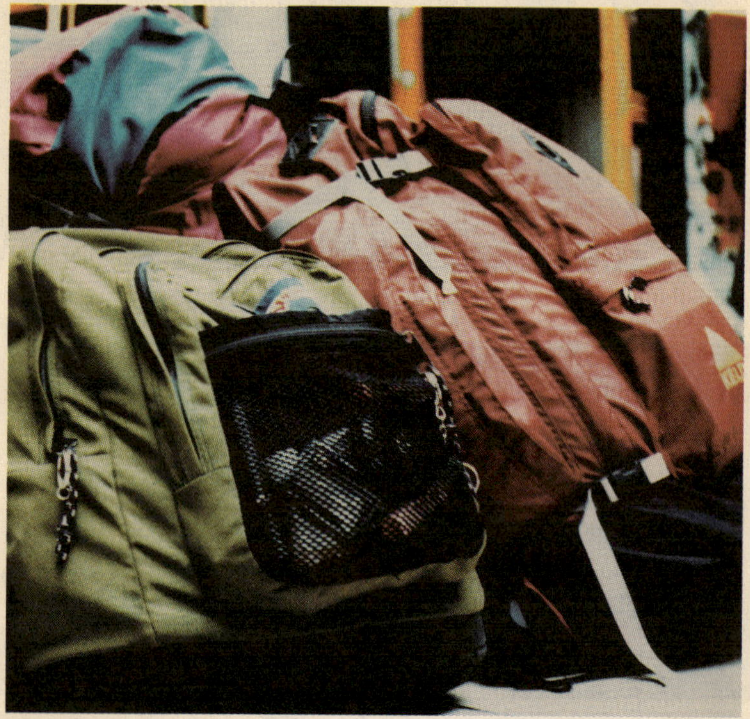

Bienvenue aux auberges – un réseau unique d'hébergement où vous pouvez passer une bonne nuit de sommeil dans un milieu accueillant et à des prix abordables.

Ce guide détaille et liste les services proposés dans les Auberges de Jeunesse affiliées à la

INTERNATIONAL YOUTH HOSTEL FEDERATION

Vous les trouverez par **ordre alphabétique, par pays et par ville.**

Dans cette introduction, nous vous proposons des renseignements généraux sur Hostelling International – les services offerts aux ajistes, les remises aux adhérents ainsi que notre engagement à garantir des normes minimales, que chaque auberge devra s'efforcer à atteindre.

Si vous avez besoin de renseignements sur les auberges du monde entier, vous pouvez **soit:**

Contacter l'Association d'auberges de jeunesse de votre pays avant votre départ

soit:

Consulter notre site Internet à **http://www.iyhf.org**

Hostelling International – Introduction

Le mouvement des Auberges de Jeunesse a été fondé en Allemagne au début du siécle et s'est rapidement étendu à d'autres pays entre les deux guerres, principalement en Europe.

Aujourd'hui, Hostelling International vous propose un choix de 4 500 centres d'hébergement dans plus de 60 pays disséminés de par le monde entier.

Dans nos auberges d'Europe, d'Asie, d'Afrique, d'Amérique et du Pacifique, nous espérons vous offrir un service constant et de haute qualité – une bonne nuit de sommeil dans un milieu accueillant, à un prix abordable. Ce guide est un recueil de renseignements sur toutes les auberges qui sont à votre disposition.

Il est maintenant possible de réserver un lit jusqu'à six mois à l'avance en utilisant le système de réservation IBN – International Booking Network – Voir les pages suivantes pour de plus amples renseignements.

PAS DE LIMITE D'ÂGE

Malgré leur nom, les Auberges de Jeunesse sont ouvertes à tous les âges, dans pratiquement tous les pays où elles sont implantées. Un nombre limité d'auberges allemandes imposent un âge limite et ce, en raison des contraintes de la législation locale.

Les jeunes de moins de 14 ans devront être accompagnés par un adulte et d'ailleurs, nombreux sont nos établissements qui proposent des chambres familiales.

La plupart des auberges acceptent les groupes et la majorité, surtout dans les grandes villes, mettent à disposition un choix d'hébergement, c'est à dire, des chambres individuelles, des chambres pour couples ou bien encore des dortoirs.

LES PRIVILÈGES DE L'ADHÉSION

Afin d'être admis à séjourner dans une auberge de jeunesse, il vous faudra devenir membre de l'Association d'Auberges de Jeunesse de votre pays. Votre carte d'adhérent vous permettra en outre de bénéficier de certains services exclusifs.

Ce guide contient la liste de tous les principaux avantages internationaux offerts aux adhérents mais vous trouverez de nombreuses autres remises et concessions dans le pays que vous désirez visiter.

Pour obtenir davantage de détails sur ces privilèges négociés au niveau national, contactez directement l'Association du pays en question, la plupart des Associations mettant à la disposition des ajistes des guides détaillés sur leur pays, qui catalogue entre autres les prestations spéciales réservées aux adhérents. S'il n'existe pas d'Association nationale dans votre pays, vous pouvez acheter une carte Hostelling International ou un Timbre de Bienvenue (Welcome Stamp) à votre arrivée à l'auberge.

Normes Garanties

Hostelling International reconnaît qu'un service et des installations de qualité constante, d'une auberge à l'autre, importent beaucoup aux gens qui voyagent avec un budget limité. Le Plan pour la Garantie des Normes en Auberges a été mis en place precisément pour vous assurer cette constance dans nos prestations, quelle que soit l'auberge où vous séjournez.

Qu'est-ce que les Normes Garanties vous apportent?

ACCUEIL

Les auberges sont ouvertes à tous, quel que soit votre âge, sexe, culture, race ou religion. Si vous n'avez pas déjà l'avantage d'être membre, vous aurez la possibilité d'aquérir, à l'auberge où vous comptez séjourner, une adhésion complète ou partielle.

Vous pouvez réserver un lit à l'avance, par fax, e-mail, courrier ordinaire ou via le système IBN.

En principe, il vous sera possible d'arriver entre 7h et 10h et entre 17h et 22h30 dans la plupart des auberges.

Si l'auberge est fermée pendant un certain temps dans la journée, vous aurez accès à un abri, à des toilettes et à un endroit où garder vos bagages. Mais surtout, vous accueillir sera la priorité du personnel de l'auberge qui s'engagera à vous fournir l'aide et l'information dont vous aurez besoin pour tirer un maximum de votre séjour.

CONFORT

Vous pouvez compter passer une bonne nuit de sommeil confortablement et trouver un nombre suffisant de douches et de sanitaires ainsi qu'une bonne réserve d'eau chaude! Là où ce n'est pas compris dans le prix de la nuité, il vous sera possible de louer des draps propres, si besoin est.

Bien qu'elles servent en général des repas, certaines auberges peuvent n'être aménagées que d'une cuisine individuelle. Dans ces cas-là, vous devriez être en mesure d'acheter des denrées de base, soit à l'auberge, soit à proximité. Les auberges mettront à votre disposition une reserve pour denrées, une surface de préparation et de cuisson et un évier pour la vaisselle.

PROPRETÉ

Où que vous soyez, vous êtes en droit d'attendre des auberges et de leur personnel un haut degré de propreté et d'hygiène.

SÉCURITÉ

Le personnel des auberges fera tout son possible pour garantir votre sécurité personnelle et celle de vos biens pendant votre séjour. Des consignes fermant à clé seront à votre disposition pour y déposer bagages et objets de valeur.

INTIMITÉ

Même si vous vous trouvez dans la même chambre que d'autres ajistes de même sexe, (à moins d'avoir reservé une chambre individuelle ou familiale), le Plan de Garantie des Normes vous promet votre intimité là où vous en avez besoin – spécialement dans les douches, salles de bain et toilettes.

Notre Engagement envers l'Environnement

CHARTE DE L'ENVIRONNEMENT

Outre ces Normes Garanties, les auberges s'engagent à adhérer à la Charte Environnementale de l'IYHF qui dicte les critères de consommation et de préservation des ressources, d'élimination des déchets et de recyclage, de défense de l'environnement et prévoit également que les auberges devront jouer un rôle dans l'éducation écologique.

Pour beaucoup de gens, ce qui caractérise l'ajisme ce sont des endroits perdus, isolés et insolites et des bâtiments très spéciaux.

Nous devons admettre, cependant, qu'il nous est difficile d'appliquer ces mêmes normes partout - au milieu de la forêt tropicale ou dans une cabane de berger isolée, par exemple. C'est pourquoi nous avons fait une exception de quelques petites auberges plus simplement equipées où le personnel ainsi que les périodes d'ouverture peuvent être limités. Ce type d'auberge sera indiqué clairement dans le guide sous l'appellation Auberge Simple (ou Simple Hostel).

La présence de ces normes dans les auberges seront contrôlées par Hostelling International et par vous, les usagers. N'hésitez pas à utiliser les cartes ou fiches-commentaires que vous trouverez dans ce guide et qui vous permettront de nous contacter plus facilement.

Le Réseau International de Réservation (IBN)

RÉSERVEZ À L'AVANCE GRÂCE À IBN

Notre réseau international de réservation (IBN) vous offre une solution simple et économique pour réserver à l'avance et à peu de frais dans plus de 300 sites-clés répartis à travers le monde.

Un symbole IBN apposé au nom d'une auberge vous signale que ce site pourra vous réserver un lit jusqu'à 6 mois avant votre départ (selon les disponibilités).

Ces auberges et les autres centres de réservation IBN, répertoriés par pays dans chacune des sections consacrées aux diverses Associations nationales, vous offrent un service unique dans le secteur de l'hébergement bon marché.

IBN vous permet:

- de régler votre séjour dans la devise du pays où vous effectuez votre réservation, avant votre départ.
- d'effectuer des réservations au cours de vos périples depuis n'importe quelle auberge ou centre de réservations IBN.
- dans la plupart des cas, de payer par carte de crédit
- dans de nombreux pays, d'appeler une seule centrale de réservation pour réserver une série de nuitées dans plusieurs auberges.

AUTRES METHODES DE RESERVATION

Vous pouvez vous présenter à l'auberge sans réservation, mais en saison haute, nous vous recommandons vivement de réserver à l'avance pour vous éviter une déception.

- Les chambres familiales sont très demandées. Quant aux groupes, ils devront toujours faire une réservation au préalable.
- Il est également possible de réserver en envoyant un fax ou un courrier directement à l'auberge concernée.
- Si vous réservez par courrier, n'oubliez pas de joindre un coupon-réponse international (que vous obtiendrez dans les bureaux de poste) ainsi qu'une enveloppe à vos nom et adresse.
- N'oubliez pas cependant, si vous réservez sans verser d'arrhes, que vous devrez arriver à l'auberge avant 18h, à moins d'avoir convenu avec l'auberge d'une heure différente pour votre arrivée.

Nous sommes sûrs que votre expérience des auberges sera agréable. Elle sera de toutes façons abordable.

Nous sommes impatients de faire votre connaissance.

Le Réseau International De Communication (ICN)

ICN est un service de communication polyvalent et économique qui a été spécialement conçu pour le voyageur individuel et indépendant. Les points de vente de la carte de communication ICN sont signalés par le symbole ICN. Cette carte vous donne accès à un grand nombre de services, à des tarifs très compétitifs. Vous pourrez, entre autres:

- utiliser la carte comme une simple carte téléphonique depuis n'importe quel téléphone.
- envoyer et recevoir des messages électroniques depuis tout kiosque ICN, implanté dans les auberges de grand passage.
- envoyer des fax à vos proches.
- consulter les renseignements disponibles sur les attractions touristiques locales, sur chacun des kiosques.
- créer votre propre boîte aux lettres pour recevoir des courriers électroniques pendant que vous voyagez.
- vérifier les disponibilités en lits dans chaque auberge IBN que vous comptez visiter (ce service deviendra opérationnel à une date ultérieure).

Avec ICN, vous pouvez maintenir le contact avec vos proches où que vous soyez. ICN constitue un progrès sans égal dans le domaine de la communication entre le voyageur et sa famille, garantissant à l'un et à l'autre un degré de sécurité et de tranquilité d'esprit, sachant qu'en cas d'urgence, il leur sera toujours possible de se contacter. **ICN est réservé exclusivement aux membres Hostelling International.**

Change Sans Commission

UNE OFFRE SPECIALE RESERVEE AUX MEMBRES HOSTELLING INTERNATIONAL

TRAVELEX – La chaîne de bureaux de change la plus prédominante dans les aéroports et autres terminaux passagers – offre aux membres Hostelling International un service très exclusif qui leur permet de reduire les frais de leurs voyages transfrontaliers. Sur simple présentation de votre carte d'adhérent Hostelling International, vous pouvez changer des devises sans commission à n'importe lequel des bureaux Travelex listés ci-dessous. **TRAVELEX**

AMERIQUE DU NORD

Canada - aéorports
Edmonton
Halifax
Winnipeg
Vancouver

USA - aéorports
Atlanta
Baltimore
Boston
Cleveland
Columbus
Detroit
Fort Lauderdale
Indianapolis
JFK (tous les terminaux)
Kansas
La Guardia
Las Vegas
Los Angeles (tous les terminaux)
Memphis
Minneapolis
Nouvelle Orléans
Newark (tous les terminaux)
Norfolk, Virginia
Omaha
Ontario, California
Palm Springs
Pittsburgh
Portland (Oregon)
Raleigh Durham
San Diego
San Francisco
Tampa

PACIFIQUE

Australie - aéorports
Brisbane International
Cairns International
Ansett Sydney
Ansett Melbourne
Ansett Brisbane
Ansett Coolangatta
Qantas Sydney
Qantas Melbourne
Qantas Brisbane
Qantas Adelaide
Qantas Perth
Qantas Coolangatta
Alice Springs
Cairns
Canberra
Hamilton Island

Nouvelle-Zélande - aéorports
Auckland
Christchurch
Queenstown
Rotorua

Cette offre unique vous permettra d'économiser des sommes considérables, surtout si vos périples vous emmènent dans plus d'un pays. *Le Buy Back Plus, une offre exclusive de Travelex: Moyennant une somme modique, nous vous rachèterons toutes les devises étrangères que vous n' aurez pas utilisées exactement au même taux qu'à l'achat, et ce, sans commission!*

Keep in touch wherever you are

Maintenez le contact – où que vous soyez • In Kontakt bleiben – wo immer Sie auch sind • ¡Manténgase en contacto – dondequiera que Ud. se encuentre!

Send and receive e-mails **Send faxes** Local travel information
Set up your own e-mail box Check accommodation availability

ICN INTERNATIONAL COMMUNICATION NETWORK

Wie Sie diesen Führer benutzen

Willkommen in der Welt von Hostelling International - dem einmaligen Netz von Unterkünften für eine gute Nachtruhe in freundlicher Umgebung - zu einem Preis, den Sie sich leisten können.

Der Führer enthält Informationen über die Ausstattungen und Leistungen der Jugendherbergen, die in der

INTERNATIONAL YOUTH HOSTEL FEDERATION

zusammengeschlossen sind.

Die Angaben sind nach **Ländern und Orten alphabetisch geordnet.**

In der Einführung finden Sie die wichtigsten Auskünfte über 'Hostelling International' – den angebotenen Gästeservice, die Vorteile Mitglied zu sein und die allen Herbergen auferlegte Verpflichtung, vorgegebene Standards zu gewährleisten.

Falls Sie weitere Informationen über Herbergen in aller Welt wünschen, können Sie sich entweder

an den Jugendherbergsverband Ihres Landes wenden

oder

unsere Internet Home Page **http://www.iyhf.org** besuchen.

Eine Einführung zu Hostelling International

Die Jugendherbergsbewegung entstand in Deutschland Anfang dieses Jahrhunderts and wuchs schnell in den Jahren zwischen den Kriegen, besonders in Europe. Heute bietet Hostelling International eine Auswahl von nahezu 4.500 Herbergen in 60 Ländern in aller Welt an.

In den Jugendherbergen Europas, Asiens, Afrikas, Nord- und Südamerikas und dem pazifischen Raum wollen wir Ihnen einen gleichbleibenden guten Service anbieten – eine erfrischende Nachtruhe in freundlicher Umgebung und preiswert dazu.

Dieser Führer enthält Angaben über die Herbergen, die Ihnen zur Wahl stehen. Heute ist es möglich, eine Übernachtung 6 Monate im voraus zu buchen unter Benutzung des "International Booking Network (IBN) Systems" – Einzelheiten dazu auf den folgenden Seiten.

KEINE ALTERSBEGRENZUNG

Jugendherbergen sind trotz ihres Namens in den meisten Ländern offen für alle Altersgruppen. Nur eine kleine Anzahl von Herbergen in Deutschland hat eine obere Altersgrenze aufgrund örtlicher Vorschriften.

Gäste unter 14 Jahren sollten von einem Erwachsenen begleitet sein und viele Herbergen bieten heute Familienzimmer an. Reisegruppen werden in den meisten Herbergen aufgenommen mit einer Auswahl an Unterbringungsmöglichkeiten: Sie finden Einzel-, Doppel- und Mehrbettzimmer in den meisten grösseren Herbergen.

VORTEILE FÜR MITGLIEDER

Um Unterkunft in einer Jugendherge zu bekommen, müssen Sie Mitglied des Jugendherbergsverbandes Ihres Landes sein. Darüberhinaus können Sie als Mitglied zusätzliche spezielle Services und Leistungen in Anspruch nehmen.

In diesem Führer sind die wichtigsten der international erhältlichen Vergünstigungen aufgeführt. Zusätzliche Preisvorteile und Rabatte können Sie jedoch im besuchten Land finden. Weitere Einzelheiten darüben finden Sie in den jeweiligen Landesführern, die von den meisten Jugendherbergsverbänden herausgegeben und von dort bezogen werden können.

Falls Ihr Land keinen eigenen Jugendherbergsverband hat, können Sie bei der Ankunft in der von Ihnen ausgewählten Herberge entweder eine "Hostelling International Card" oder einzelne "Welcome Stamps" erwerben.

Zugesicherte Standards

Hostelling International weiss, dass der preisbewusste Gast gleichbleibende Qualität und immer guten Service erwartet. Um diese Leistungen zu erreichen, haben wir die "Zugesicherten Standards" eingeführt, damit Ihnen überall in unseren Herbergen ein annehmbarer Service und entsprechende Ausstattungen angeboten werden.

Was bedeuten diese Zugesicherten Standards für Sie?

EMPFANG

In unseren Herbergen sind alle Besucher willkommen, unabhängig von Alter, Geschlecht, Kulturkreis, Rasse oder Religion. Wenn Sie der Herbergsbewegung noch nicht angehören, so können Sie in jeder Herberge die volle oder zeitlich begrenzte Mitgliedschaft erwerben.

Sie können Ihre Unterkunft im voraus buchen, entweder per Post oder per Fax, mit e-mail oder durch das IBN-System.

Normalerweise kann man in den meisten Herbergen zwischen 00.700 und 10.00 sowie 17.00 und 22.00 Uhr einchecken. Falls die Herberge tagsüber für einige Stunden geschlossen ist, können Sie auf jeden Fall Ihr Gepäck dort aufbewahren.

Am allerwichtigsten ist jedoch die herzliche Aufnahme durch das Herbergspersonal. Alle Mitarbeiter werden bemüht sein, Ihnen mit Auskünften zu helfen und Sie so zu beraten, dass Ihr Aufenthalt ein voller Erfolg wird.

KOMFORT

Sie können eine gute und komfortable Nachtruhe erwarten, genügend Duschen, WC's und Waschgelegenheiten und ausreichend warmes Wasser.

Frische Bettwäsche ist selbstverständlich, in einigen Herbergen jedoch gegen Gebühr. In den meisten Herbergen werden Mahlzeiten angeboten. Dort, wo nur Selbstversorgung möglich ist, können Sie normalerweise Ihre Grundnahrungsmittel in der Herberge oder nahebei kaufen. Alle notwendigen Einrichtungen, wie für Nahrungsmittelaufbewahrung, zur Essensvorbereitung, zum Kochen und um hinterher aufzuspülen, stehen ebenfalls zur Verfügung.

SAUBERKEIT

Wo immer Sie auch reisen, in unseren Herbergen können Sie höchste Sauberkeits- und Hygienestandards erwarten.

SICHERHEIT

Unser Personal wird bemüht sein, Ihnen während Ihres Aufenthaltes Ihre Sicherheit zu gewährleisten, zusammen mit der Fürsorge für Ihr persönliches Eigentum. Es gibt Schliessfächer für Ihr Gepäck und Ihre Wertsachen.

PRIVATSPHÄRE

Selbst wenn Sie Ihr Zimmer mit anderen Gästen desselben Geschlechts teilen (falls Sie nicht ein Familienzimmer gebucht haben), versprechen Ihnen die Zugesicherten Standards Ihre geschützte Privatsphäre dort, wo sie wichtig ist – in Duschen, Waschräumen und WC's.

Eine Verpflichtung gegenüber unser Umwelt

UMWELTCHARTA

Zusätzlich zu den Zugesicherten Standards befolgen unsere Herbergen die IYHF Umweltcharta, die vorschreibt, wie Ressourcen genutzt und gespart werden können, wie Abfallvermeidung und Recycling einzusetzen sind, wie man die natürliche Umwelt schützt und mit Erziehung das Umweltbewusstsein fördern kann.

Für viele Besucher hat eine einfache Herberge, wie man sie in abgelegenen Gegenden oder in ungewöhnlichen Gebäuden findet, einen besonderen Reiz. Wir müssen zugeben, dass es schwierig ist, den gleichen Standard in der Mitte eines Regenwaldes oder in einer einsam gelegenen Schäferhütte zu erreichen.

Es gibt daher Ausnahmen für kleine Herbergen, die nur eine einfache Ausstattung, wenig Personal und kürzere Öffnungszeiten haben. Diese Herbergen haben wir deutlich als **einfache Herberge** gekennzeichnet.

Die Standards werden von Hostelling International und von Ihnen, unseren Gästen, überwacht. Die Kommentarblätter in diesem Führer helfen Ihnen, uns zu informieren.

Das International Booking Network (IBN)

VORAUSBUCHUNGEN DURCH DAS IBN

Mit unserem Computer Buchungssystem IBN können Sie einfach und preiswert Reservierungen in über 300 der wichtigsten Herbergen rund um den Globus vornehmen.

Überall dort, wo Sie das IBN Symbol sehen, können Sie eine Unterkunft 6 Monate im voraus buchen (vorausgesetzt es sind Betten frei).

Diese Herbergen und weitere IBN Buchungszentren, die in den Ländersektionen angeführt sind, bieten damit einen Service an, der für diesen preisbewussten Unterkunftssektor einmalig ist.

- Sie können bei Reservierung in der Währung des jeweiligen Landes bezahlen, in dem Sie vor Ihrer Abreise buchen.
- Sie können während Ihrer Reise von jeder IBN Herberge oder Buchungsstelle aus reservieren.
- In vielen Fällen können Sie mit Kreditkarten bezahlen.
- In vielen Ländern gibt es Zentrale Buchungsstellen, bei denen Sie Übernachtungen für verschiedene Herbergen gleichzeitig reservieren können.

ZUSÄTZLICHE BUCHUNGSINFORMATIONEN

Sie können ohne Vorausbestellung einer Unterkunft in jeder Herberge eintreffen: Wir raten jedoch dringend – besonders in den Hauptreisezeiten – zu reservieren, um Enttäuschungen zu vermeiden.

- Dies ist besonders wichtig für Gruppenreisen und für Familienzimmer, die oft schnell vergeben sind.
- Buchen Sie bitte die ausgewählte Herberge per Fax oder Brief. Falls Sie schriftlich buchen, legen Sie bitte einen internationalen Postcoupon und einen Briefumschlag mit Ihrer Anschrift bei.
- Falls Sie ohne Anzahlung gebucht haben wird normalerweise erwartet, dass Sie vor 18.00 Uhr in der Herberge eintreffen, wenn nicht eine andere Zeit vereinbart wurde.

Wir sind überzeugt, dass Ihnen Ihr Herbergsaufenthalt gefallen wird. Auf jeden Fall können Sie sich diesen leisten! Wir freuen uns auf Ihren Besuch.

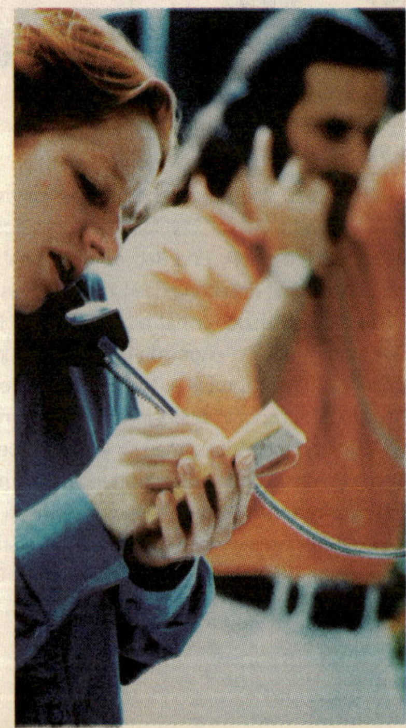

Das International Communication Network (ICN)

ICN (das internationale Kommunikationsnetz) ist ein umfangreicher, preiswerter Kommunikationsservice, der besonders für unabhängige Einzelreisende eingeführt wurde.

Wo immer Sie das ICN Symbol sehen, können Sie eine ICN Kommunikationskarte kaufen. Mit dieser Karte haben Sie für wenig Geld Zugang zu den folgenden Serviceleistungen:

- Sie können diese Karte wie eine normale Telefonkarte benutzen.
- Sie können in den Herbergen, die dem System angeschlossen sind, e-mail senden und empfangen.
- Sie können Text per Fax an Ihre Familie und Freunde schicken.
- Sie können örtliche Reiseinformationen abfragen.
- Sie können Ihren eigenen e-mail-Briefkasten einrichten, um dort eingehende Post auf Ihren Reisen zu lesen.
- Sie können sich erkundigen, ob in der Herberge Ihrer Wahl Betten frei sind – *(dieser Service wird zu einem späteren Zeitpunkt aktiviert)*.

Mit ICN bleiben Sie - wo immer Sie auch sind - in Verbindung mit Familie und Freunden.

ICN ist ein grosser Fortschritt, der Herbergsgästen sicheres reisen garantieren kann, ohne der Familie zu Haus Sorgen zu bereiten, weil diese weiss, dass Sie im Notfall immer erreichbar sind.

ICN steht exklusiv nur den Mitgliedern von Hostelling International zur Verfügung.

Gebührenfreier Devisenverkauf

EIN SONDERANGEBOT FÜR
HOSTELLING INTERNATIONAL MITGLIEDER

TRAVELEX – die weltweit grösste Spezialbank mit Wechselstuben in Flughäfen und Terminals – bietet Hostelling International Mitgliedern einen Sonderservice an, mit dem Sie bei internationalen Reisen Kosten sparen können.

Bei der Vorlage Ihres Mitgliedsausweises tauschen die folgenden Travelex-Geschäftsstellen gebührenfrei Geld um:

TRAVELEX

NORDAMERIKA

Kanada - Flughäfen
Edmonton
Halifax
Winnipeg
Vancouver

USA - Flughäfen
Atlanta
Baltimore
Boston
Cleveland
Columbus
Detroit
Fort Lauderdale
Indianapolis
JFK (alle Terminals)
Kansas
La Guardia
Las Vegas
Los Angeles (alle Terminals)
Memphis
Minneapolis
New Orleans
Newark (alle Terminals)
Norfolk, Virginia
Omaha
Ontario, California
Palm Springs
Pittsburgh
Portland (Oregon)

Raleigh Durham
San Diego
San Francisco
Tampa

PAZIFIK

Australien - Flughäfen
Brisbane International
Cairns International
Ansett Sydney
Ansett Melbourne
Ansett Brisbane
Ansett Coolangatta
Qantas Sydney
Qantas Melbourne
Qantas Brisbane
Qantas Adelaide
Qantas Perth
Qantas Coolangatta
Alice Springs
Cairns
Canberra
Hamilton Island

NEUSEELAND - Flughäfen
Queenstown

Einzelhandelsverkaufsstellen

Auckland
Christchurch
Queenstown
Roturua

Dieser super Service spart Ihnen viel Geld, besonders wenn Sie mehrere Länder besuchen.

Exklusives Travelex Rückkauf-Angebot; Für eine Minimalgebühr kaufen wir unbenutzten Devisen zum Einkaufspreis zurück, ohne kommission!

Cómo Utilizar Esta Guía

Bienvenido al mundo de Hostelling International – una red de centros de alojamiento sin igual, en los que Ud. pasará una buena noche en un ambiente acogedor a un precio asequible.

Esta guía contiene información específica sobre las instalaciones y prestaciones suministradas por los albergues juveniles afiliados a la

INTERNATIONAL YOUTH HOSTEL FEDERATION

(Federación Internacional de Albergues Juveniles)

Los albergues se encuentran listados **alfabéticamente por país y por ciudad.**

En nuestra introducción le presentamos a Hostelling International: los servicios ofrecidos a sus huéspedes, los beneficios de los que disfrutan sus socios y su adhesión a unas normas garantizadas que todos los albergues deben esforzarse en satisfacer. Si desea obtener información suplementaria sobre cualquier albergue del mundo, Ud. puede:

Contactar con la Asociación de Albergues Juveniles de su país antes de salir de viaje

o bien:

Consultar nuestra página de Internet en la dirección siguiente: **http://www.iyhf.org**

Hostelling International – Introducción

El alberguismo juvenil fue fundado en Alemania a principios de siglo y se extendió con rapidez, dentro de Europa especialmente, durante el periodo de entreguerras.

Actualmente, Hostelling International le propone un surtido de casi 4,500 centros de alojamiento repartidos por más de 60 países del mundo.

En los albergues juveniles de Europa, Asia, Africa, las Américas y el Pacífico, esperamos ofrecerle un servicio uniforme de primera calidad – una buena noche en un ambiente acogedor a un precio asequible.

Esta guía contiene información detallada sobre los albergues a su disposición. Ahora es posible reservar una cama con hasta 6 meses de antelación a través de la red internacional de reservas IBN (International Booking Network), de la cual encontrará una descripción más adelante.

PARA JOVENES DE TODAS LAS EDADES

A pesar de su nombre, los albergues juveniles están abiertos a personas de todas las edades en prácticamente todos los países. Sólo en un pequeño número de albergues alemanes existe un límite máximo de edad impuesto por la legislación regional.

Los menores de 14 años deberán ir acompañados de un adulto.

Muchos albergues hoy en día ofrecen habitaciones familiares. La mayoría aceptan grupos y disponen de varios tipos de habitación – Ud. encontrará habitaciones individuales, dobles y grandes dormitorios en casi todos los principales albergues.

AFILIACION – SUS PRIVILEGIOS

Para alojarse en un albergue juvenil, es necesario hacerse socio de la Asociación de Albergues Juveniles del país donde uno viva. Esta adhesión le concede, además, toda una serie de ventajas.

En esta guía se detallan los principales beneficios que es posible conseguir a nivel internacional, pero encontrará muchos más descuentos y ofertas en el país que Ud. visite. Para averiguar cuáles son, póngase en contacto con la Asociación de dicho país, pues casi todas las Asociaciones poseen su propia guía nacional en la que se indicarán los servicios especiales ofrecidos a los socios.

Si no existe una Asociación de Albergues Juveniles en su país, Ud. tendrá la oportunidad de adquirir un carnet Hostelling International o un "sello de bienvenida" en el albergue en el que se aloje.

Normas Garantizadas

Hostelling International es consciente de la importancia que tiene un nivel de calidad y servicio constante para los viajeros con presupuesto limitado. Por este motivo, hemos instituido nuestro Plan de Normas Garantizadas, para que Ud. pueda contar con instalaciones y prestaciones de un grado uniforme cuando se aloje en cualquiera de nuestros albergues.

¿Qué representan para Ud. las Normas Garantizadas de los albergues?

RECIBIMIENTO

Los albergues están abiertos a todos, sin distinción de edad, sexo, cultura, raza ni religión.

Si Ud. no es aún socio, podrá hacerse socio de pleno derecho o afiliarse a corto plazo en el albergue mismo.

Puede reservar una cama por correo, fax, correo electrónico o a través del sistema IBN.

Generalmente, el horario de la recepción es de 7 h. a 10 h. y de 17 h. a 22.30 h. como mínimo en casi todos los albergues. En los que estén cerrados durante parte del día, Ud. tendrá acceso a un lugar donde refugiarse y dejar su equipaje.

Ante todo, la prioridad del personal será acogerle y hacer todo lo posible por asistirle y darle la información que necesite para disfrutar de su estancia al máximo.

COMODIDAD

Ud. puede estar seguro de que pasará una buena y confortable noche, y de que dispondrá de un número adecuado de duchas, servicios y lavabos, así como de suficiente agua caliente.

En los casos en que no esté incluida en el precio de la pernoctación, será posible alquilar ropa blanca recién lavada si la necesita.

Aunque normalmente los albergues sirven comidas, en los que sólo sea posible cocinar uno mismo se podrán generalmente comprar alimentos básicos en el albergue mismo o cerca de él. Habrá un lugar donde guardar los alimentos, encimeras para la preparación de comidas, una cocina para guisar y una pila para fregar la vajilla.

LIMPIEZA

Adondequiera que viaje, Hostelling International le garantiza las más rigurosas normas de limpieza e higiene.

SEGURIDAD

El personal del albergue hará todo lo posible por proteger tanto a Ud. como sus efectos personales durante su estancia y el establecimiento dispondrá de armarios con cerrojo para su equipaje y objetos de valor.

PRIVACIDAD

Aunque puede darse que tenga que compartir una habitación con otros alberguistas del mismo sexo (a menos que haya reservado una habitación privada), nuestras Normas Garantizadas preservan su intimidad en los lugares más importantes, especialmente en las duchas, cuartos de baño y servicios.

Nuestro Compromiso Ecológico

NORMAS MEDIOAMBIENTALES

Además de estas Normas Garantizadas, los albergues se comprometen a cumplir las Normas Medioambientales de la IYHF, las cuales establecen los criterios relativos al consumo y conservación de recursos, a la eliminación de residuos y su reciclaje, a la protección de la naturaleza y a la provisión de educación medioambiental.

Para muchas personas, el atractivo de los albergues sencillos es que están situados en lugares aislados y poco corrientes, y que a menudo se encuentran en edificios muy especiales. No obstante, tenemos que admitir que es difícil mantener las mismas normas en todos los lugares – por ejemplo, en medio de la selva tropical o en una remota cabaña de pastor. Debido a estas diferencias, aplicamos algunas de nuestras normas de forma menos rigurosa en ciertos albergues pequeños y en aquellos que sólo poseen instalaciones básicas, en los cuales Ud. podrá encontrarse con un número de empleados y un horario de apertura limitados. Este tipo de albergue se halla indicado claramente como **"simple hostel"** *(albergue sencillo)*.

Las normas serán objeto de un seguimiento por parte de Hostelling International y también por parte de Ud., el usuario. Para ello, esta guía contiene impresos en los que puede enviarnos sus comentarios, ayudándole de esta forma a contactar con nosotros.

La Red Internacional de Reservas – IBN

RESERVE DE ANTEMANO A TRAVES DE IBN

Nuestro sistema informatizado de reservas constituye una forma sencilla y barata de reservar de antemano en más de 300 albergues clave del mundo.

Dondequiera que Ud. vea el símbolo IBN en esta guía, podrá reservar una cama hasta 6 meses antes de su estancia (siempre y cuando haya camas disponibles).

Estos albergues y demás centros de reservas IBN relacionados bajo cada país ofrecen un servicio sin igual en el sector del alojamiento económico, a saber:

- IBN le permite abonar sus reservas en la moneda del país en el que efectúe las mismas, antes de su viaje.
- Ud. podrá hacer reservas durante su viaje desde cualquier centro de reservas o albergue IBN.
- Generalmente, será posible pagar por tarjeta de crédito.
- En muchos países existe la posibilidad de llamar a una sola Oficina Central de Reservas para reservar de antemano pernoctaciones en varios albergues.

RESERVAS - INFORMACION SUPLEMENTARIA

Es posible llegar a un albergue sin reserva previa, pero, en temporada alta, le instamos a que reserve con antelación para no llevarse desilusiones.

- Las habitaciones familiares en particular se ocupan con rapidez y los grupos también deberán reservar con tiempo.
- Ud. puede realizar sus reservas enviando un fax o una carta al albergue deseado.
- Si reserva por correo, no se olvide de adjuntar un cupón internacional de respuesta pagada (en venta en la mayoría de las oficinas de correos) y un sobre con su nombre y dirección.
- Si realiza una reserva sin abonar un depósito, normalmente deberá llegar al albergue antes de las 18 h., a menos que haya concertado previamente otra hora de llegada.

Estamos seguros de que disfrutará de su estancia en nuestros albergues y de que no le saldrá cara la experiencia.

Esperamos tener el agrado de su visita.

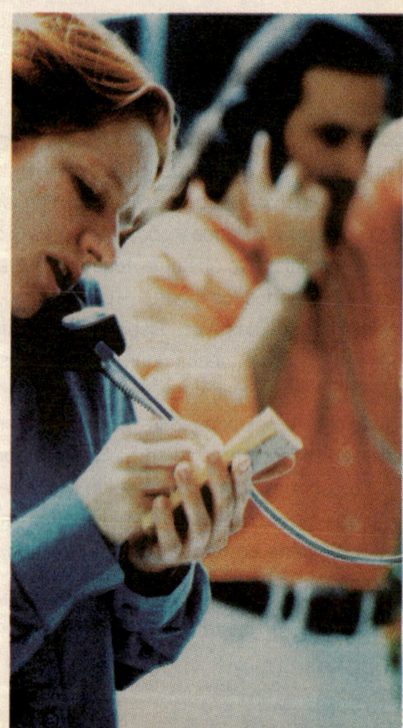

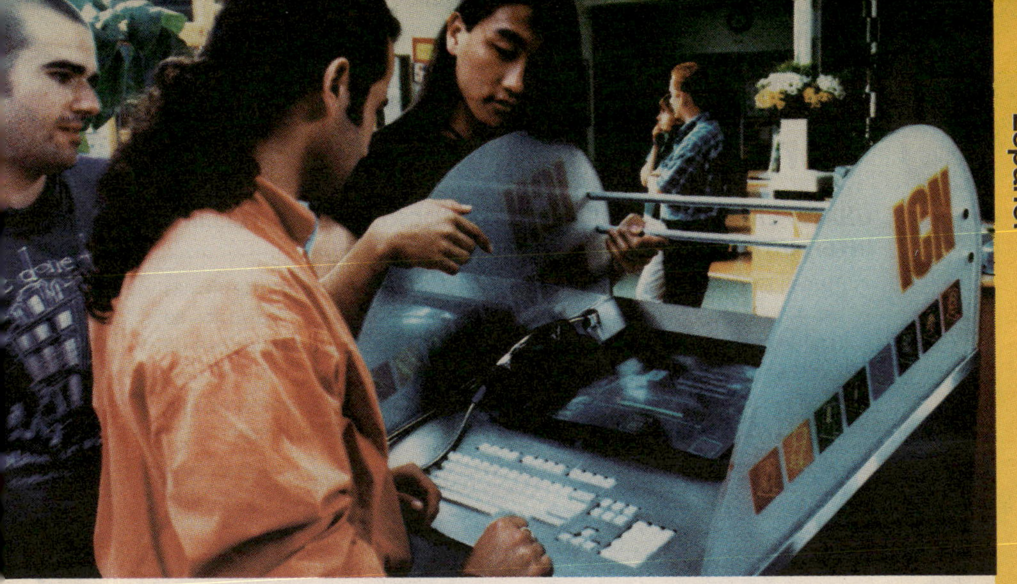

La Red Internacional de Comunicaciones – ICN

ICN es un servicio de comunicación integral y económico concebido especialmente para los viajeros independientes.

Dondequiera que Ud. vea el símbolo ICN, podrá adquirir una tarjeta de comunicación ICN. Con dicha tarjeta, le será posible utilizar una variedad de prestaciones a precios muy bajos. Ud. podrá:

- Usar la tarjeta en cualquier teléfono como una tarjeta telefónica normal.
- Enviar y recibir mensajes por correo electrónico en cualquiera de los quioscos ICN situados en los albergues clave.
- Enviar mensajes por fax a su familia y amigos.
- Conseguir información turística sobre la zona en que se encuentre en cualquier quiosco.
- Crear su propio buzón de correo electrónico en el que recibir mensajes durante su viaje.
- Averiguar si hay camas disponibles en los demás albergues IBN previstos en su itinerario. *(Este servicio estará disponible en el futuro.)*

Mediante ICN, podrá mantenerse en contacto con su familia y amigos dondequiera que Ud. se encuentre.

La seguridad y tranquilidad que ICN supone para Ud. y su familia al saber que siempre pueden contactar con Ud. en caso de emergencia representan un gran adelanto en el sector de las comunicaciones.

ICN está a la disposición exclusiva de los socios de Hostelling International.

Cambio de Divisas Gratuito

UNA OFERTA ESPECIAL PARA LOS SOCIOS DE HOSTELLING INTERNATIONAL

TRAVELEX, la compañía de cambio de divisas con el mayor número de oficinas en aeropuertos y terminales de pasajeros del mundo, ofrece a los socios de Hostelling International un servicio muy especial destinado a reducir el coste de los viajes internacionales.

Enseñando su carnet de socio, Ud. podrá cambiar divisas sin pagar comisión en cualquiera de las casas de cambio de Travelex siguientes:

NORTEAMERICA

Canadá - aeropuertos
Edmonton
Halifax
Winnipeg
Vancouver

Estados Unidos - aeropuertos
Atlanta
Baltimore
Boston
Cleveland
Columbus
Detroit
Fort Lauderdale
Indianápolis
JFK (todas las terminales)
Kansas
La Guardia
Las Vegas
Los Angeles (todas las terminales)
Menfis
Mineápolis
Nueva Orleáns
Newark (todas las terminales)
Norfolk, Virginia
Omaha
Ontario, California
Palm Springs
Pitsburgo
Portland (Oregón)
Raleigh Durham
San Diego
San Francisco
Tampa

EL PACIFICO

Australia - aeropuertos
Brisbane International
Cairns International
Ansett Sydney
Ansett Melbourne
Ansett Brisbane
Ansett Coolangatta
Qantas Sydney
Qantas Melbourne
Qantas Brisbane
Qantas Adelaide
Qantas Perth
Qantas Coolangatta
Alice Springs
Cairns
Canberra
Isla de Hamilton

Nueva Zelanda - aeropuerto
Auckland
Christchurch
Queenstown
Rotorua

Gracias a esta fabulosa oferta, Ud. se ahorrará una suma importante, sobre todo si tiene previsto viajar a más de un país. Buy Back Plus, una oferta exclusiva de Travelex: Por una suma módica, volvemos a comprar las divisas extranjeras que no haya utilizado al mismo tipo de cambio aplicado en el momento de la compra, y ¡sin comisión!

TRAVELEX 

EUROPE

Youth Hostels within Europe are listed in the Hostelling International Guide - Europe. The addresses of the full member Associations are given below:

Les AJ de l'Europe sont cataloguées dans le guide Hostelling International Guide - Europe. Les adresses des associations membres à part entière sont indiquées ci-dessous:

Die europäische JH sind im Hostelling International Guide - Europa aufgeführt. Die Adressen der vollberechtigten Mitgliedsverbände sind unten angegeben:

Los Albergues Juveniles de Europa se incluyen en la Hostelling International Guide - Europe. A continuación se encuentran las direcciones de las Asociaciones miembros de pleno derecho:

AUSTRIA:

Österreichischer Jugendherbergsverband, Hauptverband, 1010 Vienna, Schottenring 28.
☏ (1) 5335353 ℻ (1) 5350861
E-mail: oejhv-zentrale@oejhv.or.at
WWW address: http://www.oejhv.or.at

Österreichisches Jugendherbergswerk, Helferstorferstrasse 4, A-1010 Vienna.
☏/℻ (1) 5331833
E-mail: oejhw@oejhw.or.at
WWW address: http://www.oejhw.or.at/oejhw

BELGIUM:

Les Auberges de Jeunesse, Rue de la Sablonnière 28, 1000 Brussels.
☏ (2) 2195676 ℻ (2) 2191451
E-mail: auberges.jeunesse@gate71.be

Vlaamse JeugdHerbergcentrale, Van Stralenstraat 40, B-2060 Antwerp.
☏ (3) 2327218 ℻ (3) 2318126

CROATIA:

Hrvatski Ferijalni i Hostelski Savez (Croatian Youth Hostel Association), Savska cesta 5/1, 1000 Zagreb.
☏ (1) 4829296 ℻ (1) 4829294
E-mail: hfhs@alf.tel.hr

CYPRUS:

Cyprus Youth Hostel Association, 34 Th. Theodotou Street, PO Box 1328, Nicosia.
☏ (2) 442027 ℻ (2) 442896
E-mail: montis@logos.cy.net

CZECH REPUBLIC:

KMC-Club of Young Travellers, 11000 Prague 1, Karolíny Světlé 30.
☏/℻ (2) 24230633

DENMARK:

DANHOSTEL, Vesterbrogade 39, DK 1620 Copenhagen V.
☏ 31313612 ℻ 31313626
E-mail: ldv@danhostel.dk

ENGLAND & WALES:

Youth Hostels Association (England & Wales), Trevelyan House, 8 St Stephens Hill, St Albans, Hertfordshire, AL1 2DY.
☏ (1727) 855215 ℻ (1727) 844126
E-mail: YHACustomerServices@Compuserve.com

FINLAND:

Suomen Retkeilymajajärjestö-SRM, Yrjönkatu 38 B 15, 00100 Helsinki.
☏ (9) 6940377 ℻ (9) 6931349
E-mail: info@srm.inet.fi

FRANCE:

Fédération Unie des Auberges de Jeunesse, 27 rue Pajol, 75018 Paris.
☎ (1) 44898727 ✆ (1) 44898710
E-mail: fuaj@fuaj.org

GERMANY:

Deutsches Jugendherbergswerk, Hauptverband für Jugendwandern und Jugendherbergen e.V., im GILDE Zentrum, Bad Meinberger Str. 1, D-32760 Detmold.
☎ (5231) 9936-0 ✆ (5231) 993663
E-mail: info@djh.org

HUNGARY:

Magyarországi Ifjúsági Szállások Szövetsége, H-1065 Budapest V, Bajcsy-Zsilinszky ut 31.11/3.
☎/✆ (1) 3319705

ICELAND:

Bandalag Íslenskra Farfugla, Sundlaugavegur 34, 105 Reykjavík.
☎ 5538110 ✆ 5889201
E-mail: bit@islandia.is

IRELAND (NORTHERN):

Youth Hostel Association of Northern Ireland, 22 Donegall Rd, Belfast BT12 5JN.
☎ (1232) 315435 ✆ (1232) 439699
E-mail: info@hini.org.uk

IRELAND (REPUBLIC OF):

An Óige, Irish Youth Hostel Association, 61 Mountjoy St, Dublin 7.
☎ (1) 8304555 ✆ (1) 8305808
E-mail: anoige@iol.ie

ISRAEL:

Israel Youth Hostels Association, Binyanei Hauma, 1 Shazar Street, P O Box 6001, Jerusalem 91060.
☎ (2) 6558400 ✆ (2) 6558430
E-mail: iyha@netvision.net.il

ITALY:

Associazione Italiana Alberghi per la Gioventù, Via Cavour 44, 00184 Rome.
☎ 064871152 ✆ 064880492
E-mail: aig@uni.net

LUXEMBOURG:

Centrale des Auberges de Jeunesse Luxembourgeoises, 2 rue du Fort Olisy, L-2261 Luxembourg.
☎ 225588 ✆ 463987
E-mail: information@youthhostels.lu

NETHERLANDS:

Stichting Nederlandse Jeugdherberg Centrale, Prof Tulpstraat 2, 1018 HA Amsterdam.
☎ (20) 5513133 ✆ (20) 6390199

NORWAY:

Norske Vandrerhjem, Dronningensgate 26, N-0154 Oslo.
☎ 23139300 ✆ 23139350
E-mail: hostels@online.no

POLAND:

Polskie Towarzystwo Schronisk Mlodzieżowych (Polish Youth Hostel Association), ul Chocimska 28, 00-791 Warsaw.
☎ (22) 498128 ✆ (22) 498354

PORTUGAL:

MOVIJOVEM-Agencia de Turismo Jovem, Cooperativa de Interesse Público de Responsabilidade Limitada, Av. Duque d'Avila 137, 1050 Lisbon.

☎ (1) 3138820 ✆ (1) 3535982

E-mail: movijovem@mail.telepac.pt

SCOTLAND:

Scottish Youth Hostels Association, 7 Glebe Crescent, Stirling FK8 2JA.

☎ (1786) 891400 ✆ (1786) 891333

E-mail: info@syha.org.uk

SLOVENIA:

Pocitniska Zveza Slovenije, Parmova 33, 1000 Ljubljana.

☎ (61) 312156 ✆ (61) 1332219

SPAIN:

Red Española de Albergues Juveniles, c/.José Ortega y Gasset 71, Madrid 28006.

☎ (91) 3477700 ✆ (91) 4018160

E-mail: streaj@mtas.es

SWEDEN:

Svenska Turistföreningen, Stureplan 4, PO Box 25, 101 20 Stockholm.

☎ (8) 4632100 ✆ (8) 6781958

E-mail: info@stfturist.se

SWITZERLAND:

Schweizer Jugendherbergen, Schaffhauserstr 14, PO Box 161, CH 8042 Zürich.

☎ (1) 3601414 ✆ (1) 3601460

E-mail: bookingoffice@youthhostel.ch

YUGOSLAVIA (FEDERAL REPUBLIC OF):

Ferijalni savez Jugoslavije, Obilicev venac 4/III, Belgrade 11000.

☎ (11) 622956 ✆ (11) 3220762

HOSTELLING INTERNATIONAL

▲ There for everyone - young, not so young and those in the middle.▲

▲ c'est pour tout le monde -les jeunes, les moins jeunes et tous les autres.▲

▲ albergues para todos - los jóvenes, los menos jóvenes y los jóvenes de espíritu.▲

▲ für jederman - ob jung, nicht mehr ganz so jung oder die dazwischen.▲

The Euro
-a new currency is born

A new currency called the euro is born at the stroke of midnight central European time on 31 December 1998. Economic and Monetary Union in Europe will at last have been achieved.

The currencies of participating countries will cease to exist in their own right, but become "expressions" or sub-units of the euro; and in time the new currency will take its place as a world currency alongside the dollar and the yen.

WHO ?

Only members of the European Union can join the euro-zone. Of these eleven countries, Belgium, Germany, Spain, France, Ireland, Italy, Luxembourg, Netherlands, Austria, Portugal and Finland, will be adopting the new currency as from 1.1.1999. (The countries are listed in alphabetical order when written in their own language.)

The other countries (Denmark, Greece, Sweden and the United Kingdom) can join later when they are ready.

WHY ?

These countries are doing this to gain the economic advantages of having a single currency.

★ Savings on foreign exchange costs when changing one country's money into another ;
★ Greater competition between firms in different countries (for example it is easier to compare prices) ;
★ Trade between participating countries will become easier.

Furthermore the rules ensured that the countries chosen to adopt the euro on 1.1.1999 all had healthy economies with sound government finances, low inflation, stable exchange rates and low interest rates.

The countries have agreed rules to ensure that this healthy economic management is continued into the future.

The stable and healthy economic background, combined with more competition, more trade and fewer exchange costs, will help the economy prosper.

From the Youth Hosteller's point of view, the great advantage will be felt in 2002 when he or she can travel freely throughout the eleven countries of the euro-zone and use the same notes and coins everywhere. Before that, though, airline ticketing systems (and the IYHF booking system) will be able to operate in euros. This will have various advantages, for example it will make it easier to compare prices.

WHEN ?

1.1.1999	(00h00 CET) the euro is born
4.1.1999	(Monday, the first working day of the new year) all large-scale financial transactions are carried out in euros.
1999-2001	Use of the euro is optional but because notes and coins will be issued later it will be restricted to "scriptural" transactions, such as writing cheques, book-keeping, etc. Some companies, especially those with a lot of exports or imports or in the tourist industry, are expected to use the euro from early on. Others may wait until the notes and coins are issued.
1.1.2002	Euro notes and coins are introduced. Scriptural transactions will only be in the euro denomination.
30.6.2002	(But probably much earlier) old national notes and coins are withdrawn from circulation

HOW ?

An independent System of European Central Banks has been created, headquartered in Frankfurt, to run the euro-zone's monetary policy : it will set interest rates and control the issue of bank notes.

National Governments will continue to run economic policy ; they have agreed rules to make sure economic management remains healthy.

Old national currency units will be converted into euros at **fixed conversion rates** which must be used by law. These rates will be decided on 1.1.1999.

Detailed rules have been agreed on how to do these conversions so that everybody should get the same result.

If someone pays you an amount in euros **the bank** will credit your account, using the fixed conversion rates, even if your account is still in the old national currency unit, and vice versa.

When the new euro **notes and coins** are introduced in 2002 you will be able to spend your old national notes and coins in the shops as usual for a time, or you will be able to exchange old for new at your bank.

WHERE TO GET MORE INFORMATION ?

All the eleven national governments have launched their own communications campaigns. But you can try the telephone help desks and websites on the following pages for more detailed information.

Euro hotline phone numbers*

and Internet sites

Country	Number	Internet site
Germany	0180-522 1999 0180-321 2002	http://www.bundesregierung.de http://www.bundesfinanzministerium.de
Austria	0660-6363 Europe telephone (1)514 33 2226 Federal government's euro hot line	http://www.oenb.co.at/
Belgium	0800/90806 Euro forum 02/221.33.42 Euro-Desk for semi-professionals only	http://www.euro.fgov.be
Spain	902-1-1-2002	http://www.euro-mech.com
Finland	010-345 6700	http://www.vn.fi/vm/suomi/emuproj/
France	0800 01 20 02 Minitel 3615 EURO 99	http://www.finances.gouv.fr
Ireland	01/6767571 ext 5147/5146/5082 General information ECT, Finance Department	http://www.irlgov.ie.finance
	01/607 32 99 Forfas, information for professionals	http://www.emuaware.forfas.ie
	01/679 2777 ext. 4817/4148/4146 Information on tax and customs aspects of the switchover, tax receipts	http://www.revenue.ie
Italy	48 82.118 Euro bureau	http://www.tesoro.it
Luxembourg	(352) 478-2641 Help-Line 478-2608	http://www.etat.lu/FI/
Netherlands	0800 1521 Euroline	http://www.euro.nl
Portugal	being set up	http://www.dgep.pt
United Kingdom		http://www.hm-treasury.gov.uk http://www.euro.gov.uk
Sweden		http://www.regeringen.se
European Monetary Institute (European Central Bank)		http://www.ecb.int/
European Parliament		http://www.europarl.eu.int/
European Commission ★ Official euro page ★ Year 2000 and euro: IT challenges ★ Directorate General for Economic and Financial Affairs		http://www.europa.eu.int/euro/ http://www.ispo.cec.be/y2keuro/ http://europa.eu.int/comm/dg02/index_en.htm

*** Freephone numbers, except in certain countries where national phone rates apply.**

Algeria

ALGERIE

ALGERIEN

ARGELIA

Fédération Algérienne des Auberges de Jeunesse,
213 Rue Hassiba Ben Bouali, B.P. 15,
El-Annasser, 16015, Alger, Algeria

☎ (213) (2) 670321/683049
🖷 (213) (2) 683049

A copy of the Hostel Directory for this Country can be obtained from:
The National Office.

Capital:	Algiers	Population:	23,403,000
Language:	Arabic	Size:	2.381,741 sq km
Currency:	DA (dinar)		

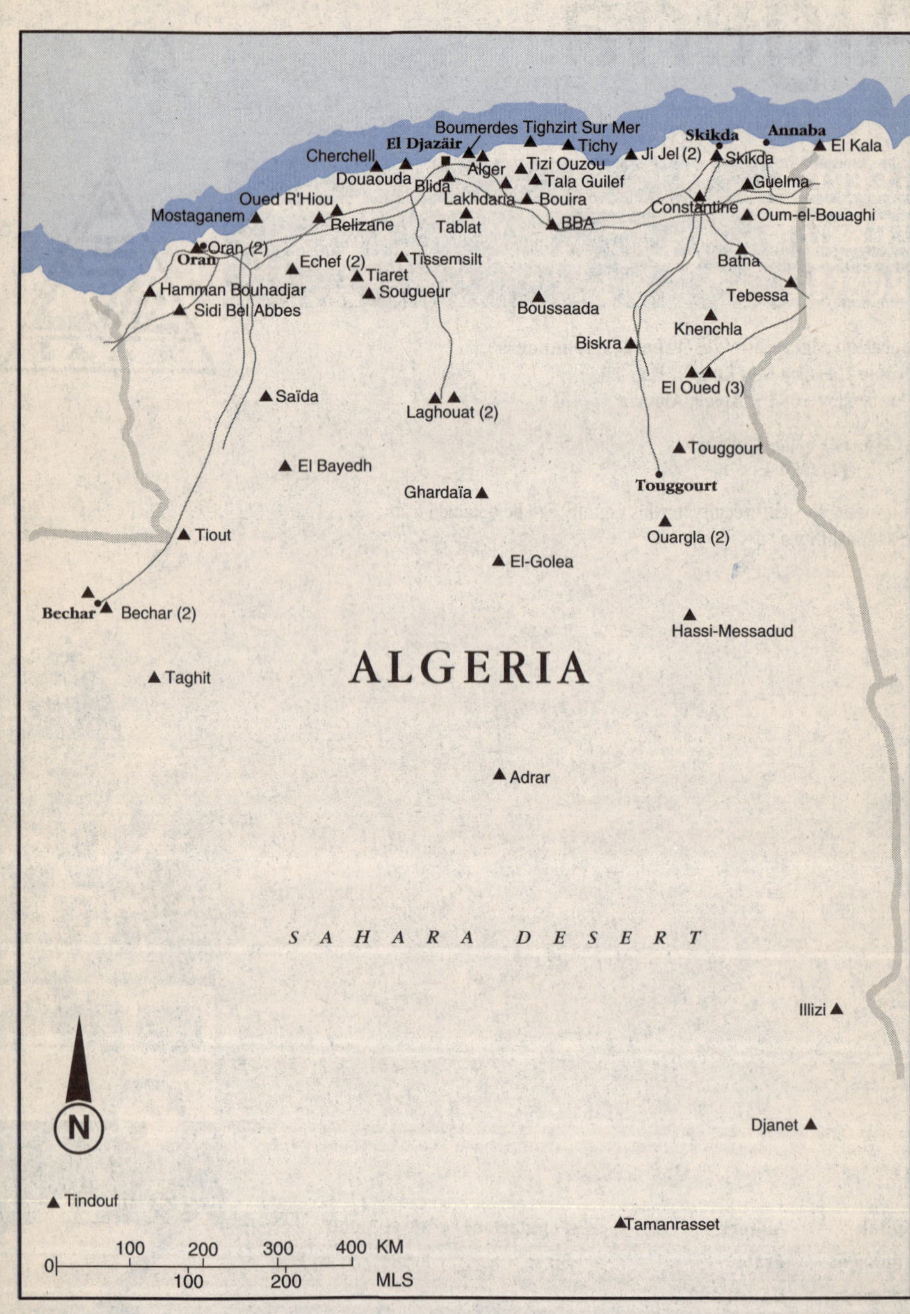

Algeria
ALGERIA
Boumerdes Tighzirt Sur Mer
El Djazäir
Cherchell
Alger
Douaouda
Blida
Tizi Ouzou
Tala Guilef
Skikda
Annaba
El Kala
Ji Jel (2)
Skikda
Guelma
Tichy
Lakhdaria
Bouira
Oued R'Hiou
Mostaganem
Relizane
Tablat
BBA
Constantine
Oum-el-Bouaghi
Oran (2)
Oran
Echef (2)
Tissemsilt
Batna
Tebessa
Hamman Bouhadjar
Tiaret
Sidi Bel Abbes
Sougueur
Boussaada
Knenchla
Biskra
El Oued (3)
Saïda
Laghouat (2)
El Bayedh
Touggourt
Ghardaïa
Touggourt
Tiout
Ouargla (2)
El-Golea
Bechar
Bechar (2)
Hassi-Messadud
Taghit
ALGERIA
Adrar
SAHARA DESERT
Illizi
N
Djanet
Tindouf
Tamanrasset
100   200   300   400 KM
0
100   200   MLS

English

ALGERIAN HOSTELS

Hostels in Algeria offer a good network for exploration of the southern part of the country and the Mediterranean coast.

Most hostels are open 10.00-12.00hrs and 17.00-22.00hrs, unless otherwise stated. Expect to pay in the region of 60DA per night plus linen hire if needed. Self-catering is available only in a limited number of hostels.

Your stay at any one hostel may be limited to three nights.

PASSPORTS AND VISAS

All visitors to Algeria must possess a valid passport and visa.

HEALTH

An International Vaccination Certificate is not required.

BANKING HOURS

Banks are open 08.30-15.30hrs Sunday-Thursday.

POST OFFICES

Opening hours are 08.00-17.00hrs Saturday-Thursday.

SHOPPING HOURS

Shops are generally open 09.00-18.00hrs.

TRAVEL

Air
Inter-Air Services offer a range of internal flights - discounts are available for travellers under 22 years.

Rail
The Algerian Railways (SNTF) operates a daily passenger service from Algiers to the principal provincial cities and also to Tunis and Morocco with sleepers.

Bus
The company SNTV is fairly cheap and modern. Other private companies provide the link between Algiers and the main towns.

Ferry
A frequent service operates between Algiers and Marseille in France.

Driving
The road system is fairly good.

TELEPHONE INFORMATION

Country Code	**213**
Main City Area Codes	
Algiers	2

Français

AUBERGES DE JEUNESSE ALGERIENNES

Le réseau d'auberges algériennes permet d'explorer la partie sud du pays et la côte méditerranéenne.

La plupart des auberges sont ouvertes de 10h à 12h et de 17h à 22h, sauf indication contraire. Une nuit vous coûtera environ 60 DA, plus location de draps le cas échéant. Quelques auberges seulement mettent une cuisine à la disposition des voyageurs.

Les séjours sont souvent limités à trois nuits dans une même auberge.

PASSEPORTS ET VISAS

Toutes les personnes se rendant en Algérie doivent être munies d'un passeport valide et d'un visa.

SOINS MEDICAUX

Il n'est pas nécessaire de se procurer un certificat international de vaccination.

HEURES D'OUVERTURE DES BANQUES

Les banques sont ouvertes de 8h30 à 15h30, du dimanche au jeudi.

BUREAUX DE POSTE

Les bureaux de poste sont ouverts de 8h à 17h, du samedi au jeudi.

HEURES D'OUVERTURE DES MAGASINS

Les magasins sont en général ouverts de 9h à 18h.

DEPLACEMENTS

Avions

Les services Inter-Air offrent toute une gamme de vols intérieurs - des remises sont disponibles pour les voyageurs de moins de 22 ans.

Trains

Les Chemins de Fer Algériens (SNTF) assurent un service passagers journalier à partir d'Alger vers les principales villes de province, et vers Tunis et le Maroc, avec des wagons-lits.

Autobus

La compagnie SNTV est assez bon marché et moderne. D'autres compagnies privées assurent la liaison entre Alger et les principales villes.

Ferry-boats

Un service fréquent assure des traversées entre Alger et Marseille, en France.

Automobiles

Le réseau routier est assez bon.

TELEPHONE

Indicatif du Pays 213
Indicatifs régionaux des Villes principales
   Alger 2

Deutsch

ALGERISCHE JUGENDHERBERGEN

Algerien hat ein gutes Netz von Jugendherbergen zur Bereisung des südlichen Landesteiles und der Mittelmeerküste.

Wenn nichts anderes angegeben ist, sind die meisten Herbergen von 10.00-12.00 Uhr und von 17.00-22.00 Uhr geöffnet. Es ist mit einem Preis von ca. 60DA pro Nacht plus, bei Bedarf, einer Gebühr für die Miete von Bettwäsche zu rechnen. Einrichtungen für Selbstversorger gibt es nur in einer beschränkten Zahl von Herbergen.

Manchmal wird der Aufenthalt in ein und derselben Herberge auf drei Übernachtungen beschränkt.

PÄSSE UND VISA

Alle Algerien-Reisenden müssen im Besitz eines gültigen Reisepasses und Visums sein.

GESUNDHEIT

Es wird kein internationales Impfzeugnis benötigt.

GESCHÄFTSSTUNDEN DER BANKEN

Banken sind sonntags bis donnerstags von 08.30-15.30 Uhr geöffnet.

POSTÄMTER

Öffnungszeiten: samstags-donnerstags 08.00-17.00 Uhr.

LADENÖFFNUNGSZEITEN

Geschäfte sind im allgemeinen von 09.00-18.00 Uhr geöffnet.

REISEN

Flugverkehr

Inter-Air Services führt eine Reihe von Inlandsflügen durch - für Reisende unter 22 Jahren gibt es eine Ermäßigung.

Eisenbahn

Die algerische Eisenbahn (SNTF) bietet einen täglichen Passagierverkehr zwischen Algier und den wichtigsten Provinzstädten und mit Schlafwagen auch nach Tunis und Marokko.

Busse

Das Busunternehmen SNTV ist verhältnismäßig billig, und die Busse sind modern. Andere private Unternehmen sorgen für die Verbindung zwischen Algier und den bedeutenden Städten.

Fähren

Zwischen Algier und Marseille in Frankreich findet ein häufiger Verkehr statt.

Autofahren

Es gibt ein verhältnismäßig gutes Straßennetz.

FERNSPRECHINFORMATIONEN

Landes-Kennzahl 213
größere Städte - Ortsnetzkennzahlen
  Algier 2

Español

ALBERGUES DE JUVENTUD ARGELINOS

Los albergues argelinos ofrecen una buena red para explorar la parte sur del país y la costa mediterránea.

La mayoría de los albergues abren de 10.00 a 12.00 horas y de 17.00 a 22.00 horas, a menos que se indique lo contrario. El precio es de aprox. 60 DA por noche, más alquiler de sábanas, si las necesita. Sólo un número limitado de albergues ofrece cocina para huéspedes.

La estancia en cualquier albergue puede verse limitada a tres noches.

PASAPORTES Y VISADOS

Todos los visitantes deben estar en posesión de un pasaporte válido y de un visado.

SANIDAD

No se requiere un Certificado Internacional de Vacunación.

HORARIO DE BANCOS

Los bancos abren de 08.30 a 15.30 horas de domingo a jueves.

OFICINAS DE CORREOS

El horario es de 08.00 a 17.00 horas de sábado a jueves.

HORARIO COMERCIAL

Las tiendas suelen abrir de 09.00 a 18.00 horas.

DESPLAZAMIENTOS

Avión

Los Servicios Inter-Air ofrecen varios vuelos internos. Existen descuentos para pasajeros menores de 22 años.

Tren

La compañía ferroviaria argelina (SNTF) opera un servicio diario para pasajeros entre Argel y las principales ciudades provinciales y también con destino a Túnez y Marruecos en coche-cama.

Autobús

La compañía SNTV es bastante barata y moderna. Otras empresas privadas proporcionan un servicio entre Argel y las principales ciudades.

Ferry

Existe un servicio frecuente entre Argel y Marsella (Francia).

Coche

La red de carreteras es bastante buena.

INFORMACION TELEFONICA

Código Nacional 213
Prefijos de las Ciudades Principales
  Argel 2

Location/Address	Telephone No. Fax No.	Beds	Opening Dates	Facilities
▲ **Adrar** Maison de Jeunes de la Wilaya, 01000 Adrar.	☎ (7) 258284	25		
△ *Alger* AJ Hassiba-Ben-Bouali, 213 Rue Hassiba-Ben-Bouali, Alger.	☎ 670032	74		
△ *Annaba* Rue Abdaoui Mouloud Cité FLN Annaba, 23000 Wilaya d'Annaba.	☎ (8) 844983	38		
▲ **Béchar** - Centre Ville Hai Essalem.	☎ (7) 810844	50		
▲ **Biskra** Cité des Moudjahidines, Biskra.	☎ (4) 714835	50		
▲ **Blida** Route du Nouveau Stade, Blida	☎ 03 416601 ☎ 03 416601	50		0.4N
△ *Bordj-Bou-Arreridj* Ave du 24 Avril, Route de Setif, Bordj-Bou-Arreridj.	☎ (213) 5699683	20		0.5E
▲ **Boumerdes** Auberge de Jeunesse, Boumerdes		50		0.2N
△ *Boussaada* Route de Biskra, BP 23, Wilaya de M'Sila.	☎ (5) 532258	50		
▲ **Cherchell** Route de Tenes, Wilaya de Tipasa.	☎ (9) 445914	50		
△ *Constantine* MJ Cité Filali, Constantine.	☎ 695461	25		
▲ **Djanet** Auberge de Jeunesse, Djanet, Wilaya D'illizi		50		0.2NE
△ *Douaouda-Marine* 23 Rue Bouzar Boulem, BP10, 42445 Wilaya de Tipaza.		40		
▲ **Elbayedh** Elbayedh Centreville.	☎ (7) 718825	50		
△ *Echlef Centre Ville* Echlef (Gare Ferroviaire).	☎ (213) 3777279	50		
▲ **El-Golea** Auberge de Jeunesse, El-Golea, Wilaya de Ghardaïa		50		
△ *El-Kala* Cité du 19 Juin, Wilaya de Tarf 36100.	☎ (8) 650534	40		
▲ **El-Oued** - Houari Boumediene AJ El-Oued, BP 151 - Zone Industrielle, Route de Tebessa, El-Oued.	☎ (4) 228196	50		
▲ **El-Oued** - AJ Taleb el Arabi El-Oued.	☎ (4) 229521	50		
▲ **Ghardaïa** Aj-Daïa-Ben-Daïa, RP 85CTR	☎ 09 871883 ☎ 09 871884	50		10S
▲ **Guelma** Rue Gahdour Tahar BP195.	☎ (8) 205953	42		

Location/Address	Telephone No. / Fax No.	Beds	Opening Dates	Facilities
▲ **Hammam Bouhadjar** Wilaya de Aïn-Temouchent.	☎ (7) 216706	100		👥 🍽 ♿ P 🖨
▲ **Hassi** Hassi - Messaoud Centre.		50		P
△ *Illizi* *AJ Tassili, Illizi 33000.*		50		🍹
△ *Jijel - AJ Taher* *Rue du 1er Novembre, Taher, Wilaya de Jijel.*	☎ (5) 960427	70		🍹 🖨
△ *Laghouat* *rue Emir Khaled, Wilaya de Laghouat.*	☎ (9) 722303	48		🍹
▲ **Laghouat** Route de Ghardaia, Laghouat.		50		👥 🍽 ♿ 🍹 P 🖨
△ *Lakhdaria* *Route de la Daira, Wilaya de Bouira 10200.*	☎ 522400	20		🍹 P
△ *Khenchela* *Auberge de Jeunesse Aïn Silone Khenchellol.*	☎ (4) 322803	80		P
▲ **Mostaganem** Plage Salamandre, Mostaganem.	☎ (6) 218984 🖷 (6) 218983	50		👥 🍽 🍹 P
△ *Nakhla* *APC Nakhla, Wilaya El-Oued 39180.*		50		🍹 P
△ *Oran* *AJ Oran, 3 rue Benadjila Lahouari, Seddikia, Wilaya d'Oran.*	☎ (6) 350245	40		🍹
△ *Oran* *AJ Oran, 19 rue Maoued Ahmed, Oran.*	☎ (6) 398026	40		
▲ **Ouargla** AJ Rose des Sables, Ave de la Palestine, Route de Ghardaïa, Ouargla.	☎ (9) 703820	40		P 🖨
▲ **Skikda** Cite Freres Saker		50		👥 🍽 ® 0.3N 🍹 P 🖨 ☕
▲ **Taghit** Wilaya de Bechar.		50		👥 🍽 ♿ 🍹 P
▲ **Tamanrasset** Ex centre culturel, Quartier Tahagart.	☎ (9) 734047	100		🍹 P
△ *Tebessa* *Cité Djebel Naouel, Route de Constantine, Tebessa.*	☎ (8) 975797	50		👥 🍽 2W P
△ *Tiaret* *AJ Machou Ahmed, Sougueur, 14000 W Tiaret.*	☎ (7) 288133	100		🍹 P 🖨
▲ **Tiaret** Auberge de Jeunesse, Centre Ville, Tiaret	☎ 07 429762	50		👥 🍽 ® 1NE ♿ P 🖨 ☕
△ *Tichy* *AJ Tichy, Wilaya de Bejaïa.*	☎ (5) 231460	40		👥 🍽 1S 🍹 P
△ *Tighzirt Sur Mer* *Tighzirt, Wilaya de Tizi-Ouzou.*	☎ (3) 258041	40		🍽 P

ALGERIA • ALGERIE • ALGERIA • ARGELIE

Location/Address	Telephone No. Fax No.	Beds	Opening Dates	Facilities
▲ **Tindouf** Tindouf Centre.	☎ (7) 932562, 932510	50	🗓	🚻 🍴 🚿 🅿
▲ **Tiout** Wilaya de Naama.	☎ (7) 761330	50	🗓	🚻 🍴 ♿ 🚿 🅿
▲ **Tissemsilt** Arib-Djillali, Tissemsilt	☎ 07 479131, 07 499592	50	🗓	🚻 🍴 Ⓡ 0.7S ♿ 🅿 🍽
▲ **Tizi-Ouzou** rue Boulila Amar, BP 456, Tizi-Ouzou.	☎ (3) 201212	50	🗓	🚿

SUPPLEMENTARY ACCOMMODATION
OUTSIDE THE ASSURED STANDARDS SCHEME

Location/Address	Telephone No.	Beds	Opening Dates	Facilities
Batna AJ Rachid Saidi, Rue des Abattoirs, Batna.	☎ (4) 553807	30	🗓	Ⓡ 🚿
Béchar ex Cantine Scolaire, Cité Riadi, 08000 Béchar.	☎ (7) 810844	50	🗓	🚿 🅿 🗄
Touggourt AJ Kheir-Eddine, Touggourt 30200, W Ouargla.	☎ (9) 674709, 673328	80	🗓	🍴 🚿 🅿 🗄

Australia

AUSTRALIE

AUSTRALIEN

AUSTRALIA

**Australian Youth Hostels Association Inc
Level 3, 10 Mallett Street, Camperdown,
New South Wales 2050, Australia.**

☎ (61) (2) 9565-1699
🖷 (61) (2) 9565-1325
E-mail: yha@yha.org.au
WWW address: http://www.yha.org.au

A copy of the Hostel Directory for this Country can be obtained from:
The National Office.

IBN Booking Centres for outward bookings

- **Adelaide** - YHA South Australia, 38 Sturt Street, Adelaide 5000, South Australia.
  ☎ (61) (8) 82315583,
  🖷 (61) (8) 82314219
- **Brisbane** - YHA Queensland,154 Roma Street, Brisbane, Queensland 4000.
  ☎ (61) (7) 32361680,
  🖷 (61) (7) 32361702
- **Melbourne** - YHA Victoria,205 King Street, Melbourne, Victoria 3000.
  ☎ (61) (3) 96707991,
  🖷 (61) (3) 96709840
- **Perth** - YHA Western Australia, 236 William Street, Northbridge, Perth, Western Australia 6003.
  ☎ (61) (8) 92275122,
  🖷 (61) (8) 92275123
- **Sydney** - YHA New South Wales,GPO Box 5276, 422 Kent Street, Sydney 2001, New South Wales.
  ☎ (61) (2) 92611111,
  🖷 (61) (2) 92611969

Capital:	**Canberra**
Language:	**English**
Currency:	**Australian dollar**

Population:	**18,600,000**
Size:	**7,686,848 sq km**

Australia

TASMANIA
Stanley
Wynyard
Devonport
George Town
Winnaleah
St Helens
Launceston
Deloraine
Great Lake
Queenstown
Bicheno
Strahan
Coles Bay
Oatlands
Swansea
Mt Field National Park
Triabunna
Derwent
Hobart
Hobart
Huon Valley
Port Arthur
Lune River
Bruny Island
Darwin
Darwin
Kakadu
Kununurra
Broome
Exmouth
L. Mackay
GIBSON DESERT
Ayers Rock
Carnarvon
Denham
WESTERN AUSTRALIA
Kalbarri
GREAT VICTORIA DESERT
Geraldton
Dongara
Kalgoorlie
Lancelin
Northam
Rottnest Island
Perth
Perth
Mundaring Weir
Fremantle
Bunbury
Dunsborough
Porongurup
Esperance
Augusta
Pemberton
Albany
200
400
600
800
1000
KM
0
200
400
600
MLS

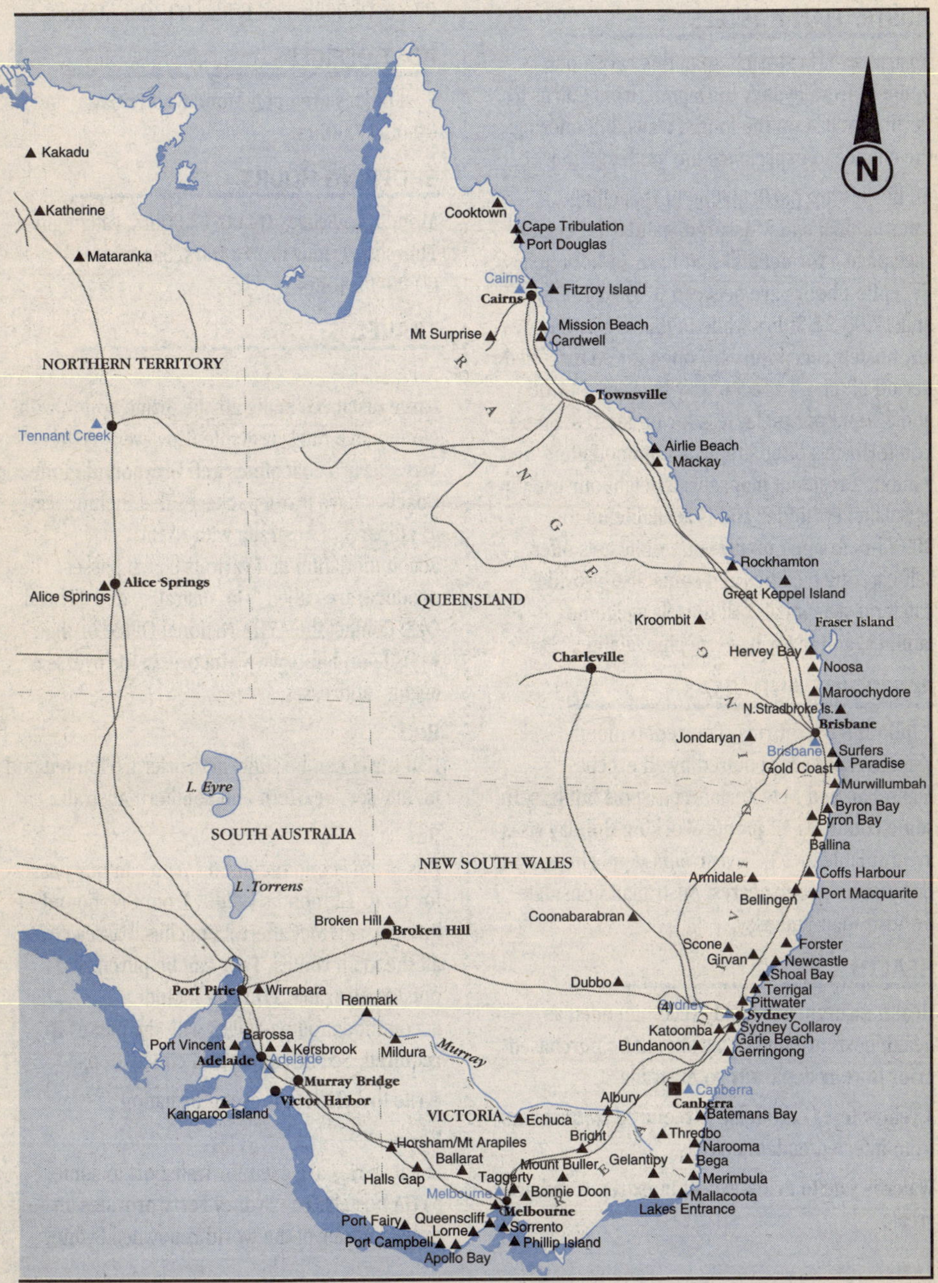

N
Kakadu
Katherine
Mataranka
NORTHERN TERRITORY
Tennant Creek
Alice Springs
Alice Springs
L. Eyre
SOUTH AUSTRALIA
L. Torrens
Port Pirie
Wirrabara
Renmark
Barossa
Port Vincent
Kersbrook
Adelaide
Adelaide
Mildura
Murray
Kangaroo Island
Murray Bridge
Victor Harbor
Horsham/Mt Arapiles
Ballarat
Halls Gap
Taggerty
Port Fairy
Queenscliff
Lorne
Port Campbell
Apollo Bay
Melbourne
Melbourne
Sorrento
Phillip Island
Bonnie Doon
VICTORIA
Echuca
Bright
Mount Buller
Gelantipy
Lakes Entrance
Cooktown
Cape Tribulation
Port Douglas
Cairns
Cairns
Fitzroy Island
Mt Surprise
Mission Beach
Cardwell
Townsville
Airlie Beach
Mackay
Rockhampton
Great Keppel Island
Fraser Island
Kroombit
Hervey Bay
Noosa
Maroochydore
N.Stradbroke Is.
Brisbane
Jondaryan
Brisbane
Surfers
Paradise
Gold Coast
Murwillumbah
Byron Bay
Byron Bay
Ballina
Coffs Harbour
Port Macquarie
Armidale
Bellingen
Coonabarabran
Scone
Forster
Girvan
Newcastle
Shoal Bay
Dubbo
Terrigal
Pittwater
Sydney
Sydney
Katoomba
Sydney Collaroy
Garie Beach
Bundanoon
Gerringong
Albury
Canberra
Canberra
Batemans Bay
Thredbo
Narooma
Bega
Merimbula
Mallacoota
QUEENSLAND
Charleville
NEW SOUTH WALES
Broken Hill
Broken Hill

English

AUSTRALIAN HOSTELS

Australian YHA Hostels span this enormous country, from Sydney to Darwin, from Cairns to Perth. Not just on the tourist trails, but offering the chance to experience the 'outback' too.

All hostels are participating in Hostelling International's new Assured Standards Scheme (see page 4 for details) and have 24 hour access. Reception hours are between 07.00-10.00hrs and 17.00-22.30hrs while in the larger 'Gateway' city hostels receptions are open for an extended period of time. Expect to pay between $11.00 and $20.00 per night, less for under 18s. Some Youth Hostels offer simple accommodation without a resident manager; a neighbour usually acts as a key holder and is available up to 20.00hrs to open up for you. All hostels offer self-catering facilities and some also provide cafeteria style meals. All hostels welcome families, and many have specific facilities.

PASSPORTS AND VISAS

A full valid passport is required. 6 month Visitors' visas are required by all except Australian and New Zealand passport holders. In some countries 12 month Working Holiday visas are available to 18-25 year olds. Apply in person or by post to your nearest Australian Consulate or Australian Embassy.

HEALTH

Health insurance is highly recommended as health costs are high. This should be purchased prior to your departure to Australia.

A yellow fever certificate is required by travellers from infected/endemic areas.

Water is safe to drink except in extreme outback areas.

BANKING HOURS

Banks are open Monday to Thursday, 09.30-16.00hrs and Friday 09.30-17.00hrs.

POST OFFICES

Post offices are open Monday to Friday, 09.00-17.00hrs.

SHOPPING HOURS

Monday to Friday, 09.00-17.00hrs. Late night Thursday/Friday to 21.00hrs. Saturday 09.00-17.30hrs.

TRAVEL

Air

Large distances make air the prime option with competitive rates available. However, AYHA, McCafferty's Coachlines and Greyhound Pioneer Coaches have travel packages that include travel to all parts of Australia with AYHA accommodation and various coach passes. These products are called "Go Australia" and "Travel Oz". Contact the AYHA National Office or their website on http://www.yha.org.au for overseas agents' addresses.

Rail

Rail travel can be slow, networks are limited and mainly serve eastern and southern Australia.

Bus

Bus is the economic option. You can buy passes for up to 12 months validity from Greyhound Pioneer and McCaffertys Coaches. Passes cover all the main routes. They can be purchased outside Australia. YHA can include accommodation packages with the passes if required. See discounts and concessions.

Write to AYHA for more information.

Ferry

Local ferries are used for transport to some AYHA hostels. The Sydney Ferry provides an excellent tour of the world renowned Sydney

Harbour. The main transport from Victoria to Tasmania is by overnight ferry.

Driving

An International Driving Licence is not required.

Hitch-Hiking

AYHA strongly recommends that you **DO NOT** hitch-hike in Australia.

TELEPHONE INFORMATION

Country Code	**61**
Main City Area Codes	
Adelaide	**8**
Brisbane	**7**
Cairns	**7**
Canberra	**2**
Darwin	**8**
Hobart	**3**
Melbourne	**3**
Perth	**8**
Sydney	**2**

Note: If phoning a hostel from within Australia add '0' in front of the area code shown in the hostel information.

Français

AUBERGES DE JEUNESSE AUSTRALIENNES

Les auberges de jeunesse Australiennes sont disséminées dans cet immense pays, de Sydney à Darwin, de Cairns à Perth, non seulement dans les régions fréquentées par les touristes mais aussi dans les coins reculés, pour vous permettre de les explorer.

Toutes les auberges participent au Plan Hostelling International pour la Garantie des Normes (voir page 12 pour plus d'informations). Elles sont également toutes ouvertes 24h sur 24. L'accueil est ouvert entre 7h00 et 10h00 et entre 17h00 et 22h30 bien que pour certaines grandes auberges dans les villes principales, la réception puisse rester ouverte au public plus longtemps. Une nuit vous coûtera entre 11 et 20 $, moins pour les moins de 18 ans. Quelques auberges offrent un logement simple, sans gérant à demeure; c'est en principe un voisin qui garde la clé et qui est disponible jusqu'à 20h pour vous faire entrer. Toutes les auberges ont des cuisines pour les voyageurs et certaines offrent des repas de style cafétéria. Toutes accueillent volontiers les familles et bon nombre d'entre elles offrent des services particuliers.

PASSEPORTS ET VISAS

Un passeport complet valide est nécessaire. Les visas temporaires de 6 mois sont nécessaires pour tous les voyageurs sauf pour ceux munis de passeports australiens et néo-zélandais. Pour certaines nationalités, des visas permettant au porteur de travailler pendant les vacances pour une durée maximale de 12 mois sont disponibles pour les jeunes de 18 à 25 ans. Adressez-vous en personne ou par écrit à votre consulat ou ambassade d'Australie le/la plus proche.

SOINS MEDICAUX

Il est vivement conseillé de souscrire à une police d'assurance maladie avant le départ pour l'Australie, car les frais médicaux sont élevés.

Un certificat de vaccination contre la fièvre jaune est obligatoire pour les voyageurs venant de régions où cette maladie sévit ou est endémique.

L'eau est potable sauf dans les régions très reculées.

HEURES D'OUVERTURE DES BANQUES

Les banques sont ouvertes du lundi au jeudi, de 9h30 à 16h et le vendredi de 9h30 à 17h.

BUREAUX DE POSTE

Les bureaux de poste sont ouverts du lundi au vendredi, de 9h à 17h.

HEURES D'OUVERTURE DES MAGASINS

Les magasins sont ouverts du lundi au vendredi, de 9h à 17h. Ils restent ouverts plus tard, jusqu'à 21h, le jeudi et le vendredi. Le samedi, ils sont ouverts de 9h à 17h30.

DEPLACEMENTS

Avions

Du fait des grandes distances à parcourir, les voyages aériens représentent la meilleure solution, et offrent des tarifs concurrentiels. Toutefois, l'AYHA (Association des Auberges de Jeunesse Australiennes), McCafferty's Coachline et Greyhound Pioneer Coaches (services de cars australiens) ont mis au point des options voyage qui comprennent des déplacements à destination de toutes les régions d'Australie avec hébergement en auberges de jeunesse AYHA et un choix de cartes-voyage en car. Ces forfaits s'appellent 'Go Australia' et 'Travel Oz'. Renseignez-vous auprès du bureau national de l'AYHA ou branchez-vous sur le site Internet de l'association (http://www.yha.org.au) pour obtenir les adresses d'agents à l'étranger.

Trains

Les services ferroviaires peuvent être lents, les réseaux sont limités et desservent surtout l'est et le sud de l'Australie.

Autobus

Les autobus représentent la solution la plus économique. Vous pouvez acheter des cartes valables 12 mois auprès de Greyhound Pioneer et McCaffertys Coaches. Les cartes sont valides pour tous les itinéraires principaux et peuvent être achetées dans d'autres pays. L'AYHA peut inclure votre hébergement dans votre forfait autobus, si vous le souhaitez. Voir la section intitulée 'Discounts and Concessions'. Ecrivez à l'AYHA pour de plus amples renseignements.

Ferry-boats

Des bateaux locaux sont utilisés pour transporter les voyageurs jusqu'à certaines auberges AYHA.

Le Sydney Ferry offre une excellente visite du port de Sydney, de renommée internationale. La traversée de Victoria jusqu'en Tasmanie se fait principalement en bateau de nuit.

Automobiles

Les permis de conduire internationaux ne sont pas nécessaires.

Auto-stop

L'AYHA vous conseille fortement de **NE PAS** faire d'auto-stop en Australie.

TELEPHONE

Indicatif du Pays   **61**
Indicatifs régionaux des Villes principales

Adélaïde	**8**
Brisbane	**7**
Cairns	**7**
Hobart	**3**
Canberra	**2**
Darwin	**8**
Melbourne	**3**
Perth	**8**
Sydney	**2**

Remarque: Pour téléphoner à une auberge depuis l'Australie, ajouter un '0' devant l'indicatif régional indiqué dans la liste des auberges.

Deutsch

AUSTRALISCHE JUGENDHERBERGEN

Die australischen YHA-Herbergen erstrecken sich über das ganze weite Land, von Sydney bis Darwin und von Cairns bis Perth. Sie befinden sich nicht nur in den Fremdenverkehrsgebieten, sondern bieten auch Gelegenheit zur Erkundung des 'Hinterlandes'.

Alle Herbergen sind 24 Stunden am Tag zugänglich und sind an dem 'Zugesicherten Standards' Plan des Hostelling International beteiligt (siehe Seite 20 für weitere Einzelheiten). Der Empfang ist von 07.00 - 10.00 Uhr und

17.00 - 22.30 Uhr geöffnet. In den großen Schlüsselherbergen, in den Stadtzentren, sind die Empfänge länger geöffnet. Es ist mit einem Preis von $11,00 bis $20,00 pro Nacht zu rechnen. Jugendliche unter 18 Jahren bezahlen weniger. Einige Herbergen bieten einfache Unterkünfte ohne einen in der Herberge wohnenden Verwalter. In diesem Fall verwahrt den Schlüssel normalerweise ein Nachbar, der bis 20.00 Uhr zur Verfügung steht, um Ihnen zu öffnen. Alle Herbergen haben Einrichtungen für Selbstversorger, und einige bieten auch Schnellgerichte an. Familien sind in sämtlichen Herbergen herzlich willkommen. Viele haben sogar besondere Einrichtungen für Familien.

PÄSSE UND VISA

Man braucht einen voll gültigen Reisepaß. Außer den Inhabern eines australischen oder neuseeländischen Reisepaß, benötigen alle Reisenden ein Besuchervisum mit einer Gültigkeit von 6 Monaten. Junge Leute im Alter von 18 bis 25 Jahren können in einigen Gegenden beim nächsten Australischen Konsulat oder bei der nächsten Australischen Botschaft persönlich oder auf dem Postweg ein 12 Monate gültiges Ferienarbeitsvisum beantragen.

GESUNDHEIT

Es empfiehlt sich sehr der Abschluß einer Krankenversicherung, da die Kosten für ärztliche Behandlung und Krankenhauskosten sehr hoch sind. Die Versicherung sollte schon vor der Abreise nach Australien abgeschlossen werden.

Von Reisenden, die aus infizierten/endemischen Gebieten kommen, wird ein Gelbfieber-Impfzeugnis verlangt.

Das Wasser kann überall, außer im äußersten Hinterland, bedenkenlos getrunken werden.

GESCHÄFTSSTUNDEN DER BANKEN

Banken sind montags bis donnerstags von 09.30-16.00 Uhr und freitags von 09.30-17.00 Uhr geöffnet.

POSTÄMTER

Postämter sind montags bis freitags von 09.00-17.00 Uhr geöffnet.

LADENÖFFNUNGSZEITEN

Montags bis freitags 09.00-17.00 Uhr, donnerstags/freitags bis 21.00 Uhr. Samstags 09.00-17.30 Uhr.

REISEN

Flugverkehr

Angesichts der großen Entfernungen sind Flugreisen, die sehr preisgünstig sind, die beste Lösung. Die AYHA, McCafferty's Coachlines und Greyhound Pioneer Coachlines bieten aber auch in allen Teilen Australiens Pauschalreisen mit AYHA-Unterkunft und verschiedenartigen Fahrkarten an. Diese Angebote heißen 'Go Australia' und 'Travel Oz'. Bitte verbinden Sie sich mit der Geschäftsstelle der australischen YHA oder ihrer Website Addresse: http://www.yha.org.au um die Adressen von Auslandsvertretungen zu bekommen .

Eisenbahn

Eisenbahnreisen sind oft langsam. Es steht nur ein beschränktes Netz zur Verfügung, das sich hauptsächlich über Ost- und Südaustralien erstreckt.

Busse

Busse sind ein preiswertes Verkehrsmittel. Greyhound Pioneer Coaches und McCaffertys verkaufen Pässe mit einer Gültigkeit bis zu 12 Monaten. Die Pässe gelten für alle Hauptstrecken. Sie können auch außerhalb Australiens gekauft werden. Auf Wunsch kann die YHA Unterkunftspauschalen in die Pässe einschließen (siehe Discounts und Concessions).

Fordern Sie bei der AYHA weitere Informationen an.

Fähren

Für die Fahrt zu einigen YHA-Herbergen werden örtliche Fähren verwendet. Die Sydney Ferry macht eine ausgezeichnete Rundfahrt durch den weltbekannten Hafen von Sydney. Das wichtigste Verkehrsmittel zwischen Victoria und Tasmania ist die Nachtfähre.

Autofahren

Es wird kein internationaler Führerschein verlangt.

Per Anhalter reisen

Die AYHA **RÄT DRINGEND DAVON AB**, in Australien per Anhalter zu reisen.

FERNSPRECHINFORMATIONEN

Landes-Kennzahl	61

größere Städte - Ortsnetzkennzahlen

Adelaide	8
Brisbane	7
Cairns	7
Canberra	2
Darwin	8
Hobart	3
Melbourne	3
Perth	8
Sydney	2

Zur Beachtung: Wenn Sie von Australien aus eine Herberge anrufen, fügen Sie vor der in den Herbergsinformationen stehenden Ortsnetzkennzahl eine '0' hinzu.

Español

ALBERGUES JUVENILES AUSTRALIANOS

Los albergues australianos están sembrados por todo este inmenso país, desde Sydney hasta Darwin y desde Cairns hasta Perth, y se encuentran no sólo en los puntos de interés turístico habituales, sino también en las zonas despobladas del interior, permitiéndole descubrir asimismo estas partes del país.

Todos los albergues participan en el nuevo Plan de Normas Garantizadas de Hostelling International (véase la página 28 para más información) y están abiertos las 24 horas del día. El horario de la recepción es de 7 h. a 10 h. y de 17 h. a 22.30 h., aunque en algunos albergues de las grandes ciudades, este horario suele ser más prolongado. Los precios oscilan entre 11 y 20 $ por noche, con tarifas reducidas para los menores de 18 años. Algunos albergues juveniles ofrecen alojamiento sencillo sin gerente residente. En éstos, un vecino suele tener la llave y se le puede pedir que abra el albergue hasta las 20 h. Todos los albergues tienen cocina para huéspedes y algunos también sirven comidas al estilo de las cafeterías. Todos ofrecen alojamiento a las familias y muchos de ellos proporcionan servicios específicos para ellas.

PASAPORTES Y VISADOS

Es necesario un pasaporte válido. Se exige un visado de visitante de 6 meses de duración a todos excepto a los titulares de pasaportes australianos o neocelandeses. Para ciertas nacionalidades, existe un visado que permite trabajar durante sus vacaciones a las personas de 18 a 25 años. Este es válido un máximo de 12 meses. Solicítelo personalmente o por correo a la embajada o consulado australianos más cercanos.

INFORMACION SANITARIA

Encarecemos a los viajeros se hagan un seguro médico antes de salir de viaje, ya que los cuidados médicos en Australia son caros.

Se exige un certificado de vacuna contra la fiebre amarilla a todos los visitantes procedentes de regiones contaminadas por esta enfermedad o donde ésta sea endémica.

El agua es potable excepto en zonas muy remotas.

HORARIO DE LOS BANCOS

Los bancos abren de lunes a jueves de 9.30 h. a 16 h. y los viernes de 9.30 h. a 17 h.

OFICINAS DE CORREOS

Las oficinas de correos abren de lunes a viernes de 9 h. a 17 h.

HORARIO COMERCIAL

Las tiendas abren de lunes a viernes de 9 h. a 17 h. Los jueves y viernes, algunas de ellas permanecen abiertas hasta las 21 h. Sábados: de 9 h. a 17.30 h.

DESPLAZAMIENTOS

Avión

Dadas las grandes distancias a recorrer, el avión es la mejor forma de transporte y las tarifas aéreas son muy competitivas. No obstante, la AYHA (Asociación de Albergues Juveniles Australianos) y las compañías de autocares McCafferty's Coachlines y Greyhound Pioneer Coaches han concertado viajes organizados por toda Australia que comprenden alojamiento en los albergues de la AYHA y diversos abonos de autocar. Estos productos son "Go Australia" y "Travel Oz". Póngase en contacto con la oficina nacional australiana de la AYHA o consulte su página en el Internet (http://www.yha.org.au) para averiguar las direcciones de los representantes de estas compañías en el extranjero.

Tren

Viajar en tren puede resultar lento, las redes son pocas y están limitadas principalmente al este y sur de Australia.

Autobús

El autobús es el medio de transporte más económico. Se puede conseguir un abono válido 12 meses para las compañías de autocares Greyhound Pioneer y McCafferty's. Este abono comprende todos los principales trayectos y es posible adquirirlo fuera de Australia. La AYHA

puede incluir el alojamiento en dicho abono si lo desea. Véase la sección 'Discounts and Concessions'.

Escriba a la AYHA para más información.

Ferry

Se utilizan barcos locales para transportar a los viajeros a algunos de los albergues de la AYHA. En el Sydney Ferry es posible realizar un excelente recorrido del mundialmente conocido puerto de Sydney. El principal medio de transporte entre Victoria y Tasmania es el ferry nocturno.

Automóvil

No es necesario tener un permiso de conducir internacional.

Autostop

La AYHA recomienda encarecidamente **NO** hacer autostop en Australia.

INFORMACION TELEFONICA

Código Nacional   **61**

Prefijos de las Ciudades Principales

Adelaide	**8**
Brisbane	**7**
Cairns	**7**
Canberra	**2**
Darwin	**8**
Hobart	**3**
Melbourne	**3**
Perth	**8**
Sydney	**2**

Nota: Para llamar a un albergue australiano desde Australia, es necesario marcar un '0' antes del prefijo indicado en la información sobre el albergue.

Discounts And Concessions

The following national and major state discounts are just a few of those available to YHA members who hold a current YHA membership card or Hostelling International Card.

Pick up a YHA Accommodation and Discount Guide which includes all the 800 discounts. This book is free for all Australian and overseas YHA members. Simply ask at any YHA hostel, YHA Membership & Travel Centre or YHA Membership Issuing Agency.

YHA Travel Insurance: 5-10% nationwide discount on all Australian and overseas travel insurance policies.

Travelex: 100% discount on commission charges for all foreign currency notes or foreign currency travellers cheques transactions. Travelex has currency exchange locations at airports all around Australia and city locations in Sydney, Melbourne, Brisbane, Cairns and Surfers Paradise. ☎ 1800 337 377 or 1800 649 565.

Eurail: Nationwide discounts for cash or cheque payments at all YHA Membership and Travel Centres.

Greyhound Pioneer: 5% off full fare Express and Pass products domestically and 15% off Pass products internationally when purchased from YHA Membership and Travel Centres.

McCafferty's Coaches: 10% discount on all McCafferty's passes and point-to-point tickets when purchased at YHA Membership & Travel Centres. 15% discount on passes and point-to-point tickets when purchased outside Australia.

Budget Rent-A-Car: Up to 30% discount. Rent a small manual car for seven days at $55.00 per day with unlimited kilometres. ☎ 1300 362 848 and quote BCD (Budget Customer Discount) number EO13609.

Avis Australia: offers members a minimum 30% off standard rates and, if applicable, a further 5% off promotional rates. Must quote No P081600 when making a reservation to receive the YHA rate. ☎ 1800 225533 or contact YHA Membership and Travel Centre.

Hertz Australia: Substantial discounts off car and commercial vehicle rentals. ☎ 133039 and quote CDP No 317961 for YHA rates. A small manual vehicle can be rented for $48 per day for 7 days.

Network Rentals: Nationwide discount from Network car and truck rentals - corporate rate (approximately 20% off). Contact YHA Membership & Travel Centres or Network offices nationally.

State Offices of AYHA as follows:-

New South Wales: 422 Kent Street, Sydney 2000
☎ (2) 92611111
✆ (2) 92611969
Northern Territory: 69 Mitchell St, Darwin 0801
☎ (8) 89816344
✆ (8) 89816674
Queensland: 154 Roma St., Brisbane 4000
☎ (7) 32361680
✆ (7) 32361702
South Australia: 38 Sturt Street, Adelaide 5000
☎ (8) 82315583
✆ (8) 82314219
Tasmania: 1st Floor, 28 Criterion Street, Hobart 7000
☎ (3) 62349617
✆ (3) 62347422
Victoria: 205 King Street, Melbourne 3000
☎ (3) 96707991
✆ (3) 96709840
Western Australia: 236 William Street, Northbridge 6003
☎ (8) 92275122
✆ (8) 92275123.

Adelaide

290 Gilles St,
Adelaide,
South Australia 5000.
☎ (8) 82236007
📠 (8) 82232888

Open Dates:	🗓
Reservations:	(IBN) (CC)
Price Range:	$14.00 ⊞
Beds:	52 - 3x² 1x⁴ 3x⁶ 3x⁶
Facilities:	♿ � ♂ 🛏 ⌨ 🖥 💼 ♣ 🅱 ⊜ ℹ 👥
Directions:	2S from city centre
✈	8km
A🚌	YH
🚂	Central 5km
🚌	171; 172
🚎	50m
Attractions:	🚴

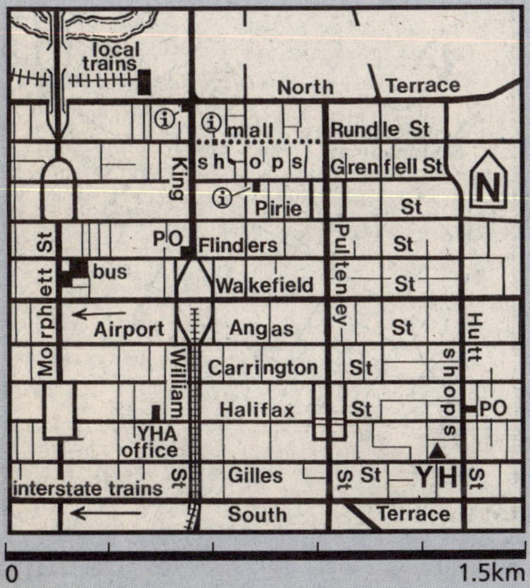

Airlie Beach

Club Habitat,
394 Shute Harbour Rd,
Airlie Beach,
Queensland 4802.
☎ (7) 49466312, (Freecall 1800 247251)
📠 (7) 49467053

Open Dates:	🗓
Open Hours:	07.00-19.00 (🕑 access to rooms)
Reservations:	(R) (CC)
Price Range:	$15.00-$19.00 ⊞
Beds:	80 - 4x² 8x³ 8x⁴ 8x⁵ 8x⁶
Facilities:	♂♂♂ 4x♂♂♂ ♂ 🛏 📺 🖥 💼 🅿 ℹ 👥
Directions:	
✈	Proserpine 45km
🚂	Proserpine 30km
🚌	200m
Attractions:	🔍 ∪ 🏊

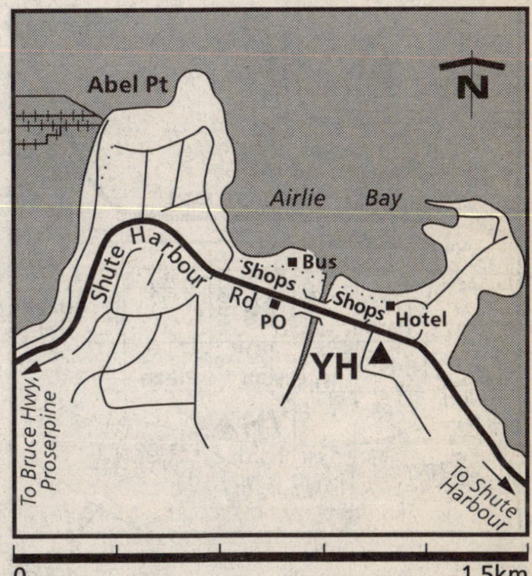

Alice Springs

Pioneer Hostel,
Corner of Parsons St and Leichhardt Terrace,
** Alice Springs,**
Northern Territory 0870.
❶ (8) 89528855
❶ (8) 89524144

Open Dates:	
Open Hours:	06.30-21.30hrs
	(Please ring if arriving after hours)
Reservations:	CC
Price Range:	$14.00 (Dorm Rate)
Beds:	62 - 13x⁴ 1x⁶ 1x⁶
Facilities:	

Directions:

✈	Alice Springs Airport 15km
A🚌	Airport Shuttle bus available ($9.00 one-way, $15.00 return)
🚂	Regular Services, "Ghan" Alice - Adelaide 2km
🚌	500m

Attractions: 🚴

Blue Mountains

66 Waratah St,
Katoomba,
New South Wales 2780.
❶ (2) 47821416
❶ (2) 47826203

Open Dates:	
Open Hours:	07.00-22.00hrs
Reservations:	R CC
Price Range:	$13.00-$25.00
Beds:	76 - 7x² 3x⁴ 4x⁶ 4x⁶
Facilities:	

Directions:

🚂	Katoomba 1km

Attractions: 🚴 🏃 ∪ ⚲3km 🏊1km

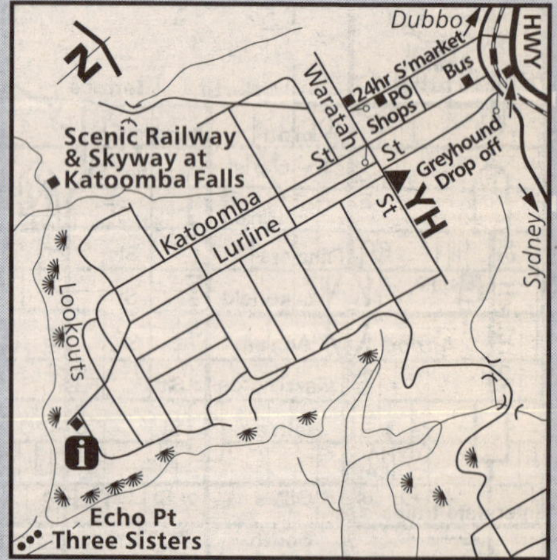

0   1.5km

0   3km

Brisbane

Brisbane City,
392 Upper Roma St,
Brisbane,
Queensland 4000.
☎ (7) 32361004
✆ (7) 32361947

Open Dates:	🗓
Open Hours:	06.30-22.30hrs (🕐 access to rooms)
Reservations:	Ⓡ ⌊IBN⌋ ⌊CC⌋
Price Range:	$16.00-$28.00 💱
Beds:	160 - 32x² 20x³ 6x⁴
Facilities:	♿ ⅲ ⅲ ☕ 🍴 🛏 📺 📖 💼 🏢 ⊜ 🅿 ℹ ♿

Directions:

✈	Brisbane International 25km
A🚌	Direct to YH
🚃	Roma Street 600m
🚌	Brisbane Transit Centre 600m ap Brisbane Transit Centre

Attractions: 🔍

Cairns - McLeod St

20-24 McLeod St,
Cairns,
Queensland 4870.
☎ (7) 40510772
✆ (7) 40313158

Open Dates:	🗓
Open Hours:	06.30-23.00hrs (🕐 access to rooms)
Reservations:	Ⓡ ⌊IBN⌋ ⌊CC⌋
Price Range:	$16.00-$19.00 💱
Beds:	170 - 16x² 10x⁶ 5x⁶
Facilities:	ⅲ 3x ⅲ 🍴 🛏 📺 📖 💼 🏢 8 🅿 ℹ ♿

Directions:

✈	Cairns International 8km
A🚌	Direct to YH
🚃	Bunda Street 200m
🚌	500m

Attractions: 🔍 ∪ 10km 🏊

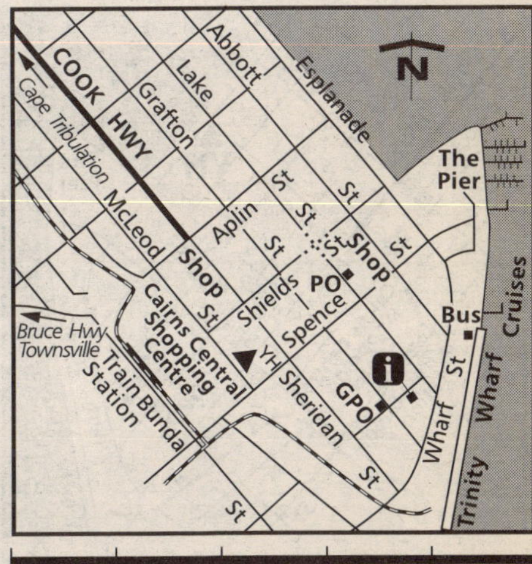

Cairns - Esplanade

93 The Esplanade,
Cairns,
Queensland 4870.
☎ (7) 40311919
✆ (7) 40314381

Open Dates:	🗓
Open Hours:	07.00-20.00hrs (⏱ access to rooms)
Reservations:	**R** ⊢CC⊣
Price Range:	$17.00-$20.00 🛏
Beds:	60 - 10x^2🛏 8x^6🛏
Facilities:	👬👬 ♂ 🛋 📺 📖 🔲 🧳 🏢 ⊜ ⓘ 🎱
Directions:	

✈	Cairns International 8km
A🚌	Direct to YH
🚂	800m
🚌	800m
Attractions:	🔍 ∪ 10km 🏊

Canberra

191 Dryandra St,
O'Connor,
Australian Capital Territory 2602.
☎ (2) 62489155
✆ (2) 62491731

Open Dates:	🗓
Open Hours:	07.00-22.00hrs
Reservations:	**R** (IBN) ⊢CC⊣
Price Range:	$17.00-$24.00 🏨
Beds:	124 - 7x^2🛏 17x^4🛏
Facilities:	👬 🍴 ♂ 🛋 📺 🔲 🏢 🅿 ⓘ ⚿ 🏔
Directions:	

✈	Canberra 14km
🚂	Kingston 10km
🚌	Jolimont Centre 5km
Attractions:	🌲 🏔 🚶 🏊 2km

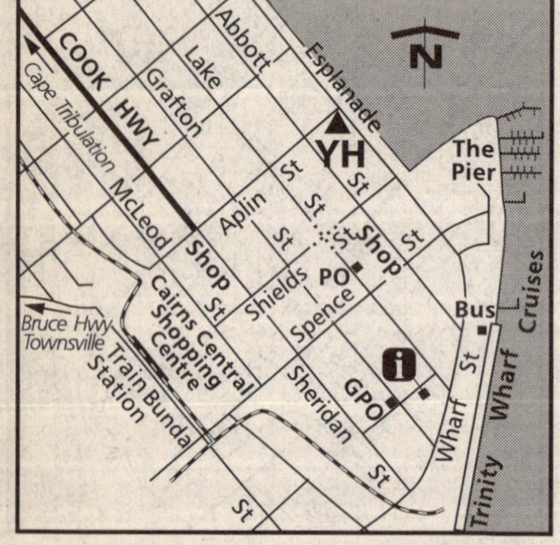

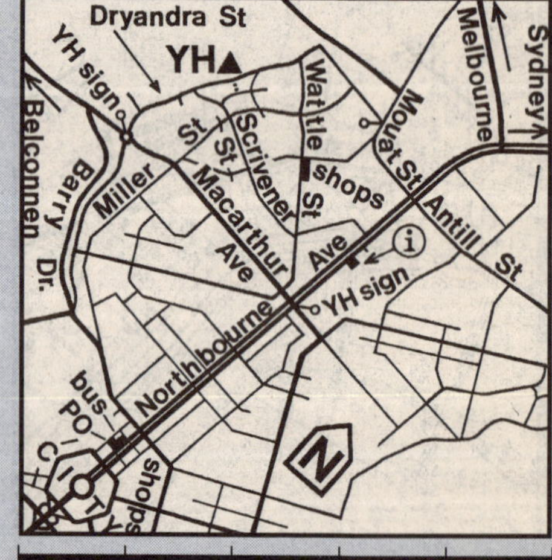

Darwin

69 Mitchell St,
Darwin,
Northern Territory.
(1,500km N of Alice Springs,
located in Darwin Transit Centre-coach and
Tour Terminus)
☎ (8) 89813995
🖷 (8) 89816674

Open Dates:	🗓
Open Hours:	⏲ Reception
Reservations:	Ⓡ IBN ⚏CC⚏
Price Range:	$15.00-$26.00 🏧
Beds:	292 - 10x¹🛏 27x²🛏 6x³🛏 49x⁴🛏 2x⁶⁺🛏
Facilities:	👥👥👤 ♿ TV 🖼 🅿 📷 🔢 ⊜ ⓘ 🎮 ♣

Directions:

✈	Darwin International 15km
A🚌	Free airport shuttle if reservation is made before arrival
🚌	Local Bus Depot 500m
🚋	Greyhound Pioneer; McCafferty's 200m

Attractions: 🚴

Fremantle

Backpackers Inn Freo,
11 Pakenham St,
Fremantle,
Western Australia 6160.
☎ (8) 94317065
🖷 (8) 93367106

Open Dates:	🗓
Open Hours:	07.00-23.00 (⏲ access)
Reservations:	Ⓡ ⚏CC⚏
Price Range:	$14.00-$17.00 🏧
Beds:	140 - 4x¹🛏 18x²🛏 12x⁴🛏 6x⁶🛏
Facilities:	♿ 👥 TV 🖨 ⚿ ⓘ 🎮

Directions:

A🚌	Bus ap hostel
🚢	Rottnest ferry - 4 mins walk
🚂	2 mins walk
🚌	2 mins walk

Attractions: 🔍 🚴 🏊

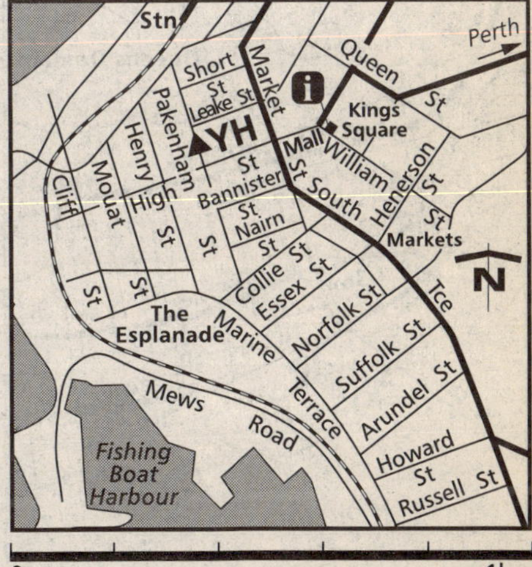

Hobart

Adelphi Court,
17 Stoke St,
New Town,
Hobart,
Tasmania 7008.
☎ (3) 62284829
✆ (3) 62782047

Open Dates:	🗓
Open Hours:	07.30-22.30hrs (16.12-15.03); 08.00-11.00; 15.00-21.30 (16.03-15.12)
Reservations:	R ⌐CC¬
Price Range:	$14.00-$19.00
Beds:	100 - 2x² 4x³ 14x⁴ 4x⁵ 1x⁶
Facilities:	††† 4x††† ▼◎(B) 🛏 💺 TV 🧺2x 🏕 🗄 🏢 P i 👪 ♿ 🔍 🌲 ⛩
Directions:	2N from city centre
✈	Hobart 18km
A🚌	Airporter ap hostel
⛴	Devonport 300km
🚌	25-42, 100, 105-128 stop 13; 15-16 stop 8A
Attractions:	🚴 🎣 1km ⛷ 1km

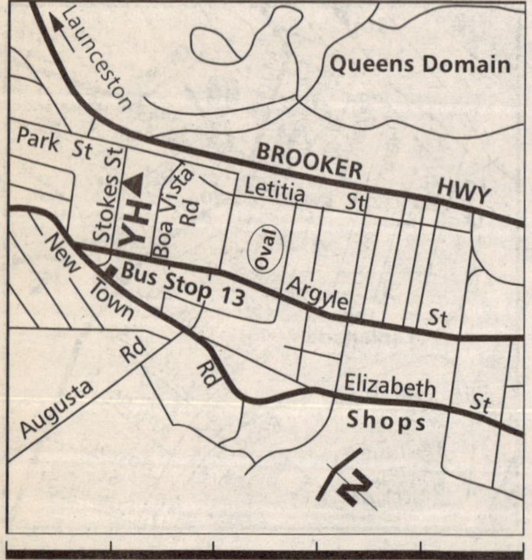

Melbourne - Queensberry Hill

Queensberry Hill YHA,
78 Howard St,
North Melbourne,
Victoria 3051.
☎ (3) 93298599
✆ (3) 93268427

Open Dates:	🗓
Open Hours:	🕐
Reservations:	IBN ⌐CC¬
Price Range:	$17.00-$18.00
Beds:	300 - 50x⁴ 2x⁶ 4x⁶
Facilities:	♿ ††† 30x††† ◎(BD) 🛏 💺 TV 🧺 🗄 🏢 8 ♿ P i 👪
Directions:	1.4N from city centre
✈	Melbourne 26km
A🚌	Skybus 100m
⛴	Station Pier 3.2km
🚂	Spencer St 1.4km
🚌	ap Franklin St
🚋	Tram 55 from William St 200m ap Queensberry St, stop 11
U	Melbourne Central 1km
Attractions:	🚴 ⛷ 1km

Melbourne -
Chapman Gardens

Chapman Gardens YHA,
76 Chapman St,
North Melbourne,
Victoria 3051.
(3) 93283595
(3) 93297863

Open Dates:	
Open Hours:	
Reservations:	CC
Price Range:	$16.00-$18.00
Beds:	100 - 40x² 2x³ 2x⁴ 2x⁶
Facilities:	

Directions:

✈	Melbourne 26km
A 🚌	Skybus 50m
🚢	Station Pier 4.2km
🚉	Spencer 2.5km
🚌	Franklin St 1.5Km; Spencer 2.5km
🚋	#57 from Elizabeth St, travel N ap Stop 18, Abbotsford St
U	Melbourne Central 1.2km

Attractions: 2km

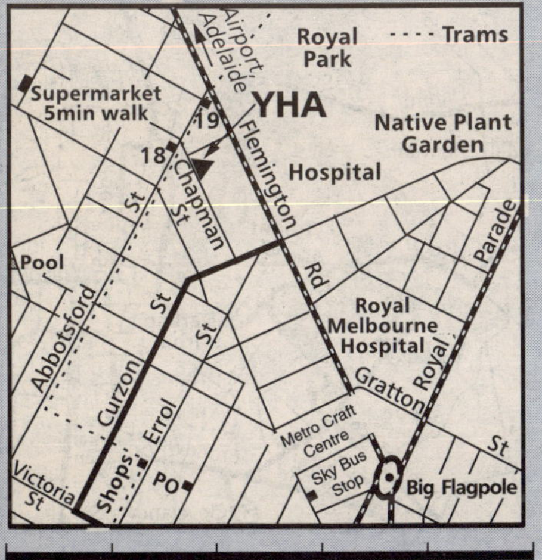

Perth - Northbridge

Northbridge YHA,
42-48 Francis St,
Perth,
Western Australia 6000.
(8) 93287794
(8) 93287794

Open Dates:	
Open Hours:	08.00-22.00hrs (may close 12.00-15.00hrs Wi only) check-in for advance bookings
Reservations:	R CC
Price Range:	$15.00-$18.00 (Free linen with weekly accommodation)
Beds:	108 - 4x² 2x⁴ 1x⁵ 8x⁶ 5x⁶
Facilities:	

Directions:

A 🚌	ap hostel
🚉	5 mins walk 200m
🚌	5 mins walk 200m

Attractions: 🚴

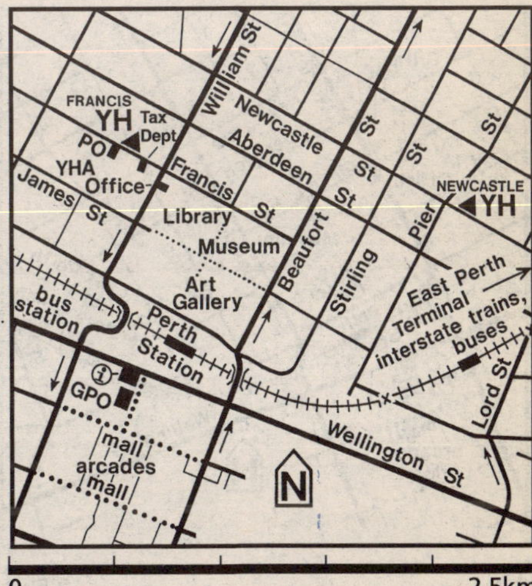

Perth - Britannia

Britannia International,
253 William St,
Perth,
Western Australia 6003.
☎ (8) 93286121
🖷 (8) 92279784

Open Dates:	
Open Hours:	
Reservations:	R IBN CC
Price Range:	$15.00-$19.00
Beds:	134 - 36x^1 25x^2 1x^3 5x^4 6x^6 4x^6
Facilities:	

Directions:

A	ap hostel
	5 mins walk
	5 mins walk from City bus station

Attractions:

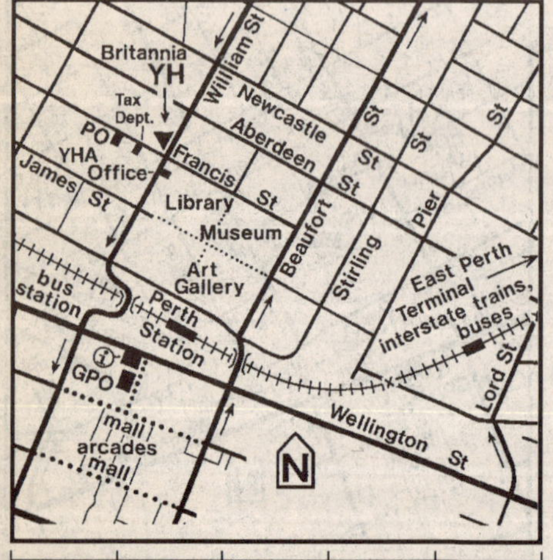

Sydney - Glebe Point

262 Glebe Point Rd,
Glebe,
New South Wales 2037.
☎ (2) 96928418
🖷 (2) 96600431

Open Dates:	
Open Hours:	07.00-19.30; 20.00-23.00hrs
Reservations:	IBN CC
Price Range:	$19.00-$25.00
Beds:	150 - 21x^2 19x^4 3x^5
Facilities:	

Directions:

✈	Sydney 16km
A	KST 16km
	Central 2.5km
	431 or 434 2.5km ap hostel 10m
U	Central Station 2.5km

Attractions: 2km

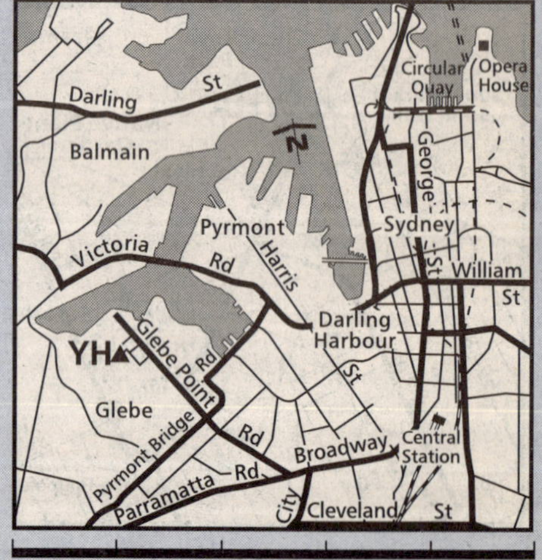

Sydney - Central

Sydney Central YHA,
11 Rawson Place. (cnr Pitt St and Rawson)
opposite Central Station
☎ (2) 92819111 ☏ (2) 92819199
ICN kiosk at hostel,
Kiosque ICN à l'auberge
ICN-Kiosk in der Herberge,
Quisco ICN en el albergue

Open Dates:	
Open Hours:	
Reservations:	IBN CC
Price Range:	$20.00-$32.50
Beds:	532 - 52x² 77x⁴ 12x⁶ 3x⁶
Facilities:	

Directions:

✈	Sydney 10km
A🚌	Airport Express 100m
🚂	Central 100m
🚌	All buses stop at Central Station 100m ap Central Station
U	Central Station 100m

Attractions: 500m

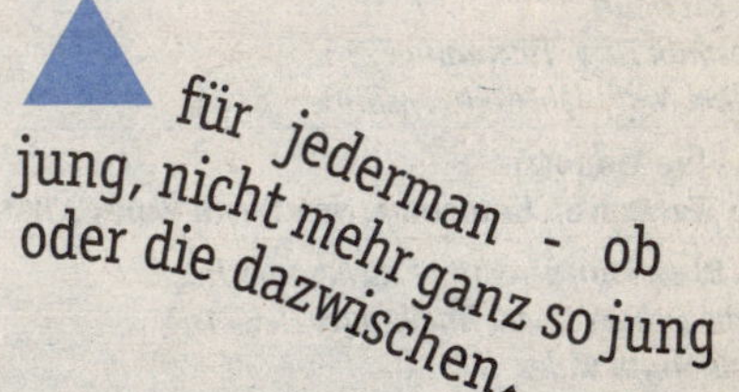

Location/Address	Telephone No. Fax No.	Beds	Opening Dates	Facilities
▲ **Adelaide** [IBN] **290 Gilles St, Adelaide, South Australia 5000.**	☎ (8) 82236007 🖷 (8) 82232888	52	🗓	🚻 2S ♿ CC 🔑 🖬
▲ **Airlie Beach** **Club Habitat, 394 Shute Harbour Rd,** **Airlie Beach, Queensland 4802.**	☎ (7) 49466312, (Freecall 1800 247251) 🖷 (7) 49467053	80	🗓	🚻 R CC 🔑 P 🖬
▲ **Albany** - Bayview YHA 49 Duke St, Albany, Western Australia 6330.	☎ (8) 98423388 🖷 (8) 98423388	63	🗓	🚻 CC 🔑 🖬
▲ **Albury-Wodonga** - Albury Motor Village YHA 372 Wagga Rd (Hume Hwy), Lavington 2641.	☎ (2) 60402999 🖷 (2) 60403160	24	🗓	🚻 4.6N CC 🔑 P 🖬
▲ **Alice Springs** **Pioneer Hostel,** **Corner of Parsons St and Leichhardt Terrace,** **Alice Springs, Northern Territory 0870.**	☎ (8) 89528855 🖷 (8) 89524144	62	🗓	🚻 CC 🔑 🖬
▲ **Apollo Bay** - Surfside Backpackers YHA Corner Great Ocean Road and Gambier Street, Apollo Bay, Victoria 3233	☎ (3) 52377263, (Freecall 1800 357263)	22	🗓	🚻 R 0.2S ♿ CC 🔑 P 🖬
▲ **Armidale** Pembroke Leisure Park, 39 Waterfall Way, Armidale, New South Wales 2350.	☎ (2) 67726470 🖷 (2) 67729804	40	🗓	CC 🔑 P 🖬
▲ **Augusta** 88 Blackwood Ave, Augusta, WA 6290. (320km S of Perth)	☎ (8) 97581290 🖷 (8) 97581291	36	🗓	🚻 R ♿ CC 🔑 P 🖬
▲ **Ballarat** Sovereign Hill Lodge YHA, Magpie St, Sovereign Hill, Ballarat, Victoria 3350.	☎ (3) 53333409, 53311944 🖷 (3) 53335861	16	🗓	🚻 R CC 🔑 P 🖬
▲ **Ballina** Traveller's Lodge, 36 Tamar St, Ballina, New South Wales 2478.	☎ (2) 66866737 🖷 (2) 66866342	18	🗓	🚻 CC 🔑 P 🖬
▲ **Batemans Bay** Batemans Bay Tourist Park, Old Princes Hwy, Batemans Bay, New South Wales 2536.	☎ (2) 44724972 🖷 (2) 44724045	22	🗓	🚻 1SE CC P 🖬
▲ **Bega** 3 Kirkland Crescent, Bega, New South Wales 2550.	☎ (2) 64923103 🖷 (2) 64922335	20	🗓	🔑 P
▲ **Bellingen** Bellingen YHA Backpackers, 2 Short St, Bellingen NSW 2454.	☎ (2) 66551116 🖷 (2) 66551358	20	🗓	🚻 0.1SE 🔑 P 🖬
△ *Bicheno* *Tasman Hwy, Tasmania 7215.* *(3km N of Bicheno township)*	☎ *(3) 63751293*	*18*	🗓	🔑 P 🖬
▲ **Blue Mountains** **66 Waratah St, Katoomba, New South Wales 2780.**	☎ (2) 47821416 🖷 (2) 47826203	76	🗓	🚻 R CC 🔑 P 🖬
△ *Blue Mountains* - Hawkesbury Heights *Hawkesbury Road, Hawksbury Heights,* *New South Wales, 2777.*	☎ *(2) 92611111*	*16*	🗓	P
▲ **Bonnie Doon** Lakeside Leisure Resort YHA, Hutchinsons Rd, Bonnie Doon, Victoria 3720.	☎ (3) 57787252 🖷 (3) 57787569	32	🗓	CC 🔑 P 🖬

Location/Address	Telephone No. Fax No.	Beds	Opening Dates	Facilities
▲ **Bright** - Bright YHA Hostel Cherry Lane, Bright, Victoria 3741.	☏ (3) 57501180 🖷 (3) 57501186	40		♠
▲ **Brisbane** ⟨IBN⟩ **Brisbane City, 392 Upper Roma St, Brisbane, Queensland 4000.**	☏ (7) 32361004 🖷 (7) 32361947	160		♠
▲ **Broken Hill** Tourist Lodge, 100 Argent St, Broken Hill, New South Wales 2880.	☏ (8) 80882086 🖷 (8) 80879551	79		♠
▲ **Broome** - The Last Resort 2 Bagot St, Broome, Western Australia 6725.	☏ (8) 91935000 🖷 (8) 91936033	100		♠
▲ **Bruny Island** "Lumeah", Quiet Corner, Main Rd, Adventure Bay, Tasmania 7150 (38km from 🛳; for transport to & from ☏ YH 1 day in advance)	☏ (3) 62931265 🖷 (3) 62931265	16		♠
▲ **Bunbury** - Backpackers Residency YHA Corner of Stirling & Moore Sts, Bunbury, Western Australia 6230.	☏ (8) 97912621 🖷 (8) 97914742	45		♠
▲ **Bundanoon** Railway Ave, Bundanoon, New South Wales 2578.	☏ (2) 48836010 🖷 (2) 48836010	37		♠
▲ **Byron Bay** - Cape Byron Hostel Cnr Byron & Middleton St, Byron Bay, New South Wales 2481.	☏ (2) 66858788, (Freecall 1800 652627) 🖷 (2) 66858814	124		♠
▲ **Byron Bay** - J's Bay Hostel 7 Carlyle Street, Byron Bay, New South Wales 2481.	☏ (2) 66858853, (Freecall 1800 678195) 🖷 (2) 66856766	100		♠
▲ **Cairns** - McLeod St ⟨IBN⟩ **20-24 McLeod St, Cairns, Queensland 4870.**	☏ (7) 40510772 🖷 (7) 40313158	170		♠
▲ **Cairns** - Esplanade **93 The Esplanade, Cairns, Queensland 4870.**	☏ (7) 40311919 🖷 (7) 40314381	60		♠
▲ **Carnarvon** Carnarvon Backpackers, 50 Olivia Terrace, Carnarvon WA 6701.	☏ (8) 99411095 🖷 (8) 99411095	60		♠
▲ **Canberra** ⟨IBN⟩ **191 Dryandra St, O'Connor, Australian Capital Territory 2602.**	☏ (2) 62489155 🖷 (2) 62491731	124		♠
▲ **Cape Tribulation** - Crocodylus Village Lot 5, Buchanan Creek Rd, Cow Bay, North Queensland 4873.	☏ (7) 40989166 🖷 (7) 40989131	110		♠
▲ **Cardwell** - Hinchinbrook Hostel 175 Bruce Hwy, Cardwell, Queensland 4849.	☏ (7) 40668648 🖷 (7) 40668910	40		♠
▲ **Coffs Harbour** 110 Albany St, Coffs Harbour, New South Wales 2450.	☏ (2) 66526462 🖷 (2) 66526462	52		♠
▲ **Coles Bay** - "Iluka Backpackers" Esplanade, Coles Bay, Tasmania 7215.	☏ (3) 62570115 🖷 (3) 62570384	32		♠

Location/Address	Telephone No. Fax No.	Beds	Opening Dates	Facilities
△ *Coles Bay - Freycinet National Park* *Coles Bay, Tasmania 7215.*	✆ c/o (3) 62349617	*10*		R ☕ P
▲ **Cooktown** Pam's Place, Cnr Boundary & Charlotte Streets, Cooktown 4871.	✆ (7) 40695166 📠 (7) 40695964	66		♦♦♦ CC ☕ P ▣
▲ **Coonabarabran** The Imperial Hotel, 70 John St, Coonabarabran, New South Wales 2357.	✆ (2) 68421023 📠 (2) 68422104	32		♦♦♦ CC ☕ P ▣
▲ **Darwin** IBN **69 Mitchell St, Darwin, Northern Territory. (1,500km N of Alice Springs, located in Darwin Transit Centre-coach and Tour Terminus)**	✆ (8) 89813995 📠 (8) 89816674	292		♦♦♦ R CC ☕ ▣
▲ **Deloraine** "Highview Lodge", 8 Blake St, Deloraine, Tasmania 7304.	✆ (3) 63622996	30		♦♦♦ ☕ P ▣
▲ **Denham** Bay Lodge, 95 Knight Terrace, Denham, Western Australia 6537.	✆ (8) 99481278 📠 (8) 99481031	22		♦♦♦ P ▣
▲ **Devonport** 'Mac Wright House', 115 Middle Rd, Devonport, Tasmania 7310.	✆ (3) 64245696 📠 (3) 64249952	42		♦♦♦ 2SW ☕ P ▣
▲ **Dongara** Dongara Backpackers, 32 Waldeck St, Dongara, Western Australia 6525. (350km N of Perth)	✆ (8) 99271581 📠 (8) 99271581	24		♦♦♦ 🍽 R CC ☕ P ▣
▲ **Dubbo** 87 Brisbane St, Dubbo, New South Wales 2830.	✆ (2) 68820922 📠 (2) 68820922	32		♦♦♦ CC ☕ P ▣
▲ **Dunsborough** Three Pines Resort, 285 Geographe Bay Rd, Quindalup, Western Australia 6282. (260km S of Perth)	✆ (8) 97553107 📠 (8) 97553107	70		♦♦♦ CC ☕ P ▣
▲ **Echuca** Echuca Gardens YHA Hostel, 103 Mitchell St, Echuca 3564, Victoria.	✆ (3) 54806522 📠 (3) 54826951	16		♦♦♦ R 0.8E CC ☕ P ▣
▲ **Esperance** Blue Waters Lodge, Goldfields Rd, Esperance, Western Australia 6450. (770km SE of Perth)	✆ (8) 90711040 📠 (8) 90711040	127		♦♦♦ CC ☕ P ▣
▲ **Exmouth** - Petes Exmouth Backpackers Cnr Murat and Turnscott Crescent, Exmouth, Western Australia 6707.	✆ (8) 99491101 📠 (8) 99491402	40		R CC ☕ P ▣
▲ **Fitzroy Island** Fitzroy Island Resort, Fitzroy Island, via Cairns, Queensland 4870.	✆ (7) 40519588 📠 (7) 40521335	118		🍽 35E CC ☕ ▣ ☕
▲ **Forster** Dolphin Lodge, 43 Head St, Forster, New South Wales 2428.	✆ (2) 65558155 📠 (2) 65558155	80		♦♦♦ R CC P ▣
▲ **Fremantle** **Backpackers Inn Freo, 11 Pakenham St, Fremantle, Western Australia 6160.**	✆ (8) 94317065 📠 (8) 93367106	140		R CC ☕ ▣

Location/Address	Telephone No. / Fax No.	Beds	Opening Dates	Facilities
△ *Garie Beach* *Royal National Park, New South Wales.* *(50km S of Sydney)*	☎ *(2) 92611111*	*12*	🗓	R
▲ **Gelantipy** Karoonda Park YHA, Gelantipy, Victoria 3885 (Via Buchan).	☎ (3) 51550220 📠 (3) 51550308	22	🗓	
▲ **Geraldtown** - Foreshore Backpackers 172 Marine Terrace, Geraldton, WA 6530	☎ (08) 99213275 📠 (08) 99213233	49	🗓	
▲ **George Town** "Travellers Lodge" 4 Elizabeth St, George Town, Tasmania 7253.	☎ (3) 63823261	18	🗓	
△ *Gerringong* *Nesta House, Fern St, Gerringong,* *New South Wales 2534.*	☎ / 📠 *(2)* *42341249*	*34*	🗓	
△ *Girvan* *via Stroud 2425, New South Wales.*	☎ *(2) 49976639*	*12*	🗓	P
▲ **Gold Coast** - Coolangatta YHA 230 Coolangatta Rd, Bilinga, Queensland 4225. (105km S of Brisbane)	☎ (7) 55367644 📠 (7) 55995436	80	🗓	R
▲ **Gold Coast** British Arms International Backpackers Resort, Mariner's Cove, 70 Seaworld Drive, Surfers Paradise, Queensland 4217.	☎ (7) 55711776, (Freecall 1800 680269) 📠 (7) 55711747	96	🗓	4N
▲ **Great Keppel Island** YHA Great Keppel Island (Keppel Haven), Great Keppel Island, Queensland 4700	☎ (7) 49275288 📠 (7) 49226040	50	🗓	R
△ *Halls Gap* *Grampians Rd, Halls Gap, Victoria 3381.*	☎ *(3) 53566221* 📠 *(3) 53566330*	*24*	🗓	
▲ **Hervey Bay** - Colonial Log Cabin Resort 820 Boat Harbour Drive, Hervey Bay, Queensland 4655.	☎ (7) 41251844 📠 (7) 41253161	90	🗓	
▲ **Hobart** **Adelphi Court, 17 Stoke St, New Town, Hobart,** **Tasmania 7008.**	☎ (3) 62284829 📠 (3) 62782047	100	🗓	R, 2N
▲ **Horsham** - Mount Arapiles "Tim's Place" YHA, Asplins Road, Quantong, Victoria.	☎ (3) 53840236 📠 (3) 53840236	25	🗓	R
▲ **Huon Valley** "Balfes Hill", Cradoc Rd, Cradoc, Tasmania 7109. (11km S of Huonville)	☎ (3) 62951551 📠 (3) 62951551	60	🗓	
▲ **Kalbarri** Kalbarri Backpackers, 2 Mortimer St, Kalbarri, Western Australia 6536. (589km N of Perth)	☎ (8) 99371430 📠 (8) 99371563	46	🗓	R
▲ **Kalgoorlie** Goldfield Backpackers, 166 Hay St, Kalgoorlie, Western Australia 6430.	☎ (8) 90911482 📠 (8) 90911484	36	🗓	
▲ **Kangaroo Island** - Penguin Walk YHA 33 Middle Tce, Penneshaw, Kangaroo Island, SA 5022	☎ (08) 85531233 📠 (08) 85531190	51	🗓	R, 110S

Location/Address	Telephone No. / Fax No.	Beds	Opening Dates	Facilities
▲ **Katherine** Palm Court Backpackers, Corner Third and Giles, Katherine, NT 0850.	☎ (8) 89722722 🖷 (8) 89711443	40		[CC] P
Katoomba ☞ **Blue Mountains**				
△ *Kersbrook* *Roachdale National Trust Property.* *(2km N of Kersbrook, 40km Adelaide)*	☎ (8) 82315583 🖷 (8) 82314219	*12*		[R] [2N] P
▲ **Kroombit** - Kroombit Tourist Park "Lochenbar", PO Box 135, Biloela, QLD 4715	☎ (7) 49922186 🖷 (7) 49924186	142		[35 E] [CC] P
▲ **Kununurra** Desert Inn, Cnr Konkerberry Drive & Tristania St, Kununurra, Western Australia 6743.	☎ (8) 91682702 🖷 (8) 91682271	28		[CC] P
▲ **Lakes Entrance** Riviera Backpackers YHA, 5 Clarkes Rd, Lakes Entrance 3909.	☎ (3) 51552444 🖷 (3) 51554558	56		[1 NE] [CC] P
▲ **Lancelin** Lancelin Lodge, 10 Hopkins St, Lancelin, Western Australia 6044.	☎ (8) 96552020 🖷 (8) 96552021	40		[CC] P
▲ **Lorne** Great Ocean Rd Backpackers YHA, 10 Erskine Ave, Lorne, Victoria 3232. (142km SW from Melbourne)	☎ (3) 52891809 🖷 (3) 52892508	22		[CC] P
▲ **Lune River** Main Rd, Lune River, Tasmania 7109.	☎ (3) 62983163; 62983117	20		P
▲ **Mackay** - Larrikin Lodge 32 Peel St, Mackay, Queensland 4740.	☎ (7) 49513728 🖷 (7) 49572978	22		P
▲ **Mallacoota** Mallacoota Lodge YHA, 51-55 Maurice Ave, Mallacoota 3892.	☎ (3) 51580455 🖷 (3) 51580453	12		[CC] P
▲ **Maroochydore** - Maroochydore YHA Backpackers 24 Schirrmann Drive, Maroochydore, Queensland 4558. (112km N of Brisbane)	☎ (7) 54433151 🖷 (7) 54433151	48		[CC] P
△ *Mataranka* *Mataranka Homestead, Mataranka,* *Northern Territory 0852.*	☎ (8) 89754544 🖷 (8) 89754580	*18*		[CC] P
▲ **Melbourne** - Queensberry Hill [IBN] **Queensberry Hill YHA, 78 Howard St,** **North Melbourne, Victoria 3051.**	☎ (3) 93298599 🖷 (3) 93268427	300		[1.4 N] [CC] P
▲ **Melbourne** - Chapman Gardens **Chapman Gardens YHA, 76 Chapman St,** **North Melbourne, Victoria 3051.**	☎ (3) 93283595 🖷 (3) 93297863	100		[CC] P
▲ **Merimbula** Wandarrah Lodge, 8 Marine Parade, Merimbula, New South Wales 2548.	☎ (2) 64953503 🖷 (2) 64953163	44		[R] [CC] P
▲ **Mildura** Rosemont Guest House YHA, 154 Madden Ave, Mildura 3500, Victoria. (560Km NW of Melbourne)	☎ (3) 50231535 🖷 (3) 50231535	10		[CC] P

Location/Address	Telephone No. Fax No.	Beds	Opening Dates	Facilities
▲ **Mission Beach** - Treehouse Bingil Bay Rd, Mission Beach, North Queensland 4854.	☏ (7) 40687137 🖷 (7) 40687028	60		[CC] ♂ P 🗄
▲ **Mount Field National Park** Main Rd, Mt Field National Park, Tasmania 7140.	☏ (3) 62881369	23		♁♁♁ ♂ P 🗄
▲ **Mt Buller** YHA Hostel Lodge, The Avenue, Mt Buller Alpine Village, Victoria 3723. (240km NE Melbourne)	☏ (3) 57776181 🖷 (3) 57776691	45	Jun–Oct	♁♁♁ Ⓡ [CC] ♂ 🗄
▲ **Mt Surprise** - Undara Experience Swags Tent Village, Lava Lodge, Undara, Queensland 4871. 270km West of Cairns.	☏ (7) 40971411 🖷 (7) 40971450	72		♁♁♁ ⵝⵣ Ⓡ [CC] ♂ P 🗄 ☕
▲ **Mt Warning** 1 Tumbulgum Rd, Murwillumbah, New South Wales 2484.	☏ (2) 66723763	24		[CC] ♂ P 🗄
▲ **Narooma** - Bluewater Lodge YHA 11-13 Riverside Drive, Narooma, NSW 2546.	☏ (2) 44764440 🖷 (2) 44763492	20		♁♁♁ 1N [CC] ♂ P 🗄
▲ **Newcastle** - Newcastle Beach YHA Backpackers 20 Pacific St, Newcastle, New South Wales 2291.	☏ (2) 49253944	100		[CC] ♂ 🗄
▲ **Noosa Heads** Halse Lodge Guest House, 2 Halse Lane, Noosa Heads, Queensland 4567.	☏ (7) 54473377, (Freecall 1800 242567) 🖷 (7) 54472929	74		ⵝⵣ [CC] ♂ P 🗄
▲ **North Stradbroke Island** Stradbroke Island Guesthouse, 1 East Coast Rd, Point Lookout, Queensland 4183.	☏ (7) 34098888 🖷 (7) 34098588	56		♁♁♁ [CC] ♂ P 🗄
△ *Oatlands* *9 Wellington St, Oatlands, Tasmania 7205.* *(80km N of Hobart)*	☏ *(3) 62541320*	*10*		♂ P 🗄
▲ **Pemberton** 'Pimelea Chalets', Stirling Rd, Pemberton, Western Australia 6260.	☏ (8) 97761153 🖷 (8) 97761819	63		♁♁♁ [CC] ♂ P 🗄
▲ **Perth** - Northbridge **Northbridge YHA, 42-48 Francis St, Perth, Western Australia 6000.**	☏ (8) 93287794 🖷 (8) 93287794	108		Ⓡ [CC] ♂ 🗄
▲ **Perth** - Britannia ⒾⒷⓃ **Britannia International, 253 William St, Perth, Western Australia 6003.**	☏ (8) 93286121 🖷 (8) 92279784	134		♁♁♁ Ⓡ ♿ [CC] ♂ 🗄
▲ **Perth Hills** Djaril-Mari YHA, Mundaring Weir Rd, Mundaring Weir, Western Australia 6073. (40km E of Perth-located in midst of bushland)	☏ (8) 92951809 🖷 (8) 92951809	36		♁♁♁ ⵝⵣ ♂ P
▲ **Phillip Island (Cowes)** Amaroo Park YHA, 97 Church St, Cowes, Phillip Island, Victoria 3922.	☏ (3) 59522548 🖷 (3) 59523620	50		♁♁♁ ⵝⵣ [CC] ♂ P 🗄 ☕
▲ **Porongurup** Porongurup Backpackers, Porongurup Rd, Porongurup, Western Australia 6324.	☏ (8) 98531110 🖷 (8) 98531116	15		♁♁♁ ⵝⵣ [CC] ♂ P 🗄

Location/Address	Telephone No. Fax No.	Beds	Opening Dates	Facilities
▲ **Port Arthur** Champ St, Port Arthur, Tasmania 7182. (100km S of Hobart)	☎ (3) 62502311	44		
▲ **Port Campbell** Port Campbell YHA, 18 Tregea St, Port Campbell 3269.	☎ (3) 55986305 ✆ (3) 55986305	38		0.1 W
▲ **Port Douglas** - Port O'Call Lodge Port St, Port Douglas, Queensland 4871.	☎ (7) 40995422 ✆ (7) 40995495	95		
▲ **Port Fairy** Port Fairy YHA Hostel, 8 Cox St, Port Fairy, Victoria 3284. (290km SW of Melbourne)	☎ (3) 55682468 ✆ (3) 55682302	50		
▲ **Port Macquarie** 40 Church St, Port Macquarie, New South Wales 2444.	☎ (2) 65835512 ✆ (2) 65835512	30		
▲ **Port Vincent** On Girl Guide property, Port Vincent, South Australia. (190km Adelaide)	☎ (8) 88537285, 88537030	45		
▲ **Queenscliff** - The Queenscliff Inn YHA Hostel 59 Hesse St, Queenscliff, Victoria 3225	☎ (3) 52584600 ✆ (3) 52581591	28		
△ *Renmark* *Renmark Holiday Hostel, Sixteenth St, Renmark 5341.*	☎ *(8) 85866937, (8) 85866839 after hrs)*	8		
▲ **Rockhampton** 60 MacFarlane St, North Rockhampton, Queensland 4701.	☎ (7) 49275288 ✆ (7) 49226040	52		
▲ **Rottnest Island** Rottnest YH, Kingstown Barracks, Western Australia 6161. (10km W of Perth)	☎ (8) 93729780 ✆ (8) 92925141	54		10 W
▲ **Sandy Creek** Pimpala Road, Barossa Valley, South Australia.	☎ (8) 85244135 (08.00-17.00hrs daily) ✆ (8) 82314219	16		
△ *Scone* *1151 Segenhoe Road, Scone, New South Wales 2337.*	☎ *(2) 65452072* ✆ *(2) 65452072*	24		
▲ **Shoal Bay** Shoal Bay YHA, 61 Beachfront Rd, Shoal Bay, New South Wales 2315.	☎ (2) 49842315 ✆ (2) 49841052	18		
▲ **Sorrento** Sorrento YHA Hostel, 3 Miranda St, Sorrento, Victoria 3943.	☎ (3) 59844323 ✆ (3) 59844323	30		
▲ **St Helens** 5 Cameron St, St Helens, Tasmania 7216.	☎ (3) 63761661	22		
▲ **Stanley** Wharf Rd, c/- Caravan Park, Stanley, Tasmania 7331.	☎ (3) 64581266 ✆ (3) 64581266	12		
▲ **Strahan** Harvey St, Strahan, Tasmania 7468.	☎ (3) 64717255 ✆ (3) 64717513	60		
▲ **Swansea** 5 Franklin St, Swansea, Tasmania.	☎ (3) 62578367	20		

Location/Address	Telephone No. Fax No.	Beds	Opening Dates	Facilities
▲ **Sydney** Sydney Beachouse, 4 Collaroy St, Collaroy Beach, New South Wales 2097.	☎ (2) 99811177 ✆ (2) 99811114	200		
▲ **Sydney** - Glebe Point [IBN] **262 Glebe Point Rd, Glebe,** **New South Wales 2037.**	☎ (2) 96928418 ✆ (2) 96600431	150		
▲ **Sydney** - Pittwater Halls Wharf, via Church Point, New South Wales 2105. (30km N of Sydney, W shore of Pittwater)	☎ (2) 99992196 ✆ (2) 99974296	32		
▲ **Sydney** - Central [IBN] **Sydney Central YHA,** **11 Rawson Place. (cnr Pitt St and Rawson)** **opposite Central Station**	☎ (2) 92819111 ✆ (2) 92819199	532		
△ *Taggerty* *Australian Bush Settlement YHA, Taggerty,* *RMB 2618 Alexandra, Maroondah Hwy, Victoria.* *(104km NE of Melbourne)*	☎ *(3) 57747378* ✆ *(3) 57747442*	*30*		
▲ **Tennant Creek** [IBN] 12 Davidson St, Tennant Creek, Northern Territory.	☎ (8) 89622207 ✆ (8) 89623188	27		
▲ **Terrigal** Terrigal Beach Lodge, 12 Campbell Crescent, Terrigal, New South Wales 2260.	☎ (2) 43853330 ✆ (2) 43853330	36		
▲ **Thredbo** 8 Jack Adams Path, Thredbo Alpine Village, New South Wales 2625.	☎ (2) 64576376 ✆ (2) 64576043	52		
▲ **Triabunna** Spencer St, Triabunna, Tasmania 7190.	☎ (3) 62573439	34		
▲ **Winnaleah** 'Merlinkei' Farm Hostel, 524 Racecourse Rd, Winnaleah, Tasmania 7265.	☎ (3) 63542152 ✆ (3) 63541000	22		
▲ **Wirrabara** Wirrabara State Forest, Wirrabara, Flinders Ranges, South Australia. (250km N of Adelaide SA)	☎ (8) 85684158	20		
▲ **Wynyard** 36 Dodgin St, Wynyard, Tasmania 7325.	☎ (3) 64422013	28		

SUPPLEMENTARY ACCOMMODATION
OUTSIDE THE ASSURED STANDARDS SCHEME

Location/Address	Telephone No. Fax No.	Beds	Opening Dates	Facilities
Kakadu National Park Gagudju Lodge Cooinda, Kakadu Hwy, NT 0886 PO Box 696 Jabiru NT 0886.	☎ (8) 89790145 ✆ (8) 89790148	76		

HOSTELLING INTERNATIONAL

Make your credit card bookings at these centres
Réservez par cartes de crédit aux centres suivants
Buchen Sie mit Kreditkarte in folgenden Buchungszentren
Reserve por tarjeta de crédito en los siguientes centros

English

Australia	☎ (2) 9261 1111
Canada	☎ (800) 663 5777
England & Wales	☎ (1629) 581 418
France	☎ (1) 44 89 87 27
Northern Ireland	☎ (1232) 324 733
Republic of Ireland	☎ (1) 830 1766
New Zealand	☎ (9) 303 9524
Scotland	☎ (541) 553 255
Switzerland	☎ (1) 360 1414
USA	☎ (202) 783 6161

Français

Angleterre & Pays de Galles	☎ (1692) 581 418
Australie	☎ (2) 9261 1111
Canada	☎ (800) 663 5777
Écosse	☎ (541) 553 255
États-Unis	☎ (202) 783 6161
France	☎ (1) 44 89 87 27
Irlande du Nord	☎ (1232) 324 733
Nouvelle-Zélande	☎ (9) 303 9524
République d'Irlande	☎ (1) 830 1766
Suisse	☎ (1) 360 1414

Deutsch

Australien	☎ (2) 9261 1111
England & Wales	☎ (1629) 581 418
Frankreich	☎ (1) 44 89 87 27
Irland	☎ (1) 830 1766
Kanada	☎ (800) 663 5777
Neuseeland	☎ (9) 303 9524
Nordirland	☎ (1232) 324 733
Schottland	☎ (541) 553 255
Schweiz	☎ (1) 360 1414
USA	☎ (202) 783 6161

Español

Australia	☎ (2) 9261 1111
Canadá	☎ (800) 663 5777
Escocia	☎ (541) 553 255
Estados Unidos	☎ (202) 783 6161
Francia	☎ (1) 44 89 87 27
Inglaterra y Gales	☎ (1629) 581 418
Irlanda del Norte	☎ (1232) 324 733
Nueva Zelanda	☎ (9) 303 9524
República de Irlanda	☎ (1) 830 1766
Suiza	☎ (1) 360 1414

Bahrain

BAHREIN
BAHRAIN
BAHRAIN

Bahrain Youth Hostels Society,
P.O. Box 2455,
H No.1105, R No.4225,
Block 342, Manama, Bahrain.

☎ (973) 727170
TX 8738 SHABAB BN
📠 (973) 7299190

Office Hours: 08.00-13.00; 15.00-22.30hrs

Capital:	Manama	Population:	515,000
Language:	Arabic, English	Size:	691 sq km
Currency:	Bd (Dinar)		

Bahrain

PERSIAN GULF
Al-Manamah
Al-Manamah
BAHRAIN
SAUDI
ARABIA
QATAR
Dukhan
N
10   20   30   KM
0
10   20   MLS

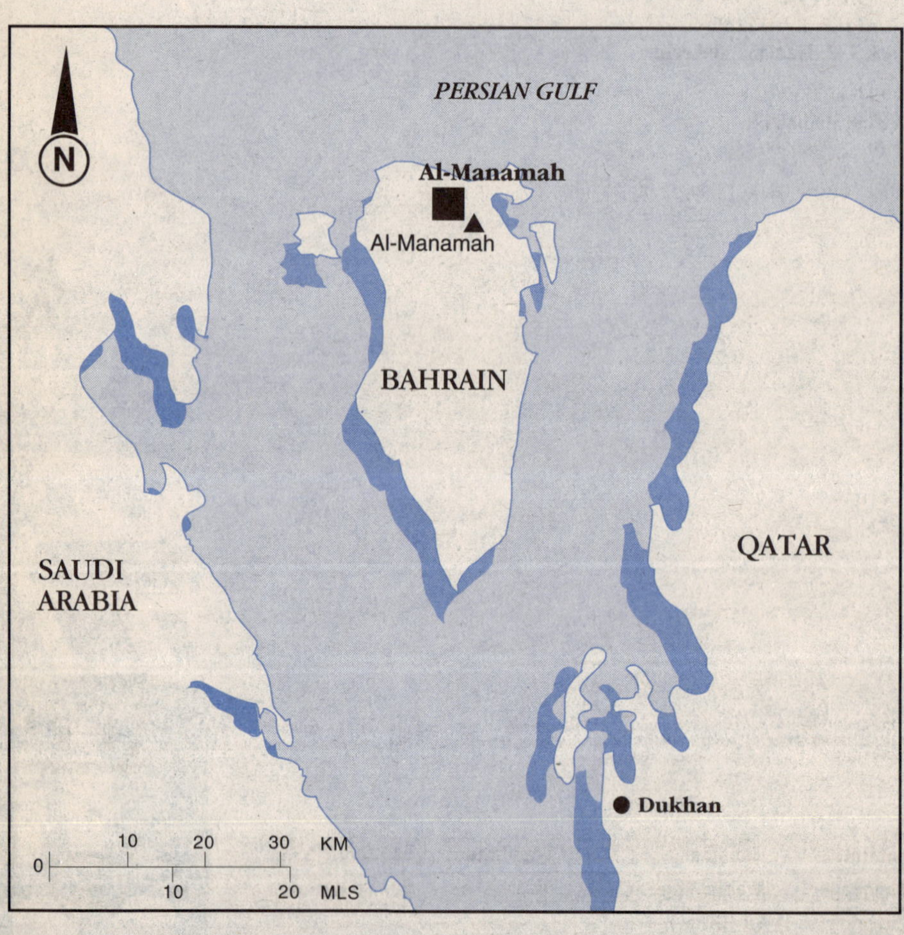

English

BAHRAIN YOUTH HOSTELS

As Bahrain has only two Youth Hostels it is vital to book at least 15 days in advance. Priority is given to younger members and the length of stay is limited to 6 nights.

TELEPHONE INFORMATION

Country Code 973
Main City Area Codes
   area code required

Français

AUBERGES DE JEUNESSE AU BAHREÏN

Le Bahreïn n'ayant que deux auberges de jeunesse, il est absolument nécessaire de réserver au moins 15 jours à l'avance. Priorité est donnée aux jeunes membres et les séjours sont limités à 6 nuits.

TELEPHONE

Indicatif du Pays 973
Indicatifs régionaux des Villes principales
   Pas d'indicatif régional requis

Deutsch

JUGENDHERBERGEN IN BAHRAIN

Da Bahrain nur zwei Jugendherbergen hat, muß man sich unbedingt mindestens 15 Tage im voraus anmelden. Jüngere Mitglieder werden bevorzugt aufgenommen, und die Länge des Aufenthalts ist auf 6 Übernachtungen beschränkt.

FERNSPRECHINFORMATIONEN

Landes-Kennzahl 973
größere Städte - Ortsnetzkennzahlen
   keine Ortsnetzkennzahl erforderlich

Español

ALBERGUES DE JUVENTUD DE BAHREIN

Como Bahrein sólo tiene dos albergues, es esencial hacer la reserva por lo menos con quince días de antelación. Tienen prioridad los más jóvenes y la estancia está limitada a seis noches.

INFORMACION TELEFONICA

Código Nacional 973
Prefijos de las Ciudades Principales
   No hace falta prefijo

Location/Address	Telephone No. Fax No.	Beds	Opening Dates	Facilities
▲ **Manama** Al-Juffair YH, Building 1105, Rd 4225, Block 342, PO Box 2455, Manama.	☎ 727170 ✆ 729919		🗐	
▲ **Muharraq** Al-Muharraq YH, Building 116, Rd 375, Block 450, PO Box 2455, Muharraq.	☎ 320015 ✆ 729919		🗐	

use International Communications Network (ICN) at major hostels to send and receive e-mail, set up e-mail box, send faxes, make International phone calls, surf the Web – all at low, low prices using the ICN Communications Card

Utilisez le Réseau International de Communication (ICN), dans nos plus grandes auberges pour envoyer et recevoir du courrier électronique, ouvrir une boîte à lettres électronique, transmettre des fax, appeler l'étranger, surfer sur l'internet – le tout à prix très très concurrentiels, grâce à la Carte de Communication ICN

benutzen Sie das International Communications Network (ICN) in Hauptherbergen, um e-mail zu senden und zu empfangen, e-mail Briefkästen einzurichten, Faxe zu schicken, international zu telefonieren oder "Surf the Net" – und das alles mit der ICN Kommunikationskarte zu günstigsten Preisen!

utilice la Red Internacional de Comunicaciones ICN en los principales albergues para transmitir y recibir mensajes electrónicos, establecer un buzón de correo electrónico, enviar facsímiles, realizar llamadas telefónicas internacionales, navegar por la red de Internet – todo a precios muy, muy económicos – mediante la Tarjeta de Comunicación ICN.

Brazil

BRESIL
BRASILIEN
BRASIL

**Federação Brasileira dos Albergues da Juventude,
Rua General Dionísio 63, Botafogo - Rio de Janeiro
CEP: 22271-050, Brazil.**

(55) (21) 2860303
(55) (21) 2865652
E-mail: info@hostel.org.br
WWW address: http://www.hostel.org.br

A copy of the Hostel Directory for this Country can be obtained from:
**Federação Brasileira de Albergues da Juventude,
Rua da Assembléia,
10-1616 Rio de Janeiro-RJ**

IBN Booking Centres for outward bookings

- **Rio de Janeiro** - Regional Office,
  Rua da Assembléia 10, Sala 1616
  (55) (21) 5312234
  (55) (21) 5311943
- **São Paulo** - Regional Office,
  Rua Sete de Abril, 386 Cj.22, CEP
  01044-908, São Paulo/SP.
  / (55) (11) 2580388
- **Porto Alegre** - Rio Grande du Sul
  Assoc., Rua dos Andradas, 1137 S.
  214 / (55) (51) 2265380
- **Curitiba** - Regional Office,
  Rua Padre Agostinho 645, Mercês
  (55) (41) 2332746
  (55) (41) 2332834

Capital:	Brasilia	Population:	140,340,000
Language:	Portuguese	Size:	511,965 sq km
Currency:	R$ (Real)		

Brazil

COLOMBIA
ECUADOR
Quito
PERU
Lima
AMAZONAS
ACRE
Rio Branco
Porto Velho
RONDONIA
BOLIVIA
La Paz
L. Titicaca
L. Poopo
Cuzco
PACIFIC OCEAN
Antofagasta
CHILE
N
Cordoba
AMAPÁ
Macará
Negro
Japurá
Amazon
Ucayali
Manus
Amazonas
Madeira
Belem
São Luis
PARÁ
Tocantins
BRAZIL
MATO GROSSO
Cuiabá
MATO GROSSO DO SUL
Campogrande
Paraguay
PARAGUAY
Pilcomayo River
Asuncion
Paraná
PARANA
Uruguay
RIO GRANDE DO SUL
Paraná
Salto Grande Dam
ATLANTIC OCEAN
CEARA
Fortaleza
Fortaleza
MARANHAO
Teresina
RIO GRANDE DO NORTE
Natal
João Pessoa
PARAIBA
Olinda
Recife
PIAUI
PERNAMBUCO
ALAGGAS
Maceió
Maceió
SERGIPE
Aracajœ
Salvador (2)
Salvador
DISTRITO FEDERAL
BAHIA
Brasília
Ilhéus
MINAS GERAIS
Belo Horizonte
Belo Horizonte
ESPIRTO SANTO
Guarapari
Cabofrio
SAO PAULO
Serra Negra
Itatiáia
Caraguatatuba
Pindamonhangaba
Campos de Jordão
Rio de Janeiro
Sao Paulo
Sao Paulo
Ubatuba
Rio de Janeiro
Guarujá
Curitiba
SANTA CATARINA
Florianópolis (2)
Florianópolis
Bento Gonçalves
Torres
Canela
Pôrto Alegre
Tramandai
400   800   1200   KMS
0
200   400   600   MLS

English

BRAZILIAN HOSTELS

The hostels in Brazil have different prices based on standards. Rates vary from R$ 7.50-14.00.

Hostels have on average around 50 beds and are all very cosy. Most hostels are open 24hrs, leaving you free to samba until the small hours!

PASSPORTS AND VISAS

Visa requirements vary so contact the Brazilian Embassy or Consulate in your own country before travelling.

HEALTH

Vaccinations are not required.

BANKING HOURS

National and exchange banks are open 10.00-16.00hrs.

SHOPPING HOURS

Shops are generally open Monday to Saturday, 09.00-18.00hrs. (Malls 10.00-22.00hrs).

TRAVEL

Travel is mostly by road. For long distances, the most convenient and economical method is to use the excellent bus service.

Air

Brazilian Airlines, Varig, offers an air pass permitting travel throughout Brazil for 21 consecutive days, visiting 5 cities, allowing 2 transfers, without mileage limit. Contact the Brazil Youth Hostel Federation for up-to-date information.

Bus

Brazil has an excellent bus network with budget prices. Bus stations are in all cities.

TELEPHONE INFORMATION

Country Code	**55**
Main City Area Codes	
Recife	**81**
Rio de Janeiro	**21**
Salvador	**71**
São Paulo	**11**

Français

AUBERGES DE JEUNESSE BRÉSILIENNES

Le prix de l'hébergement dans les auberges brésiliennes varie en fonction de la qualité des prestations. Les tarifs vont de 7,50 à 14.00 $R.

Les auberges disposent en moyenne de 50 lits et sont toutes très confortables. La plupart des auberges sont ouvertes 24 heures sur 24, ce qui vous permet de danser la samba jusqu'au petit matin!

PASSEPORTS ET VISAS

L'obtention d'un visa n'est pas tourjours nécessaire. Contactez l'Embassade ou le Consulat Brésiliens dans votre pays avant de commencer votre voyage.

SOINS MEDICAUX

Les vaccinations ne sont pas obligatoires.

HEURES D'OUVERTURE DES BANQUES

Les banques nationales et internationales sont ouvertes de 10h à 16h00.

HEURES D'OUVERTURE DES MAGASINS

Les magasins sont généralement ouverts du Lundi au Samedi entre 9h et 18h. (Centres commerciaux: 10h - 22h).

DEPLACEMENTS

Le transport se fait surtout par route. Pour les longues distances, le moyen le plus éfficace et économique de voyager est d'utiliser l'excellent service d'autocar.

Avions

La Ligne Aérienne Brésilienne, Varig, offre une carte d'abonnement aérienne qui permet de voyager à travers le Brésil pour un séjour de 21 jours consécutifs, de visiter 5 villes, et de faire 2 transferts, pour un kilométrage illimité.

Autobus

Le Brésil dispose d'un excellent réseau d'autocars dont les prix sont très compétitifs. Vous trouverez des gares routières dans toutes les villes.

TELEPHONE

Indicatif du Pays   **55**
Indicatifs régionaux des Villes principales
    Recife   **81**
    Rio de Janeiro   **21**
    Salvador   **71**
    São Paulo   **11**

Deutsch

BRASILIANISCHE JUGENDHERBERGEN

Die Jugendherbergen in Brasilien haben unterschiedliche Preise die auf Standarte basiert sind. Es ist mit einem Preis von R$ 7.50 - 14.00 zu rechnen.

Die meisten Jugendherbergen haben ungefähr 50 Betten, alle sind sehr komfortabel und 24 Stunden geöffnet, so daß Sie bis in die frühen Morgenstunden tanzen können!

PÄSSE UND VISA

Ein Visum ist unterschiedlich je nach Land erforderlich. Es wird empfohlen, daß Sie sich vor der Reise mit der Botschaft ihres Landes in Verbindung setzen.

GESUNDHEIT

Impfungen sind nicht benötigt.

GESCHÄFTSSTUNDEN DER BANKEN

Volksbanken und Wechselbanken sind von 10.00 Uhr bis 16.00 Uhr geöffnet.

LADENÖFFNUNGSZEITEN

Geschäfte sind im allgemeinen von Montag bis Samstag geöffnet (09.00-18.00 Uhr). Geschäftszentrum 10.00-22.00 Uhr geöffnet.

REISEN

Reiseverkehr ist meistens auf der Straße. Für Fernreisen ist es am günstigen und am billigsten, die ausgezeichneten Busverbindungen zu nutzen.

Flugverkehr

Die brasilianischen Fluglinien, Varig, bieten einen Flugausweis an, der das Reisen während 21 aufeinanderfolgenden Tagen durch ganz Brasilien, 5 Stadtbesuche und 2 Umsteigemöglichkeiten erlaubt, ohne Höchstkilometerzahl. Bitte setzen Sie sich mit der Brasilianische YHA in Verbindung.

Busse

Brasil hat ausgezeichnete Busverbindungen, die auch sehr günstig sind. Busbahnhöfe befinden sich in allen Städten.

FERNSPRECHINFORMATIONEN

Landes-Kennzahl   **55**
größere Städte - Ortsnetzkennzahlen
    Recife   **81**
    Rio de Janeiro   **21**
    Salvador   **71**
    São Paulo   **11**

Español

ALBERGUES JUVENILES BRASILEÑOS

Los precios de los albergues brasileños varían según la calidad de sus prestaciones. Las tarifas oscilan entre 7,50 y 14 \$R.

Los albergues son todos muy acogedores y tienen un promedio de 50 camas. La mayoría están abiertos las 24 horas del día, ¡así es que Ud. puede irse a bailar la samba hasta el amanecer!

PASAPORTES Y VISADOS

La necesidad de obtener un visado depende de su nacionalidad. Rogamos se ponga en contacto con la embajada o el consulado brasileños en su propio país antes de viajar.

ASISTENCIA MEDICA

No es necesaria ninguna vacuna.

HORARIO DE LOS BANCOS

Los bancos nacionales y los de cambio de divisas están abiertos de 10 h. a 16 h.

HORARIO COMERCIAL

Generalmente, las tiendas están abiertas de lunes a sábado, de 9 h. a 18 h. (Centros comerciales: 10 h. - 22 h.).

DESPLAZAMIENTOS

Los desplazamientos se realizan principalmente por carretera. La manera más económica y práctica de efectuar largos recorridos es mediante el excelente servicio de autocares.

Avión

La línea aérea brasileña Varig ofrece un abono aéreo que permite viajar por Brasil durante 21 días consecutivos, visitando un total de 5 ciudades, sin límite de kilometraje y efectuando 2 transbordos. Rogamos se ponga en contacto con la Federación Brasileña de Albergues Juveniles para obtener información actualizada.

Autobús

Brasil tiene una excelente red de autocares con tarifas asequibles. Encontrará estaciones de autocar en todas las ciudades.

INFORMACION TELEFONICA

Código Nacional   **55**

Prefijos de las Ciudades Principales

Recife	**81**
Río de Janeiro	**21**
Salvador	**71**
São Paulo	**11**

Rio de Janeiro

**Rua General Dionísio 63,
Botafogo,
22271-050 Rio de Janeiro,
RJ.**

☎ (21) 2860303,
✆ (21) 2865652

Open Dates:	
Open Hours:	
Reservations:	ⓡ (IBN) ⊂CC⊃
Price Range:	$14.00-18.00
Beds:	70 - 1x² 2x⁴ 1x⁵ 6x⁶ 2x⁶
Facilities:	(B) 1x

Directions:	8S from city centre
✈	Internacional 20km
⛴	Do RJ 11km
🚌	172, 176, 409 500m
Ⓤ	Botafogo 1.5km
Attractions:	

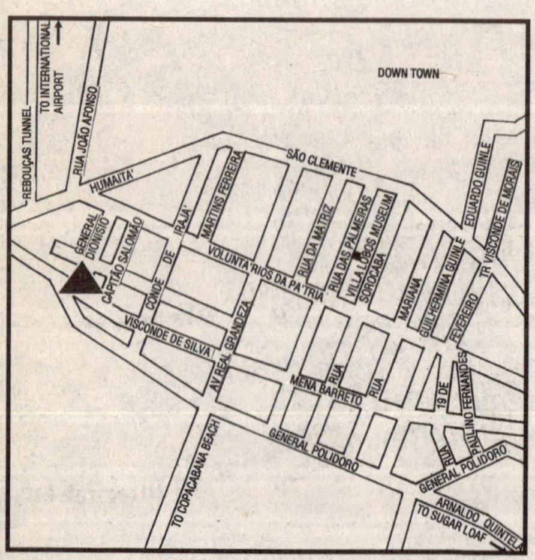

▲ There for everyone - young, not so young and those in the middle ▲

▲ c'est pour tout le monde - les jeunes, les moins jeunes et tous les autres ▲

▲ albergues para todos - los jóvenes, los menos jóvenes y los jóvenes de espíritu ▲

▲ für jederman - ob jung, nicht mehr ganz so jung oder die dazwischen ▲

Location/Address	Telephone No. Fax No.	Beds	Opening Dates	Facilities
△ *Angra dos Reis* *AJ Pousada Rio Bracuí, Estrada Santa Rita 4,* *Bracuí, Angra dos Reis/RJ, CEP 23900-000.*	(243) 631234 (243) 631234	40		R P
▲ **Bahia** - AJ Do Porto Rua Barão do Sergy 197, Barra-Salvador, Bahia. CEP 40140-040.	(071) 2478228 (071) 2478228	50		[5N]
△ *Barra do Piraí* *AJ Barra do Piraí-Dorândia,* *Estrada Fazenda Santa Rita, 1876 Dorândia,* *Barra do Piraí, Rio de Janeiro State. CEP 27160-000.*	(244) 425323	28		R P
△ *Belo Horizonte* *Chalé Mineiro, Rua Santa Luzia 288,* *30260-120 Belo Horizonte, MG.*	(31) 4671576	54		[3E] P
△ *Belo Horizonte* - AJ Pousadinha Mineira *Rua Araxá, 514-Floresta-Belo Horizonte-MG,* *CEP 31110-280*	(031) 4448205 (031) 4424488	78		
▲ **Bento Gonçalves** AJ Pousada Casa Mia, Travessa Niterói 71, 95700-000 Bento Gonçalves, RS.	(54) 4511215	54		R P
▲ **Bonito** - AJ de Bonito Rua Lucio Borralho, 716 - Villa Donária - Bonito - MS, CEP 79290-000	(067) 2551462 (067) 2551462	56		P
▲ **Búzios** - AJ Praia dos Amores Av Bento Ribeiro Dantas, 92 - Praia da Tartaruga - Búzios - RJ. CEP 28905-000.	(246) 232422	50		R [1N]
▲ **Cabo Frio** AJ São Lucas de Cabo Frio, Rua Goiás 266, Jardim Excelsior, 28915-170 Cabo Frio, RJ.	(246) 453037	36		R P
▲ **Canela** AJ Pousada do Viajante, Rua Ernesto Urbani 132, 95680-000 Canela, RS.	(54) 2822017	40		R [0.2S] P
△ *Caraguatatuba* *AJ Recanto das Andorinhas,* *Rua Engº João Fonseca 112, 11660-200* *Caraguatatuba, SP.*	(124) 221862	35		R P
▲ **Curitiba** [IBN] Rua Padre Agostinho 645, Mercês 80430-050, Curitiba, PR.	(41) 2332746 (41) 2332834	60		[3W] P
▲ **Florianópolis** - Canasvieiras R.Dr.João de Oliveira, 100, Florianópolis / SC-CEP:88054-120.	(48) 2251692 (48) 2251692	140		R P
▲ **Florianópolis** - Ilha de Santa Catarina Rua Duarte Schutel 227, 88015-640 Florianópolis, SC.	(48) 2253781 (48) 2251692	70		R [4N] P
▲ **Foz do Iguacú** Hostal Paudimar, Rod das Cataratas KM 6, Remanso Grande, Foz do Iguacú, PR 85863-000.	(45) 5722430 (45) 5722430	80		P

Location/Address	Telephone No. / Fax No.	Beds	Opening Dates	Facilities
▲ **Guarapari** AJ Guaralbergue, Avenida F, Quadra 40, Itapebussu, 29200- 000 Guarapari, ES.	☎ (27) 2610475 📠 (27) 2610475	100		⑂ ❍ Ⓡ 0.8S P
△ *Guarujá* *Rua das Camélias, 10 - Praia da Enseada - Guarujá, SP-CEP:11441-110.*	☎ *(013) 3517779*	46		⑂ Ⓡ 2NE P
▲ **Ilha Bela** - AJ Ilha Bela Av Cel José Vicente Faria Lima, 1243 Perequê, Ilha Bela/SP, CEP 11630-000.	☎ (012) 4728353 📠 (012) 4728353	65		⑂ ❍ 4S ♿ CC P ☕
△ *Ilha Grande* *Av Presidente Vargas 13, Praia do Abraão, CEP:20271-021, Angra dos Reis, RJ.*	☎ *(21) 2646147*	42		⑂ ❍ Ⓡ
▲ **Ilhéus** AJ Fazenda Tororomba, Rua Luiz Eduardo Magalhães S/N - Centro - Olivença - Ilhéus - BA, CEP:45650-000.	☎ (73) 2691139 📠 (73) 2691139	100		⑂ ❍ Ⓡ 5S ♿ P
△ *Maceió* *Nossa Casa, Rua Prefeito Abdon Arroxeles 327, Ponta Verde, 57035-380 Maceió, AL.*	☎ *(82) 2312246*	75		⑂ Ⓡ 6S ♿ P
▲ **Monteverde** - AJ Torre Branca Rua Pau Brasil, 28 - Monteverde - Camanducia MG, CEP 37653-000	☎ (035) 4381833 📠 (035) 4381833	66		⑂ ❍ 1S ♿ CC P ☕
▲ **Natal** - Lua Cheia Rua Dr Manoel Augusto Bezerra de Araújo, 500 Ponta Negra, Natal, R/N, CP 59090-430.	☎ (84) 2363696 📠 (84) 2363696	80		⑂ ❍ Ⓡ P
▲ **Olinda** Cheiro do Mar, Ave Ministro Marcos Freire 95, 53030-000 Olinda, PE.	☎ (81) 4290101	46		⑂ ❍ Ⓡ 1.5S P
▲ **Pindamonhangaba** AJ Recanto Tropical, R. DR Joáo Romeirão, 92, 12400-000 Pindamonhangaba, SP.	☎ (122) 422737	24		⑂ ❍ Ⓡ P
▲ **Porto Seguro** AJ Maracaia, Rodovia BR-367, Km 77, 5, 45820-000 Coroa Vermelha, Santa Cruz de Cabrália, BA.	☎ (73) 8721155 📠 (73) 8721156	180		⑂ ❍ Ⓡ 15N P
▲ **Porto Seguro** - AJ Porto Seguro R. Cova da Moça, 720 - Trevo de Porto Seguro - BA, CEP 45810-000.	☎ (73) 2881742 📠 (73) 2881742	80		⑂ ❍ Ⓡ
▲ **Praia do Forte** - AJ Praia do Forte Rua da Aurora No. 3, Praia do Forte/BA, CEP 48280-000	☎ (071) 8761094 📠 (071) 8761094	62		⑂ 0.2S ♿ P ☕
▲ **Rio de Janeiro** IBN **Rua General Dionísio 63, Botafogo, 22271-050 Rio de Janeiro, RJ.**	☎ (21) 2860303, 📠 (21) 2865652	70		⑂ ❍ Ⓡ 8S ♿ CC P
▲ **Salvador** - Casa Grande Rua Minas Gerais 122, Pituba, 41830-020 Salvador, BA.	☎ (71) 2480527 📠 (71) 2480527	50		⑂ ❍ Ⓡ 5N P

Location/Address	Telephone No. Fax No.	Beds	Opening Dates	Facilities
▲ **Salvador** - Do Pelô Rua Ribeiro dos Santos 5, Salvador, BA, CEP 40030-020.	☏ (71) 2428061, 📠 (71) 2428061	60		♐♐ ⊘ R ▣
▲ **São Paulo** Magdalena Tagliaferro, Estrada Turística do Jaraguá 651, Parque Estadual do Jaraguá, 05161-000 São Paulo, SP.	☏ (11) 2580388 📠 (11) 2580388	55		♐♐ R 18W CC P ▣
▲ **São Paulo** - AJ Praça Da Árvore Rua Pageú, 266 - Saúde - São Paulo - SP, CEP 04139-000	☏ (011) 50715148 📠 (011) 50715148	40		♐♐ ⊘ R 0.5NE CC ▣
▲ **São Roque** - AJ Palhoça Est da Bela Vista, 154- São Roque - SP, CEP 18130-000	☏ (011) 4254363	40		♐♐ ⊘ P ▣
▲ **Serra Negra** Estância Clube Veranêio, Rodovia Serra Negra, Águas de Lindóia, CEP:13970-000, SP: 156km Serra Negra.	☏ (19) 8922155	54		♐♐ ⊘ R 3E P ▣
▲ **Socorro** AJ Paschoalino Sígolo, Rua Antonio Leopoldino 215, 13960-000 Socorro, SP.	☏ (11) 2580388 📠 (11) 2580388	18		R 0.5S CC P ▣
▲ **Torres** AJ São Domingos, Rua Julio de Castilhos 875, 95560-000 Torres, RS.	☏ (51) 6641865 📠 (51) 6641022	150		♐♐ R P ▣
△ *Ubatuba* *AJ Cora Coralina, Rodovia Oswaldo Cruz, 89km,* *11680-000 Ubatuba, SP.*	☏ *(11) 2580388* 📠 *(11) 2580388*	*26*		♐♐ ⊘ R 6W CC P ▣

SUPPLEMENTARY ACCOMMODATION
OUTSIDE THE ASSURED STANDARDS SCHEME

Location/Address	Telephone No. Fax No.	Beds	Opening Dates	Facilities
Itatiaia AJ Ipê Amarelo, Rua João Mauricio de Macedo Costa 352, 27580-000 Itatiaia, RJ.	☏ (243) 521232	45		♐♐ ⊘ R 1E ♿ P ▣

HOSTELLING INTERNATIONAL

Make your credit card bookings at these centres
Réservez par cartes de crédit aux centres suivants
Buchen Sie mit Kreditkarte in folgenden Buchungszentren
Reserve por tarjeta de crédito en los siguientes centros

English

Australia	☎ (2) 9261 1111
Canada	☎ (800) 663 5777
England & Wales	☎ (1629) 581 418
France	☎ (1) 44 89 87 27
Northern Ireland	☎ (1232) 324 733
Republic of Ireland	☎ (1) 830 1766
New Zealand	☎ (9) 303 9524
Scotland	☎ (541) 553 255
Switzerland	☎ (1) 360 1414
USA	☎ (202) 783 6161

Français

Angleterre & Pays de Galles	☎ (1692) 581 418
Australie	☎ (2) 9261 1111
Canada	☎ (800) 663 5777
Écosse	☎ (541) 553 255
États-Unis	☎ (202) 783 6161
France	☎ (1) 44 89 87 27
Irlande du Nord	☎ (1232) 324 733
Nouvelle-Zélande	☎ (9) 303 9524
République d'Irlande	☎ (1) 830 1766
Suisse	☎ (1) 360 1414

Deutsch

Australien	☎ (2) 9261 1111
England & Wales	☎ (1629) 581 418
Frankreich	☎ (1) 44 89 87 27
Irland	☎ (1) 830 1766
Kanada	☎ (800) 663 5777
Neuseeland	☎ (9) 303 9524
Nordirland	☎ (1232) 324 733
Schottland	☎ (541) 553 255
Schweiz	☎ (1) 360 1414
USA	☎ (202) 783 6161

Español

Australia	☎ (2) 9261 1111
Canadá	☎ (800) 663 5777
Escocia	☎ (541) 553 255
Estados Unidos	☎ (202) 783 6161
Francia	☎ (1) 44 89 87 27
Inglaterra y Gales	☎ (1629) 581 418
Irlanda del Norte	☎ (1232) 324 733
Nueva Zelanda	☎ (9) 303 9524
República de Irlanda	☎ (1) 830 1766
Suiza	☎ (1) 360 1414

Canada

CANADA
KANADA
CANADA

**Hostelling International - Canada (National Office),
205 Catherine St, Suite 400, Ottawa,
Ontario K2P 1C3, Canada.**

☎ (1) (613) 237-7884
🖷 (1) (613) 237-7868
E-mail: info@hostellingintl.ca
WWW Address: www.hostellingintl.ca

A copy of the Hostel Directory for this Country can be obtained from:
The National Office, any hostel or regional office.

IBN Booking Centres for outward bookings

- **Edmonton**- Travel Shop, 10926-88th Avenue,Edmonton, Alberta, T6G 0Z1
  ☎ (1) (403) 4393089,
  🖷 (1) (403) 4337781
- **Montréal**- Tourisme Jeunesse, 4545 Pierre de Coubertin,CP 1000 Succursale M, Montréal, Québec H1V 3R2.
  ☎ (1) (514) 2523117,
  🖷 (1) (514) 2523119.
- **Ottawa**- *via National Office above.*
- **Vancouver**- Regional Office,134 Abbott Street, Suite 402, Vancouver, British Columbia.
  ☎ (1) (604) 6847101,
  🖷 (1) (604) 6847181.

Capital:	Ottawa	Population:	29,955,000
Language:	English, French	Size:	9,976,139 sq km
Currency:	$ (dollar)		

Canada

Great Bear Lake
NORTHWEST TERRITORIES
Dawson City
YUKON
Yellow Knife
Mackenzie
Great Slave Lake
Whitehorse
N
ALBERTA
BRITISH COLUMBIA
Edmonton
Edmonton
Jasper
Jasper
Maligne Canyon
Mount Edith Cavell
Athabasca Falls
Beauty Creek
Rampart Creek
Hilda Creek
Nordegg
Mosquito Creek
Lake Louise
Whiskey Jack
Castle Mountain
Calgary
Banff
Calgary
Yoho Nat'l Park
Ribbon Creek
Powell River
Whistler
Squilax
Kamloops
Big White
Fernie
Vancouver
Kelowna
Vancouver
Vancouver (2)
Penticton
Nelson
Victoria
Saltspring
Rossland
Island
Victoria
UNITED STATES OF AMERICA
200
400
600
KM
0
100
200
300
MLS

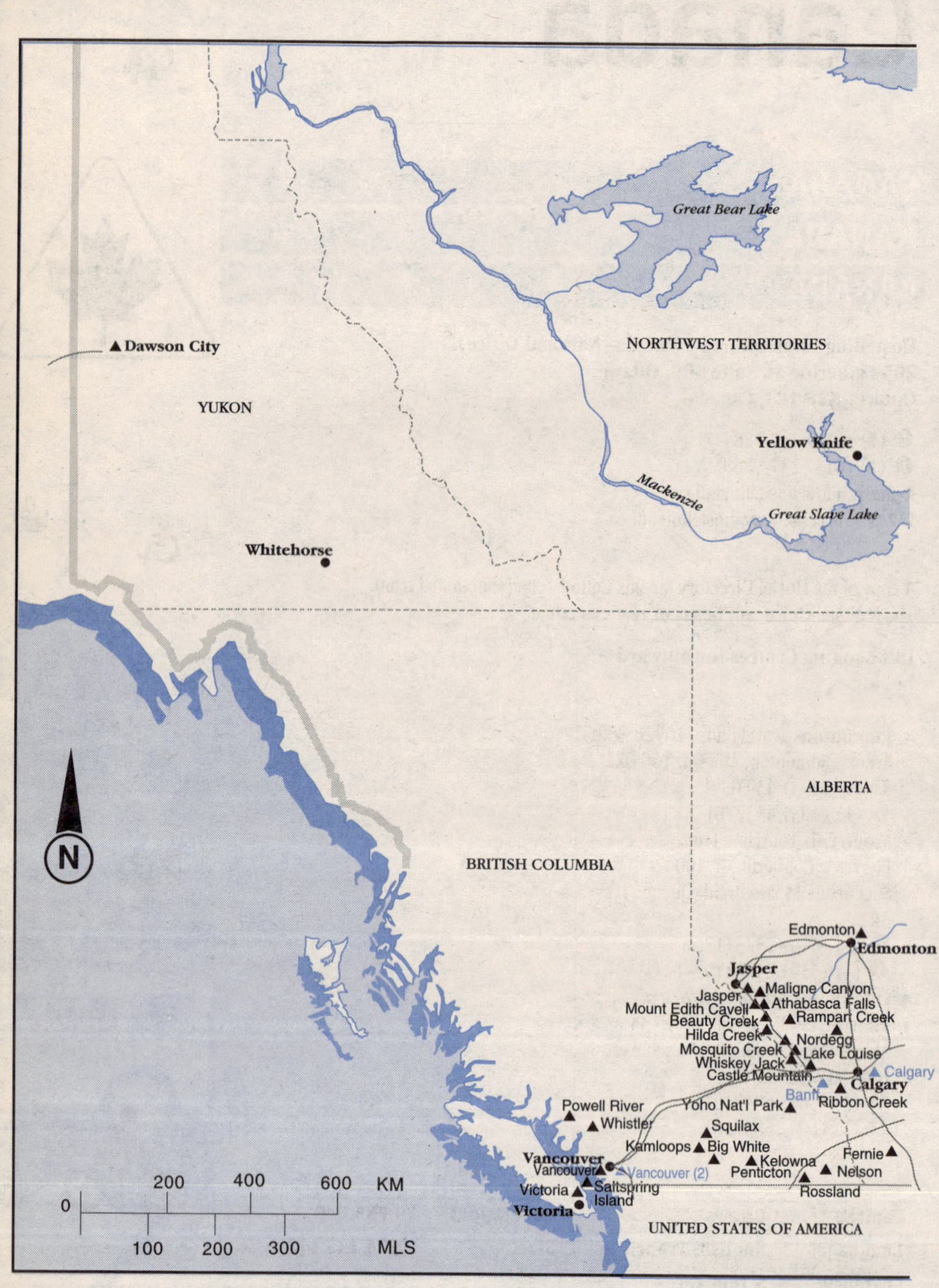

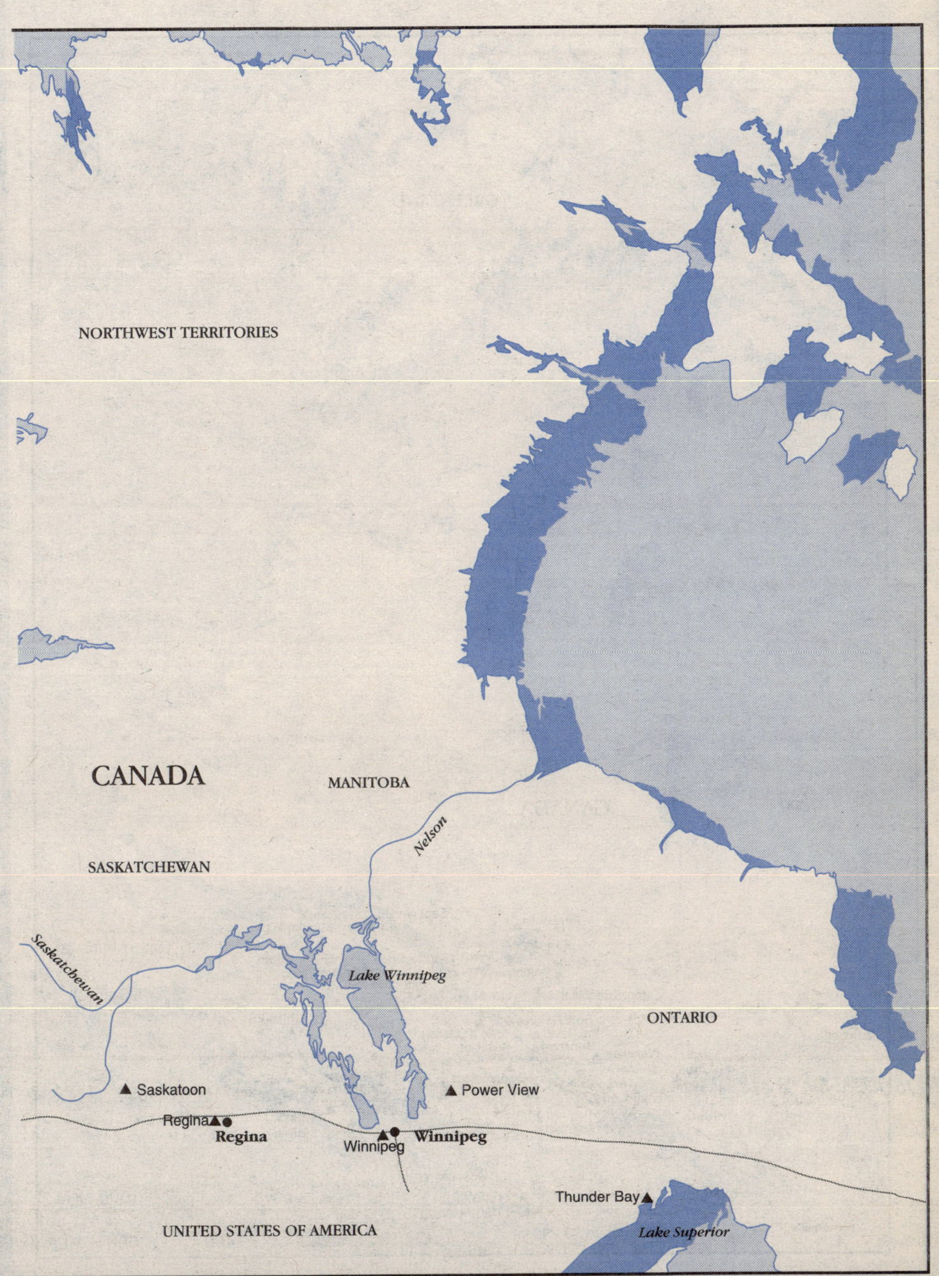
NORTHWEST TERRITORIES
CANADA
MANITOBA
SASKATCHEWAN
Nelson
Saskatchewan
Lake Winnipeg
ONTARIO
Saskatoon
Regina
Regina
Power View
Winnipeg
Winnipeg
Thunder Bay
UNITED STATES OF AMERICA
Lake Superior

Canada

N
GREENLAND
HUDSON BAY
QUEBEC
NEWFOUNDLAND
ONTARIO
CANADA
GULF OF ST. LAWRENCE
NEWFOUNDLAND
Thunder Bay
Peribonka
Sept Iles
Sainte-Anne-des-Monts
St Jean Lake
Saguenay River
Cap Aux Os
Lake Superior
La Togue
Jonquière
Tadoussac
Pointe-a-la-Garde
Campbellton
Saint-Luce-Sur-Mer
Mont Tremblant
Quebec
Quebec
Rivière-du-Loup
Nelson
Charlottetown
St John's
Sault Ste Marie
Fort Colouge
Trois Rivieres
Ile d'Orleans
NEW BRUNSWICK
Marquette
Ottawa
Val David
Racine
Wentworth
Wakefield
Montreal
MAINE
Alma
Montreal
Fredericton
Lake Huron
Orillia
Ottawa
St John
Halifax
Halifax
Barrie
Ottawa
Magog/Orford
NOVA SCOTIA
MICHIGAN
Peterborough
St. Lawrence
VERMONT
Toronto
Kingston
Annapolis Royal
La Have
Toronto
Lake Ontario
NEW YORK
South Milford
Niagara
NEW HAMPSHIRE
Lake Michigan
Detroit
Buffalo
Lake Eire
Hudson
Boston
Chicago
MASSACHUSETTS
Cleveland
RHODE ISLAND
PENNSYLVANIA
CONNECTICUT
Indianapolis
Pittsburgh
New York
500   1000 KM
0
200   400   600   MLS

English

CANADIAN HOSTELS

Hostels in all of Canada's major gateway cities and resort locations are open 24 hours. Most hostels offer full day and late night access all year round. Some hostels close during the day, between 10.00 and 17.00hrs, and some are seasonal hostels open only during the summer months - check individual entries for details.

Canada's 73 hostels cover almost everywhere you could want to visit and the variety is mind-boggling - take your pick from a lighthouse, a historic county jailhouse, a log cabin in the mountains, a refurbished dairy barn, a historic courthouse or a modern urban facility. Break away from the crowd and explore the wilderness, or live it up in the bright lights of the big city.

Expect to pay between $9.00 and $22.50 per night (based on shared accommodation), plus linen hire if needed. Private rooms are available at many locations and incur a slight surcharge. Down sleeping bags are recommended for hostels located in parks, especially Canada's Rockies, where night-time temperatures can be cool, even in summer. Major centres offer great value meals in their cafés or cafeterias. Self-catering kitchens are provided unless otherwise stated. Canada's hostels are pleased to provide non-smoking facilities for the comfort of all guests.

Many hostels offer activity programmes, especially during the summer months. Some organize outings such as walking tours, visits to local events and attractions, hiking trips and nature walks. Others work with reputable local operators to offer exciting programmes such as white water rafting, horseback riding, canoeing and whale watching. Each hostel will have full details of schedules and costs - enquire upon arrival.

To help give a wide coverage Hostelling International-Canada co-operates with private householders and other organizations to provide special types of hostels as follows:

HH Home Hostel
Limited number of beds in a private home, with basic hostel facilities. Meals or shared kitchen may be provided by the owner.

SA Supplementary Accommodation
eg YMCA, YWCA, University residence etc. Some will be without self-catering facilities.

PASSPORTS AND VISAS

A valid passport is required for travel in Canada from all countries but the United States (valid driver's licence suffices).

All visitors must have a return or onward ticket.

The maximum length of stay is 3 months unless indicated otherwise on your passport. For some countries it can be up to 6 months. Contact the Canadian High Commission or Embassy in order to check validity periods and whether or not you will require a visa.

HEALTH

Currently no vaccinations are required for travel in Canada.

BANKING HOURS

Normal banking hours in Canada are 10.00-17.00hrs, Monday to Friday. Most locations, especially those downtown or in tourist centres, have extended hours including evenings and weekends.

POST OFFICES

The normal opening hours for post offices throughout Canada are 09.30-17.00hrs (extended hours may exist in some locations).

SHOPPING HOURS

Normal hours for shopping throughout Canada are 09.00-17.00hrs. Many stores have extended hours one or two nights per week. Some cities also allow Sunday shopping. Tourist centres tend to offer extended hours.

TRAVEL

Rail

VIA Rail Canada offers the Canrail pass to international travellers. There are adult and youth rates as well as high and low season. Ask your travel agent for more information on pass options and validity. Canadians can also purchase within Canada.

Bus

GO Canada combines unlimited Greyhound bus travel with a 15 or 30 night hostel voucher package which is valid throughout Hostelling International-Canada's 73 hostel network. The bus pass includes extensive routes across Canada. GO Canada offers excellent flexibility and value to travellers wanting an affordable and fun Canadian holiday experience. This package is available year round and must be purchased prior to arrival in Canada. Domestic passes (sold in Canada) are also available, however, for the best value the GO Canada package is advised. Contact your local association office, travel agent or Hostelling International-Canada for more information.

Driving

Non-residents must have either a United States or International Driver's Licence. Car rental is available for visitors 25 years and over. With a major credit card, some rental firms go as low as 21 years. Check with the individual outlet.

TELEPHONE INFORMATION

Country Code	1
Main City Area Codes	
Calgary	403
Edmonton	403
Halifax	902
Montréal	514
Québec City	418
Toronto	416
Vancouver	604
Ottawa	613

Français

AUBERGES DE JEUNESSE CANADIENNES

Les auberges situées dans toutes les grandes villes d'accueil du Canada et les principaux lieux touristiques sont ouvertes jour et nuit. La plupart des auberges reçoivent les voyageurs toute la journée et jusqu'à une heure tardive toute l'année. Certaines auberges ferment dans la journée, entre 10h et 17h, et d'autres sont saisonnières et n'ouvrent que les mois d'été - voir la liste pour plus de renseignements.

Les 73 auberges du Canada se trouvent dans presque tous les endroits que l'on puisse souhaiter visiter et sont d'une variété stupéfiante - choisissez parmi un phare, une prison historique provinciale, une cabane en rondins de bois dans la montagne, une étable rénovée, qui abritait autrefois des vaches laitières, ou un bâtiment moderne en ville. Laissez les foules derrière vous et explorez les régions sauvages, ou bien allez vous amuser à la ville.

Une nuit vous coûtera entre 9 et 22.50 $ (sur la base d'un hébergement en commun; de nombreuses auberges offrent des chambres individuelles pour un petit supplément), plus location de draps le cas échéant. Les sacs de couchage en plumes ou duvet sont recommandés pour les auberges situées dans les parcs, surtout ceux des Montagnes Rocheuses, où la température nocturne peut être fraîche, même en été. Les centres principaux servent des repas très bon marché dans leurs cafés ou cafétérias. Il y a aussi des cuisines pour les voyageurs, sauf indication contraire. En outre, certaines salles sont réservées aux non-fumeurs pour le confort de tous les voyageurs.

Un grand nombre d'auberges mettent sur pied des programmes d'activités, surtout pendant les mois d'été. Certaines organisent des sorties: excursions à pied, visites de lieux d'intérêt et de manifestations locales, randonnées et promenades dans la nature. D'autres s'associent avec des organisations locales professionnelles pour offrir des programmes passionnants: descentes de rapides en radeau, randonnées à cheval, canoë et sorties à la découverte des baleines. Chaque auberge est en mesure de fournir des renseignements complets sur les programmes et les prix - informez-vous à votre arrivée.

Afin d'étendre le réseau d'auberges internationales le plus possible, le Canada coopère avec des particuliers et d'autres organisations et peut offrir des types spéciaux d'auberges comme suit:-

HH Home Hostel
Un nombre limité de lits chez l'habitant, avec des installations d'auberge simples. Il se peut que le propriétaire fournisse les repas ou accepte de partager sa cuisine.

SA Supplementary Accommodation
Par exemple, YMCA, YWCA, campus universitaire, etc. Certains établissements sont sans cuisine.

PASSEPORTS ET VISAS

Tous les visiteurs étrangers doivent être munis d'un passeport valide pour entrer dans le pays sauf les citoyens des Etats-Unis, pour lesquels un permis de conduire valide suffit.

Tous les visiteurs doivent avoir un billet indiquant leur intention soit de retourner dans leur pays soit de continuer leur voyage.

La durée maximale d'un séjour est de 3 mois sauf indication contraire sur le passeport. Pour certains pays, la durée maximale est de 6 mois. Renseignez-vous auprès du haut commissaire canadien ou de l'ambassade afin de vous assurer des périodes de validité et de savoir s'il vous faut un visa ou non.

SOINS MEDICAUX

A présent, aucune vaccination n'est nécessaire pour se rendre au Canada.

HEURES D'OUVERTURE DES BANQUES

Les banques canadiennes sont normalement ouvertes de 10h à 17h, du lundi au vendredi. La plupart d'entre elles, surtout celles qui sont situées dans les villes ou dans les centres touristiques, sont ouvertes plus longtemps, soirs et weekends y compris.

BUREAUX DE POSTE

Les bureaux de poste sont normalement ouverts, dans tout le pays, de 9h30 à 17h (parfois plus longtemps dans certains endroits).

HEURES D'OUVERTURE DES MAGASINS

Les magasins sont normalement ouverts, dans tout le pays, de 9h à 17h. De nombreux magasins ouvrent plus tard un ou deux soirs par semaine. L'ouverture des magasins le dimanche est autorisée dans certaines grandes villes. Les magasins ont tendance à ouvrir plus longtemps dans les centres touristiques.

DEPLACEMENTS

Trains
VIA Rail Canada offre la carte Canrail aux voyageurs internationaux. Il existe des tarifs différents pour les jeunes et les adultes et également en fonction de la saison. Renseignez-vous auprès de votre agence de

voyages pour en savoir plus sur les options et les périodes de validité. Les Canadiens peuvent également acheter cette carte sur le territoire canadien.

Autobus

Go Canada est un forfait qui comprend votre transport illimité en cars Greyhound et un avoir pour 15 ou 30 nuitées en auberge, valable sur l'ensemble du réseau d'auberges Hostelling-International-Canada. Go Canada offre une grande flexibilité et un excellent rapport qualité-prix aux voyageurs désireux de passer d'agréables et distrayantes vacances au Canada sans se ruiner. Ce forfait est disponible toute l'année mais vous devrez vous le procurer avant votre arrivée au Canada. Des cartes nationales (vendues au Canada) sont également disponibles mais nous vous conseillons de choisir Go Canada, beaucoup plus avantageux. Conctatez le bureau de votre Association nationale ou régionale, votre agence de voyage ou Hostelling-International Canada pour plus d'informations.

Automobiles

Les personnes non domiciliées au Canada doivent être munies d'un permis de conduire délivré aux Etats-Unis ou d'un permis de conduire international. Les conducteurs de 25 ans ou plus peuvent louer des voitures mais certaines agences de location acceptent de louer des voitures aux conducteurs de 21 ans sur production d'une carte de crédit de réputation internationale. Vérifiez auprès des agences.

TELEPHONE

Indicatif du Pays	**1**
Indicatifs régionaux des Villes principales	
Calgary	403
Edmonton	403
Halifax	902
Montréal	514
Ville de Québec	418
Toronto	416
Vancouver	604
Ottawa	613

Deutsch

KANADISCHE HERBERGEN

In allen größeren Einreisestädten und an bekannten Urlaubsorten sind die Herbergen in Kanada 24 Stunden geöffnet. Die meisten Herbergen sind ganzjährig den ganzen Tag über und auch spät nachts zugänglich. Einige schließen tagsüber zwischen 10.00 und 17.00 Uhr. Es gibt auch Saisonherbergen, die nur in den Sommermonaten geöffnet sind - siehe Angaben der einzelnen Herbergen.

Die 73 Herbergen, die es in Kanada gibt, erstrecken sich praktisch über alle Landesteile, die von Reisenden besucht werden. Das Angebot ist überaus vielseitig - es gibt einen Leuchtturm, ein historisches Gefängnis, eine Holzhütte in den Bergen, eine modernisierte Molkereischeune, ein historisches Gerichtsgebäude und modern eingerichtete Herbergen in der Stadt. Ob Sie dem hektischen Trubel entrinnen und die wilde Natur erforschen wollen, oder ob Sie vom Lichtermeer der Großstadt angezogen werden - Sie finden genau das, was Sie suchen.

Es ist mit einem Preis von $9,00-$22,50 pro Nacht zu rechnen. Diese Preise basieren auf gemeinsamer Unterkunft. Dazu kommt bei Bedarf noch die Gebühr für die Miete von

Bettwäsche. Privatzimmer stehen in vielen Standorten zur Verfügung, und dafür bezahlt man einen kleinen Zuschlag. Für Herbergen in Parks, besonders in den kanadischen Rockies, wo die nächtlichen Temperaturen selbst im Sommer recht niedrig sein können, wird ein Daunen-Schlafsack empfohlen. Die größeren Herbergen bieten in ihren Schnellgaststätten oder Cafeterias sehr preiswerte Mahlzeiten an. Wenn nichts anderes angegeben ist, gibt es auch Küchen für Selbstversorger. Die kanadischen Herbergen stellen auch gerne Nichtraucherzimmer zur Verfügung, damit sich alle Gäste wohlfühlen können.

Viele Herbergen bieten Aktivitätsprogramme, besonders im Sommer. Einige veranstalten Ausflüge, zum Beispiel Wanderungen, Besuche örtlicher Veranstaltungen und Sehenswürdigkeiten, Wanderreisen und naturkundliche Führungen. Andere bieten in Zusammenarbeit mit renommierten örtlichen Firmen erlebnisreiche Programme, wie Wildwasser-Rafting, Reiten, Kanufahren und die Beobachtung von Walfischen. Jede Herberge kann über ihre Programme und die Kosten genau Auskunft geben - bitte erkundigen Sie sich nach der Ankunft.

Um mit einem breiten Angebot aufwarten zu können, arbeitet Kanada mit Familien und anderen Organisationen zusammen, so daß auch die folgenden speziellen Unterkünfte angeboten werden können:

HH Home Hostel (Familienherberge)
Eine beschränkte Zahl von Betten bei einer Familie, die die gleichen Grundeinrichtungen bietet wie eine Herberge. Dazu gehören manchmal auch Mahlzeiten oder Küchenbenutzung.

SA Supplementary Accommodation (zusätzliche Unterkünfte)
Beispiele: Unterkünfte des Christlichen Vereins Junger Männer (YMCA) oder des Christlichen Vereins Junger Frauen (YWCA), Studenten-Wohnheime usw. zum Teil ohne Einrichtungen für Selbstversorger.

PÄSSE UND VISA

Zum Bereisen Kanadas brauchen Staatsangehörige aller Länder, mit Ausnahme der USA (die nur einen gültigen Führerschein benötigen) einen gültigen Reisepaß.

Alle Reisenden müssen im Besitz eines Tickets für ihre Heim- oder Weiterreise sein.

Sofern im Paß nichts anderes angegeben ist, beträgt die Höchstaufenthaltsdauer 3 Monate. Für Staatsangehörige gewisser Länder kann sie aber auch bis zu 6 Monate betragen. Bitte erkundigen Sie sich bei der Hohen Kommission Kanadas oder Botschaft nach der Gültigkeit und ob Sie ein Visum benötigen.

GESUNDHEIT

Zur Zeit werden für Reisen in Kanada keine Impfungen verlangt.

GESCHÄFTSSTUNDEN DER BANKEN

Die Banken sind in Kanada gewöhnlich montags bis freitags von 10.00-17.00 Uhr geöffnet. Die meisten Banken, besonders in Stadtzentren oder Fremdenverkehrsorten, haben aber verlängerte Geschäftsstunden, besonders am Abend oder am Wochenende.

POSTÄMTER

Postämter sind in ganz Kanada gewöhnlich von 09.30-17.00 Uhr geöffnet (an gewissen Orten auch länger).

LADENÖFFNUNGSZEITEN

Die Geschäfte sind in ganz Kanada gewöhnlich von 09.00-17.00 Uhr geöffnet. Viele schließen aber an einem oder zwei Abenden in der Woche erst später. In gewissen Städten kann man sogar am Sonntag einkaufen. An Fremdenverkehrsorten sind die Geschäfte gewöhnlich länger geöffnet.

REISEN

Eisenbahn

VIA Rail Canada bietet internationalen Reisenden den Canrail-Paß. Es gibt Hochsaison- und Vor- bzw. Nachsaisonpreise sowie Preise für Erwachsene und Jugendliche. Bitte wenden Sie sich an ein Reisebüro wegen näherer Auskunft über Gültigkeit usw. Kanadier können auch den Canrailpaß in Kanada kaufen.

Busse

Der GO-Canada Paß bietet unbegrenztes Reisen mit den Greyhound Bussen sowie einen für 15 oder 30 Tage gültigen Übernachtungsgutschein. Der Gutschein ist für jede der 73 Jugendherbergen in dem ganzen Netz von Hostelling International-Canada gültig. GO-Canada bietet Reisenden, die eine preiswerte und vergnügliche Urlaubserfahrung in Kanada möchten, ausgezeichnete Flexibilität. Dieses Angebot ist das ganze Jahr über erhältlich, aber man muß es vor Ankunft in Kanada kaufen. Die Inlandsversion (Verkauf in Kanada) ist auch erhältlich, aber um Geld zu sparen, empfiehlt sich der Kauf des GO-Canada-Angebotes. Wenden Sie sich an Ihren Jugendherbergsverband, Reisebüro oder Hostelling International-Canada für nähere Auskünfte.

Autofahren

Wer nicht in Kanada wohnhaft ist, muß entweder im Besitz eines US- oder eines internationalen Führerscheins sein. Reisende im Alter von über 25 Jahren können ein Fahrzeug mieten. Einige Mietwagen-Unternehmen sind auch bereit, jüngeren Leuten bis zu einem Mindestalter von 21 Jahren ein Fahrzeug zu vermieten, sofern sie mit einer bekannten Kreditkarte bezahlen. Erkundigen Sie sich in der jeweiligen Mietstation.

FERNSPRECHINFORMATIONEN

Landes-Kennzahl	**1**
größere Städte - Ortsnetzkennzahlen	
Calgary	**403**
Edmonton	**403**
Halifax	**902**
Montréal	**514**
Québec City	**418**
Toronto	**416**
Vancouver	**604**
Ottawa	**613**

Español

ALBERGUES DE JUVENTUD CANADIENSES

Los albergues que se encuentran en los principales puntos de entrada al país y lugares turísticos están abiertos las 24 horas del día. La mayoría de los albergues ofrece acceso durante todo el día hasta tarde durante todo el año. Algunos cierran durante el día, entre las 10.00 y las 17.00 horas, y algunos son de temporada, por lo que sólo abren en los meses de verano. Verifique los datos de cada uno.

Los 73 albergues de Canadá cubren casi todos los lugares que uno quiera visitar, ofreciendo una diversidad excepcional. Elija entre un faro, una cárcel provincial histórica, una cabaña en las montañas, una granja lechera reformada, un juzgado histórico o un moderno edificio urbano. Aléjese de las multitudes y explore la naturaleza, o disfrute al ritmo de las grandes ciudades.

Se paga alrededor de $9,00 y $22,50 por noche en alojamiento compartido, además del alquiler de ropa de cama, de necesitarla. Muchos albergues ofrecen habitaciones privadas pagando un pequeño suplemento. Se recomienda llevar un saco de dormir de plumón a los albergues que se encuentren en parques, sobre todo en las

Montañas Rocosas del Canadá, donde la temperatura de noche puede ser fresca incluso en verano. Los centros más importantes sirven buena comida a precios muy razonables en sus cafeterías. A menos que se indique lo contrario, los albergues ofrecen cocina para huéspedes. Los albergues de Canadá se complacen en ofrecer instalaciones para no fumadores para mayor comodidad de todos los huéspedes.

Muchos albergues cuentan con programas de actividades, sobre todo en los meses de verano. Algunos organizan excursiones, visitas a acontecimientos y atracciones locales y paseos por la naturaleza. Otros colaboran con operadores locales de confianza para ofrecer actividades de especial interés como rafting en aguas rápidas, equitación, piragüismo y observación de ballenas. Cada albergue dispone de información completa sobre las opciones y su coste. Pregunten a su llegada.

Para poder ofrecer albergues en más puntos del país, Hostelling International-Canada colabora con propietarios de casas particulares y otras organizaciones para poner a disposición de los visitantes los siguientes tipos de alojamiento:

Símbolo utilizado

HH Home Hostel
Número limitado de camas en una casa particular con servicios básicos tipo albergue. El propietario puede servir comidas u ofrecer compartir la cocina.

SA Supplementary Accommodation
P.ej. YMCA, YWCA, residencias universitarias, etc. Algunas no disponen de cocina para huéspedes.

PASAPORTES Y VISADOS

Para viajar a Canadá se exige un pasaporte válido a los ciudadanos de todos los países excepto de los Estados Unidos (para los que basta un permiso de conducir vigente).

Todos los visitantes deben tener un billete de ida y de vuelta.

La estancia máxima permitida es de 3 meses a menos que el pasaporte indique lo contrario. Para los ciudadanos de algunos países, la estancia puede ser de hasta 6 meses. Póngase en contacto con el Alto Comisionado de Canadá o la Embajada para confirmar los períodos de validez y la necesidad o no de un visado.

SANIDAD

En la actualidad no se requieren vacunas para viajar a Canadá.

HORARIO DE BANCOS

En Canadá el horario habitual de los bancos es de 10.00 a 17.00 horas de lunes a viernes. En muchos sitios, sobre todo céntricos y turísticos, tienen un horario más prolongado, hasta última hora de la tarde y los fines de semana.

OFICINAS DE CORREOS

El horario habitual de las oficinas de correos de todo Canadá es de 09.30 a 17.00 horas (que podrá ser más protongado en determinados lugares).

HORARIO COMERCIAL

El horario comercial habitual en todo Canadá es de 09.00 a 17.00 horas. Muchas tiendas abren hasta más tarde una o dos veces a la semana. En algunas ciudades también abren los domingos. Los centros turísticos tienden a ofrecer un horario más prolongado.

DESPLAZAMIENTOS

Tren
VIA Rail Canadá ofrece el abono Canrail a los viajeros internacionales. Existen tarifas para adultos y jóvenes, así como de temporada alta y baja. Diríjase a su agencia de viajes para más información sobre las opciones y validez del abono. Los canadienses también pueden comprar el abono dentro del Canadá.

Autobús
El abono GO Canada combina un número

ilimitado de viajes en autobuses de la compañía Greyhound con un vale de 15 ó 30 noches válido para todos los albergues de la red de 73 albergues Hostelling International Canadá. El abono GO Canada ofrece una gran flexibilidad a buen precio a los viajeros en busca de vacaciones divertidas y al alcance de su bolsillo en el Canadá. Este abono se puede conseguir todo el año y debe comprarse antes de entrar en el Canadá. También existen otros abonos nacionales (que se venden en el Canadá), pero GO Canada es el más recomendable a nivel de precios. Para más información, diríjase a la oficina local de su asociación, a su agencia de viajes o a Hostelling International Canadá.

Coche

Los no residentes deben tener un permiso de conducir estadounidense o internacional. Los visitantes de 25 años de edad o más pueden alquilar coches. Si se dispone de una tarjeta de crédito, algunas compañías los alquilan a partir de los 21 años. Confírmelo con el establecimiento.

INFORMACION TELEFONICA

Código Nacional	**1**
Prefijos de las Ciudades Principales	
Calgary	**403**
Edmonton	**403**
Halifax	**902**
Montreal	**514**
Ciudad de Quebec	**418**
Toronto	**416**
Vancouver	**604**
Ottawa	**613**

Discounts And Concessions

Your Hostelling International membership card buys you a wide range of discounts at or near hostels, cutting entrance fees, fares, eating out, equipment and activity costs. Check the North American Hostelling International Guide for a full listing.

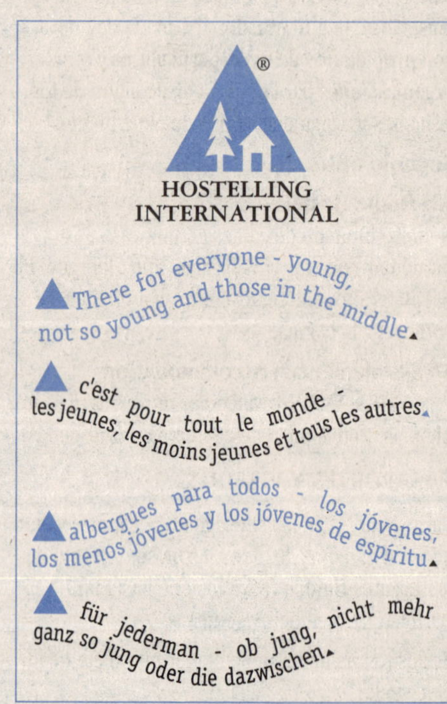

Banff -
Banff International

PO Box 1358,
807 Coyote Road,
Banff,
Alberta,
T0L 0C0.
☎ (403) 7624122
📠 (403) 7623441

Open Dates:	🗓
Open Hours:	🕐
Reservations:	R IBN CC
Price Range:	$19.00-23.00 (Dorm); $50-58 (Private rooms)
Beds:	216 - 7x³ 24x⁴ 2x⁵ 12x⁶
Facilities:	7x 1x

Directions:

✈	Calgary International 160km
A🚌	Brewster/Greyhound 3km

Attractions: 2640m+ 3km

Halifax

Halifax Heritage House Hostel,
1253 Barrington St,
Halifax,
Nova Scotia B3J 1Y3.
☎ (902) 4223863
📠 (902) 4223863

Open Dates:	🗓
Open Hours:	08.00-12.00; 15.00-22.00hrs
Reservations:	R IBN CC
Price Range:	$15.00
Beds:	70 - 2x¹ 1x² 4x⁴ 4x⁶ 3x⁶
Facilities:	1x (B)

Directions:

✈	Halifax International
⛴	Halifax Harbour 1km
🚂	500m
🚌	Asadian Bus Depot 4km ap Terminal
🚎	#7, #9 100m ap South & Barrington Streets

Attractions: 🚴

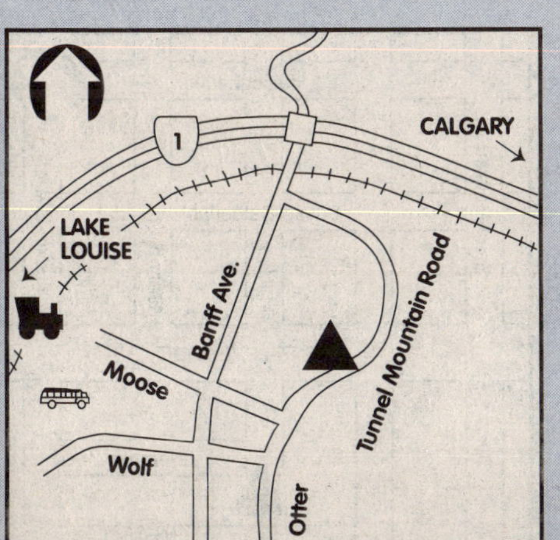

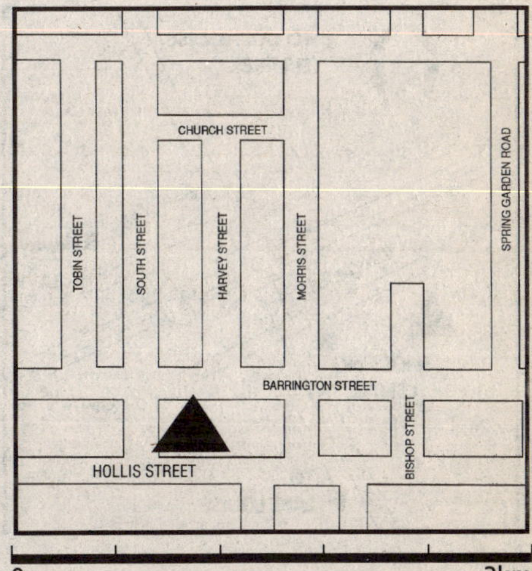

Lake Louise

Village Rd,
Box 115,
Lake Louise,
Alberta T0L 1E0.
t (403) 5222200
f (403) 5222253

Open Dates:	
Open Hours:	
Reservations:	**R** CC
Price Range:	$20.25-30.25
Beds:	150 - 7x1 5x2 4x3 34x4 6x5
Facilities:	40x 1x
Directions:	

✈	Calgary International 200km
A🚌	Airporter 500m
🚌	Greyhound 500m
Attractions:	1500m 4km 1km

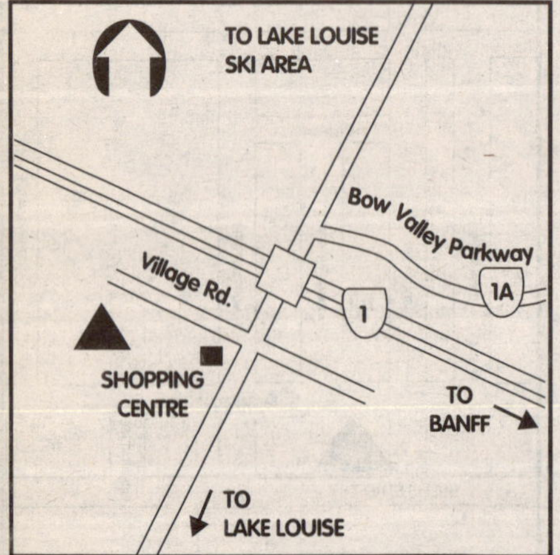

Montréal

1030,
Rue Mackay,
Montréal,
Québec H3G 2H1.
t (514) 8433317
f (514) 9343251

Open Dates:	
Open Hours:	
Reservations:	**R** IBN CC
Price Range:	$18.50-22.50
Beds:	246 - 15x2 3x3 24x4 8x6 6x6+
Facilities:	39x (B)
Directions:	

✈	Dorval 12km
A🚌	Hostel door
🚆	Central 100m
U	Lucien L'Allier 200m

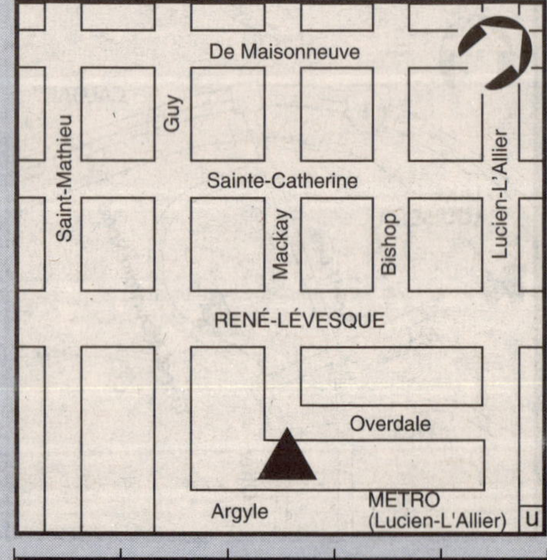

Ottawa

**International,
75 Nicholas St,
Ottawa,
Ontario K1N 7B9.**
☎ (613) 2352595
🖷 (613) 5692131

Open Dates: 🗓9
Open Hours: ☺ (01.04-31.10); 07.00-02.00hrs
(01.11-31.03)
Reservations: Ⓡ ⒤ⒷⓃ ⒸⒸ
Price Range: $17.00-21.00 🛏
Beds: 148 - 1x² 12x⁴ 9x⁶ 4x⁶
Facilities: ⅰⅰⅰ 3x ⅰⅰⅰ ♿ 🛏 📺 🔲 🏢 8 🅿 ⅰ ❀ 🔍 🏫

Directions: 0.1E from city centre
✈ Ottawa International 15km
A🚌 to Novotel Hotel 50m
🚂 via Rail 3.2km
🚌 #95 from 🚂 3.2km, Voyageur
Colonial #4 100m ap Rideau Center
100m

Attractions: ⛰ 🚴 🚶

Québec

**Centre International de Séjour de Québec,
19 rue Ste Ursule,
 Québec G1R 4E1.**
☎ (418) 6940755
🖷 (418) 6942278

Open Dates: 🗓9
Open Hours: ☺
Reservations: Ⓡ ⒤ⒷⓃ ⒸⒸ
Price Range: $15.00-49.98 🛏
Beds: 245 - 6x¹ 6x² 4x³ 33x⁴ 1x⁵ 5x⁶ 4x⁶
Facilities: ⅰⅰⅰ 🍽 ♿ 🛏 📺 🔲 🌊 2x ✈ 🔲 💼 🏫 8 ⅰ ⛷ 🔍 🏫

Directions:
✈ Quebec City International 15km
A🚌 La Quebecoise 20km
⛴ Quebec - Levis Ferry 2km
🚂 Gare du Palais 1km
🚌 Bus from 🚂 and 🚌; #800 or
#25 200m ap Terminus Place
d'Vouville

Attractions: 🚴 🎣 🔍2km 🏊2km

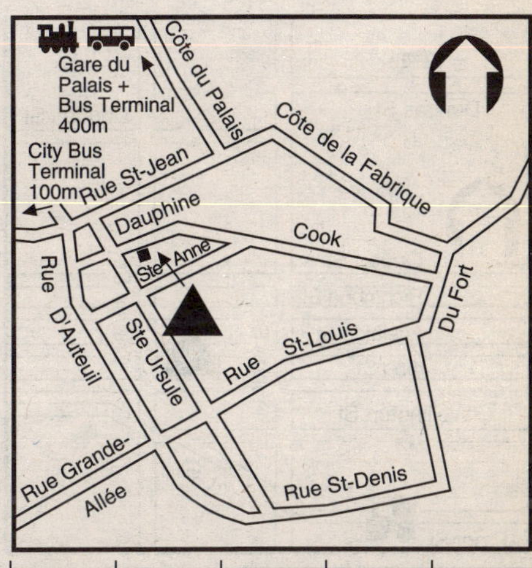

Toronto

HI-Toronto,
76 Church Street,
Toronto,
Ontario M5C 2G1.
☎ **(416) 9714440 or 1-800 6684487**
(416) 9714088

Open Dates: 🗓

Open Hours: 🕐

Reservations: R   IBN   CC

Price Range: $17.95-20.09 🏨

Beds: 170 - 7x² 7x³ 14x⁴ 7x⁶ 7x⁶⁺

Facilities: 21x 🛁 TV 📺 1x 🔟 🖼 🍴 8 ♿ ⬆ ℹ 👪

Directions:

✈ Pearson International 30km

A🚌 From all terminals

🚂 Union 500m

U King Station

Attractions: 🚴

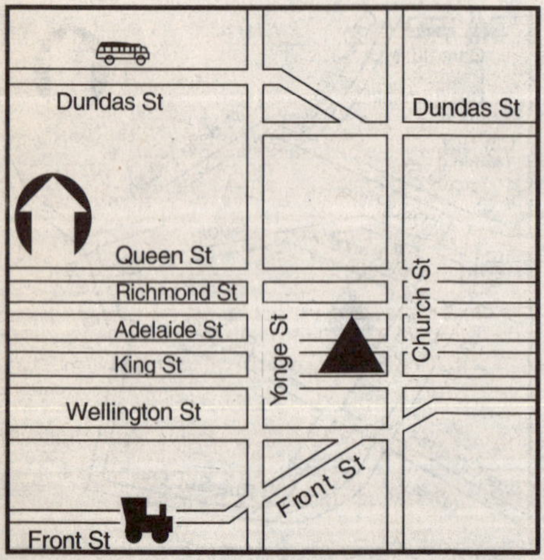

Vancouver

Downtown,
1114 Burnaby St,
Vancouver,
BC,
V6E 1P1.
☎ **(604) 6844565**
(604) 6844540

Open Dates: 🗓

Open Hours: 🕐

Reservations: R   IBN   CC

Price Range: $19.95 🏨

Beds: 223 - 44x⁴

Facilities: ♿ 23x 🛁 TV 📺 1x 🔟 🖼 8 ⬆ P ℹ 👪 🌿

Directions:

✈ Vancouver International 15km

A🚌 Parkhill Hotel 25m

⛴ Tsawwassen 32km

🚂 Pacific Central 2.5km

🚌 #6 2.5km ap Thurlow & Davie

U Granville 1.5km

Attractions: 🏞 🏕 🔍 🚴 🎿 1230m 🏊 🏃 1.5km 🏊 50m

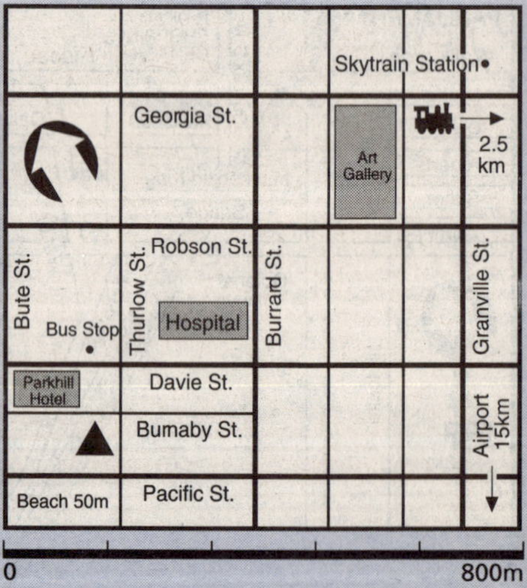

Victoria

516 Yates St,
Victoria,
BC,
V8W 1K8.
☎ (250) 3854511
🖶 (250) 3853232

Open Dates:	🗓
Open Hours:	07.00-02.30hrs
Reservations:	**R** ⊂CC⊃
Price Range:	$16.00
Beds:	110 - 2x² 1x⁴ 1x⁶ 4x⁶
Facilities:	♿ 🏻 2x 🛆 📺 ▣ ▣ 8 ⓘ

Directions:

✈	Victoria 28km
A🚌	Shuttle to door
⛴	Swartz Bay 32km, Victoria 700m
🚂	E+N Via 200m
🚌	#70 280m ap Yates & Douglas

Attractions: 🔍 ⚲ 🏊

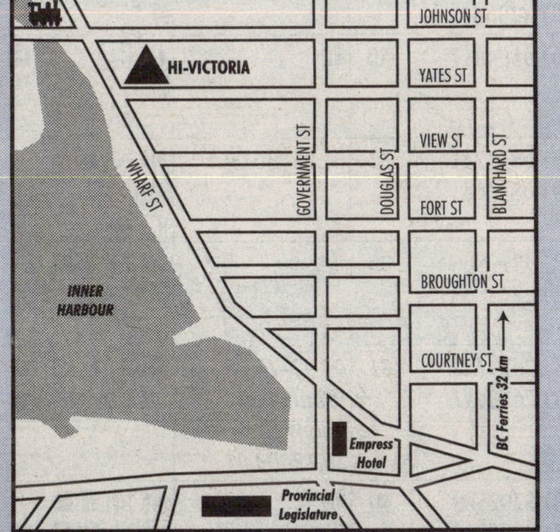

Winnipeg

Ivey House International Hostel,
210 Maryland St,
Winnipeg,
Manitoba R3G 1L6.
☎ (204) 7723022
🖶 (204) 7841133

Open Dates:	🗓
Open Hours:	08.00-10..hrs; 16.00-24.00hrs
Reservations:	**R** ⊂CC⊃
Price Range:	$14.00
Beds:	38 - 2x² 6x⁴ 1x⁵
Facilities:	🏻 1x 🛆 📺 ▣ ▣ 8 P ⓘ

Directions: 3E from city centre

✈	Winnipeg International 7km
🚂	Via 2km
🚌	#29 500m ap 29 Sherbrook 500m

Attractions: 🚴 ⛵ 1km

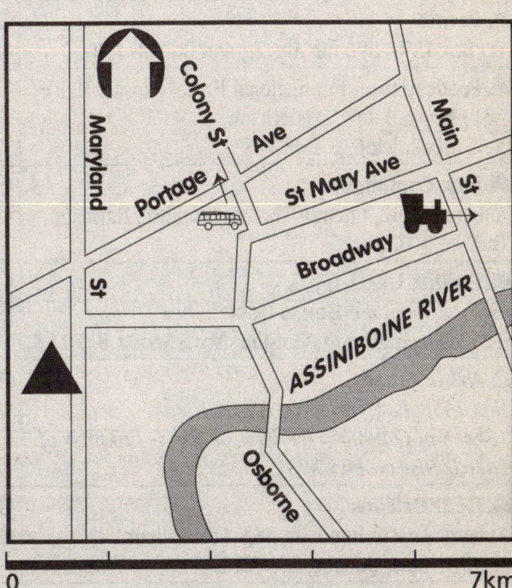

Location/Address	Telephone No. / Fax No.	Beds	Opening Dates	Facilities
▲ **Alma** Fundy National Park Hostel, General Delivery, PO Box 122, Alma, New Brunswick E0A 1B0 (S on Trans-Canada #2 linked by Rte 114).	☎ (506) 8872216 🖷 (506) 8872226	28	01.06–01.09	👪 R ♿ CC 🚿 P
▲ **Banff** - Banff International (IBN) **PO Box 1358, 807 Coyote Road, Banff, Alberta, T0L 0C0.**	☎ (403) 7624122 🖷 (403) 7623441	216	🗓	👪 🍴 R CC 🚿 P 🖨 ☕
▲ **Barrie** - Georgian Green Summer Hostel 148 Bell Farm Rd, Barrie, ON LYM 5K5	☎ (705) 7350772 🖷 (705) 7398615	48	01.05–15.08	👪 R 5NE 🚿 P 🖨
▲ **Big White** - Samesun Hostel 7660 Porcupine Rd, Big White Ski Resort, Kelowna BC V1X 4K5 (near Kelowna, very top of Big White).	☎ (250) 7657050 🖷 (250) 7657050	42	15.10–30.04	👪 45SE CC 🚿 P 🖨
▲ **Calgary** - Calgary International (IBN) 520-7th Ave, SE Calgary, Alberta T2G 0J6.	☎ (403) 2698239 🖷 (403) 2666227	120	🗓	👪 R ♿ CC 🚿 P 🖨
▲ **Campbellton** 1 Ritchie St, P.O. Box 100, Campbellton, New Brunswick E3N 3G1.	☎ (506) 7597044 🖷 (506) 7597403	20	07.06–14.08	🍴 R 🚿
▲ **Cap-Aux-Os** 2095 Boul Grande-Grève, Cap-Aux-Os, Québec G0E 1J0.	☎ (418) 8925153 🖷 (418) 8925292	48	01.05–01.11	👪 🍴 R ♿ CC 🚿 P 🖨
△ *Castle Mountain* *Box 1358, Banff, AB T0L 0C0 (on hwy #1A, 1.5km E of the junction with hwy #1 & #93 S)*	☎ *(403) 7624122* 🖷 *(403) 7623441*	*36*	*11.08–10.12*	👪 R CC 🚿 P
▲ **Charlottetown** 153 Mount Edward Rd, Charlottetown, PEI, C1A 7N4.	☎ (902) 8949696 🖷 (902) 6286424	52	01.06–07.09	👪 ♿ CC 🚿 P
△ *Dawson City* *River Hostel, PO Box 32, Dawson City, Yukon Y0B 1G0.*	☎ *(867) 9936823*	*28*	*15.05–01.10*	👪 🍴 ♿ 🚿 P
▲ **Edmonton** 10647-81 Ave Edmonton, AB T6E 1Y1	☎ (780) 9886836 🖷 (780) 9888698	104	🗓	👪 CC 🚿 🖨
▲ **Fernie** PO Box 1899, 892 6th Ave, Fernie, BC V0B 1M0.	☎ (250) 4236811 🖷 (250) 4236812	62	🗓	👪 CC 🚿 P 🖨
▲ **Fredericton** - International Hostel (Rosary Hall) 621 Churchill Row, Fredericton, New Brunswick E3B 1M3	☎ (506) 4504417	40	🗓	👪 1E 🚿 P 🖨
▲ **Fort Coulonge** Auberge Esprit, Chemin Thomas Lefebure, Davidson, Quebec, J0X 1R0	☎ (819) 6833241 🖷 (819) 6833641	32	01.05–30.09	👪 🍴 R 3W ♿ CC 🚿 P
▲ **Halifax** (IBN) **Halifax Heritage House Hostel, 1253 Barrington St, Halifax, Nova Scotia B3J 1Y3.**	☎ (902) 4223863 🖷 (902) 4223863	70	🗓	👪 🍴 R CC 🚿 P
△ *Hilda Creek* *Box 1358, Banff, Alberta T0L 0C0 (8km S of Columbia Icefields Centre & 120km N of Lake Louise on hwy #93)*	☎ *(403) 7624122* 🖷 *(403) 7623441*	*21*	*01.02–15.05 (Thurs–Sat only); 26.12–03.01*	R CC 🚿
▲ **Ile D'Orléans** Auberge Le P'tit Bonheur, 183, Côte Lafleur, Ile D'Orléans, Quebec, G0A 3W0.	☎ (418) 8292588 🖷 (418) 8290900	40	🗓	👪 🍴 R 1W CC 🚿 P 🖨

Location/Address	Telephone No. Fax No.	Beds	Opening Dates	Facilities
△ *Jasper National Park* - *Maligne Canyon Hostel* *Box 387, Jasper, Alberta T0E 1E0.* *(11km E of Jasper on Maligne Lake Rd,* *SE from Hwy #16)*	☎ *(780) 8523215* 📠 *(780) 8525560*	*24*	🗓	R ⒸⒸ 🍴 P
△ *Jasper National Park* - *Mount Edith Cavell Hostel* *Box 387, Jasper, Alberta T0E 1E0.* *(from Jasper Townsite: 9km S on Hwy #93,* *turn right on Hwy 93A for 5km to Mount Edith Cave* *ll turnoff, follow rd 13km)*	☎ *(780) 8523215* 📠 *(780) 8525560*	*32*	🗓	R ⒸⒸ 🍴 P
△ *Jasper National Park* - *Athabasca Falls Hostel* *Box 387, Jasper, Alberta T0E 1E0.* *(32km S of Jasper on the E side,* *200m past Athabasca Falls - turn off Hwy #93)*	☎ *(780) 8523215* 📠 *(780) 8525560*	*40*	🗓	R ⒸⒸ 🍴 P
△ *Jasper National Park* - *Beauty Creek Hostel* *Box 387, Jasper, Alberta T0E 1E0.* *(87km S of Jasper & 17km N of* *Columbia Icefield Centre on W side of Hwy #93)*	☎ *(780) 8523215* 📠 *(780) 8525560*	*24*		R ⒸⒸ 🍴 P
▲ **Jasper National Park** - Jasper International Hostel Box 387, Jasper, Alberta T0E 1E0. (3km S of Jasper on Hwy 93, right on Whistler's Mountain Rd: follow for 4km)	☎ *(780) 8523215* 📠 *(780) 8525560*	80	🗓	👪 ⒸⒸ 🍴 P
▲ **Kamloops** 7 West Seymour St, Kamloops, BC V2C 1E4. (on TransCanada Hwy, half-way between Banff & Vancouver)	☎ *(250) 8287991* 📠 *(250) 8282442*	72	🗓	👪 R 0.1E ⒸⒸ 🍴 P 🔒
▲ **Kelowna** Kelowna Samesun Motel Hostel, 245 Harvey Ave, Kelowna, British Columbia, V1Y 6C2.	☎ / 📠 *(250)* *7639814*	34	🗓	👪 0.1E ♿ ⒸⒸ 🍴 P 🔒
▲ **Kingston** Louise House, 329 Johnson St, Kingston, ONT, K7L 1Y6.	☎ *(613) 5318237* 📠 *(613) 3851707*	51	01.05–31.08	👪 🍽 R 0.2N ⒸⒸ 🍴 P 🔒
△ *La Have* *La Have Marine Hostel, PO Box 92, La Have,* *Nova Scotia, B0R 1C0.*	☎ *(902) 6882908* 📠 *(902) 6881083*	*8*	*01.06–01.10*	👪 ⒸⒸ 🍴 P 🔒
▲ **La Tuque** Auberge la Residence 352, Avenue Brown, La Tuque, Quebec G9X 2W4	☎ *(819) 5239267* 📠 *(819) 5233678*	49	🗓	👪 🍴 P 🔒
▲ **Lake Louise** **Village Rd, Box 115, Lake Louise,** **Alberta T0L 1E0.**	☎ *(403) 5222200* 📠 *(403) 5222253*	150	🗓	👪 🍽 R ♿ ⒸⒸ 🍴 P 🔒 ☕
▲ **Magog-Orford** Auberge La Grande Fugue, Route 141 Nord, Magog, Canton d'Orford, Québec J1X 3W3. (Located in Parc du Mont Orford)	☎ *(819) 8438595* 📠 *(819) 8437274*	180	01.05–31.10	👪 🍽 R 5N ⒸⒸ 🍴 P
▲ **Montréal** IBN **1030, Rue Mackay, Montréal, Québec H3G 2H1.**	☎ *(514) 8433317* 📠 *(514) 9343251*	246	🗓	👪 🍽 R ⒸⒸ 🍴 P 🔒

Location/Address	Telephone No. Fax No.	Beds	Opening Dates	Facilities
▲ **Mont-Tremblant Village** Auberge Internationale du Mont-Tremblant 2213, Chemin Principal BP1001, Mont Tremblant, Quebec JOT 1ZO	☎ (819) 4256008 ✆ (819) 4253760	81	🗓	� 🍴 Ⓡ 0.5NE ⌷CC⌷ ☛ P 🔒 ☕
△ *Mosquito Creek* *Banff National Park, Alberta.* *(27 km N of Lake Louise on Hwy #93, 211km S of Jasper)*	☎ *(403) 7624122* ✆ *(403) 7623441*	*38*	*26.12–03.01 (Closed Mon & Tues 13.10–15.05)*	� Ⓡ ⌷CC⌷ ☛ P
▲ **Nelson** Dancing Bear Inn, 171 Baker St, Nelson, BC V1L 4H1.	☎ (250) 3527573 ✆ (250) 3529818	35	🗓	� Ⓡ ⌷CC⌷ ☛ P 🔒
▲ **Nelson** Beaubear Manor, Nelson, New Brunswick E0C 1T0.	☎ (506) 6223036	24	🗓	� ☛ P
▲ **Niagara Falls** 4549 Cataract Avenue, Niagara, Ontario, L2E 3M2.	☎ (905) 3570770, 1-888 7490058 ✆ (905) 3577673	81	🗓	� Ⓡ ⌷CC⌷ ☛ P 🔒
▲ **Nordegg** Shunda Creek Hostel, General Delivery, Nordegg, Alberta T0M 2H0. (located 3km N of Hwy 11 on the Shunda Creek Recreation Area Rd, 87km E of Banff National Park and 94km W of Rocky Mountain House)	☎ (403) 7212140 ✆ (403) 7212140	48	🗓	� ⌷CC⌷ ☛ P 🔒
▲ **Ottawa** ⌷IBN⌷ **International, 75 Nicholas St, Ottawa, Ontario K1N 7B9.**	☎ (613) 2352595 ✆ (613) 5692131	148	🗓	� Ⓡ 0.1E ⌷CC⌷ ☛ P 🔒
▲ **Ottawa** - Regina Guesthouse Hostel 205 Charlotte Street, Ottawa, Ontario, K1N 8K7	☎ (613) 2410908 ✆ (613) 2412141	56	01.05–28.08	� Ⓡ 1E ⌷CC⌷ ☛ P 🔒
▲ **Penticton** 464 Ellis St, Penticton, BC V2A 4M2.	☎ (250) 4923992 ✆ (250) 4928755	47	🗓	� Ⓡ 0.2E ♿ ⌷CC⌷ ☛ P 🔒
▲ **Péribonka** Auberge Ile-Du-Repos de Péribonka, 105 Ile-du-Repos Rd, C P 38, Ste-Monique de Honfleur, Lac Saint-Jean, Québec G0W 2T0.	☎ (418) 3475649 ✆ (418) 3474810	54	🗓	� 🍴 Ⓡ 5E ♿ ⌷CC⌷ P 🔒 ☕
▲ **Peterborough** - Severn Court Summer Hostel 555 Wilfred Drive, Peterborough, ON K9K 1W1	☎ (705) 7401150 ✆ (705) 7400944	48	01.05–23.08	� Ⓡ 8SW ♿ ⌷CC⌷ ☛ P 🔒
▲ **Pointe-à-la-Garde** Auberge Le Château Bahia, 152 Boul. Perron, Pointe-à-la-Garde, Québec G0C 2M0.	☎ (418) 7882048 ✆ (418) 7882048	48	🗓	� 🍴 Ⓡ 3E ⌷CC⌷ ☛ P 🔒
△ *Powell River* *Fiddlehead Farm, PO Box 421, Powell River, BC V8A 5C2. (extremely remote area: make* Ⓡ *at least one week in advance to ensure pick-up by private boat from the bus, Comox ferry or Powell Lake Marina.)*	☎ *(604) 4833018* ✆ *(604) 4853832*	*18*	*01.03–15.10*	� 🍴 Ⓡ
△ *Powerview* *Maskwa Project, Box 130, Powerview, Winnipeg R0E 1P0, Manitoba.*	☎ *(204) 3674390*	*35*	🗓	Ⓡ ☛ P

Location/Address	Telephone No. Fax No.	Beds	Opening Dates	Facilities
▲ Québec **IBN** **Centre International de Séjour de Québec,** **19 rue Ste Ursule, Québec G1R 4E1.**	☎ (418) 6940755 ⊜ (418) 6942278	245	🗓	🍴 R CC 🚿 📠
▲ Racine Auberge de la Grande Ligne, 318 Ch de la Grande Ligne, Racine, Québec J0E 1Y0.	☎ (514) 5323177 ⊜ (514) 5324082	25	🗓	👪 🍴 R 🚿 P 📠
△ *Rampart Creek* *Box 1358, Banff, AB, TOL OCO* *(95km N of Lake Louise & 34km S of* *the Columbia Icefield Centre on hwy #93*	☎ *(403) 7624122* ⊜ *(403) 7623441*	*30*	*13.10–15.05 (Fri – Tues only); 16.05–12.10*	R CC 🚿 P
▲ Regina Turgeon International Hostel, 2310 McIntyre St, Regina, Saskatchewan S4P 2S2.	☎ (306) 7918165	39	01.02–24.12	👪 CC 🚿 P 📠
△ *Ribbon Creek* *Alberta, Box 1358, Banff AB, TOL OCO* *(70km W of Calgary on Trans* *Canada hwy at Kananaskis turn off (hwy #40 S)* *follow signs to Kananaskis village)*	☎ *(403) 7624122* ⊜ *(403) 7623441*	47	*08.11–12.10 (Closed Tuesdays* 🗓*)*	👪 R CC 🚿 P 📠
▲ Rivière du Loup Auberge Internationale de Rivière du Loup, 46 Hotel de Ville, Rivière du Loup, Québec G5R 1L5. (200km to Québec City)	☎ (418) 8627566 ⊜ (418) 8621843	65	🗓	👪 🍴 R CC 🚿 P 📠
▲ Rossland Mountain Shadow Hostel, 2125 Columbia Avenue, Box 100, Rossland, BC, V0G 1Y0.	☎ (250) 3627160 ⊜ (250) 3627150	40	🗓	👪 R CC 🚿 P 📠
▲ Sainte-Anne-des-Monts Auberge L'Echourie, 295 1e Avenue Sainte-Anne-des-Monts, Quesbec G0E 2G0	☎ (418) 7631555 ⊜ (418) 8925292	85	🗓	👪 🍴 R 2E CC 🚿 P 📠 ☕
▲ Sainte-Luce-sur-Mer Auberge le Roupillon du Capitaine 147, Route du Fleuve, Sainte-Luce, Quebec G0K 1P0	☎ (418) 7395152 ⊜ (418) 7395152	15	🗓	👪 🍴 R 0.5W 🚿 P 📠
▲ Salt Spring Island 640 Cusheon Lake Rd, Salt Spring Island, BC V8K 2C2.	☎ (250) 5374149 ⊜ (250) 5374149 (☎ before faxing)	35	01.03–15.11	👪 R CC 🚿 P
▲ Sept-Iles Auberge Internationale Le Tangon, 555 Cartier, CP 902, Sept-Iles, Québec G4R 4L2.	☎ (418) 9628180 (Su) ⊜ (418) 9628180	50	01.04–31.12	👪 🍴 R CC 🚿 P 📠
▲ Shuswap Lakes Squilax General Store & Caboose Hostel, Rural Route #2, S-2-C11, Chase, BC V0E 1M0.	☎ (250) 6752977 ⊜ (250) 6752977	23	🗓	👪 R CC 🚿 P 📠
△ *South Milford* - *Raven Haven Hostel* *P.O. Box 100, Annapolis Royal, Nova Scotia,* *B0S 1A0*	☎ *(902) 5327320* ⊜ *(902) 5322096*	6	🗓	👪 R 22S ♿ CC 🚿 P
▲ Tadoussac - La Maison Majorique 158 Bateau-Passeur, Tadoussac, Québec G0T 2A0.	☎ (418) 2354372 ⊜ (418) 2354608	64	🗓	👪 🍴 R ♿ CC 🚿 P 📠
▲ Tadoussac - La Maison Alexis 389, Des Pionniers, Tadoussac, G0T 2A0.	☎ (418) 2354372 ⊜ (418) 2354608	33	🗓	👪 R ♿ 🚿 P 📠

Location/Address	Telephone No. / Fax No.	Beds	Opening Dates	Facilities
▲ **Toronto** [IBN] **HI-Toronto, 76 Church Street, Toronto, Ontario M5C 2G1.**	☎ (416) 9714440 or 1-800 6684487 📠 (416) 9714088	170	🗓	
▲ **Trois Rivières** Auberge Internationale la Flottille, 497 Radisson, Trois Rivières, Québec G9A 2C7.	☎ (819) 3788010 📠 (819) 3784334	45	🗓	
▲ **Val David** Le Chalet Beaumont, 1451 Beaumont, Val David, Québec J0T 2N0.	☎ (819) 3221972 📠 (819) 3223793	65	🗓	
▲ **Vancouver** - Jericho Beach [IBN] 1515 Discovery St (Jericho Park), Vancouver, BC V6R 4K5.	☎ (604) 2243208 📠 (604) 2244852	286	🗓	
▲ **Vancouver** [IBN] **Downtown, 1114 Burnaby St, Vancouver, BC, V6E 1P1.**	☎ (604) 6844565 📠 (604) 6844540	223	🗓	
▲ **Victoria** **516 Yates St, Victoria, BC, V8W 1K8.**	☎ (250) 3854511 📠 (250) 3853232	110	🗓	
▲ **Wakefield** Sentiers Carman Trails, Carman Rd West, PO Box R3, RA RR#3 Wakefield, Quebec, J0X 3G0.	☎ (819) 4593180 📠 (819) 4592113	22	🗓	15W
▲ **Waterton Lakes National Park** The Lodge at Waterton Lakes, Corner of Cameron Falls Drive & Windflower Ave, in Waterton townsite.	☎ (403) 8592150/2151 📠 (403) 8592229	22	🗓	
△ *Wentworth* *RR #1, Wentworth, Nova Scotia B0M 1Z0.* *(Route 104 (Trans-Canada) to Wentworth Valley; exit on Valley Rd - follow signs to YH)*	☎ *(902) 5482379* 📠 *(902) 5482389*	*25*	🗓	
△ *Whiskey Jack* *Yoho National Park, BC. (near Alberta border, 27km W of Lake Louise on Hwy #1 (Trans-Canada), 13km W along Yoho Valley Rd from Kicking Horse Camp Ground)*	☎ *(403) 7624122* 📠 *(403) 7623441*	*27*	*15.06–13.10*	
▲ **Whistler** PO Box 128, 5678 Alta Lake Rd, Whistler, BC V0N 1B0. (121km N of Vancouver on Hwy 99, turn off on Alta Lake Rd, continue 5km)	☎ (604) 9325492 📠 (604) 9324687	32	🗓	
▲ **Winnipeg** **Ivey House International Hostel, 210 Maryland St, Winnipeg, Manitoba R3G 1L6.**	☎ (204) 7723022 📠 (204) 7841133	38	🗓	3E

SUPPLEMENTARY ACCOMMODATION
OUTSIDE THE ASSURED STANDARDS SCHEME

Location/Address	Telephone No. / Fax No.	Beds	Opening Dates	Facilities
Orillia HH Orillia Home Hostel, 198 Borland St East, Orillia, Ontario L3V 2C3.	☎ (705) 3250970 📠 (705) 3259826	9	🗓	

Location/Address	Telephone No. Fax No.	Beds	Opening Dates	Facilities
Saskatoon Patricia Hotel, 345 2nd Ave N, Saskatoon, Saskatchewan S7K 2B8.	☎ (306) 2428861	20	🗐	⫩ ⊚ ᴄᴄ ℗ ⬚
Sault Ste Marie The Algonquin Hotel, 864 Queen St E, Sault Ste Marie, Ontario P6A 2B4.	☎ (705) 2532311	45	🗐	⫩ ⊚ 🔒 ℗
Thunder Bay Sibley Hall Residence, 960 William St, Thunder Bay, Ontario P7C 4W1.	☎ (807) 4756381	100	10.05–10.08	⫩ ⊚ Ⓡ ℗ ⬚

use International Communications Network (ICN) at major hostels to send and receive e-mail, set up e-mail box, send faxes, make International phone calls, surf the Web – all at low, low prices using the ICN Communications Card

Utilisez le Réseau International de Communication (ICN), dans nos plus grandes auberges pour envoyer et recevoir du courrier électronique, ouvrir une boîte à lettres électronique, transmettre des fax, appeler l'étranger, surfer sur l'internet – le tout à prix très très concurrentiels, grâce à la Carte de Communication ICN

benutzen Sie das International Communications Network (ICN) in Hauptherbergen, um e-mail zu senden und zu empfangen, e-mail Briefkästen einzurichten, Faxe zu schicken, international zu telefonieren oder "Surf the Net" – und das alles mit der ICN Kommunikationskarte zu günstigsten Preisen!

utilice la Red Internacional de Comunicaciones ICN en los principales albergues para transmitir y recibir mensajes electrónicos, establecer un buzón de correo electrónico, enviar facsímiles, realizar llamadas telefónicas internacionales, navegar por la red de Internet – todo a precios muy, muy económicos – mediante la Tarjeta de Comunicación ICN.

Know Where You're Going?

Wherever you're headed, **Rough Guides** show you the way, on and off the beaten track.. We give you the best places to stay and eat on your **budget**, plus all the inside background and info to make your **trip** a great experience.

ROUGH GUIDES

Travel Guides to more than 100 destinations worldwide from Amsterdam to Zimbabwe.

AT ALL BOOKSTORES • DISTRIBUTED BY PENGUIN

www.roughguides.com

Check out our Web site for unrivalled travel information on the Internet.

Plan ahead by accessing the full text of our major titles, make travel reservations and keep up to date with the latest news in the Traveller's Journal or by subscribing to our free newsletter ROUGH*NEWS* - packed with stories from Rough Guide writers.

Chile

CHILI
CHILE
CHILE

Asociación Chilena de Albergues Turísticos Juveniles
Hernando de Aguirre 201 of 602,
Providencia,
Santiago, Chile.

 (2) 2333220
 (2) 2332555
E-mail: histgoch@hostelling.co.cl
         achatj@hostelling.co.cl
WWW address: http://www.hostelling.co.cl

Travel Section:
Student Flight Center
Hernando de Aguirre #201, OF 401.
Providencia,
Santiago, Chile.

 (2) 3350395
 (2) 3350394
E-mail: stflictr@ctc-mundo.net

A copy of the Hostel Directory for this Country can be obtained from:
The National Office.

IBN Booking Centre for outward bookings

• **Santiago**, *via National Office above.*

Capital:	Santiago	Population:	14,000,000
Language:	Spanish	Size:	756,945 sq km
Currency:	$ peso		

Chile

N
L. Poopo
BOLIVIA
PARAGUAY
Paraguay
Bermejo
BRAZIL
Paraná
São Paulo
Asuncion
Cúitaba
Antofagasta
CHILE
Isla de Pascua
(Easter Island)
Florianápolis
Uruguay
PACIFIC OCEAN
Porto Alegre
La Serenà
Viña del Mar
Cordoba
Paraná
Mendoza
URUGUAY
Santiago
Santiago
Rosário
Chillan
Salto del Laja
Buenos Aires
Montevideo
Temuco
Temuco
ARGENTINA
Bahía Blanca
ATLANTIC OCEAN
Pucon
Valdivia
Valdivia
Frutillar
Pta Montt
Ancud
FALKLAND ISLANDS (UK)
Punta
Arenas
TIERRA DEL FUEGO
DRAKE PASSAGE
0
200
400
400
800 KM
MLS
ANDES

English

CHILE HOSTELS

13 Youth Hostels open up Chile as a very interesting destination.

Expect to pay between 4500-9000 peso (US\$ 10.00-20.00) per night unless otherwise stated. Hostels are open 24hrs. You may find your stay limited to 5 consecutive nights in any one hostel in high season. Self-catering facilities are available in Salto del Laja, Temuco and Frutillar.

PASSPORTS AND VISAS

Only some countries need passports, the majority of Latin American countries need only identity cards.

BANKING HOURS

09.00-14.00hrs.

POST OFFICES

09.00-16.00hrs.

SHOPPING HOURS

10.00-21.00hrs.

TRAVEL

Air
The country's main cities are connected by air.

Rail
Santiago is well connected with the south of the country by rail.

Bus
Bus services link Santiago with both the north and the south.

Driving
An international driving licence is required.

TELEPHONE INFORMATION

Country Code	**56**
Main City Area Codes	
Concepción	41
Santiago	2
Valparaiso	32
Punta Arenas	61

Français

AUBERGES DE JEUNESSE CHILIENNES

13 auberges de jeunesse font du Chili une destination très intéressante.

Une nuit vous coûtera entre 4500-9000 peso (10 et 20 \$US) sauf indication contraire. Les auberges sont ouvertes 24 heures sur 24. Il est possible que votre séjour dans une auberge soit limité à 5 nuits consécutives en pleine saison. Les auberges de Salto del Laja, Temuco, Frutillar, offrent la possibilité de cuisiner.

PASSEPORTS ET VISAS

Seulement quelques pays ont besoin d'un passeport. La majorité des pays d'Amérique Latine n'ont besoin que d'une carte d'identité.

HEURES D'OUVERTURE DES BANQUES

Les banques sont ouvertes de 9h à 14h.

BUREAUX DE POSTE

Les bureaux de poste sont ouverts de 9h à 16h.

HEURES D'OUVERTURE DES MAGASINS

Les magasins sont ouverts de 10h à 21h.

DEPLACEMENTS

Avions
Les villes principales du pays sont desservies par des compagnies aériennes.

Trains
Santiago est bien relié par chemin de fer au sud du pays.

Autobus

Des services d'autobus relient Santiago au nord et au sud du pays.

Aubomobiles

Les conducteurs doivent être munis d'un permis de conduire international.

TELEPHONE

Indicatif du Pays	**56**
Indicatifs régionaux des Villes principales	
Concepción	41
Santiago	2
Valparaiso	32
Punta Arenas	61

Deutsch

JUGENDHERBERGEN IN CHILE

13 Jugendherbergen erschließen Chile dem Reisenden als sehr interessantes Reiseziel.

Es ist mit einem Preis von 4500-9000 peso (US$ 10-20) pro Nacht, wenn nicht anders angegeben, zu rechnen. Die Herbergen sind 24 Stunden geöffnet. In der Hochsaison wird manchmal der Aufenthalt auf 5 aufeinanderfolgende Übernachtungen in der gleichen Herberge beschränkt. Einrichtungen für Selbstversorger gibt es nur auf der Salto del Laja, Temuco, Frutillar.

PÄSSE UND VISA

Nur einige Länder brauchen Pässe. Die meisten lateinamerikanischen Länder brauchen nur einen Identitätsnachweis für die Einreise nach Chile.

GESCHÄFTSSTUNDEN DER BANKEN

09.00-14.00 Uhr.

POSTÄMTER

09.00-16.00 Uhr.

LADENÖFFNUNGSZEITEN

10.00-21.00 Uhr.

REISEN

Flugverkehr

Die wichtigsten Städte des Landes sind mit dem Flugzeug zu erreichen.

Eisenbahn

Zwischen Santiago und dem südlichen Landesteil gibt es gute Eisenbahnverbindungen.

Busse

Zwischen Santiago und dem Norden und Süden des Landes gibt es einen Busverkehr.

Autofahren

Man braucht einen internationalen Führerschein.

FERNSPRECHINFORMATIONEN

Landes-Kennzahl	**56**
größere Städte - Ortsnetzkennzahlen	
Concepción	41
Santiago	2
Valparaiso	32
Punta Arenas	61

Español

ALBERGUES DE JUVENTUD CHILENOS

13 albergues juveniles revelan a Chile como destino de gran interés.

Los precios oscilan entre 4500-9000 pesos (10-20 dólares US) por noche. Los albergues están abiertos las 24 horas del día. La estancia se puede ver limitada a 5 noches consecutivas en el mismo albergue durante la temporada alta. Sólo los albergues de Salto del Laja, Temuco y Frutillar ofrecen cocina para huéspedes.

PASAPORTES Y VISADOS

Solamente algunos países necesitan pasaporte. La mayoría de los países latinoamericanos necesitan solamente carnet de identidad.

HORARIO DE BANCOS

De 09.00 a 14.00 horas.

OFICINAS DE CORREOS

De 09.00 a 16.00 horas.

HORARIO COMERCIAL

De 10.00 a 21.00 horas.

DESPLAZAMIENTOS

Avión

Las principales ciudades del país están conectadas por avión.

Tren

La ciudad de Santiago está bien conectada con el sur del país por tren.

Autobús

Servicios de autobús conectan Santiago tanto con el norte como con el sur.

Coche

Se requiere un permiso de conducir internacional.

INFORMACION TELEFONICA

Código Nacional	**56**
Prefijos de las Ciudades Principales	
Concepción	**41**
Santiago	**2**
Valparaiso	**32**
Punta Arenas	**61**

Assured Standards – visited by our Liaison team and by you the guest – tell us when we don't measure up (reply slips at the end of this Guide)▸

des Normes Garanties, par les visites de notre Equipe de Liaison et par vous, les usagers – faites-le nous savoir quand nous ne sommes pas à la hauteur (Fiches-commentaires à la fin du Guide)▸

Zugesicherte Standards – beurteilt von unserem Liaison Team und von Ihnen, unserem Gast – sagen Sie es uns, wenn wir Sie enttäuschen (Antwortkarten hinten im Führer)▸

Normas Garantizadas – comprobadas por nuestro Equipo de Enlace y por Ud., el usuario – si fallamos en algo, díganoslo (al final de esta Guía encontrará nuestras hojas de comentarios)▸

Santiago

**Cienfuegos 151,
Santiago de Chile.**
☎ (2) 6718532
✆ (2) 6728880

Open Dates:	🗓
Open Hours:	🕐
Reservations:	Ⓡ [IBN] [CC]
Price Range:	$4500-5500
Beds:	120 - 2x² 20x⁴ 6x⁶
Facilities:	� of icons... 🍴🍵🛏📺📖1x🍽🔒♿8 P ℹ♿❀⚠🔍

Directions:

✈	Arturo Merino Benitez 21km
A🚌	Centropuerto 500m; Tour Express 500m
⛴	Valparaiso 120km
🚆	Estacion Central 1km
🚌	2 blocks
Ⓤ	1, 2 Los Heroes 300m; Santa Ana Station, Line 2 400m

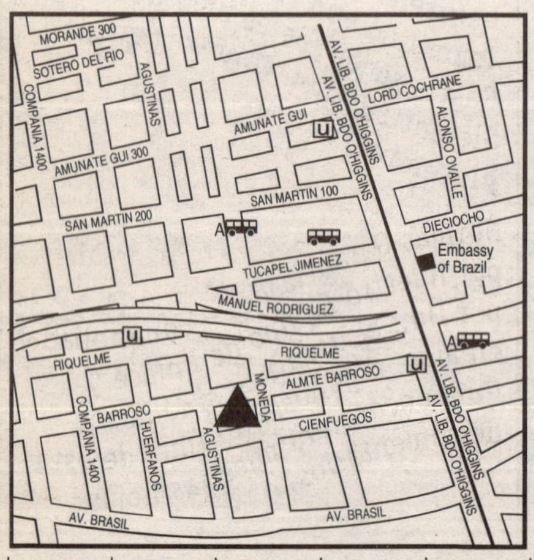

▲ There for everyone - young, not so young and those in the middle.▲

▲ c'est pour tout le monde -les jeunes, les moins jeunes et tous les autres.▲

▲ albergues para todos - los jóvenes, los menos jóvenes y los jóvenes de espíritu.▲

▲ für jederman - ob jung, nicht mehr ganz so jung oder die dazwischen.▲

Location/Address	Telephone No. / Fax No.	Beds	Opening Dates	Facilities
△ **Ancud** - *Hospedaje Vista Al Mar*	☎ (65) 622617 🖷 (65) 622617	26		0.5 SE
△ **Chillan** - *Complejo Turistico "Las Trancas"* *Km 73.5 Camino a las Termas de Chillan, Chillan*	☎ (42) 213764 🖷 (42) 222582	36		73.3 SE
△ **Frutillar** *Residencial Winkler, Phillipi 1155, Frutillar.*	☎ (65) 421388	28		
△ **Isla de Pascua** *Residencial "Kona Tau", Avaripua S/N.*	☎ 321	16		
△ **Pucon** *Hosteria ¡Ècole!, General Urrutia 592, Pucon.*	☎ (45) 441675 🖷 (45) 441660	47		
△ **Puerto Montt** - *Hostal Independencia I* *Independencia 167, Puerto Montt*	☎ (65) 277949 🖷 (65) 277949	20		
△ **Puerto Montt** - *Hostal Independencia II* *Angelmo 2196, Puerto Montt*	☎ (65) 257938	22		
△ **Punta Arenas** *Pasaje Darwin 175, Punta Arenas.*	☎ (61) 248543 🖷 (61) 248543	12		
△ **Salto del Laja** *Panamericana Sur 485,* *Complejo Turístico (Holiday Centre),* *Los Manantiales.*	☎ (43) 314275 🖷 (43) 314275			
△ **Santiago** IBN **Cienfuegos 151, Santiago de Chile.**	☎ (2) 6718532 🖷 (2) 6728880	120		
△ **La Serena** *Residencial Limmat, Lautaro 914 La Serena.*	☎ (51) 211373 🖷 (51) 211373	20		0.5 W
△ **Temuco** - *Residencial Temuco* *Manuel Rodriguez 1341, 2º Piso.*	☎ (45) 233721 🖷 (45) 233721	20		
△ **Valdivia** - *Residencial Germania* *Picarte 873, Valdivia.*	☎ (63) 212405	34		

HOSTELLING INTERNATIONAL

...not just a cheap bed, but a cheaper ticket, meal, insurance package (see your national Association for details...)

pas simplement un lit bon marché, mais aussi un billet, un repas, un forfait assurance moins chers (contactez votre Association nationale pour plus de renseignements...)

nicht nur ein preiswertes Bett, sondern auch preisgünstigere Eintrittskarten, Mahlzeiten und Reiseversicherungen (mehr darüber von den nationalen Mitgliedsverbänden...).

no sólo alojamiento a precios asequibles, sino también billetes, comidas y seguros más económicos (para más información, diríjase a su Asociación nacional...)

HOSTELLING INTERNATIONAL

Make your credit card bookings at these centres

Réservez par cartes de crédit aux centres suivants

Buchen Sie mit Kreditkarte in folgenden Buchungszentren

Reserve por tarjeta de crédito en los siguientes centros

English

Australia	☎ (2) 9261 1111
Canada	☎ (800) 663 5777
England & Wales	☎ (1629) 581 418
France	☎ (1) 44 89 87 27
Northern Ireland	☎ (1232) 324 733
Republic of Ireland	☎ (1) 830 1766
New Zealand	☎ (9) 303 9524
Scotland	☎ (541) 553 255
Switzerland	☎ (1) 360 1414
USA	☎ (202) 783 6161

Français

Angleterre & Pays de Galles	☎ (1692) 581 418
Australie	☎ (2) 9261 1111
Canada	☎ (800) 663 5777
Écosse	☎ (541) 553 255
États-Unis	☎ (202) 783 6161
France	☎ (1) 44 89 87 27
Irlande du Nord	☎ (1232) 324 733
Nouvelle-Zélande	☎ (9) 303 9524
République d'Irlande	☎ (1) 830 1766
Suisse	☎ (1) 360 1414

Deutsch

Australien	☎ (2) 9261 1111
England & Wales	☎ (1629) 581 418
Frankreich	☎ (1) 44 89 87 27
Irland	☎ (1) 830 1766
Kanada	☎ (800) 663 5777
Neuseeland	☎ (9) 303 9524
Nordirland	☎ (1232) 324 733
Schottland	☎ (541) 553 255
Schweiz	☎ (1) 360 1414
USA	☎ (202) 783 6161

Español

Australia	☎ (2) 9261 1111
Canadá	☎ (800) 663 5777
Escocia	☎ (541) 553 255
Estados Unidos	☎ (202) 783 6161
Francia	☎ (1) 44 89 87 27
Inglaterra y Gales	☎ (1629) 581 418
Irlanda del Norte	☎ (1232) 324 733
Nueva Zelanda	☎ (9) 303 9524
República de Irlanda	☎ (1) 830 1766
Suiza	☎ (1) 360 1414

CHINA (People's Republic of)

CHINE (République Populaire de)

CHINA (Volksrepublik)

CHINA (República Popular)

Guangdong Province

Guangdong Province Tourism Bureau,
185, Huanshi Xi Road,
Guangzhou,
China.

☏ (86) (20) 86677422
🖷 (86) (20) 86665039

Capital:	Guangzhou	Currency:	Yuan (Renminbi)
Language:	Mandarin, Cantonese	Population:	70,000,000
		Size:	180,000 sq km

Hong Kong (Special Administrative Region - SAR)

Hong Kong Youth Hostels Association,
Room 225, Block 19,
Shek Kip Mei Estate,
Sham Shui Po, Kowloon,
Hong Kong.

☏ (852) 2788 1638
🖷 (852) 2788 3105

A copy of the Hostel Directory for this region can be obtained from:
The National Office.

Capital:	Hong Kong	Population:	6,421,300
Language:	Cantonese, English, Mandarin	Size:	1,094 sq km
Currency:	HK$		

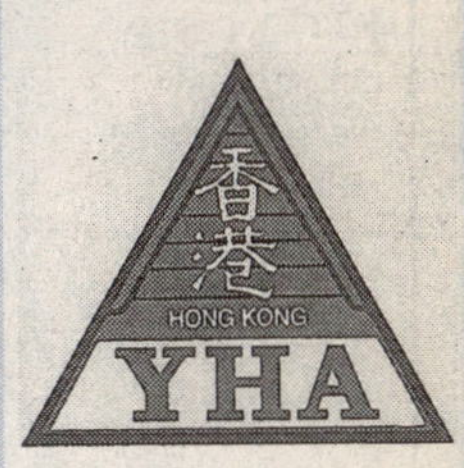

China (People's Republic of)

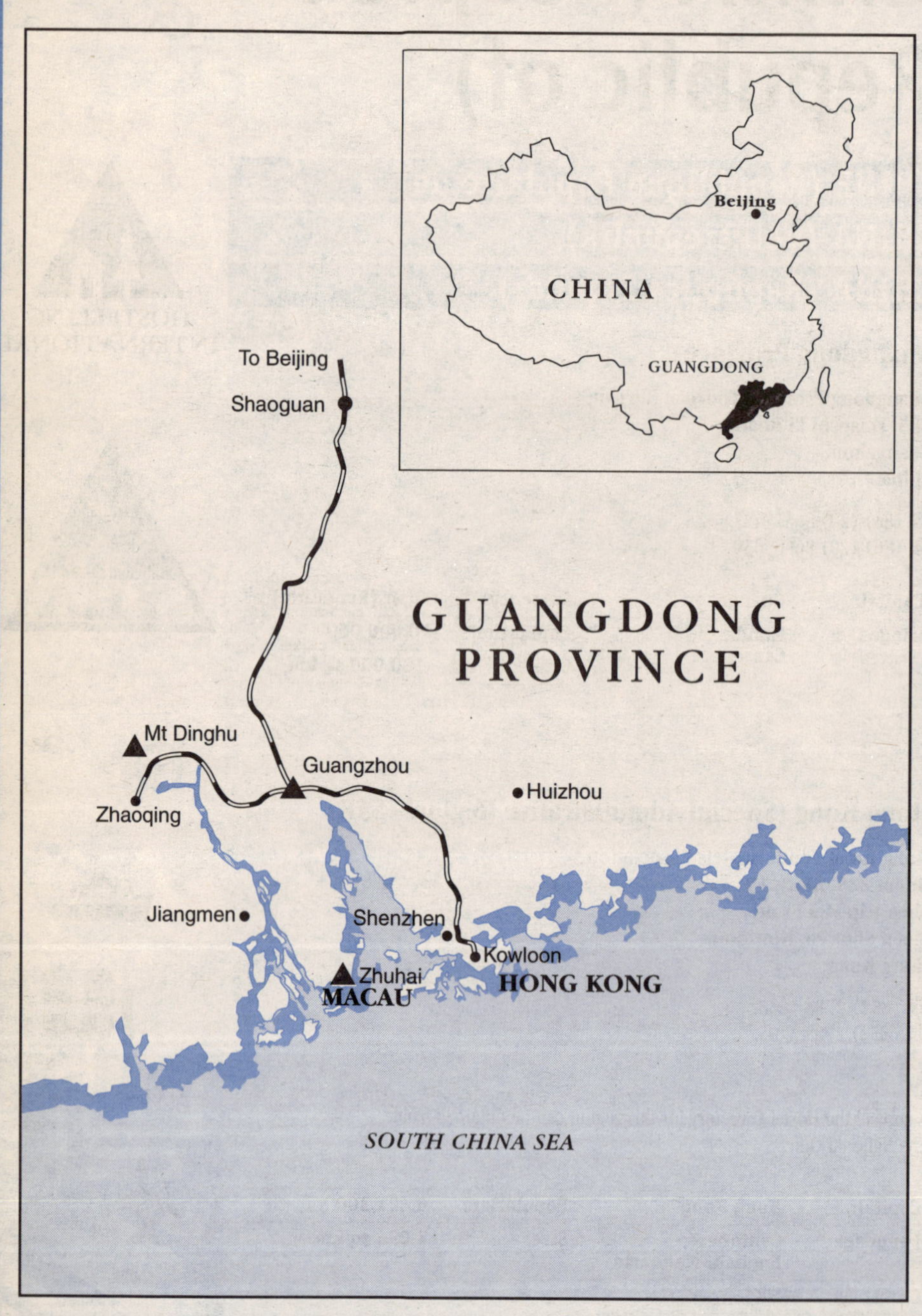

English

GUANGDONG PROVINCE

HOSTELS

Guangdong Province is a prosperous province in southern mainland China, and its capital city Guangzhou is the gateway for trade and tourism in the region.

There are three hostels in Guangdong Province (at time of going to press) which are under the co-ordination of Hotel Management Division of the Guangdong Provincial Tourism Bureau. The Guangzhou Hostel is centrally located in the city, and offers air conditioned, en suite facilities. The Zhuhai Hostel is located in the Zhuhai Holiday Resort, and guests are entitled to use the resort's recreational facilities. There is a direct bus service between Zhuhai and Macao, and a direct ferry service between Zhuhai and Hong Kong. Mt Dinghu Hostel is located in the Mt Dinghu nature reserve, near Zhaoqing, which is famous for its rare flora. Seven Stars Crags are also located in the nearby area.

Expect to pay between US$ 5-10. Breakfast, dinner and linen are included in the price.

PASSPORTS & VISAS

A valid passport and a visa is required for entry into any province of the People's Republic of China. Visas are available worldwide from Chinese Embassies and Consulates and through specialist tour operators and visa agents. Apply as far in advance as possible.

HEALTH

Medical insurance is advisable. Medical costs are low, and facilities in the large cities are good. For minor complaints, most towns have a pharmacy which can suggest remedies, and doctors who offer both traditional Chinese or Western medicine. Vaccination requirements are subject to change at short notice – check with your doctor well in advance of departure. Travellers arriving from an infected or epidemic area may be asked to produce valid certificates of inoculation.

BANKING & CURRENCY

Banks are open 09.30 – 12.00 hrs and 14.00 – 17.00 hrs Monday to Friday; 09.00 – 17.00 hrs Saturday. Banks are closed for the first 3 days of the Chinese New Year, with reduced opening hours for the next 11 days. The Chinese currency Yuan Renminbi (RMB) is not traded outside China. Import and export of local currency is prohibited. Travellers cheques may be exchanged at banks and hotels. Major credit cards are valid in major cities in designated establishments.

POST OFFICES

Main Post Offices are open 7 days a week 08.00–18.00 hrs. Smaller offices close at lunch times and weekends.

TRAVEL

Guangdong Province (Guangzhou) is accessible by air, ferry, train and bus from Hong Kong. Major routes also connect Guangzhou to Beijing and other major Chinese cities.

TELEPHONE INFORMATION

Country Code	**86**
Area Code	
Guangzhou	**20**

Français

PROVINCE DE GUANGDONG

AUBERGES DE JEUNESSE

La Province de Guangdong est une province prospère du Sud de la Chine continentale dont la capitale, Guangzhou, est la plaque-tournante touristique et commerciale.

Il existe trois auberges dans la Province de Guangdong (au moment où nous mettons sous presse), qui sont toutes sous le contrôle de la Division de Gestion Hôtelière de la Direction touristique de la Province de Guangdong. L'Auberge de Guangzhou jouit d'une position centrale dans la ville et offre des chambres climatisées avec salle de bains attenante. L'Auberge de Zhulai est située dans la station de vacances de Zhulai et toutes les installations de détente qui s'y trouvent sont mises à la disposition des ajistes. Il y a un service de cars direct entre Zhulai et Macao, ainsi qu'une ligne directe de ferry entre Zhulai et Hong-Kong. L'Auberge de Mt Dinghu est implantée dans la réserve naturelle du même nom, près de Zhaoqing, qui est renommée pour son unique flore. Les "Rochers des 7 étoiles" se trouvent également non loin de là.

Une nuit vous coûtera entre 5 et 10$US, le petit déjeuner, dîner et location de draps étant compris dans le prix.

PASSEPORTS ET VISAS

Il vous faudra un passeport en cours de validité et un visa pour entrer dans toute province de la République Populaire de Chine. Les visas peuvent s'obtenir auprès des ambassades et des consulats chinois ou auprès de certaines agences de voyages ou d'agents spécialisés. Il est recommandé de faire sa demande le plus tôt possible.

SOINS MEDICAUX

Il est conseillé de souscrire à une police d'assurance maladie. Les frais médicaux sont relativement peu onéreux et les équipements hospitaliers dans les grandes agglomérations sont de bonne qualité. Pour les moindres maux, la plupart des villes ont une pharmacie, qui pourra vous recommander des remèdes, et des

médecins qui dispensent des soins selon la médecine traditionnelle chinoise ou la médecine occidentale. La nature des vaccinations requises pourra changer à la dernière minute – il est donc conseillé de vous renseigner auprès de votre médecin longtemps avant votre départ. Il sera peut-être demandé aux voyageurs en provenance d'une région où une épidémie ou une maladie infectieuse sévit de présenter un certificat valide de vaccination.

BANQUES ET CHANGE

Les banques sont ouvertes de 9h30 à 12h et de 14h à 17h du lundi au vendredi, et de 9h à 17h le samedi. Elles ferment complètement les trois premiers jours du Nouvel An chinois et, pour les 11 jours suivants, les heures d'ouverture sont limitées. La monnaie chinoise, le Yuan Renminbi (RMB) n'est pas disponible en dehors de Chine. L'importation et l'exportation de la devise chinoise est interdite. Les chèques de voyages peuvent être changés dans les banques ou les hôtels. Les principales cartes de crédits sont acceptées dans certains établissements des grandes agglomérations.

BUREAUX DE POSTE

Les bureaux de poste principaux sont ouverts 7 jours sur 7 de 8h à 18h. Les plus petits ferment à midi et le week-end.

DEPLACEMENTS

La Province de Guangdong (Guangzhou) est accessible par avion, ferry, train et autocar depuis Hong-Kong. Des axes principaux relient également Guangzhou et Beijing, ainsi que d'autres grandes villes chinoises.

TELEPHONE

Indicatif du Pays   **86**
Indicatifs régionaux des Villes principales
  Guangzhou   **20**

Deutsch

GUANGDONG PROVINCE

JUGENDHERBERGEN

Die Guangdong Province ist eine gedeihende Provinz im südlichen Festland Chinas. Für Tourismus und Handel ist die Hauptstadt Guangzhou das Tor in die Region.

In der Guangdong Province gibt es drei Herbergen (zur Zeit der Fertigstellung dieser Ausgabe), die dem Tourismusbüro der Guangdong Province - Abteilung für Hotelmanagement - unterstehen. Die Guangzhou-Herberge befindet sich im Stadtzentrum und bietet klimatisierte, mit Bad und WC ausgestattete Einrichtungen. Im Urlaubsort Zhuhai gibt es die Zhuhai-Herberge. Dort ist den Gästen der Zugang zu allen Freizeiteinrichtungen des Urlaubsortes gewährt. Es besteht eine direkte Busverbindung zwischen Zhuhai und Macao sowie eine direkte Fährverbindung zwischen Zhuhai und Hong Kong. Die Mt Dinghu Herberge befindet sich im Mt Dinghu Naturreservat in der Nähe von Zhaoqing, das für seine seltene Flora berühmt ist. Im umliegenden Gebiet kann man ebenso die Schluchten "Seven Stars Crags" besichtigen.

Es ist mit einem Übernachtungspreis von 5-10 US$ zu rechnen. Frühstück, Abendbrot und Bettwäsche sind im Preis inbegriffen.

REISEPÄSSE UND VISA

Ein gültiger Reisepaß und ein Visum werden für die Einreise in jede Provinz der Volksrepublik China benötigt. Visa werden weltweit von Chinesischen Botschaften und Konsulaten, sowie durch spezialisierte Reiseveranstalter und Einreisebehörden zur Verfügung gestellt. Es wird empfohlen, die Anträge frühstmöglich im voraus zu stellen.

GESUNDHEIT

Eine Krankenversicherung ist ratsam. Die Arzthonorare sind gering und medizinische Einrichtungen in Großstädten gut. Für kleinere Beschwerden haben die meisten Städte Apotheken, die Medikamente empfehlen können, sowie Ärzte, die sich sowohl der traditionellen chinesischen als auch der modernen westlichen Medizin bedienen. Da die Impfanforderungen oft kurzfristigen Änderungen unterliegen, sollten Sie rechtzeitig vor Abfahrt Ihren Arzt konsultieren. Reisende aus Gebieten mit Infektionen oder Epidemien, können bei ihrer Ankunft gebeten werden, eine gültige Impfbescheinigung vorzulegen.

GESCHÄFTSZEITEN DER BANKEN UND WÄHRUNG

Die Banken sind Montag bis Freitag von 9.30 – 12.00 Uhr und 14.00 – 17.00 Uhr, am Samstag von 9.00 – 17.00 Uhr geöffnet. Sie sind für die ersten 3 Tage des Neuen Chinesischen Jahres geschlossen. In den darauffolgenden 11 Tagen haben die Banken verkürzte Öffnungszeiten. Die chinesische Währung Yuan Renminbi (RMB) wird nicht außerhalb Chinas gehandelt. Der Import und Export in einheimischer Währung ist verboten. Reiseschecks können bei Banken und Hotels eingelöst werden. Die bedeutendsten Kreditkarten werden in gekennzeichneten Einrichtungen in den größten Städten akzeptiert.

POSTÄMTER

Die Hauptpostämter sind 7 Tage in der Woche von 8.00 – 18.00 Uhr geöffnet. Kleinere Ämter schließen um die Mittagszeit und an den Wochenenden.

REISEN

Die Guangdong Province (Guangzhou) ist von Hong Kong aus mit dem Flugzeug, der Fähre, dem Zug und dem Bus erreichbar. Die Hauptrouten verbinden ebenso Guangzhou mit

Beijing und mit anderen wichtigen Städten Chinas.

FERNSPRECHINFORMATIONEN

Landes-Kennzahl	**86**
größere Städte - Ortsnetzkennzahlen	
Guangzhou	**20**

Español

PROVINCIA DE GUANGDONG

ALBERGUES JUVENILES

La Provincia de Guangdong es una región próspera del sur de la China continental y su capital, Guangzhou, es la puerta de entrada del comercio y turismo de la comarca.

Existen tres albergues en la Provincia de Guangdong (al cierre de la edición) que se encuentran bajo la dirección de la División de Gestión Hotelera de la Oficina de Turismo Provincial de Guangdong. El albergue de Guangzhou, situado en el centro de la ciudad, está dotado de climatización y habitaciones con baño. El albergue de Zhuhai está ubicado en el Centro Turístico del mismo nombre, cuyas instalaciones recreativas están a la disposición de los huéspedes del albergue. Un servicio directo de autobuses enlaza Zhuahi con Macao y una línea de ferrys, también directa, comunica Zhuahi con Hong-Kong. El tercer albergue se encuentra en Monte Dinghu, reserva natural famosa por su insólita flora y emplazada cerca de Zhaoqing. Los Riscos de las Siete Estrellas también se hallan en esa zona.

Los precios oscilan entre 5 y 10 $USA e incluyen desayuno, cena y sábanas.

PASAPORTES Y VISADOS

Se requieren un pasaporte vigente y un visado para entrar en cualquier provincia de la República Popular China. Los visados son expedidos por las embajadas y consulados chinos de todos los países, y pueden también tramitarse a través de los tour operadores especializados y de las agencias dedicadas a la obtención de visados. Solicite su visado lo antes posible.

INFORMACION SANITARIA

Es recomendable hacerse un seguro médico. Los honorarios médicos no son elevados y los servicios sanitarios de las grandes ciudades son buenos. Para las afecciones de poca gravedad, la mayoría de las poblaciones disponen de una farmacia donde le podrán recomendar algún remedio y de médicos que ejercen tanto la medicina tradicional china como la occidental. Las vacunas que se necesitan cambian a menudo – infórmese en su centro de salud con suficiente antelación. Es posible que se exija a los viajeros procedentes de regiones contaminadas por enfermedades contagiosas o donde estas sean endémicas que presenten certificados de vacunación vigentes.

HORARIO DE LOS BANCOS Y CAMBIO DE DIVISAS

Los bancos abren de 9.30 h. a 12 h. y de 14 h. a 17 h. de lunes a viernes, y de 9 h. a 17 h. los sábados. Estos cierran los 3 primeros días del Año Nuevo Chino y tienen un horario reducido durante los 11 días siguientes. La unidad monetaria china, el Yuan Renminbi (RMB), no se vende fuera de la China. La importación y exportación de divisas chinas está prohibida. Es posible cambiar cheques de viajero en los bancos y hoteles. En las grandes ciudades se aceptan las principales tarjetas de crédito en los establecimientos que así lo indiquen.

OFICINAS DE CORREOS

Las oficinas de correos centrales abren los 7 días de la semana de 8 h. a 18 h. Las sucursales cierran al mediodía y los fines de semana.

DESPLAZAMIENTOS

Para llegar a la Provincia de Guangdong (a Guangzhou) es preciso desplazarse por avión, ferry, ferrocarril o autobús desde Hong-Kong. También es posible trasladarse de Guangzhou a Beijing y otras grandes ciudades chinas por los principales medios de transporte.

INFORMACION TELEFONICA

Código Nacional   **86**
Prefijos de las Ciudades Principales
  Guangzhou   **20**

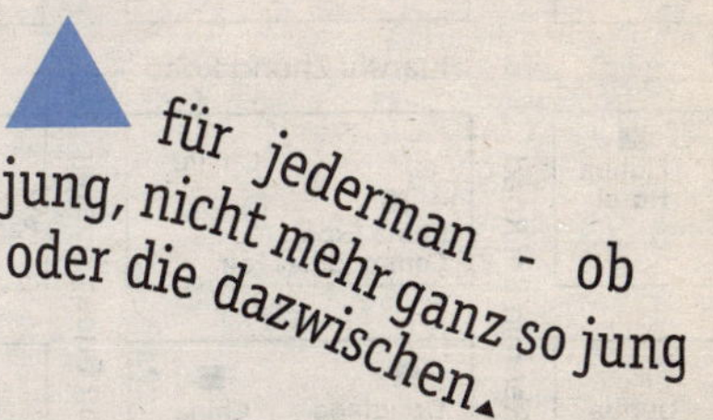

Guangzhou –
City Youth Hostel

**179, Huanshi Xi Road,
Guangzhou**
☏ (20) 86666889
✆ (20) 86679787

Open Dates:	🗓
Open Hours:	🕑
Reservations:	**R** **CC**
Price Range:	RMB 68-168 🏠
Beds:	217- 91x^1 48x^2 10x^3
Facilities:	▥ ▥ 🍽 ☕ ▥ 📺 💼 ⬛ 🔢 ⊜ ↕ 🅿 ℹ ♿

Directions:

✈	Baigun 4km
A🚌	Special Line 50m
⛴	Zhoutouzui 20km
🚂	Guangzhou 200m
🚌	122, 133, 30, 812, 210, 240, 218, 191 250m ap Caonuan Park

Attractions: 🏊 3km

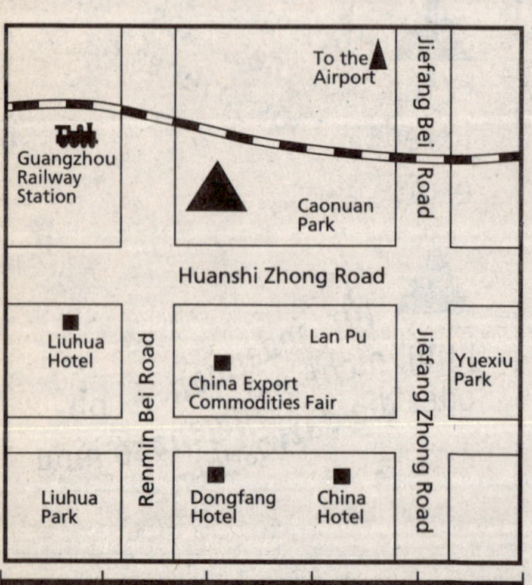

Assured Standards – visited by our Liaison team and by you the guest – tell us when we don't measure up (reply slips at the end of this Guide) ▸

des Normes Garanties, par les visites de notre Equipe de Liaison et par vous, les usagers – faites-le nous savoir quand nous ne sommes pas à la hauteur (Fiches-commentaires à la fin du Guide) ▸

Zugesicherte Standards – beurteilt von unserem Liaison Team und von Ihnen, unserem Gast – sagen Sie es uns, wenn wir Sie enttäuschen (Antwortkarten hinten im Führer) ▸

Normas Garantizadas – comprobadas por nuestro Equipo de Enlace y por Ud., el usuario – si fallamos en algo, díganoslo (al final de esta Guía encontrará nuestras hojas de comentarios) ▸

Location/Address	Telephone No. Fax No.	Beds	Opening Dates	Facilities
▲ **Guangzhou** - City Youth Hostel 179, Huanshi Xi Road, Guangzhou	☏ (20) 86666889 ✆ (20) 86679787	217		

SUPPLEMENTARY ACCOMMODATION
OUTSIDE THE ASSURED STANDARDS SCHEME

Location/Address	Telephone No. Fax No.	Beds	Opening Dates	Facilities
Mt. Dinghu - International Youth Hostel Mt. Dinghu, Zhaoqing, Guangdong Province	☏ (758) 2621668 ✆ (758) 2621665	100		
Zhuhai - International Youth Hostel 51 Hua Shan, Zhuhai Special Economic Zone, Guangdong Province	☏ (756) 3332038, 3332036	120		

HOSTELLING INTERNATIONAL

IBN INTERNATIONAL BOOKING NETWORK

make your credit card booking at these centres:-

Australia	☎ (2) 9261 1111
Canada	☎ (800) 663 5777
England & Wales	☎ (1629) 581 418
France	☎ (1) 44 89 87 27
Northern Ireland	☎ (1232) 324 733
Republic of Ireland	☎ (1) 830 1766
New Zealand	☎ (9) 303 9524
Scotland	☎ (541) 553 255
Switzerland	☎ (1) 360 1414
USA	☎ (202) 783 6161

réservez par cartes de crédit aux centres suivants:-

Angleterre & Pays de Galles	☎ (1692) 581 418
Australie	☎ (2) 9261 1111
Canada	☎ (800) 663 5777
Écosse	☎ (541) 553 255
États-Unis	☎ (202) 783 6161
France	☎ (1) 44 89 87 27
Irlande du Nord	☎ (1232) 324 733
Nouvelle-Zélande	☎ (9) 303 9524
République d'Irlande	☎ (1) 830 1766
Suisse	☎ (1) 360 1414

buchen Sie mit Kreditkarte in folgenden Buchungszentren:-

Australien	☎ (2) 9261 1111
England & Wales	☎ (1629) 581 418
Frankreich	☎ (1) 44 89 87 27
Irland	☎ (1) 830 1766
Kanada	☎ (800) 663 5777
Neuseeland	☎ (9) 303 9524
Nordirland	☎ (1232) 324 733
Schottland	☎ (541) 553 255
Schweiz	☎ (1) 360 1414
USA	☎ (202) 783 6161

reserve por tarjeta de crédito en los siguientes centros:-

Australia	☎ (2) 9261 1111
Canadá	☎ (800) 663 5777
Escocia	☎ (541) 553 255
Estados Unidos	☎ (202) 783 6161
Francia	☎ (1) 44 89 87 27
Inglaterra y Gales	☎ (1629) 581 418
Irlanda del Norte	☎ (1232) 324 733
Nueva Zelanda	☎ (9) 303 9524
República de Irlanda	☎ (1) 830 1766
Suiza	☎ (1) 360 1414

China (People's Republic of)

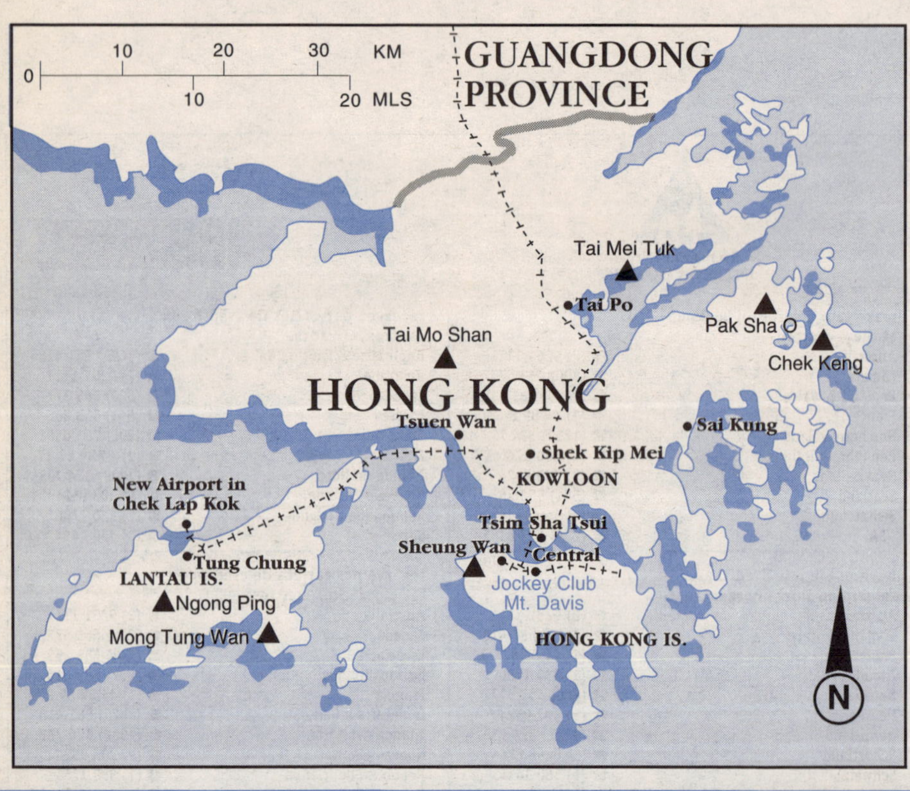

English

HONG KONG

HOSTELS

Many travellers think of Hong Kong as providing a purely urban travel experience. Hong Kong Youth Hostels give you the opportunity to get out into the countryside and explore the real Hong Kong.

Jockey Club Mt. Davis Youth Hostel can be booked through IBN, or by calling the hostel direct from the airport. In addition, all hostels can be booked through Head Office at Shek Kip Mei either by fax, by writing or by telephoning during office hours (Monday-Friday 09.30-17.30hrs; Saturday 09.30-13.00hrs).

Hostels are open from 07.00-10.00hrs and 16.00-23.00hrs with the exception of Jockey Club Mt. Davis Youth Hostel and the S.G. Davis Hostel (the nearest hostel to the new airport in Chek Lap Kok) which is open all day from 07.00-23.00hrs. A provision for earlier check-in at 14.00hrs is made on Saturdays and the day before any public holiday. Some hostels close mid week for one or two days, so do check that the hostel is open when you want to visit it.

All Hong Kong Youth Hostels have self-catering kitchens and barbecue facilities but do not serve meals. Overnight accommodation prices for Hostels within the "Assured Standards Scheme" will vary according to location and facilities. The range is from HK\$35-HK\$120 (This price range is correct at the time of printing, and may be subject to change during the year). Overnight fees are shown under each entry, these relate to over 18s, there are reductions for younger visitors.

Before leaving the airport pick up an HKYHA map and a shuttle bus schedule of Jockey Club Mt. Davis Youth Hostel from the Hong Kong Tourist Association counter in the arrival hall.

PASSPORTS AND VISAS

Few visitors need visas but an onward or return ticket is required. Visa-free stays vary from one week up to six months depending upon nationality. Some nationalities require a minimum 6 months validity in their passports. Enquire at your nearest Consulate General of China for full details.

HEALTH

Insurance cover is recommended as hospitals and medical treatment is expensive. Travellers who have come from an infected or epidemic area may be asked to produce valid certificates of inoculation.

BANKING HOURS

Banks operate 5½ days a week. Travellers cheques and foreign bank notes can be encashed 7 days a week in Tsim Sha Tsui at Money Exchanges but commission rates vary widely. Always check rates and charges before parting with money.

POST OFFICES

Post offices also operate 5½ days a week from 08.00-18.00hrs Monday-Friday and 08.00-14.00hrs on Saturdays.

TRAVEL

Air

The brand new US\$9 billion Hong Kong International Airport in Chek Lap Kok, Lantau Island provides an excellent standard of airport services and is well connected to all major cities of the world.

Hong Kong is too small for local flights. The extensive network of railways, buses, ferries and trams enable you to go to almost any part of the territory by public transport.

Ferry

The Star and Hong Kong Ferry Company provide services between Hong Kong Island and Kowloon. Ferries to Lantau depart from the Outlying Districts Ferry Pier in Central.

Rail

The Mass Transit Railway (MTR) runs 5 underground lines that link up urban Hong Kong, Kowloon and the northern part of Lantau Island. The Kowloon Canton Railway (KCR) runs electric trains from Kowloon to Lo Wu on the boundary between Hong Kong and Mainland China. There are also 3 tram lines.

Bus

Hong Kong is extremely well served with buses, minibuses and more than 17,500 taxis. Some traffic restrictions exist on the picking up and setting down of passengers in urban areas.

Driving

Driving is not recommended. Other forms of public transport are cheap, efficient and convenient.

TELEPHONE INFORMATION

Country Code   852
Main City Area Codes
   No area code

Français

HONG-KONG

AUBERGES DE JEUNESSE

De nombreux voyageurs ont tendance à penser qu'Hong-Kong n'a que les agréments d'une ville à leur offrir. Les auberges de Hong-Kong vous prouveront le contraire en vous permettant de sortir de la ville, en campagne et d'explorer le vrai Hong-Kong.

Il est possible de réserver Ma Wui Hall par l'intermédiaire d'IBN ou en appelant l'auberge directement depuis l'aéroport. Pour réserver les autres auberges, adressez-vous au bureau national de l'Association à Shek Kip Mei soit par fax soit par écrit, ou bien encore en téléphonant du lundi au vendredi de 9h 30 à 17h 30, et le samedi de 9h 30 à 13h.

Les auberges sont ouvertes de 7h à 10h et de 16h à 23h à l'exception de Jockey Club Mt. Davis YH qui est ouvert toute la journée de 7h à 23h. Le samedi et le jour qui précède un jour férié, l'accueil se fait à partir de 14h. Il est possible que les heures d'ouverture de l'Auberge S.G. Davis, qui est maintenant l'auberge la plus proche du nouvel aéroport de Chek Lap Kok, soient prolongées en 1999. Contactez l'auberge ou le bureau de l'association pour des renseignements plus à jour. Certaines auberges ferment en milieu de semaine sur une ou deux journées; il est donc prudent de vérifier au préalable que l'auberge sera ouverte quand vous voudrez y passer quelque temps.

Toutes les auberges d'Hong-Kong sont équipées d'une cuisine ajiste et d'un barbecue. En revanche, elles ne servent pas de repas. Le prix de la nuitée dans les auberges au "Plan de Garantie des Normes" pourra être compris, selon le lieu et la qualitié des prestations offertes, entre HK$35-HK$120 (ces chiffres sont corrects à l'heure où nous mettons sous presse, mais pourront être ajustés au cours de l'année). Vous trouverez le prix des nuitées dans le paragraphe consacré à chaque auberge. Ces prix ne s'appliquent qu'aux plus de 18 ans, les plus jeunes ajistes bénéficiant de tarifs réduits.

Avant de quitter l'aéroport, procurez-vous un plan HKYHA et un horaire du bus qui fait la navette entre Jockey Club Mt. Davis YH et Hong-Kong au comptoir de l'Association de Tourisme (Tourism Association) dans le hall d'arrivée.

PASSEPORTS ET VISAS

Peu de visiteurs ont besoin d'un visa, mais il vous faudra présenter un billet retour ou pour une autre destination. Vous pouvez séjourner à Hong-Kong sans visa pour une durée allant d'une semaine à 6 mois selon votre nationalité. Pour certaines nationalités, les passeports devront avoir une validité de 6 mois. Renseignez-vous auprès du Consulat Général de Chine le plus proche pour un complément d'information.

SOINS MEDICAUX

Il est conseillé de souscrire à une police d'assurance du fait des coûts élevés des services hospitaliers et des traitements médicaux. Il pourra être sollicité des voyageurs en provenance de régions où sévissent des infections ou des épidémies de fournir un certificat valide de vaccination.

HEURES D'OUVERTURE DES BANQUES

Les banques sont ouvertes 5 jours et demi par semaine. Les chèques de voyage et les billets de banque étrangers peuvent être échangés 7 jours sur 7 au Money Exchanges de Tsim Sha Tsui, mais les commissions varient considérablement. Vérifiez toujours les taux de change et le montant des commissions avant de remettre votre argent à qui que ce soit.

BUREAUX DE POSTE

Les bureaux de poste sont ouverts 5 jours et demi par semaine de 8h00 à 18h00 du lundi au vendredi et de 8h00 à 14h00 le samedi.

DEPLACEMENTS

Avions

Le tout nouvel aéroport international de Hong-Kong, dont la construction à Chek Lap Kok, sur l'île de Lantau, a coûté 9 milliards de dollars US, met à la disposition des voyageurs de nombreux services de très haute qualité. Il est également très bien relié à toutes les grandes villes du monde.

Hong-Kong est trop petite pour les vols intérieurs. L'important réseau de transport en commun (trains, bus, ferries et tramways) vous permet de vous rendre facilement dans n'importe quelle partie du territoire.

Ferry-boats

Deux compagnies maritimes, Star et Hong-Kong Ferry, assurent des navettes entre l'île de Hong-Kong et Kowloon. Les ferry-boats à destination de Lautau partent du "Outlying Districts Ferry Services Pier", à Central.

Trains

Le Mass Transit Railway (MTR) assure 5 lignes de métro qui relient Hong-Kong, Kowloon et le nord de l'Ile de Lantau. Le Kowloon Canton Railway (KCR) assure un service de trains entre Kowloon et Lo Wu, à la frontière entre Hong-Kong et la Chine continentale, sur une ligne électrifiée. Il existe également 3 lignes de tramway.

Autobus

Hong-Kong est bien desservie par les autobus et les minibus. Il y a en outre plus de 17 500 taxis. Certaines restrictions sont en vigueur en ce qui concerne la prise en charge et la dépose des passagers.

Automobiles

Nous ne vous conseillons pas de conduire, étant donné que les autres moyens de transport sont bon marché, efficaces et pratiques.

TELEPHONE

Indicatif du Pays   **852**
Indicatifs régionaux des Villes principales
    Pas d'indicatif régional

Deutsch

HONG KONG

JUGENDHERBERGEN

Viele Reisende glauben, daß Hong Kong nur ein städtisches Reiseerlebnis bieten kann. Wenn man Jugendherbergen benutzt, hat man die Möglichkeit, aufs Land zu fahren sowie etwas vom richtigen Hong Kong zu sehen.

Reservierungen der Jockey Club Mt. Davis Jugendherberge kann man entweder durch IBN buchen oder rufen Sie die Herberge direkt am Flughafen an. Außerdem kann man sich bei allen Jugendherbergen per Telefax, schriftlich oder telefonisch in der Hauptgeschäftsstelle in Shek Kip Mei anmelden. (Öffnungszeiten der Hauptgeschäftsstelle: Montag bis Freitag 09.30 - 17.30 Uhr, Samstags 09.30 - 13.00 Uhr).

Mit der Ausnahme von der Jockey Club Mt. Davis Jugendherberge und der S.G. Davis Herberge (die Herberge, die in der Nähe des neuen Flughafens Chek Lap Kok ist), die ganztags zwischen 7.00 - 23.00 Uhr geöffnet sind, sind alle Jugendherbergen zwischen 7.00 - 10.00 Uhr und 16.00 - 23.00 Uhr geöffnet. Samstags und vor einem Feiertag kann man sich früher anmelden (ab 14.00 Uhr). Einige Jugendherbergen schließen mittwöchentlich für ein oder zwei Tage. Es empfiehlt sich deshalb, immer im voraus anzurufen.

Jugendherbergen in Hong Kong bieten keine Mahlzeiten an, aber alle Jugendherbergen stellen Selbstversorgungsmöglichkeiten und B-B-Qs zur Verfügung. Übernachtungpreise schwanken abhängig von Ort und Ausstattung. Die Preisspanne reicht von HK$35-HK$120 (Diese Preisspanne ist bei Drucktermin genau und kann sich während des Jahres ändern). Die Übernachtungspreise gelten für Reisende über 18 Jahre; es gibt Rabatte für jungere Gäste. Raballe atter Gäste.

Holen sie sich vor Verlassen des Flughafens eine HKYHA-Karte und einen Pendelbusfahrplan für die Jockey Club Mt. Davis Jugendherberge vom Tourismusverbandschalter in der Empfangshalle.

PÄSSE UND VISA

Nur wenige Besucher brauchen Visa, aber man benötigt eine Weiter- oder Rückfahrkarte. Abhängig von der Staatsangehörigkeit, kann man bis zu 6 Monaten ohne Visum im Land bleiben. Einige Nationalitäten brauchen eine Paßgültigkeit von mindestens 6 Monaten. Bitte erkundigen Sie sich beim Konsulat General von China nach Einzelheiten.

GESUNDHEIT

Krankenhäuser- und Arzthonorare sind sehr hoch. Es wird daher dringend zu einer privaten Versicherung geraten. Reisende aus Gebieten, in denen Epidemien herrschen, müssen für die betreffenden Krankheiten im Besitz eines internationalen Impfzeugnisses sein.

GESCHÄFTSSTUNDEN DER BANKEN

Banken sind im allgemeinen 5 Tage in der Woche geöffnet. Man kann Reiseschecks und Devisen 7 Tage in der Woche bei den Wechselstuben in Tsim Sha Tsui umtauschen, aber die Provisionsgebühren sind sehr unterschiedlich. Es empfiehlt sich immer, den Kurs und die Provisionsgebühren zu vergleichen.

POSTÄMTER

Auch Postämter sind 5 Tage in der Woche geöffnet. Montags bis freitags 8.00 - 18.00 Uhr und samstags 8.00 - 14.00 Uhr.

REISEN

Flugverkehr

Der brandneue US $9 Billionen Hong Kong internationle Flughafen in Chek Lap Kok, Lantau Island, verfügt über gute Serviceleistungen, und es gibt gute Flugverbindungen zu allen größeren Städten der Welt.

Für örtliche Flüge ist Hong Kong zu klein. Das weitverbreitete Netz von Zügen, Bussen, Fähren und Straßenbahnen bietet ihnen die Möglichkeit zu fast allen Teilen des Gebietes mit öffentlichen Verkehrsmitteln zu gelangen.

Fähren

Zwei Fährboot-Unternehmen ('The Star' und 'Hong Kong Ferry Company') betreiben einen Pendelverkehr zwischen der Insel von Hong Kong und Kowloon. Fährboote nach Lantau fahren vom 'Outlying Districts Ferry Services Pier' in Central ab.

Eisenbahn

Die Mass Transit Railway (MTR) betreibt 5 U-Bahnlinien, die Hong Kong, Kowloon und den nördlichen Teil der Lantau Insel miteinander verbinden. Die Kowloon Canton Railway (KCR) unterhält elektrische Züge vom Bahnhof Kowloon bis zur Grenze von Hong Kong und Festland China. Es gibt auch 3 Straßenbahnlinien.

Busse

In Hong Kong verkehren viele Busse und Minibusse. Außerdem gibt es mehr als 17.500 zugelassene Taxen. In einigen Gegenden der Stadt können Fahrgäste nur bedingt aufgenommen bzw. abgesetzt werden.

Autofahren

Da andere Verkehrsmittel billig, leistungsfähig und bequem sind, empfiehlt es sich nicht, selbst einen Wagen zu steuern.

FERNSPRECHINFORMATIONEN

Landes-Kennzahl   852
größere Städte - Ortsnetzkennzahlen
   Keine Ortsnetzkennzahl

Español

HONG-KONG

ALBERGUES JUVENILES

Muchos viajeros piensan que Hong-Kong sólo ofrece una experiencia turística urbana. Sin embargo, los albergues juveniles de Hong-Kong le brindan la oportunidad de salir al campo y explorar la verdadera Hong-Kong.

Las reservas para el albergue Jockey Club Mt. Davis pueden hacerse por medio de la red IBN o llamando directamente al albergue desde el aeropuerto. Además, es posible reservar en todos los albergues a través de la Oficina Central de Skek Kip Mei por fax, por correo o por teléfono en horas de oficina (de lunes a viernes de 9.30 h. a 17.30 h. y los sábados de 9.30 h. a 13.30 h.).

Los albergues están abiertos de 7 h. a 10 h. y de 16 h. a 23 h. excepto Jockey Club Mt. Davis, el cual está abierto todo el día de 7 h. a 23 h. Los sábados y vísperas de fiestas, el registro de viajeros se efectúa más temprano, a partir de las 14 h. Es posible que se extienda el horario del S.G. Davis, el albergue más cercano al nuevo aeropuerto de Chek Lap Kok, en 1999 - póngase en contacto con el albergue o con la oficina de la asociación nacional para más información. Algunos albergues cierran uno o dos días entre semana. Por lo tanto, asegúrese de que el albergue esté abierto cuando usted desee alojarse en él.

Se puede cocinar en todos los albergues de Hong-Kong y también tienen parrillas, pero no sirven comidas. Los precios por noche en los albergues que se adhieren al "Plan de las Normas Garantizadas" varían según el emplazamiento y las prestaciones ofrecidas. Estos ocilan entre HK$35-HK$120 (los precios indicados son correctos al cierre de la edición, pero podrán modificarse durante el transcurso del año). El precio indicado para cada albergue es por noche para personas mayores de 18 años, pero existen descuentos para los visitantes más jóvenes.

Antes de salir del aeropuerto, consiga un mapa HKYHA y el horario del autobús regular que enlaza Jockey Club Mt. Davis con Hong-Kong en el mostrador de la Oficina de Turismo, en la sala de llegadas.

PASAPORTES Y VISADOS

Pocos visitantes necesitan visado, pero se les exige un billete de vuelta o con otro destino. La duración de las estancias sin visado oscila entre una semana y seis meses, según su nacionalidad. Para ciertas nacionalidades, los pasaportes deberán tener una validez de seis meses como mínimo. Infórmese en el Consulado General de China más cercano.

ASISTENCIA MEDICA

Se recomienda hacerse un seguro médico, dado que los hospitales y los cuidados médicos son muy caros. Es posible que se exija a los visitantes provenientes de zonas contaminadas por enfermedades contagiosas o donde estas sean endémicas un certificado de vacunación vigente.

HORARIO DE LOS BANCOS

Los bancos abren 5 días y medio a la semana. En las oficinas de cambio de Tsim Sha Tsui, las cuales están abiertas los 7 días de la semana, es posible cambiar cheques de viajero y divisas, pero las comisiones varían mucho de un lugar a otro. Compruebe siempre los tipos de cambio y el importe de las comisiones antes de realizar la transacción.

OFICINAS DE CORREOS

Las oficinas de correos también abren 5 días y medio a la semana, de 8 h. a 18 h. de lunes a viernes y de 8 h. a 14 h. los sábados.

DESPLAZAMIENTOS

Avión
El flamante Aeropuerto Internacional de Hong-Kong situado en Chek Lap Kok, en la isla de Lantau, cuya construcción ha costado 9 billones de $USA, tiene una buena red aérea con vuelos a todas las principales ciudades del mundo.

Hong-Kong no tiene vuelos nacionales por ser demasiado pequeña, pero la amplia red de ferrocarriles, autobuses, ferrys y tranvías le permitirá desplazarse a casi cualquier parte del territorio por transporte público.

Ferry
Existen dos compañías de ferry, The Star y Hong Kong Ferry Company, las cuales enlazan la isla de Hong-Kong con Kowloon. Los ferrys que van a Lantau salen del muelle del servicio de ferry de largos recorridos (Outlying Districts Ferry Services Pier), en Central.

Tren
El Mass Transit Railway (MTR) posee 5 líneas de metro que enlazan el centro urbano de Hong-Kong con Kowloon y el norte de la isla de Lantau. La red ferroviaria Kowloon Canton Railway (KCR) tiene un servicio de ferrocarril entre Kowloon y Lo Wu, en la frontera que separa Hong-Kong de la China continental, sobre una línea electrificada. Existen también 3 líneas de tranvía.

Autobús
Hong-Kong posee un excelente servicio de autobuses (algunos dejan de funcionar a las 19 h.) y de microbuses y más de 17.500 taxis. En el centro, existen ciertas restricciones en cuanto a la subida y bajada de pasajeros.

Automóvil
No le recomendamos el coche, ya que los demás medios de transporte son económicos, eficaces y prácticos.

INFORMACION TELEFONICA

Código Nacional   852
Prefijos de las Ciudades Principales
  No existen prefijos

Hong Kong

**Jockey Club Mt. Davis Youth Hostel
(formerly Ma Wui Hall),
Top of Mt Davis Path,
off Victoria Rd,
Kennedy Town,
Hong Kong Island.**

☎ (852) 2817 5715
✆ (852) 2788 3105

Open Dates:	🗓
Open Hours:	07.00-23.00 hrs
Reservations:	**R** **IBN**
Price Range:	HK$65-120 🛏
Beds:	111 - 6x² 1x³ 10x⁴ 1x⁶ 4x⁶
Facilities:	♚ 17x👪 ☎ TV 🍴 📷 8 ⊜
Directions:	4W from city centre
✈	Hong Kong International
A🚌	S61/S51 to Tung Chung AR Station & MTR ap Sheung Wan & taxi or hostel shuttle bus to hostel

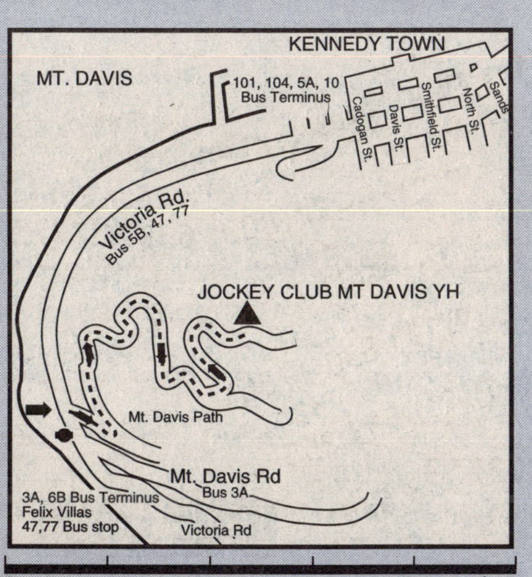

There for everyone - young, not so young and those in the middle.

c'est pour tout le monde - les jeunes, les moins jeunes et tous les autres.

albergues para todos - los jóvenes, los menos jóvenes y los jóvenes de espíritu.

für jederman - ob jung, nicht mehr ganz so jung oder die dazwischen.

CHINA (People's Republic of) • CHINE (République Populaire de)

Location/Address	Telephone No. Fax No.	Beds	Opening Dates	Facilities
△ *Chek Keng* *Bradbury Hall, Chek Keng, Sai Kung,* *New Territories.*	☎ (852) 2328 2458 📠 (852) 2788 3105	100	🗓9	R ☕
▲ Hong Kong [IBN] **Jockey Club Mt. Davis Youth Hostel** **(formerly Ma Wui Hall), Top of Mt Davis Path,** **off Victoria Rd, Kennedy Town,** **Hong Kong Island.**	☎ (852) 2817 5715 📠 (852) 2788 3105	111	🗓9	� R 4W ☕ 🗄
△ *Mong Tung Wan* *Jockey Club Mong Tung Wan Hostel,* *Mong Tung Wan, Lantau Island.*	☎ (852) 2984 1389 📠 (852) 2788 3105	88	🗓9	R ☕
△ *Ngong Ping* *S G Davis YH, Ngong Ping, Lantau Island.*	☎ (852) 2985 5610 📠 (852) 2788 3105	52	🗓9	♟ R ☕
△ *Pak Sha O* *Pak Sha O YH, Hoi Ha Rd, Pak Sha O, Sai Kung,* *New Territories.*	☎ (852) 2328 2327 📠 (852) 2788 3105	112	🗓9	R ☕
△ *Tai Mei Tuk* *Bradbury Lodge,66 Tai Mei Tuk Road, Tai Mei Tuk,* *Tai Po, New Territories.*	☎ (852) 2662 5123 📠 (852) 2788 3105	94	🗓9	♟ R ♿ ☕ 🗄
△ *Tai Mo Shan* *Sze Lok Yuen, Off Tai Mo Shan Rd, Tsuen Wan,* *New Territories.*	☎ (852) 2488 8188 📠 (852) 2788 3105	92	🗓9	R ☕

Costa Rica

COSTA RICA

COSTA RICA

COSTA RICA

Red Costarricense de Albergues Juveniles,
PO Box 1355-1002, Paseo de los Estudiantes
Avenida Central, Calles 29 y 31
San José, Costa Rica.

☎ (506) 2348186,
   (506) 2244085,
   (506) 2536588
✆ (506) 2244085
E-mail: recajhi@sol.racsa.co.cr
WWW address: http://www.hostels.com/cr.html

A copy of the Hostel Directory for this Country can be obtained from:
The National Office.

Capital:	San José	Population:	3,500,000
Language:	Spanish	Size:	51,100 sq km
Currency:	colón		

Costa Rica

NICARAGUA
R San Juan
CARIBBEAN SEA
Guanacaste-Rincón de la Vieja
Guanacaste-Guanacaste Hotel
Arenal
Monteverde Finca Valverde
Liberia
R Tempisque
Puerto Limon
Puntarenas
San Jose
R Grande de Tárcales
Toruma
Cartago
COSTA RICA
PANAMA
PACIFIC OCEAN
R Grande de Térraba
N
400   800   KM
0
200   400   MLS

English

COSTA RICAN HOSTELS

In Costa Rica our hostels try to follow ecological conservation regulations based on the sustainable development principle, in harmony with nature. Each hostel is in a strategic location which makes the most of national parks, beaches and cities. Most have double, triple or family rooms with bed linen, towels and soap included in the price. Overnight accommodation prices for Hostels within the "Assured Standards Scheme" will vary according to location and facilities. The range is from US$ 10.00-US$ 35.00 (This price range is accurate at the time of printing, and may be subject to change during the year). Reservations can be made by phone, fax, e-mail or mail, directly to the hostel. Each hostel has something different to offer: hiking tours, cycling, white water rafting, Spanish courses and a tropical paradise waiting to be discovered.

PASSPORTS AND VISAS

Visa requirements vary according to nationality. Check with the Costa Rican Embassy or Consulate in your own country before travelling.

HEALTH

Drinking water in some beach areas should be purified. Malaria Prophylaxis is recommended in banana zones or areas close to the Nicaraguan border.

BANKING HOURS

State banks are open Monday to Friday 08.30-15.00 hrs. and private banks open Monday to Friday 09.00-18.00 hrs.

POST OFFICES

Post offices are open Monday to Friday 08.00-17.00hrs and can be used to send and receive faxes, money orders and mail.

SHOPPING HOURS

Shops are open all week 09.00-18.00hrs. Supermarkets are open every day 10.00-21.00hrs and the "Pulperias" (general stores) are open every day 05.30-18.00hrs. The Farmers' markets are open on Saturday and Sunday mornings.

TRAVEL

Air
You can reach Costa Rica with all main airlines worldwide, making connections mainly in the U.S.A. There are also several national airlines which provide domestic regular and charter flights.

Bus
Bus services are private throughout the country. Our main office can provide you with timetables to any destination.

Ferry
Ferry is the best way to get to the Nicoya Peninsula from Punta Arenas or points east and south.

Driving
We recommend 4x4 during the rainy season and for hostels in the mountains or if wanting to watch turtle egg-laying.

TELEPHONE INFORMATION

Country Code   **506**
Main City Area Codes
  No area codes

Français

AUBERGES DE JEUNESSE COSTARICIENNES

Au Costa Rica, nos auberges essayent de suivre des normes écologiques de conservation basées sur une notion d'équilibre entre le développement de l'activité humaine et l'environnement, c'est-à-dire en harmonie avec la nature. Chaque auberge se trouve dans un emplacement privilégié pour vous permettre de profiter au maximum des parcs nationaux, des plages et des villes. La plupart ont des chambres à 2 ou 3 lits ou des chambres familiales et le prix de la nuitée comprend la location des draps, des serviettes de toilette et du savon. Dans les auberges appartenant au "Plan de Ganrantie des Normes" il pourra être compris, selon le lieu et la qualité des prestations offertes, entre US$ 10.00-US$ 35.00 (ces chiffres sont corrects à l'heure où nous mettons sous presse mais pourront être ajustés au cours de l'année). Vous pouvez réserver par téléphone, fax, courrier ordinaire ou électronique, en vous adressant directement à l'auberge. Chaque auberge a quelque chose de différent à offrir: excursions, randonnées à vélo, rafting en eaux vives et beaucoup d'autres sports, cours d'espagnol et un paradis tropical qui ne demande qu'à être découvert.

PASSEPORTS ET VISAS

Il n'est pas toujours nécessaire d'obtenir un visa. Consultez l'Embassade ou le Consulat costaricien de votre pays avant d'entamer votre voyage.

SOINS MEDICAUX

Aux environs de certaines plages, il est recommandé de purifier l'eau avant de la boire. Il est également recommandé de prendre des mesures de prévention contre la malaria dans les régions de bananiers ou dans les régions proches de la frontière nicaraguayenne.

HEURES D'OUVERTURE DES BANQUES

Les banques d'état sont ouvertes de 08h30 à 15h00 du lundi au vendredi tandis que les banques privées sont ouvertes de 09h00 à 18h00 également du lundi au vendredi.

BUREAUX DE POSTE

Les bureaux de poste sont ouverts du lundi au vendredi de 08h00 à 17h00 et l'on peut y

envoyer et recevoir des fax, des mandats ou du courrier.

HEURES D'OUVERTURE DES MAGASINS

Les magasins sont ouverts toute la semaine de 9h à 18h. Les supermarchés sont ouverts tous les jours de 10h à 21h et les "Pulperias" (grands magasins) sont ouverts tous les jours de 5h30 à 18h. Les marchés fermiers ont lieu les samedi et dimanche matins.

DEPLACEMENTS

Avions

Il est possible de se rendre au Costa Rica avec la plupart des principales compagnies aériennes internationales qui font la liaison principalement avec les USA. En outre il existe plusieurs compagnies nationales qui proposent des vols charters intérieurs réguliers.

Autobus

Les services de bus sont assurés par des compagnies privées partout dans le pays. Notre bureau principal pourra vous fournir les horaires de ces bus pour n'importe quelle destination.

Ferry-boats

Le ferry est le meilleur moyen de se rendre à la Péninsule de Nicoya à partir de Punta Arenas ou à partir de l'est et le sud.

Automobiles

Nous vous recommandons les véhicules à quatre roues motrices pendant la saison des pluies et pour vous rendre aux auberges de montagne ou bien encore si vous désirez aller observer les tortues pendant la ponte des oeufs.

TELEPHONE

Indicatif du Pays   506
Indicatifs régionaux des Villes principales
     Pas d'indicatifs régionaux

Deutsch

JUGENDHERBERGEN IN COSTA RICA

In Costa Rica versuchen unsere Jugendherbergen ökologische Naturschutzvorschriften zu befolgen. Sie ruhen auf menschlichen Aktivitäten in Umwelt und Natur. Jede Herberge ist ein günstiger Standort für das Erleben von National Parks, Stränden und Städten. Die meisten haben Doppel, Dreier- oder Familienzimmer. Bettwäsche, Handtücher und Seife sind im Preis inbegriffen. Übernachtungspreise schwanken abhängig von Ort und Ausstattung. Die Preisspanne reicht von US\$ 10.00-US\$ 35.00 (Diese Preisspanne ist bei Drucktermin genau und kann sich während des Jahres ändern). Reservierung kann man telefonisch, durch Fax, e-mail oder schriftlich machen, direkt mit der Herberge oder durch IBN, wo es angebracht ist. Jede Herberge hat etwas anderes anzubieten: Wanderreisen, Radfahren, einen Spanischkurs besuchen; Wildwasser-Rafting, Vulkantouren, Kajak, Surfen, Vögel beobachten, Thermalbäder, Wasserfälle, Tauchtouren und auch ein tropisches Paradies erwartet Sie, um entdeckt zu werden.

PÄSSE UND VISA

Die Visaanforderungen sind unterschiedlich nach Nationalität. Nehmen Sie also vor Antritt der Reise Kontakt mit der Botschaft oder einem Konsulat von Costa Rica in Ihrem Lande auf.

GESUNDHEIT

In gewissen Strandbereichen muß das Trinkwasser gereinigt werden. In Bananenzonen oder Gebieten in der Nähe der nicaraguanischen Grenze wird eine Malaria-Prophylaxe empfohlen.

GESCHÄFTSSTUNDEN DER BANKEN

Für komplizierte Bankgeschäfte sind die Banken von 09.00-15.00 Uhr geöffnet. In den Zentralfilialen in San José sind sie zur Einlösung von Schecks von 08.30-18.00 Uhr geöffnet.

POSTÄMTER

Postämter sind montags bis freitags von 08.00-17.00 Uhr geöffnet. Man kann auch Faxinformationen, Zahlungsanweisungen und Post aussenden und empfangen.

LADENÖFFNUNGSZEITEN

Die Geschäfte sind montags bis sonntags von 09.00-18.00 Uhr und samstags von 09.00-12.00 Uhr geöffnet. Supermärkte sind täglich von 10.00-21.00 Uhr und die "Pulperias" (allgemeine Geschäfte) täglich von 05.30-18.00 Uhr geöffnet. Die Bauernmärkte sind samstags und sonntags am Vormittag geöffnet.

REISEN

Flugverkehr
Man kann Costa Rica mit allen internationalen Fluggesellschaften erreichen, hauptsächlich mit Anschluß in die USA. Es gibt verschiedene nationale Fluglinien, die innerhalb des Landes fliegen und Charterflüge.

Busse
Busreisedienste sind privat im ganzen Land. Unser Hauptbüro kann Ihnen mit Fahrplänen für jeden Bestimmungsort aushelfen.

Fähren
Zur Halbinsel Nicoya gelangt man von Punta Arenas oder verschiedenen Häfen im Osten und Süden aus am besten mit der Fähre.

Autofahren
Es wird ein vierrädiges Fahrzeug während der Regenzeit und für die Herbergen in den Bergen empfohlen, oder wenn man Schildkröten bei der Eiablage beobachten möchte.

FERNSPRECHINFORMATIONEN

Landes-Kennzahl   506
größere Städte - Ortsnetzkennzahlen
   Keine Ortsnetzkennzahlen

Español

ALBERGUES JUVENILES COSTARRICENSES

En Costa Rica nuestros albergues se esfuerzan por seguir normas ecológicas de conservación basadas en el principio del equilibrio entre el desarrollo de la actividad del hombre y el medio ambiente, es decir, en armonía con la naturaleza. Cada albergue está estratégicamente ubicado para lograr un mejor aprovechamiento de los parques nacionales, playas y ciudades. La mayoría de ellos ofrecen habitaciones dobles, triples o familiares, con sábanas, toallas y jabón incluidos en el precio. Los precios de los albergues que se adhieren al "Plan de las Normas Garantizadas" varían según el emplazamiento y las prestaciones ofrecidas. Estos oscilan entre US$ 10.00-US$ 35.00 (los precios indicados son correctos al cierre de la edición, pero podrán modificarse durante el transcurso del año). Puede hacer sus reservas contactando directamente el albergue por teléfono, fax, correo electrónico o correo normal. Cada albergue tiene algo diferente que ofrecerle: excursiones a pie y en bicicleta, rafting (navegación en balsa en aguas rápidas) y otras muchas actividades deportivas y visitas turísticas, así como cursos de español y un paraíso tropical que espera ser descubierto por usted.

PASAPORTES Y VISADOS

La necesidad de visado varía según la nacionalidad. Rogamos se ponga en contacto con la embajada o el consulado costarricenses de su propio país antes de viajar.

ASISTENCIA MEDICA

Es preciso depurar el agua en algunas zonas de playa antes de beberla. Recomendamos medicarse contra la malaria en zonas bananeras y en lugares próximos a la frontera con Nicaragua.

HORARIO DE LOS BANCOS

Los bancos estatales trabajan de lunes a viernes de 8.30 h. a 15 h. y los privados de lunes a viernes de 9 h. a 18 h.

OFICINAS DE CORREOS

Las oficinas de correos abren de lunes a viernes, de 8 h. a 17 h. En ellas se pueden enviar y recibir facsímiles, giros postales y correo.

HORARIO COMERCIAL

Las tiendas abren toda la semana de 9 h. a 18 h. Los supermercados abren todos los días de 10 h. a 21 h. y las "pulperías" (almacenes generales) abren a diario de 5.30 h. a 18 h. Los mercadillos de los campesinos son los sábados y domingos por la mañana.

DESPLAZAMIENTOS

Avión

Se puede llegar a Costa Rica utilizando las principales líneas aéreas del mundo, con conexiones principalmente en los Estados Unidos. A nivel nacional, existen varias compañías que realizan vuelos regulares y chárter.

Autobús

El servicio de autobuses es privado en todo el país. En nuestras oficinas centrales, le podemos suministrar horarios para el lugar que Ud. desee.

Ferry

El ferry es la mejor forma de llegar a la Península de Nicoya desde Punta Arenas o desde el este y el sur.

Automóvil

Recomendamos un automóvil de tracción integral (4x4) para sus visitas durante la estación lluviosa y a los albergues de montaña o para observar el desove de las tortugas.

INFORMACION TELEFONICA

Código Nacional   **506**
Prefijos de las Ciudades Principales
  No existen prefijos regionales

Location/Address	Telephone No. Fax No.	Beds	Opening Dates	Facilities
▲ **Arenal** Cabinas Rossi, 1Km West, La Fortuna, Road to the Volcano	☎ 4799023 ✆ 4799414	40		ŧ†ŧ ¶⊙ R 1W ♿ CC ♂ P
▲ **Finca Valverde** 250mts SE Banco Nacional	☎ 6455157 ✆ 6455216	48		ŧ†ŧ ¶⊙ R 0.3 SE ♿ CC P 🗖 ♨
▲ **Guanacaste** - Rincón de la Vieja Hostel Liberia, Guanacaste. (300km from San José; active volcano)	☎ 695553; 2568206 ✆ 2244085	50		ŧ†ŧ ¶⊙ R 27 NE CC P 🗖
▲ **Guanacaste** - Hotel Guanacaste Liberia, Guanacaste.	☎ 6662287; 6660085 or RECAJ 2244085 ✆ 6662287	68		ŧ†ŧ ¶⊙ R 0.5 W CC ♂ P
▲ **Puntarenas** - Hotel Cabinas San Isidro 700mts West Sanabria Hospital, El Roble (Pacific Beach), 100Kms from San José	☎ 2805200, 6630031 or RECAJ 2348186 ✆ 2244611 or 2244085	300		ŧ†ŧ ¶⊙ R 10 W ♿ CC ♂ P ♨
▲ **San José** - Toruma Toruma Hostel, Avenida Central, calle 29 y 31, San José.	☎ 2348186 ✆ 2244085	87		ŧ†ŧ 2E CC P

HOSTELLING INTERNATIONAL

Make your credit card bookings at these centres
Réservez par cartes de crédit aux centres suivants
Buchen Sie mit Kreditkarte in folgenden Buchungszentren
Reserve por tarjeta de crédito en los siguientes centros

English

Australia	☎ (2) 9261 1111
Canada	☎ (800) 663 5777
England & Wales	☎ (1629) 581 418
France	☎ (1) 44 89 87 27
Northern Ireland	☎ (1232) 324 733
Republic of Ireland	☎ (1) 830 1766
New Zealand	☎ (9) 303 9524
Scotland	☎ (541) 553 255
Switzerland	☎ (1) 360 1414
USA	☎ (202) 783 6161

Français

Angleterre & Pays de Galles	☎ (1692) 581 418
Australie	☎ (2) 9261 1111
Canada	☎ (800) 663 5777
Écosse	☎ (541) 553 255
États-Unis	☎ (202) 783 6161
France	☎ (1) 44 89 87 27
Irlande du Nord	☎ (1232) 324 733
Nouvelle-Zélande	☎ (9) 303 9524
République d'Irlande	☎ (1) 830 1766
Suisse	☎ (1) 360 1414

Deutsch

Australien	☎ (2) 9261 1111
England & Wales	☎ (1629) 581 418
Frankreich	☎ (1) 44 89 87 27
Irland	☎ (1) 830 1766
Kanada	☎ (800) 663 5777
Neuseeland	☎ (9) 303 9524
Nordirland	☎ (1232) 324 733
Schottland	☎ (541) 553 255
Schweiz	☎ (1) 360 1414
USA	☎ (202) 783 6161

Español

Australia	☎ (2) 9261 1111
Canadá	☎ (800) 663 5777
Escocia	☎ (541) 553 255
Estados Unidos	☎ (202) 783 6161
Francia	☎ (1) 44 89 87 27
Inglaterra y Gales	☎ (1629) 581 418
Irlanda del Norte	☎ (1232) 324 733
Nueva Zelanda	☎ (9) 303 9524
República de Irlanda	☎ (1) 830 1766
Suiza	☎ (1) 360 1414

Ecuador

EQUATEUR
ECUADOR
ECUADOR

**Asociación Ecuatoriana de Albergues,
Pinto 325 y Reina Victoria, Quito,
Ecuador.**
☎ (593) (2) 543995
✆ (593) (2) 508221
Email: ecuatori@pi.pro.ec

Office Hours: Monday-Friday, 09.00-13.00hrs,
15.00-19.00hrs

A copy of the Hostel Directory for this Country can be obtained from:
The National Office.

Travel Section: Asociación Ecuatoriana de Albergues,
German Aleman y Pasaje a N. 105, Quito, Ecuador.

☎ (593) (2) 9459900
✆ (593) (2) 9459900

Capital:	Quito	**Population:**	12,200,000
Language:	Spanish/Quichua	**Size:**	270,000 sq km
Currency:	$ Sucre		

Ecuador

San Cristobal
GALAPAGOS ISLANDS
COLOMBIA
Tulcan
Atacames
Ibarra
Guallupe
Otavalo
Quito
Cayambe
Quito
Bahia
Pasochoa Forest
San Vicente
Baños
Riobamba
Puerto Lopez
Misahulli
Guayaquil
Salango
ECUADOR
Salinas
Cuenca
PACIFIC OCEAN
Villabamba
PERU

English

ECUADOREAN HOSTELS

Most hostels are situated in Ecuador's main cities and in the more tourist-orientated areas of the Sierra, the Coast, Amazonia and the Galápogos, all of which possess a wealth of natural beauty and cultural interest.

The hostels offer travellers twin, triple, rooms with double beds and group rooms, many of these with private bathrooms, and also bedroom suites; there is no need to hire sheets. Most hostels are open 24 hours a day and prices range from US$ 5.00 to US$ 10.00 (26.000-53.000 Sucre) including breakfast.

PASSPORTS AND VISAS

Visa requirements in Ecuador vary according to nationality; you should contact the Ecuadorian Embassy or Consulate in your own country to obtain precise information on entry to Ecuador.

HEALTH

No inoculations are required.

BANKING HOURS

The National Banking System is open from 09.00-18.00hrs Monday-Friday, 09.00-13.00hrs, Saturday/Sunday.

SHOPPING HOURS

Normally open from 09.00-20.30hrs Monday-Saturday, 09.00-13.00hrs Sunday.

TRAVEL

Most transport is by main road, on long distance journeys.

Air
Daily flights are available with Ecuatoriana, SAETA, SAN, TAME and AEROGAL covering the country's main cities.

Rail
The train is used particularly to cover the tourist routes through attractive valleys and roadways, both in the mountain areas and on the Ecuadorian coast. There are railway stations in Quito, Ibarra and Riobamba.

Bus
Ecuador has an excellent, modern bus and coach service covering all of the country's main tourist locations and cities; there are bus stations in all cities and towns.

TELEPHONE INFORMATION

Country Code	**593**
Main City Area Codes	
Quito	02
Guayaquil	04
Cuenca	07
Baños	03
Galápagos	05

Français

AUBERGES DE JEUNESSE EQUATORIENNES

La plupart des auberges sont situées dans les villes principales de l'Equateur et dans les régions plus axées sur le tourisme comme la Sierra, la côte, l'Amazonie et les îles Galapagos, toutes ces régions possédant une abondance de beautés naturelles et de richesses d'intérêt culturel.

Les auberges offrent aux voyageurs des chambres à 2, 3 ou 4 lits ou des chambres pour groupe, un grande nombre d'entre elles ayant leurs salles de bain privées, ainsi que des chambres avec lits pour 2 personnes; il n'est pas nécessaire de louer des draps. La plupart des auberges sont ouvertes 24 heures sur 24 et les prix varient de 5 $US à 10 $US (26.000-53.000 Sucre), petit déjeuner inclus.

PASSEPORTS ET VISAS

L'obtention d'un visa est obligatoire selon les nationalités. Nous vous conseillons de prendre contact avec l'Ambassade ou le Consulat équatorien de votre propre pays pour obtenir des informations précises sur les conditions d'entrée en Equateur.

SOINS MEDICAUX

Aucune inoculation spéciale n'est requise.

HEURES D'OUVERTURE DES BANQUES

Le systéme bancaire national est ouvert de 9h à 18h, du vendredi et le samedi et le dimanche de 9h à 13h.

HEURES D'OUVERTURE DES MAGASINS

Les magasins sont ouverts normalement de 9h à 20h30 du lundi au samedi et le dimanche de 9h à 13h.

DEPLACEMENTS

Les déplacements se font principalement par route, pour les longs trajets.

Avions

Des vols journaliers sont disponibles par l'intermédiaire des compagnies Ecuatoriana, SAETA, TAME, SAN et AEROGAL, qui relient les principales villes du pays.

Trains

Le train est particulièrement utilisé sur les parcours touristiques à travers de ravissantes vallées tant dans les régions montagneuses que sur la côte éqatorienne. Il y a des gares de chemin de fer à Quito, Ibarra et Riobamba.

Autobus

L'Equateur possède un service excellent et moderne de bus et de cars qui relie toutes les localités touristiques principales et toutes les villes du pays; il y a des stations d'autobus dans toutes les villes et bourgades du pays.

TELEPHONE

Indicatif du Pays	**42**
Indicatifs régionaux des Villes principales	
Quito	2
Guayaquil	04
Cuenca	07
Baños	03
Galápagos	05

Deutsch

JUGENDHERBERGEN IN ECUADOR

Die meisten Herbergen befinden sich in den Großstädten Ecuadors sowie in den von den Touristen stärker aufgesuchten Regionen wie der Sierra, der Küste, im Amazonasgebiet und auf den Galápagos-Inseln. Diese kulturell interessanten Regionen zeichnen sich alle durch ihren natürlichen Charme aus.

Die Herbergen bieten den Reisenden Zwei-, Drei- oder Vierbettzimmer sowie Gruppenzimmer an, viele mit eigenem Badezimmer, sowie ganze Suites; Bettlaken sind im Preis inbegriffen. Die meisten Jugendherberge sind rund um die Uhr geöffnet. Ihre Preise liegen bei US\$ 5,00 bis US\$ 10,00 (26.000-53.000 Sucre) inklusive Frühstück.

PÄSSE UND VISA

Die in Ecuador gültigen Visabestimmungen hängen von der jeweiligen Nationalität ab. Bitte informieren Sie sich vor Ihrer Abreise bei der ecuadorianischen Botschaft oder dem Konsulat in Ihrem Land über den aktuellen Stand der Einreisebedingungen für Ecuador.

GESUNDHEIT

Impfungen sind nicht erforderlich.

GESCHÄFTSSTUNDEN DER BANKEN

Die Banken sind montags bis freitags von 09.00-18.00 Uhr und samstags und sonntags von 09.00-13.00 Uhr geöffnet.

GESCHÄFTSÖFFNUNGSZEITEN

Die Geschäfte sind in der Regel montags bis samstags von 09.00-20.30 Uhr und sonntags von 09.00-13.00 Uhr geöffnet.

REISEN

Gerade bei langen Überlandfahrten geht es über die Hauptstraßen.

Flugverkehr

Ecuatoriana, SAETA, SAN, TAME und AEROGAL bieten tägliche Flüge zu Großstädten des Landes an.

Züge

Züge verkehren überwiegend auf den Touristenstrecken, durch reizvolle Täler und über die Höhen der Bergregionen und entlang der Küste Ecuadors. Es gibt in Quito, Ibarra und Riobamba Bahnhöfe.

Busse

In Ecuador verkehren zwischen allen großen Touristenattraktionen und den Großstädten höchst komfortable moderne Busse und Reisebusse; alle Städte und Großstädte haben Busbahnhöfe.

FERNSPRECHINFORMATIONEN

Landes-Kennzahl	**593**
größere Städte - Ortsnetzkennzahlen	
Quito	2
Guayaquil	04
Cuenca	07
Baños	03
Galápagos	05

Español

ALBERGUES DE JUVENTUD ECUATORIANOS

La mayoría de los albergues juveniles se encuentran en las principales ciudades del Ecuador y en las zonas más turísticas de la sierra, costa, Amazonia y en las islas Galápagos, todos ellos lugares famosos por su riqueza natural y cultural.

Los albergues juveniles ofrecen al pasajero habitaciones dobles, triples, cuádruples y para grupos, muchas de ellas con baño, así como suites matrimoniales. No hay necesidad de alquilar sábanas. La mayoría de los albergues permanecen abiertos las 24 horas del día y tienen un precio que va de los US$ 5,00 a los US$ 10,00 (26.000-53.000 Sucres), tarifa que incluye el desayuno.

PASAPORTES Y VISADOS

La necesidad de obtener un visado varía según la nacionalidad. Es necesario ponerse en contacto con la Embajada o Consulado Ecuatoriano en su país para obtener con precisión los datos de acceso al Ecuador.

SANIDAD

No se requiere ninguna vacuna.

HORARIO DE BANCOS

El sistema bancario nacional está abierto desde las 09.00 a 18.00 horas de lunes a viernes, y los sábados y domingos de 09.00 a 13.00 horas.

HORARIO COMERCIAL

Normalmente, las tiendas abren de 09.00 a 20.30 horas de lunes a sábado y los domingos de 09.00 a 13.00 horas.

DESPLAZAMIENTOS

El transporte se realiza sobre todo por carretera para largos recorridos.

Avión

Ecuatoriana, SAETA, SAN, TAME y AEROGAL tienen vuelos diarios a las principales ciudades del país.

Tren

El tren se utiliza especialmente para realizar trayectos turísticos por hermosos valles y senderos, tanto de la serranía como de la costa ecuatoriana. Existen estaciones de tren en Quito, Ibarra y Riobamba.

Autobús

Ecuador posee un excelente y moderno servicio de autobuses que cubre todos los puntos turísticos y ciudades importantes del país. Hay estaciones de autobús en todas las ciudades.

INFORMACION TELEFONICA

Código Nacional	**593**
Prefijos de las Ciudades Principales	
Quito	2
Guayaquil	04
Cuenca	07
Baños	03
Galápagos	05

Discounts And Concessions

There are more than 400 discount points in Ecuador on land transport services, tourist services, restaurants, craft shops, bars, etc.

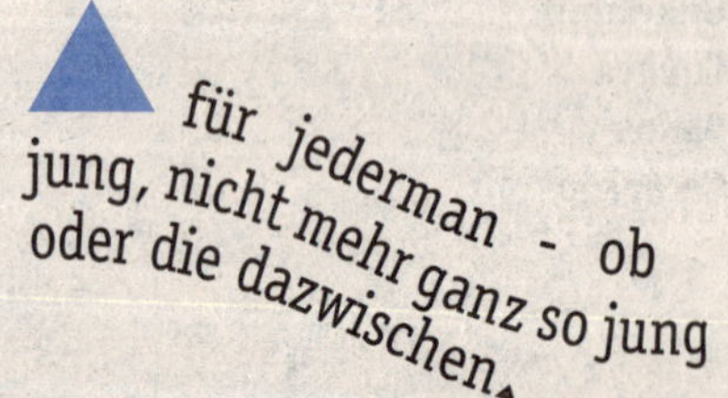

Quito

Joaquin Pinto 325 y Reina Victoria.
☎ (5932) 543995
📠 (5932) 508221

Open Dates:	🗓
Open Hours:	🕐
Reservations:	**R** **IBN** **CC**
Price Range:	$8.00-10.00 **BB**inc 🖳
Beds:	80 - 2x²🛏 6x³🛏 7x⁴🛏 1x⁵🛏 2x⁶🛏
Facilities:	👥 3x👥🍴 ⦿(B) ✆ TV 🔲 🧳 🛒 P 🛈 👤♿ ♨
Directions:	1 SE from city centre
✈	Mariscal Sucre 5km
🚂	8km
🚌	#1 & #2 300m
🚋	500m

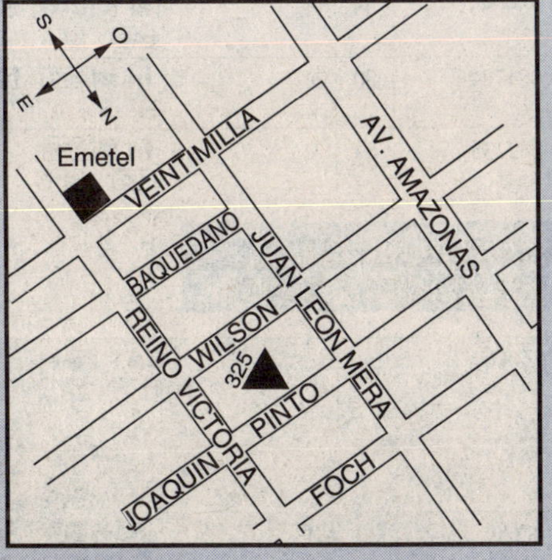

Assured Standards – visited by our Liaison team and by you the guest – tell us when we don't measure up (reply slips at the end of this Guide) ▸

des Normes Garanties, par les visites de notre Equipe de Liaison et par vous, les usagers – faites-le nous savoir quand nous ne sommes pas à la hauteur (Fiches-commentaires à la fin du Guide) ▸

Zugesicherte Standards – beurteilt von unserem Liaison Team und von Ihnen, unserem Gast – sagen Sie es uns, wenn wir Sie enttäuschen (Antwortkarten hinten im Führer) ▸

Normas Garantizadas – comprobadas por nuestro Equipo de Enlace y por Ud., el usuario – si fallamos en algo, díganoslo (al final de esta Guía encontrará nuestras hojas de comentarios) ▸

Location/Address	Telephone No. / Fax No.	Beds	Opening Dates	Facilities
▲ **Bahia** Bahia Hotel, Malecón Alberto Santos Y Vinueza.	☎ (5) 690823, 690509 fax (5) 690823	70		👪 ⦿ R CC P
△ *Cabañas Del Rio Yambala* *Vilcabamba.*	☎ *(7) 673186* *fax (7) 673186*	*52*		👪 ⦿ R
△ *Casa Mar* *Parroquia Charapoto. (Junto Empresa de Telecomunicaciones)*	☎ *(2) 223340, 433156* *fax (2) 223340*	70		👪 ⦿ R CC P
▲ **Cuenca** Macondo, Casilla 597, Tarqui 11-64, Cuenca.	☎ (7) 831198 fax (7) 833593	20		👪 ⦿ R ♿
▲ **Gästehaus (Ambato)** Shyris 557 y Nary Pillahuaso Ambato.	☎ (3) 847349, 843188	30		👪 CC P
▲ **Guayaquil** Ecuahogar, Av Isidro Ayora, (Sauces I), Frente al Banco Ecuatoriano de la Vivienda MZF31 V 20, Guayaquil.	☎ (5934) 248357 fax (5934) 248341	40		⦿ P
▲ **Ibarra** Casona de los Lagos, Sucre 350 y Grijalva, Ibarra, Imbabura.	☎ 951629, 957844	70		👪 ⦿ R CC P
▲ **Otavalo** - Jatun Pacha Av 31 de Octubre 19 y Panamericana.	☎ (6) 921168, 922223 fax (6) 922871	20		👪 0.4 SW ♿ CC P
△ *Pasochoa* *National Park (Amaguaña), Quito.*	☎ *(2) 543995, 226271* *fax (2) 543995*	*16*		R P
▲ **Quito** IBN **Joaquin Pinto 325 y Reina Victoria.**	☎ (5932) 543995 fax (5932) 508221	80		👪 R 1 SE CC P
▲ **Riobamba** Hotel Manabi, Colon 1958 y Olmedo.	☎ (3) 967967, 967305, 967978	72		👪 ⦿ CC P
▲ **Salango (Manabi)** Piquero Patas Azules.	☎ (4) 202033 fax (4) 202033	113		👪 ⦿ R CC P
▲ **Santo Domingo** Valle Hermoso 24Km via Esmeraldas.	☎ (2) 759095	45		👪 ⦿ 28 NW ♿ CC P
▲ **Tulcan** - Hostel Alejandra Sucre y Quito.	☎ (6) 981784	80		👪 ⦿ CC P
▲ **Tulcan** - Hotel Los Alpes Av Juan Ramon Arellano.	☎ (6) 982235	84		👪 ⦿ 1 NW CC P

SUPPLEMENTARY ACCOMMODATION
OUTSIDE THE ASSURED STANDARDS SCHEME

Location/Address	Telephone No. / Fax No.	Beds	Opening Dates	Facilities
Baños Hostal Isla de Baños, Calle Th Halflans 1-31 y Montalvo.	☎ (3) 740609	30		👪 ⦿ R CC P
Cayambe Bolivar 23 Y Ascazubi, Cayambe.	☎ (2) 500321	35		👪 ⦿ R CC P
El Tolondro Guallupe.	☎ (2) 226602 fax (2) 226602	20		👪 ⦿ R ♿ P

Location/Address	Telephone No. Fax No.	Beds	Opening Dates	Facilities
Misahualli Hotel Misahualli.	☎ (2) 520043 ✆ (2) 454146	24	▥	�f♗ ⍾ R CC
Puerto Lopez - Albergue Cueva del Oso Alejo Lascano #116, Y Juan Montalud	☎ 593 5 604124 ✆ 593 5 604200	18	▥	♙ ⍾ R ♒ P ▤ ☕
Villas Nuevo Amanecer Playa De Atacames, Junto A Sanbaye.	☎ (2) 527208, 402591, (6) 731170 ✆ (2) 527208	120	▥	♙ ⍾ ♿ CC P

HOSTELLING INTERNATIONAL

use International Communications Network (ICN) at major hostels to send and receive e-mail, set up e-mail box, send faxes, make International phone calls, surf the Web – all at low, low prices using the ICN Communications Card

Utilisez le Réseau International de Communication (ICN), dans nos plus grandes auberges pour envoyer et recevoir du courrier électronique, ouvrir une boîte à lettres électronique, transmettre des fax, appeler l'étranger, surfer sur l'internet – le tout à prix très très concurrentiels, grâce à la Carte de Communication ICN

benutzen Sie das International Communications Network (ICN) in Hauptherbergen, um e-mail zu senden und zu empfangen, e-mail Briefkästen einzurichten, Faxe zu schicken, international zu telefonieren oder "Surf the Net" – und das alles mit der ICN Kommunikationskarte zu günstigsten Preisen!

utilice la Red Internacional de Comunicaciones ICN en los principales albergues para transmitir y recibir mensajes electrónicos, establecer un buzón de correo electrónico, enviar facsímiles, realizar llamadas telefónicas internacionales, navegar por la red de Internet – todo a precios muy, muy económicos – mediante la Tarjeta de Comunicación ICN.

Egypt

**Egyptian Youth Hostels Association,
1 El-Ibrahimy Street, Garden City,
Cairo, Egypt.**

(20) (2) 3561448, 3540527
(20) (2) 3550329
E-mail: eyhahi@idsci.gov.eg
WWW Address: http://www.members.xoom.com/eyha

Office Hours: Sat-Thurs 08.30-15.30hrs

Travel Section: Egyptian Youth Travel Bureau,
7 Dr Abdel Hamid Saiid St, Maarouf,
Cairo, Egypt.
(20) (2) 779773
(20) (2) 5758099

A copy of the Hostel Directory for this country can be obtained from
The National Office.

Capital:	Cairo	Population:	60,000,000
Language:	Arabic	Size:	1,001,449 sq km
Currency:	LE (Egyptian £)		

Egypt

As-Sallum
Matruh
Alexandria
Tanta
Damanhur
Al-Qahirah
Cairo
Fayoum
Port Said
Al Arish
ISRAEL
Ismailia
Suez
EGYPT
Nile
Sharm El Sheikh
Assyout
Souhag
Hurghada
Luxor
Aswan
Aswan
Nasir Lake
N
SUDAN
50
100
150 KMS
0
50
MLS

English

EGYPTIAN HOSTELS

Whether it is the mystery of the pyramids, the Nile sunset or the bustle of Cairo, there is a hostel to help you get there.

Hostels are open 24hrs. Expect to pay in the region of 5.10 LE to 25.10 LE (US$ 1.50-7.40) for one night's bed and breakfast. There are self-catering facilities everywhere except Aswan, Assyout, Damanhour, El Fayoum, Sohag and Tant.

PASSPORTS AND VISAS

Visas are required and must be valid for 3 months from date of issue and for 30 days' stay. Visas can be obtained at point of entry or in some Egyptian diplomatic missions for a fee.

HEALTH

Innoculation requirements must be met.

BANKING HOURS

Normal banking hours are weekdays 08.30-14.00hrs. Banks are off on Saturdays and Fridays.

POST OFFICES

Post offices are open weekdays 08.30-14.00hrs.

SHOPPING HOURS

Shops are normally open weekdays 10.00-21.00hrs.

TRAVEL

Rail
Trains are available from Cairo to all major cities.

Bus
The network of buses covers the whole country.

Ferry
There are ferry services from the Mediterranean ports to Alexandria.

Driving
Hire cars are available.

TELEPHONE INFORMATION

Country Code — 20

Main City Area Codes

Alexandria	3
Aswan	97
Cairo	2
Hurghada	65
Ismailia	64
Luxor	95
Sharmel-shiek	62

Français

AUBERGES DE JEUNESSE EGYPTIENNES

Que vous vouliez voir les mystérieuses pyramides, un coucher de soleil sur le Nile ou faire l'expérience de la vie affairée du Caire, il se trouve toujours une auberge pour vous aider à y parvenir.

Les auberges sont ouvertes 24 heures. Une nuit et le petit déjeuner vous coûteront environ 5.10 LE et 25.10 LE (US$ 1.50-7.40). Il est possible de faire la cuisine soi-même partout sauf à El Fayoum, Tantah, Aswan, Sohay, Assyorat et Damasshour.

PASSEPORTS ET VISAS

Les visas sont nécessaires et doivent être valides 3 mois à partir de leur date d'émission et pour un séjour de 30 jours. Ils peuvent être obtenus à l'entrée dans le pays ou dans certaines missions diplomatiques égyptiennes, moyennant un paiement.

SOINS MEDICAUX

Les exigences concernant les vaccinations doivent être satisfaites.

HEURES D'OUVERTURE DES BANQUES

Les banques sont fermées le samedi et le vendredi.

BUREAUX DE POSTE

Les bureaux de poste sont ouverts en semaine de 8h30 à 14h.

HEURES D'OUVERTURE DES MAGASINS

Les magasins sont en principe ouverts en semaine de 10h à 21h.

DEPLACEMENTS

Trains

Les trains desservent toutes les grandes villes à partir du Caire.

Autobus

Le réseau d'autobus dessert tout le pays.

Ferry-boats

Les services maritimes relient les ports méditerranéens à Alexandrie.

Automobiles

Il est possible de se procurer des voitures de location.

TELEPHONE

Indicatif du Pays	20
Indicatifs régionaux des Villes principales	
Alexandrie	**3**
Aswan	**97**
Le Caire	**2**
Hurghada	**65**
Ismailia	**64**
Luxor	**95**
Sharmel-shiek	**62**

Deutsch

ÄGYPTISCHE JUGENDHERBERGEN

Ob Sie das Geheimnis der Pyramiden kennenlernen, den Sonnenuntergang am Nil bewundern oder das Leben und Treiben in Kairo erleben wollen, Sie finden bestimmt in der Nähe eine Jugendherberge.

Die Herbergen sind 24 Stunden geöffnet. Es ist mit einem Preis von 5.10 LE-25.10 LE (US$ 1.50-7.40) pro Übernachtung mit Frühstück zu rechnen. Überall, außer in Aswan, Assyorat, Damasshour, el-Faijum, Sohay und Tant, gibt es auch Einrichtungen für Selbstversorger.

PÄSSE UND VISA

Es wird ein Visum benötigt, das vom Tag der Ausstellung an für einen Aufenthalt von 30 Tagen 3 Monate gültig sein muß. Das Visum kann bei der Einreise oder in einer ägyptischen diplomatischen Mission gegen eine Gebühr erworben werden.

GESUNDHEIT

Die Impfvorschriften müssen erfüllt werden.

GESCHÄFTSSTUNDEN DER BANKEN

Banken sind freitags und samstags geschlossen.

POSTÄMTER

Die Postämter sind werktags von 08.30-14.00 Uhr geöffnet.

LADENÖFFNUNGSZEITEN

Die Geschäfte sind im allgemeinen werktags von 10.00-21.00 Uhr geöffnet.

REISEN

Eisenbahn

Zwischen Kairo und allen größeren Städten gibt es einen Zugverkehr.

Busse

Das Busnetz erstreckt sich über das ganze Land.

Fähren

Von den Mittelmeerhäfen nach Alexandria gibt es einen Fährenverkehr.

Autofahren

Es gibt Mietwägen.

FERNSPRECHINFORMATIONEN

Landes-Kennzahl	20
größere Städte - Ortsnetzkennzahlen	
Alexandria	3
Aswan	97
Kairo	2
Hurghada	65
Ismailia	64
Luxor	95
Sharmel-shiek	62

Español

ALBERGUES DE JUVENTUD EGIPCIOS

Tanto si desea ver las misteriosas pirámides, una puesta de sol sobre el Nilo o el bullicio del Cairo, siempre habrá un albergue donde alojarse.

Los albergues abren las 24 horas del día. Suelen cobrar unas 5,10 LE-25,10 LE (US$ 1,50-7,40) por noche con desayuno. Disponen de cocina para huéspedes excepto en Aswan, Assyorat, Damasshour, El Fayoum, Sohay y Tant.

PASAPORTES Y VISADOS

Se requiere un visado válido 3 meses a partir de la fecha de expedición y para una estancia de 30 días. Se pueden obtener visados en el punto de entrada al país y en algunas misiones diplomáticas egipcias abonando una suma.

SANIDAD

Deben cumplirse los requisitos de vacunación.

HORARIO DE BANCOS

Los bancos están cerrados los sábados y los viernes.

OFICINAS DE CORREOS

Las oficinas de correos abren los días laborables de 08.30 a 14.00 horas.

HORARIO COMERCIAL

Las tiendas suelen abrir los días laborables de 10.00 a 21.00 horas.

DESPLAZAMIENTOS

Tren

Existen servicios de tren desde El Cairo a las principales ciudades.

Autobús

La red de autobuses cubre todo el país.

Ferry

Hay servicios de ferry desde los puertos del Mediterráneo a Alejandría.

Coche

Se pueden alquilar coches.

INFORMACION TELEFONICA

Código Nacional	20
Prefijos de las Ciudades Principales	
Alejandría	3
Aswan	97
El Cairo	2
Hurghada	65
Ismailia	64
Luxor	95
Sharmel-shiek	62

Discounts And Concessions

Your membership entitles you to discounts on rail travel and some shops, check with the travel office.

Cairo

**135 Abdel Aziz Al Saoud St, El Manial,
Kobri El Gamaa (University Bridge),
Cairo.**

☏ (2) 3640729
✆ (2) 3684107

Open Dates:	🗓9
Open Hours:	🕐
Reservations:	R CC
Price Range:	LE 20.1, US$6.00 BB inc 🍴🍴
Beds:	167 - 11x³ 19x⁶
Facilities:	👪 11x👪🍴 ⛱ 📺 📖 2x 🛏 ▫ 💼 8 P i ♿ ♨ 🔍
Directions:	2S from city centre
✈	Cairo 35km
A🚌	4km
🚂	6km
🚌	357 100m
U	Sayda Zeimah 500m
Attractions:	↻1km ⚲1km ⚓1km

١٣٥ شارع عبد العزيز آل سعـــود

بجوار كوبرى الجامعـة ـــ القاهرة

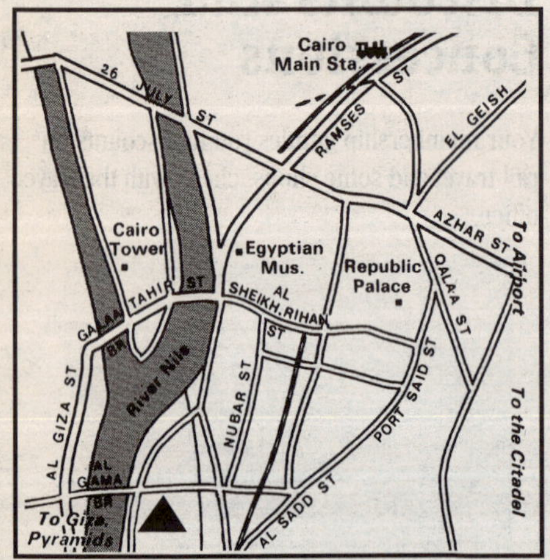

▲ There for everyone - young, not so young and those in the middle ▲

▲ c'est pour tout le monde - les jeunes, les moins jeunes et tous les autres ▲

▲ albergues para todos - los jóvenes, los menos jóvenes y los jóvenes de espíritu ▲

▲ für jederman - ob jung, nicht mehr ganz so jung oder die dazwischen ▲

Location/Address	Telephone No. Fax No.	Beds	Opening Dates	Facilities
▲ **Alexandria** 32 Port Said St, Shatbi, Raml, Alexandria.	☎ (3) 5975459 🖷 (3) 5964759	200		2NE
△ *Assyout* Bldg 503 El Walidia, Assyout.	☎ (88) 324846	40		
▲ **Cairo** **135 Abdel Aziz Al Saoud St, El Manial,** **Kobri El Gamaa (University Bridge), Cairo.**	☎ (2) 3640729 🖷 (2) 3684107	167		R 2S CC
△ *Damanhour* 9 El Shaheed Gawad Hosni St, Damanhour.	☎ (045) 317824	30		
△ *El Fayoum* Lux Housing Block of Flats, Hadaka, Block 7, Flat No 7, 8, Fayoum.	☎ (084) 350005	24		
△ *Hurghada* New Tourist Centre, Hurghada.	☎ (065) 444137	45		
▲ **Hurghada** Hurghada Torestic Area.	☎ (065) 544989	200		
▲ **Hurghada** Hurghada Hostel, Hurghada Road, Beside Water Wheel Living Museum, Cairo	☎ (065) 454989	200		R ♿
▲ **Ismailia** Emara Touristic Rd, Temsah Lake.	☎ (64) 322850 🖷 (64) 331429	200		
△ *Luxor* 16 Maabad El Karnak St, near the Education and Administration Centre: approach via City Gate nearest to airport.	☎ (95) 372139 🖷 (95) 370539	275		
△ *Mersa Matrouh* behind 4 El Galaa St, Salloum Rd, Mersa Matrouh.	☎ (3) 932331	52		
▲ **Port Said** El Amin St & Kornaish (near Sport Stadium), Port Said.	☎ (066) 228702 🖷 (66) 226432	210		
▲ **Sharm-El-Sheikh** PO 46619: 290km SE of Suez.	☎ (062) 660317 🖷 (062) 660317	120		
△ *Sohag* 5 Port Said St, Sohag.	☎ (93) 324395	28		
▲ **Sohag** Assyout Sohag Road in front of Elmanzalawy Factory.	☎ (093) 311430	110		CC
△ *Tanta* Shobra Malas, Mahala El Kobra Rd, Tanta.	☎ (40) 348689	24	24hrs	

SUPPLEMENTARY ACCOMMODATION OUTSIDE THE ASSURED STANDARDS SCHEME

Location/Address	Telephone No. Fax No.	Beds	Opening Dates	Facilities
Aswan 96 Abtaal El Tahrir St, Aswan.	☎ (097) 322313	80		
Suez Sharia Tariq El Horia (near Sport Stadium), PO 171, Suez.	☎ (62) 221945	105		

Make your credit card bookings at these centres
Réservez par cartes de crédit aux centres suivants
Buchen Sie mit Kreditkarte in folgenden Buchungszentren
Reserve por tarjeta de crédito en los siguientes centros

English

Australia	☎ (2) 9261 1111
Canada	☎ (800) 663 5777
England & Wales	☎ (1629) 581 418
France	☎ (1) 44 89 87 27
Northern Ireland	☎ (1232) 324 733
Republic of Ireland	☎ (1) 830 1766
New Zealand	☎ (9) 303 9524
Scotland	☎ (541) 553 255
Switzerland	☎ (1) 360 1414
USA	☎ (202) 783 6161

Français

Angleterre & Pays de Galles	☎ (1692) 581 418
Australie	☎ (2) 9261 1111
Canada	☎ (800) 663 5777
Écosse	☎ (541) 553 255
États-Unis	☎ (202) 783 6161
France	☎ (1) 44 89 87 27
Irlande du Nord	☎ (1232) 324 733
Nouvelle-Zélande	☎ (9) 303 9524
République d'Irlande	☎ (1) 830 1766
Suisse	☎ (1) 360 1414

Deutsch

Australien	☎ (2) 9261 1111
England & Wales	☎ (1629) 581 418
Frankreich	☎ (1) 44 89 87 27
Irland	☎ (1) 830 1766
Kanada	☎ (800) 663 5777
Neuseeland	☎ (9) 303 9524
Nordirland	☎ (1232) 324 733
Schottland	☎ (541) 553 255
Schweiz	☎ (1) 360 1414
USA	☎ (202) 783 6161

Español

Australia	☎ (2) 9261 1111
Canadá	☎ (800) 663 5777
Escocia	☎ (541) 553 255
Estados Unidos	☎ (202) 783 6161
Francia	☎ (1) 44 89 87 27
Inglaterra y Gales	☎ (1629) 581 418
Irlanda del Norte	☎ (1232) 324 733
Nueva Zelanda	☎ (9) 303 9524
República de Irlanda	☎ (1) 830 1766
Suiza	☎ (1) 360 1414

India

Youth Hostels Association of India,
5 Nyaya Marg, Chanakyapuri,
New Delhi 110 021, India.

☎ (91) (11) 6871969, 6110250
✆ (91) (11) 6113469
Telegraphic address: 'Youthostel, New Delhi 110 021'
E-mail: yhostel@del2.vsnl.net.in

A copy of the Hostel Directory for this Country can be obtained from:
The National Office.

Capital:	New Delhi	Population:	965,607,000
Language:	Hindi	Size:	3,287,590 sq km
Currency:	Rs (rupee)		

India

Patnitop
Dalhousie
Rup Nagar
Panchkula
Kurukshetra
Nainital
Delhi
Agra
Jodhpur
Jaipur
Namchi
Naharlagun
Shillong
Patna
Tura
Imphal
Kankroli
Aizawl
Gandhinagar
Vadodra
Bhopal
Aurangabad
Puri
Gopalpur on Sea
Hassan
Panaji
Tirupati
Mysore
Chennai
Calicut
Pondicherry
Port Blair
Tiruchirapalli
Cochin
Vellanad
Trivendrum
Scale 1:25,000,000
km 100 0 100 300 500 km

English

INDIAN HOSTELS

India's 37 Youth Hostels seldom offer self-catering, but who would want to miss the diversity of cuisine that the country has to offer? Smaller than average, with as few as 7 beds, it is always wise to book in advance. Other accommodation options may be very limited, but include government rest houses, tourist and dak bungalows, and in a few centres of YMCA and YWCA.

Expect to pay in the region of Rs20-50 per night. Family tariff varies. Take your own sheet or down sleeping bag. The new air-conditioned Delhi Youth Hostel is open 24hrs but the remaining hostels are open 07.00-22.00hrs unless otherwise stated.

PASSPORTS AND VISAS

A valid passport is required.

HEALTH

Government hospitals provide emergency treatment throughout India.

BANKING HOURS

10.00-14.00hrs Monday to Friday, 10.00-12.00hrs Saturday.

POST OFFICES

10.00-17.00hrs.

SHOPPING HOURS

10.00-19.00hrs.

TRAVEL

Air
Regular domestic air services operated by Indian Airlines and some private airlines connect all major places of tourist interest, cities and towns.

Rail
Indian Railways provide one of the best modes of cheap travel in India, with connections to major locations.

Bus
The various State Government Transport Departments provide regular bus services to places of tourist interest. The Indian Tourism Department has regular conducted sight seeing tours which are economical and comfortable.

Driving
A driving licence is essential for driving any vehicle.

TELEPHONE INFORMATION

Country Code	91
Main City Area Codes	
Bombay	22
Calcutta	33
Madras	44
New Delhi	11

Français

AUBERGES DE JEUNESSE INDIENNES

Les 37 auberges de jeunesse en Inde sont rarement équipées de cuisines pour les voyageurs, mais qui souhaiterait ne pas faire l'expérience de la cuisine variée que ce pays a à offrir? Il est toujours prudent de réserver à l'avance, les auberges étant de dimensions plus petites que la normale, avec seulement 7 lits quelquefois. A part les auberges, les autres possibilités d'hébergement sont plutôt limitées, mais on peut citer les maisons de repos gouvernementales, les bungalows pour touristes et voyageurs et quelques YMCA et YWCA.

Une nuit vous coûtera entre 20 et 50Rs. Les tarifs familles varient d'une auberge à l'autre. Apportez votre propre drap ou votre sac de couchage. L'auberge de New Delhi, qui est maintenant équipée d'un dispositif de climatisation, est ouverte 24 heures sur 24 tandis que le reste des auberges indiennes sont ouvertes de 7h à 22h sauf indication contraire.

PASSEPORTS ET VISAS

Un passeport valide est nécessaire.

SOINS MEDICAUX

Les hôpitaux gouvernementaux assurent des traitements d'urgence dans toute l'Inde.

HEURES D'OUVERTURE DES BANQUES

Les banques sont ouvertes de 10h à 14h du lundi au vendredi et de 10h à 12h le samedi.

BUREAUX DE POSTE

Les bureaux de poste sont ouverts de 10h à 17h.

HEURES D'OUVERTURE DES MAGASINS

Les magasins sont ouverts de 10h à 19h.

DEPLACEMENTS

Avions

Des vols intérieurs réguliers assurés par Indian Airlines et certaines lignes aériennes privées relient toutes les villes et grands centres et tous les lieux touristiques principaux.

Trains

Indian Railways (les chemins de fer indiens) représentent l'une des meilleures façons de voyager en Inde à peu de frais, avec des correspondances à destination des lieux principaux.

Autobus

Les divers services de transports gouvernementaux assurent des services d'autobus réguliers à destination de lieux d'intérêt touristique. Le Ministère indien du Tourisme organise régulièrement des visites guidées qui sont bon marché et confortables.

Automobiles

Il est nécessaire d'avoir un permis pour conduire tout véhicule.

TELEPHONE

Indicatif du Pays	91
Indicatifs régionaux des Villes principales	
Bombay	22
Calcutta	33
Madras	44
New Delhi	11

Deutsch

INDISCHE JUGENDHERBERGEN

Die 37 Jugendherbergen, die es in Indien gibt, bieten nur selten Einrichtungen für Selbstversorger, aber wer möchte sich auch die Vielfalt der einheimischen Küche entgehen lassen? Da die Herbergen kleiner sind als eine durchschnittliche Jugendherberge, oft sogar nur 7 Betten haben, ist Vorausbuchung immer ratsam. Andere Unterkunftsmöglichkeiten sind sehr beschränkt. Es gibt jedoch auch staatliche Rasthäuser, Touristen- und Dak-Bungalows und an einigen Orten Unterkünfte des Christlichen Vereins junger Männer (YMCA) bzw. des Christlichen Vereins junger Frauen (YWCA).

Es ist mit einem Preis von R20-50 pro Nacht zu rechnen. Der Tarif für Familienunterkunft ist von Herberge zu Herberge verschieden. Ein eigenes Laken oder ein Daunen-Schlafsack ist mitzubringen. Die Herbergen sind von 07.00-22.00 Uhr (wenn nicht anders angegeben) geöffnet. New Delhi Jugendherberge, die auch Unterkunft mit Klimaanlage hat, ist ganztägig geöffnet.

PÄSSE UND VISA

Man braucht einen gültigen Reisepaß.

GESUNDHEIT

Staatliche Krankenhäuser bieten in ganz Indien Behandlung in Notfällen.

GESCHÄFTSSTUNDEN DER BANKEN

Montags bis freitags 10.00-14.00 Uhr, samstags 10.00-12.00 Uhr.

POSTÄMTER

10.00-17.00 Uhr.

LADENÖFFNUNGSZEITEN

10.00-19.00 Uhr.

REISEN

Flugverkehr

Indian Airlines betreibt einen inländischen Linienverkehr, und einige private Fluggesellschaften fliegen an alle Orte von besonderem Interesse für den Fremdenverkehr und in andere größere Städte.

Eisenbahn

Die Eisenbahn ist eines der besten Verkehrsmittel für billiges Reisen in Indien. Es gibt Anschlüsse zu den meisten größeren Orten.

Busse

Die verschiedenen staatlichen Verkehrsabteilungen bieten einen Linienbusverkehr an Orte von besonderem Interesse für den Fremdenverkehr. Das indische Fremdenverkehrsamt führt regelmäßig geführte Besichtigungsfahrten durch, die billig und bequem sind.

Autofahren

Wer ein Fahrzeug führen will, muß im Besitz eines Führerscheins sein.

FERNSPRECHINFORMATIONEN

Landes-Kennzahl	91
größere Städte - Ortsnetzkennzahlen	
Bombay	22
Kalkutta	33
Madras	44
Neu-Delhi	11

Español

ALBERGUES JUVENILES INDIOS

Los 36 albergues juveniles de la India no suelen ofrecer cocina para huéspedes, pero ¿quién se perdería la diversidad culinaria que el país ofrece? Siendo albergues más bien pequeños, algunos con sólo 7 camas, se recomienda reservar con antelación. Otras alternativas de alojamiento, si bien muy limitadas, son las residencias estatales, bungalows turísticos y "dak", y algunos centros de la YMCA y YWCA.

Los precios oscilan entre 20 y 50 Rs por noche. Las tarifas familiares varían de un albergue a otro. Llévese su propio saco de dormir o sábanas. Los albergues abren de 7 h. a 22 h. a menos que se indique otro horario en la guía. El albergue climatizado de Nueva Delhi está abierto las 24 horas del día.

PASAPORTES Y VISADOS

Se requiere un pasaporte válido.

ASISTENCIA MEDICA

Los hospitales estatales ofrecen servicio de urgencias en todo el país.

HORARIO DE LOS BANCOS

De 10 h. a 14.00 h. de lunes a viernes, de 10 h. a 12 h. los sábados.

OFICINAS DE CORREOS

De 10 h. a 17 h.

HORARIO COMERCIAL

De 10 h. a 19 h.

DESPLAZAMIENTOS

Avión

Los servicios regulares nacionales operados por Indian Airlines y algunas compañías privadas tienen vuelos a todos los lugares de interés turístico y ciudades.

Tren

Los servicios de la compañía ferroviaria india constituyen una de las mejores maneras de viajar por poco dinero en el país, ofreciendo conexiones con todos los puntos de interés.

Autobús

Los distintos Departamentos Gubernamentales de Transporte ofrecen servicios regulares de autobús a los lugares de interés turístico. El Departamento de Turismo de la India ofrece excursiones turísticas que resultan baratas y cómodas.

Coche

Un permiso de conducir es imprescindible para conducir cualquier vehículo.

INFORMACION TELEFONICA

Código Nacional	**91**
Prefijos de las Ciudades Principales	
Bombay	22
Calcuta	33
Madrás	44
Nueva Delhi	11

Assured Standards – visited by our Liaison team and by you the guest – tell us when we don't measure up (reply slips at the end of this Guide)▶

des Normes Garanties, par les visites de notre Equipe de Liaison et par vous, les usagers – faites-le nous savoir quand nous ne sommes pas à la hauteur (Fiches-commentaires à la fin du Guide)▶

Zugesicherte Standards – beurteilt von unserem Liaison Team und von Ihnen, unserem Gast – sagen Sie es uns, wenn wir Sie enttäuschen (Antwortkarten hinten im Führer)▶

Normas Garantizadas – comprobadas por nuestro Equipo de Enlace y por Ud., el usuario – si fallamos en algo, díganoslo (al final de esta Guía encontrará nuestras hojas de comentarios)▶

New Delhi

**International YH,
5 Nyaya Marg,
Chanakyapuri,
New Delhi 110021.**
☎ (11) 6116285
☏ (11) 6113469

Open Dates:	
Open Hours:	
Reservations:	**R**
Price Range:	Rs 50-250 (Dormitory); Rs250-700 (Rooms)
Beds:	160
Facilities:	♿ ♨ 4x ♨ ▯ ☎ ▥ TV ▤ ▥ 2x ⚑ ▥ ▣ ⑧ ⊜ ⇳ P ⓘ ⚑ ⚘ ⌂ ♣

Directions:

✈	Indira Gandhi International 20km
🚆	New Delhi 8km, Delhi Main 11km
🚌	620, 640, 680, 710, 720 ap Chanakyapuri Police Station, New Delhi

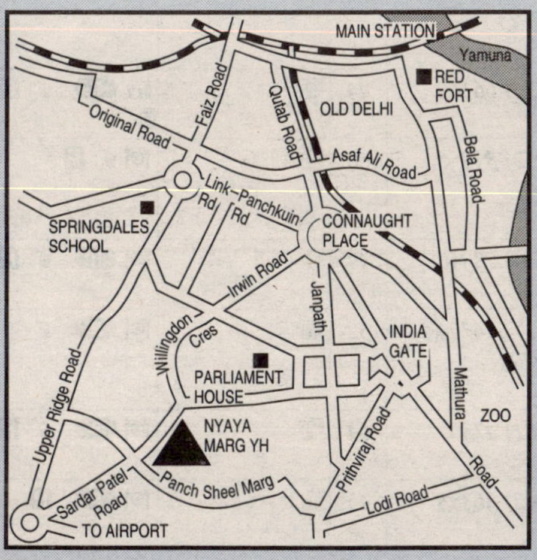

There for everyone
- young, not so young
and those in the middle▲

c'est pour tout le
monde - les jeunes, les moins
jeunes et tous les autres▲

albergues para todos
- los jóvenes, los menos
jóvenes y los jóvenes de
espíritu▲

für jederman - ob
jung, nicht mehr ganz so jung
oder die dazwischen▲

Location/Address	Telephone No. / Fax No.	Beds	Opening Dates	Facilities
△ **Agra** Sanjay Place, M G Rd, Agra 282002.	☎ (562) 354462	86		
△ **Aizawl** Luangmual, Aizawal, Mizoram 796 009.	☎ (389) 832243	120		
△ **Aurangabad** Padampura Corner, Station Rd, Aurangabad 431005, Maharashtra.	☎ (240) 334892	60		
△ **Bhopal** North TT Nagar, Bhopal 462003, Madhya Pradesh.	☎ (755) 553670	60		
△ **Calicut (Kozhikode)** East Hill, P.O. West Hill, Calicut - 673005, Kerala.	☎ (495) 58354	40		
△ **Chennai** Indira Nagar, Chennai - 600 020, Tamil Nadu.	☎ (44) 4420233	46		
△ **Cochin** NGO Qrts Junction Thrikkakara, Distt Ernakulam, Cochin, Kerala.	☎ (484) 422808, 424399	53		
△ **Dalhousie** Near bus-stand, Dalhousie 176304, Himachal Pradesh.	☎ (1899) 42189 ✆ (1899) 40929	42		
△ **Gandhinagar** Opposite Government Arts & Science College, Gandhinagar 382016, Gujarat.	☎ (2712) 22364	42		
△ **Gopalpur-on-Sea** Gopalpur-on-Sea, Distt, Ganjam 761002, Orissa.	☎ (6621) 82324	18		
△ **Imphal** Khuman Lampak, Imphal 795001, Imphal.	☎ (3852) 223423	44		
△ **Jaipur** Bhagwan Das Road, Near S.M.S Stadium, Jaipur 302004, Rajasthan.	☎ (141) 518330	62		
△ **Jodhpur** Circuit House Road, Ratanada, Jodhpur 342011, Rajasthan.	☎ (291) 620210, 629123	60		
△ **Hassan** Besides Dist. Stadium, Hassan 573201, Karnataka.	☎ (8172) 66168	44		
△ **Kankroli** Shri Dwarkesh Hotel, Mukherji Choraya, Bhilwara Rd, Kankroli 313324, Rajasthan.	☎ (2952) 359	60		
△ **Kurukshetra** Pipli Kurukshetra 132118, Haryana.	☎ (1744) 23340	44		
△ **Mysore** HUDCO, II Stage, Gangothri Layout, Mysore 570009, Karnataka.	☎ (821) 544704, 27479	52		
△ **Naharlagun** PO Naharlagun, 791110 Arunachal Pradesh.	☎ (3781) 4730	64		
△ **Nainital** Ardwell, Mallital, Nainital 263001, Uttar Pradesh.	☎ (5942) 36353	45		

Location/Address	Telephone No. Fax No.	Beds	Opening Dates	Facilities
△ **Namchi** Namchi 737126 Sikkim.	☎ (3595) 63774	44		▯O▯ Ⓡ 🍸 🅿
△ **New Delhi** **International YH, 5 Nyaya Marg,** **Chanakyapuri, New Delhi 110021.**	☎ (11) 6116285 🖷 (11) 6113469	160		♦♦ ▯O▯ Ⓡ ♿ 🍸 🅿 ▯
△ **Panaji** Miramar, Panaji 403001, Goa.	☎ (832) 225433	55		Ⓡ 🅿
△ **Panchkula** Ambala Kalka Rd, Sector 3, Panchkula, Dist Ambala 133001, Haryana.	☎ (172) 566423	45		▯O▯ Ⓡ 🍸 🅿
△ **Patna** Fraser Road, South to Maurya Hotel, Patna GPO, Patna 800 001, Bihar.		50		♦♦ ▯O▯ 🅿
△ **Patnitop** PO Kud 182142, Dist Udhampur, J&K.		44		▯O▯ Ⓡ 🍸 🅿
△ **Pondicherry** Solai Nagar, Muthialpet, Pondicherry 605003.	☎ (413) 33495	60		▯O▯ 🍸 🅿
△ **Port Blair** Aberdeen Bazar, PO 744104, Andaman and Nicobar Islands.	☎ (3192) 32459, 30521	38		▯O▯ 🅿
△ **Puri** Chakratirtha Rd, Puri 752002, Orissa.	☎ (6752) 22424	45		▯O▯ Ⓡ 🍸 🅿
△ **Rup Nagar (Ropar)** Nr New Bus Stand, Opposite Nehru Stadium, Rup Nagar (Ropar), 140001 Punjab.	☎ (1881) 20350	50		🅿
△ **Shillong** Opposite Central Telegraph Office, Vivekananda Marg, Shillong 793001, Meghalaya.	☎ (364) 224382, 222246	56		♦♦ ▯O▯ Ⓡ 🍸
△ **Tiruchirapalli** Near Anna Stadium, Kaja Malai, Tiruchirapalli 620 023, Tamil Nadu.	☎ (431) 421508	46		3E 🅿
△ **Tirupati** Near Reserve Police Quarters, M R Palle, Tirupati - 517 502, Andhra Pradesh.	☎ (8574) 50300	46		▯O▯ 1.5S 🍸 🅿 ▯
△ **Trivandrum (Thiruvananthapuram)** Nr Boat Club, Veli, Trivandrum 695021, Kerala.	☎ (471) 501230	46		🍸 🅿
△ **Tura** Stadium Area, P.O. Chandmari (Lower), West Garo Hills. Tura 794002 Meghalaya.	☎ (3651) 32126	50		▯O▯ 🅿
△ **Vadodra** Behind VUDA Office, BMC Shopping Centre, Fatehganj, Vadodra 390002 Gujrat.	☎ (265) 23626	25		▯O▯ Ⓡ 🅿
△ **Vellanad** Mitra Niketan Hostel, PO Vellanad 695543, Dist Trivandrum, Kerala.	☎ (47288) 451564	7		▯O▯ 🍸 🅿

The International Student Identity Card
ISIC
International Student Identity Card
Carte d'étudiant internationale / Carné internacional de estudiante
STUDENT
Studies at / Étudiant à / Est. de Enseñanza
University of London
Name / Nom / Nombre
SAHLAS, M.
Born / Né(e) le / Nacido/a el
23/06/1974
Validity / Validité / Validez
09/1998 - 12/1999
UNESCO
ISIC
Your world Your card
• Only internationally accepted proof of students status
• Worldwide students discounts and benefits
• Reductions on air and land travel
• Global Telecommunications Package
• 24 Hour Help Line Assistance
• 3 million cardholders in over 90 countries
• Endorsed by UNESCO
For more information contact: The ISIC Association
PO Box 15857, 1001 NJ Amsterdam, The Netherlands, www.istc.org

Japan

JAPON
JAPAN
JAPON

Japan Youth Hostels, Inc,
Suidobashi Nishiguchi Kaikan,
2-20-7, Misaki-cho, Chiyoda-ku, Tokyo 101-0061, Japan.

📞 (81) (3) 3288-1417 📠 (81) (3) 3288-1248

Travel Section: Suidōbashi-nishiguchi-kaikan, 2F 2-20-7 Misaki-cho, Chiyoda-ku, Tokyo 101-0061, Japan.

📞 (81) (3) 3288-0260
📠 (81) (3) 3288-1490
E-mail: jyh@znet.or.jp
WWW address: http://www.znet.or.jp/˜jyh

A copy of the Hostel Directory for this Country can be obtained from:
The National Office.

IBN Booking Centres for outward bookings

- **Kyoto**, Kyoto Youth Hostel Association, 29 Uzumasa-Nakayama-cho, Ukyo-ku, Kyoto 616-8191.
  📞 (81) (75) 4629185,
  📠 (81) (75) 4622289.
- **Nagoya-Aichi**, Aichi Youth Hostel Association, Aichiken Seinen Kaiken, 18-8-Sakae 1 Chome, Naka-ku, Nagoya-shi 460.
  📞 (81) (52) 2216080,
  📠 (81) (52) 2216057.
- **Osaka**, Osaka Youth Hostel Association, 8-110 Namba-naka 2, Naniwa-ku, Osaka 556.
  📞 (81) (6) 6338621,
  📠 (81) (6) 6340751.

- **Tokyo** -Japan Youth Hostels Inc, *via Travel Section Office above.*
- **Tokyo** -Tokyo Youth Hostels Association, Saiwai Bldg, 4 Gobancho, Chiyoda-ku, Tokyo 102.
  📞 (81) (3) 32610191,
  📠 (81) (3) 32610190.
- **Tokyo** -Yoyogi, c/o Tokyo-Yoyogi Youth Hostel, 3-1 Yoyogi Kamizono-cho, Shibuya-ku, 31, Tokyo 151.
  📞 (81) (3) 34679163,
  📠 (81) (3) 34679417.

Capital:	Tokyo	Population:	125,864,000
Language:	Japanese	Size:	377,780 sq km
Currency:	¥ (yen)		

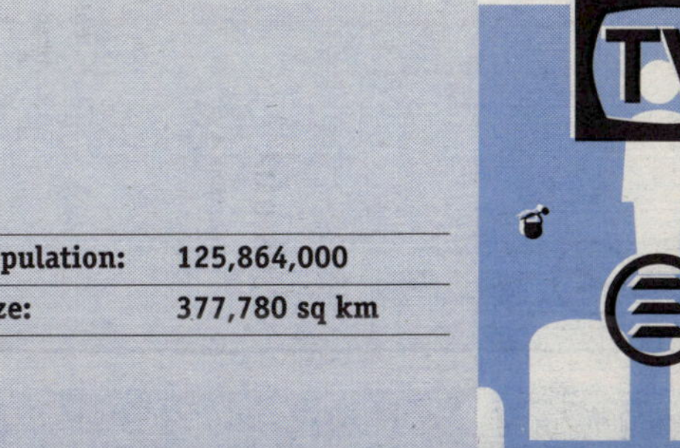

"""

Japan

Omachi
Hotaka
Matsumoto
Kanazawa
Gokayama
Eihei-ji Hida
Norikura-kogen
Kiso-fukushima
Inuyama
Nagoya
Hamana-ko
Fukui
Gifu
Omi-hachiman
Omi-Yasu
Kyoto (3)
Kamo
Matsuzaka
Ise
Kanazawa
Biwa-ko
Nara
Kawachi-nagano
Ikoma
Yoshino
Koyasan
Kumano
Shingu
Amanohashidate
Wakasa
Miyama
Otsu
Kyoto
Ashiya
Osaka
Kobe
Yuasa
Hongu
Taiji
Shiono-misaki
Kawanishi
Awaji-shima
Tanabe
Hamasaka
Hyonosen
Nihombara
Kurayoshi
Okayama
Kurashiki
Shodo-shima
Washu
Muroto
SHIKOKU
Obake-koboke
Takamatsu
Tokushima
Ikeda
Kochi
Matsue
Taisha
Tachikue-kyo
Nima
Miyoshi
Yano
Kasaoka
Hiroshima
Sefoda
Iyo-mishima
Tadotsu
Takamatsu
Ashizuri
OKI-SHOTO
Hagi
Akiyoshi
Iwakuni
Yamaguchi
Ube
Hiroshima
Tsuwano
Toyota
Kitakyushu
Iizuka
Dazaifu
Matsuyama
Kunisaki-hanto
Yaba-kei
Shimantogawa
Sukumo
Uwajima
Iyo-Ozu
KYUSHU
Yufuin
Aso
Takamori
Takachiho
Miyazaki
Nichinan
Toi-misaki
Miyakonojo
Kirishima
Sakurajima
Nejime
Setaka
Saga
Kumamoto
Kagoshima
Ibusuki
Yakushima
Takeo
Shimabara
Amakusa
Nagasaki
Hiradoguch
Kitakyushu
Fukuoka
Nagasaki
TSUSHIMA
Tsushima
N
Okinawa (3)
Miyakojima
Ishigaki-jima
Iriomote
KM
MLS
0   50   100 150 200
0   50   100

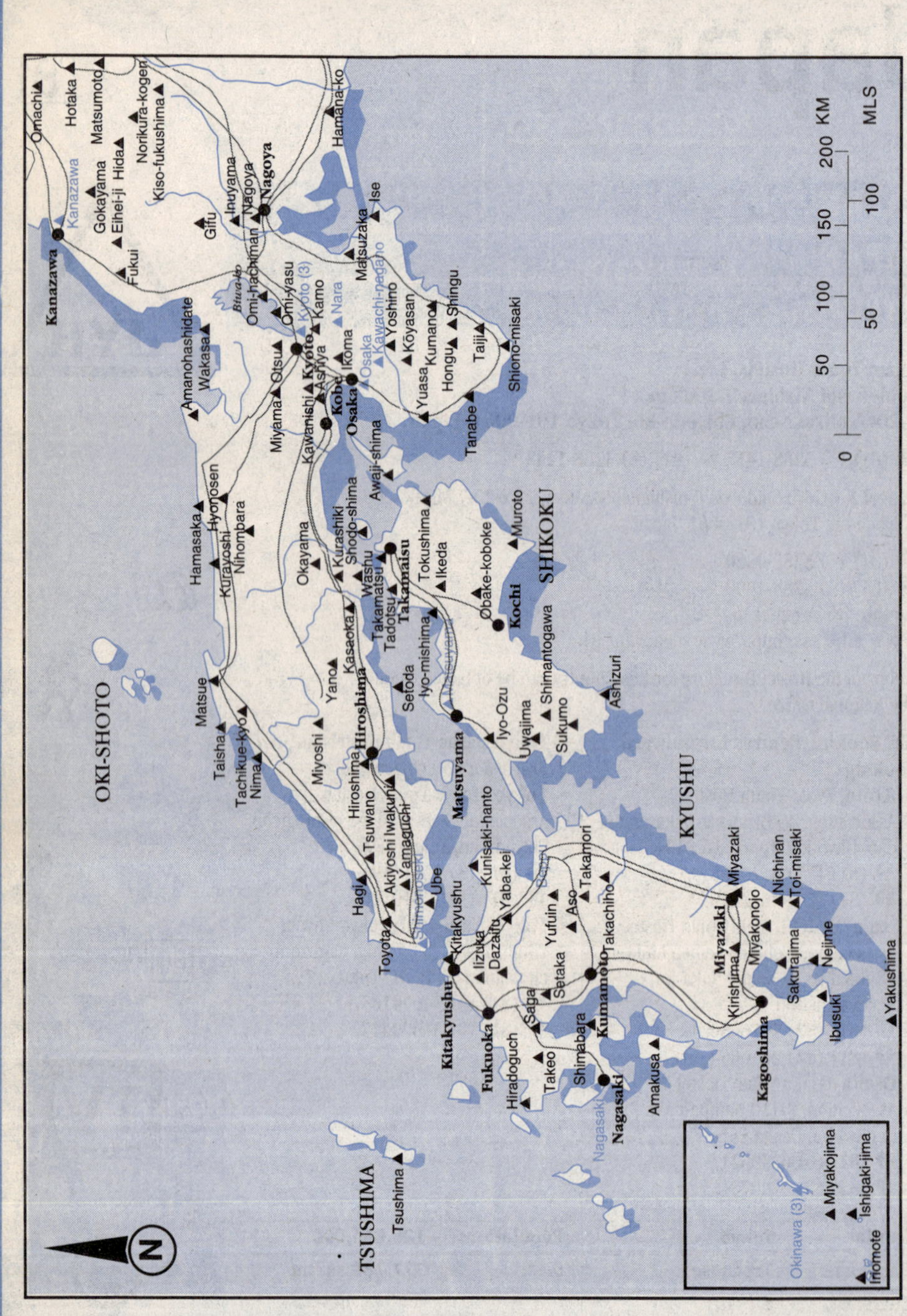

Japan

Japan
50 100 150 200 KM
0
50 100 MLS
N
Shimokita
Aomori
Misawa
Hirosaki
Oirase
Oyu
Towada
Hachimantai
Shizukuishi
Tazawa-ko
Morioka
Akita
Morioka
Hanamaki
Tono
Kisakata
Hiraizumi
Rikuzen-takata
Karakuwa
Sendai
Matsushima
Yamagata
Sendai
SADO
Niigata
HONSHU
Aizu
Bandai
Aizu-Takada
Fukushima
Noto
Wajima
Minazuki
Uchiura
Muika machi
Taira
Tomari
Kusatsu
Nikko
Hakuba
Togakushi
Manza
Nikko-imaichi
Toyama
Omachi
Nagano
Ueda
Haruna
Kanazawa
Gokayama
Hotaka
Komoro
Norikura-Kōgen
Matsumoto
Mito
Fukui
Eihei-ji
Hida
Shirakaba-ko
Chichibu
Tsuchiura
Suwa
Kamakita
Kiso-fukushima
Kiyosato
Mitake
Kobuckizawa
Kofu
Isawa
Tokyo
Narita
Gifu
Hakone
Chiba
Fuji-san
Yokohama
Biwa-ko
Inuyama
Shimojō
Kujukuri
Omi-
hachiman
Nagoya
Hokono-ko
Kamakura
Nagoya
Asuke
Jogashima
Ohara
Shitara
Ito
Toi
Shuzenji
Matsuzaki
Kawazu
Hamana-ko
Omaezaki
Shimo-kamo
Ise
Shingu
Tokyo
IZU ISLANDS
Hachijo Is.
Aogashima Is.
Tori Is.
Muko Is.
OGASAWARA
ISLANDS
Chichi Is.
Haha Is.
JAPAN

Japan

N
50 100 150 200 KM
0
50 100 MLS
Rebun
Rishir
Wakkanai
Haboro
Ishikari
Shiokari
Shiretoko Iwaobetsu
Saroma
Rausu
Abashiri
Shari
Fukagawa
Asahikawa
Koshimizu
Bihoro
Mashu-ko
Soun-kyo
Biei
Kamikawa
Kussharo-Genya
Akan
Nukabira
Toro
Shakotan
Sahoro
Kushiro
Nemuro
Otaru
Obihiro
Niseko
Sapporo
Sapporo
Ikeda
Shikotsu-ko
Shimamaki
Tomakomai
Toya
Kitayuzawa
Monbetsu
HOKKAIDO
Noboribetsu
Niikappu
Muroran
Erimo
Hakodate
Hakodate

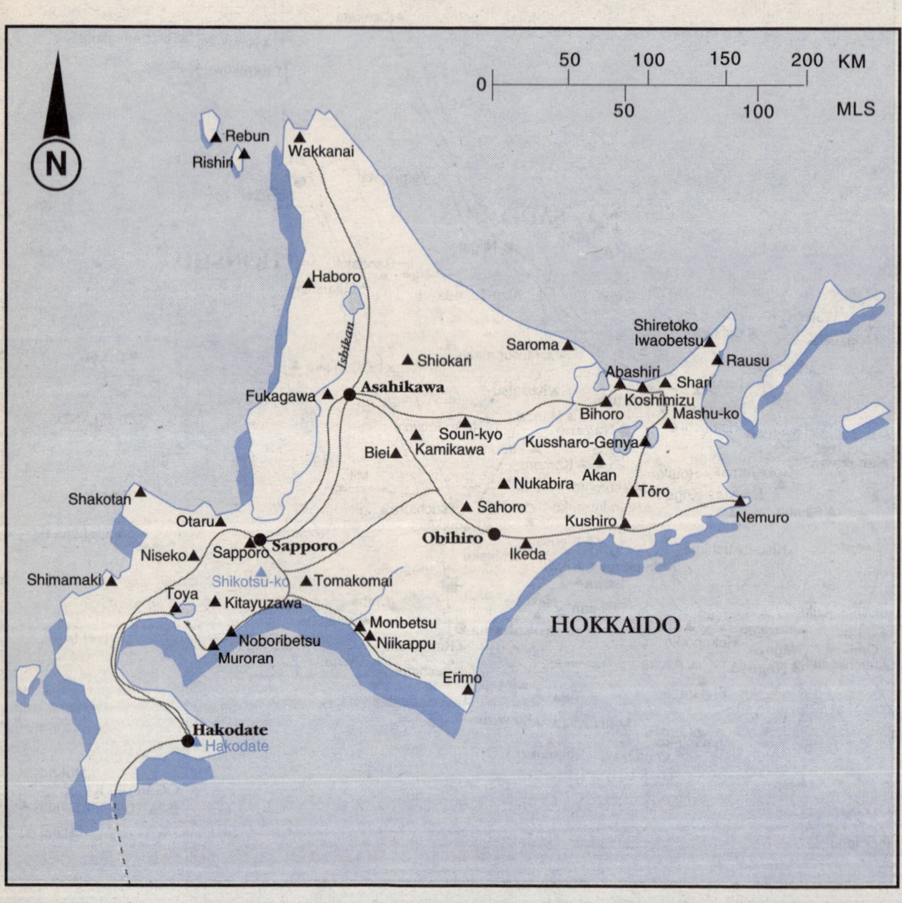

English

JAPANESE HOSTELS

Japan can be a very expensive place to stay, but its comprehensive network of Youth Hostels puts it within reach of budget travellers. Hostels reflect the Japanese culture and offer a unique experience.

Expect to pay 1,500-3,200 ¥ (Youth Guest House up to 5,000), less for under 15's, plus 5% tax. It is essential to book in advance, through IBN or direct with the hostel by letter or telephone.

Some hostels have bedrooms in Japanese style, the rooms are floored with 'tatami' or grass-root mats, and a mattress and quilt will be laid out at night to sleep on. Most hostels do have western style beds.

Meals are available at most hostels, but need to be ordered in advance. A few have self-catering, be prepared for a small charge to cover utensils.

PASSPORTS AND VISAS

Entry visas are not necessary for nationals of the following countries: Argentina, Austria, Belgium, Canada, Chile, Colombia, Costa Rica, Croatia, Cyprus, Denmark, Finland, France, Germany, Greece, Hungary, Iceland, Ireland, Israel, Italy, Luxembourg, Malta, Mexico, Netherlands, New Zealand, Norway, Portugal, Singapore, Slovenia, Spain, Sweden, Switzerland, Tunisia, Turkey, United Kingdom, Uruguay, USA.

HEALTH

Medical fees are very expensive, so private insurance is highly recommended.

BANKING HOURS

09.00-15.00hrs Monday to Friday.

POST OFFICES

09.00-17.00hrs Monday to Friday.

SHOPPING HOURS

10.00-19.00hrs.

TRAVEL

Air

A good airline network operates throughout the country.

Rail

A metro service operates in the main cities. A "Japan Rail Pass", comparatively economical, is available to foreign tourists and allows unlimited travel for periods of 7, 14 or 21 days. This pass must be purchased before arrival in Japan. Contact a Japanese Tourist Authority for details.

Bus

Bus services operate in the main cities, and there is a good long distance coach service.

Driving

Cars keep to the left. An International Driver's Licence is necessary.

TELEPHONE INFORMATION

Country Code	81
Main City Area Codes	
Hiroshima	82
Kyoto	75
Nara	742
Osaka	6
Tokyo	3

Français

AUBERGES DE JEUNESSE JAPONAISES

Séjourner au Japon peut revenir très cher, mais son réseau étendu d'auberges de jeunesse le rend abordable aux voyageurs restreints par leur budget. Les auberges reflètent la culture japonaise et offrent une expérience unique.

Une nuit vous coûtera entre 1500 et 3200 ¥ (et jusqu'à 5 000 dans les pensions pour jeunes), moins pour les moins de 15 ans, plus 5% de taxe. Il est nécessaire de réserver à l'avance, par IBN ou en contactant l'auberge directement par lettre ou téléphone.

Quelques auberges proposent des chambres de style japonais; le sol est fait de 'tatami' ou des tapis tressés et un matelas et un duvet sont posés la nuit pour dormir. La plupart des auberges disposent de lits de style occidental.

La plupart des auberges servent des repas, mais ceux-ci doivent être commandés à l'avance. Quelques-unes ont une cuisine pour les voyageurs; une petite contribution vous sera demandée si vous vous servez des ustensiles.

PASSEPORTS ET VISAS

Les visas d'entrée ne sont pas nécessaires pour les citoyens des pays suivants: Argentine, Autriche, Allemagne, Belgique, Canada, Chili, Chypre, Colombie, Costa Rica, Croatie, Danemark, Etats-Unis d'Amérique, Finlande, France, Grèce, Hongrie, Islande, Irlande, Israël, Italie, Luxembourg, Malte, Mexique, Nouvelle-Zélande, Norvège, Pays-Bas, Portugal, Royaume-Uni, Singapour, Slovénie, Espagne, Suède, Suisse, Tunisie, Turquie, Uruguay.

SOINS MEDICAUX

Les frais médicaux étant très chers, nous vous conseillons vivement de souscrire à une police d'assurance maladie.

HEURES D'OUVERTURE DES BANQUES

Les banques sont ouvertes de 9h à 15h du lundi au vendredi.

BUREAUX DE POSTE

Les bureaux de poste sont ouverts de 9h à 17h du lundi au vendredi.

HEURES D'OUVERTURE DES MAGASINS

Les magasins sont ouverts de 10h à 19h.

DEPLACEMENTS

Avions

Une bonne ligne aérienne est en service dans tout le pays.

Trains

Un réseau de métro est en service dans les villes principales. Les touristes étrangers peuvent se procurer une carte "Japan Rail Pass", relativement économique, qui leur permettra de se déplacer autant qu'ils le voudront pendant des périodes de 7, 14 ou 21 jours. Cette carte doit être achetée avant d'arriver au Japon. Renseignez-vous auprès des autorités touristiques japonaises.

Autobus

Des autobus sont en service dans les grandes villes, et il y a un bon service de cars pour les longs trajets.

Automobiles

La conduite est à gauche et les conducteurs doivent être munis d'un permis de conduire international.

TELEPHONE

Indicatif du Pays	**81**
Indicatifs régionaux des Villes principales	
Hiroshima	**82**
Kyoto	**75**
Nara	**742**
Osaka	**6**
Tokyo	**3**

Deutsch

JAPANISCHE JUGENDHERBERGEN

Japan kann sehr teuer sein, aber sein umfangreiches Jugendherbergsnetz macht es auch für Reisende mit kleinem Geldbeutel erschwinglich. Die Herbergen reflektieren die japanische Kultur. Sie bieten ein einmaliges Erlebnis.

Es ist mit einem Preis von 1.500-3.200 ¥ (in einem Jugendgästehaus mit bis zu 5.000 ¥) plus 5 % Steuer zu rechnen. Jugendliche unter 15 Jahren zahlen weniger. Voranmeldung über IBN oder schriftlich oder telefonisch direkt bei der betreffenden Herberge ist unerläßlich.

Einige Jugendherbergen haben Schlafzimmer im japanischen Stil; die Zimmer sind mit 'Tatami' oder Binsenmatten ausgelegt. Eine Matratze und eine Steppdecke werden nachts zum Schlafen ausgebreitet. Fast alle Herbergen haben westliche Betten.

In den meisten Herbergen gibt es Mahlzeiten, die aber vorbestellt werden müssen. Einige haben auch Einrichtungen für Selbstversorger, für die im allgemeinen eine kleine Benutzungsgebühr erhoben wird.

PÄSSE UND VISA

Staatsbürger der folgenden Länder brauchen kein Einreisevisum: Argentinien, Österreich, Belgien, Kanada, Chile, Kolumbien, Costa Rica, Zypern, Dänemark, Finnland, Frankreich, Deutschland, Griechenland, Ungarn, Island, Irland, Israel, Italien, Kroatien, Luxemburg, Malta, Mexiko, Niederlande, Neuseeland, Norwegen, Portugal, Singapur, Spanien, Schweden, Schweiz, Slowenien, Tunesien, Türkei, Vereinigtes Königreich, Uruguay, USA.

GESUNDHEIT

Arzthonorare sind sehr hoch. Es wird daher dringend zu einer privaten Versicherung geraten.

GESCHÄFTSSTUNDEN DER BANKEN

Montags bis freitags 09.00-15.00 Uhr.

POSTÄMTER

Montags bis freitags 09.00-17.00 Uhr.

LADENÖFFNUNGSZEITEN

10.00-19.00 Uhr.

REISEN

Flugverkehr
Die Flugverbindungen sind im ganzen Land sehr gut.

Eisenbahn
Die bedeutendsten Städte haben ein U-Bahn-System. Für ausländische Touristen gibt es einen "Japan Rail Pass", der für 7, 14 oder 21 Tage Anspruch auf unbeschränktes Reisen gewährt und relativ günstig ist. Dieser Paß muß vor der Ankunft in Japan gekauft werden. Nähere

Auskunft erteilt jedes japanische Fremdenverkehrsamt.

Busse
In den bedeutendsten Städten verkehren Busse, und es gibt auch ein gutes Netz von Fernverkehrsbussen.

Autofahren
In Japan herrscht Linksverkehr. Man braucht einen internationalen Führerschein.

FERNSPRECHINFORMATIONEN

Landes-Kennzahl	**81**
größere Städte - Ortsnetzkennzahlen	
Hiroshima	**82**
Kyoto	**75**
Nara	**742**
Osaka	**6**
Tokio	**3**

Español

ALBERGUES JUVENILES JAPONESES

Japón puede resultar un lugar muy caro para hospedarse, pero su amplia red de albergues juveniles lo pone al alcance de viajeros con poco presupuesto. Los albergues reflejan la cultura japonesa y ofrecen una experiencia única.

Tendrá que pagar unos 1.500 - 3.200 ¥ (en las pensiones para jóvenes pagará hasta 5.000 ¥), más 5% de impuesto. Los viajeros de menos de 15 años pagarán menos. Es preciso reservar con antelación a través de IBN, o bien por teléfono o por carta directamente al albergue.

Algunos albergues tienen dormitorios de estilo japonés; los cuartos están recubiertos de 'tatami' o estera de junco sobre la que se ponen edredones y colchones por la noche para dormir. Casi todos los albergues tienen camas de estilo occidental.

La mayoría de ellos sirven comidas, pero hay que encargarlas con antelación. Algunos albergues tienen cocina, pero cobrarán un pequeño suplemento por los utensilios.

PASAPORTES Y VISADOS

No necesitan visado de entrada al país los ciudadanos de los siguientes países: Alemania, Argentina, Austria, Bélgica, Canadá, Chile, Chipre, Colombia, Costa Rica, Croacia, Dinamarca, Eslovenia, España, Estados Unidos, Finlandia, Francia, Grecia, Hungría, Irlanda, Islandia, Israel, Italia, Luxemburgo, Malta, México, Nueva Zelanda, Noruega, Países Bajos, Portugal, Reino Unido, Singapur, Suecia, Suiza, Túnez, Turquía y Uruguay.

ASISTENCIA MEDICA

Los honorarios de los médicos son muy elevados, así es que lo mejor es hacerse un seguro médico.

HORARIO DE LOS BANCOS

De 9 h. a 15 h. de lunes a viernes.

OFICINAS DE CORREOS

De 9 h. a 17 h. de lunes a viernes.

HORARIO COMERCIAL

De 10 a 19 h.

DESPLAZAMIENTOS

Avión

El país cuenta con una buena infraestructura aérea.

Tren

Hay metro en las ciudades principales. Existe un billete especial, relativamente económico, denominado "Japan Rail Pass" a disposición de los turistas extranjeros. Con él podrá viajar de forma ilimitada durante períodos de 7, 14 o 21 días. Este billete debe adquirirse antes de llegar al Japón. Consulte a algún centro turístico japonés para más información al respecto.

Autobús

En las ciudades principales hay servicios de autobuses y una buena red de autocares para largos recorridos.

Automóvil

Se conduce por la izquierda. Es preciso tener un permiso de conducir internacional.

INFORMACION TELEFONICA

Código Nacional   **81**
Prefijos de las Ciudades Principales
  Hiroshima   **82**
  Kioto   **75**
  Nara   **742**
  Osaka   **6**
  Tokio   **3**

Discounts And Concessions

Your Hostelling International membership card buys you a wide range of discounts at or near hostels, cutting entrance fees, fares, eating out, equipment and activity costs. In addition the following nationally available discounts apply on travel and car hire:

Nissan-Rent-A-Car, and Japaren: 20% discount on all bookings.
SOGO Department Stores: 5% discount on sale items.

Hiroshima

Hiroshima YH,
1-13-6 Ushita-shin-machi,
Higashi-ku Hiroshima-shi,
Hiroshima-ken 732-0068.
📞 (82) 2215343
📠 (82) 2215377

Open Dates:	🗓
Open Hours:	07.00-10.00hrs; 15.00-22.00hrs
Price Range:	¥1770 (¥1510 for under 18's)
Beds:	104 - 5x² 1x⁴ 10x⁶ 3x⁶⁺
Facilities:	♦♦♦ 🍽 (BD) 🛏 60x 🔒 📷 ⊜ P 🅿 ♻ 🌳

Directions:	③NW from city centre
✈	Hiroshima 50km
A🚌	No number 50km
⛴	Hiroshima Port 8km
🚂	Hiroshima 4km
🚌	Lots of buses go to Ushita ap Ushita-Shinmachi-Ichōme
🚋	No number 700m ap Ushita
Attractions:	🏊

Kyoto

Utano YH,
29 Uzumasa Nakayama-cho,
Ukyō-ku,
Kyoto-shi,
Kyoto-fu 616-8191.
📞 (75) 4622288
📠 (75) 4622289

Open Dates:	🗓
Open Hours:	07.00-22.30hrs
Reservations:	IBN CC
Price Range:	¥2650 (¥2150 for under 18's)
Beds:	168 - 3x² 2x⁵ 19x⁶⁺
Facilities:	♦♦♦ 🍽 (BD) 🛏 TV 📺 🔒 📷 🎰 8 ⊜ P 🅿 ♻ 🔍

Directions:	⑧NW from city centre
✈	Kansai International 100km
🚂	JR Hanazono 4km
🚌	#26 from Kyoto 🚂 ap Youth Hostel-mae 50m
Attractions:	🚴 🚶

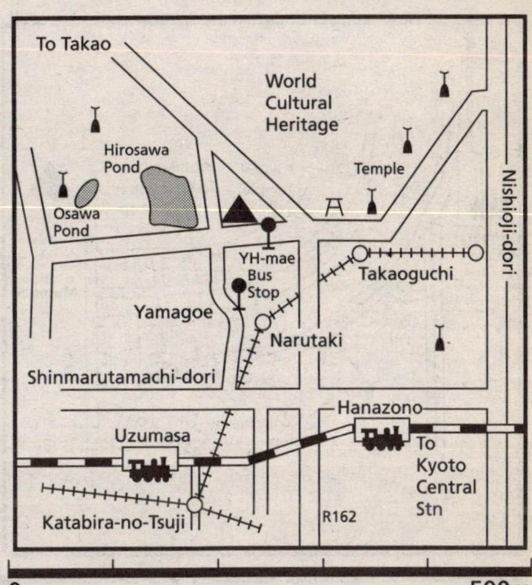

JAPAN • JAPON

Nagasaki

Nagasaki YH,
1-1-16 Tateyama,
Nagasaki-shi,
Nagasaki-ken 850-0007.
☎ (95) 8235032
🖷 (95) 8234321

Open Dates:	03.01-28.12
Open Hours:	07.00-10.00hrs; 15.00-22.00hrs
Reservations:	IBN
Price Range:	¥3000 BBinc
Beds:	122 - 15x⁶
Facilities:	5x 5x (B) TV 1x
Directions:	1NE from city centre
✈	Nagasaki Airport 40km
A🚌	Airport Limousine Bus 40km
⛴	Nagasaki 2km
🚂	Nagasaki 1km
Attractions:	3km

Narita

Skycourt Narita YGH,
161 Shinden,
Taieimachi,
Katorigun,
Chiba-ken 287-0224.
☎ (478) 736211
🖷 (478) 736212

Open Dates:	
Open Hours:	
Reservations:	IBN CC
Price Range:	¥4200
Beds:	125 - 80x¹ 15x² 5x³
Facilities:	(BD) TV 1x P
Directions:	62E from city centre
✈	Narita 10km
A🚌	#14 (Terminal 1); #26 (Terminal 2) 10km
⛴	Kisarazu 70km
🚂	Narita-Kūkō Terminal 2 5.5km
Attractions:	

Osaka

Osaka International YH,
1-5, Hagoromo-koen,
Takaishi-shi,
Osaka 592-0002.
☏ (722) 658539
✆ (722) 673682

Open Dates:	01.01-17.05; 21.05-15.11; 19.11-31.12
Open Hours:	15.00-23.00hrs
Reservations:	IBN CC
Price Range:	¥3150
Beds:	220 - 4x² 6x⁴ 29x⁶ 1x⁶ᵗʰ
Facilities:	7x 5x ...

Directions:

✈	Kansai International 25km
⛴	Osaka Ferry Port 20km
🚂	Hagoromo 1km
Attractions:	500m 500m

Tokyo - Yoyogi

Yoyogi YH,
c/o National Olympics Memorial Youth
Center,
3-1 Yoyogi Kami-zono-cho,
Shibuya-ku,
Tokyo 151-0052.
☏ (3) 34679163
✆ (3) 34679417

Open Dates:	05.01-27.12
Open Hours:	07.00-09.00hrs; 17.00-20.00hrs
Reservations:	IBN CC
Price Range:	¥3000
Beds:	60 - 60x¹
Facilities:	...
Directions:	7W from city centre
✈	Narita 70km
A🚌	Limousine bus to Shinjyuku 70km
🚂	Sangubashi Odakyu Line 500m
U	Yoyogi-Kōen, Chiyoda Line 800m

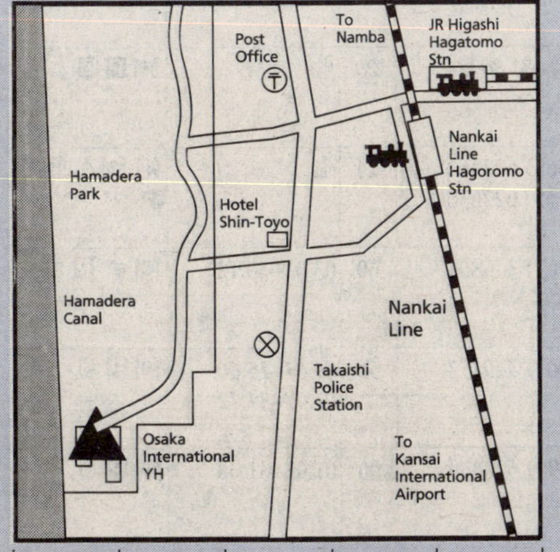

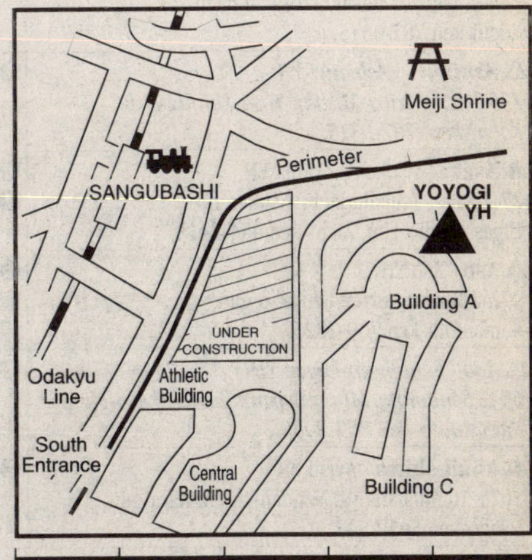

Location/Address	Telephone No. Fax No.	Beds	Opening Dates	Facilities
▲ **Abashiri** - Ryuhyo-no-oka YH 22-6 Meiji, Abashiri-shi, Hokkaido 093-0085.	☎ (152) 438558	28	🗓	⑪ P ▣
▲ **Abashiri** - Genseikaen YH 208-2 Kita-hama, Abashiri-shi, Hokkaido 099-3112.	☎ (152) 462630	44	25.01–09.04	⑪ P ▣
▲ **Aizu-no-sato YH** 36 Hatakeda, Kofune, Aizu-shiokawa-cho Yama-gun, Fukushima-ken 969-3532.	☎ (241) 272054	14	07.01–23.12	P
▲ **Aizu Takada-Aizuno YH** 88 Kakiyashiki, Terazaki, Aizu-Takada-machi, Onuma-gun, Fukushima-ken 969-6271.	☎ (242) 551020	18	🗓	⑪ P ▣
△ *Akan Angel YH* *5-1 Shurikomabetsu, Akan-Kohan, Akan-cho,* *Akan-gun, Hokkaido 085-0463.*	☎ *(154) 672309*	*90*	🗓	⑪ P ▣
▲ **Akiyoshidai YH** 4236-1, Akiyoshi, Shuho-cho, Mine-gun, Yamaguchi-ken, 754-0511.	☎ (8376) 20341	55	01.01–16.01; 01.02–31.12	⑪ 🍴 P ▣
△ *Amakusa YH* *180 Hondo, Hondo-cho, Hondo-shi,* *Kumamoto-ken 863-0003.*	☎ *(969) 223085*	*30*	🗓	⑪ 🍴 P ▣
▲ **Amanohashidate** - Amanohashidate YH 905 Nakano, Miyazu-shi, Kyoto-fu 629-2232.	☎ (772) 270121	60	🗓	⑪ P ▣
△ *Amanohashidate* - Kanko-kaikan *22 Ogaki, Miyazu-shi, Kyoto-fu 629-2242.*	☎ *(772) 270046*	*11*	🗓	⑪ P
▲ **Asahikawa YH** 18-chome, 7-jo, Kamui, Asahikawa-shi, Hokkaido, 070-8017.	☎ (166) 612800	50	🗓	⑪ P ▣
▲ **Ashiya-Rokko-Ashiya YH** 40-30 Okuike-minami-cho, Ashiya-shi, Hyogo-ken 659-0004.	☎ (797) 380109	90	10.01–20.12	⑪ P ▣
▲ **Ashizuri** - Kongōfuku-ji YH 214-1 Ashizuri-misaki, Tosa-shimizu-shi, Kōchi-ken 787-0315.	☎ (8808) 80038	80	10.01–12.08; 17.08–31.12	⑪ P ▣
△ *Ashizuri* - Ashizuri YH *1351-3, Ashizuri-Misaki, Tosa-Shimizu-shi,* *Kochi-ken, 787-0315.*	☎ *(8808) 80324*	*20*	🗓	⑪ P ▣
▲ **Asuke** - Asuke Satoyama YH 27-2 Saka, Tsubakidachi, Asuke-cho, Higashikamo-gun, Aichi-ken 444-2419.	☎ (565) 622462 📠 (565) 622636	24	🗓	👫 ⑪ ♿ P ▣ ☕
▲ **Aso** - Aso YH 922-2 Bochu, Aso-machi, Aso-gun, Kumamoto-ken 869-2225.	☎ (967) 340804	60	03.01–30.12	⑪ 🍴 P ▣
△ *Aso* - Senomoto-kōgen YH *6332 Senomoto, Minami-oguni-machi, Aso-gun,* *Kumamoto-ken 869-2400.*	☎ *(967) 440157*	*56*	01.01–15.06; 01.07–31.12	⑪ P ▣
▲ **Awaji-shima** - Awaji YH 2624-16 Ama-shioya, Nandan-cho Mihara-gun, Hyogo-ken 565-0543.	☎ (799) 520460	90	01.03–31.08	⑪ P ▣

Location/Address	Telephone No. Fax No.	Beds	Opening Dates	Facilities
▲ **Bandai** - Ura-Bandai YH Goshiki-numa, Ura-bandai, Azuma-kyoku, Fukushima-ken 969-2701.	☎ (241) 322811	100	20.04–20.11	⊖ P
▲ **Beppu YH** IBN 2 Kankaiji-onsen, Beppu-shi, Oita-ken 874-0822.	☎ (977) 234116	95		⊖ P
▲ **Biei** - Bibaushi Liberty YH Shigaichi, Bibaushi, Biei-cho, Kamikawa-gun, Hokkaido 071-0472.	☎ (166) 952141	20		⊖ CC P
▲ **Biei** - Potato no Oka YH Ōmura Murayama, Biei-cho, Kamikawa-gun, Hokkaido, 071-0218.	☎ (166) 923255	30		⊖ R P
▲ **Bihoro YH** 31 Moto-machi, Bihoro-cho, Abashiri-gun, Hokkaido 092-0063.	☎ (1527) 32560	80	01.01–15.01; 20.05–05.11; 16.11–31.12	⊖
▲ **Chiba-shi YH** 955 Yasashido-cho, Midori-ku, Chiba-shi, Chiba-ken 267-0062.	☎ (43) 2941850	60	06.01–28.12	⊖ P
▲ **Dazaifu YH** 1-18-1 Sanjo, Dazaifu-shi, Fukuoka-ken 818-0111.	☎ (92) 9228740	24		⊖ P
▲ **Eihei-ji** - Monzen Yamaguchi-so YH 22-3 Shihi, Eihei-ji-machi, Yoshida-gun, Fukui-ken 910-1228.	☎ (776) 633123	28		⊖ P
△ *Erimo* - *Erimo-Misaki YH* *236-6 Erimo-misaki, Erimo-machi, Horo-izumi-gun, Hokkaido 058-0342.*	☎ *(1466) 31144*	*70*		⊖ CC P
△ *Fuji-san* - *Fuji-yoshida YH* *339 2-chome, Shimo-yoshida-hon-cho, Fuji-yoshida-shi 403-0004, Yamanashi-ken.*	☎ *(555) 220533*	*30*	*04.01–29.12*	⊖ P
▲ **Fuji-san** - Kawaguchi-ko YH 2128 Funazu, Kawaguchi-ko-machi, Minami-tsuru-gun 401-0301.	☎ (555) 721431	50	20.03–05.11	⊖ P
△ *Fuji-san* - *Fujinomiya Fumoto-no-ie YH* *251 Sugita, Fujinomiya-shi, Shizuoka-ken 418-0021.*	☎ *(544) 274314*	*8*	*01.01–31.08; 01.10–31.12*	
▲ **Fuji-san** - Gotemba YH 3857 Higashiyama, Gotemba-shi, Shizuoka-ken 412-0024.	☎ (550) 823045	52		⊖ P
▲ **Fuji-san** - Yamanaka-ko Iiz YGH Asahigaoka, Yamanakako-mura, Minami-Tsuru-gun, Yamanashi-ken, 401-0500.	☎ (555) 620020	100		⊖ P
▲ **Fukagawa** - Irumu-no-Oka YH 546-2, Otoe, Otoe-cho, Fukagawa-shi, Hokkaido, 074-1273.	☎ (164) 251000	14		⊖ P
▲ **Fukui** - Fukuiken Seinenkan YH 3-11-17 Ōte, Fukui-shi, Fukui-ken 910-0005.	☎ (776) 225920	32		P
▲ **Fukuoka** - Shikano-shima-sō YH 1526-2, Shikano-shima, Higashi-ku, Fukuoka-shi, Fukuoka-ken, 811-0323.	☎ (92) 6030009	50		⊖ 20 NW P

Location/Address	Telephone No. Fax No.	Beds	Opening Dates	Facilities
▲ **Fukushima** - Azuma-kogen Star Hunt YH Takayu-onsen, 1-49 Jin-no-mori, Machiniwasaka, Fukushima-shi, Fukushima-ken 960-2261.	☎ (245) 911412	96		⏵⏴ ⌖ ⌂⌂
▲ **Fukushima** - YGH Atoma 15-2, Funaishi, Sakuramoto, Fukushima-shi, Fukushima-ken 960-2151.	☎ (24) 5912523	30		⏵⏴ ⌂⌂
▲ **Furano** - Rokugō Frarin YH 1, Higashi-Rokugo, Furano-shi, Hokkaido, 076-0162.	☎ (167) 292172	25		⏵⏴ ⌂⌂
▲ **Gifu YH** 4716-17 Kamikanoyama, Gifu-shi, Gifu-ken 500-8121.	☎ (58) 2636631	60	04.01–28.12	⏵⏴ ⌂⌂
▲ **Gokayama** - Ecchu Gokayama YH 24 Oze, Kamitaira-mura, Higashi- tonami-gun, Toyama-ken 939-1971.	☎ (763) 673331	20	01.03–30.11	⏵⏴ ⌂⌂
▲ **Haboro** - Haboro Yuho YH 260 Sakae-machi, Haboro-cho, Tomamae-gun, Hokkaido 078-4123.	☎ (1646) 22146 🖷 (1646) 22146	23	01.01-31.10; 01.12-31.12	⏵⏴ ⌂⌂
▲ **Hachimantai YH** 5-2 Midorigaoka, Matsuo-mura, Iwate-gun, Iwate-ken 028-7304.	☎ (195) 782031	70		⏵⏴ ⌂⌂
▲ **Hagi YH** 109-22 Horinouchi, Hagi-shi, Yamaguchi-ken 758-0057.	☎ (838) 220733	68	01–15.01; 10.02–31.12	⏵⏴ ⌂⌂
▲ **Hakodate YGH** (IBN) 17-6 Hourai-cho, Hakodate-shi, Hokkaido 040-0043.	☎ (138) 267892	45		⏵⏴ ⌂⌂
▲ **Hakone** - Hakone Lake Villa YH 103-354, Oshiba, Motohakone, Hakone-machi, Ashigara-shimo-gun, Kanagawa-ken, 250-0522.	☎ (460) 31610	20		⏵⏴ ⌂⌂
▲ **Hakone** - Sengokuhara YH 912, Sengokuhara, Hakone-machi, Ashigara-shimo-gun, Kanagawa-ken, 250-0631.	☎ (460) 48966	27		⌀ ⌂
▲ **Hakuba** - Hakuba-no-sato Schondorf YH Tsugaike-kogen, Otari-mura, Kita Azumi-gun Nagano-ken 399-9400.	☎ (261) 833011	37		⏵⏴ ⌂
▲ **Hamana-ko YH** 223-2 Uchiyama, Arai-machi, Hamana-gun, Shizuoka-ken 431-0304.	☎ (53) 5940670	80		⏵⏴ ⌂⌂
▲ **Hamasaka** - Hamasaka YH Shiroyama-enchi, Hamasaka-cho, Mikata- gun, Hyogo-ken 669-6701.	☎ (796) 821282	80	01–20.01; 10.02–31.12	⏵⏴ ⌂⌂
▲ **Hamasaka** - Moroyose-so YH 461 Moroyose, Hamasaka-cho, Mikata-gun, Hyogo-ken 669-6753.	☎ (796) 821279	40		⏵⏴ ⌂⌂
▲ **Hanamaki Nara-no-sato YH** 10-16-1 Takamatsu, Hanamaki-shi, Iwate-ken 025-0014.	☎ (198) 312341	17		⏵⏴ ⌂⌂
▲ **Haruna-kogen YH** 845 Haruna-san, Haruna-machi, Gumma-gun, Gumma-ken 370-3341.	☎ (273) 749300	48		⏵⏴ ⌂⌂

Location/Address	Telephone No. Fax No.	Beds	Opening Dates	Facilities
▲ **Hida Furukawa YH** 180 Shimpo, Furukawa-chō, Yoshiki-gun, Gifu-ken 509-4272.	☎ (577) 752979	22		⑨ P ▣
▲ **Hiraizumi** - Motsu-ji YH 58 Osawa, Hiraizumi-machi, Nishi-iwai-gun, Iwate-ken 029-4102.	☎ (191) 462331	40	04.01–29.12	⑨ P ▣
▲ **Hirosaki YH** 11 Mori-machi, Hirosaki-shi, Aomori-ken 036-8205.	☎ (172) 337066	24		⑨ P ▣
▲ **Hiroshima** **Hiroshima YH, 1-13-6 Ushita-shin-machi, Higashi-ku Hiroshima-shi, Hiroshima-ken 732-0068.**	☎ (82) 2215343 ℻ (82) 2215377	104		⑨ 3NW P ▣
▲ **Hiroshima** - Hiroshima Bayside Saka YH 401-8 Ueda, Kōgai-Sakamachi, Hiroshima-shi, Hiroshima-ken 731-4335.	☎ (82) 8850700	12		⑨ 13SE P ▣
▲ **Hiroshima** - Higashi Hiroshima YH 3148 Hara, Happonmatsu-machi, Higashi Hiroshima-shi, Hiroshima-ken 739-0151.	☎ (824) 290305	27		⑨ 15E P ▣
▲ **Hiroshima** - Miyajima-guchi YH 1-4-14 Miyajima-guchi, Ono-machi, Saeki-gun, Hiroshima-ken 739-0411.	☎ (829) 561444	30		⑨
▲ **Hotaka** - Azumino Pastoraru YH Ariake-Toyosato, Hotaka-cho, Minami-azumi-gun, Nagano-ken 399-8301.	☎ (263) 836170	32	01–16.01; 08.02–31.12	P ▣
▲ **Hyōnosen** - Wakasa Hyonosen YH 631-10 Tsukuyone, Wakasa-cho, Yazu-gun, Tottori-ken 680-0728.	☎ (858) 821700, 820980	96	01.01–15.06; 01.07–31.12	P ▣
△ *Ibusuki - Tamaya YH* *5-27-8 Yuno-hama, Ibusuki-shi, Kagoshima-ken 891-0406.*	☎ *(993) 223553*	*35*		⑨ P ▣
▲ **Ibusuki** - Yunosato YH 2-38-20, Omure, Ibusuki-shi, Kagoshima-ken 891-0401.	☎ (993) 225680	20		⑨ P ▣
▲ **Iizuka Yakiyama-Kōgen YH** 1270-14 Yakiyama, Iizuka-shi, Fukuoka-ken 820-0047.	☎ (948) 226385	90	01.01–30.11; 10–31.12	20E P ▣
▲ **Ikeda** - Awa-Ikeda YH 3798, Sako, Nishiyama, Ikeda-cho, Miyoshi-gun, Tokushima-ken, 778-0040.	☎ (883) 725277	21		P
▲ **Ikoma** - Senko-ji YH 188 Narukawa, Heguri-cho, Ikoma-gun, Nara-ken 636-0945.	☎ (745) 450652	30		⑨ P ▣
▲ **Inuyama International YH** 162-1, Tsugao-Himuro, Inuyama-shi, Aichi-ken, 484-0091.	☎ (568) 611111	80	04.01–27.12	ⓡ P ▣
▲ **Iriomote** - Irumote-sō YH 870 Uehara, Taketomi-cho, Yaeyama-gun, Okinawa-ken 907-1541.	☎ (9808) 56255	45		⑨ P ▣

Location/Address	Telephone No. Fax No.	Beds	Opening Dates	Facilities
▲ **Iriomote** - Iriomote-jima Midori-sō YH 572-5 Uehara, Taketomi-cho, Yaeyama-gun, Okinawa-ken 907-1541.	☎ (9808) 56526	32	🗓	⭤ P 🔲
▲ **Isawa** - Onsen YH 106-2 Yamasaki, Isawa-machi, Higashi-yatsushiro-gun, Yamanashi-ken 406-0022.	☎ (552) 622110	36	🗓	⭤ ⭑ P 🔲
▲ **Ise** - Ise-shima YH 1219-82 Anagawa, Isobe-cho, Shima-gun, Mie-ken 517-0213.	☎ (5995) 50226	80	🗓	⭤ P 🔲
▲ **Ise** - Taikō-ji YH 1659 Ei, Futami- cho, Watarai-gun, Mie-ken 519-0602.	☎ (596) 432283	28	🗓	⭤ ⭑ 🔲
▲ **Ishigaki-jima** - Trek Ishigaki-jima YH 165-12 Hoshino, Ishigaki-shi, Okinawa-ken 907-0241.	☎ (9808) 68257	12	04.01–29.12	⭤ P
▲ **Itō** - Izu-Kogen Aoikaze YH 1250-34, Yawatano, Ito-shi, Shizuoka-ken, 413-0232.	☎ (557) 513785	15	🗓	⭤ P 🔲
▲ **Itō YH** Komuroyama-kōen 1260-125, Kawana, Itō-shi, Shizuoka-ken 414-0044.	☎ (557) 450224	100	🗓	⭤ ⭑ P 🔲
▲ **Iwakuni YH** 1-10-46 Yokoyama-cho, Iwakuni-shi, Yama- guchi-ken 741-0081.	☎ (827) 431092	60	05.01–28.12	⭤ ⭑ P 🔲
▲ **Iyo-mishima-Shi** - Hasendera YH 3214 Sangawa-cho, Iyo-mishima-shi, Ehime-ken 799-0431.	☎ (896) 250202	50	06.01–09.06; 01.07–12.08; 17.08–29.12	⭤ ⭑ P 🔲
▲ **Jōgashima YH** 121 Yoroshi, Jogashima, Misaki-cho, Miura-shi, Kanagawa-ken 238-0237.	☎ (468) 813893	104	🗓	⭤ ⭑ P 🔲
▲ **Kamakitako** - Lake View YH 86-1 Gongen-dō, Moroyama-machi, Iruma- gun, Saitama-ken 350-0454.	☎ (492) 940219	48	🗓	⭤ ⭑ P 🔲
▲ **Kamakura** - Kagetsu-en YH 27-9 Sakanoshita, Kamakura-shi, Kanagawa-ken 248-0021.	☎ (467) 251238	30	🗓	⭤ P
△ *Kamikawa-Daisetsu-zan* - *Shirakaba-so YH Asahidake-onsen, 1418, Higashikawa-cho, Kamikawa-gun, Hokkaido 071-0372.*	☎ *(166) 972246*	46	🗓	⭤ P 🔲
▲ **Kanazawa** - Kanazawa YH **(IBN)** Utatsuyama-koen, 37 Suehiro-cho, Kanazawa-shi, Ishikawa-ken 920-0833.	☎ (76) 2523414	80	01–31.01; 15.02–31.12	⭤ ⊂CC⊃ ⭑ P 🔲
▲ **Kanazawa** - Matsui YH 1-9-3 Kata-machi, Kanazawa-shi, Ishikawa-ken 920-0981.	☎ (76) 2210275	15	🗓	⭤ P 🔲
▲ **Karakuwa** - Riasu Karakuwa YH 2-8 Nakai, Karakuwa-machi, Motoyoshi-gun, Miyagi-ken 988-0563.	☎ (226) 322490	28	🗓	⭤ ⭑ P 🔲

Location/Address	Telephone No. Fax No.	Beds	Opening Dates	Facilities
▲ **Karuizawa** - Windy Bell Kitakaruizawa YH 1053 Kanbara, Tsumagoi-mura, Agatsuma-gun, Gumma-ken, 377-1615.	☎ (279) 865180	18		⑪ Ⓟ 🔒
▲ **Kasaoka** - Kasaoka-ya YH 5658 Nishi-hon-machi, Kasaoka-shi, Okayama-ken 714-0081.	☎ (865) 634188	21	04.01–30.12	⑪ Ⓟ 🔒
▲ **Kawachi-nagano YH** [IBN] 1305-2 Amano-cho, Kawachi-nagano-shi, Osaka-fu 586-0086.	☎ (721) 531010	80	01–31.01; 06.02–31.05; 06.06–31.12	⑪ Ⓟ 🔒
△ *Kawanishi - Inagawa Sansō YH* *1-21-9 Yato, Kawanishi-shi, Hyogo-ken 666-0131.*	☎ (727) 513565	*20*		⑪ 🍴 Ⓟ 🔒
▲ **Kawazu** - Amagi Harris Court YH 28-1 Nashimoto, Kawazu-machi, Kamo-gun, Shizuoka-ken 413-0501.	☎ (558) 357253	42		⑪ Ⓟ 🔒
△ *Kirishima Jingumae YH* *2459 Taguchi, Kirishima-cho, Aira-gun, Kagoshima-ken 889-4201.*	☎ (995) 571188	*30*	*04.01–30.12*	⑪ Ⓟ 🔒
▲ **Kisakata** - Kisakata Seinen-no-ie YH 19-2 Iriko no ma, Kisakata-machi, Yuri-gun, Akita-ken 018-0108.	☎ (184) 433154	52		⑪ Ⓟ 🔒
▲ **Kiso-Fukushima-Kiso Ryojoan YH** 634 Shinkai, Kiso-fukushima-machi, Kiso-gun, Nagano-ken 397-0002.	☎ (264) 237716	30	01.01–27.11; 11–31.12	⑪ 🍴 Ⓟ 🔒
▲ **Kita-kyūshū YH** Hobashira-shizenkoen, 7 Hobashira, Yahata-higashi-ku, Kita-kyūshū-shi, Fukuoka-ken 805-0056.	☎ (93) 6818142	56	01.01–31.05; 15.06–31.12	⑪ Ⓟ 🔒
▲ **Kitayuzawa YH** 50 Kitayuzawa-onsen-cho, Otaki-mura, Usu-gun, Hokkaido 052-0316.	☎ (142) 686552	40		⑪ [CC] Ⓟ 🔒
▲ **Kiyosato YH** 3545 Kiyosato, Takane-cho, Kita-koma-gun, Yamanashi-ken 407-0301.	☎ (551) 482125	50		⑪ Ⓟ
▲ **Kobe** - Kobe Tarumi YH 5-58, Kaigan-dori, Tarumi-ku, Kobe-shi, Hyogo, 655-0036.	☎ (78) 7072133	28		⑪ 🍴 Ⓟ 🔒
▲ **Kobuchizawa-Yatsugatake Pony YH** 3332-495, Kamisasao, Kobuchizawa-cho, Kita Koma-gun, Yamanashi-ken 408-0041.	☎ (551) 364044	15	20.03–30.11	⑪ Ⓟ 🔒
▲ **Kōfu** - Kōfu Highland YH 1355 Kamiobina-machi, Kōfu-shi, Yamanashi-ken 400-1101.	☎ (552) 518020	50		⑪ [CC] Ⓟ 🔒
▲ **Komoro YH** 3876-4, Minami-ga-hara, Komoro-shi, Nagano-ken, 384-0063	☎ (267) 235732	40		⑪ Ⓟ 🔒
▲ **Koshimizu** - Ohotsuku Koshimizu YH 137-4 Hama-koshimizu, Koshimizu-machi, Shari-gun, Hokkaido 099-3452.	☎ (152) 642011	75	01.01–31.10; 15–31.12	⑪ 🍴 Ⓟ 🔒

Location/Address	Telephone No. Fax No.	Beds	Opening Dates	Facilities
▲ **Koyasan** - Koyasan YH 628, Koyasan, Koya-cho, Ito-gun, Wakayama-ken, 648-0211.	☎ (736) 563889	13	01–10.01; 20.02–31.12	▯ P ▯
▲ **Kujūkuri-hama-Shirako YH** 2722 Sorigane, Shirako-machi, Chōsei- gun, Chiba-ken 299-4203.	☎ (475) 332254	20	▯	▯ P ▯
▲ **Kumamoto** - Suizenji YH 1-2-20 Hakusan, Kumamoto-shi, Kumamoto-ken 860-0959.	☎ (96) 3719193	20	03.01–29.12	▯
▲ **Kumano** - Kumano-shi Seinen-no-ie YH 2-13 Haichigi, Arima-cho, Kumano-shi, Mie-ken 519-4325.	☎ (5978) 90800	12	04.01–28.12	▯ P ▯
▲ **Kumano-hongū** - Kajika-so YH 1408 Kawayu, Hongū-machi, Higashi-muro-gun, Wakayama-ken 647-1711.	☎ (735) 420518	30	▯	▯ P ▯
▲ **Kunisaki-hantō** - Kunimi YH 3750 Imi, Kunimi-cho, Higashi-kunisaki-gun, Oita-ken 872-1401.	☎ (978) 820104	60	01.01–06.11; 17.11–31.12	▯ CC ▯ P ▯
▲ **Kurashiki YH** 1537-1 Mukaiyama, Kurashiki-shi, Okayama- ken 710-0044.	☎ (86) 4227355	60	▯	▯ P ▯
▲ **Kurayoshi** - Kōhō-ji YH 195 Shimoasozu, Hawai-cho, Tōhaku-gun, Tottori-ken 682-07.	☎ (858) 352054	35	▯	▯ ▯ P ▯
▲ **Kusatsu** - Kusatsu-kogen YH Tengu-yama-shita, Kusatsu, Kusatsu-machi, Agatsuma-gun, Gumma-ken 377-1711.	☎ (279) 883895	96	▯	▯ P ▯
▲ **Kushiro** - Hoshino-Makiba YH 7-23 Kawakita-cho, Kushiro-shi, Hokkaido 085-0003.	☎ (154) 230852	44	01.01–20.10; 20–31.12	▯
▲ **Kushiro** - Kushiro Shitsugen Toro YH 7 Toro, Shibecha-cho, Kawakami-gun, Hokkaido 088-2261.	☎ (1548) 72510	14	▯	▯ P ▯
▲ **Kussharo** - Kussharo-Genya YGH 443-1 Kussharo-genya, Teshikaga-cho, Kawakami-gun, Hokkaido 088-3341.	☎ (1548) 42609	28	▯	▯ P ▯
▲ **Kyoto** - Higashiyama YH (IBN) 112 Goken-cho, Shirakawa-bashi, San-jō-dōri, Higashiyama-ku, Kyotō-shi, Kyoto-fu 605-0036.	☎ (75) 7618135	150	▯	▯ 4NE P ▯
▲ **Kyoto** (IBN) **Utano YH, 29 Uzumasa Nakayama-cho, Ukyō-ku, Kyoto-shi, Kyoto-fu 616-8191.**	☎ (75) 4622288 🖷 (75) 4622289	168	▯	▯ 8NW CC ▯ P ▯
▲ **Kyoto** - Kitayama YH (IBN) Koetsuji-han, Takagamine, Kita-ku, Kyoto-shi, Kyoto-fu 603-8478.	☎ (75) 4925345	43	30.01–29.12	▯ 8N CC P ▯
▲ **Mashū-ko YH** 883 Genya, Teshikaga-machi, Kawakami-gun, Hokkaido 088-3222.	☎ (1548) 23098	104	01.01–30.11; 21–31.12	▯ P ▯

Location/Address	Telephone No. Fax No.	Beds	Opening Dates	Facilities
▲ **Matsue** - Lakeside YH 1546 Kososhi-machi, Matsue-shi, Shimane-ken 690-0151.	☎ (852) 368620	50	01–10.01; 21.01–31.12	� P
▲ **Matsumoto** - Asama Onsen YH 1-7-15 Asama Onsen, Matsumoto-shi, Nagano-ken 390-0303.	☎ (263) 461335	110	04.01–27.12	P
▲ **Matsushima** - Pila Matsushima YH ⓘⒷⓃ 89-48 Minami-akazaki, Nobiru, Naruse-machi, Monou-gun, Miyagi-ken 981-0411.	☎ (225) 882220	100		P
▲ **Matsuyama YH** ⓘⒷⓃ 22-3 Himezuka Otsu, Dogo, Matsuyama-shi, Ehime-ken 790-2502.	☎ (89) 9336366 ✆ (89) 9336378	70		P
▲ **Matsuzaki** - Sanyo-so YH 73-1 Naka, Matsuzaki-machi, Kamo-gun, Shizuoka-ken 410-3626.	☎ (558) 420408	63		P
▲ **Misawa** - Kawayo Green YH Kawayo-green-farm, 3331 Mukaiyama, Shimoda-machi, Kamikita-gun, Aomori-ken 039-2151.	☎ (178) 562756	30	01–05.01; 06.02–31.12	P
△ *Mitake YH* *57 Mitake-san, Ōme-shi, Tokyo 198-0175.*	☎ *(428) 788774*	*30*		
▲ **Mito** - Kairakuen YH 1-1-18, Midori-cho, Mito-shi, Ibaraki-ken 310-0034.	☎ (29) 2261388	61	04.01–28.12	P
▲ **Miyakojima YH** 1325-3, Shimozato, Hirara-shi, Okinawa-ken, 906-0013	☎ (9807) 37700	40		P
▲ **Miyakonojō YH** 6361-1, Tohoku-cho, Miyakonojō-shi, Miyazaki-ken 885-0004.	☎ (986) 380022	13		P
▲ **Miyama** - Heimat YH 57 Nakasai, Kobuchiko, Miyama-cho, Kitakuwata-gun, Kyoto-fu 601-0775.	☎ (771) 750997	13		Ⓡ P
▲ **Miyazaki** - Miyazaki-ken Fujin-kaikan YH 1-3-10 Asahi, Miyazaki-shi, Miyazaki-ken 880-0803.	☎ (985) 245785	20	04.01–29.12	P
▲ **Miyazaki** - Aoshima YH 1-11, Aoshima Nishi, Miyazaki-shi, Miyazaki-ken 889-2163.	☎ (985) 651657	60		P
▲ **Miyoshi YH** Terato, Miyoshi-machi, Miyoshi-shi, Hiroshima-ken 728-0021.	☎ (824) 631759	20	04.01–12.08; 17.08–28.12	P
▲ **Monbetsu** - Toyosato-Muminmura YH 115 Toyosato, Monbetsu-cho, Saru-gun, Hokkaido, 059-2126	☎ (1456) 26388	24		P
▲ **Morioka YH** 1-9-41 Takamatsu, Morioka-shi, Iwate-ken 020-0114.	☎ (19) 6622220	70		P
▲ **Muika-machi** - Muika-machi Onsen International YH 1920-1 Oguriyama, Muika-machi, Minami-uonuma-gun, Niigata-ken 949-6636.	☎ (257) 722842	180		Ⓒ P

Location/Address	Telephone No. Fax No.	Beds	Opening Dates	Facilities
▲ **Muroran YH** 3-12-2 Miyuki-cho, Muroran-shi, Hokkaido 050-0084.	☎ (143) 443357	74	01–15.01; 27.01–31.12	▢
△ *Muroto - Hotsumisaki-ji YH* *4058-1 Muroto-misaki-machi, Muroto-shi,* *Kochi-ken 781-71.*	☎ (8872) 30024	*150*		
▲ **Nagasaki** [IBN] **Nagasaki YH, 1-1-16 Tateyama, Nagasaki-shi,** **Nagasaki-ken 850-0007.**	☎ (95) 8235032 ☎ (95) 8234321	122	04.01–28.12	1 NE P
▲ **Nagasaki** - Uragami-ga-oka YH 26-27 Joei-cho, Nagasaki-shi, Nagasaki-ken 850-8034.	☎ (95) 8478473	56	03.01–28.12	3 NW P
▲ **Nagoya** - Aichi-ken Seinenkaikan YH 1-18-8 Sakae, Naka-ku, Nagoya-shi, Aichi-ken 460-0008.	☎ (52) 2216001	50	05.01–27.12	1 SE P
▲ **Nagoya** - Nagoya YH 1-50 Kameiri, Tashiro-cho, Chikusa-ku, Nagoya-shi, Aichi-ken 464-0803.	☎ (52) 7819845	93	04.01–28.12	10 E P
▲ **Nara** - Nara YH [IBN] 1716 Hōren-cho, Nara-shi, Nara-ken 630.	☎ (742) 221334	200		P
▲ **Nara** - Nara-ken Seishōnen-kaikan YH 72-7 Ikenokami, Handa-hirakicho, Nara-shi, Nara-ken 630-8111.	☎ (742) 225540	58	04.01–28.12	P
▲ **Narita** [IBN] **Skycourt Narita YGH, 161 Shinden, Taieimachi,** **Katorigun, Chiba-ken 287-0224.**	☎ (478) 736211 ☎ (478) 736212	125		R 62 E CC P
▲ **Nejime** - Kinko-wan South Road YH 718-2, Kawaminami, Nejime-cho, Kimotsuki-gun, Kagoshima-ken, 893-2502	☎ (9942) 45632	18		R P
▲ **Nemuro Tomoshiri YH** 4-9, Koyo-cho, Nemuro-shi, Hokkaido 087-0004	☎ (1532) 22825	24	26.04–31.10	P
▲ **Nichinan-kaigan YH** 2348 Koo, Kumaya, Nichinan-shi, Miyazaki-ken 889-0023.	☎ (987) 270113	58		P
▲ **Nihonbara Kogen YH** 158 Ichiba, Shōboku-cho, Katsuta-gun, Okayama-ken 708-1206.	☎ (868) 362165	30		P
▲ **Niikappu** - Funhorse-in-Niikappu YH 489, Takae, Niikappu-cho, Niikappu-gun, Hokkaido, 059-2413.	☎ (1464) 72317	56	01.03–31.10	P
▲ **Nikko** - Daiyagawa YH 1075 Naka-hatsuishi-machi, Nikko-shi, Tochigi-ken 321-1402.	☎ (288) 541974	26	01–24.01; 01.02–31.12	
△ *Nikko - Nikko YH* [IBN] *2854 Tokorono, Nikko-shi, Tochigi-ken 321-1421.*	☎ *(288) 541013*	*48*	*04.01–28.12*	P
▲ **Nikko** - Green Road Nikko Suginamiki YH 2112-7 Kiwadajima, Imaichi-shi, Tochigi-ken 321-2375.	☎ (288) 260951	30		P

Location/Address	Telephone No. Fax No.	Beds	Opening Dates	Facilities
△ *Nima* - *Jofuku-ji YH* *1114 Nima-machi, Nima-cho, Nima-gun,* *Shimane-ken 699-2301.*	☎ *(8548) 83019*	*15*	⑨	⑪ ⌐ P ⊡
▲ **Niseko** - Niseko Annupuri YH 479-4, Niseko, Niseko-cho, Abuta-gun, Hokkaido, 048-1511.	☎ (136) 582084	18	01.01–31.03; 28.04–03.11	⑪ P ⊡
▲ **Niseko** - Niseko Kōgen YH 336, Niseko, Niseko-cho, Abuta-gun, Hokkaido, 048-1511.	☎ (136) 441171	29	01.01–08.04; 25.04–31.10; 01–31.12	⑪ P ⊡
▲ **Nishi-Tosa** - Shimanto-gawa YH 493-2, Hage, Nishi-Tosa-mura, Hata-gun, Kochi-ken, 787-1323.	☎ (880) 541352	12	⑨	⑪ P ⊡
△ *Noboribetsu* - *Kanefuku YH* *132 Noboribetsu Onsen, Noboribetsu-shi,* *Hokkaido 059-0551.*	☎ *(143) 842565*	*26*	*08.01–24.12*	⑪ P ⊡
▲ **Norikura-Kōgen** - Onsen YH Norikura-kōgen, Azumi-mura, Minami-Azumi-gun, Nagano-ken, 390-1513.	☎ (263) 932748	42	⑨	⑪ P ⊡
△ *Noto Minazuki-Wan YH* *Minazuki, Monzen-machi, Fugeshi-gun,* *Ishikawa-ken 927-2271.*	☎ *(768) 462022*	*15*	⑨	⑪ P
▲ **Noto Uchiura-Noto** - Isaribi YH Yo 51-6 Ogi, Uchiura-machi, Suzu-gun, Ishikawa-ken 927-0553.	☎ (768) 740150	20	⑨	⑪ P
▲ **Nukabira** - Higashi Taisetsu Nukabira YH Nukabira-Onsen, Kamishihoro-cho, Kato-gun, Hokkaido 080-1403.	☎ (1564) 42004	22	⑨	⑪ P ⊡
▲ **Oboke-Koboke/Jofuku-ji YH** 158 Aō, Ōtoyo-machi, Nagaoka-gun, Kōchi-ken 789-0167.	☎ (887) 740301	30	⑨	⑪ P ⊡
▲ **Ogasawara YH** 46-12 Nishi-machi, Chichi-jima, Ogasawara-mura, Tokyo 100-2101.	☎ (4998) 22692	33	⑨	⑪ ⊡
▲ **Ohara** - Seaside-Ohara YH 2122-27, Idoya, Iwafune, Ohara-machi, Isumi-gun, Chiba-ken, 298-0011	☎ (470) 628735	12	⑨	⑪ P ⊡
▲ **Oirase YH** Yakiyama, Towada-ko-machi, Kamikita-gun, Aomori-ken 034-0301.	☎ (176) 742031	40	⑨	⑪ P ⊡
▲ **Okayama** - Okayama-ken Seinen Kaikan YH 1-7-6 Tsukura-cho, Okayama-shi, Okayama-ken 700-0014.	☎ (86) 2520651	50	⑨	⑪ P ⊡
▲ **Okinawa** - City Front Harumi YH ⒾⒷⓃ 2-22-10 Tomari, Naha-shi, Okinawa-ken 900-0012.	☎ (98) 8673218	40	⑨	⑪ P ⊡
▲ **Okinawa** - Okinawa International YH 51 Onoyama-cho, Naha-shi, Okinawa-ken 900-0026.	☎ (98) 8570073	200	01–07.01; 19.01–31.12	⑪ ⒸⒸ P ⊡

Location/Address	Telephone No. Fax No.	Beds	Opening Dates	Facilities
▲ **Okinawa** - Minami-Onna Toropical YH 6486-3 Onna, Onna-son, Kunigami-gun, Okinawa-ken 904-0411.	☎ (98) 9661088 ✆ (98) 9661133	14	🗓	⑩ Ⓟ ▣
▲ **Okuchichibu Lake View YH** 3755 Otaki, Otaki-mura, Chichibu-gun, Saitama-ken 369-1901.	☎ (494) 550056	40	🗓	⑩ Ⓟ ▣
▲ **Ōmachi** - Hakuba-Sanroku-Onsen YH 10594 Taira, Ōmachi-shi, Nagano-ken 398-0001.	☎ (261) 221820	48	🗓	⑩ Ⓟ ▣
▲ **Omaezaki YH** 43-7 Omaezaki, Omaezaki-cho, Haibara-gun, Shizuoka-ken 421-0601.	☎ (548) 634518	36	🗓	⑩ Ⓟ ▣
▲ **Ōmi** - Ōmi Hachiman YH 610 Maruyama-cho, Ōmi-hachiman-shi, Shiga-ken 523-0805.	☎ (748) 322938	30	🗓	⑩ Ⓟ ▣
▲ **Ōmi** - yasu-Ōmi-Kibōgaoka YH 978 Kita-sakura, Yasumachi, Yasu-gun, Shiga-ken 520-2321.	☎ (77) 5872201	122	🗓	⑩ Ⓟ ▣
▲ **Ōsaka** - Hattori Ryokuchi YH 1-3 Hattori-ryokuchi, Toyonaka-shi, Ōsaka-fu 560-0873.	☎ (6) 8620600	92	04.01–27.12	⑩ 6N Ⓟ ▣
▲ **Osaka** IBN **Osaka International YH, 1-5, Hagoromo-koen,** **Takaishi-shi, Osaka 592-0002.**	☎ (722) 658539 ✆ (722) 673682	220	01.01–17.05; 21.05–15.11; 19.11–31.12	♦♦ ⑩ ₢₢ ✿ Ⓟ ▣
▲ **Osaka** - Osaka-shiritsu Nagai YH 1-1, Nagai-koen, Higashi-Sumiyoshi-ku, Osaka-shi, 546-0034.	☎ (6) 6995631	100	05.01–27.12	♦♦ ⑩ Ⓟ ▣
△ *Otaru Tenguyama YH* *2-16-22 Mogami, Otaru-shi, Hokkaido 047-0023.*	☎ *(134) 341474*	*51*	🗓	⑩ ₢₢ Ⓟ ▣
▲ **Ōtsu** - Ōtsu YH Centre 18-1 Yamagami-cho, Ōtsu-shi, Shiga-ken 520-0038.	☎ (77) 528009	308	🗓	⑩ Ⓟ ▣
▲ **Ōtsu** - Saikyō-ji YH 5-13-1 Sakamoto, Ōtsu-shi, Shiga-ken 520-0113.	☎ (77) 5780013	15	🗓	⑩ Ⓟ
▲ **Ōyu** - Ōyu Onsen Kuromori YH 63 Kaminoyu, Towada-ōyu, Kazuno-shi, Akita-ken 018-5421.	☎ (186) 372144	30	🗓	⑩ Ⓟ ▣
△ *Rausu YH* *4 Hon-cho, Rausu-machi, Menashi-gun,* *Hokkaido 086-1833.*	☎ *(1538) 72145*	*66*	*01.02–31.10*	⑩ Ⓟ ▣
▲ **Rebun** - Momoiwa-sō YH Motochi, Kabuka, Rebun-cho, Rebun-gun, Hokkaido 097-1201.	☎ (1638) 61390, 61421	68	01.06–30.09	⑩ ✿ Ⓟ ▣
▲ **Rikuzen-takata YH** 1000 Takata-Matsubara, Rikuzen-takata-shi, Iwate-ken 029-2204.	☎ (192) 554246	68	01.01–05.06; 16.06–31.12	⑩ Ⓟ ▣
▲ **Rishiri Green Hill YH** 35-3 Fujino, Oshidomari, Rishiri-Fuji-cho, Rishiri-gun, Hokkaido 097-0101.	☎ (1638) 22507	46	01.04–30.09	⑩ Ⓟ ▣

Location/Address	Telephone No. Fax No.	Beds	Opening Dates	Facilities
△ *Sado-ga-shima - Kazashima-kan YH* *397 Katanoo, Ryōtsu-shi, Niigata-ken 952-3542.*	✆ (259) 292003	14	01.03–30.11	⦿ P ▣
△ *Sado-ga-shima - Sado-Hakusan YH* *Yamada, Sawada-machi, Sado-gun,* *Niigata-ken 952-1321.*	✆ (259) 524422	14	🔁	⦿ P
▲ **Sado-ga-shima** - Sado Belle Mer YH 369-4 Himezu, Aikawa-machi, Sado-gun, Niigata-ken 952-2134.	✆ (259) 752011	26	🔁	⦿ P ▣
△ *Sado-ga-shima - Sotokaifu YH* *131 Iwaya-guchi, Aikawa-machi, Sado-gun,* *Niigata-ken 952-2201.*	✆ (259) 782911	20	🔁	⦿ ☕ P ▣
△ *Sado-ga-shima - Ogi-sakuma-so YH* *1562 Ogi-cho, Sado-gun, Niigata-ken 952-0604.*	✆ (259) 862565	13	01.03–30.11	⦿ P ▣
▲ **Sado-ga-shima** - Green Village YH 750-4 Uriuiya, Niibo-mura, Sado-gun, Niigata-ken 952-0106.	✆ (259) 222719	20	01–03.01; 01.03–31.12	⦿ P ▣
▲ **Saga** - Saga-ken Seinen Kaikan YH 1-21-50 Hinode, Saga-shi, Saga-ken 849-0923.	✆ (952) 312328	56	04.01–27.12	⦿ P ▣
▲ **Sahoro YH** 26 2-chome, 4-Jō-minami, shintokuchō, Kamikawa-gun, Hokkaido 081-0014.	✆ (1566) 46550	17	01.01–06.04; 25.04–10.11; 01.12–31.12	⦿ P ▣
▲ **Sakurajima YH** 189 Yokoyama, Sakurajima-cho, Kagoshima-gun, Kagoshima-ken 891-1419.	✆ (99) 2932150	100	🔁	⦿ P ▣
▲ **Sapporo** - Sapporo House YH 3-1 Nishi 6-chome, Kita 6-jō, Kita-ku, Sapporo-shi, Hokkaido 060-0806.	✆ (11) 7264235	135	02.01–30.12	⦿ [0.3W] ▣
▲ **Sapporo** - Sapporo Lions YH 4-15 18-chome, 1-jō, Miyanomori, Chū ō-ku, Sapporo-shi, Hokkaido 064-0951.	✆ (11) 6114709	88	🔁	⦿ [7SW] P ▣
▲ **Sapporo** - Sapporo-Miyagaoka YH 1-1 14-chome, 1-jo, Miyanomori, Chū ō-ku, Sapporo-shi, Hokkaido 064-0951.	✆ (11) 6432781	52	01.07–30.09	⦿ [4S] P ▣
▲ **Saroma-kohan YH** Saroma-kohan, Hama-Saroma, Saroma-cho, Tokoro-gun, Hokkaido 093-0423.	✆ (1587) 62515	60	01.01–15.05; 20.05–09.11; 20.11–31.12	⦿ CC ☕ P ▣
▲ **Sendai** - Dōchūan YH IBN 31 Kitayashiki, Ōnoda, Taihaku-ku, Sendai-shi, Miyagi-ken 982-0014.	✆ (22) 2470511	40	01.01–05.06; 21.06–05.11; 21.11–31.12	⦿ ☕ P ▣
▲ **Sendai** - Maple-Sendai-YH 1-9-35 Kashiwagi, Aoba-ku, Sendai-shi, Miyagi-ken 981-0933.	✆ (22) 2343922	23	🔁	⦿ ☕ P ▣
▲ **Sendai** - Sendai-Chitose YH 6-3-8 Odawara, Aoba-ku, Sendai-shi, Miyagi-ken 983-0003.	✆ (22) 2226329	50	🔁	⦿ P ▣
▲ **Setaka** - Runowaru YH 1380-3 Sakae-machi, Shimonosho, Setaka-machi, Yamato- gun, Fukuoka-ken 835-0024.	✆ (944) 622423	15	05.01–28.12	⦿ P ▣

JAPAN • JAPON

Location/Address	Telephone No. Fax No.	Beds	Opening Dates	Facilities
▲ **Setoda** - Setoda YH 668-1 Setoda-machi, Toyoda-gun, Hiroshima-ken 722-2411.	☎ (8452) 70224	89		⫲ P 🔲
▲ **Setoda** - Ikuchi-jima Seaside YH 58 Tarumi, Setoda-machi, Toyoda-gun, Hiroshima-ken 722-2404.	☎ (8452) 73137	28		⫲ P 🔲
△ *Shakotan YH* *297 Yobetsu-cho, Shakotan-machi, Shakotan-gun, Hokkaido 046-0322.*	☎ *(135) 465051*	*117*		⫲ ⚲ P
▲ **Shari** - Kiyosato Ihatov YH 282 Kōyō, Kiyosato-cho, Shari-gun, Hokkaido 099-4403.	☎ (1522) 53995	24		⫲ ⚲ P 🔲
▲ **Shikotsu-ko YH** (IBN) Shikotsu-kohan, Chitose-shi, Hokkaido 066-0281.	☎ (123) 252311	108	01.01–30.11; 11–31.12	⫲ ⚲ P 🔲
△ *Shimabara YH* *7938 Shimo-kawashiri-machi Shimabara-shi, Nagasaki-ken 855-0861.*	☎ *(957) 624451*	*48*		⫲ P 🔲
▲ **Shimamaki YH** 21, Chihase, Shimamaki-mura, Shimamaki-gun, Hokkaido, 048-0631	☎ (1367) 45264	23		⫲ P 🔲
△ *Shimojo Land YH* *7852-98, Mutsusawa, Shimajo-mura, Shimoina-gun, Nagano-ken 399-2101.*	☎ *(260) 272714*	*12*		⚲ P 🔲
▲ **Shimo-kamo-Gensu YH** 289 Shimo-kamo, Minami-izu-machi, Kamo-gun, Shizuoka-ken 415-0303.	☎ (558) 620035	25		⫲ P
▲ **Shimokita** - Wakinosawa YH 41 Senokawame, Wakinosawa-mura, Shimokita-gun, Aomori-ken 039-5311.	☎ (175) 442341	30	03.01–29.12	⫲ P 🔲
▲ **Shimonoseki Hinoyama YH** (IBN) 3-47 Mimosusogawa-machi, Shimonoseki-shi, Yamaguchi-ken 751-0813.	☎ (832) 223753	52		⫲ P 🔲
▲ **Shingū** - Hayatama YH 1-1-9 Kamihon-machi, Shingū-shi, Wakayama-ken 647-0003.	☎ (735) 222309	13	02.01–30.12	⫲ P 🔲
△ *Shiokari* - *Onsen YH* *3 Shiokari, Wassamu-cho, Kamikawa-gun, Hokkaido 098-0125.*	☎ *(16532) 2168*	*30*		⫲ P 🔲
▲ **Shiono-misaki** - Misaki Lodge YH 2864-1 Shiono-misaki, Kushimoto-cho, Nishimuro-gun, Wakayama-ken 649-3502.	☎ (7356) 21474	27		⫲ ⚲ P 🔲
▲ **Shirakaba-ko** - Shirakaba-ko YH 3418 Kitayama, Chino-shi, Nagano-ken 391-0301.	☎ (266) 682031	70		⫲ P 🔲
▲ **Shirakaba-ko** - Tateshina Shirakaba-kōgen YH 1020 Megamiko-dori, Tateshina-machi, Kitasaku-gun, Nagano-ken 384-2309.	☎ (267) 556601	70		⫲ P 🔲
▲ **Shirakaba-ko** - Tateshina Kuraine YH 5890 Kitayama, Chino-shi, Nagano-ken 391-0301.	☎ (266) 772077	14		⫲ P

Location/Address	Telephone No. / Fax No.	Beds	Opening Dates	Facilities
▲ **Shiretoko** - Iwaobetsu YH Iwaobetsu, Shari-machi, Shari-gun, Hokkaido 099-4356.	✆ (1522) 42311	91	01.02–25.03; 29.04–24.10	⑩ P ▣
▲ **Shizukuishi YH** 19-1, Hayasaka, Dai-10-Chiwari, Nagayama, Shizukuishi-cho, Iwate-gun, Iwate-ken 020-0585	✆ (19) 6932854	17	▣	⑩ P ▣
▲ **Shōdoshima Olive YH** Olive-mura, Uchinomi-cho, Shozu-gun, Kagawa-ken 761-4434.	✆ (879) 826161	120	▣	⑩ P ▣
▲ **Shuzenji** - Shuzenji YH **IBN** 4279-152 Shuzenji-machi, Shuzenji, Tagata-gun, Shizuoka-ken 410-2416.	✆ (558) 721222	120	01–17.01; 23.01–29.05; 04.06–31.12	⑩ CC P ▣
▲ **Shuzenji** - Kiya-ryokan YH 388 Warabo, Naka-izu-cho, Tagata-gun, Shizuoka-ken 410-2564.	✆ (558) 830146	20	▣	⑩ P ▣
▲ **Sōun-kyō YH** Sōun-kyō, Kamikawa machi, Kamikawa-gun, Hokkaido 078-1701.	✆ (1658) 53418	75	▣	⑩ P ▣
▲ **Sukumo YH** 196 Kamiari, Hashigami-machi, Sukumo-shi, Kochi-ken 788-0044.	✆ (880) 640233	28	▣	⑩ ☕ P ▣
▲ **Suwa-ko** - Youpen House YH 8932-2 Takagi, Shimo-suwa-machi, Suwa-gun, Nagano-ken 393-0033.	✆ (266) 277075	30	▣	⑩ P ▣
▲ **Tachikue-kyō YH** Tachikue, Ottachi-machi, Izumo-shi, Shimane-ken 693-0393.	✆ (853) 450102	30	▣	⑩ P
△ *Tadotsu - Kaigan-ji YH* *997 Nishi-shirakata, Tadotsu-cho, Nakatado-gun,* *Kagawa-ken 764-0037.*	✆ *(877) 333333*	*150*	*04.01–12.08;* *16.08–30.12*	⑩ P ▣
▲ **Taiji YH** 599-2 Taiji-machi, Higashimuro-gun, Wakayama-ken 649-5171.	✆ (7355) 92636	14	10.02–10.05; 10.07–10.11	⑩ P
▲ **Taira YH** 26 Kamanodai, Taira Shimokabeya, Iwaki-shi, Fukushima-ken 970-0101.	✆ (246) 347581	58	06.01–27.12	⑩ ☕ P ▣
▲ **Taisha** - Ebisuya YH Shinmon-dōri, Taisha-machi, Hinokawa-gun, Shimane-ken 699-0711.	✆ (853) 532157	28	▣	⑩ P ▣
▲ **Takachiho** - Takachiho YH 5899-2 Mitai, Takachiho-cho, Nishi-Usuki-gun, Miyazaki-ken 882-1101.	✆ (982) 723021	28	▣	⑩ P ▣
▲ **Takachiho** - Yamatoya YH 1148 Mitai, Takachiho-cho, Nishi-Usuki-gun, Miyazaki-ken 882-1101.	✆ (982) 722243, 723808	15	▣	⑩ P
△ *Takamatsu Yashima-Sanso YH* *77-4 Yashima-naka-machi, Takamatsu-shi,* *Kagawa-ken 760-0112.*	✆ *(878) 412318,* *416010*	*50*	▣	⑩ ▣

Location/Address	Telephone No. Fax No.	Beds	Opening Dates	Facilities
▲ **Takamori** - Murataya Ryokan YH 1672 Takamori, Takamori-machi, Aso-gun, Kumamoto-ken 869-1602.	☎ (9676) 20066	30		🍴 P
▲ **Takayama-Hida** - Takayama Tensho-ji YH 83, Tenshoji-cho, Takayama-shi, Gifu-ken, 506-0832	☎ (577) 326345	95		🍴 P
▲ **Takeo Onsen YH** Nagashima, Takeo-machi, Takeo-shi, Saga-ken 843-0021.	☎ (954) 222490	80	01.01–19.05; 11.06–31.12	🍴 P
▲ **Tanabe** - Ohgigahama YH 35-1, Shinyashiki-cho, Tanabe-shi, Wakayama-ken, 646-0033	☎ (739) 223433	15		
▲ **Tazawa-ko YH** 33-8 Kami-ishikami, Obonai, Tazawa-ko-machi, Senboku-gun, Akita-ken 014-1201.	☎ (187) 431281	37		🍴 P
▲ **Togakushi-Kogen-Yokokura YH** 3347, Chūsha, Togakushi-mura, Kami-minochi-gun, Nagano-ken 381-4100.	☎ (26) 2542030	50		🍴 P
△ *Toi - Takasagoya-ryokan YH* *790-1 Toi, Toi-machi, Tagata-gun, Shizuoka-ken 410-3302.*	☎ *(558) 980200*	*25*		🍴 P
△ *Toi-misaki YH* *Toi-misaki, Kushima-shi, Miyazaki-ken 888-0222.*	☎ *(987) 761397*	*30*		🍴 P
▲ **Tokachi-Ikeda Kitanokotan YH** 99-4 Toshibetsu-nishi-machi, Ikeda-cho, Nakagawa-gun, Hokkaido 083-0031.	☎ (1557) 23666	14	01–15.01; 28.01–04.04; 21.04–10.05; 22.05–05.11; 23–31.12	🍴 P
▲ **Tokushima YH** 7-1 Hama, Ohara-machi, Tokushima-shi, Tokushima-ken 770-8012.	☎ (886) 631505	60		🍴 CC P
▲ **Tokyo** - Yoyogi YH IBN **c/o National Olympics Memorial Youth Center, 3-1 Yoyogi Kami-zono-cho, Shibuya-ku, Tokyo 151-0052.**	☎ (3) 34679163 ☎ (3) 34679417	60	05.01–27.12	7W CC
▲ **Tokyo** - International YH Central Plaza 18F, 1-1, Kagura gashi, Shinjuku-ku, Tokyo 162-0823.	☎ (3) 32351107	158	04.01–28.12	🍴 4NW
▲ **Tokyo** - Skycourt Koiwa YGH IBN 6-11-4, Kita Koiwa, Edogawa-ku, Tokyo 133-0051	☎ (3) 36724411 ☎ (3) 36724400	37		CC
▲ **Tokyo** - Skycourt Asakusa YGH 6-35-8 Asakusa, Taito-ku, Tokyo, 111-0032.	☎ (3) 38754411 ☎ (3) 38754941	28		🍴 CC P
▲ **Tomakomai** - Utonai-ko YH 150-3 Uenae, Tomakomai-shi, Hokkaido 059-1365.	☎ (144) 582153	68		🍴 P
▲ **Tomari-Toyama** - Tenkyo-ji YH 913 Ōienoshō, Asahi-machi, Shimo-niikawa-gun, Toyama-ken 939-0722.	☎ (765) 833339	25		🍴 P

Location/Address	Telephone No. Fax No.	Beds	Opening Dates	Facilities
▲ **Tōno YH** 13-39-5, Tsuchibuchi, Tsuchibuchi-cho, Tōno-shi, Iwate-ken 028-0555.	(198) 628736	28		
▲ **Toya-ko** - Shōwa-shinzan YH 103 Sō-betsu-onsen, Sōbetsu-chō, Usu-gun, Hokkaido 052-0103.	(142) 752283	67		
▲ **Toyama YH** 3377 Matsushita, Hamakurosaki, Toyama-shi, Toyama-ken 931-8414.	(764) 379010	41	04.01–27.12	
▲ **Tsuchiura Masuo YH** 1-7-14 Komatsu, Tsuchiura-shi, Ibaraki-ken 330-0823.	(298) 214430	10	04.01–28.12	
▲ **Tsushima-Seizan-ji YH** 1453 Kokubu, Izuhara-machi, Shimoagata-gun, Nagasaki-ken 817-0022.	(9205) 20444	16		
▲ **Tsuwano YH** 819-ko Washihara, Tsuwano-machi, Kanoashi-gun, Shimane-ken, 699-5613.	(8567) 20373	28		
△ *Ube Tokiwa-kohan YH* *Hiraki, 654 Takahata, Kami-ube, Ube-shi, Yamaguchi-ken 755-0452.*	(836) 213613	60		
▲ **Ueda** - Mahoroba YH 40-1, Bessho-Onsen, Ueda-shi, Nagano-ken, 386-1431.	(268) 385229	19		
▲ **Uwajima** - Uwajima YH Atagokōen, Uwajima-shi, Ehime-ken 798-0045.	(895) 227177	38		
▲ **Wajima** - Sosogi-kajiyama YH 4-1 Sosogi-kibe, Machino-machi, Wajima-shi, Ishikawa-ken 928-0206.	(768) 321145	30	04.01–12.08; 19.08–29.12	
△ *Wajima* - *Wajima Chōraku-ji YH* *7-104 Shimbashi-dori, Wajima-shi, Ishikawa-ken 928-0061.*	(768) 220663	50	05.01–30.03; 05.04–30.12	
▲ **Wakasa** - Mihamaso YH 19-92 Hayase, Mihama-cho, Mikata-gun, Fukui-ken 919-1124.	(770) 320301	14		
▲ **Wakkanai** - Wakkanai YH 3-9-1 Komadori, Wakkanai-shi, Hokkaido 097-0003.	(162) 237162	68		
▲ **Wakkanai** - Wakkanai Moshiripa YH 2-9-5 Chuo, Wakkanai-shi, Hokkaido 097-0022.	(162) 240180	34		
▲ **Washū-zan YH** 1666-1 Obatake, Kurashiki-shi, Okayama-ken 711-0924.	(86) 4799280	60	04.01–27.12	
▲ **Yabakei** - Yamaguniya YH 1933-1 Ao-no-dōmon, Hon-yabakei-machi, Shimoke-gun, Oita-ken 871-0202.	(979) 522008	30	03.01–30.12	
▲ **Yakushima** - Yakushima YH 258-24, Hirauchi, Yaku-cho, Kumage-gun, Kagoshima-ken 891-4406.	(9974) 73751	19		

Location/Address	Telephone No. Fax No.	Beds	Opening Dates	Facilities
▲ **Yamagata YH** 293-3 Kurosawa, Yamagata-shi, Yamagata-ken 990-2311.	☎ (236) 883201	20	▣	⊠ℙ▣
▲ **Yamaguchi** - Jinjo-ji YH 624 Era, Toyota- cho, Toyoura-gun, Yamaguchi-ken 750-0452.	☎ (8376) 60286	40	▣	⊠⌁ ℙ▣
▲ **Yamaguchi** - Yamaguichi YH 801 Miyano-kami, Yamaguchi-shi, Yamaguchi-ken 753-0001.	☎ (839) 280057	30	01–09.01; 26.01–19.06; 06.07–31.12	⊠⌁ ℙ▣
▲ **Yano** - Shizen-no-mori M.G. YH 470-1 Yano-onsen, Jyōge-cho, Kōnu-gun, Hiroshima-ken 729-3423.	☎ (847) 623244	24	▣	⊠ℙ
▲ **Yokohama** - Kanagawa YH [IBN] 1 Momijigaoka, Nishi-ku, Yokohama-shi, Kanagawa-ken 220-0044.	☎ (45) 2416503	67	▣	⊠▣
▲ **Yoshino-Yama** -Kizo-in YH 1254 Yoshino-yama, Yoshino-machi, Yoshino-gun, Nara-ken 639-3115.	☎ (7463) 23014	90	01.03–24.12	⊠ℙ▣
▲ **Yuasa** - Arida Orange YH 809 Suhara, Yuasa-machi, Arida-gun, Wakayama-ken 643-0005.	☎ (737) 624536	30	▣	⊠ℙ▣
▲ **Yufuin YH** 441-29, Kawakami, Yufuin-cho, Oita-gun, Oita-ken, 879-5102	☎ (977) 843734	21	▣	⊠ℙ▣

HOSTELLING INTERNATIONAL

Kenya

KENYA

KENYA

KENIA

**Kenya Youth Hostels Association,
PO Box 48661, Nairobi, Kenya.**

**Secretariat: Nairobi Youth Hostel,
Ralph Bunche Road near Nairobi Hospital,
PO Box 48661, Nairobi, Kenya.**

☎ (254) (2) 721765
🖷 (254) (2) 724862

A copy of the Hostel Directory for this Country can be obtained from:
The National Office.

Capital:	Nairobi	Population:	21,061,000
Language:	English/Swahili	Size:	582,646 sq km
Currency:	Ksh (shilling)		

Kenya

SUDAN
ETHIOPIA
L. Rudolf
UGANDA
KENYA
L. Victoria
Mt Kenya
Nairobi
Nairobi
TANZANIA
Mombasa
N
0
100
200
300
400 KM
100
200
MLS
Dar es Salaam

English

KENYA HOSTELS

Expect to pay around Ksh 100-500 per night. Bring your own down sleeping bag except where indicated. Hostels are open 06.30-23.00hrs. Meals are not normally provided.

PASSPORTS AND VISAS

A valid passport is required. Commonwealth citizens do not require a visa.

HEALTH

Travellers should be immunized against yellow fever, typhoid and cholera. Anti-malarial medication is also recommended.

BANKING HOURS

Banks are open 09.00-15.00hrs Monday to Friday. In addition they open on the first and last Saturday from 09.00 to 11.00hrs.

POST OFFICES

Post office hours are 08.00-17.00hrs Monday to Friday and 08.00-12.00hrs at weekends. Free temporary mailing addresses are available (post restante) in Nairobi's main post office, and telephone "credit cards" are available for purchase.

SHOPPING HOURS

08.30-18.00hrs. Most shops are closed on Sundays and public holidays.

TRAVEL

Rail
Second class rail travel is very satisfactory. Advance booking is recommended for all trains.

Bus
Bus services operate to most areas. Advance booking is recommended for long distance buses. Small minibuses (Matatus) operate in urban areas.

TELEPHONE INFORMATION

Country Code	254
Main City Area Codes	
Mombasa	11
Nairobi	2

Français

AUBERGES DE JEUNESSE KENYANES

Une nuit vous coûtera entre 100 et 500 SHK. Apportez votre sac de couchage sauf indication contraire. Les auberges sont ouvertes de 6h30 à 23h. Elles ne servent en principe pas de repas.

PASSEPORTS ET VISAS

Un passeport valide est nécessaire. Les citoyens du Commonwealth n'ont pas besoin de visa.

SOINS MEDICAUX

Les voyageurs doivent être immunisés contre la fièvre jaune, la typhoïde et le choléra. Il est aussi conseillé de prendre des médicaments contre la malaria.

HEURES D'OUVERTURE DES BANQUES

Les banques sont ouvertes de 9h à 15h du lundi au vendredi. En outre, elles ouvrent le premier et le dernier samedi de 9h à 11h.

BUREAUX DE POSTE

Les bureaux de poste ouvrent de 8h à 17h du lundi au vendredi et de 8h à 12h le weekend. Il est possible d'obtenir des adresses temporaires gratuites (poste restante) à la poste principale de Nairobi, et des 'cartes de crédit' pour téléphone sont également en vente.

HEURES D'OUVERTURE DES MAGASINS

Les magasins ouvrent de 8h30 à 18h. La plupart des magasins sont fermés le dimanche et les jours fériés.

DEPLACEMENTS

Trains

Les voyages en deuxième classe sont tout à fait satisfaisants. Il est recommandé de réserver à l'avance pour tous les trains.

Autobus

Des services de bus fonctionnent dans la plupart des régions. Il est conseillé de réserver à l'avance pour les voyages sur grande distance. Des minibus (Matatus) sont en service dans les zones urbaines.

TELEPHONE

Indicatif du Pays   254
Indicatifs régionaux des Villes principales
   Mombasa   11
   Nairobi   2

Deutsch

JUGENDHERBERGEN IN KENYA

Es ist mit einem Preis von ca. KSh 100-500 pro Nacht zu rechnen. Sofern nichts anderes angegeben ist, ist ein eigener Daunen-Schlafsack mitzubringen. Die Herbergen sind von 06.30-23.00 Uhr geöffnet. Normalerweise gibt es keine Mahlzeiten.

PÄSSE UND VISA

Man braucht einen gültigen Reisepaß. Staatsangehörige eines Commonwealth-Staates brauchen kein Visum.

GESUNDHEIT

Reisende sollten sich gegen Gelbfieber, Typhus und Cholera impfen lassen. Es wird auch die Einnahme von Antimalariamitteln empfohlen.

GESCHÄFTSSTUNDEN DER BANKEN

Banken sind montags bis freitags von 09.00-15.00 Uhr und am ersten und letzten Samstag des Monats von 09.00-11.00 Uhr geöffnet.

POSTÄMTER

Postämter sind montags bis freitags von 08.00-17.00 Uhr und am Wochenende von 08.00-12.00 Uhr geöffnet. Auf der Hauptpost von Nairobi gibt es kostenlos vorübergehende Postlagerungsadressen (poste restante). Telefon-"Kreditkarten" können käuflich erworben werden.

LADENÖFFNUNGSZEITEN

08.30-18.00 Uhr. An Sonn- und Feiertagen sind die meisten Geschäfte geschlossen.

REISEN

Eisenbahn

In der 2. Klasse kann man sehr gut mit der Eisenbahn fahren. Für alle Züge sind Vorausbuchungen empfehlenswert.

Busse

In den meisten Gebieten gibt es einen Busverkehr. Für Fernverkehrsbusse ist Vorausbuchung ratsam. In Stadtgebieten verkehren kleine Minibusse (Matatus).

FERNSPRECHINFORMATIONEN

Landes-Kennzahl   254
größere Städte - Ortsnetzkennzahlen
   Mombasa   11
   Nairobi   2

Español

ALBERGUES DE JUVENTUD KENIANOS

Pagará alrededor de Ksh 100-500 por noche. Lleve su propio saco de dormir, salvo si se indica lo contrario. Los albergues abren de 06.30 a 23.00 horas. No suelen servirse comidas.

PASAPORTES Y VISADOS

Se requiere un pasaporte válido. Los ciudadanos de la Commonwealth no necesitan visado.

SANIDAD

Los visitantes deben vacunarse contra la fiebre amarilla, la fiebre tifoidea y el cólera. También se recomienda la medicación contra la malaria.

HORARIO DE BANCOS

Los bancos abren de 09.00 a 15.00 horas de lunes a viernes. Además, abren el primer y último sábado de cada mes de 09.00 a 11.00 horas.

OFICINAS DE CORREOS

El horario de las oficinas de correos es de 08.00 a 17.00 horas de lunes a viernes y de 08.00 a 12.00 horas los fines de semana. En la sede principal de correos de Nairobi, se puede conseguir una dirección temporal gratuita (lista de correos/poste restante) y se pueden comprar 'tarjetas de crédito' telefónicas.

HORARIO COMERCIAL

De 08.30 a 18.00 horas. La mayoría de las tiendas cierran los domingos y festivos.

DESPLAZAMIENTOS

Tren

Los servicios ferroviarios en segunda clase son muy satisfactorios. Se recomienda reservar con antelación para todos los trenes.

Autobús

Existen servicios de autobús hacia casi todas las zonas. Se recomienda reservar con antelación para trayectos de largo recorrido. En las zonas urbanas operan pequeños microbuses (Matatus).

INFORMACION TELEFONICA

Código Nacional	**254**
Prefijos de las Ciudades Principales	
Mombasa	**11**
Nairobi	**2**

HOSTELLING
INTERNATIONAL

Assured Standards – visited by our Liaison team and by you the guest – tell us when we don't measure up (reply slips at the end of this Guide)▸

des Normes Garanties, par les visites de notre Equipe de Liaison et par vous, les usagers – faites-le nous savoir quand nous ne sommes pas à la hauteur (Fiches-commentaires à la fin du Guide)◂

Zugesicherte Standards – beurteilt von unserem Liaison Team und von Ihnen, unserem Gast – sagen Sie es uns, wenn wir Sie enttäuschen (Antwortkarten hinten im Führer)▸

Normas Garantizadas – comprobadas por nuestro Equipo de Enlace y por Ud., el usuario – si fallamos en algo, díganoslo (al final de esta Guía encontrará nuestras hojas de comentarios)◂

Nairobi

**Ralph Bunche Rd,
PO Box 48661,
Nairobi. (near Nairobi hospital; GPO 2km)**
☎ 721765
🖷 724862

Open Dates:	🗐
Open Hours:	06.30-23.30hrs
Reservations:	(R) (IBN)
Price Range:	$5.50-8.00
Beds:	96 - 8x² 4x³ 3x⁴ 3x⁶
Facilities:	♦♦♦ 2x♦♦♦ ⦿ ☌ ▣ TV ▣▣ ▣ ▦ 8 P ⓘ ☺

Directions:

✈	Jomo Kenyatta International 18km
A🚌	Stage Coach #34 18km
🚈	Central 3km
🚌	111, 4, 8, 42, 40, 28 & 135 both Stage Coach & Matatus Mini Coach 3km ap Traffic Police HQ
Attractions:	⛰▲ ∪5km ⚓500m ⚓500m

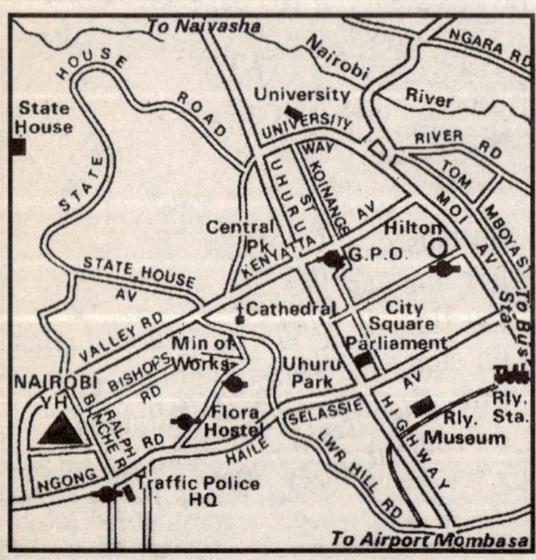

▲ There for everyone - young, not so young and those in the middle. ▲

▲ c'est pour tout le monde -les jeunes, les moins jeunes et tous les autres. ▲

▲ albergues para todos - los jóvenes, los menos jóvenes y los jóvenes de espíritu. ▲

▲ für jederman - ob jung, nicht mehr ganz so jung oder die dazwischen. ▲

Location/Address	Telephone No. Fax No.	Beds	Opening Dates	Facilities
△ *Mt Kenya* *PO Box 274, Naro Moru, Nyeri.*	☎ (176) 62412	38		⚲ 🅿
▲ Nairobi IBN Ralph Bunche Rd, PO Box 48661, Nairobi. (near Nairobi hospital; GPO 2km)	☎ 721765 🖷 724862	96		♙ ℡ Ⓡ ⚲ 🅿

HOSTELLING
INTERNATIONAL

use International Communications Network (ICN) at major hostels to send and receive
e-mail, set up e-mail box, send faxes, make International phone calls, surf the Web
– all at low, low prices using the ICN Communications Card

Utilisez le Réseau International de Communication (ICN), dans nos plus
grandes auberges pour envoyer et recevoir du courrier électronique, ouvrir une boîte
à lettres électronique, transmettre des fax, appeler l'étranger, surfer sur l'internet –
le tout à prix très très concurrentiels, grâce à la Carte de Communication ICN

benutzen Sie das International Communications Network (ICN) in Hauptherbergen,
um e-mail zu senden und zu empfangen, e-mail Briefkästen einzurichten, Faxe zu
schicken, international zu telefonieren oder "Surf the Net" – und das alles mit der
ICN Kommunikationskarte zu günstigsten Preisen!

utilice la Red Internacional de Comunicaciones ICN en los principales albergues para
transmitir y recibir mensajes electrónicos, establecer un buzón de correo electrónico,
enviar facsímiles, realizar llamadas telefónicas internacionales, navegar por la red
de Internet – todo a precios muy, muy económicos – mediante la Tarjeta de
Comunicación ICN.

South Korea

COREE DU SUD

SÜDKOREA

COREA DEL SUR

**Korea Youth Hostels Association,
Rm 408, Juksun Hyundai Building 80
Juksun-Dong, Jongro-Ku,
Seoul 110-052,
South Korea.**

☎ (82) (2) 7253031
📠 (82) (2) 7253113
E-mail: inform@kyha.or.kr
WWW Address: http://www.kyha.or.kr

A copy of the Hostel Directory for this Country can be obtained from:
The National Office.

**IBN Booking Centre for outward
bookings**

- **Seoul** - Korea, *via National Office
  above*

Capital:	Seoul		Population:	44,850,000
Language:	Korean		Size:	99,200 sq km
Currency:	Won			

South Korea

Sulaksan
Naksan
Pochun Bears Town
Kangchon
Ilyoung Shalom
Kwanglim
Kanghwa Namsan
Chung Pyung Academi
Koyang
Kanghwa
Daemyung Hongchun
Kyongin
Dunnae
Seoul
Yang Pyong
Olympic Parktel
Yong Pyong
Yeoju Flowerland
Wonju Hwaseung
Everland
Sobacksan
Eumsung
Suanbo Sajo Maeul
Sokrisan Heungwoon
West Sea
Kyeryongsan Kwangmyong
Buyeo
Yusong
Chilgok Choil
Chilgok Academy
Kyongju
Kyongju Bulkuksa
Jun Ju
Kyongju-Shilla
SOUTH KOREA
Youngchysan
Pusan
Dongsung
Kwangsan-Gu
Haenam
Namhae
Ullungdo
Tokdo
East Sea
Cheju
Chejudo
SOUTH KOREA

English

SOUTH KOREAN HOSTELS

Explore this fast developing country and get off the beaten track. The Youth Hostels are busy so you need to book in advance, directly with the hostel, although KYHA are happy to help you with your booking.

Expect to pay in the region of 4,000-13,500 WON including linen hire. Many Youth Hostels serve meals which may have to be booked in advance. Self-catering facilities are also available with a small charge for fuel.

PASSPORTS AND VISAS

Most countries have their own Embassy or Consulate in Seoul to help travellers. Most visitors with confirmed outbound tickets may stay for up to 3 months without a visa, although this does not apply to certain nationalities. Longer stays require a visa, although some countries have reciprocal visa exemption agreements with South Korea - check before you travel.

HEALTH

Travellers can receive medical treatment 24 hours a day. The manager of a Youth Hostel can arrange for a doctor or ambulance.

BANKING HOURS

Banks are open for business weekdays 09.30-16.30hrs and Saturday 09.30-13.30hrs.

POST OFFICES

Open weekdays 09.00-17.00hrs; Saturdays 09.00-13.00hrs. Closed Sundays and Public Holidays.

SHOPPING HOURS

Major department stores are open 10.30-19.30hrs including Sundays, smaller shops tend to be open from early morning until late evening.

TRAVEL

Air
Several airlines serve Korea.

Rail
The Korean National Railroad provides an extensive network of railways. Seoul has an excellent metro system.

Bus
Express buses operate between main cities and resorts.

Ferry
There is a regular sea service to Pusan, Korea's second largest city and principal port.

Driving
Taxis are plentiful and relatively inexpensive in Korea.

TELEPHONE INFORMATION

Country Code	**82**
Main City Area Codes	
Pusan	51
Seoul	2

Français

AUBERGES DE JEUNESSE SUD-COREENNES

Explorez ce pays en plein développement et sortez des sentiers battus. Les auberges reçoivent beaucoup de monde et il vous faudra donc réserver à l'avance, en vous adressant directement à l'auberge, mais KYHA (l'association des auberges de jeunesse coréennes) se fera un plaisir de vous aider à réserver.

Une nuit vous coûtera entre 4 000 et 13 500 WON, location de draps comprise. La plupart des auberges servent des repas, qu'il faudra quelquefois commander à l'avance. Il est possible de faire sa propre cuisine, moyennant un petit supplément pour l'énergie consommée.

PASSEPORTS ET VISAS

La plupart des pays ont leur propre Ambassade ou Consulat à Séoul pour aider les voyageurs. La plupart des visiteurs en possession d'un billet valide pour un autre pays peuvent séjourner dans le pays pour un maximum de 3 mois sans visa, bien que cela ne s'applique pas à certaines nationalités. Des séjours plus longs nécessitent l'obtention d'un visa, bien que certains pays aient des accords réciproques d'exemption de visas avec la Corée du Sud - vérifier les règlements avant de partir.

SOINS MEDICAUX

Les voyageurs peuvent recevoir un traitement médical pendant 24 heures. Les gérants des auberges de jeunesse feront le nécessaire au cas où un docteur ou une ambulance seraient requis.

HEURES D'OUVERTURE DES BANQUES

Les banques sont ouvertes en semaine de 9h30 à 16h30 et le samedi de 9h30 à 13h30.

BUREAUX DE POSTE

Ils sont ouverts en semaine du 9h à 17h; le samedi de 9h à 13h. Fermés le dimanche et les jours fériés.

HEURES D'OUVERTURE DES MAGASINS

Les grands magasins principaux sont ouverts de 10h30 à 19h30, dimanche y compris; les plus petits magasins ont tendance à ouvrir tôt le matin jusque tard le soir.

DEPLACEMENTS

Avions

La Corée est desservie par plusieurs lignes aériennes.

Trains

Le réseau des Chemins de fer nationaux coréens (Korean National Railroad) est étendu. Séoul possède un réseau de métro excellent.

Autobus

Des bus express relient les villes et les lieux touristiques principaux.

Ferry-boats

Un service maritime régulier dessert Pusan, port principal et deuxième ville de Corée.

Automobiles

Les taxis sont nombreux et assez bon marché en Corée.

TELEPHONE

Indicatif du Pays   **82**
Indicatifs régionaux des Villes principales
   Pusan   **51**
   Séoul   **2**

Deutsch

SÜDKOREANISCHE JUGENDHERBERGEN

Es lohnt sich, dieses sich schnell entwickelnde Land näher zu erkunden und auch unbekanntere Gebiete zu bereisen. Die Jugendherbergen sind immer sehr belegt, so daß man sich direkt bei der Herberge im voraus anmelden muß. Die KYHA ist aber gerne bei der Reservierung behilflich.

Es ist mit einem Preis von 4.000-13.500 WON, einschließlich Miete von Bettwäsche, zu rechnen. Viele Jugendherbergen bieten im voraus gebuchte Mahlzeiten an, während Selbstversorgerküche mit einer Gebühr für Nebenkosten auch vorhanden ist.

PÄSSE UND VISA

Die meisten Länder haben in Seoul eine eigene Botschaft oder ein eigenes Konsulat, wo man Reisenden können gerne behilflich ist. Die meisten Reisenden mit einem bestätigten Ticket für die Weiter- oder Rückreise bis zu 3 Monate lang ohne Visum im Land bleiben. Auf bestimmte Staatsangehörigkeiten trifft das jedoch nicht zu. Für einen längeren Aufenthalt wird ein Visum benötigt, aber mit einigen Staaten hat Südkorea gegenseitige Visumsbefreiungsverträge geschlossen. Bitte erkundigen Sie sich vor Ihrer Abreise.

GESUNDHEIT

Reisende können 24 Stunden ärztlich behandelt werden. Der Verwalter einer Jugendherberge kann einen Arzt oder Krankenwagen rufen.

GESCHÄFTSSTUNDEN DER BANKEN

Banken sind für Bankgeschäfte werktags von 09.30-16.30 Uhr und samstags von 09.30-13.30 Uhr geöffnet.

POSTÄMTER

Geöffnet wochentags 09.00-17.00 Uhr und samstags 09.00-13.00 Uhr. Geschlossen an Sonn-und Feiertagen.

LADENÖFFNUNGSZEITEN

Die größeren Warenhäuser sind auch sonntags von 10.30-19.30 Uhr geöffnet. Kleinere Geschäfte sind im allgemeinen vom frühen Morgen bis zum späten Abend geöffnet.

REISEN

Flugverkehr
In Korea gibt es mehrere Fluggesellschaften.

Eisenbahn
Die Koreanische Nationaleisenbahn verfügt über ein umfangreiches Streckennetz. Seoul hat ein erstklassiges U-Bahn-System.

Busse
Zwischen den wichtigsten Städten und anderen sehenswerten Orten verkehren Expreßbusse.

Fähren
Nach Pusan, der zweitgrößten Stadt Koreas, die auch die wichtigste Hafenstadt ist, wird auf dem Seeweg ein Fähren-Linienverkehr geboten.

Autofahren
Es gibt viele Taxis, die in Korea verhältnismäßig billig sind.

FERNSPRECHINFORMATIONEN

Landes-Kennzahl   **82**
größere Städte - Ortsnetzkennzahlen
   Pusan   **51**
   Seoul   **2**

Español

ALBERGUES JUVENILES SURCOREANOS

Explore este país en pleno desarrollo sin limitarse al itinerario turístico. Los albergues juveniles siempre están concurridos, por lo cual es necesario reservar con antelación dirigiéndose directamente al albergue, aunque la KYHA (la Asociación Coreana de Albergues Juveniles) tendrá mucho gusto en ayudarle a realizar su reserva.

Una noche le costará entre 4.000 y 13.500 WON incluyendo el alquiler de las sábanas. Muchos albergues sirven comidas, aunque es posible que sea necesario reservarlas de antemano. También disponen de una cocina en la que los huéspedes pueden prepararse sus propias comidas, por el uso de la cual le cobrarán una pequeña cantidad en concepto de gastos de combustible.

PASAPORTES Y VISADOS

Casi todos los países poseen su propia embajada o consulado en Seúl para ayudar a los viajeros. La mayoría de los visitantes portadores de un billete confirmado de salida para otro país podrán quedarse un máximo de 3 meses sin visado, pero esto no es aplicable a ciertas nacionalidades. Para estancias más prolongadas sí es necesario un visado, aunque algunos países mantienen acuerdos mutuos de exención de visado con Corea del Sur. Infórmese antes de su viaje.

ASISTENCIA MEDICA

Los visitantes pueden recibir tratamiento médico las 24 horas del día. Los encargados de los albergues pueden solicitar los servicios de un médico o ambulancia.

HORARIO DE LOS BANCOS

Los bancos abren los días laborables de 9.30 h. a 16.30 h. y los sábados de 9.30 h. a 13.30 h.

OFICINAS DE CORREOS

Las oficinas de correos abren los días laborables de 9 h. a 17 h. y los sábados de 9 h. a 13 h. Todas ellas cierran los domingos y fiestas.

HORARIO COMERCIAL

Los grandes almacenes abren de 10.30 h. a 19.30 h., domingos inclusive. Las tiendas más pequeñas suelen abrir por la mañana temprano y cerrar a última hora de la tarde.

DESPLAZAMIENTOS

Avión

Corea dispone de varias líneas aéreas.

Tren

La compañía ferroviaria nacional de Corea (Korean National Railroad) cuenta con una amplia red de ferrocarriles. Seúl disfruta de un excelente servicio de metro.

Autobús

Varios servicios directos de autobús enlazan las principales ciudades y centros turísticos.

Ferry

Existe un servicio marítimo regular para Pusán, la segunda ciudad más grande de Corea y su principal puerto.

Automóvil

En Corea los taxis son numerosos y relativamente baratos.

INFORMACION TELEFONICA

Código Nacional	**82**
Prefijos de las Ciudades Principales	
Pusán	51
Seúl	2

Discounts And Concessions

Guided Tours: 10% reduction on groups of 30 or more. Booked 3 months in advance.

Assured Standards – visited by our Liaison team and by you the guest – tell us when we don't measure up (reply slips at the end of this Guide) ▲

des Normes Garanties, par les visites de notre Equipe de Liaison et par vous, les usagers – faites-le nous savoir quand nous ne sommes pas à la hauteur (Fiches-commentaires à la fin du Guide) ▲

Zugesicherte Standards – beurteilt von unserem Liaison Team und von Ihnen, unserem Gast – sagen Sie es uns, wenn wir Sie enttäuschen (Antwortkarten hinten im Führer) ▲

Normas Garantizadas – comprobadas por nuestro Equipo de Enlace y por Ud., el usuario – si fallamos en algo, díganoslo (al final de esta Guía encontrará nuestras hojas de comentarios) ▲

Buyeo

Buyeo YH,
105-1 Kukyo-ri,
Buyeo-Eup,
Buyeo-Gun,
Choongnam-Do 323-800.
❶ (463) 8353102
❻ (463) 8353791

Open Dates:	🗓
Open Hours:	🕐
Reservations:	ⓡ ⌐CC⌐
Price Range:	8900 💶
Beds:	582 - 8x² 26x⁶ 11x⁶
Facilities:	16x 🛉🛉🛉 🍴 ☕ 🛏 📺 2x 🍷 🔦 🏢 🔒 ⬇ 🅿 ℹ ♿ ❀ 🏡

Directions:

✈	Kunsan 50km
A🚌	Baekma Airport Bus 50km
🚂	Nonsan 30km
🚌	Kumnam Bus 500m ap Kumnam Bus Terminal

Attractions: 🌲 ⛰ 🔍 🏃 🏊

Seoul

Seoul Olympic Parktel YH,
88 Bangyi-Dong,
Songpa-Ku,
Seoul 138-050.
❶ (2) 4102114
❻ (2) 4102100

Open Dates:	🗓
Open Hours:	🕐
Reservations:	ⓡ ⌐CC⌐
Price Range:	11000 💶
Beds:	967 - 9x¹ 84x² 52x³ 20x⁴ 20x⁵ 10x⁶
Facilities:	♿ 🛉🛉🛉 180x 🛉🛉 🍴 ☕ 🛏 📺 🎮 20x 🍷 🔦 📷 🏢 🔒 ⬇ ⬆ 🅿 ℹ ♿ ❀ ⛩ 🏡 🏤

Directions: 25 SE from city centre

✈	Kimpo 40km
A🚌	600 or Kal Limousine line 4 40km
🚌	569, 568, 212, 21, 813, 16, 70 100m ap Olympic Park
Ⓤ	Sungnae 300m

Attractions: 🌲 ⛰ 🚴 🏃 🔍 500m 🏊

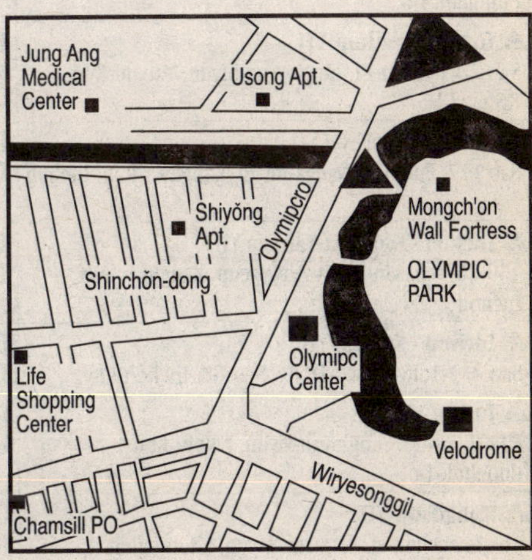

Location/Address	Telephone No. / Fax No.	Beds	Opening Dates	Facilities
▲ **Buyeo** **Buyeo YH, 105-1 Kukyo-ri, Buyeo-Eup, Buyeo-Gun, Choongnam-Do 323-800.**	☎ (463) 8353102 ✆ (463) 8353791	582		
▲ **Cheju YH** 483, Nameup-ri, Awol-eup, Bukcheju-kun, Cheju-do	☎ (64) 7998811 ✆ (64) 7998821	498		15S
△ *Chilgok Academy YH* *349-1, Namyool-Ri, Sukjeong-Myun, Chilgok-Kun, Kyongbuk.*	☎ (545) 9759966 ✆ (545) 9759967	*121*		10.2SE
△ *Chilkok choil YH* *164, Yongsu-Ri, Gasan-Myun, Chilkok-kun, Kyoungbuk-Do.*	☎ (545) 9750602 ✆ (53) 3536572	*106*		
▲ **Chung Pyung** - Academy YH San 18, Duckhyun-Ri, Sang-Myun, Gapyung-kun, kyunggi-Do.	☎ (356) 845500 ✆ (356) 855600	318		
▲ **Daejon** - Yusong YH 671-4, Kyesan-Dong, Yusong-Gu, Daejon-Si.	☎ (42) 8229591 ✆ (42) 8239965	240		7E
▲ **Daemyong Hongchun YH** 125-1, Palbong-ri, Seo-myun, Hongchun-kun, Kangwon-do	☎ (366) 4348311 ✆ (366) 4358304	1307		32W
▲ **Dunnae YH** 1140, Sapkyo-Ri, Dunnae-Myun, Heuingsung-kun, Kangwon-Do.	☎ (372) 3436488 ✆ (372) 3436487	898		4NE
△ *Eumsung YH* *San 49-1, Saengkeuk-Myun, Eumsung-kun, Chungbuk-Do.*	☎ (446) 8777802 ✆ (446) 8818539	*198*		
▲ **Everland YH** 310, Jeondae-ri, Pokok-myun, Yongin-shi, Kyonggi-do	☎ (335) 209727 ✆ (335) 209727	585		15N
▲ **Haenam YH** San 7-10, Kurim-Ri, Samsan-Myun, Haenam-kun, Chunnam-Do.	☎ (634) 5330170	250		
▲ **Ilyoung Shalom YH** San 72, Ilyoung-Ri, Jangheung-Myun, Yangju-Kun, Kyonggi-Do.	☎ (351) 428011 ✆ (351) 427085	217		7SE
▲ **Inchon** - Kanghwa YH San 177, Euipo-ri, Naega-myun, Kanghwa-kun, Inchon	☎ (32) 9338891/ 2 ✆ (32) 9339335	354		0.4S
▲ **Inchon** - Kanghwa Namsan YH 439-16, Namsan-ri, Kanghwa-eup, Kanghwa-kun, Inchon	☎ (32) 9347777 ✆ (32) 9347782	400		2NE
▲ **Inchon** - Kyongin YH San 253-1, Kyongseo-Dong, Seo-Gu, Inchon-City.	☎ (32) 5797195 ✆ (32) 5797198	840		28.5S
▲ **Jun Ju YH** 712-2, Sin-Ri, Sangkwan-Hyun, Wanju-Kun, Chunbuk-Do.	☎ (652) 2320150 ✆ (652) 2320155	181		
▲ **Kangchon YH** 366 Kangchon-Ri, Namsan-Myun, Choonchun-Si, Kangwon-Do.	☎ (361) 2621201 ✆ (361) 2621204	196		17W

Location/Address	Telephone No. Fax No.	Beds	Opening Dates	Facilities
△ *Koyang YH* *278-3, Koyang-Dong, Koyang-Si, Kyonggi-Do 411-830.*	☎ *(344) 629049* ✆ *(344) 629579*	*200*		20 NW
▲ **Kwangju-Kwangsangu YH** 38-3 Songhak-Dong, Kwangsan-Gu, Kwangju-Si.	☎ (62) 9434378 ✆ (62) 9434379	130		22 S
▲ **Kyeryongsan-Kwangmyong YH** 136, Jungjang-Ri, Kyeryong-Myun, Kongju-Si, Chungnam-Do.	☎ (416) 8564666 ✆ (416) 8564660	530		11 NE
▲ **Kyongju** - Bulkuksa YH 530-3, Jinhyon-Dong, Kyongju-Si, Kyongbuk-Do.	☎ (561) 7460826 ✆ (561) 746-7805	750		11 SE
▲ **Kyongju** - Kyongju YH 470-2, Choonghyo-Dong, Kyongju-City, Kyongbuk-Do.	☎ (561) 421771 ✆ (561) 420535	248		5.5 W
▲ **Kyongiu** - Shilla YH 611-11, Jinhyun-dong, Kyongju-shi, Kyongbuk-do	☎ (561) 7487333 ✆ (561) 7487334	473		10 SE
▲ **Naksan YH** 30-1, Jeonjin-Ri, Kangheun-Myun, Yangyang-Kun, Kang-wondo.	☎ (396) 6723416 ✆ (396) 6723418	400		
▲ **Namhae YH** 140-1 Keumsong-Ri, Samdong-Myun, Namhae-kun, Kyongnam.	☎ (594) 8674510 ✆ (594) 8674511	300		
▲ **Pochun** - Bears Town YH 295 Sohak-Ri, Naechon-Myun, Pochun-kun, Kyonggi-Do.	☎ (357) 322534 ✆ (357) 339060	600		
▲ **Pochun** - Kwanglim YH 456, Jikdong-ri, Soheul-eup, Pochun-kun, Kyonggi-do	☎ (357) 5440515; 5440518 ✆ (357) 5440519	454		10 S
▲ **Pusan** - Dongsung YH 206-11 Songjeong-Dong, Haewoondae-Gu, Pusan City.	☎ (51) 7038466 ✆ (51) 7450256	141		25 NE
▲ **Seoul** **Seoul Olympic Parktel YH, 88 Bangyi-Dong, Songpa-Ku, Seoul 138-050.**	☎ (2) 4102114 ✆ (2) 4102100	967		25 SE
▲ **Sokrisan Hungwoon YH** 238, Sangpan-ri, Naesokri-myun, Boeun-kun, Chungbuk-do	☎ (433) 5425999 ✆ (433) 5433634	511		16 NE
▲ **Sobacksan YH** San 23-6, Chundong-ri, Danyang-eup, Danyang-kun, Chungbuk-do	☎ (444) 4215555; 4215557 ✆ (444) 4213860	1370		8 E
▲ **Suanbo Sajo Maeul YH** 641, Oncheon-Ri, Sangmo-Myun, Joongwon-Ku, Chungbuk, Suanbo.	☎ (441) 8460750 ✆ (441) 8461789	736		0.8 NE
▲ **Sulaksan YH** 246-77, Sulak-Dong, Sokcho-si, Kangwon-Do.	☎ (392) 6367115 ✆ (392) 6367107	844		
▲ **Wonju Hwaseung YH** San 2-4, Wolsong-Ri, Jijong-Myun, Wonju-Si, Kangwon-Do.	☎ (371) 7323700 ✆ (371) 7327665	418		10 S

Location/Address	Telephone No. Fax No.	Beds	Opening Dates	Facilities
▲ **Yeoju Flowerland YH** 444-5, Yongeun-Ri, Neungso-Myun, Yeoju-Kun, Kyonggi-Do.	☎ (337) 841717 🖷 (337) 840625	620		♗ ⁏◍ Ⓡ 10E ♿ ♁ P
▲ **Yongpyong YH** Yong Pyeong YH, Dragon Valley Resort, 130 Yongsan-Ri, Doam-Myun, Pyungchang-kun, Kangwon-Do.	☎ (374) 355757 🖷 (374) 350160	470		♗ ⁏◍ Ⓡ 50 W ⊂CC⊃ ♁ P ⊡
△ *Youngchysan YH* *13-2, Soonji-Ri, Habuk-Myun, Yangsan-Kun, Kyongnam-Do.*	☎ (523) 3836462 🖷 (523) 3827222	200		♗ ⁏◍ Ⓡ ♁ P

SUPPLEMENTARY ACCOMMODATION
OUTSIDE THE ASSURED STANDARDS SCHEME

Location/Address	Telephone No. Fax No.	Beds	Opening Dates	Facilities
Yangpyong YH San 2, Seoksan-ri, Danwol-myun, Yangpyong-kun, Kyonggi-do	☎ (338) 747800 🖷 (338) 747815	1180		♗ ⁏◍ Ⓡ 40 W ♁ P ☕

Libya

LIBYE

LIBYEN

LIBIA

Libyan Youth Hostel Association,
69 Amr Ben Al-Aas Street, PO Box 10322,
Tripoli, Al-Jamahiriya, Libya.

☎ (218) (21) 4445171
✆ (218) (21) 3330118

A copy of the Hostel Directory for this Country can be obtained from:
The National Office.

Capital:	Tripoli	Population:	4,000,000
Language:	Arabic	Size:	1,759,540 sq km
Currency:	LD (Libyan Dinar)		

Libya

Zwarah
Surman
Elimil
Tarabulus
Sabrata
Tripoli (2)
Ezhra
Ezzawya
Al Khums
Shahat
(Cyrene)
Misratah
El-Marj
Benghazi
Derna
Gharyan
Derj
Zentan
Bani Walid
Sirt
Ghadamis
Waddan
Hun
LIBYA
Sabha
Fejeaj (Ubari Area)
Ghat
Omm Al-Araneb
Murzuk
S A H A R A   D E S E R T
NIGER
CHAD
N
250
500
750
KMS
0
200
400
MLS

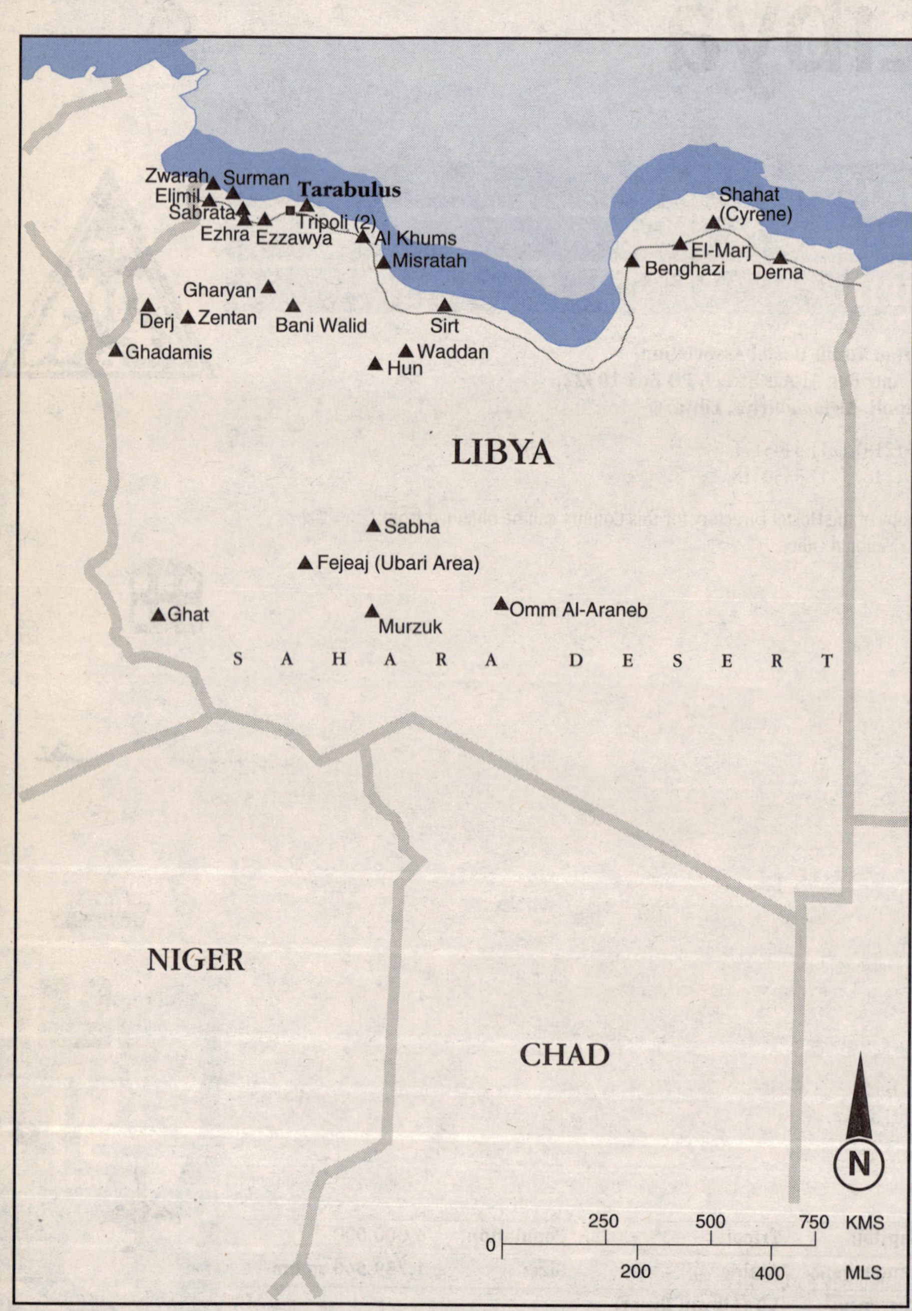

English

LIBYAN HOSTELS

Hostels are open 06.00-10.00hrs and 14.00-23.00hrs except for Tripoli-Gergarish which is open 07.00-24.00hrs. Expect to pay in the region of 3.00-5.00 LD, including sheets.

In key city hostels and during peak periods the maximum length of stay at any hostel is 3 nights.

PASSPORTS AND VISAS

All visitors must have an entry visa to the country, except visitors from Arabic countries. A valid passport and two passport size photographs are required. All Libyan Embassies and Consulates will grant a visitors visa on the same day. An Arabic translation of the passport information is required.

The Libyan/Tunisian Border is open from the Libyan side and visitors to/from Tunis can enter Libya without a visa, however, this rule is subject to change without prior notice.

HEALTH

Medical treatment is free of charge in public hospitals and clinics.

BANKING HOURS

Banks are open Saturday to Thursday from 08.00hrs until 14.00hrs.

POST OFFICES

Post offices are open seven days a week from 08.00hrs until 20.00hrs.

International phone offices are open 24 hours every day.

SHOPPING HOURS

Shops are generally open Saturday to Thursday 08.00-14.00hrs and 16.00-21.00hrs. Friday 09.00-13.00hrs.

TRAVEL

Air

Direct flights are available from all European airports. Flights within Libya are operated by Libyan Arab Airlines.

Bus

Direct bus services are available from Tripoli to Tunis, Alger, Casablanca, Cairo, Alexandria and Amman.

Ferry

Passenger and car ferry services from Malta, Tunis, Cairo, Casablanca, Azmir, Alexandria, and Genoa call at Tripoli.

Driving

It is possible to drive on the Libyan highways, along the Mediterranean coast from Morocco to Egypt. Visitors with cars should possess a valid International Driving license. Use of the vehicle within Libyan territory should not exceed 3 months.

TELEPHONE INFORMATION

Country Code	**218**
Main City Area Codes	
Tobruk	**87**
Tripoli	**21**

Français

AUBERGES DE JEUNESSE LIBYENNES

Les auberges sont en général ouvertes de 6h à 10h et de 14h à 23h, sauf celle de Tripoli-Gergarish, qui est ouverte de 7h à 24h. Une nuit vous coutera entre 3.00-5.00 LD, location de draps comprise.

Dans les auberges très fréquentées, situées dans les grandes villes, et dans toutes les auberges pendant les périodes de pointe, la durée maximale d'un séjour est de 3 nuits.

PASSEPORTS ET VISAS

Tous les visiteurs doivent être munis d'un visa d'entrée, sauf les citoyens des pays arabes. Un passeport valide et deux photos pour passeports sont requis. Toutes les ambassades et tous les consulats de Libye accordent des visas de tourisme le jour même.

La frontière libyenne/tunisienne est ouverte du côté de la Libye et les visiteurs pour/en provenance de Tunis, peuvent entrer en Libye sans visa, mais ce règlement est susceptible de changer sans préavis.

SOINS MEDICAUX

Les traitements médicaux sont gratuits dans les hôpitaux et cliniques publiques.

HEURES D'OUVERTURE DES BANQUES

Les banques sont ouvertes du samedi au jeudi de 8h à 14h.

BUREAUX DE POSTE

Les bureaux de poste sont ouverts sept jours sur sept de 8h à 20h.

Les bureaux téléphoniques internationaux sont ouverts 24 heures sur 24 tous les jours.

HEURES D'OUVERTURE DES MAGASINS

Les magasins sont en principe ouverts du samedi au jeudi de 8h à 14h et de 16h à 21h.

DEPLACEMENTS

Avions

Des vols directs partent de tous les aéroports européens. Les vols intérieurs sont assurés par Libyan Arab Airlines.

Autobus

Des services de bus directs sont assurés à partir de Tripoli à destination de Tunis, d'Alger, de Casablanca, du Caire, d'Alexandrie et d'Amman.

Ferry-boats

Les traversées pour passagers et véhicules à partir de Malte, de Tunis, du Caire, de Casablanca, d'Azmir, d'Alexandrie et de Gênes passent par Tripoli.

Automobiles

Il est possible d'emprunter les autoroutes libyennes, le long de la côte méditerranéenne, du Maroc en Egypte.

TELEPHONE

Indicatif du Pays	**218**
Indicatifs régionaux des Villes principales	
Tobrouk	87
Tripoli	21

Deutsch

LIBYSCHE JUGENDHERBERGEN

Die Herbergen sind von 06.00-10.00 Uhr und von 14.00-23.00 Uhr geöffnet, außer der in Tripolis-Gergarish, die von 07.00-24.00 Uhr geöffnet ist. Es ist mit einem Preis von ca. 3.00-5.00 LD, einschließlich Bettlaken, zu rechnen.

In größeren Städten und während der Hauptsaison beschränkt sich der Höchstaufenthalt in einer Herberge auf 3 Übernachtungen.

PÄSSE UND VISA

Alle Besucher, es sei denn sie kommen aus arabischen Ländern, müssen im Besitz eines Einreisevisums sein. Man braucht einen gültigen Reisepaß und zwei Paßfotos. Alle libyschen Botschaften und Konsulate gewähren auf Antrag noch am gleichen Tag ein Visum.

Die Grenze zwischen Libyen und Tunesien ist auf der libyschen Seite offen. Aus Tunis kommende oder nach Tunis gehende Reisende können ohne Visum nach Libyen einreisen oder das Land wieder verlassen. Diese Vorschrift kann sich jedoch unangekündigt ändern.

GESUNDHEIT

In öffentlichen Krankenhäusern und Kliniken ist ärztliche Behandlung kostenlos.

GESCHÄFTSSTUNDEN DER BANKEN

Banken sind samstags bis donnerstags von 08.00 bis 14.00 Uhr geöffnet.

POSTÄMTER

Postämter sind an sieben Tagen der Woche von 08.00 bis 20.00 Uhr geöffnet.

Fernsprechämter sind für Auslandsgespräche 24 Stunden am Tag geöffnet.

LADENÖFFNUNGSZEITEN

Die Geschäfte sind im allgemeinen samstags bis donnerstags von 08.00-14.00 Uhr und von 16.00-21.00 Uhr geöffnet.

REISEN

Flugverkehr

Von allen europäischen Flughäfen aus gibt es Direktflüge. Innerhalb Libyens betreibt Libyan Arab Airlines einen Flugverkehr.

Busse

Von Tripolis nach Tunis, Algier, Casablanca, Kairo, Alexandria und Amman gibt es einen direkten Busverkehr.

Fähren

Von Malta, Tunis, Kairo, Casablanca, Azmir, Alexandria und Genua aus gibt es einen Passagier- und Autofährenverkehr, der über Tripolis führt.

Autofahren

Auf libyschen Straßen kann man von Marokko nach Ägypten an der Mittelmeerküste entlang fahren.

FERNSPRECHINFORMATIONEN

Landes-Kennzahl   **218**
größere Städte - Ortsnetzkennzahlen

    Tobruk   **87**
    Tripolis   **21**

Español

ALBERGUES DE JUVENTUD LIBIOS

Los albergues están abiertos de 06.00 a 10.00 horas y de 14.00 a 23.00 horas, excepto el Gergarish de Trípoli, que abre de 07.00 a 24.00 horas. Pagará alrededor de 3,00-5,00 LD y las sábanas están incluidas en el precio.

En los albergues de las ciudades importantes y en temporada alta, la estancia máxima es de 3 noches.

PASAPORTES Y VISADOS

Todos los turistas deberán tener visado de entrada al país, excepto los procedentes de los países árabes. Es obligatorio un pasaporte válido y deberá presentar dos fotografías tamaño carné. Todos los consulados y las embajadas libias expiden visados el mismo día en que se solicita.

La frontera de Libia con Túnez está abierta por la parte libia y todos los visitantes que se dirijan a Túnez o procedan de allí pueden entrar en Libia sin visado, aunque puede haber cambios sin previo aviso.

SANIDAD

Se ofrece asistencia médica gratuita tanto en los hospitales públicos como en las clínicas.

HORARIO DE BANCOS

Los bancos abren de sábado a jueves de 08.00 a 14.00 horas.

OFICINAS DE CORREOS

Las oficinas de correos abren los siete días de la semana de 08.00 a 20.00 horas.

Las oficinas en las que se pueden hacer llamadas telefónicas internacionales están abiertas las 24 horas del día.

HORARIO COMERCIAL

Las tiendas suelen abrir de sábado a jueves de 08.00 a 14.00 horas y de 16.00 a 21.00 horas.

DESPLAZAMIENTOS

Avión

Hay vuelos directos desde todos los aeropuertos europeos. Los vuelos nacionales están a cargo de las líneas aéreas libio-árabes.

Autobús

Hay servicio directo de autocar desde Trípoli a Túnez, Argel, Casablanca, El Cairo, Alejandría y Ammán.

Ferry

Hay servicios de ferry para pasajeros y coches procedentes de Malta, Túnez, El Cairo, Casablanca, Azmir, Alejandría y Génova, todos con parada en Trípoli.

Coche

Siguiendo las autopistas libias, se puede recorrer la costa del Mediterráneo desde Marruecos hasta Egipto.

INFORMACION TELEFONICA

Código Nacional	218
Prefijos de las Ciudades Principales	
Tobruk	87
Trípoli	21

HOSTELLING INTERNATIONAL

Assured Standards – visited by our Liaison team and by you the guest – tell us when we don't measure up (reply slips at the end of this Guide) ▶

des Normes Garanties, par les visites de notre Equipe de Liaison et par vous, les usagers – faites-le nous savoir quand nous ne sommes pas à la hauteur (Fiches-commentaires à la fin du Guide) ▶

Zugesicherte Standards – beurteilt von unserem Liaison Team und von Ihnen, unserem Gast – sagen Sie es uns, wenn wir Sie enttäuschen (Antwortkarten hinten im Führer) ▶

Normas Garantizadas – comprobadas por nuestro Equipo de Enlace y por Ud., el usuario – si fallamos en algo, díganoslo (al final de esta Guía encontrará nuestras hojas de comentarios) ▶

Location/Address	Telephone No. / Fax No.	Beds	Opening Dates	Facilities
▲ **Al Khums** Alkhums Sport Center SW.	☎ (31) 20888, 21881-2	160		3 SW
△ *Banī Walid* *YH, the former Banī Walid Hotel, Banī Walid.*	☎ *(322) 2415*	*30*		
▲ **Bengazi** Sport City Bengazi SW.	☎ (61) 95961	200		(R) 1 SW
△ *Derj* *Derj YH.*		*20*		0.5 W
△ *El Jmil* *El Jmil City Centre.*	☎ *(281) 2127*	*25*		
▲ **El-Marj** YH, El-Marg Town.	☎ (67) 3669	60		
▲ **Elzahra YH** Elzahra City Centre.	☎ (272) 2993	20		
▲ **Ezzawya** YH, Ezzawya City: Tripoli 40km W.	☎ (23) 23119	80		
▲ **Fejeaj (Ubari Area)** Fejeaj YH, People's Housing Project: Village of Fejeaj.	☎ (728) 2902	40		
▲ **Ghadamis** YH, Ghadamis.	☎ (484) 2023	120		(R) 1 SE
△ *Hun* *Hun YH.*	☎ *(57) 2040*	*50*		
▲ **Misratah** YH, Misratah.	☎ (51) 642435	120		(R) 4 W
▲ **Murzuk YH** Murzuk City Centre.	☎ (725) 2301	50		
△ *Omm Al-Araneb* *YH, Omm Al-Araneb: near Murzuq.*	☎ *(72) 62228*	*30*		
▲ **Sabha** Jamal Abdel Naser ST, Sabha.	☎ (71) 621178	160		(R) 3 E
▲ **Sabrata** YH, Sabrata: Tripoli 68km.	☎ (24) 2821 ✆ (23) 29082	160		(R) 1 NW
▲ **Shahat (Cyrene)** The former Cyrene (Shahat) Tourist Hotel.	☎ (851) 2102	200		(R) 2 NW
▲ **Sirt** YH, Cost Rd, Sirt.	☎ (54) 61391, 61825	120		(R) 2 N
▲ **Surman** YH, Surman.	☎ (273) 2581	50		2 N
▲ **Tripoli** Gergarish Rd, Km 5, Tripoli.	☎ (21) 76694 ✆ (21) 75034	200		(R) 5 S
▲ **Tripoli** 69 Amru Ben Al-Aas St, Tripoli.	☎ (21) 4445171 ✆ (21) 3330118	120		
▲ **Waddan** YH, Waddan.	☎ (581) 2329, 2267	160		(R)
▲ **Yafrin** YH, Yafrin: centre of city.	☎ (421) 2394	45		

Location/Address	Telephone No. Fax No.	Beds	Opening Dates	Facilities
▲ **Zentan** YH, Zentan: centre of city.	☎ (451) 2826	30		❙�◎❙ ℙ
△ *Zwarah* *Zwarah YH.*	☎ *(25) 21012*	30		❙◎❙ 1NE ℙ

**SUPPLEMENTARY ACCOMMODATION
OUTSIDE THE ASSURED STANDARDS SCHEME**

Location/Address	Telephone No. Fax No.	Beds	Opening Dates	Facilities
Gharyan YH, Gharyan.	☎ (41) 31491	120		❙❙❙ ❙◎❙ Ⓡ 2NE 🔒 ℙ

Malaysia

MALAISIE
MALAYSIA
MALASIA

**Malaysian Youth Hostels Association,
KL International Youth Hostel,
21, Jalan Kampung Attap, 50460 Kuala Lumpur,
Malaysia.**

☏ (60) (3) 2736870/71
✆ (60) (3) 2741115
E-mail: myha@pd.jaring.my

A copy of the Hostel Directory for this Country can be obtained from:
The National Office.

**IBN Booking Centre for outward
bookings**

- **Kuala Lumpur - MSL Travel
  Centre,** 66 Jalan Putra, 50350 Kuala
  Lumpur.
  ☏ (60) (3) 4424722
  ✆ (60) (3) 4433707.

Capital: Kuala Lumpur	**Currency:** RM (Malaysian Ringgit)
Language: Malay, English widely spoken	**Population:** 18,000,000
	Size: 330,434 sq km

Malaysia

Georgetown
MALAYSIA
Fraser's Hill
Kuala Lumpur (2)
Kuala Lumpur
Port Dickson
Melaka
Singapore
SUMATRA
KEPULAUAN
RIAU
N
50   100   150   200 KM
0
50   100   MLS

English

MALAYSIAN HOSTELS

Whether it is the bright lights of Kuala Lumpur or Penang, or the simplicity of Melaka Beach, Malaysia's 5 Youth Hostels provide a unique insight into this country.

Meals are not normally provided, but can be arranged. Hostels are generally open 07.00-23.00hrs.

Overnight accommodation prices for Hostels withing the "Assured Standards Scheme" will vary according to location and facilities. The range is from RM 10.00-25.00 (This price range is accurate at the time of printing, and may be subject to change during the year).

TELEPHONE INFORMATION

Country Code	60
Main City Area Codes	
Kuala Lumpur	3
Penang	4

Français

AUBERGES DE JEUNESSE MALAISES

Que ce soit l'effervescence de Kuala Lumpur ou de Penang, ou la simplicité de Melaka Beach qui vous attirent, les 5 auberges de jeunesse de Malaisie vous donneront un aperçu unique de ce pays.

Les auberges ne servent en principe pas de repas, mais peuvent s'en occuper. Elles sont en général ouvertes de 7h à 23h.

Le prix de la nuitée dans les auberges appartenant au "Plan de Garantie des Normes" pourra être compris, selon le lieu et la qualité des prestations offertes, entre RM 10,00-25,00 (ces chiffres sont corrects à l'heure où nous mettons sous presse mais pourront être adjustés au cours de l'année).

TELEPHONE

Indicatif du Pays	60
Indicatifs régionaux des Villes principales	
Kuala Lumpur	3
Penang	4

Deutsch

MALAYSISCHE JUGENDHERBERGEN

Ob im Lichtermeer von Kuala Lumpur oder Penang oder am einfachen Strand von Melaka, die 5 Jugendherbergen, in Malaysia, bieten einen einmaligen Einblick in dieses Land.

Normalerweise werden keine Mahlzeiten geboten, aber auf Wunsch läßt sich auch das arrangieren. Die Herbergen sind im allgemeinen von 07.00-23.00 Uhr geöffnet.

Übernachtungpreise schwanken abhängig von Ort und Ausstattung. Die Preisspanne reicht von RM 10.00-25.00 (Diese Preisspanne ist bei Drucktermin genau und kann sich während des Jahres ändern).

FERNSPRECHINFORMATIONEN

Landes-Kennzahl	60
größere Städte - Ortsnetzkennzahlen	
Kuala Lumpur	3
Penang	4

Español

ALBERGUES DE JUVENTUD MALAYOS

Ya sea en el esplendor de Kuala Lumpur o Peneng, o en la sencillez de la Playa de Melaka, los 5 albergues de juventud malayos ofrecen siempre una perspectiva única del país.

Generalmente no se sirven comidas, aunque se puede llegar a un acuerdo. Los albergues suelen estar abiertos de 07.00 a 23.00 horas.

Los precios por noche en los albergues que se adhieren al "Plan de las Normas Garantizadas" varían seguin el emplazamiento y las prestaciones ofrecidas. Estos oscilan entre RM 10,00 y 25,00 (los precios indicados son correctos al cierre de la edición, pero podrán modificarse durante el transcurso del año).

INFORMACION TELEFONICA

Código Nacional   **60**
Prefijos de las Ciudades Principales
    Kuala Lumpur   **3**
    Peneng   **4**

HOSTELLING INTERNATIONAL

▲ There for everyone - young, not so young and those in the middle ▲

▲ c'est pour tout le monde - les jeunes, les moins jeunes et tous les autres ▲

▲ albergues para todos - los jóvenes, los menos jóvenes y los jóvenes de espíritu ▲

▲ für jederman - ob jung, nicht mehr ganz so jung oder die dazwischen ▲

Kuala Lumpur - International YH

**21 Jalan Kampung Attap,
50460 Kuala Lumpur.**
(3) 2736870/71
(3) 2741115

Open Dates:	
Open Hours:	07.00-23.59hrs
Reservations:	R IBN CC
Price Range:	RM 20.00
Beds:	72 - 6x^4 3x^6 3x^{6+}
Facilities:	6x
Directions:	2SE from city centre
✈	50km
🚉	1km
🚌	1km

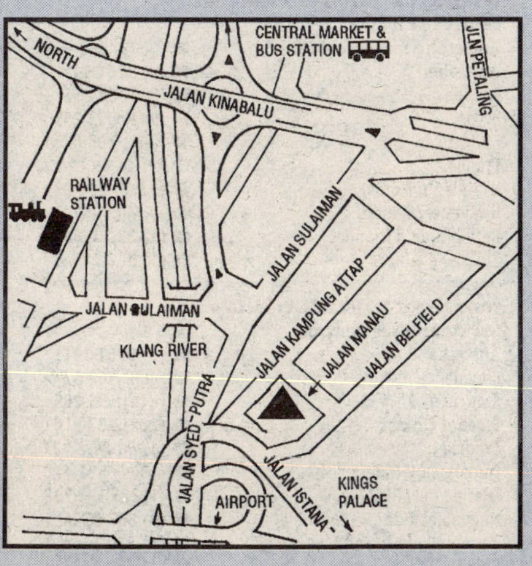

Assured Standards – visited by our Liaison team and by you the guest – tell us when we don't measure up (reply slips at the end of this Guide) ▲

des Normes Garanties, par les visites de notre Equipe de Liaison et par vous, les usagers – faites-le nous savoir quand nous ne sommes pas à la hauteur (Fiches-commentaires à la fin du Guide) ▲

Zugesicherte Standards – beurteilt von unserem Liaison Team und von Ihnen, unserem Gast – sagen Sie es uns, wenn wir Sie enttäuschen (Antwortkarten hinten im Führer) ▲

Normas Garantizadas – comprobadas por nuestro Equipo de Enlace y por Ud., el usuario – si fallamos en algo, díganoslo (al final de esta Guía encontrará nuestras hojas de comentarios) ▲

Location/Address	Telephone No. Fax No.	Beds	Opening Dates	Facilities
△ *Fraser's Hill* *Michaels Apartment, MC G/5 Taman Setia,* *49000 Bukit Fraser.*	☎ *(9) 3622443* ✆ *(9) 3622443*	*12*	📷	♦♦♦ ☞ Ⓟ
▲ **Kuala Lumpur** - International YH ⟨IBN⟩ **21 Jalan Kampung Attap, 50460 Kuala Lumpur.**	☎ (3) 2736870/ 71 ✆ (3) 2741115	72	📷	♦♦♦ Ⓡ 2SE ⊂CC⊃ Ⓟ
▲ **Kuala Lumpur** - International Youth Centre Jalan Tenteram, Bandar Tun Razak, Cheras, 56000 Kuala Lumpur.	☎ (3) 9719204	240	📷	♦♦♦ Ⓡ Ⓟ
▲ **Melaka** ⟨IBN⟩ 341 Taman Melaka Paya, 75000 Melaka. (next to Malacca Club)	☎ (6) 2827915	56	📷	♦♦♦ Ⓟ 📷
▲ **Port Dickson** km 6, Jalan Pantai, 71000 Port Dickson.	☎ (6) 6472188	64	📷	♦♦♦ Ⓟ 📷

HOSTELLING INTERNATIONAL

IBN INTERNATIONAL BOOKING NETWORK

make your credit card booking at these centres:-		**réservez par cartes de crédit aux centres suivants:-**	
Australia	☎ (2) 9261 1111	Angleterre & Pays de Galles	☎ (1692) 581 418
Canada	☎ (800) 663 5777	Australie	☎ (2) 9261 1111
England & Wales	☎ (1629) 581 418	Canada	☎ (800) 663 5777
France	☎ (1) 44 89 87 27	Écosse	☎ (541) 553 255
Northern Ireland	☎ (1232) 324 733	États-Unis	☎ (202) 783 6161
Republic of Ireland	☎ (1) 830 1766	France	☎ (1) 44 89 87 27
New Zealand	☎ (9) 303 9524	Irlande du Nord	☎ (1232) 324 733
Scotland	☎ (541) 553 255	Nouvelle-Zélande	☎ (9) 303 9524
Switzerland	☎ (1) 360 1414	République d'Irlande	☎ (1) 830 1766
USA	☎ (202) 783 6161	Suisse	☎ (1) 360 1414

buchen Sie mit Kreditkarte in folgenden Buchungszentren:-		**reserve por tarjeta de crédito en los siguientes centros:-**	
Australien	☎ (2) 9261 1111	Australia	☎ (2) 9261 1111
England & Wales	☎ (1629) 581 418	Canadá	☎ (800) 663 5777
Frankreich	☎ (1) 44 89 87 27	Escocia	☎ (541) 553 255
Irland	☎ (1) 830 1766	Estados Unidos	☎ (202) 783 6161
Kanada	☎ (800) 663 5777	Francia	☎ (1) 44 89 87 27
Neuseeland	☎ (9) 303 9524	Inglaterra y Gales	☎ (1629) 581 418
Nordirland	☎ (1232) 324 733	Irlanda del Norte	☎ (1232) 324 733
Schottland	☎ (541) 553 255	Nueva Zelanda	☎ (9) 303 9524
Schweiz	☎ (1) 360 1414	República de Irlanda	☎ (1) 830 1766
USA	☎ (202) 783 6161	Suiza	☎ (1) 360 1414

Morocco

MAROC
MAROKKO
MARRUECOS

Fédération Royale Marocaine des Auberges de Jeunes,
Parc de la Ligue Arabe,
BP No 15998,
Casa-Principale,
Casablanca 21000,
Morocco.

☎ (212) (2) 470952
✆ (212) (2) 227677

Office Hours: 08.30-12.00hrs & 08.30-15.00hrs (Su)
08.30-12.00hrs & 14.00-18.00hrs (Wi)

A copy of the Hostel Directory for this Country can be obtained from:
The National Office.

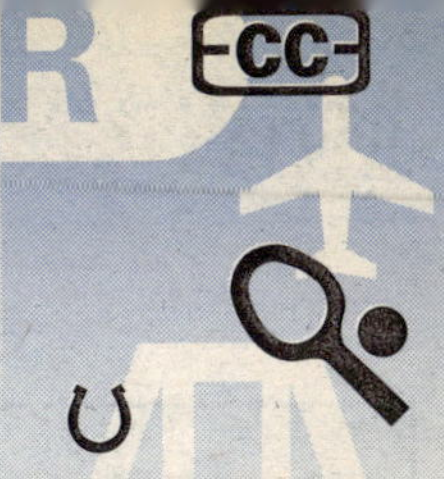

Capital:	Rabat	**Population:**	26,073,717
Language:	Arabic	**Size:**	710,850 sq km
Currency:	Dh (dirham)		

Morocco

SPAIN
Tanger
Tanger
Chefchaouen
Rabat
Rabat
Fes
Casablanca
Meknes
Casablanca
Azrou
MOROCCO
Marrakech
Marrakech
Asni
ALGERIA
Laayoune
MAURITANIA
MALI
100 200 300 400 KMS
0
100 200 MLS
N

English

MOROCCAN HOSTELS

Priority is given to people under 30 years of age. Visitors may stay for more than three nights provided this does not exclude new arrivals. Hostel opening times are 08.00-10.00hrs, 12.00-16.00hrs and 18.30-24.00hrs between 1 July and 30 September and 08.00-10.00hrs, 12.00-15.00hrs and 18.00-22.30/23.00hrs at all other times of the year.

Expect to pay in the region of 25-60 DH, plus linen hire if needed.

TRAVEL

Rail
The Moroccan train service is fast and comfortable.

Bus
The national bus line (CTM) provides a good network service.

Ferry
Morocco has a good ferry service plus hydrofoils. From Algeciras there are four ferries a day to Tangier in summer.

TELEPHONE INFORMATION

Country Code	**212**
Main City Area Codes	
Meknès	5
Tangier	9
Casablanca	2
Rabat	7
Marakesh	4

Français

AUBERGES DE JEUNESSE MAROCAINES

Priorité est donnée aux voyageurs de moins de 30 ans. Des séjours de plus de trois nuits sont possibles pourvu qu'il y ait assez de place pour les nouveaux venus. Les auberges ouvrent de 8h à 10h, de 12h à 16h et de 18h30 à 24h, du 1er juillet au 30 septembre. Le reste de l'année, elles sont ouvertes de 8h à 10h, de 12h à 15h et de 18h à 22h30/23h.

Une nuit vous coûtera entre 25 et 60 DH, plus location de draps le cas échéant.

DEPLACEMENTS

Trains
Les trains marocains sont rapides et confortables.

Autobus
La compagnie nationale d'autobus CTM assure de bons services sur son réseau.

Ferry-boats
Les ferry-boats et les hydrofoils assurent un bon service. En été, quatre ferry-boats par jour partent d'Algésiras à destination de Tanger.

TELEPHONE

Indicatif du Pays	**212**
Indicatifs régionaux des Villes principales	
Meknès	5
Tanger	9
Casablanca	2
Rabat	7
Marakesh	4

Deutsch

MAROKKANISCHE JUGENDHERBERGEN

Junge Leute unter 30 Jahren werden bevorzugt aufgenommen. Besucher können auch länger als drei Nächte bleiben, wenn dadurch keine Neuankömmlinge abgewiesen werden müssen. Die Herbergen sind vom 1. Juli-30. September von 08.00-10.00 Uhr, von 12.00-16.00 Uhr und von 18.30-24.00 Uhr und zu allen anderen Jahreszeiten von 08.00-10.00 Uhr, von

12.00-15.00 Uhr und von 18.00-22.30/23.00 Uhr geöffnet.

Es ist mit einem Preis von ca. 25-60 DH plus, bei Bedarf, einer Leihgebühr für Bettwäsche zu rechnen.

REISEN

Eisenbahn
Die marokkanische Eisenbahn ist schnell und bequem.

Busse
Das staatliche Busunternehmen (CTM) bietet einen guten Linienverkehr.

Fähren
Marokko bietet gute Fährenverbindungen und auch einen guten Tragflügelbootverkehr. Von Algeciras aus fahren im Sommer täglich vier Fähren nach Tanger.

FERNSPRECHINFORMATIONEN

Landes-Kennzahl	212
größere Städte - Ortsnetzkennzahlen	
Meknès	5
Tanger	9
Casablanca	2
Rabat	7
Marakesh	4

Español

ALBERGUES DE JUVENTUD MARROQUIES

Tienen prioridad los menores de 30 años. Los visitantes pueden permanecer más de tres noches siempre y cuando la duración de su estancia no impida nuevas llegadas. Las horas de apertura de los albergues son de 08.00 a 10.00 horas, de 12.00 a 16.00 horas y de 18.30 a 24.00 horas, del 1° de julio al 30 de septiembre. El resto del año abren de 08.00 a 10.00 horas, de 12.00 a 15.00 horas y de 18.00 a 22.30/23.00 horas.

Los precios oscilan entre 25 y 60 dirhams, más alquiler de sábanas si le hacen falta.

DESPLAZAMIENTOS

Tren
El servicio de trenes marroquí es rápido y cómodo.

Autobús
La línea nacional de autocares (CTM) ofrece una amplia red de servicios.

Ferry
Marruecos tiene un buen servicio de ferrys y de hidrodeslizadores. En verano hay cuatro ferrys diarios de Algeciras a Tánger. Siempre y cuando la duración de su astancia.

INFORMACION TELEFONICA

Código Nacional	212
Prefijos de las Ciudades Principales	
Meknés	5
Tánger	9
Casablanca	2
Rabat	7
Marakesh	4

Location/Address	Telephone No. Fax No.	Beds	Opening Dates	Facilities
▲ **Azrou** Route de Midelt, Ifrane, BP 147 (Moyen Atlas).	☎ (05) 563733	40	🗓9	♂
▲ **Casablanca** 6 Place Ahmed Al Bidaoui, Ville Ancienne, Casablanca	☎ (2) 22 0551 🖷 (2) 227677	80	🗓9	♟ ⑲ Ⓡ ♂
▲ **Fes** 18 Rue Abdeslam Seghrini, Ville Nouvelle, Fes.	☎ (05) 624085	40	🗓9	♟ ⑲ ♂
▲ **Laayoune** Laayoune Complexe Sportif, Laayoune, Sakiat Alhamra.	☎ (08) 893402	40	🗓9	♂
▲ **Marrakech** Rue El Jahed, Quartier Industriel (near camp site), Marrakech.	☎ (04) 447713	50	🗓9	♟ ⑲ Ⓡ ♂
▲ **Meknès** Boulvard Okba Ben Nafii, Meknès (near Transatlantique Hotel).	☎ (05) 524698	60	🗓9	♟ ⑲ ♂
▲ **Rabat** 43 Rue Marassa, Bab El Had, Rabat, BP 488 RP Rabat.	☎ (07) 725769	50	🗓9	⑲ ♂
▲ **Tanger** 8 rue El Antaki, Av d'Espagne, Tanger.	☎ (09) 946127	50	🗓9	Ⓡ

SUPPLEMENTARY ACCOMMODATION
OUTSIDE THE ASSURED STANDARDS SCHEME

Location/Address	Telephone No. Fax No.	Beds	Opening Dates	Facilities
Asni Route d'Amlil par Marrakech, Asni (Grand Atlas).	☎ (04) 447713	40	🗓9	♂
Chefchaouen Pres du Camping Municipal, Chefchaouen	☎ (09) 986031	30	🗓9	⑲ ♂

…not just a cheap bed, but a cheaper ticket, meal, insurance package (see your national Association for details…)

…pas simplement un lit bon marché, mais aussi un billet, un repas, un forfait assurance moins chers (contactez votre Association nationale pour plus de renseignements…)

…nicht nur ein preiswertes Bett, sondern auch preisgünstigere Eintrittskarten, Mahlzeiten und Reiseversicherungen (mehr darüber von den nationalen Mitgliedsverbänden…).

…no sólo alojamiento a precios asequibles, sino también billetes, comidas y seguros más económicos (para más información, diríjase a su Asociación nacional…)

Make your credit card bookings at these centres
Réservez par cartes de crédit aux centres suivants
Buchen Sie mit Kreditkarte in folgenden Buchungszentren
Reserve por tarjeta de crédito en los siguientes centros

English

Australia	☎ (2) 9261 1111
Canada	☎ (800) 663 5777
England & Wales	☎ (1629) 581 418
France	☎ (1) 44 89 87 27
Northern Ireland	☎ (1232) 324 733
Republic of Ireland	☎ (1) 830 1766
New Zealand	☎ (9) 303 9524
Scotland	☎ (541) 553 255
Switzerland	☎ (1) 360 1414
USA	☎ (202) 783 6161

Français

Angleterre & Pays de Galles	☎ (1692) 581 418
Australie	☎ (2) 9261 1111
Canada	☎ (800) 663 5777
Écosse	☎ (541) 553 255
États-Unis	☎ (202) 783 6161
France	☎ (1) 44 89 87 27
Irlande du Nord	☎ (1232) 324 733
Nouvelle-Zélande	☎ (9) 303 9524
République d'Irlande	☎ (1) 830 1766
Suisse	☎ (1) 360 1414

Deutsch

Australien	☎ (2) 9261 1111
England & Wales	☎ (1629) 581 418
Frankreich	☎ (1) 44 89 87 27
Irland	☎ (1) 830 1766
Kanada	☎ (800) 663 5777
Neuseeland	☎ (9) 303 9524
Nordirland	☎ (1232) 324 733
Schottland	☎ (541) 553 255
Schweiz	☎ (1) 360 1414
USA	☎ (202) 783 6161

Español

Australia	☎ (2) 9261 1111
Canadá	☎ (800) 663 5777
Escocia	☎ (541) 553 255
Estados Unidos	☎ (202) 783 6161
Francia	☎ (1) 44 89 87 27
Inglaterra y Gales	☎ (1629) 581 418
Irlanda del Norte	☎ (1232) 324 733
Nueva Zelanda	☎ (9) 303 9524
República de Irlanda	☎ (1) 830 1766
Suiza	☎ (1) 360 1414

New Zealand

HOSTELLING
INTERNATIONAL
YHA NEW ZEALAND

Youth Hostels Association of New Zealand, Inc
PO Box 436,
Christchurch,
New Zealand

☏ (64) (3) 3799970
🖷 (64) (3) 3654476
E-mail: info@yha.org.nz
WWW address: http://www.yha.org.nz

Auckland City YHA National Reservation Centre
Cnr City Rd and Liverpool St,
PO Box 68-149,
Auckland,
New Zealand

☏ (64) (9) 3039524
🖷 (64) (9) 3039525
Email: book@yha.org.nz

A copy of the Hostel Directory for this Country can be obtained from:
The National Office.

IBN Booking Centre for outward bookings

- Auckland - USIT YHA Travel Centre,18 Shortland St, Auckland, New Zealand.

Capital:	Wellington	Population:	3,500,000
Language:	English	Size:	268,676 sq km
Currency:	NZ$		

New Zealand

Pukenui
Kaitaia
Kerikeri
Opononi
Paihia
Whangarei
Dargaville
Waiheke Island
Coromandel
Auckland (2)
Opoutere
Thames
Te Aroha
NORTH ISLAND
Hamilton
Tauranga
Rotorua
Waitomo Caves
Lake Taupo
Taupo
Gisborne
New Plymouth
Turangi
Ohakune
Napier
Wanganui
NEW ZEALAND
Palmerston North
Kenepuru
Masterton
Havelock
Kaitoke
Nelson
Picton
Wellington
Westport
St Arnaud
Hanmer Springs
Kaikoura
Greymouth
SOUTH ISLAND
Arthur's Pass
Okarito
Springfield
Franz Josef
Christchurch (2)
Haast
Mt Cook
Tekapo
Timaru
Milford
Wanaka
Queenstown
Oamaru
Alexandra
Te Anau
Dunedin
Invercargill

English

NEW ZEALAND HOSTELS

New Zealand has 57 hostels, all participating in Hostelling International's new Assured Standards Scheme (see page 4 for details) and ideally positioned for exploration of North and South Islands. Don't miss Mount Cook hostel, with its dramatic views of New Zealand's highest mountains, or Auckland City, offering twin room accommodation throughout! Not only are New Zealand's hostels particularly well equipped (try the hot pool at Rotorua!), they are in central city locations, and in unique settings in National Parks or near activities and idyllic scenery.

Hostels are open 24 hours, although you will find the majority are not staffed between 10.00 and 17.00hrs. Expect to pay between NZ$ 14.00 and NZ$ 19.00 including bedding and linen, reduced prices for under 18s. You can also use your own sleeping bag, if you prefer. Hostels provide excellent self-catering facilities, including pots, plates and cutlery etc.

PASSPORTS AND VISAS

Passports are required for all visitors and must be valid for at least 3 months beyond the date the visitor intends leaving the country.

Check with the New Zealand Consulate or Embassy in your own country for details of visa requirements.

HEALTH

Insurance is recommended. Health services are not free. Water is safe to drink except from lakes and streams unless boiled or treated.

BANKING HOURS

Normal banking hours in New Zealand are 09.30-16.30hrs, Monday to Friday, except public holidays.

POST OFFICES

Monday to Friday, 08.30-17.00hrs.

SHOPPING HOURS

Monday to Friday 09.00-17.30hrs, Saturday 09.00-16.00 and Sunday 10.00-13.00hrs.

TRAVEL

Air
All cities and major towns are serviced by domestic flights.

Rail
Trains operate throughout the country.

Bus
Coaches operate throughout the country.

Ferry
A ferry service connects North and South Islands. Ferries also operate to Waiheke Island and Great Barrier Reef and from Invercargill to Stewart Island.

TELEPHONE INFORMATION

Country Code	**64**
Main City Area Codes	
Auckland	**9**
Christchurch	**3**
Dunedin	**3**
Rotorua	**7**
Wellington	**4**

Français

AUBERGES DE JEUNESSE NEO-ZELANDAISES

Il y a 57 auberges en Nouvelle-Zélande, toutes font partie du nouveau Projet de Hostelling International des Normes Garanties (voir page 12 pour les détails) et sont idéalement situées pour explorer l'île du Nord et l'île du Sud. Ne manquez pas l'auberge de Mount Cook, d'où vous pourrez admirer le panorama spectaculaire des montagnes les plus hautes de Nouvelle-Zélande, ou celle d'Auckland City, qui est entièrement équipée de chambres à deux lits! Les auberges néo-zélandaises ne sont pas seulement particulièrement bien aménagées (essayez la piscine chauffée à Rotorua!), elles sont également bien situées, au cœur des villes ou dans les cadres uniques des Parcs Nationaux prés des centres d'activités ou au beau milieu de paysages idylliques.

Les auberges sont ouvertes 24 heures sur 24, mais vous trouverez que le personnel n'est pas sur place dans la plupart d'entre elles entre 10h et 17h. Une nuit vous coûtera entre 14 et 19 $NZ, location de draps comprise; réductions pour les moins de 18 ans. Vous pouvez également utiliser votre sac de couchage si vous préférez. Les auberges ont à votre disposition d'excellentes installations pour faire votre cuisine et fournissent également la vaisselle, les couverts etc.

PASSEPORTS ET VISAS

Tous les visiteurs doivent être munis d'un passeport, qui doit être valide au moins trois mois au-delà de la date à laquelle le visiteur compte quitter le pays.

Adressez-vous au consulat ou à l'embassade néo-zélandaise de votre pays pour savoir si vous devez vous munir d'un visa.

SOINS MEDICAUX

Il est recommandé de s'assurer. Les services de santé ne sont pas gratuits. L'eau peut être bue sans danger sauf si elle provient d'un lac ou d'un ruisseau, auquel cas elle devra être bouillie ou traitée.

HEURES D'OUVERTURE DES BANQUES

Les banques sont normalement ouvertes de 9h30 à 16h30, du lundi au vendredi, sauf pendant les jours fériés.

BUREAUX DE POSTE

Les bureaux de poste sont ouverts du lundi au vendredi, de 8h30 à 17h.

HEURES D'OUVERTURE DES MAGASINS

Les magasins sont ouverts du lundi au vendredi, de 9h à 17h30, le samedi de 9h à 16h et le dimanche de 10h à 13h.

DEPLACEMENTS

Avions

Toutes les grandes villes et villes principales sont desservies par des vols intérieurs.

Trains

Les trains desservent tout le pays.

Autobus

Des cars desservent tout le pays.

Ferry-boats

Une ligne maritime relie l'île du Nord à celle du Sud. Des bateaux assurent également un service à destination de l'île Waiheke et du Grand Récif Corallien et depuis Invercargill jusqu'à l'île Stewart.

TELEPHONE

Indicatif du Pays	**64**
Indicatifs régionaux des Villes principales	
Auckland	**9**
Christchurch	**3**
Dunedin	**3**
Rotorua	**7**
Wellington	**4**

Deutsch

NEUSEELÄNDISCHE JUGENDHERBERGEN

Neuseeland hat 57 Herbergen, die zum Kennenlernen der Nordinsel und der Südinsel ideal gelegen sind. Sie sind dem 'Assured Standards' Schema der Hostelling International angeschlossen (siehe Seite 20). Lassen Sie sich die Jugendherberge von Mount Cook nicht entgehen, denn von dort bietet sich ein phantastischer Blick auf die höchsten Berge Neuseelands. Es lohnt sich auch, die Jugendherberge in Auckland City, die nur Doppelzimmer bietet, zu besuchen. Die neuseeländischen Herbergen sind nicht nur besonders gut eingerichtet (probieren Sie einmal den Hotpool in Rotorua aus!), sondern oft auch in Stadtzentren, und in einzigartiger Umgebung in Nationalparks oder nahe Aktiverholungsgebieten und idyllischer Landschaft.

Die Herbergen sind 24 Stunden geöffnet, aber in den meisten ist zwischen 10.00 und 17.00 Uhr kein Personal vorhanden. Es ist mit einem Preis von NZ\$ 14,00 und 19,00, einschließlich Bettwäsche, zu rechnen. Jugendliche unter 18 Jahren bezahlen ermäßigte Preise. Wer will, kann auch seinen eigenen Daunen-Schlafsack verwenden. In den Herbergen sind hervorragende Einrichtungen für Selbstversorger die Norm (einschließlich Geschirr, Töpfe usw).

PÄSSE UND VISA

Alle Reisenden benötigen einen Reisepaß, der mindestens 3 Monate über den Tag, an dem die betreffende Person das Land wieder verlassen will, hinaus gültig sein muß.

Es wird empfohlen sich mit dem Neuseeländischen Konsulat oder der Botschaft Ihres Landes in Verbindung zu setzen um nähere Einzelheiten zu erfahren.

GESUNDHEIT

Es ist ratsam, eine Versicherung abzuschließen. Es gibt keinen kostenlosen Gesundheitsdienst. Das Wasser kann unbesorgt getrunken werden. Wenn es aber aus Seen oder Bächen stammt, sollte man es abkochen oder vorbehandeln.

GESCHÄFTSSTUNDEN DER BANKEN

Bankschalter sind in Neuseeland gewöhnlich montags bis freitags, außer an Feiertagen, von 09.30-16.30 Uhr geöffnet.

POSTÄMTER

Montags bis freitags von 08.30-17.00 Uhr.

LADENÖFFNUNGSZEITEN

Montags bis freitags von 09.00-17.30 Uhr, samstags von 09.00-16.00 Uhr, sonntags von 10.00-13.00 Uhr.

REISEN

Flugverkehr

In alle Großstädte und viele andere größere Städte gibt es einen inländischen Flugverkehr.

Eisenbahn

Der Zugverkehr erstreckt sich über das ganze Land.

Busse

Im ganzen Land verkehren Reisebusse.

Fähren

Die Nordinsel und die Südinsel sind durch einen Fährenverkehr miteinander verbunden. Fähren verkehren auch nach Waiheke Island und zum Großen Barriereriff und von Invercargill nach Stewart Island.

FERNSPRECHINFORMATIONEN

Landes-Kennzahl	**64**
größere Städte - Ortsnetzkennzahlen	
Auckland	**9**
Christchurch	**3**
Dunedin	**3**
Rotorua	**7**
Wellington	**4**

Español

ALBERGUES DE JUVENTUD NEOZELANDESES

Nueva Zelanda cuenta con más de 57 albergues que participan en el nuevo Plan de Hostelling International de Normas Garantizadas (ver página 28 para más información) y están idealmente situados para explorar tanto la Isla del Norte como la del Sur. No se pierda el albergue de Mount Cook, con su espectacular vista de las montañas más altas de Nueva Zelanda, ni el de Auckland City, que ofrece alojamiento solamente en habitaciones dobles. Los albergues de Nueva Zelanda no sólo están especialmente bien equipados (¡pruebe la piscina de agua caliente en Rotorua!), sino que se encuentran tanto en el centro de las ciudades como en el marco único de los Parques Nacionales o cerca de centros de actividades y de paisajes magníficos.

Los albergues abren las 24 horas del día, si bien la mayoría no tienen personal que atienda al público entre las 10.00 y las 17.00 horas. Los precios oscilan entre NZ$ 14,00 y 19,00 incluyendo el alquiler de sábanas, con precios reducidos para menores de 18 años. Si lo prefiere, también puede utilizar su propio saco de dormir. Los albergues tienen excelentes cocinas para huéspedes con cacharros, platos y cubiertos, etc.

PASAPORTES Y VISADOS

Todos los visitantes deben llevar un pasaporte que sea válido por lo menos 3 meses después de la fecha en que el visitante tenga previsto dejar el país.

Pregunte en el Consulado o Embajada neocelandeses en su propio país si necesita visado.

SANIDAD

Se recomienda hacerse un seguro. Los servicios sanitarios no son gratuitos. El agua es potable excepto en los lagos y ríos, en cuyo caso se debe hervir o tratar debidamente.

HORARIO DE BANCOS

En Nueva Zelanda los bancos abren normalmente de 09.30 a 16.30 horas de lunes a viernes excepto días festivos.

OFICINAS DE CORREOS

De lunes a viernes de 08.30 a 17.00 horas.

HORARIO COMERCIAL

De lunes a viernes de 09.00 a 17.30 horas, sábado de 09.00 a 16.00 horas y domingo de 10.00 a 13.00 horas.

DESPLAZAMIENTOS

Avión

Todas las ciudades y principales poblaciones están conectadas por vuelos nacionales.

Tren

Los trenes operan en todo el país.

Autobús

Los autocares operan en todo el país.

Ferry

Un servicio de ferry conecta la Isla del Norte con la del Sur. Los ferrys también van a la isla de Waiheke y al Arrecife de la Gran Barrera, y van desde Invercargill a la Isla Stewart.

INFORMACION TELEFONICA

Código Nacional	**64**
Prefijos de las Ciudades Principales	
Auckland	9
Christchurch	3
Dunedin	3
Rotorua	7
Wellington	4

Discounts And Concessions

Air New Zealand: 50% off domestic standby to international travellers (special conditions apply).
Ansett Flights: 50% off domestic standby to international travellers (special conditions apply).
Coach Services: 20%-30% off all coach travel.
Tranz Rail: 30% discount on train travel
Airport Shuttle: Special rates to hostels from Christchurch, Auckland and Wellington (via Rail/Ferry)
Backpacker buses: 5% off

For full details of national and local concessions, pick up a copy of the guide or check the notice board at hostels.

Assured Standards – visited by our Liaison team and by you the guest – tell us when we don't measure up (reply slips at the end of this Guide)▶

des Normes Garanties, par les visites de notre Equipe de Liaison et par vous, les usagers – faites-le nous savoir quand nous ne sommes pas à la hauteur (Fiches-commentaires à la fin du Guide)◀

Zugesicherte Standards – beurteilt von unserem Liaison Team und von Ihnen, unserem Gast – sagen Sie es uns, wenn wir Sie enttäuschen (Antwortkarten hinten im Führer)▶

Normas Garantizadas – comprobadas por nuestro Equipo de Enlace y por Ud., el usuario – si fallamos en algo, díganoslo (al final de esta Guía encontrará nuestras hojas de comentarios)◀

NEW ZEALAND • NOUVELLE ZELANDE

Auckland

**Corner City Rd & Liverpool St,
Auckland.**
☎ (9) 3092802
🖷 (9) 3735083

Open Dates:	
Open Hours:	
Reservations:	R · IBN · CC
Price Range:	$19-22
Beds:	156 - 3x^1 45x^2 2x^3 4x^4 2x^5 1x^6
Facilities:	♿ ♦♦♦ 2x♦♦♦ ⦿ (BD) ☕ ▦ ⚏ TV ▣ ▦ ▦ ⬍ ⓘ ⚇ ⌂ ♦♦

Directions:

✈	Auckland International 25km
⛴	Princes Wharf 1km
🚌	Linkbus

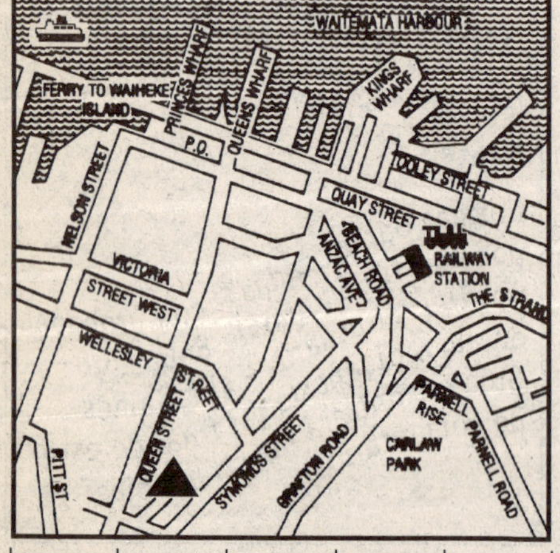

Christchurch – City Central

**273 Manchester St,
Christchurch.**
☎ (3) 3799535
🖷 (3) 3799537

Open Dates:	
Open Hours:	
Reservations:	R · IBN · CC
Price Range:	$18-20
Beds:	129 - 19x^2 2x^3 15x^4 4x^5
Facilities:	♿ ♦♦♦ 15x♦♦♦ ⦿ ⚏ TV ▣ ▦ 🅱 ⊜ P ⓘ ⚇ ♦♦

Directions: 0.5 NE from city centre

✈	Christchurch International 8km
A🚌	Shuttle
🚕	Addington 3km
🚌	Airport Bus 500m

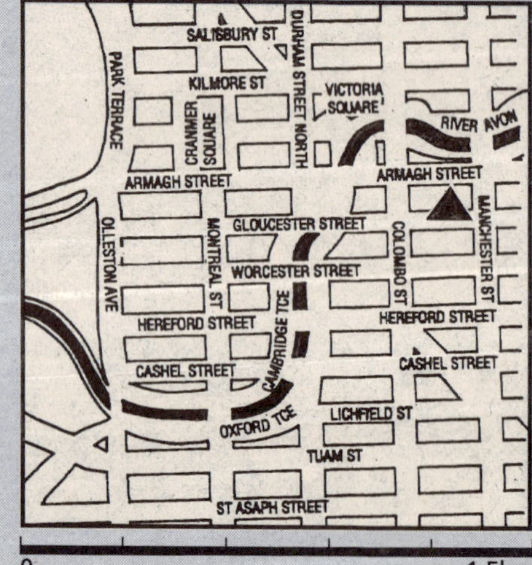

Franz Josef

2-4 Cron St,
PO Box 12,
Franz Josef Village.
📞 (3) 7520754
📠 (3) 7520080

Open Dates:	
Open Hours:	
Reservations:	R CC
Price Range:	$16.00-18.00
Beds:	60 - 4x² 1x³ 7x⁴ 1x⁵ 1x⁶ 1x⁶
Facilities:	

Directions:

InterCity 300m ap YH

Attractions: 6km 12km

Mount Cook

Mount Cook National Park.
📞 (3) 4351820
📠 (3) 4351821

Open Dates:	
Open Hours:	
Reservations:	R CC
Price Range:	$20-23
Beds:	70 - 2x¹ 5x² 1x⁴ 1x⁶ 6x⁶
Facilities:	

Directions:

✈ Mt Cook 5.5km
A🚌 Mt Cook Line Shuttle
🚌 Mt Cook Line & Intercity

Attractions: 25km 200m 10km

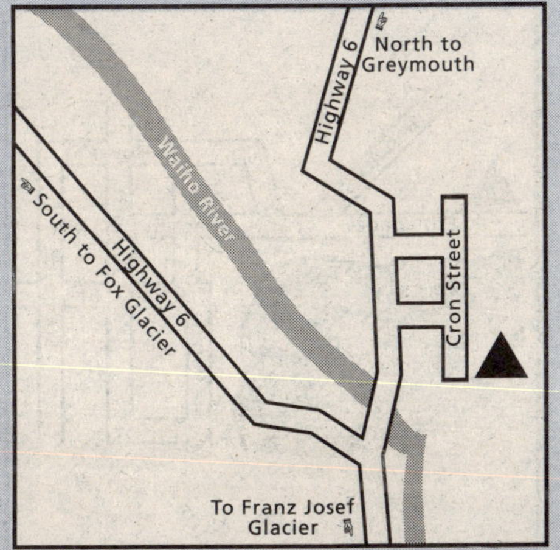

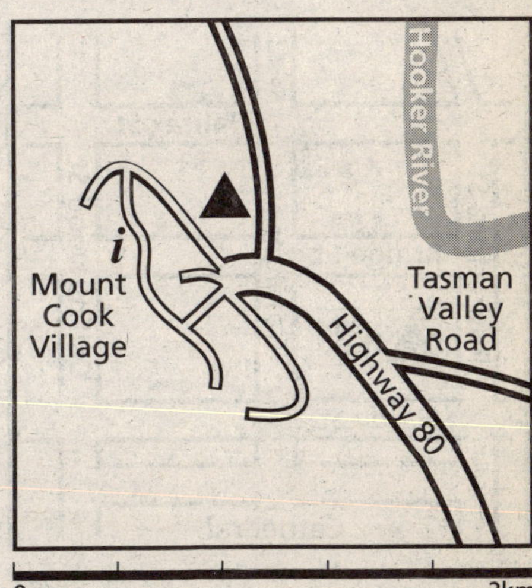

Nelson - Central YHA

**59 Rutherford St,
Nelson.**
☎ (3) 5459988
🖷 (3) 5459989

Open Dates:	🗓9
Open Hours:	🕐
Reservations:	Ⓡ ⌐CC⌐
Price Range:	$18, $20, $28 🗐
Beds:	90 - 1x^1 19x^2 3x^3 5x^4 3x^5 1x^{6+}
Facilities:	♿ ♦♦♦ 6x♦♦♦ 🛁 🛏 📺 🍳 ▣ 💼 ⌂ ▣8 ▣ i 🔌 🏠

Directions:

✈	Nelson 7km
A🚌	Supershuttle (to door)
🚌	Central Terminal 100m

Attractions: 🌲 ⛰ 🔍 🎿 1800m 🏃 ↻17km 🏊 2km

Queenstown

**88 & 90 Lake Esplanade,
Queenstown.**
☎ (3) 4428413
🖷 (3) 4426561

Open Dates:	🗓9
Open Hours:	🕐
Reservations:	Ⓡ ⟨IBN⟩ ⌐CC⌐
Price Range:	$18-21 🗐
Beds:	144 - 17x^2 4x^3 4x^4 1x^5 3x^6 7x^{6+}
Facilities:	♦♦♦ 4x♦♦♦ 🛁 🛏 📺 🍳 ▣ 💼 ⌂ 8 🅿 i 🔌 🏠

Directions:

✈	Queenstown 10km
A🚌	Airport Shuttle 10km
🚌	ap Intercity

Attractions: 🌲 ⛰ 🔍 🎿 1620m 🚣 🏃 ↻6km

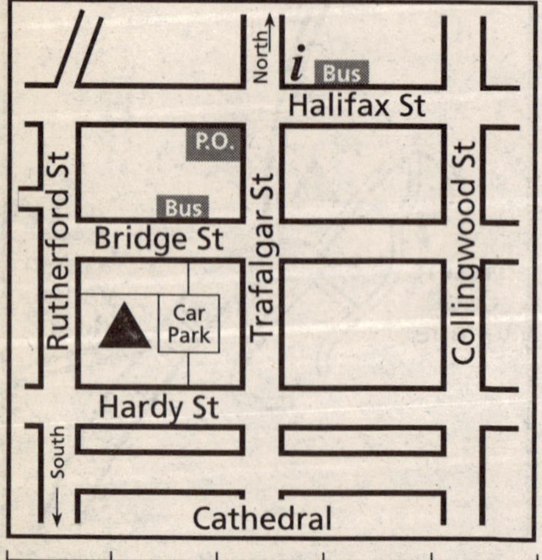

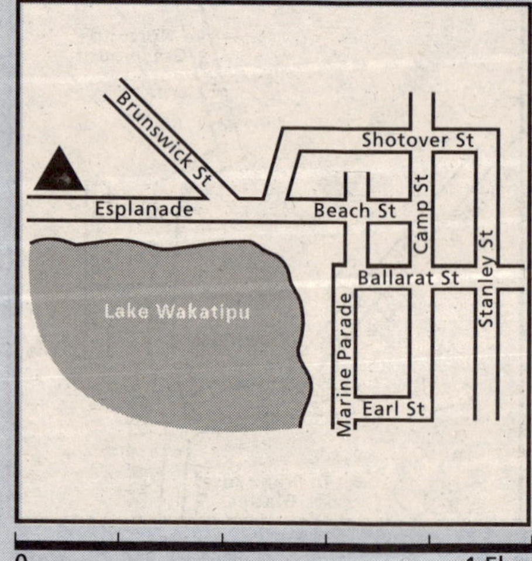

Rotorua - Colonial Inn

1271 Hinemaru St,
Rotorua
(7) 3476810
(7) 3491426

Open Dates:	9
Open Hours:	
Reservations:	R IBN CC
Price Range:	$17-20
Beds:	73 - 5x2 2x3 9x4 1x5 1x6 1x6+
Facilities:	19x TV 8 P i
Directions:	
✈	Rotorua 6km
Train	Rotorua 6km
Bus	1km
Attractions:	3km 3km

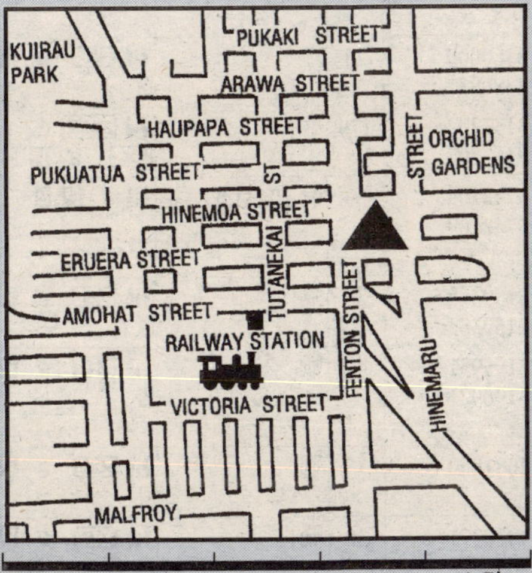

Wellington

Corner Wakefield St and Cambridge Terrace,
Wellington.
(4) 8017280
(4) 8017278

Open Dates:	9
Open Hours:	
Reservations:	R IBN CC
Price Range:	$17-19
Beds:	114 - 3x1 15x4 4x6
Facilities:	6x TV 8 P i
Directions:	1 W from city centre
✈	Wellington 15km
A Bus	Shuttle (to door)
Ferry	Inter-Islander Ferry Terminal 5km
Train	Wellington 3km
Bus	InterCity; Newmans 3km
Attractions:	3km 1km

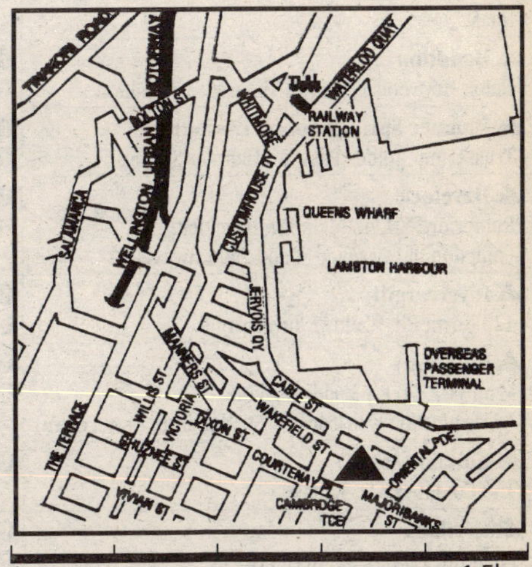

NEW ZEALAND • NOUVELLE ZELANDE

Location/Address	Telephone No. / Fax No.	Beds	Opening Dates	Facilities
▲ **Alexandra (Assoc)** Two Bob Backpackers, 4 Dunorling St, Alexandra.	(3) 4488152	35		
▲ **Arthurs Pass** Sir Arthur Dudley Dobson Memorial Hostel, Arthurs Pass : (opposite store).	(3) 3189230	24		CC
▲ **Auckland** [IBN] **Corner City Rd & Liverpool St, Auckland.**	(9) 3092802 (9) 3735083	156		R / CC
▲ **Auckland** [IBN] 2 Churton St, Parnell, Auckland.	(9) 3793731 (9) 3584143	65		1E / CC
▲ **Christchurch** - Rolleston House [IBN] Corner Worcester Blvd and Rolleston Ave, Christchurch.	(3) 3666564 (3) 3655589	54		0.5 S / CC / P
▲ **Christchurch** - City Central [IBN] **273 Manchester St, Christchurch.**	(3) 3799535 (3) 3799537	129		R / 0.5 NE / CC / P
▲ **Coromandel (Assoc)** Tidewater Tourist Park Hostel, 270 Tiki Rd, Coromandel.	(7) 8668888 (7) 8667231	20		CC / P
▲ **Dargaville (Assoc)** The Greenhouse Hostel, 13 Portland St, Dargaville.	(9) 4396342	22		CC / P
▲ **Dunedin** Stafford Gables YH, 71 Stafford St, Dunedin.	(3) 4741919 (3) 4741919	61		1 SW / CC / P
▲ **Franz Josef** **2-4 Cron St, PO Box 12, Franz Josef Village.**	(3) 7520754 (3) 7520080	60		R / CC / P
▲ **Gisborne** 32 Harris St, Gisborne. (Corner of Wainui Rd)	(6) 8673269 (6) 8673296	38		CC / P
▲ **Greymouth** Kainga-ra Hostel, 15 Alexander St, Greymouth.	(3) 7684951 (3) 7684951	41		CC / P
▲ **Haast (Assoc)** Highway Accommodation, Marks Rd, PO Box 11, Haast.	(3) 7500703 (3) 7500718	43		CC / P
▲ **Hamilton** Helen Heywood YH, 1190 Victoria St, Hamilton.	(7) 8380009 (7) 8380837	24		CC / P
▲ **Hanmer Springs Forest (Assoc)** Trust Camp, Jollies Pass Rd, Hanmer Springs.	(3) 3157202 (3) 3157202	170		2.5 NW / CC / P
▲ **Havelock** Rutherford YH, 46 Main Rd, Havelock. (Junction of Lawrence St and State Hwy No 6)	(3) 5742104 (3) 5742109	34	01.10–31.05	P
▲ **Invercargill** 122 North Rd, Waikiwi, Invercargill.	(3) 2159344 (3) 2159382	33		CC / P
▲ **Kaikoura** Maui YH, 270 Esplanade, Kaikoura. (Near junction with Torquay St, 2km from town centre)	(3) 3195931 (3) 3196921	41		CC / P
▲ **Kaitaia (Assoc)** 160 Commerce St, Kaitaia.	(9) 4081840	35		CC / P
▲ **Kerikeri** Main Rd, PO Box 62, Kerikeri.	(9) 4079391 (9) 4079328	30		CC / P

Location/Address	Telephone No. Fax No.	Beds	Opening Dates	Facilities
△ *Kenepuru* *Mary's Holiday Cottage, RD2, Waitaria Bay, Kenepuru Sound, Marlborough Sounds.*	☎ *(3) 5734660*	9	📅	🍳 P 🔲
▲ **Masterton (Assoc)** Backpackers, 22 Victoria St, Masterton.	☎ (6) 3772228	18	📅	P 🔲
▲ **Milford (Assoc)** "Milford Wanderer" Boat. Milford Harbour, PO Box 1, Te Anau Milford Sound.	☎ (3) 2497416 Freephone (0800) 656501 📠 (3) 2497022	61	📅	⇄ ⑲ CC P 🔲
▲ **Mount Cook** **Mount Cook National Park.**	☎ (3) 4351820 📠 (3) 4351821	70	📅	⇄ R CC 🍳 P 🔲
▲ **Napier** 277 Marine Pde, Napier.	☎ (6) 8357039 📠 (6) 8357039	40	📅	⇄ CC 🍳 🔲
▲ **Nelson** - Central YHA **59 Rutherford St, Nelson.**	☎ (3) 5459988 📠 (3) 5459989	90	📅	⇄ R ♿ CC 🍳 🔲
▲ **New Plymouth** Egmont Lodge - 12 Clawton St, New Plymouth.	☎ (6) 7535720 📠 (6) 7535782	32	📅	⇄ R 🍳 P 🔲
▲ **Oamaru** Red Kettle Seasonal Hostel, 2 Reed St, Oamaru.	☎ (3) 4345008	20	01.10–31.05	⇄ CC 🍳 🔲
▲ **Ohakune** 15 Clyde St, Ohakune.	☎ (6) 3858724 📠 (6) 3858724	30	📅	⇄ CC 🍳 P 🔲
▲ **Okarito (Assoc)** PO Box 24, Whataroa, South Westland.	☎ (3) 7534124	10	📅	🍳 P
▲ **Opononi** Okopako Lodge, PO Box 99, Opononi	☎ (9) 4058815	20	📅	⇄ CC 🍳 P
▲ **Opoutere** Main Road, Opoutere	☎ (7) 8659072 📠 (7) 8656172	36	📅	⇄ CC 🍳 P 🔲
▲ **Paihia Lodge Eleven (Assoc)** Cnr Kings Rd and MacMurray Rd, Paiha Bay of Islands.	☎ (9) 4027487 📠 (9) 4027487	50	📅	⇄ CC P 🔲
▲ **Palmerston North (Assoc)** Peppertree Hostel, 121 Grey St, Palmerston North.	☎ (6) 3554054 📠 (6) 3554063	35	📅	🍳 P 🔲
▲ **Picton (Assoc)** Wedgwood House, 10 Dublin St, Picton.	☎ (3) 5737797 📠 (3) 5736426	20	📅	⇄ R CC 🍳 P 🔲
▲ **Pukenui (Assoc)** Cnr State Highway 1 & Wharf Road, Houhora, Rd4, Kaitaia	☎ (09) 4098837 📠 (09) 4098704	16	📅	⇄ CC 🍳 P 🔲
▲ **Queenstown** IBN **88 & 90 Lake Esplanade, Queenstown.**	☎ (3) 4428413 📠 (3) 4426561	144	📅	⇄ R CC 🍳 P 🔲
▲ **Rotorua** - Colonial Inn IBN **1271 Hinemaru St, Rotorua**	☎ (7) 3476810 📠 (7) 3491426	73	📅	⇄ R ♿ CC 🍳 P 🔲
▲ **Springfield (Assoc)** Smylie's Hostel and Ski Lodge Hostel, Main Rd, Springfield.	☎ (3) 3184740 📠 (3) 3184740	18	📅	⇄ CC P 🔲
▲ **St Arnaud (Assoc)** The Yellow House, Private Bag, St Arnaud, Nelson Lakes National Park.	☎ (3) 5211887 📠 (3) 5211882	36	📅	⇄ CC 🍳 P 🔲

Location/Address	Telephone No. Fax No.	Beds	Opening Dates	Facilities
▲ **Taupo (Assoc)** Action Down Under Hostel, 56 Kaimanawa St, Taupo.	(7) 3783311	47		
▲ **Tauranga** Waireinga YH, 171 Elizabeth St, Tauranga.	(7) 5785064 (7) 5785064	29		CC
▲ **Te Anau** 220-224 Milford Rd, Te Anau. (1km N from PO on Hwy No 97)	(3) 2497847 (3) 2497823	44		CC
▲ **Te Aroha** Miro St, PO Box 72, Te Aroha.	(7) 8848739	13		
▲ **Tekapo** Tekapo YH, Simpson Lane, Lake Tekapo.	(3) 6806857 (3) 6806664	24		CC
▲ **Thames (Assoc)** Dickson Holiday Park, Victoria St, Box 242, Thames.	(7) 8687308 (7) 8687319	28		CC
▲ **Timaru (Assoc)** Timaru Backpackers, 44 Evans St, Timaru.	(3) 6845067 (3) 6845706	35		1S CC
▲ **Turangi (Assoc)** Turangi Club Habitat, 25 Ohuanga Rd, Turangi.	(7) 3867492 (7) 3860106	212		CC
▲ **Waiheke Island** Onetangi YH, Seaview Rd, Onetangi, Waiheke Island.	(9) 3728971 (9) 3728971	40		CC
▲ **Waitomo Caves (Assoc)** Waitomo Caves Hostel, Private Bag 501, Waitomo Caves Village, Otorohanga.	(7) 8788204 (7) 8788205	43		CC
▲ **Wanaka** 181 Upton St, Wanaka.	(3) 4437405 (3) 4437405	37		CC
▲ **Wanganui (Assoc)** The Riverside Inn, 2 Plymouth St, Wanganui.	(6) 3472529 (6) 3472529	22		CC
▲ **Wellington** IBN **Corner Wakefield St and Cambridge Terrace, Wellington.**	(4) 8017280 (4) 8017278	114		R 1W CC
△ *Wellington* *Marchant Rd, Cnr SH2, Upper Hutt, Kaitoke.* *(46km N Wellington, 100m from bridge)*	(4) 5264626	20		CC
▲ **Westport (Assoc)** Marg's YHA, 56 Russell St, Wesport.	(3) 7898627 (3) 7898396	56		CC
▲ **Whangarei** 52 Punga Grove Ave, Whangarei.	(9) 4388954 (9) 4388954	20		CC

English

FIJIAN HOSTELS

Youth Hostel Association members can benefit from discounted accommodation when they visit Fiji. New Zealand YHA, on behalf of the International Youth Hostel Federation has negotiated 'approved accommodation' agreements with privately owned facilities in Fiji. Only the facilities listed here have YHA's approval. Facilities are regularly inspected.

OVERNIGHT TARIFFS ARE AT THE DISCRETION OF THE INDIVIDUAL OPERATOR. CURRENTLY BUNKROOM TARIFFS RANGE FROM FIJI$ 8-$15 PER NIGHT. YHA MEMBERS WILL BE SUPPLIED WITH RECOMMENDED ACCOMMODATION (See YHANZ Accommodation Guide).

The Fiji Visitor's Bureau at Nadi International Airport offers YHA members assistance and information.

Français

AUBERGES FIDJIENNES

Les adhérents peuvent bénéficier de réductions pendant leur visite aux îles Fidi. L'Association néo-zélandaise a négocié, au nom de l'IYHF, des accords d'hébergement accrédité' avec des organisations privées aux îles Fidi. Seuls les établissements cités ici ont l'approbation de l'Association. Ils sont régulièrement inspectés.

LES PRIX DE L'HEBERGEMENT RESTENT A LA DISCRETION DES RESPONSABLES INDIVIDUELS. LES PRIX S'ECHELONNENT ACTUELLEMENT ENTRE 8 ET 15 DOLLARS FIDIENS PAR NUIT. SERONT FOURNIES

AUX MEMBRES DE YHANZ DES INFORMATIONS SUR LES LOGEMENTS RECOMMANDES (voir le Guide de Logement de YHANZ).

Le bureau des visiteurs à l'aéroport international de Nadi offre aux adhérents toute assistance et information.

Deutsch

FIJIAN HOSTELS

Mitglieder des Jugendherbergsverbands haben die Möglichkeit verbilligter Unterkunft bei einem Besuch der Fidschi-Inseln. Die YHA Neuseelands hat namens des Internationalen Jugendherbergsverbands Vereinbarungen betreffend 'empfohlener Unterkunft' mit im Privatbesitz befindlichen Einrichtungen in Fidschi getroffen. Nur die unten verzeichneten Einrichtungen haben Genehmigung des YHA. Sie werden regelmäßig kontrolliert.

ÜBERNACHTUNGSGEBÜHREN SIND DEM EINZELNEN BETREIBER ANHEIMGESTELLT. DERZEIT IST DER TARIF FÜR EINEN SCHLAFSTELLENPLATZ FIDSCHI $8-15 PRO NACHT. YHA-MITGLIEDER WERDEN IN EMPFOHLENER UNTERKUNFT BEHERBERGT SEIN (siehe YHANZ UNTERKUNFTS-BROCHURE).

Das Fiji Visitor's Bureau am Nadi Internationalen Flughafen erteilt YHA Mitgliedern Hilfe und Auskunft.

Español

ALBERGUES JUVERNILES DE LAS ISLAS FIJI

Los socios pueden obtener descuentos durante su visita a las islas Fiji. La YHANZ (la Asociación neocelandesa) ha negociado, en nombre de la Federación Internacional de Albergues Juveniles, acuerdos de 'alojamiento aprobado' con los propietarios de alojamientos privados de Fiji. La Asociación solamente ha aprobado los alojamientos que aparecen a continuación y que se inspeccionan regularmente.

EL PRECIO POR NOCHE ES A DISCRECION DE CADA DUEÑO. LOS PRECIOS ACTUALES, EN HABITACIONES CON LITERAS, OSCILAN ENTRE 8 Y 15 DOLARES DE FIJI POR NOCHE. SE INFORMARA A LOS MIEMBROS DE YHANZ SOBRE LOS ALOJAMIENTOS RECOMENDADOS (véase la Guía de Alojamiento de YHANZ).

La Oficina de Turismo de Fiji, en el aeropuerto internacional de Nadi, ofrece ayuda e información a los miembros de la Asociación.

Location/Address	Telephone No. Fax No.	Beds	Opening Dates	Facilities

SUPPLEMENTARY ACCOMMODATION OUTSIDE THE ASSURED STANDARDS SCHEME

Location/Address	Telephone No. Fax No.	Beds	Opening Dates	Facilities
Cathay Hotel Lautoka Lautoka Fiji	(679) 660566 (679) 660136			♦♦♦ ⑩ ECC P
Club Fiji Resort Nadi Bay, Fiji	(679) 700622 (679) 720350	40		♦♦♦ ⑩ ECC P
Saweni Beach Apartment Hotel Lautoka Fiji	(679) 661777 (679) 660136	40		♦♦♦ ECC P
South Seas Private Hotel 6 Williamson Rd, Government Buildings, Suva	(679) 312296 (679) 340236	80		♦♦♦ ECC P ⓘ
Travel Inn Suva 19 Gorrie St, Government Buildings, Suva, Fiji	(679) 304254 (679) 340236	40		♦♦♦ ECC
Tubakula Beach Bungalows and Beach Club Queens Hwy, Coral Coast, Sigatoka	(679) 500097 (679) 340236	40		♦♦♦ Ⓡ ECC P ⓘ

HOSTELLING INTERNATIONAL

not just a cheap bed, but a cheaper ticket, meal, insurance package (see your national Association for details...)

pas simplement un lit bon marché, mais aussi un billet, un repas, un forfait assurance moins chers (contactez votre Association nationale pour plus de renseignements...)

nicht nur ein preiswertes Bett, sondern auch preisgünstigere Eintrittskarten, Mahlzeiten und Reiseversicherungen (mehr darüber von den nationalen Mitgliedsverbänden...).

no sólo alojamiento a precios asequibles, sino también billetes, comidas y seguros más económicos (para más información, diríjase a su Asociación nacional...)

Pakistan

PAKISTAN

PAKISTAN

PAKISTAN

**Pakistan Youth Hostels Association,
Shaheed-e-Millat Road, (Near Akhbar Market), Aabparà,
Sector G-6/4, Islamabad, Pakistan.**

☎ (92) (51) 826899
TX54475 SENAT Pak
🖷 (92) (51) 9206417

A copy of the Hostel Directory for this Country can be obtained from:
Pakistan Youth Hostels Association,
Youth Hostel, Lahore-110-B-3,
Firdous Market,
Gulberg-III, Lahore.

Capital:	Islamabad	Population:	131,600,000
Language:	Urdu/English	Size:	803,943 sq km
Currency:	Rs (rupee)		

Pakistan

RUSSIA
CHINA
AFGHANISTAN
Sharan
Batakundi
Naran
Abbottabad
Bhurban
(Murree)
Peshawar
Taxila
Khanaspur (Ayubia)
Islamabad
Islamabad
Kitas
Lahore
Lahore
Quetta
Multan
Indus
Delhi
IRAN
PAKISTAN
INDIA
Hyderabad
Karachi
Ahmadabad
Bombay
N
0
100
200
200
300
400
600 KM
MLS

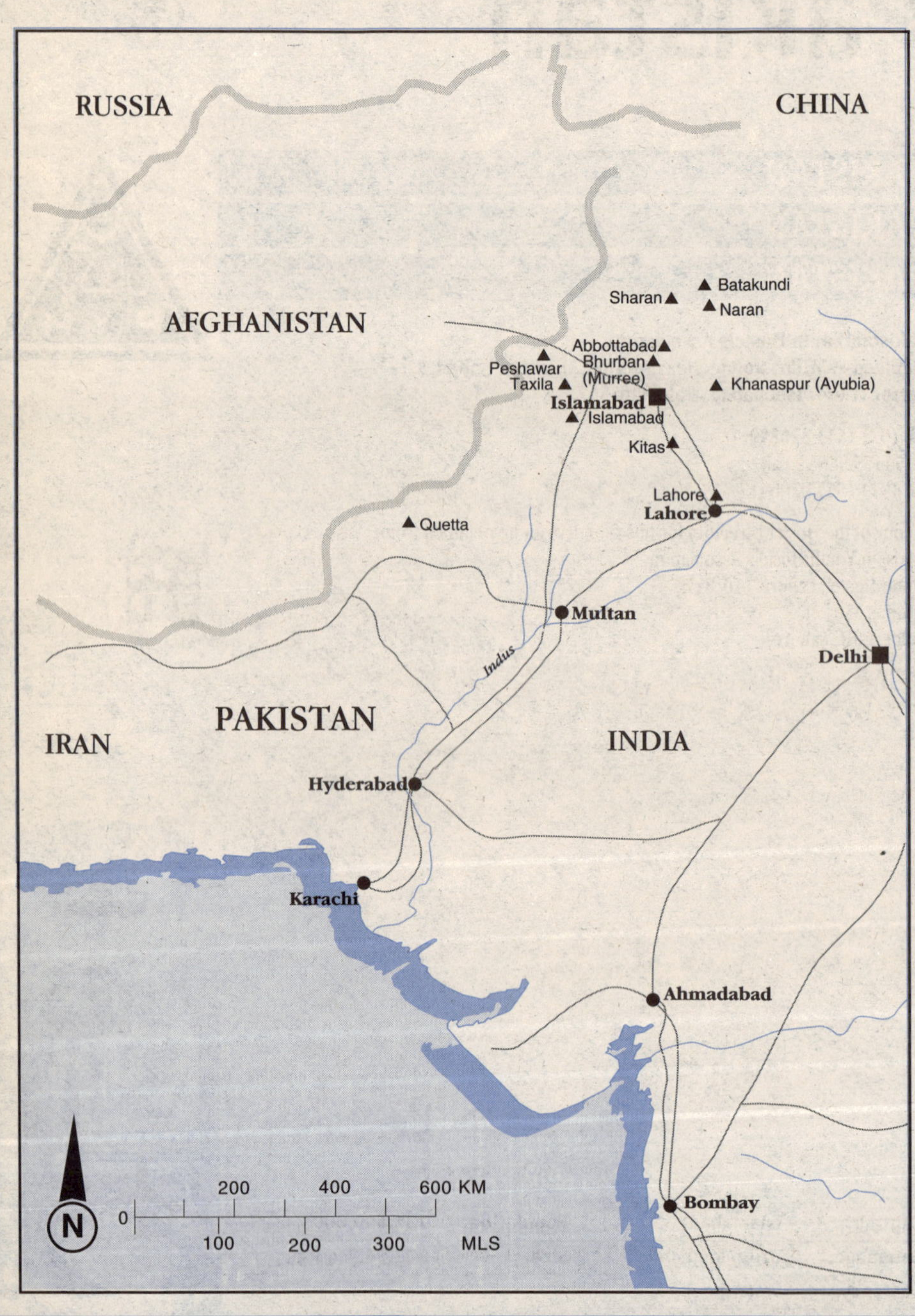

English

PAKISTAN HOSTELS

The network of facilities available to members in Pakistan includes a wide range of government rest houses, and is particularly well known for the extensive accommodation in the mountain area to the north of the country.

Expect to pay Rs 45-55, Rs 30 if you are a student, plus linen hire if needed. Charges are also made for parking bicycles or motor vehicles. Meals are not provided at Youth Hostels, but all have self-catering facilities, for which a small charge is made to cover the cost of fuel.

Hostels are open 06.00-09.00hrs and 17.00-22.00hrs.

PASSPORTS AND VISAS

All foreigners entering Pakistan need a passport. Visas are also required from nationals of countries which have not been specifically exempted from this requirement.

HEALTH

Vaccinations/inoculations against cholera, yellow fever etc and valid certificates to that effect are necessary for visitors coming from endemic areas.

BANKING HOURS

Monday-Thursday + Saturday, 09.00-13.00hrs; Friday 09.00-12.00hrs.

POST OFFICES

09.00-15.00hrs, every day except Sunday.

SHOPPING HOURS

09.00-20.00hrs, every day except Sunday.

TRAVEL

Air
Air transportation, although expensive, is the easiest and most convenient mode of travel for long journeys between the big cities.

Rail
There is an extensive railway network which connects almost all cities and towns, and is a cheaper mode of transport than air.

Bus
A frequent bus service is available. Taxis and rickshaws are alternatives for shorter journeys and jeeps can be hired in the mountainous areas.

Driving
An International Driver's Licence is necessary. Traffic keeps to the left.

A tourist may import a motor vehicle free of duty under a Carnet de passage en Douane, for a period of up to 3 months, provided he/she gives an undertaking at the place of entry that the ownership of the vehicle will not be transferred during his/her stay in Pakistan.

The road network is also very suitable for cycling.

TELEPHONE INFORMATION

Country Code	92
Main City Area Codes	
Islamabad	51
Lahore	42
Peshawar	521

Français

AUBERGES DE JEUNESSE PAKISTANAISES

Parmi les types d'hébergement offerts aux adhérents visitant le Pakistan se trouve tout un réseau de maisons de repos publiques, et le grand choix d'établissements existant de la région montagneuse située au nord du pays est particulièrement bien connu.

Une nuit vous coûtera entre 45 et 55 RUPP, 30 RUPP si vous êtes étudiant, plus location de draps le cas échéant. Vous devrez également payer pour garer votre bicyclette ou véhicule. Les auberges de jeunesse ne servent pas de repas mais toutes sont équipées de cuisines pour les voyageurs. Une petite contribution à la consommation d'énergie vous sera demandée.

Les auberges de jeunesse sont ouvertes de 6h à 9h et de 17h à 22h.

PASSEPORTS ET VISAS

Tous les étrangers entrant au Pakistan doivent être munis d'un passeport. Les visas sont aussi requis par les citoyens des pays qui n'en sont pas spécifiquement exempts.

SOINS MEDICAUX

Les voyageurs venant de pays où le choléra, la fièvre jaune etc sont endémiques doivent être munis d'un certificat de vaccination prouvant qu'ils ont été vaccinés contre ces maladies.

HEURES D'OUVERTURE DES BANQUES

Les banques sont ouvertes du lundi au jeudi ainsi que le samedi, de 9h à 13h, et le vendredi de 9h à 12h.

BUREAUX DE POSTE

Les bureaux de poste sont ouverts de 9h à 15h tous les jours sauf le dimanche.

HEURES D'OUVERTURE DES MAGASINS

Les magasins sont ouverts de 9h à 20h tous les jours, sauf le dimanche.

DEPLACEMENTS

Avions

Les transports aériens, bien que chers, représentent la façon la plus facile et la plus pratique de se déplacer, pour couvrir les longues distances qui séparent les grandes villes.

Trains

Le réseau ferroviaire est très étendu et relie presque toutes les villes et grandes villes, tout en étant moins cher que les transports aériens.

Autobus

Les bus sont fréquents. Pour les trajets plus courts, les taxis et les pousse-pousse sont une solution et il est possible de louer des jeeps dans les régions montagneuses.

Automobiles

Les conducteurs doivent avoir un permis de conduire international. La conduite est à gauche.

Les touristes peuvent importer un véhicule, sans payer de taxe, avec un Carnet de passage en Douane, pour une période de 3 mois maximum, à condition de garantir, au point d'arrivée dans le pays, qu'ils en resteront le propriétaire et que le véhicule ne sera pas transféré à un tiers pendant leur séjour au Pakistan.

Le réseau routier se prête également très bien au cyclisme.

TELEPHONE

Indicatif du Pays	**92**
Indicatifs régionaux des Villes principales	
Islamabad	**51**
Lahore	**42**
Peshawar	**521**

Deutsch

PAKISTANISCHE JUGENDHERBERGEN

Zum pakistanischen Herbergsnetz gehören auch mehrere staatliche Rasthäuser. Besonders in der Gebirgsgegend im Norden des Landes gibt es zahlreiche Unterkünfte.

Es ist mit einem Preis von Rs 45-55 oder für Studenten Rs 30, plus, bei Bedarf, einer Gebühr für die Miete von Bettwäsche zu rechnen. Auch für das Parken von Fahrrädern oder Kraftfahrzeugen wird eine Gebühr erhoben. In Jugendherbergen gibt es keine Mahlzeiten, aber alle haben Einrichtungen für Selbstversorger, für die zur Deckung der Brennstoffkosten eine kleine Gebühr berechnet wird.

Jugendherbergen sind von 06.00-09.00 Uhr und von 17.00-22.00 Uhr geöffnet.

PÄSSE UND VISA

Alle nach Pakistan einreisenden Ausländer brauchen einen Reisepaß. Staatsangehörige von Ländern, die von dieser Vorschrift nicht ausdrücklich ausgenommen sind, benötigen außerdem ein Visum.

GESUNDHEIT

Wer aus endemischen Gebieten kommt, muß gegen Cholera, Gelbfieber usw. geimpft sein und ein gültiges Impfzeugnis vorweisen können.

GESCHÄFTSSTUNDEN DER BANKEN

Montag-Donnerstag und Samstag von 09.00-13.00 Uhr, Freitag von 09.00-12.00 Uhr.

POSTÄMTER

Täglich, außer sonntags, von 09.00-15.00 Uhr.

LADENÖFFNUNGSZEITEN

Täglich, außer sonntags, von 09.00-20.00 Uhr.

REISEN

Flugverkehr
Obwohl das Fliegen teuer ist, ist es für lange Reisen zwischen großen Städten die einfachste und bequemste Reisemöglichkeit.

Eisenbahn
Es gibt ein ausgedehntes Schienennetz mit Anschlüssen in alle Städte. Die Eisenbahn ist ein billigeres Verkehrsmittel als das Flugzeug.

Busse
Es gibt einen Busverkehr mit häufigen Verbindungen. Für kürzere Reisen kann man auch ein Taxi oder eine Rikscha nehmen. Für Fahrten in Gebirgsgegenden kann man einen Jeep mieten.

Autofahren
Man braucht einen internationalen Führerschein. In Pakistan herrscht Linksverkehr.

Touristen können mit einem Carnet de Passage en Douane für bis zu 3 Monate ein Kraftfahrzeug zollfrei einführen, sofern sie sich bei der Einreise verpflichten, das Eigentum an dem Fahrzeug während ihres Aufenthalts in Pakistan nicht auf eine andere Person zu übertragen.

Das Straßennetz eignet sich auch gut zum Radfahren.

FERNSPRECHINFORMATIONEN

Landes-Kennzahl	**92**
größere Städte - Ortsnetzkennzahlen	
Islamabad	**51**
Lahore	**42**
Peshawar	**521**

Español

ALBERGUES DE JUVENTUD PAQUISTANIES

La red de instalaciones que ofrece Pakistán incluye una gran variedad de casas de reposo del gobierno, famosas especialmente por las muchas posibilidades de alojamiento en la zona montañosa, al norte del país.

Pagará alrededor de 45-55 rupias y 30 si es estudiante. Se cobra aparte el alquiler de sábanas, si las necesita. El aparcamiento de bicicletas o de vehículos también es aparte. Los albergues de juventud no ofrecen comidas, aunque todos tienen instalaciones de cocina, por las que cobran un pequeño suplemento para cubrir los gastos de combustible.

Los albergues están abiertos de 06.00 a 09.00 horas y de 17.00 a 22.00 horas.

PASAPORTES Y VISADOS

Todos los extranjeros necesitan pasaporte para entrar en Pakistán. También necesitan visado los ciudadanos de los países que no estén específicamente exentos de este requisito.

SANIDAD

Hay que vacunarse contra la fiebre amarilla, el cólera, etc. Además, tendrán que llevar los certificados correspondientes los visitantes procedentes de zonas en las que estas enfermedades sean endémicas.

HORARIO DE BANCOS

De domingo a jueves y los sábados de 09.30 a 13.00 horas; los viernes de 09.00 a 12.00 horas.

CASAS DE CORREO

De 09.00 a 15.00 horas todos los días menos los domingos.

HORARIO COMERCIAL

De 09.00 a 20.00 horas todos los días menos los domingos.

DESPLAZAMIENTOS

Avión

El transporte aéreo, aunque resulte caro, es la forma más sencilla y cómoda de recorrer largas distancias entre grandes ciudades.

Tren

Hay una extensa red ferroviaria que comunica casi todas las grandes ciudades y poblaciones; resulta más barato que el transporte aéreo.

Autobús

Hay servicio regular de autobuses. Los taxis y los cochecillos tirados por un hombre son otras posibilidades para los trayectos más cortos. En las zonas montañosas se puede alquilar un jeep.

Coche

Es necesario el carnet de conducir internacional. Se circula por la izquierda.

Los turistas pueden llevar su vehículo sin pagar impuestos con el Carnet de Passage en Douane, por un período de hasta tres meses, siempre que a la entrada se comprometa a no venderlo durante su estancia en Pakistán.

La red de carreteras es muy apropiada para el ciclismo.

INFORMACION TELEFONICA

Código Nacional	**92**
Prefijos de las Ciudades Principales	
Islamabad	51
Lahore	42
Peshawar	521

Assured Standards – visited by our Liaison team and by you the guest – tell us when we don't measure up (reply slips at the end of this Guide)▲

des Normes Garanties, par les visites de notre Equipe de Liaison et par vous, les usagers – faites-le nous savoir quand nous ne sommes pas à la hauteur (Fiches-commentaires à la fin du Guide)▲

Zugesicherte Standards – beurteilt von unserem Liaison Team und von Ihnen, unserem Gast – sagen Sie es uns, wenn wir Sie enttäuschen (Antwortkarten hinten im Führer)▲

Normas Garantizadas – comprobadas por nuestro Equipo de Enlace y por Ud., el usuario – si fallamos en algo, díganoslo (al final de esta Guía encontrará nuestras hojas de comentarios)▲

Location/Address	Telephone No. Fax No.	Beds	Opening Dates	Facilities
▲ **Abbottabad** 4.8km N of town on rd to Balakot (Mansehra Rd): Mandian Stop near Burn Hall School and Government Degree College.		50		
△ *Batakundi* *17.6km from Naran*		25	01.06–15.10	
△ *Bhurban (Murree)* *Opposite Pearl Continental Hotel, 12.8km from Murree.*		32		
▲ **Islamabad** Adjoining Akhbar Market, Shaheed-e-Millat Rd, Aabpara, Sector G-6/4, Islamabad.	☎ (51) 826899 🖷 (51) 9206417	100		
▲ **Khanaspur (Ayubia)** 27km from Murree on Murree-Abbottabad Rd (rd junction at Kooza Gali, 24km from Murree).		32	01.04–25.12	
▲ **Lahore** 110-B-3, Gulberg-III, near Firdaus Market.	☎ 878201	100		
▲ **Peshawar** Plot No 37, Block B/1, Phase V, Jamrod Road, Hayatabad.	☎ 813581	50		
▲ **Quetta** Inside Ayub Stadium, Chaman Phatik, Quetta.		50		
△ *Sharan* *Post Office, Paras, Kaghan Valley: 11km from Paras, YH on left after crossing River Kunhar.*		25	01.06–15.10	
▲ **Taxila** Near Taxila Museum.		35		

SUPPLEMENTARY ACCOMMODATION OUTSIDE THE ASSURED STANDARDS SCHEME

Location/Address	Telephone No. Fax No.	Beds	Opening Dates	Facilities
Kitas 1.6km from Choa Saiden Shah on Choa Saiden Shah-Kalar Kahar Rd, District Chakwal.		35		
Naran 3km before the Naran Village; on the right side of the main rd from Balakot.		32	01.06–15.10	

Rest Houses (RH)

The Pakistan Youth Hostels Association offers a network of Government Rest houses which are open to youth hostellers. This is supplementary accomodation outside the Assured Standards Scheme. Please contact the National Office for details.

HOSTELLING
INTERNATIONAL

Make your credit card bookings at these centres
Réservez par cartes de crédit aux centres suivants
Buchen Sie mit Kreditkarte in folgenden Buchungszentren
Reserve por tarjeta de crédito en los siguientes centros

English

Australia	☎ (2) 9261 1111
Canada	☎ (800) 663 5777
England & Wales	☎ (1629) 581 418
France	☎ (1) 44 89 87 27
Northern Ireland	☎ (1232) 324 733
Republic of Ireland	☎ (1) 830 1766
New Zealand	☎ (9) 303 9524
Scotland	☎ (541) 553 255
Switzerland	☎ (1) 360 1414
USA	☎ (202) 783 6161

Français

Angleterre & Pays de Galles	☎ (1692) 581 41
Australie	☎ (2) 9261 111
Canada	☎ (800) 663 57
Écosse	☎ (541) 553 25
États-Unis	☎ (202) 783 61
France	☎ (1) 44 89 87
Irlande du Nord	☎ (1232) 324 7
Nouvelle-Zélande	☎ (9) 303 9524
République d'Irlande	☎ (1) 830 1766
Suisse	☎ (1) 360 1414

Deutsch

Australien	☎ (2) 9261 1111
England & Wales	☎ (1629) 581 418
Frankreich	☎ (1) 44 89 87 27
Irland	☎ (1) 830 1766
Kanada	☎ (800) 663 5777
Neuseeland	☎ (9) 303 9524
Nordirland	☎ (1232) 324 733
Schottland	☎ (541) 553 255
Schweiz	☎ (1) 360 1414
USA	☎ (202) 783 6161

Español

Australia	☎ (2) 9261 1111
Canadá	☎ (800) 663 577
Escocia	☎ (541) 553 255
Estados Unidos	☎ (202) 783 616
Francia	☎ (1) 44 89 87
Inglaterra y Gales	☎ (1629) 581 41
Irlanda del Norte	☎ (1232) 324 73
Nueva Zelanda	☎ (9) 303 9524
República de Irlanda	☎ (1) 830 1766
Suiza	☎ (1) 360 1414

Peru

PEROU
PERU
PERU

**Asociación Peruana de Albergues Turísticos Juveniles,
Avda Casimiro Ulloa 328, San Antonio,
Miraflores, Lima 18,
Peru.**

☎ (51) (1) 2423068
🖷 (51) (1) 4448187
E-mail: hostell@mail.cosapidata.com.pe

A copy of the Hostel Directory for this Country can be obtained from:
The National Office.

**IBN Booking Centre for outward
bookings**

- **Lima**, *via National Office above*

Capital:	Lima		Population:	23,834,000
Language:	Spanish		Size:	1,285,215 sq km
Currency:	S/. (Sol)			

Peru

COLOMBIA
Quito
ECUADOR
Japurá
Yarapa River
Yanayacu River
Iquitos (3)
Rio Amazonas
Zorritos
PERU
N
Mancora
Ucayali
AMAZONAS
Cajamarca
Tarapoto
Chiclayo
Pacasmayo
Callejon Huaylas
Trujillo
Caraz
Huaraz (3)
Chavin de Huantar
D
ACRE
Rio Branco
Villa Rica
Ocopa
Lima
Lima
Huancayo
Ayacucho
Cerro Azul
Puerto Maldonado (2)
E
Pisco
Cuzco
Cuzco (2)
Ica
Nazca
Andahua
Majes
L. Titicaca
Arequipa
Chucuito
S
La Paz
L. Poopo

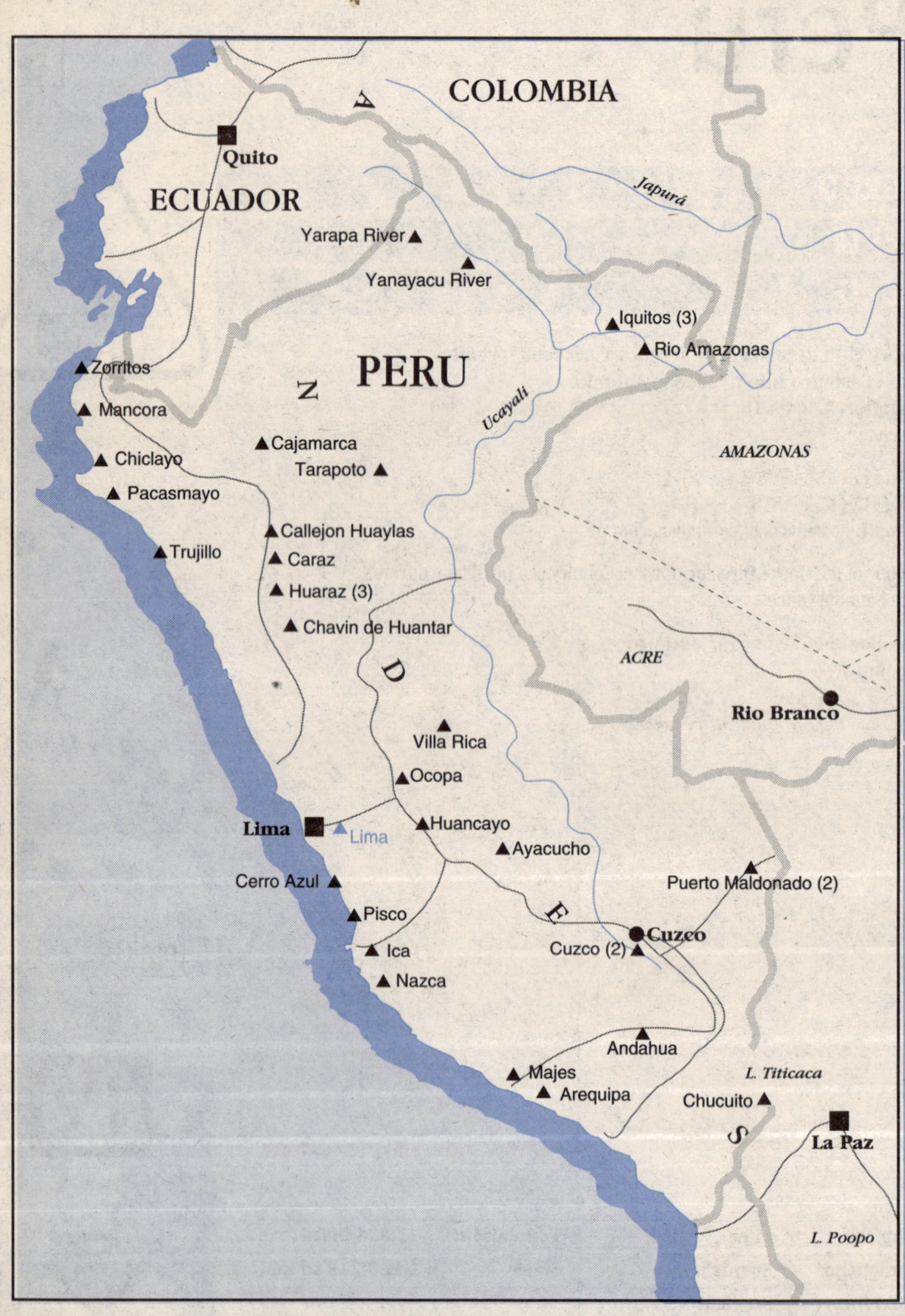

English

PERUVIAN HOSTELS

The 33 Peruvian Youth Hostels have excellent recreational facilities and are open 24 hours. All have family rooms.

Expect to pay in the region of S/10.00-S/30.00 (US$ 5.00-10.00 + tax) per night including sheets. Most hostels have cheap cafeterias, otherwise self-catering is available.

PASSPORTS AND VISAS

Visitors from some African countries need a visa for entry to Peru. Most other nationals need only a valid passport.

HEALTH

Visitors from Asian countries where cholera and yellow fever are endemic require vaccinations.

BANKING HOURS

09.00-17.00hrs.

POST OFFICES

09.00-17.00hrs.

SHOPPING HOURS

11.00-20.00hrs.

TRAVEL

Air
Frequent domestic flights are operated by Peru's airlines, Aeroperu, Aero Continente.

Rail
There are no train connections between Lima and Cuzco.

Bus
Bus routes run throughout the country.

TELEPHONE INFORMATION

Country Code	51
Main City Area Codes	
Lima	1

Français

AUBERGES DE JEUNESSE PERUVIENNES

Les 33 auberges péruviennes, ouvertes 24 heures sur 24, disposent d'excellentes installations pour le sport et les loisirs et toutes sont équipées de chambres familiales.

Une nuit vous coûtera entre S/10.00-S/30.00 (5 et 10 $US + taxe), draps compris. La plupart des auberges ont des cafétérias bon marché, ou sont équipées de cuisines pour les voyageurs.

PASSEPORTS ET VISAS

Les citoyens de certains pays africains doivent être munis d'un visa pour entrer au Pérou. Pour les citoyens de la plupart des autres pays, un passeport valide suffit.

SOINS MEDICAUX

Les citoyens de pays asiatiques dans lesquels le choléra et la fièvre jaune sont endémiques doivent être vaccinés.

HEURES D'OUVERTURE DES BANQUES

Les banques sont ouvertes de 9h à 17h.

BUREAUX DE POSTE

Les bureaux de poste sont ouverts de 9h à 17h.

HEURES D'OUVERTURE DES MAGASINS

Les magasins sont ouverts de 11h à 20h.

DEPLACEMENTS

Avions
Les lignes aériennes péruviennes Aeroperu et Aero Continente assurent toutes des vols intérieurs fréquents.

Trains
Il n'y a pas de train entre Lima et Cuzco.

Autobus
Des lignes d'autobus sillonnent tout le pays.

TELEPHONE

Indicatif du Pays   **51**
Indicatifs régionaux des Villes principales
   Lima   **1**

Deutsch

PERUANISCHE JUGENDHERBERGEN

Die ungefähr 33 peruanischen Jugendherbergen verfügen über ausgezeichnete Erholungseinrichtungen und sind 24 Stunden geöffnet. Alle haben Familienräume.

Es ist mit einem Übernachtungspreis von S/10.00-S/30.00 (US$ 5,00-10,00 plus Steuer), einschließlich Laken, zu rechnen. Die meisten Herbergen haben eine billige Cafeteria. Sonst sind Einrichtungen für Selbstversorger vorhanden.

PÄSSE UND VISA

Besucher aus einigen afrikanischen Ländern brauchen für die Einreise nach Peru ein Visum. Staatsbürger der meisten anderen Länder brauchen nur einen gültigen Reisepaß.

GESUNDHEIT

Besucher aus asiatischen Ländern, in denen Cholera und Gelbfieber endemisch sind, müssen geimpft sein.

GESCHÄFTSSTUNDEN DER BANKEN

09.00-17.00 Uhr.

POSTÄMTER

09.00-17.00 Uhr.

LADENÖFFNUNGSZEITEN

11.00-20.00 Uhr.

REISEN

Flugverkehr
Die peruanischen Fluggesellschaften Aeroperu und Aero Continente betreiben einen inländischen Flugverkehr mit häufigen Verbindungen.

Eisenbahn
Zwischen Lima und Cuzco gibt es keine Eisenbahnverbindung.

Busse
Busse verkehren im ganzen Land.

FERNSPRECHINFORMATIONEN

Landes-Kennzahl   **51**
größere Städte - Ortsnetzkennzahlen
   Lima   **1**

Español

ALBERGUES DE JUVENTUD PERUANOS

Hay alrededor de 33 albergues en el Perú, con excelentes instalaciones de recreo. Están abiertos las 24 horas del día. Todos tienen habitaciones familiares.

Pagará de S/10,00-S/30,00 (5 a 10 dólares) por noche más impuesto, sábanas incluidas. La mayor parte de los albergues tienen cafeterías baratas. Si no, ofrecen instalaciones para cocinar.

PASAPORTES Y VISADOS

Necesitan visado para entrar en Perú los visitantes de algunos países africanos y asiáticos. En casi todos los demás casos, sólo hace falta un pasaporte en regla.

SANIDAD

Necesitan vacunas los visitantes de los países asiáticos donde el cólera y la fiebre amarilla sean enfermedades endémicas.

HORARIO DE BANCOS

De 09.00 a 17.00 horas.

OFICINAS DE CORREOS

De 09.00 a 17.00 horas.

HORARIO COMERCIAL

De 11.00 a 20.00 horas.

DESPLAZAMIENTOS

Avión

Las líneas aéreas peruanas Aeroperú y Aero
Continente ofrecen vuelos nacionales frecuentes.

Tren

No hay servicio de trenes entre Lima y Cuzco.

Autobús

Los autocares recorren todo el país.

INFORMACION TELEFONICA

Código Nacional   51
Prefijos de las Ciudades Principales
  Lima   1

There for everyone
- young, not so young
and those in the middle▲

c'est pour tout le
monde -les jeunes, les moins
jeunes et tous les autres.▲

albergues para todos
- los jóvenes, los menos
jóvenes y los jóvenes de
espíritu▲

für jederman - ob
jung, nicht mehr ganz so jung
oder die dazwischen.▲

Lima

**AJ Turístico Internacional,
Av Casimiro Ulloa 328,
Miraflores,
Lima 18.**

☎ (1) 4465488
✆ (1) 4448187

Open Dates:	🗓
Open Hours:	🕐
Reservations:	(R) (IBN) (CC)
Price Range:	US$9.00-10.00 📖
Beds:	100 - 3x² 10x⁴ 1x⁵ 2x⁶
Facilities:	� ♁ ⑩ (B) 🛏 📺 1x 🍽 🔲 ⌨ ♿ 🅿 ⓘ 🎱 ⚓

Directions:

✈	Jorge Chavez 15km
A🚌	S 100m
🚌	S, P, 3M, 20, 10 100m ap Puente Benavides 100m

Attractions: 🔍 ⚲2km 🏊2km

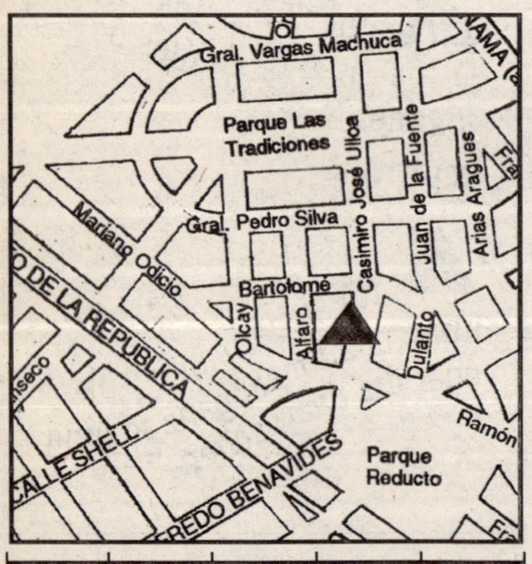

Assured Standards – visited by our Liaison team and by you the guest – tell us when we don't measure up (reply slips at the end of this Guide) ▲

des Normes Garanties, par les visites de notre Equipe de Liaison et par vous, les usagers – faites-le nous savoir quand nous ne sommes pas à la hauteur (Fiches-commentaires à la fin du Guide) ▲

Zugesicherte Standards – beurteilt von unserem Liaison Team und von Ihnen, unserem Gast – sagen Sie es uns, wenn wir Sie enttäuschen (Antwortkarten hinten im Führer) ▲

Normas Garantizadas – comprobadas por nuestro Equipo de Enlace y por Ud., el usuario – si fallamos en algo, díganoslo (al final de esta Guía encontrará nuestras hojas de comentarios) ▲

Location/Address	Telephone No. Fax No.	Beds	Opening Dates	Facilities
△ *Andahua* *AJ del valle de los Volcanes,* *Barrio de Huancarqui s/n Plaza de Armas,* *Provincia de Castilla Arequipa.*	(54) 471221 (54) 471221	15		
▲ **Amazonas River** Amazonas Sinchicuy Lodge, Amazonas River. (jungle hostel)	(1) 2417576 (1) 4467946	70		30N CC
▲ **Arequipa** Albergue Internacional el Misti, Av Salaverry 302 Vallecito, Arequipa.	(54) 245760 (54) 245760	26		
▲ **Ayacucho** AJ El Marques de Valdelirios, Alameda Bolognesi 720/24, Ayacucho. (Alt 2000m)	(64) 813908 (64) 814014	40		CC
▲ **Cajamarca** AJ Baños del Inca, Plaza de Armas S/N Baños del Inca.	(44) 827385 (44) 822800	100		R
▲ **Caraz** - A.J. Los Pinos Parque San Martin No.103, La Merced, Caraz	(44) 791130 (44) 791130	25		
△ *Cerro Azul* *AJ "Las Olas de Cerro Azul", Jiron Comercio 455,* *Cerro Azul.*	(1) 3450985 (1) 3451097	50		
▲ **Chavin de Huantar** - A J Montecarlo Jr. 17 de Enero N.101 Plaza de Armas.	(44) 754014	70		R
▲ **Chiclayo** - A.J. Turistico de Chiclayo Calle Manuel Arteaga 690 Urb. Los Libertadores	(74) 236628/ 273442	20		
△ *Chucuito* *AJ Las Cabañas, Jr. Tarapaca 538,* *Distrito de Chucuito.*	(54) 351276	30		R 18N
▲ **Cuzco** - Maison de la Jeunesse Avda. El Sol Cdra, 5 Pasaje Grace, Edificio San Jorge, Cusco.	(84) 235617 (1) 4464395	35		R CC
▲ **Cuzco** - Alberge Municipal Av. Kiskapata 240, Barrio de San Cristobal.	(84) 252506 (84) 252506	64		R
△ *Huancayo* *Albergue Los Andenes del Inti,* *Jr. Lima 354 Piso 9 Huancayo.*	(64) 234745; (64) 223785 (64) 234143	25		R CC
△ *Huaraz* - *La Montañesa* *Av A B Leguia 290 Centenario.*	(44) 721287	45		R
▲ **Huaraz** - Eccame Km 18, Huaraz aeropeurto de Anta	(44) 721933 (44) 721933	40		
△ *Huaraz* - *Alpes Andes Casa de Guias* *Parque Ginebra 286 Casa de Guias.*	(44) 721811 (44) 722306	58		R
△ *Ica* *Albergue Colonial Inn, Calle Lima 262 Ica.*	(34) 215582 (34) 235416	57		R
▲ **Iquitos** AJ Ambassador, Calle Pevas 260, Iquitos.	(94) 231618 (94) 238684	48		R CC
▲ **Iquitos** - A.J. Tambo Amazonico Lodge Yarapa River (180 km de Iquitos)	(1) 2417576 (1) 4467946	20		180NE CC

Location/Address	Telephone No. / Fax No.	Beds	Opening Dates	Facilities
▲ **Iquitos**- Amazon River, A.J. Tambo Yanayacu Lodge Yanayacu River	☎ (1) 2417576 ✆ (1) 4467946	20		ⅰⅰⅰ ⅼ⊙ⅼ 60 NE · ⌐CC⌐ · ☕
▲ **Lima** [IBN] **AJ Turístico Internacional,** **Av Casimiro Ulloa 328, Miraflores, Lima 18.**	☎ (1) 4465488 ✆ (1) 4448187	100		ⅰⅰⅰ ⅼ⊙ⅼ ® · ⌐CC⌐ ☞ P ▣
▲ **Ocopa** Hostel "Santa Rosa de Ocopa", Convento de Ocopa via Central Concepcion.	☎ (64) 210217	72		ⅰⅰⅰ ⅼ⊙ⅼ P ▣
△ *Pacasmayo* *AJ Sol y Mar, Sarmiento 112, Pacasmayo.*	☎ *(44) 521440* ✆ *(44) 222508*	*20*		ⅰⅰⅰ ® P ▣
▲ **Pisco** AJ Pisco Playa, Jr José Balta No 639, Pisco Playa.	☎ (34) 532492	60		ⅰⅰⅰ ® ☞ P ▣
▲ **Piura** - La Posada de Mancora Barrio Industrial s/n Mancora	☎ (74) 858328 ✆ (74) 858212	40		ⅰⅰⅰ ⅼ⊙ⅼ 0.2 N ☞ P ▣ ☕
▲ **Puerto Maldonado** - "Iñapari" Avda. Areopuerto Km.5 "La Joya" - Pto. Maldonado, Casilla #32 Madre de Dios.	☎ (84) 572575 ✆ (84) 572155	30		ⅰⅰⅰ ⅼ⊙ⅼ ® P ▣
▲ **Puerto Maldonado** - "AJ Ecoamazonia Lodge" Bajo Rio Madre de Dios Km. 30	☎ (84) 242244, 236159 ✆ (44) 225068	90		ⅰⅰⅰ ⅼ⊙ⅼ ® ⌐CC⌐
▲ **Río Majes** Albergue Turistico Majes River, Valle del Majes, Central Ongoro.	☎ (54) 471221 ✆ (54) 255819	40		ⅰⅰⅰ ⅼ⊙ⅼ ® ▣
▲ **Tarapoto** "Puerto Palmeras", Km 3, Marginal Sur, Tarapoto San Martin, Puerto Maldonado.	☎ (94) 523978 ✆ (94) 523980	30		ⅰⅰⅰ ⅼ⊙ⅼ ® ♿ ⌐CC⌐ ☞ P ▣
▲ **Trujillo** - Centro Vacacional El Parque Autopista Huanchaco, poste N.62, Trujillo	☎ (44) 654317; (44) 203712	70		ⅰⅰⅰ ⅼ⊙ⅼ 0.5 N ☞ P ▣ ☕
△ *Villa Rica* *Av Leopoldo Krause 451, Villa Rica, Oxapampa.*	☎ *(64) 530204*	*50*		ⅰⅰⅰ ⅼ⊙ⅼ ® P ▣
△ *Zorritos* *AJ La Casa del Grillo, Los Pinos,* *563 Zorritos-Tumbes: (1235km).*	☎ *(1) 4465488* ✆ *(1) 4448187*	*42*		ⅰⅰⅰ ⅼ⊙ⅼ ☞ P ▣

SUPPLEMENTARY ACCOMMODATION
OUTSIDE THE ASSURED STANDARDS SCHEME

Location/Address	Telephone No. / Fax No.	Beds	Opening Dates	Facilities
Nazca AJ Alegria, Jr Lima No 166, Nazca.	☎ (34) 522702 ☎ (34) 522444	80		ⅰⅰⅰ ® ☞ ▣ ☕

Philippines

PHILIPPINES

PHILIPPINEN

FILIPINAS

**Youth & Student Hostel Foundation of the
Philippines, (YSHFP)
4227-9 Tomas Claudio St.,
Parañaque 1700, Baclaran,
Metro Manila,
Philippines.**

**ⓣ (63) (2) 832 0680, 832 2112
TX41316 YSTAPHIL PM
ⓕ (63) (2) 8322263**

A copy of the Hostel Directory for this Country can be obtained from:
The National Office.

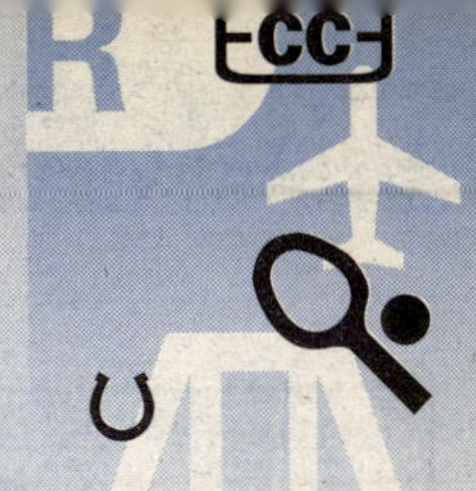

Capital:	Manila	Population:	63,000,000
Language:	Pilipino/English	Size:	300,000 sq km
Currency:	Peso		

Philippines

English

PHILIPPINE HOSTELS

Your Hostelling International card gives you access not only to Youth Hostels in the Philippines, but to other types of budget accommodation.

Expect to pay P 120-400, including linen hire. Self-catering is not usually available, but meals are served at most hostels. Hostels are open 24 hours.

PASSPORTS AND VISAS

A valid passport is required by all travellers.

Visas can be obtained from any Philippines diplomatic or consular office abroad. Visas are not required by bona fide tourists for a stay of up to 21 days provided they have a valid passport and air or sea tickets for their onward or return journey.

HEALTH

Yellow fever vaccination is required upon arrival of passengers from infected areas except for children under one year who are subject to isolation when needed.

BANKING HOURS

Banks are open Monday to Friday 09.00-15.00hrs.

POST OFFICES

Post offices are open weekdays 08.00-12.00hrs and 13.00-17.00hrs. Main post offices offer a 24 hour cable service. Stamps are also sold in some government offices, hotels, universities and commercial establishments.

SHOPPING HOURS

Most shops are open 09.00/10.00-19.00/20.00hrs, Monday to Saturday. Some are open on Sundays until midday and those geared to the tourist trade are usually open all day.

TRAVEL

Rail
The main railway links Manila to Legaspi, in the south.

Bus
Buses operate and taxis are available.

Ferry
Inter-island ships with first class accommodation connect the major island ports.

Driving
The rule of the road is the same for cyclists and motorists: keep to the right. Petrol is readily available in most parts of the country.

TELEPHONE INFORMATION

Country Code	**63**
Main City Area Codes	
Manila	**2**

Français

AUBERGES DE JEUNESSE PHILIPPINES

Votre carte Hostelling International vous permet d'utiliser non seulement les auberges de jeunesse dans les Philippines mais aussi d'autres types d'hébergement bon marché.

Une nuit vous coûtera entre 120 et 400 $PHI, location de draps comprise. Il n'est pas souvent possible de faire sa propre cuisine, mais la plupart des auberges servent des repas. Les auberges sont ouvertes 24 heures sur 24.

PASSEPORTS ET VISAS

Tous les voyageurs doivent être munis d'un passeport valide.

Les visas peuvent être obtenus auprès de tout bureau diplomatique ou consulaire des Philippines à l'étranger. Les vrais touristes souhaitant rester dans le pays pendant un maximum de 21 jours n'ont pas besoin de visa du moment où ils sont munis d'un passeport valide et d'un billet d'avion ou de bateau soit pour continuer leur voyage soit pour rentrer dans leur pays.

SOINS MEDICAUX

Les voyageurs arrivant de régions où sévit la fièvre jaune devront être vaccinés à leur arrivée, sauf les enfants de moins d'un an, qui seront isolés si besoin est.

HEURES D'OUVERTURE DES BANQUES

Les banques sont ouvertes du lundi au vendredi de 9h à 15h.

BUREAUX DE POSTE

Les bureaux de poste sont ouverts en semaine de 8h à 12h et de 13h à 17h. Les bureaux principaux offrent un service télégraphique 24 heures sur 24. Les timbres sont aussi en vente dans certains bureaux gouvernementaux, hôtels, universités et commerces.

HEURES D'OUVERTURE DES MAGASINS

La plupart des magasins sont ouverts de 9h/10h à 19h/20h, du lundi au samedi. Certains sont ouverts le dimanche jusqu'à midi et ceux qui vivent du tourisme sont en général ouverts toute la journée.

DEPLACEMENTS

Trains
Le réseau principal relie Manille à Legaspi, au sud.

Autobus
Il y a un service d'autobus, ainsi que des taxis.

Ferry-boats
Un service de bateaux tout confort relie les îles, avec escales dans les ports principaux.

Automobiles
Le code de la route est le même pour les cyclistes et les automobilistes: tenez la droite. Il est facile de se procurer de l'essence dans la plupart des régions.

TELEPHONE

Indicatif du Pays 63
Indicatifs régionaux des Villes principales
  Manille 2

Deutsch

PHILIPPINISCHE JUGENDHERBERGEN

Mit Ihrem Jugendherbergsausweis werden Sie nicht nur in den philippinischen Jugendherbergen aufgenommen, sondern es stehen Ihnen auch andere preiswerte Unterkünfte zur Verfügung.

Es ist mit einem Preis von P 120-400, einschließlich Bettwäsche, zu rechnen. Im allgemeinen gibt es keine Einrichtungen für Selbstversorger, aber in den meisten Herbergen werden Mahlzeiten serviert. Die Herbergen sind 24 Stunden geöffnet.

PÄSSE UND VISA

Alle Reisenden brauchen einen gültigen Reisepaß.

Ein Visum kann von jeder diplomatischen oder konsularischen Vertretung der Philippinen im Ausland beschafft werden. Touristen brauchen für einen Aufenthalt von bis zu 21 Tagen kein Visum, sofern sie im Besitz eines gültigen Reisepasses und eines Flugtickets oder einer Schiffskarte für die Weiter- oder Rückreise sind.

GESUNDHEIT

Von Passagieren, die aus infizierten Gebieten kommen, wird bei der Ankunft eine Gelbfieberimpfung verlangt. Kinder unter einem Jahr sind davon ausgenommen, werden aber ggf. isoliert.

GESCHÄFTSSTUNDEN DER BANKEN

Die Banken sind montags bis freitags von 09.00-15.00 Uhr geöffnet.

POSTÄMTER

Postämter sind werktags von 08.00-12.00 Uhr und von 13.00-17.00 Uhr geöffnet. Hauptpostämter bieten einen 24stündigen Kabelservice. Briefmarken werden auch von gewissen Behörden, Hotels, Universitäten und Gewerbebetrieben verkauft.

LADENÖFFNUNGSZEITEN

Die meisten Geschäfte sind montags bis samstags von 09.00/10.00-19.00/20.00 Uhr geöffnet. Einige sind auch sonntags bis um die Mittagszeit geöffnet, und auf das Geschäft mit Touristen spezialisierte Geschäfte sind im allgemeinen ganztägig geöffnet.

REISEN

Eisenbahn

Die Haupteisenbahn verbindet Manila und Legaspi im Süden.

Busse

Es gibt einen Busverkehr und auch Taxis.

Fähren

Zwischen den wichtigsten Inselhäfen verkehren Schiffe, auf denen die Passagiere erstklassig untergebracht sind.

Autofahren

Für Fahrrad- und Autofahrer gelten die gleichen Verkehrsvorschriften: immer rechts bleiben. In den meisten Landesteilen kann man leicht Benzin bekommen.

FERNSPRECHINFORMATIONEN

Landes-Kennzahl	**63**
größere Städte - Ortsnetzkennzahlen	
Manila	**2**

Español

ALBERGUES DE JUVENTUD FILIPINOS

Su tarjeta de Hostelling International le da acceso no sólo a los albergues de juventud de Filipinas, sino también a otros tipos de alojamiento económico.

Los precios oscilan entre 120-400 dólares filipinos incluyendo alquiler de sábanas. Los albergues no suelen disponer de cocina para huéspedes, pero muchos sirven comidas. Los albergues están abiertos las 24 horas del día.

PASAPORTES Y VISADOS

Todos los visitantes deberán ir provistos de un pasaporte válido.

Se pueden conseguir visados en cualquier oficina diplomática o consular en el extranjero. No se exige visado a los turistas que sean genuinos para una estancia de hasta 21 días, siempre que tengan un pasaporte válido y billetes de avión o de barco para su viaje de vuelta o de continuación.

SANIDAD

Necesitarán estar vacunados contra la fiebre amarilla los pasajeros que provengan de áreas contaminadas, excepto en el caso de los niños menores de un año, a los que se pondrá en cuarentena si es necesario.

HORARIO DE BANCOS

Los bancos abren de lunes a viernes de 09.00 a 15.00 horas.

OFICINAS DE CORREOS

Las oficinas de correos abren los días laborables de 08.00 a 12.00 horas y de 13.00 a 17.00 horas. Las oficinas centrales ofrecen un servicio telegráfico las 24 horas del día. También se venden sellos en algunas oficinas gubernamentales, hoteles, universidades y establecimientos comerciales.

HORARIO COMERCIAL

La mayor parte de las tiendas abre de 09.00/10.00 a 19.00/20.00 horas de lunes a sábado. Algunas abren los domingos hasta mediodía y las orientadas al turismo suelen abrir todo el día.

DESPLAZAMIENTOS

Tren

La principal línea de tren enlaza Manila con Legaspi, en el sur.

Autobús

Existen servicios de autobús y de taxi.

Ferry

Los puertos de las principales islas están conectados por barcos con servicio de primera clase.

Coche

La regla a seguir en la carretera es igual para los ciclistas y los conductores: circular siempre por la derecha. Se puede conseguir gasolina en la mayor parte del país.

INFORMACION TELEFONICA

Código Nacional	63
Prefijos de las Ciudades Principales	
Manila	2

Assured Standards – visited by our Liaison team and by you the guest – tell us when we don't measure up (reply slips at the end of this Guide) ▶

des Normes Garanties, par les visites de notre Equipe de Liaison et par vous, les usagers – faites-le nous savoir quand nous ne sommes pas à la hauteur (Fiches-commentaires à la fin du Guide) ▶

Zugesicherte Standards – beurteilt von unserem Liaison Team und von Ihnen, unserem Gast – sagen Sie es uns, wenn wir Sie enttäuschen (Antwortkarten hinten im Führer) ▶

Normas Garantizadas – comprobadas por nuestro Equipo de Enlace y por Ud., el usuario – si fallamos en algo, díganoslo (al final de esta Guía encontrará nuestras hojas de comentarios) ▶

Manila -
International YH

4227 T,
Claudio St,
Roxas Blvd,
Parañaque: (behind the Excelsior Building).
☎ (2) 8320680, 8322112
✆ (2) 8322263

Open Dates:	
Open Hours:	
Price Range:	120.00-200.00
Beds:	158 - 2x⁴ 4x⁶ 6x⁶
Facilities:	♦♦♦ ♦♦ ⑩ ☕ ▦ TV 🗄 1x 🍷 ⑤ 🧳 ⚏ 🔟 ⊜ P i ♿ ✿

Directions:

✈	Ninoy Aquino International 2km
🚂	Baclaran Lrt 1km

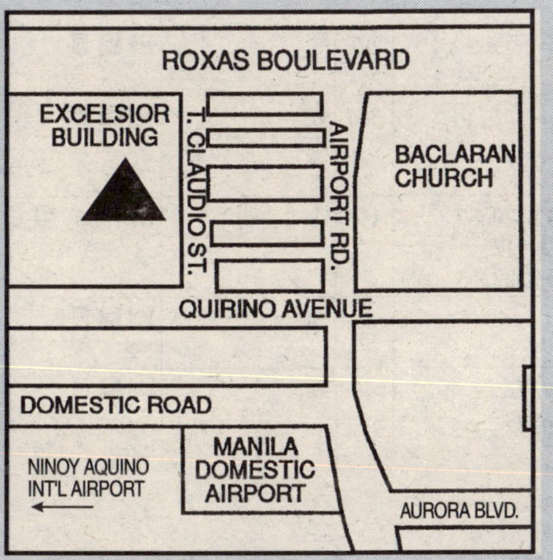

HOSTELLING INTERNATIONAL

There for everyone - young, not so young and those in the middle▲

c'est pour tout le monde - les jeunes, les moins jeunes et tous les autres▲

albergues para todos - los jóvenes, los menos jóvenes y los jóvenes de espíritu▲

für jederman - ob jung, nicht mehr ganz so jung oder die dazwischen▲

Location/Address	Telephone No. / Fax No.	Beds	Opening Dates	Facilities
△ **Alaminos** Kilometre One YH, Hundred Islands, Lucap, Alaminos, Pangasinan.		30		
△ **Baguio City** - Corfu Village 92 cor Leonard Wood cor Brent Rd and Gen Luna Sts, Baguio City	☏ 2969	50		
△ **Baguio City** - YMCA Hostel Post Office Loop, Session Rd.	☏ 4424766	30		
△ **Baguio City** - Teachers Camp Dormitory and Cottages, Leonard Wood Rd.	☏ 4423517	150		
△ **Baguio City** - Baden Powell Hall 26 Grosvenor Park Rd.	☏ 4225836	150		
△ **Banaue** - Banaue YH Banaue, Ifugao.		60		
△ **Banaue** - Banaue View Beyer-Luglug YH, Banaue, Ifugao.		30		
△ **Cagayan Valley** - Callao Cave YH Peñablanca, Cagayan.		60		
△ **Cagayan Valley** - Villa Margarita YH Busilac, Bayombong, Nueva Vizcaya.		50		
△ **Cebu** - YMCA 61 Osmena Blvd.	☏ 92031	70		
△ **Corregidor** Corregidor Island.		60		
△ **Ilocos Coast** - D'Coral Beach Resort Piao Sur, Currimao: (25km S of Laoag).	☏ 221133	100		
△ **La Unión** - Seabreeze Campsite Paringao, Bauang: (5km S of San Fernando).	☏ 413530	30		
△ **Legaspi City** - Reyes Beach Resort Eto Domingo, Albay.		50		
△ **Legaspi City** - Guillermo's Pension House Karangalan Blvd, Tabaco, Albay.		40		
△ **Malolos** Hiyasng Bulacan Convention Center Hostel, Malolos, Bulacan Province.		300		
▲ **Manila** - International YH **4227 T, Claudio St, Roxas Blvd,** **Parañaque: (behind the Excelsior Building).**	☏ (2) 8320680, 8322112 ℻ (2) 8322263	158		
△ **Mount Province** St Joseph's Rest House, Sagada, Mountain Province.		80		
△ **San Pablo City** Sampaloc Lake YH, Schetelig Ave, Efarca Village, San Pablo City, Laguna.	☏ 984797, 808943	40		

Qatar

QATAR

KATAR

QATAR

**Qatar Youth Hostels Association,
PO Box 9660, Doha, Qatar.**

☎ (974) 867180, 866402
📠 (974) 863968

A copy of the Hostel Directory for this Country can be obtained from:
Qatar Youth Hostel Association, Doha Al-Lakta. Makka Street.

Capital:	Doha	Population:	532,719
Language:	Arabic	Size:	11,427 sq km
Currency:	Qatari riyal		

Qatar

IRAN
BAHRAIN
PERSIAN GULF
Al-Shamal
Jamilia
Doha (2) Wakra
QATAR
UNITED ARAB EMIRATES
SAUDI ARABIA
50   100   150   KM
0
25   50   75   MLS
N

English

QATAR HOSTELS

Youth Hostels in Qatar are always for one sex only - but that's the culture. They have excellent sports facilities, including swimming pools and gymnasia.

Qatar has five Youth Hostels, two in Doha, one of which is the only hostel for females.

Expect to pay around 40 QR for one night or 100 QR for full board.

PASSPORTS AND VISAS

Visas are required.

HEALTH

No vaccination or health certificates are required.

BANKING HOURS

07.30-12.00hrs.

POST OFFICES

07.30-20.00hrs. A post office at the airport provides a 24 hour service.

SHOPPING HOURS

08.00-11.30hrs and 15.30-21.00hrs.

TRAVEL

There are several points of entry to Qatar: by air through Doha International Airport; by sea through the ports of Doha and Umm Said; by overland entry through Abu Samra, the frontier point with Saudi Arabia and Soda Nathil on the joint border with the United Arab Emirates.

Driving

A valid International Driver's Licence is required.

TELEPHONE INFORMATION

Country Code   **974**
Main City Area Codes
   No area code required

Français

AUBERGES DE JEUNESSE AU QATAR

Les auberges de jeunesse au Qatar sont toujours pour hommes ou femmes uniquement, conformément à la culture de ce pays. Elles ont de très bonnes installations sportives, avec des piscines et des gymnases.

Il y a cinq auberges au Qatar, deux à Doha, dont l'une est pour femmes uniquement.

Une nuit vous coûtera environ 40 QR, ou 100 QR pour pension complète.

PASSEPORTS ET VISAS

Un visa est nécessaire.

SOINS MEDICAUX

Aucune vaccination ni aucun certificat de santé ne sont nécessaires.

HEURES D'OUVERTURE DES BANQUES

Les banques sont ouvertes de 7h30 à 12h00.

BUREAUX DE POSTE

Les bureaux de poste sont ouverts de 7h30 à 20h. Un bureau de poste situé à l'aéroport international de Doha est ouvert 24 heures sur 24.

HEURES D'OUVERTURE DES MAGASINS

Les magasins sont ouverts de 8h à 11h30 et de 15h30 à 21h.

DEPLACEMENTS

Il y a plusieurs points d'arrivée au Qatar: par air, à l'aéroport international de Doha; par mer, aux ports de Doha et d'Oum Saïd; par terre, en passant par Abou Samra, à la frontière avec l'Arabie Saoudite, et par Soda Nathil, à la frontière commune avec les Emirats arabes unis.

Automobiles

Un permis de conduire international valide est nécessaire.

TELEPHONE

Indicatif du Pays   **974**
Indicatifs régionaux des Villes principales
  Pas d'indicatif régional nécessaire

Deutsch

KATARISCHE JUGENDHERBERGEN

Wie es der Kultur des Landes entspricht, sind die Jugendherbergen in Katar immer nach Geschlechtern getrennt. Sie verfügen über ausgezeichnete Sportanlagen, wie Schwimmbäder und Turnhallen.

Katar hat fünf Jugendherbergen, zwei in Doha, wovon eine die einzige Herberge für Frauen ist.

Es ist mit einem Preis von ca. 40 QR pro Übernachtung oder 100 QR für Vollpension zu rechnen.

PÄSSE UND VISA

Es wird ein Visum benötigt.

GESUNDHEIT

Es werden keine Impf- oder Gesundheitszeugnisse verlangt.

GESCHÄFTSSTUNDEN DER BANKEN

07.30-12.00 Uhr.

POSTÄMTER

07.30-20.00 Uhr. Auf dem Flughafen gibt es ein Postamt, das 24 Stunden geöffnet ist.

LADENÖFFNUNGSZEITEN

08.00-11.30 Uhr und 15.30-21.00 Uhr.

REISEN

Man kann über verschiedene Orte nach Katar einreisen: mit dem Flugzeug über den internationalen Flughafen Doha; mit dem Schiff über die Häfen Doha und Umm Said; auf dem Landweg über Abu Samra an der Grenze zu Saudi-Arabien und über Soda Nathil an der gemeinsamen Grenze mit den Vereinigten Arabischen Emiraten.

Autofahren

Man braucht einen gültigen internationalen Führerschein.

FERNSPRECHINFORMATIONEN

Landes-Kennzahl   **974**
größere Städte - Ortsnetzkennzahlen
  Keine Ortsnetzkennzahl erforderlich

Español

ALBERGUES DE JUVENTUD DE QATAR

Los albergues de juventud de Qatar son sólo para hombres o sólo para mujeres, pero esa es la cultura de todo el país. Tienen excelentes instalaciones deportivas que incluyen piscinas y gimnasios.

Qatar tiene cinco albergues de juventud, dos de ellos en Doha, uno de los cuales es el único albergue para mujeres.

El precio es de aprox. 40 QR por noche ó 100 QR con pensión completa.

PASAPORTES Y VISADOS

Se requiere visado.

SANIDAD

No se requieren vacunas ni certificados sanitarios.

HORARIO DE LOS BANCOS

De 07.30 a 12.00 horas.

OFICINAS DE CORREOS

De 07.30 a 20.00 horas. Existe una oficina de correos en el aeropuerto que está abierta las 24 horas del día.

HORARIO COMERCIAL

De 08.00 a 11.30 y de 15.30 a 21.00 horas.

DESPLAZAMIENTOS

Hay varios puntos de entrada a Qatar: por avión, a través del aeropuerto internacional de Doha; por mar, a través de los puertos de Doha y Umm Said; por tierra, a través de Abu Samra, el punto fronterizo con Arabia Saudí, y a través de Soda Nathil, en la frontera con los Emiratos Arabes Unidos.

Coche

Se requiere un permiso internacional de conducir válido.

INFORMACION TELEFONICA

Código Nacional   **974**
Prefijos de las Ciudades Principales
   No se requieren prefijos.

Assured Standards – visited by our Liaison team and by you the guest – tell us when we don't measure up (reply slips at the end of this Guide) ▶

des Normes Garanties, par les visites de notre Equipe de Liaison et par vous, les usagers – faites-le nous savoir quand nous ne sommes pas à la hauteur (Fiches-commentaires à la fin du Guide) ▶

Zugesicherte Standards – beurteilt von unserem Liaison Team und von Ihnen, unserem Gast – sagen Sie es uns, wenn wir Sie enttäuschen (Antwortkarten hinten im Führer) ▶

Normas Garantizadas – comprobadas por nuestro Equipo de Enlace y por Ud., el usuario – si fallamos en algo, díganoslo (al final de esta Guía encontrará nuestras hojas de comentarios) ▶

Doha

Doha YH,
Al-Lakta Makka Street.
☎ 867180; 866402
📠 863968

Open Dates:	🗓️
Open Hours:	🕐
Reservations:	Ⓡ
Price Range:	US$ 11.00 📖
Beds:	60 - 11x^1 22x^2 33x^3 44x^4
Facilities:	👪 🍽 📺 📷 1x 🍴 🔌 🖼 🏢 Ⓑ ⊜ 🅿 ℹ️ ♿ 📐 🔍 🏬 🚶

Directions:

✈	Doha International 12km
🚢	Doha 10km

Attractions: 🎡 〰️ 16km ⚲ 4km 🏊 8km

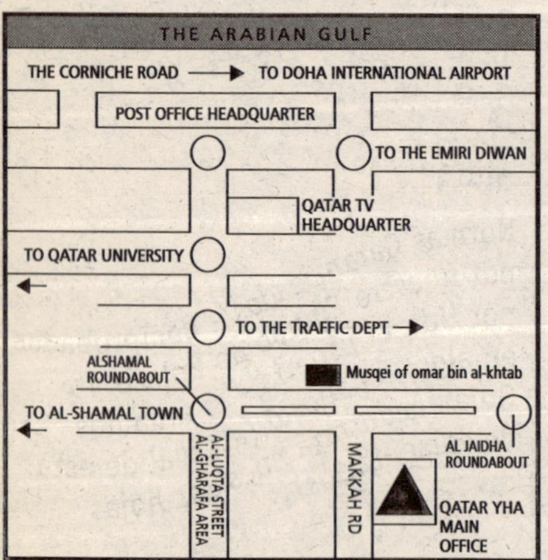

HOSTELLING INTERNATIONAL

▲ There for everyone - young, not so young and those in the middle.▲

▲ c'est pour tout le monde -les jeunes, les moins jeunes et tous les autres.▲

▲ albergues para todos - los jóvenes, los menos jóvenes y los jóvenes de espíritu.▲

▲ für jederman - ob jung, nicht mehr ganz so jung oder die dazwischen.▲

Location/Address	Telephone No. Fax No.	Beds	Opening Dates	Facilities
▲ **Al-Jamilia** Al-Ahli Sports Club Building, Al-Jamilia Town.	☎ 672122	50	🗓	🅿 👤
▲ **Al-Shamal** Al-Shamal Sports Club Building, Al-Shamal Town.	☎ 731307	50	🗓	🅿 👤
▲ **Al-Wakra** YH, Al-Wakra Sports Club Building, Al-Wakra Town.	☎ 841010	50	🗓	🅿 👤
▲ **Doha** **Doha YH, Al-Lakta Makka Street.**	☎ 867180; 866402 ✆ 863968	60	🗓	🍴 Ⓡ 🅿 🗄 👤
▲ **Doha** Doha YH, Al-Murabaa. (Behind the Traffic Department Building)	☎ 863968	50	🗓	🅿 👤

HOSTELLING
INTERNATIONAL

use International Communications Network (ICN) at major hostels to send and receive e-mail, set up e-mail box, send faxes, make International phone calls, surf the Web – all at low, low prices using the ICN Communications Card

Utilisez le Réseau International de Communication (ICN), dans nos plus grandes auberges pour envoyer et recevoir du courrier électronique, ouvrir une boîte à lettres électronique, transmettre des fax, appeler l'étranger, surfer sur l'internet – le tout à prix très très concurrentiels, grâce à la Carte de Communication ICN

benutzen Sie das International Communications Network (ICN) in Hauptherbergen, um e-mail zu senden und zu empfangen, e-mail Briefkästen einzurichten, Faxe zu schicken, international zu telefonieren oder "Surf the Net" – und das alles mit der ICN Kommunikationskarte zu günstigsten Preisen!

utilice la Red Internacional de Comunicaciones ICN en los principales albergues para transmitir y recibir mensajes electrónicos, establecer un buzón de correo electrónico, enviar facsímiles, realizar llamadas telefónicas internacionales, navegar por la red de Internet – todo a precios muy, muy económicos – mediante la Tarjeta de Comunicación ICN.

HOSTELLING INTERNATIONAL

Make your credit card bookings at these centres
Réservez par cartes de crédit aux centres suivants
Buchen Sie mit Kreditkarte in folgenden Buchungszentren
Reserve por tarjeta de crédito en los siguientes centros

English

Australia	☎ (2) 9261 1111
Canada	☎ (800) 663 5777
England & Wales	☎ (1629) 581 418
France	☎ (1) 44 89 87 27
Northern Ireland	☎ (1232) 324 733
Republic of Ireland	☎ (1) 830 1766
New Zealand	☎ (9) 303 9524
Scotland	☎ (541) 553 255
Switzerland	☎ (1) 360 1414
USA	☎ (202) 783 6161

Français

Angleterre & Pays de Galles	☎ (1692) 581 418
Australie	☎ (2) 9261 1111
Canada	☎ (800) 663 5777
Écosse	☎ (541) 553 255
États-Unis	☎ (202) 783 6161
France	☎ (1) 44 89 87 27
Irlande du Nord	☎ (1232) 324 733
Nouvelle-Zélande	☎ (9) 303 9524
République d'Irlande	☎ (1) 830 1766
Suisse	☎ (1) 360 1414

Deutsch

Australien	☎ (2) 9261 1111
England & Wales	☎ (1629) 581 418
Frankreich	☎ (1) 44 89 87 27
Irland	☎ (1) 830 1766
Kanada	☎ (800) 663 5777
Neuseeland	☎ (9) 303 9524
Nordirland	☎ (1232) 324 733
Schottland	☎ (541) 553 255
Schweiz	☎ (1) 360 1414
USA	☎ (202) 783 6161

Español

Australia	☎ (2) 9261 1111
Canadá	☎ (800) 663 5777
Escocia	☎ (541) 553 255
Estados Unidos	☎ (202) 783 6161
Francia	☎ (1) 44 89 87 27
Inglaterra y Gales	☎ (1629) 581 418
Irlanda del Norte	☎ (1232) 324 733
Nueva Zelanda	☎ (9) 303 9524
República de Irlanda	☎ (1) 830 1766
Suiza	☎ (1) 360 1414

Saudi Arabia

ARABIE SAOUDITE
SAUDI-ARABIEN
ARABIA SAUDI

**Saudi Arabian Youth Hostels Association
Alshehab Alghassni St. Alnmouzajiyah District,
North Almurabb'h, Riyadh 11451,
Kingdom of Saudi Arabia.**

**☎ (966) (1) 4055552, 4051478
TX 406560 SAYHAR SJ
🖷 (966) (1) 4021079**

A copy of the Hostel Directory for this Country can be obtained from:
The National Office.

Capital:	Riyadh	Population:	16,929,294
Language:	Arabic	Size:	2,240,000 sq km
Currency:	SR (Saudi riyal)		

Saudi Arabia

English

SAUDI ARABIAN HOSTELS

Youth Hostels in Saudi Arabia are always for one sex only, but that is the culture of the country. They have excellent sports facilities, including swimming pools and gymnasia.

Expect to pay in the region of 8.00 SR for over 20s or 6.00 SR for under 20s for an overnight. Add about 30.00 SR per day for full board.

NOTE: HOSTELS LISTED ARE FOR MALES ONLY. Separate information on female hostels is available from the national office.

PASSPORTS AND VISAS

A visa is necessary for entry into Saudi Arabia.

HEALTH

An international health card is essential.

BANKING HOURS

08.00-12.00hrs and 16.00-20.00hrs.

POST OFFICES

08.00-17.00hrs.

SHOPPING HOURS

08.00-23.00hrs.

TRAVEL

Rail
Only a local rail network is available.

Bus
Public transport available.

Driving
A valid driver's licence is required.

TELEPHONE INFORMATION

Country Code	966
Main City Area Codes	
Jeddah	2
Riyadh	1
Dammam	3

Français

AUBERGES DE JEUNESSE SAOUDIENNES

Les auberges de jeunesse d'Arabie Saoudite ne sont jamais mixtes, en vue de la culture de ce pays. Elles ont d'excellentes installations sportives, y compris des piscines et des gymnases.

Une nuit vous coûtera environ 8 RLAS pour les personnes de plus de 20 ans et 6 RLAS pour les moins de 20 ans. Pour la pension complète, ajoutez environ 30 RLAS par jour.

REMARQUE: LES AUBERGES FIGURANT SUR LA LISTE SONT POUR HOMMES UNIQUEMENT. Pour tout renseignement sur les auberges pour femmes, s'adresser au bureau national.

PASSEPORTS ET VISAS

Les visas sont nécessaires pour entrer en Arabie Saoudite.

SOINS MEDICAUX

Les cartes de santé internationales sont obligatoires.

HEURES D'OUVERTURE DES BANQUES

Les banques sont ouvertes de 8h à 12h et de 16h à 20h.

BUREAUX DE POSTE

Les bureaux de poste sont ouverts de 8h à 17h.

HEURES D'OUVERTURE DES MAGASINS

Les magasins sont ouverts de 8h à 23h.

DÉPLACEMENTS

Trains

Il n'existe qu'un réseau ferroviaire local.

Bus

Transport en commun également disponible.

Automobiles

Un permis de conduire valide est nécessaire.

TELEPHONE

Indicatif du Pays 966

Indicatifs régionaux des Villes principales

Djedda	2
Riad	1
Dammam	3

Deutsch

SAUDI-ARABISCHE JUGENDHERBERGEN

Wie es der Kultur des Landes entspricht, sind die Jugendherbergen in Saudi-Arabien immer nach Geschlechtern getrennt. Sie verfügen über ausgezeichnete Sportanlagen, wie z.B. Schwimmbäder und Turnhallen.

Wer über 20 Jahre alt ist, muß mit einem Übernachtungspreis von ca. 8,00 SR rechnen, während Jugendliche unter 20 Jahren ca. 6,00 SR bezahlen. Für Vollpension gibt es eine Gebühr von 30,00 SR pro Tag.

ZUR BEACHTUNG: DIE AUFGEFÜHRTEN JUGENDHERBERGEN NEHMEN NUR MÄNNER AUF. Die Landesgeschäftsstelle erteilt Auskunft über Jugendherbergen, die Frauen aufnehmen.

PÄSSE UND VISA

Für die Einreise nach Saudi-Arabien braucht man ein Visum.

GESUNDHEIT

Es wird ein internationaler Gesundheitsausweis verlangt.

GESCHÄFTSSTUNDEN DER BANKEN

08.00-12.00 Uhr und 16.00-20.00 Uhr.

POSTÄMTER

08.00-17.00 Uhr.

LADENÖFFNUNGSZEITEN

08.00-23.00 Uhr.

REISEN

Eisenbahn

Es gibt nur ein örtliches Schienennetz.

Busse

Öffentliche Verkehrsmittel stehen zur Verfügung.

Autofahren

Man braucht einen gültigen Führerschein.

FERNSPRECHINFORMATIONEN

Landes-Kennzahl 966

größere Städte - Ortsnetzkennzahlen

Djidda	2
Riad	1
Dammam	3

Español

ALBERGUES DE JUVENTUD SAUDIES

Los albergues de juventud de Arabia Saudí son sólo para hombres o sólo para mujeres, pero esa es la cultura de todo el país. Tienen excelentes instalaciones deportivas, incluyendo piscinas y gimnasios.

El precio es de alrededor de 8,00 SR para mayores de 20 años y 6,00 SR para menores de 20 años por noche. La pensión completa cuesta unos 30,00 SR más por día.

NOTA: LOS ALBERGUES QUE FIGURAN EN LA LISTA SON SOLO PARA HOMBRES. Para información sobre albergues para mujeres, diríjase a la oficina nacional.

PASAPORTES Y VISADOS

Se requiere visado para entrar en Arabia Saudí.

SANIDAD

Es imprescindible una tarjeta internacional de salud.

HORARIO DE BANCOS

De 08.00 a 12.00 horas y de 16.00 a 20.00 horas.

OFICINAS DE CORREOS

De 08.00 a 17,00 horas.

HORARIO COMERCIAL

De 08.00 a 23.00 horas.

DESPLAZAMIENTOS

Tren

Sólo existe una red ferroviaria local.

Autobús

Existe un servicio de transporte público.

Coche

Se necesita un permiso de conducir válido.

INFORMACION TELEFONICA

Código Nacional 966
Prefijos de las Ciudades Principales
   Yidda 2
   Ryad 1
   Dammam 3

HOSTELLING
INTERNATIONAL

There for everyone - young, not so young and those in the middle.

c'est pour tout le monde -les jeunes, les moins jeunes et tous les autres.

albergues para todos - los jóvenes, los menos jóvenes y los jóvenes de espíritu.

für jederman - ob jung, nicht mehr ganz so jung oder die dazwischen.

Riyadh

Riyadh YH,
PO Box 2359,
Riyadh 11451,
West King Fahd Rd,
Opposite New Passport Building,
Alshehab Alghassanist.
📞 (1) 4055552, 4051478
📠 (1) 4051376

Open Dates:	
Open Hours:	07.00-23.30hrs
Reservations:	**R**
Price Range:	SR 6-8
Beds:	270 - 4x¹ 2x² 20x³ 36x⁴ 4x⁶⁺
Facilities:	

Directions:

✈	Kjng Khalid International 40km
🚉	Riyadh 7km
🚌	#7 & #8 50m

Attractions:

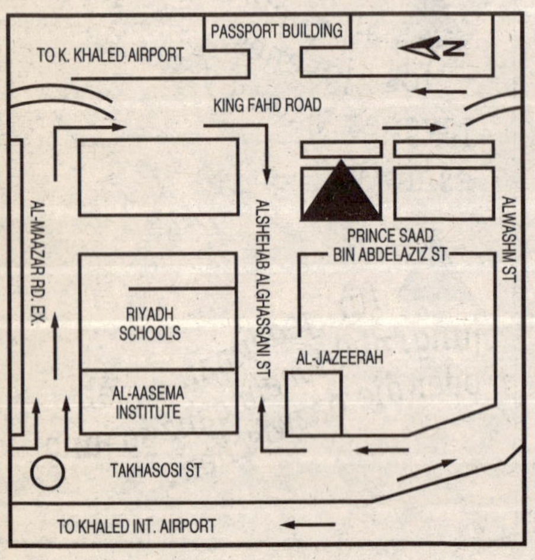

Assured Standards – visited by our Liaison team and by you the guest – tell us when we don't measure up (reply slips at the end of this Guide) ►

des Normes Garanties, par les visites de notre Equipe de Liaison et par vous, les usagers – faites-le nous savoir quand nous ne sommes pas à la hauteur (Fiches-commentaires à la fin du Guide) ►

Zugesicherte Standards – beurteilt von unserem Liaison Team und von Ihnen, unserem Gast – sagen Sie es uns, wenn wir Sie enttäuschen (Antwortkarten hinten im Führer) ►

Normas Garantizadas – comprobadas por nuestro Equipo de Enlace y por Ud., el usuario – si fallamos en algo, díganoslo (al final de esta Guía encontrará nuestras hojas de comentarios) ►

Location/Address	Telephone No. / Fax No.	Beds	Opening Dates	Facilities
△ *Albahah Area* *Albahah YH, PO Box 652, Sporting City, Albahah,* *Alaqeeq Rd, Albahah.*	☎ (7) 7250732, 7250368 🖶 (7) 7251988	*120*	🈵	
▲ **Aljouf Area** Sakaka-Aljouf YH, PO Box 211, Sakaka Kingfahd St (Almwasalat), Aljouf.	☎ (4) 6241883 🖶 (4) 6248341	70	🈵	
△ *Alkharj Governorate* *YH, PO Box 521, Military Base Rd,* *Next to Sporting Sho'la Club Stadium, Alkharj.*	☎ (1) 5485545 🖶 (1) 5485765	75	🈵	
▲ **Almadinah Area** YH, Prince Moh Bin Abdelaziz Sporting City, Alaziziyyah District, Almadinah.	☎ (4) 8474092 🖶 (4) 8474244	150	🈵	
▲ **Almajma'h Governorate** YH, PO Box 179, Sporting City - the Main Rd, Almajma'h.	☎ (6) 4323028 🖶 (6) 4321675	65	🈵	
▲ **Alqasseem Area** - Buraidah - Alqaseem YH, PO Box 949, Prince Abdallah Bin Abdelaziz Sporting City, Braidah, Alsafraa, Alqasseem.	☎ (6) 3812361 🖶 (6) 3813007	180	🈵	
△ *Arrass Governorate* *YH, 1986, Northern Alshifa-Riyadh Rd.*	☎ (6) 3333315 🖶 (6) 3336387	*50*	🈵	
▲ **Aseer Area** - Abha YH, PO Box 182, Prince Sultan Bin Abdelaziz Sporting City, Almahalah, Abha.	☎ (7) 2270503 🖶 (7) 2270503	150	🈵	
▲ **Eastern Area** - Dammam YH, PO Box 2822, Dammam 31461, Dammam.-Khobar Rd, adjacent to Gymnasium.	☎ (3) 8575358, 8575384 🖶 (3) 8579524	200	🈵	
▲ **Eastern Area** - Alahsa Governorate YH, Prince Abdallah Bin Galawi Sporting City, Alkhalidiyyah District, Hufuf, Alahsa.	☎ (3) 5800028 🖶 (3) 5800692	120	🈵	
▲ **Hail Area** YH, Prince Abdelaziz Bin Musaed Bin Galawi Sporting City, Hail: airport district.	☎ (6) 5325734 🖶 (6) 5331485	120	🈵	
▲ **Jazan Area** - Jazan YH, 1981, PO Box 319, Jazan Sporting City, Prince Abdullah Rd, Jizan.	☎ (7) 3221875, 3170954 🖶 (7) 3221646	65	🈵	
▲ **Jeddah Governorate** YH, PO Box 8486, Jeddah 21482, Makkah Rd, K7 West Stadium, Jeddah.	☎ (2) 6886632, 6886692 🖶 (2) 6887112	200	🈵	
▲ **Makkah Area** - Makkah YH, 1979, PO Box 5403 King Abdelaziz Sporting City-Al-Sharai, Old Taif Rd, Opposite Jo'ranah Bridge, Makkah.	☎ (2) 5240414 🖶 (2) 5240966	135	🈵	
△ *Najran Area* - *Najran* *YH, 1982, PO Box 155, Alfaisaliyyah,* *Opposite Najran Secondary School, Najran.*	☎ (7) 5222433, 5221668 🖶 (7) 5225019	*60*	🈵	

Location/Address	Telephone No. Fax No.	Beds	Opening Dates	Facilities
▲ **Riyadh** **Riyadh YH, PO Box 2359, Riyadh 11451,** **West King Fahd Rd, Opposite** **New Passport Building, Alshehab Alghassanist.**	☎ (1) 4055552, 4051478 🖷 (1) 4051376	270	🗓	⑩ Ⓡ ♿ ☕ Ⓟ 🗄 ⚲
△ *Shaqraa Governorate* *YH, Al Rowdah District, Alarbaeen St,* *West Alwashm Club, Shaqraa.*	☎ (01) 6220200 🖷 (01) 6220200	50	🗓	⑩ ☕ Ⓟ 🗄 ⚲
▲ **Tabouk Area** - Tabouk YH, King Fahd Sporting City, Amman Rd, Tabouk.	☎ (4) 4226308 🖷 (4) 4221668	50	🗓	⑩ ☕ Ⓟ 🗄 ⚲
▲ **Taif Governorate** YH, King Fahd Sporting City, Hawiyyah, Taif.	☎ (2) 7252000, 7253400 🖷 (2) 7253400	160	🗓	⑩ ☕ Ⓟ 🗄 ⚲

SUPPLEMENTARY ACCOMMODATION
OUTSIDE THE ASSURED STANDARDS SCHEME

| **Algateef** - Algateef Governorate
 Algateef Sport City, Eastern Area | ☎ (03) 8360900
 🖷 (03) 8361008 | 60 | 🗓 | ⑩ Ⓡ ♿ ☕
 Ⓟ 🗄 ☕ ⚲ |

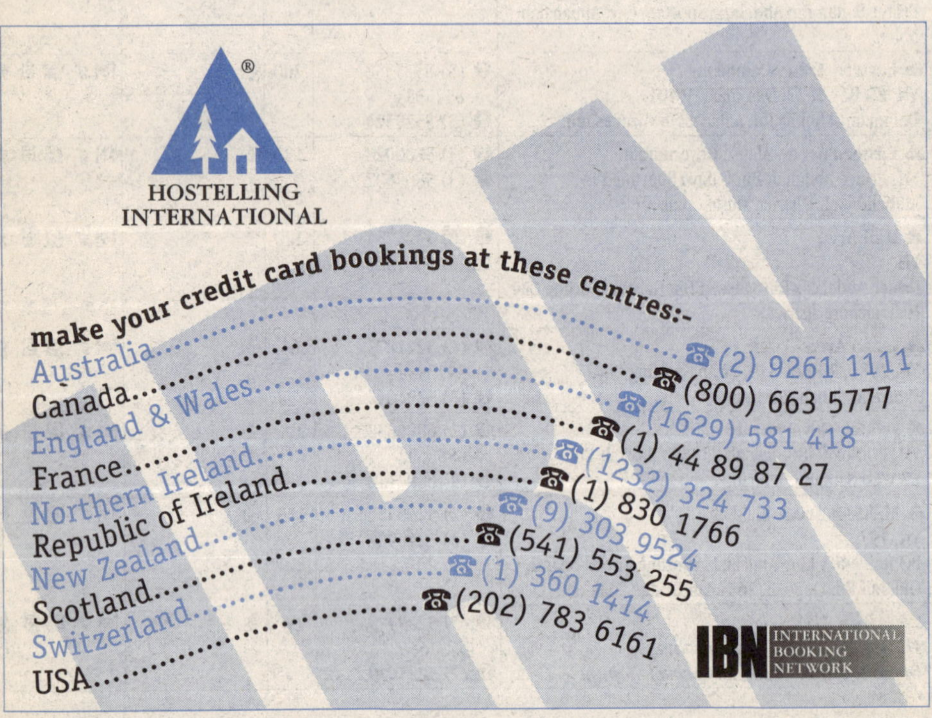

South Africa

SOUTH AFRICA

AFRIQUE DU SUD

SÜDAFRIKA

SURAFRICA

HOSTELLING INTERNATIONAL

**Hostelling International-South Africa,
PO Box 4402, Cape Town 8000, South Africa.**

Head Office Address: 3rd Floor, St. Georges House, 73 St. Georges Mall,
Cape Town 8001, South Africa.

- ☎ (27) (21) 424-2511
- ✆ (27) (21) 424-4119
- **E-mail:** info@hisa.org.za
- **WWW address:** http://www.hisa.org.za

A copy of the Hostel Directory for this Country can be obtained from:
The National Office.

**IBN Booking Centres for outward
bookings**

- **Cape Town**, *via National Office
  above*.
- **Durban** - Africa Wonderland
  Tours,19 Smith St, Durban.
  - ☎ (31) 3324944
  - ✆ (31) 3324551
- **Johannesburg** - Africa Wonderland
  Tours,4 College St, 2094 Fairview,
  Johannesburg.
  - ☎ (11) 6148743
  - ✆ (11) 6142823

Capitals:	Cape Town - Legislative: Pretoria - Administrative: Bloemfontein - Judicial

Language:	English/Afrikaans/ Zulu/Xhosa
Currency:	Rand
Population:	37,859,000
Size:	1,127,200 sq km

South Africa

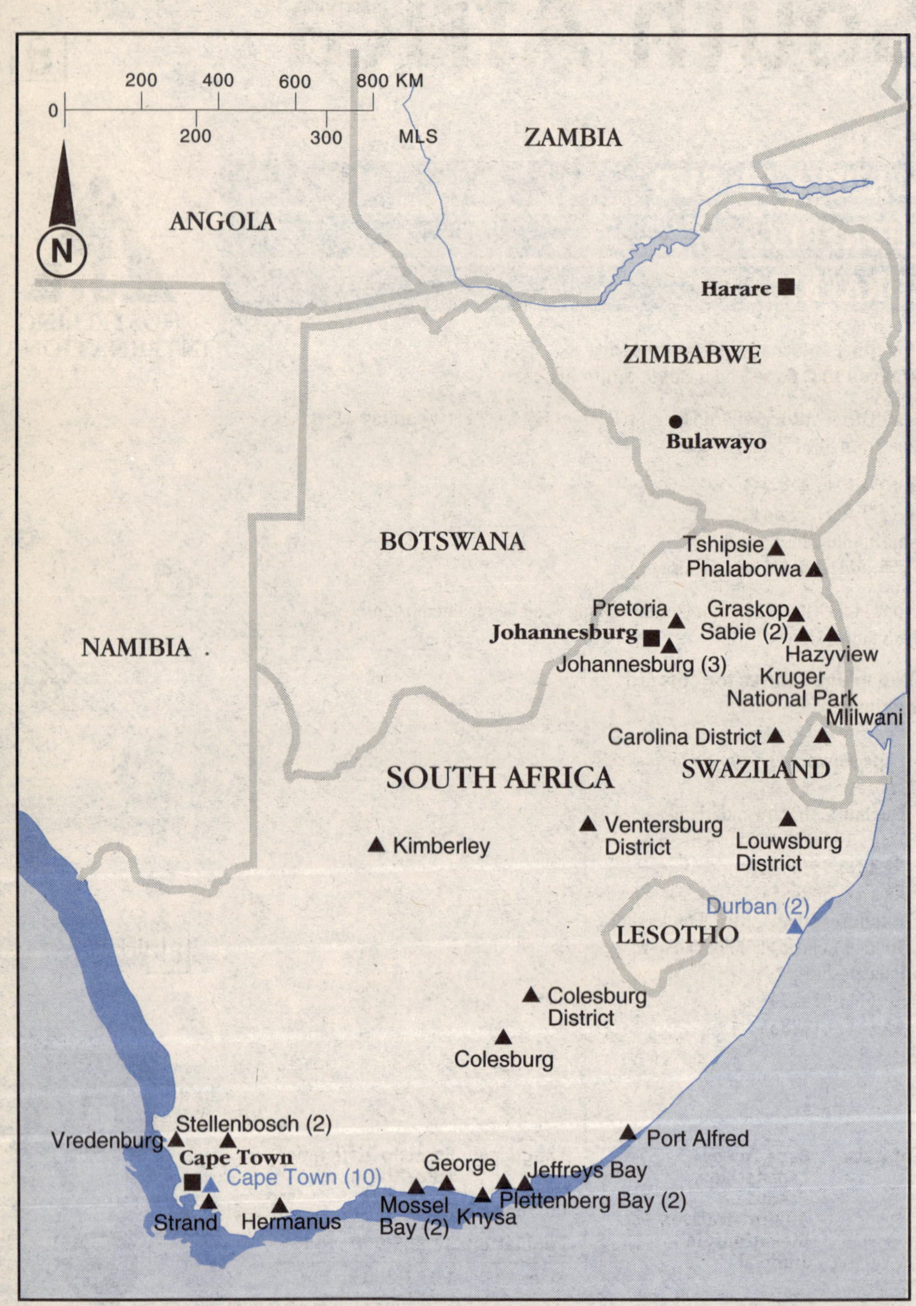

English

SOUTH AFRICAN HOSTELS

South Africa offers a unique opportunity to view the culture, as well as the beautiful scenery of this country first hand.

Hostel reception hours vary but all hostels have 24hr access. All have well equipped self-catering facilities and a few may provide meals, check with individual hostel entry. Prices range from R 35.00-150.00 per night depending on size of room, excluding bedding.

Booking is advisable during the high season, November-February and during school holidays. Book via the International Booking Network (IBN) or the Central Booking Office:
☎ (27) (21) 424 4119;
E-mail: reservations@hisa.org.za

PASSPORTS AND VISAS

Check with the South African Consulate or Embassy in your own country for details of passport and visa requirements.

HEALTH

Visitors to the Kruger National Park and bush areas are advised to take anti-malaria medication, before, during and after their visit. Medicines are sold at pharmacies which are open until approximately 20.00hrs in the major cities. Doctors consulting rooms are generally open 08.00-17.00hrs. Check with your hostel manager. If you are admitted to hospital you will be asked to pay up front unless you are a resident with full medical cover. You are strongly advised to take out adequate medical insurance cover before travelling to South Africa.

BANKING HOURS

Monday to Friday 09.00-15.30hrs and Saturday 09.00-11.00hrs.

POST OFFICES

Monday to Friday 08.00-16.30hrs and Saturday 08.00-12.00hrs.

TRAVEL

Air
All major cities and towns are served by domestic flights (SA Airways, British Airways, Comair, SA Express, Sun Air and SA Airlink). International airports at Johannesburg, Cape Town and Durban.

Rail
Trains operate between main cities and towns. The distance between centres is great but it is a reasonably inexpensive way to travel.

Bus
There is a large network of services linking all main cities and towns. Translux Express offer excellent backpacker travel passes based on the number of kilometres travelled, which are available directly from HISA or YHA Travel outlets.

Driving
Driving is on the left side of the road. An international driving licence is essential. Highways and roads are excellent and clearly marked. Wearing of seat bealts is compulsory. Speed limit is 60kmph in city centres and suburbs/highways 120kmph.

TELEPHONE INFORMATION

Country Code	**27**
Main City Area Codes	
Johannesburg	**11**
Pretoria	**12**
Cape Town	**21**
Durban	**31**
Port Elizabeth	**41**

When dialling within South Africa dial "0" before area code.

SOUTH AFRICA • AFRIQUE DU SUD

Français

AUBERGES DE JEUNESSE SUDAFRICAINES

Les Auberges de Jeunesse Sudafricaines vous offrent une occasion unique de découvrir de première main la culture de ce pays ainsi que la beauté de ses paysages.

Les heures d'accueil des auberges sont variables mais toutes les auberges sont ouvertes toute la journée. Elles sont toutes bien équipées pour permettre aux voyageurs de cuisiner et certaines servent des repas; reportez-vous au paragraphe consacré à chaque auberge. Une nuit vous coûtera, selon la taille des chambres, entre 35 et 150 R, draps non-compris.

Il est conseillé de réserver pendant la pleine saison, de novembre à février et pendant les vacances scolaires.

Réservez par IBN, le Réseau International de Réservation, ou par fax, en contactant la centrale de réservation au

❶ (27) (21) 424-4119 ou par **e-mail:** reservations@hisa.org.za.

PASSEPORTS ET VISAS

Pour savoir si vous devez vous munir d'un passeport ou d'un visa, adressez-vous au Consulat ou à l'Ambassade d'Afrique du Sud dans votre pays.

SOINS MEDICAUX

Il est conseillé aux voyageurs se rendant au parc national Kruger de prendre des médicaments contre la malaria avant, pendant et après leur visite. Les médicaments sont en vente dans les pharmacies qui sont ouvertes jusqu'à environ 20h00 dans les grandes villes. Les cabinets médicaux sont en principe ouverts de 8h00 à 17h00. Renseignez-vous auprès du directeur d'auberge. Si vous êtes admis à l'hôpital, vous devrez payer d'avance à moins d'être résident et

de bénéficier d'une couverture médicale complète. Il est fortement recommandé de souscrire à une police d'assurance-santé adéquate avant de vous rendre en Afrique du Sud.

HEURES D'OUVERTURE DES BANQUES

Les banques sont ouvertes du lundi au vendredi de 9h à 15h30, et le samedi de 9h à 11h.

BUREAUX DE POSTE

Les bureaux de poste sont ouverts du lundi au vendredi de 8h à 16h30, et le samedi de 8h à 12h.

DEPLACEMENTS

Avions

Toutes les grandes villes et les villes moyennes sont desservies par des vols intérieurs (S.A. Airways, British Airways, Comair, S.A. Express, Sun Air et SA Airlink). Il y a des aéroports internationaux à Johannesburg, à Durban et au Cap.

Trains

Les grandes villes et les villes moyennes sont reliées par un réseau ferroviaire. Malgré les grandes distances, le train offre la possibilité de voyager relativement économiquement.

Autobus

Le pays dispose d'un vaste réseau, qui relie la plupart des grandes villes et villes moyennes. Translux Express offre d'excellentes cartes-forfaits pour routards, qui sont basées sur le nombre de kilomètres parcourus et qui sont disponibles auprès des bureaux de HISA ou des points de ventes YHA Travel.

Automobiles

La conduite est à gauche. Les permis de conduire internationaux sont obligatoires. Les routes et autoroutes sont excellentes et très bien signalisées. Le port de la ceinture de sécurité est obligatoire. Les limitations de vitesse sont de

60km/h dans les centres-villes et en banlieue et de 120km/h sur les autoroutes.

TELEPHONE

Indicatif du Pays   **27**
Indicatifs régionaux des Villes principales
 Johannesburg **11**
 Pretoria   **12**
 Le Cap   **21**
 Durban   **31**
 Port Elizabeth **41**

Pour téléphoner à l'intérieur du pays, ajoutez un zéro devant l'indicatif régional.

Deutsch

JUGENDHERBERGEN IN SÜDAFRIKA

Südafrika bietet eine einmalige Gelegenheit zum Kennenlernen der Kultur und der wunderschönen Landschaft.

Die Öffnungszeiten sind unterschiedlich, aber alle Jugendherbergen sind 24 Stunden am Tag geöffnet. Alle verfügen über Einrichtungen für Selbstversorger, und in einigen werden auch Mahlzeiten angeboten. Bitte erkundigen Sie sich bei der Herberge. Die Preise liegen zwischen R 35,00 und R 150,00 pro Nacht ausschließlich Bettwäsche, je nach der Größe des Zimmers.

In der Hochsaison, November - Februar, und während der Schulferien ist eine Voranmeldung erforderlich.

Reservieren Sie einen Platz durch IBN oder das zentrale Buchungsbüro unter
ⓕ (27)(21)424-4119 oder
e-mail: reservations@hisa.org.za

PÄSSE UND VISA

Erkundigen Sie sich nach den Paß- und Visumsvorschriften beim Südafrikanischen Konsulat oder bei der Südafrikanischen Botschaft in Ihrem Land.

GESUNDHEIT

Wer den Kruger National Park und Busch Gebiete besucht, sollte vor, während und nach seinem Besuch Antimalariamittel nehmen. Apotheken verkaufen Medikamente und im allgemeinen sind sie bis 20.00 Uhr in den größeren Städten geöffnet. Ärztliche Sprechstunden sind normalerweise von 08.00-17.00 Uhr. Bitte erkundigen Sie sich bei den Herbergseltern. Wenn Sie in ein Krankenhaus gehen müssen, müssen Sie sofort dafür bezahlen, sofern Sie nicht ein Einwohner mit Krankenversicherung sind. Es empfiehlt sich, vor der Abreise nach Südafrika, eine Versicherung abzuschließen.

GESCHÄFTSSTUNDEN DER BANKEN

Montags bis freitags von 09.00-15.30 Uhr und samstags von 09.00-11.00 Uhr.

POSTÄMTER

Montags bis freitags von 08.00-16.30 Uhr und samstags von 08.00-12.00 Uhr.

REISEN

Flugverkehr
Inlandsflüge gibt es in alle größeren Städten (S.A. Airways, British Airways, Comair, SA Express, Sun Air und SA Airlink). In Johannesburg, Durban und Kapstadt gibt es einen internationalen Flughafen.

Eisenbahn
Zwischen größeren Städten gibt es einen Zugverkehr. Die Entfernungen sind sehr groß, aber die Eisenbahn ist relativ billig.

Busse
Busse verkehren zwischen allen großen Städten auf verschiedenen Routen. Translux Express bietet ausgezeichnete Backpacker Pässe, die an der Anzahl der Kilometer basiert sind, und direkt von HISA oder YHA Travel Outlets erhältlich sind.

Autofahren
Es herrscht Linksverkehr. Man braucht einen

internationalen Führerschein. Die Straßen sind ausgezeichnet und deutlich beschildert. Man muß immer einen Sicherheitsgurt tragen. Die Geschwindigkeitsbegrenzung ist 60 Km/ph in Stadtzentren und Vororten und 120 Km/ph auf den Autobahnen.

FERNSPRECHINFORMATIONEN

Landes-Kennzahl	**27**

größere Städte - Ortsnetzkennzahlen

Johannesburg	**11**
Pretoria	**12**
Kapstadt	**21**
Durban	**31**
Port Elizabeth	**41**

Innerhalb Südafrikas ist vor der Ortsnetzkennzahl eine "0" zu wählen.

Español

ALBERGUES JUVENILES SUDAFRICANOS

Africa del Sur le ofrece una ocasión única de descubrir Ud. mismo la cultura de este país, así como sus maravillosos paisajes.

El horario de recepción de los albergues varía, pero todos están abiertos las 24 horas del día. Todos están bien equipados para cocinar uno mismo y algunos sirven comidas, lo cual está indicado en la información sobre cada albergue en particular. Los precios oscilan entre 35 y 150 rands por noche, según el tamaño de la habitación, y no incluyen la ropa de cama.

Se recomienda reservar con antelación durante la temporada alta, es decir, de diciembre a febrero, y durante las vacaciones escolares. Reserve a través de la Red Internacional de Reservas (IBN) o de la Oficina Central de Reservas por:

🕿 (27) (21) 424-4119 o por
e-mail: reservations@hisa.org.za.

PASAPORTES Y VISADOS

Infórmese en la embajada o consulado de Sudáfrica de su país sobre los requisitos relativos a pasaportes y visados.

ASISTENCIA MEDICA

Se recomienda a quienes deseen visitar el parque natural de Kruger y zonas montesas se mediquen contra la malaria antes, durante y después de su estancia. Se pueden comprar medicinas en las farmacias, las cuales están abiertas hasta las 20 h. aproximadamente en las grandes ciudades. Los consultorios médicos están generalmente abiertos de 8 h. a 17 h. Confírmelo con el director del albergue. Si necesita ingresar en un hospital, le exigirán que pague por adelantado a menos que Ud. sea residente con derecho a asistencia médica. Por lo tanto, le recomendamos se haga un seguro de enfermedad adecuado antes de viajar a Sudáfrica.

HORARIO DE LOS BANCOS

De lunes a viernes de 9 h. a 15.30 h. y los sábados de 9 h. a 11 h.

OFICINAS DE CORREOS

De lunes a viernes de 8 h. a 16.30 h. y los sábados de 8 h. a 12 h.

DESPLAZAMIENTOS

Avión

Todas las principales ciudades del país están unidas por vuelos nacionales (SA Airways, British Airways, Comair, SA Express, Sun Air y SA Airlink). Los aeropuertos internacionales están en Johannesburgo, Durbán y Ciudad del Cabo.

Tren

Las grandes ciudades y poblaciones más importantes están enlazadas por una red de ferrocarriles. A pesar de que las distancias son grandes, el tren es un modo de transporte bastante económico.

Autobús

Existe una extensa red de servicios que enlazan las ciudades y poblaciones más importantes. Translux Express ofrece abonos para mochileros basados en el kilometraje recorrido. Estos se pueden conseguir directamente en las oficinas de HISA y en los puntos de ventas de YHA Travel.

Automóvil

Se conduce por la izquierda. Es obligatorio poseer un permiso de conducir internacional. Las autopistas y carreteras son excelentes y están muy bien señalizadas. Es obligatorio ponerse el cinturón de seguridad. Los límites de velocidad son de 60 km/h. en el centro de las ciudades y zonas residenciales, y de 120 km/h. en las autopistas.

INFORMACION TELEFONICA

Código Nacional	**27**
Prefijos de las Ciudades Principales	
Johannesburgo	**11**
Pretoria	**12**
Ciudad del Cabo	**21**
Durbán	**31**
Puerto Elizabeth	**41**

Para hacer llamadas dentro de Sudáfrica, marque un "0" antes del prefijo.

Discounts And Concessions

Special backpacker tours and travel passes available from HISA national office in Cape Town or HISA Agents worldwide. Special discounts and concessions available to every hosteller booking via the International Booking Network (IBN) or booking any one of HISA'S special travel related tours and packages.

Discounts include overland safaris, restaurants, boat trips, pony treks and much more. Contact HISA

ℹ (27) (21) 424 4119

E-mail: info@hisa.org.za for your nearest Agent.

Assured Standards – visited by our Liaison team and by you the guest – tell us when we don't measure up (reply slips at the end of this Guide) ▶

des Normes Garanties, par les visites de notre Equipe de Liaison et par vous, les usagers – faites-le nous savoir quand nous ne sommes pas à la hauteur (Fiches-commentaires à la fin du Guide) ◀

Zugesicherte Standards – beurteilt von unserem Liaison Team und von Ihnen, unserem Gast – sagen Sie es uns, wenn wir Sie enttäuschen (Antwortkarten hinten im Führer) ▶

Normas Garantizadas – comprobadas por nuestro Equipo de Enlace y por Ud., el usuario – si fallamos en algo, díganoslo (al final de esta Guía encontrará nuestras hojas de comentarios) ◀

Cape Town - Ashanti Lodge

11 Hof St Gardens,
Cape Town 8001,
Western Cape.
☎ (21) 4238721;(21) 4249832
✆ (21) 4238790

Open Dates:	9
Open Hours:	09.30-21.00hrs (access)
Reservations:	IBN CC
Price Range:	R45.00-150.00
Beds:	89 - 1x¹ 11x² 5x⁶ 4x⁶⁺
Facilities:	

Directions:	1.5 SW from city centre
✈	Cape Town International 20km
A🚌	To City Centre 1.5km
⛴	Cape Town Harbour 2km
🚂	Cape Town Central 1.5km
🚌	Oranjezicht bus from Adderley St 1.5km ap Mount Nelson Hotel 200m

Attractions: 🔍 🚴 ≈10m 🏊

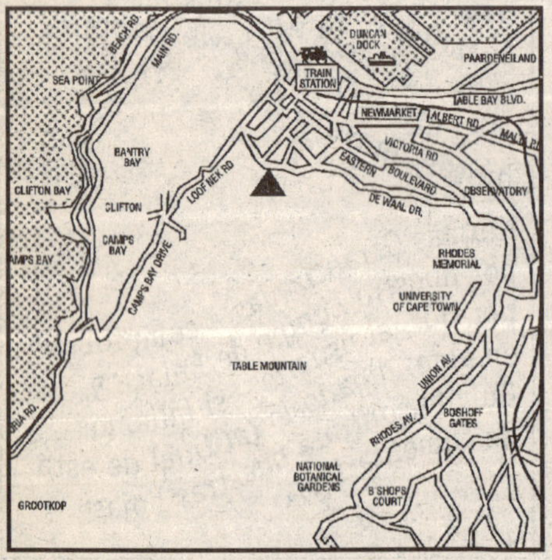

Cape Town - Zebra Crossing Backpackers Lodge

82 New Church St,
Cape Town 8001,
Western Cape.
☎ (21) 4221265;(21) 4239841
✆ (21) 4221265

Open Dates:	9
Open Hours:	08.00-20.00hrs (access)
Reservations:	IBN
Price Range:	R38.00-140.00
Beds:	60 - 4x¹ 10x² 2x⁶ 3x⁶⁺
Facilities:	

Directions:	1.5 SW from city centre
✈	Cape Town International 20km
A🚌	To City Centre 1.5km
⛴	Cape Town Harbour 2km
🚂	Cape Town Central 1.5km
🚌	Kloofnek bus from Adderley St 50m ap At stop no.68

Attractions: 🔍

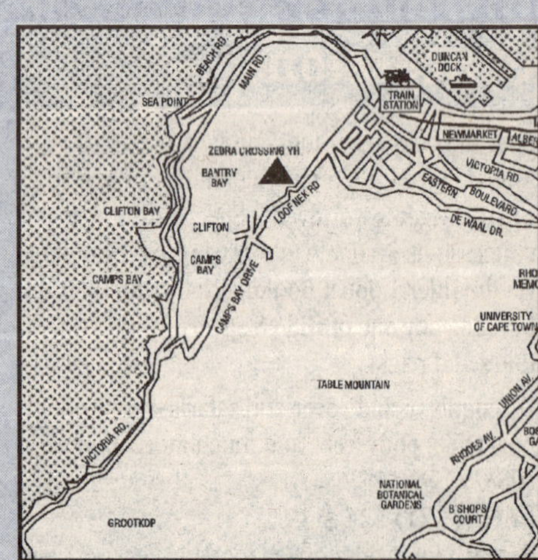

Durban - Tekweni Backpackers Hostel

169 Ninth Ave,
Morningside,
Durban 4001,
Kwazulu/Natal.
☎ (31) 3031433, (31) 3033339 (Guests)
🖷 (31) 3034369

Open Dates:	
Open Hours:	08.00-24.00hrs (access)
Price Range:	R42.00-110.00
Beds:	46 - 2x² 4x⁶ 2x⁶
Facilities:	
Directions:	4N from city centre
✈	Durban International 20km
A🚌	To City Centre 4km
⛴	Durban 5km
🚂	Durban Central 3km
🚌	Mitchell Park; Musgrave Rd; Mynah Bus ap Florida Rd opposite Hotel California 50m
Attractions:	

Johannesburg - Backpackers Ritz

1A North Rd,
Dunkeld West,
Johannesburg 2196,
Gauteng.
☎ (11) 3257125, (11) 3257379 (Guests)
🖷 (11) 3270233

Open Dates:	
Open Hours:	07.00-22.00hrs (access)
Reservations:	IBN CC
Price Range:	R40.00-140.00
Beds:	70 - 3x¹ 8x² 1x³ 3x⁶
Facilities:	
Directions:	
✈	Johannesburg International 32km
A🚌	To City Centre 7.5km
🚂	Johannesburg Park 7.5km
🚌	73, 80, 80b from Eloff St 7.5km ap Dunkeld West Shopping Centre 150m
Attractions:	

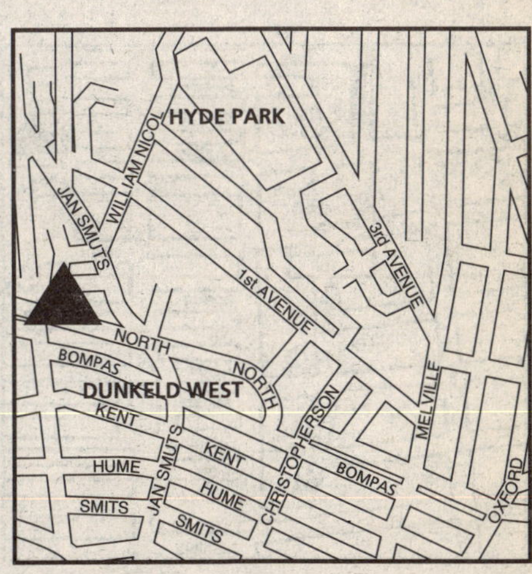

Knysna

Highfield Backpackers,
2 Graham St,
Knysna 6570,
Western Cape.
☎ (445) 826266
📠 (445) 24012

Open Dates:	🗓
Open Hours:	08.00-20.00hrs (🕐 access)
Price Range:	R35.00-100.00
Beds:	42 - 7x^2 1x^4 1x^6 2x^6
Facilities:	††† 2x††† �📶 (BD) ☞ ☕ ⌂ TV 📖

Directions:

✈	George 60km
A🚌	Direct to Hostel
🚂	Knysna 1.5km
🚌	Intercity bus 500m
Attractions:	🔍 🚴 🏃 ∪14km 🏊

Messina District - Tshipise Backpackers Lodge

(Aventura Eco Tshipise Resort,
just past Messina between the R525 and
R508),
P.O.Box 4,
Tshipise 0901,
Northern Province
☎ (15539) 624
📠 (15539) 724

Open Dates:	🗓
Open Hours:	07.00-20.00hrs (🕐 access)
Reservations:	⊡CC⊡
Price Range:	R35.00-100.00
Beds:	56 - 12x^2 6x^4
Facilities:	♿ ††† 6x††† 📶 ☞ ☕ ⌂ TV 1x
Attractions:	🌲 ⛺ 🏃 ∪ 🎣 🏊

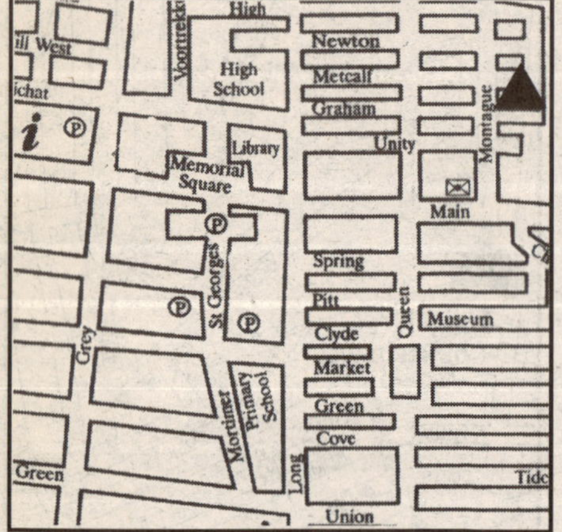

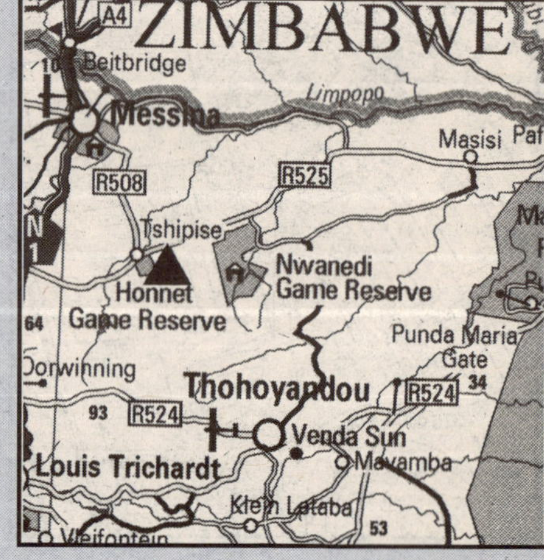

Location/Address	Telephone No. / Fax No.	Beds	Opening Dates	Facilities
▲ **Cape Town** - Abe Bailey [IBN] 11 Maynard Rd, Muizenburg, Cape Town 7945, Western Cape.	☎ (21) 7882301 7884283 (Guests) ✆ (21) 7882301	46	🗓9	♙ ⍾ 26S ⌕
▲ **Cape Town** - Albergo for Backpackers [IBN] 5 Beckham St, Cape Town 8001, Western Cape.	☎ (21) 4221849; (21) 239828 ✆ (21) 4230515	47	🗓9	♙ 1.5SW ⌕ P ⍿
▲ **Cape Town** - Ashanti Lodge [IBN] **11 Hof St Gardens, Cape Town 8001, Western Cape.**	☎ (21) 4238721; (21) 4249832 ✆ (21) 4238790	89	🗓9	♙ ⍾ 1.5SW CC ⌕ P ⍿ ☕
▲ **Cape Town** - Cloudbreak Backpackers Lodge [IBN] 219 Upper Buitenkant St, Cape Town 8001, Western Cape.	☎ (21) 4616892, (21) 455301 (Guests) ✆ (21) 4611458	46	🗓9	♙ 1.5SW ⌕ P ☕
▲ **Cape Town** - City Slickers 25 Rose St/Cnr Hout St, Cape Town 8001, Western Cape.	☎ (21) 4222357 ✆ (21) 4222355	48	🗓9	♙ 1W ⌕ ⍿ ☕
▲ **Cape Town** - Green Elephant Backpackers 57 Milton Rd, Observatory, Cape Town, 7925, Western Cape	☎ (21) 4486359 ✆ (21) 4486359	36	🗓9	♙ ⍾ 8S CC ⌕ ☕
△ *Cape Town - Overseas Visitors Club* *230 Upper Long St, Cape Town 8001, Western Cape.*	☎ *(21) 4246800;* *(21) 4239832* ✆ *(21) 4234870*	*18*	🗓9	1SE CC ⌕
▲ **Cape Town** - Stans Halt The Glen, Camps Bay, Cape Town 8001, Western Cape.	☎ (21) 4389037, 4381405 (Guests) ✆ (21) 4389037	30	🗓9	⍾ 5SW ⌕ P
▲ **Cape Town** - Riverview Backpackers 5 Anson Rd, Observatory, Cape Town 7925, Western Cape.	☎ (21) 4479056; (21) 4475936 ✆ (21) 4475192	60	🗓9	♙ ⍾ 8S CC ⌕ P ☕
▲ **Cape Town** - Zebra Crossing Backpackers Lodge [IBN] **82 New Church St, Cape Town 8001, Western Cape.**	☎ (21) 4221265; (21) 4239841 ✆ (21) 4221265	60	🗓9	♙ ⍾ 1.5SW ⌕ P ⍿ ☕
▲ **Carolina District** - Badplaas Backpackers (Aventura Spa Badplaas, just off the R38, Carolina District), P.O.Box 15, Badplaas 1190, Mpumalanga	☎ (17) 8441022 ✆ (17) 8441445	100	🗓9	♙ ⍾ ♿ CC ⌕ P ⍿ ☕
△ *Colesburg - Colesburg Backpackers* *39 Church St, Colesburg 9795, Northern Cape.*	☎ *(51) 7530582*	*30*	🗓9	♙ ⍾ ⌕ P ⍿
▲ **Colesburg District** - Midwaters Lodge Adventura Midwaters Resort, Pvt Bag X10, Gariep Dam 9922, Northern Cape.	☎ (051) 7540045 ✆ (051) 7540135	100	🗓9	⍾ ♿ CC ⌕ P ⍿ ☕
▲ **Durban** - Beach Hostel [IBN] 19 Smith St, Durban 4001, Kwazulu/Natal.	☎ (31) 3324945, 3682594 (Guests) ✆ (31) 3681720	60	🗓9	♙ CC ⌕ ⍿ ☕
▲ **Durban** - Tekweni Backpackers Hostel **169 Ninth Ave, Morningside, Durban 4001, Kwazulu/Natal.**	☎ (31) 3031433, (31) 3033339 (Guests) ✆ (31) 3034369	46	🗓9	4N ⌕ P ⍿ ☕

Location/Address	Telephone No. Fax No.	Beds	Opening Dates	Facilities
△ *George* - *Sunshine Backpackers* *103 Merriman Street, George 6530, Western Cape.*	☎ *(44) 8730424* ✆ *(44) 8730424*	20		👫 🚿 P
▲ **Graskop** - Canyon Backpackers (Aventura Elo Blydepoort, Blyde River, Canyon Nature Reserve, Graskop), Pvt. Bag X368, Ohrigstad 1122, Mpumalanga.	☎ (13) 7698005 ✆ (13) 7698059	70		👫 🍽 ♿ CC 🚿 P 🗄 ☕
△ *Hermanus* *Zoete Inval Backpackers, 23 Main Rd,* *Hermanus 7200, Western Cape.*	☎ *(283) 21242* ✆ *(283) 21242*	14		1W 🚿 P 🗄
▲ **Jeffreys Bay** Jeffreys Bay Backpackers, 12 Jeffrey St, Jeffreys Bay 6330, Eastern Cape.	☎ (423) 2931379; 2931021 ✆ (423) 961763	34		👫 🚿 P 🗄 ☕
▲ **Johannesburg** - Backpackers Ritz IBN **1A North Rd, Dunkeld West,** **Johannesburg 2196, Gauteng.**	☎ (11) 3257125, (11) 3257379 (Guests) ✆ (11) 3270233	70		👫 CC 🚿 P 🗄 ☕
△ *Johannesburg* - *Keke Kuena Hostel* *55, 1st street, Bez Valley, Johannesburg 2001.*	☎ *(11) 6142555* ✆ *(11) 6142497*	44		👫 3SE 🚿 ☕
△ *Johannesburg* - *Ranch Hostel* *Inchanga Road, Witkoppen, Johannesburg 2021,* *Gauteng.*	☎ *(11) 7081304;* *7081310* ✆ *(11) 7081464*	28		👫 26N CC 🚿 P 🗄
▲ **Kimberley** Gum Tree Lodge, Bloemfontein Rd, Kimberley 8301, Northern Cape.	☎ (531) 828577 ✆ (531) 815409	128		👫 🍽 5E CC 🚿 P 🗄 ☕
▲ **Knysna** **Highfield Backpackers, 2 Graham St,** **Knysna 6570, Western Cape.**	☎ (445) 826266 ✆ (445) 24012	42		👫 🍽 🚿 P 🗄 ☕
▲ **Kruger National Park** Kruger Park Backpackers, Main Numbi Gate Rd, Hazyview, 1242, Mpumalanga.	☎ (13) 7377224 ✆ (13) 7377224	42		👫 🚿 P 🗄 ☕
△ *Louwsburg District* - *Paradise Backpackers* *Farm* *(Off the R69 between Pongola and Vryheid),* *P.O.Box 1034, Pongola 3170, Kwazulu/Natal.*	☎ *(034) 4141033* ✆ *(034) 4141033*	32		👫 🍽 ♿ 🚿 P 🗄 ☕
▲ **Messina District** - Tshipise Backpackers Lodge **(Aventura Eco Tshipise Resort,** **just past Messina between the R525 and R508),** **P.O.Box 4, Tshipise 0901, Northern Province**	☎ (15539) 624 ✆ (15539) 724	56		👫 🍽 ♿ CC 🚿 P 🗄 ☕
△ *Mossel Bay* *Mossel Bay Backpackers, 1 Marsh St,* *Mossel Bay 6500, Western Cape.*	☎ *(444) 913182* ✆ *(444) 913182*	17		👫 🍽 🚿 P
△ *Mossel Bay* - *Santos Express Backpackers* *Santos Rd, Mossel Bay, 6511 Western Cape*	☎ *(444) 911995* ✆ *(444) 911995*	24		👫 🍽 R 1SE 🚿 ☕
△ *Phalaborwa* *Elephant Walk Backpackers, 30 Anna Scheepers St,* *Phalaborwa 1390, Northern Province.*	☎ *(1524) 4758* ✆ *(1524) 4758*	26		🍽 CC 🚿 P 🗄

Location/Address	Telephone No. Fax No.	Beds	Opening Dates	Facilities
▲ **Plettenberg Bay** Albergo for Backpackers, 8 Church St, Plettenberg Bay 6600, Western Cape.	☏ (4457) 34434 🖷 (21) 4230515	38		
▲ **Pletternberg Bay** - Nothando Backpackers 5 Wilder St, Plettenberg Bay 6600, Western Cape.	☏ (4457) 30220 🖷 (4457) 30220	28		
△ *Port Alfred - Sherwood Shack Backpackers* *(Just off the R72 along Trappers and Shaw Park Rd),* *P.O. Box 215, Port Alfred 6170, Eastern Cape.*	☏ *(46) 6751090* 🖷 *(46) 6751090*	*24*		[22 W]
△ *Pretoria* *Mazuri Backpackers Lodge, 503 Reitz St, Sunnyside,* *Pretoria 0001, Gauteng.*	☏ *(12) 3437782* 🖷 *(12) 3437782*	*18*		
△ *Sabie* *Jock of the Bushveld, Main St, Sabie 1260,* *Mpumalanga.*	☏ *(13) 7642178,* *(13) 7641097* *(Guests)* 🖷 *(13) 7643215*	*20*		
▲ **Sabie** - Sabie Vallee Backpackers No. 6, Six St, Sabie 1260, Mpumalanga	☏ (13) 7642182 🖷 (13) 7641362	36		
▲ **Stellenbosch** - Stumble Inn Backpackers 12 Market St, Stellenbosch 7600, Western Cape.	☏ (21) 8874049, 8872627 (Guests) 🖷 (21) 8874049	40		
△ *Stellenbosch - Backpackers Inn* *First Floor, De Wet Centre, Church St,* *Stellenbosch 7600, Western Cape*	☏ *(21) 8872020* 🖷 *(21) 8872010*	*52*		
▲ **Strand** - Highfield Backpackers 44 Sarel Cilliers St, Cnr. Fagen St, Strand, 7140 Western Cape	☏ (21) 8535565 🖷 (21) 8535565	26		
△ *Swaziland* *Sondzela Backpackers Lodge,* *Mlilwane Wildlife Sanctuary, Ezulwini Valley,* *PO Box 234, Mbabane, Kingdom of Swaziland.*	☏ *(09268) 61165* 🖷 *(268) 40957*	*26*		
▲ **Ventersburg District** - Goldfields Backpackers (Aventura Aldam Resort along the N1 between Kroonstad and Winburg), Pvt. Bag X6, Ventersburg 9450, Free State.	☏ (5777) 4077 🖷 (5777) 4078	60		
△ *Vredenburg - Windstone Backpackers* *(Next to Langeenheid Station on the R45,* *Hopefield Rd, West Coast), P.O. Box 320,* *Vredenburg 7380, Western Cape.*	☏ *(22) 7661645* 🖷 *(22) 7661645*	*28*		

Sudan

SOUDAN
SUDAN
SUDAN

Sudanese Youth Hostels Association,
House No 66, Street No 47
Khartoum East
PO Box 1705, Khartoum, Sudan.

☎ (249) (11) 722087
📠 (249) (11) 771504

A copy of the Hostel Directory for this Country can be obtained from:
The National Office.

Capital:	Khartoum	Population:	27,000,000
Language:	Arabic	Size:	2,505,813 sq km
Currency:	£S (Sudanese £)		

Sudan

LIBYA
EGYPT
RED SEA
CHAD
SUDAN
Nile
Port Sudan
Bur Sudan
Kassala
Al-Khartum
Khartoum
ARITERIA
Wad Medani
Elobied
Elrosaris
Blue Nile
ETHIOPIA
CENTRAL
AFRICA
White Nile
L. Rudolf
ZAIRE
UGANDA
KENYA
N
Nairobi
200   400   600 KM
0
100   200   300   MLS

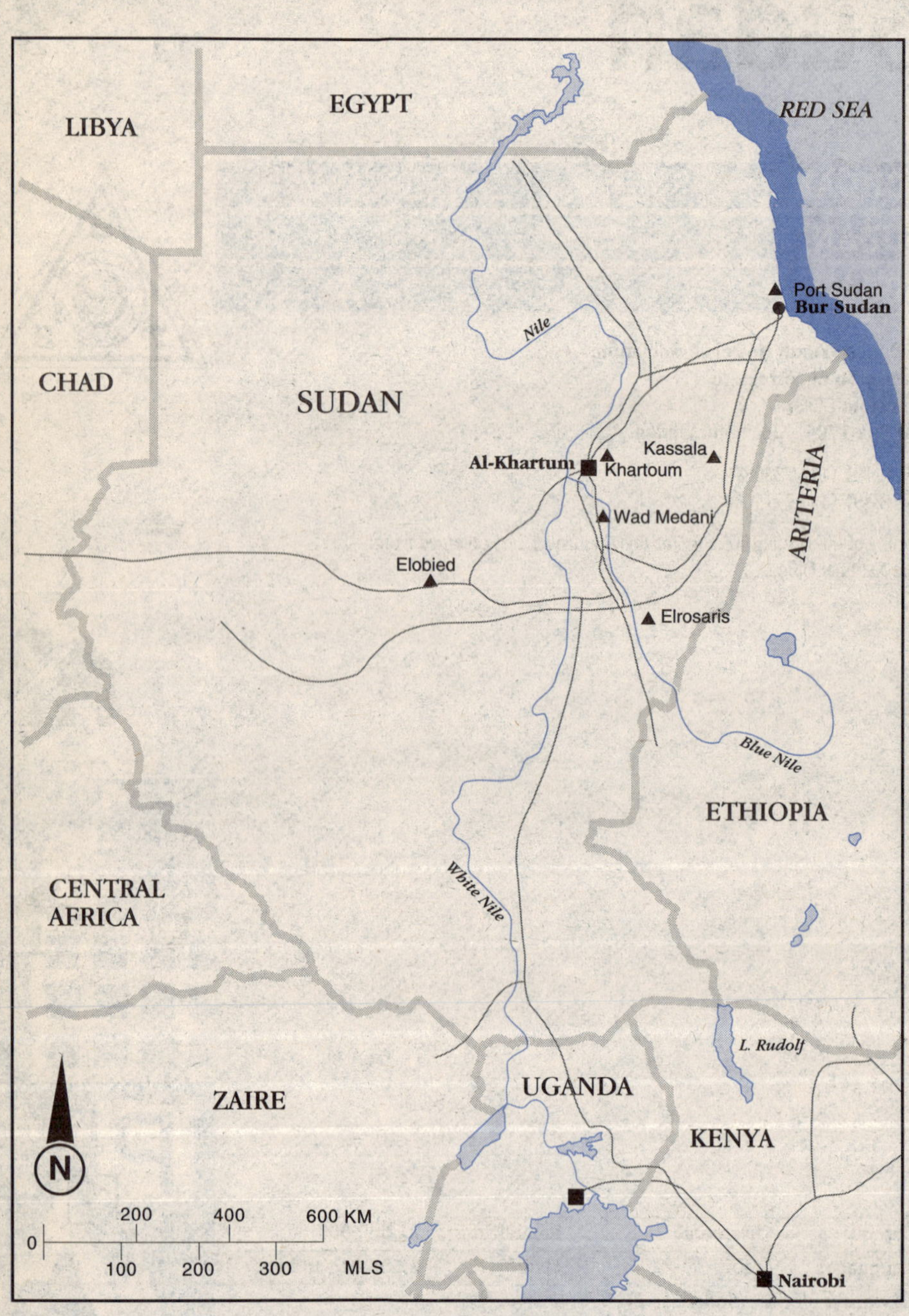

English

SUDANESE HOSTELS

Youth Hostels in Sudan are mainly used by university and high school students. The minimum age is 12 years. There is no maximum age limit, but priority is given to travellers under 30 years old, walkers and cyclists. Khartoum Youth Hostel is able to offer private family accommodation.

Hostels are open 07.00-10.00hrs and 14.00-22/23.00hrs. Expect to pay in the region of £S 3000-6000 per night. Self-catering is only available in Khartoum and also Port Sudan and meals are not provided by hostels.

PASSPORTS AND VISAS

Residents of all Arab countries, Eritreans and Ethiopians are permitted to enter Sudan without a visa. Other nationals should obtain an entry visa from the Sudanese Embassy in their own country.

HEALTH

A health certificate is no longer officially required.

BANKING HOURS

08.00-12.00hrs.

POST OFFICES

08.00-13.00hrs and 17.00-18.00hrs.

SHOPPING HOURS

08.00-17.00hrs.

TRAVEL

Air
Sudan Airways provides services between Khartoum and the important towns of Sudan.

Rail
A rail network operates throughout the country, except the Darfour, Upper Nile and Equatoria Regions.

Bus
There is a regular bus service in Khartoum as well as regular district-based services.

Driving
Yellow taxis operate in Khartoum at reasonable rates. Self-drive cars can be hired from local firms in major towns.

TELEPHONE INFORMATION

Country Code	**249**
Main City Area Codes	
Khartoum	**11**

Français

AUBERGES DE JEUNESSE SOUDANAISES

Les auberges de jeunesse soudanaises sont surtout utilisées par les étudiants des collèges et universités. L'âge minimum est 12 ans. Il n'y a pas d'âge limite maximum, mais les voyageurs de moins de 30 ans, les randonneurs et les cyclistes sont prioritaires. L'auberge de Jeunesse de Khartoum posséde des chambres familiales privées.

Les auberges sont ouvertes de 7h à 10h et de 14h à 22/23h. Une nuit vous coûtera entre 3000 et 6000 £S. Il n'y a possibilité de cuisiner qu'à Khartoum et à l'auberge de jeunesse de Port-Soudan. Aucune auberge ne fournit de repas.

PASSEPORTS ET VISAS

Les citoyens de tous les pays arabes, les Erythréens et les Ethiopiens ont le droit de rentrer au Soudan sans visa. Les citoyens d'autres pays doivent obtenir un visa auprès de l'Ambassade soudanaise dans leur propre pays.

SOINS MEDICAUX

Les certificats de santé ne sont plus officiellement requis.

HEURES D'OUVERTURE DES BANQUES

Les banques sont ouvertes de 8h à 12h.

BUREAUX DE POSTE

Les bureaux de poste sont ouverts de 8h à 13h et de 17h à 18h.

HEURES D'OUVERTURE DES MAGASINS

Les magasins sont ouverts de 8h à 17h.

DEPLACEMENTS

Avions

Sudan Airways assurent des services entre Khartoum et les grandes villes du Soudan.

Trains

Les trains desservent tout le pays, à l'exception des régions du Darfour, du Haut-Nil et d'Equatoria.

Autobus

Un service d'autobus régulier dessert la ville de Khartoum et il y a également des services réguliers régionaux.

Automobiles

Des taxis jaunes sont en service à Khartoum et leurs tarifs sont raisonnables. Il est possible de louer des voitures auprès d'agences locales dans les grandes villes.

TELEPHONE

Indicatif du Pays	**249**
Indicatifs régionaux des Villes principales	
Khartoum	11

Deutsch

SUDANESISCHE JUGENDHERBERGEN

Jugendherbergen werden im Sudan hauptsächlich von Studenten benutzt. Das Mindestalter ist 12 Jahre. Eine obere Altersgrenze gibt es nicht, aber Reisende, die jünger sind als 30 Jahre, Wanderer und Radfahrer werden bevorzugt aufgenommen.

Khartoum Youth Hostel haben Familienzimmer zur Verfügung.

Die Herbergen sind von 7.00-10.00 Uhr und von 14.00-22/23.00 Uhr geöffnet. Es ist mit einem Preis von ca. £S 3000-6000 pro Nacht zu rechnen. Einrichtungen für Selbstversorger gibt es nur in Khartoum. In den Herbergen gibt es keine Mahlzeiten.

PÄSSE UND VISA

Bewohner aller arabischen Länder, Eriträer und Äthiopier können ohne ein Visum in den Sudan einreisen. Andere Staatsbürger sollten sich von der Sudanesischen Botschaft in ihrem eigenen Land ein Einreisevisum beschaffen.

GESUNDHEIT

Offiziell wird heute kein Gesundheitszeugnis mehr verlangt.

GESCHÄFTSSTUNDEN DER BANKEN

8.00-12.00 Uhr.

POSTÄMTER

8.00-13.00 Uhr und 17.00-18.00 Uhr.

LADENÖFFNUNGSZEITEN

8.00-17.00 Uhr.

REISEN

Flugverkehr

Sudan Airways verkehrt zwischen Khartum und den wichtigsten Städten des Landes.

Eisenbahn

Das Eisenbahnnetz erstreckt sich über das ganze Land mit Ausnahme der Gebiete Darbur, Oberer Nil und Equatoria.

Busse

In Khartum und in den einzelnen Bezirken gibt es einen Linienbusverkehr.

Autofahren

Die gelben Taxis sind in Khartum sehr preiswert. In größeren Städten kann man sich bei örtlichen Mietwagen-Unternehmen einen Wagen mieten.

FERNSPRECHINFORMATIONEN

Landes-Kennzahl   **249**
größere Städte - Ortsnetzkennzahlen
   Khartum   **11**

Español

ALBERGUES DE JUVENTUD SUDANESES

Los albergues de juventud de Sudán son utilizados principalmente por estudiantes universitarios y de enseñanza secundaria. La edad mínima es de 12 años. No existe una edad máxima, si bien se da prioridad a los viajeros de menos de 30 años, a los excursionistas y a los ciclistas. El albergue juvenil de Jartum tiene habitaciones familiares.

Los albergues abren de 07.00 a 10.00 horas y de 14.00 a 22/23.00 horas y cuestan alrededor de £S 3000-6000 por noche. Sólo Jartum y Port Sudan disponen de cocina para huéspedes y ninguno de ellos sirve comidas.

PASAPORTES Y VISADOS

Los residentes de todos los países árabes, eritreos y etíopes pueden entrar en Sudán sin visado. Los ciudadanos de otros países deben obtener un visado de entrada en la Embajada de Sudán de su propio país.

SANIDAD

Ya no se requiere oficialmente un certificado sanitario.

HORARIO DE BANCOS

De 08.00 a 12.00 horas.

OFICINAS DE CORREOS

De 08.00 a 13.00 horas y de 17.00 a 18.00 horas.

HORARIO COMERCIAL

De 08.00 a 17.00 horas.

DESPLAZAMIENTOS

Avión
Sudan Airways ofrece vuelos entre Jartum y las principales ciudades de Sudán.

Tren
Existe una red ferroviaria que cubre todo el país excepto las regiones de Darfour, Alto Nilo y Ecuatoria.

Autobús
Hay un servicio regular de autobuses en Jartum, así como varios servicios regulares regionales.

Coche
En Jartum se pueden encontrar taxis amarillos a precios razonables. Se pueden alquilar coches sin conductor en compañías locales en las principales ciudades.

INFORMACION TELEFONICA

Código Nacional   **249**
Prefijos de las Ciudades Principales
   Jartum   **11**

Discounts And Concessions

Sudan Airways offer members a discount of 30% off flights to all their destinations.

Location/Address	Telephone No. Fax No.	Beds	Opening Dates	Facilities
△ **Kassala** c/o Ministry of Youth & Sports Kassala, Kassala State: near centre of town.	☎ 2251-2550	60	🗓	℞ ♿ 🅿 📥
▲ **Khartoum** House No 66, St 47, Khartoum East (Souk Two), PO Box No 1705 Khartoum.	☎ (11) 722087 📠 (11) 460475	80	🗓	🚻 ℞ ♿ ☞ 🅿 📥
▲ **Port Sudan** Salabona, Port Sudan YH, Red Sea State, PO Box No 829, Port Sudan.	☎ 23478-22362	80	🗓	℞ ♿ 🅿 📥
△ **Wad Medani** c/o Ministry of Youth & Sports, Wad Medani, Gazeira State: town centre 3km.		60	🗓	℞ ♿ 🅿 📥

SUPPLEMENTARY ACCOMMODATION OUTSIDE THE ASSURED STANDARDS SCHEME

Location/Address	Telephone No. Fax No.	Beds	Opening Dates	Facilities
Elobied PO Box 338, Elobied, North Kordofan State.	☎ 2843-2732	40	🗓	
Elrosaris Elnile St, Blue Nile Province: c/o Ministry of Youth & Sports, Youth Office.		60	🗓	℞ ♿ 🅿 📥

HOSTELLING INTERNATIONAL

not just a cheap bed, but a cheaper ticket, meal, insurance package (see your national Association for details...)

pas simplement un lit bon marché, mais aussi un billet, un repas, un forfait assurance moins chers (contactez votre Association nationale pour plus de renseignements...)

nicht nur ein preiswertes Bett, sondern auch preisgünstigere Eintrittskarten, Mahlzeiten und Reiseversicherungen (mehr darüber von den nationalen Mitgliedsverbänden...).

no sólo alojamiento a precios asequibles, sino también billetes, comidas y seguros más económicos (para más información, diríjase a su Asociación nacional...)

Thailand

THAÏLANDE
THAILAND
TAILANDIA

**Thai Youth Hostels Association,
25/14 Phitsanulok Road,
Dusit, Bangkok 10300, Thailand.**

☏ (66) (2) 628-7413-5
🖷 (66) (2) 628-7416

A copy of the Hostel Directory for this Country can be obtained from:
Thai Youth Hostels Association.

IBN Booking Centre

- **Bangkok** - *via National Office
  above*

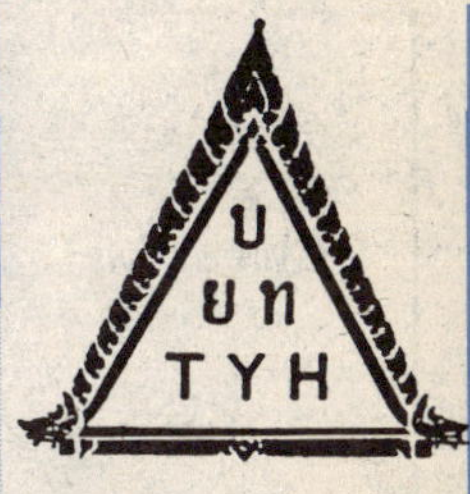

Capital:	Bangkok	Population:	66,000,000
Language:	Thai	Size:	500,000 sq km
Currency:	baht		

Thailand

LAOS
N
Chieng Mai
Viangchan
Tak
Mekong
THAILAND
Phitsanulok
Lop Buri
Nakhon Ratchasima
Ayutthaya
Krung Thep
(Bangkok)
Bangkok (2)
KAMPUCHIA
Rayong
Phnom
Penh
Prachuap Khiri Khan
50   100   150   200   KM
0
50   100   MLS

English

THAI HOSTELS

There are 2 hostels in Bangkok and 8 in the rest of the country.

Expect to pay around 120-400 Baht per night, plus sheet hire. There are self-catering facilities in only 2 hostels but cafeteria meals are always available.

PASSPORTS AND VISAS

A valid passport is required. Visitors can enjoy a stay of up to 30 days without a visa. Visas can be obtained for visits of 30, 60 or 90 day periods.

HEALTH

No vaccinations are required, unless you come from or are passing through a contaminated area. There is no free emergency medical care.

BANKING HOURS

09.30-15.30hrs Monday to Friday.

POST OFFICES

08.30-16.30hrs Monday to Friday,
08.30-12.00hrs Saturday.

SHOPPING HOURS

10.00-21.00hrs seven days a week.

TRAVEL

Air
Bangkok is the main point of entry to Thailand as most visitors arrive at the Don Muang International Airport.

Rail
Regular rail services link Singapore and Bangkok. The State Railway of Thailand runs express, fast and ordinary train services throughout the country at very reasonable fares.

Bus
Coaches and city buses are available.

Ferry
A motor boat service operates along the Chao Phraya river between Nonthaburi and Thanon Tok (Bangkok only).

Driving
An International Driver's Licence is required. Driving is on the left-hand side. International driving regulations apply.

TELEPHONE INFORMATION

Country Code   66
Main City Area Codes
  Bangkok   2

Français

AUBERGES DE JEUNESSE THAÏLANDAISES

Il y a 2 auberges à Bangkok et 8 dans le reste du pays.

Une nuit vous coûtera entre 120 et 400 Baht, plus location de draps. Deux auberges seulement mettent une cuisine à la disposition des individuels mais toutes servent des repas de style cafétéria.

PASSEPORTS ET VISAS

Un passeport valide est nécessaire. Les visiteurs ont le droit de séjourner pendant un maximum de 30 jours sans visa. Il est possible d'obtenir des visas pour des périodes de 30, 60 ou 90 jours.

SOINS MEDICAUX

Aucune vaccination n'est nécessaire sauf si vous venez d'une région contaminée ou si vous en traversez une. Il n'y a pas de soins médicaux d'urgence gratuits.

HEURES D'OUVERTURE DES BANQUES

Les banques sont ouvertes du lundi au vendredi, de 9h30 à 15h30.

BUREAUX DE POSTE

Les bureaux de poste sont ouverts du lundi au vendredi, de 8h30 à 16h30 et le samedi de 8h30 à 12h.

HEURES D'OUVERTURE DES MAGASINS

Les magasins sont ouverts de 10h à 21h sept jours sur sept.

DEPLACEMENTS

Avions

Bangkok est le lieu d'arrivée principal en Thaïlande, vu que la plupart des visiteurs arrivent à l'aéroport international de Don Muang.

Trains

Des services réguliers relient Singapour à Bangkok. Les Chemins de Fer d'Etat de Thaïlande assurent des services express, rapides et ordinaires dans tout le pays à des prix très raisonnables.

Autobus

Il y a des cars et des autobus urbains.

Ferry-boats

Des bateaux à moteur sont en service le long de la Chao Phraya entre Nonthaburi et Thanon Tok (Bangkok uniquement).

Automobiles

Un permis de conduire international est nécessaire. La conduite est à gauche. Le code de la route international est en vigueur.

TELEPHONE

Indicatif du Pays	66
Indicatifs régionaux des Villes principales	
Bangkok	2

Deutsch

THAILÄNDISCHE JUGENDHERBERGEN

In Bangkok gibt es 2 Jugendherbergen und im übrigen Land 8.

Es ist mit einem Preis von ca. 120-400 Baht pro Nacht plus Miete für Bettlaken zu rechnen. Es gibt nur 2 Herbergen mit Einrichtungen für Selbstversorger. Snacks sind immer erhältlich.

PÄSSE UND VISA

Es wird ein gültiger Reisepaß verlangt. Reisende können ohne ein Visum bis zu 30 Tage im Land bleiben. Es gibt Visa für 30, 60 oder 90 Tage.

GESUNDHEIT

Reisende, die nicht aus Gebieten kommen, in denen Epedemien herrschen, und sich auch auf der Durchreise nicht in einem solchen Gebiet befanden, brauchen sich nicht impfen zu lassen. Es gibt auch in Notfällen keine kostenlose ärztliche Behandlung.

GESCHÄFTSSTUNDEN DER BANKEN

Montags bis freitags 9.30-15.30 Uhr.

POSTÄMTER

Montags bis freitags 8.30-16.30 Uhr, samstags 8.30-12.00 Uhr.

LADENÖFFNUNGSZEITEN

An allen sieben Wochentagen von 10.00-21.00 Uhr.

REISEN

Flugverkehr

Die meisten Reisenden kommen auf dem internationalen Flughafen Don Muang in Bangkok an.

Eisenbahn

Ein Eisenbahn-Linienverkehr verbindet Singapur und Bangkok. Die Staatliche Eisenbahn von Thailand betreibt im ganzen Land einen sehr preiswerten Expreß-, Schnell- und Personenzugverkehr.

Busse

Es gibt Reisebusse und Busse im Stadtverkehr.

Fähren

Auf dem Chao Phraya gibt es zwischen

Nonthaburi und Thanon Tok (nur Bangkok) einen Motorbootverkehr.

Autofahren

Man braucht einen internationalen Führerschein. In Thailand herrscht Linksverkehr, und es gelten internationale Verkehrsvorschriften.

FERNSPRECHINFORMATIONEN

Landes-Kennzahl   66
größere Städte - Ortsnetzkennzahlen
   Bangkok   2

Español

ALBERGUES DE JUVENTUD TAILANDESES

Hay 2 albergues en Bangkok y 8 en el resto del país.

Los precios oscilan entre 120-400 Baht por noche, además del alquiler de las sábanas. Solamente 2 albergues disponen de cocina para huéspedes, pero todos sirven comida de cafetería.

PASAPORTES Y VISADOS

Se requiere un pasaporte válido. Los visitantes pueden disfrutar de una estancia de hasta 30 días sin visado. Se pueden obtener visados para visitas de 30, 60 y 90 días.

SANIDAD

No se requieren vacunas a menos que el visitante provenga o pase por una zona contaminada. No existe ningún servicio gratuito de asistencia médica de urgencias.

HORARIO DE BANCOS

De 09.30 a 15.30 horas de lunes a viernes.

OFICINAS DE CORREOS

De 08.30 a 16.30 horas de lunes a viernes, de 08.30 a 12.00 horas los sábados.

HORARIO COMERCIAL

De 10.00 a 21.00 horas los siete días de la semana.

DESPLAZAMIENTOS

Avión

Bangkok es el principal punto de entrada a Tailandia, ya que la mayoría de los visitantes llegan al aeropuerto internacional de Don Muang.

Tren

Servicios regulares de tren conectan Singapur con Bangkok. La compañía ferroviaria estatal de Tailandia opera servicios de trenes expresos, rápidos y ordinarios por todo el país a precios muy razonables.

Autobús

Existen autocares y autobuses urbanos.

Ferry

A lo largo del río Chao Phraya, entre Nonthaburi y Thanon Tok, funciona un servicio de lancha motora (sólo Bangkok).

Coche

Se requiere un permiso de conducir internacional. Se circula por la izquierda y siguiendo el reglamento internacional.

INFORMACION TELEFONICA

Código Nacional   66
Prefijos de las Ciudades Principales
   Bangkok   2

Bangkok -
International YH

25/2 Phitsanulok Rd,
Sisao Theves,
Dusit,
Bangkok 10300.
☎ (2) 2810361, 2820950
🖷 (2) 6287416

Open Dates:	🗐
Open Hours:	🕒
Reservations:	Ⓡ IBN
Price Range:	120-400 🗎
Beds:	63 - 4x^1 🛏 21x^2 🛏 4x^6 🛏
Facilities:	♙♙♙ 3x♙♙♙ 🍽 ♨ 📺 🧺 ▣ 🖼 🎱 ⊜ 🅿 ℹ ⚃

Directions:

✈	Donmuang International
A🚌	Airbus from ✈ to Sanamluang, then #43 ● Thammasat University Unit to last destination
🚌	#16, 23, 72, 99 and Air Con #5

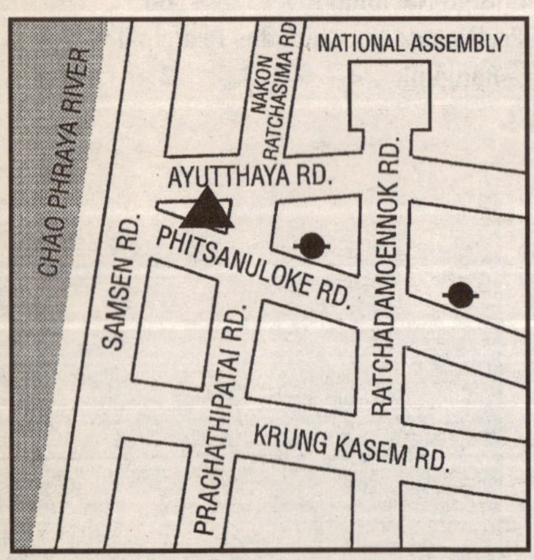

▲ There for everyone - young, not so young and those in the middle.▲

▲ c'est pour tout le monde -les jeunes, les moins jeunes et tous les autres.▲

▲ albergues para todos - los jóvenes, los menos jóvenes y los jóvenes de espíritu.▲

▲ für jederman - ob jung, nicht mehr ganz so jung oder die dazwischen.▲

Location/Address	Telephone No. Fax No.	Beds	Opening Dates	Facilities
△ *Ayutthaya* Ban Na-Wang Youth Hostel, T. 69/1 Tambon, Thawasukri, Amphor Pranakornsriayuthaya, Ayuthaya 13000.	☎ (35) 251806, 252061	10		P
▲ **Bangkok** - International YH [IBN] **25/2 Phitsanulok Rd, Sisao Theves, Dusit, Bangkok 10300.**	☎ (2) 2810361, 2820950 ✆ (2) 6287416	63		
△ *Bangkok* - Bansabuy 8/137 Soi Sahakorn 15, Ladphrao 71, Bangkok 10230.	☎ (2) 5390150, 9329200 ✆ (2) 5384387	42		
△ *Bantak Youth Hostel* Sunset Villa Bantak Youth Hostel, 9/1M10, T, Taktok A. Bantak, Tak 63120.	☎ (55) 591286 ✆ (55) 591286	8		
△ *Chieng Mai* Chieng Mai (Chang Klan), 'City Hostel', 21/8 Chang Klan Rd, Mooban Oon-Ruen, Chieng Mai 50100.	☎ (53) 276737, 204025 ✆ (53) 204025, 204516	40		
△ *Lop Buri YH* (Ban Vimolrat) 5/19 Moo 3. Naressuan Rd, Amphor Mueng, Lop Buri 15000.	☎ (36) 613731-3, 613390	20		
△ *Nakhorn Ratchasima* Phimai YH, 214 Chomsudasadet Rd, Phimai, Nakhorn Ratchasima 30110.	☎ (44) 471918	10		
△ *Phitsanulok YH* 38 Sa-Nam-Bin Rd, Phitsanulok 65000.	☎ (55) 242060, 210862 to 4 ✆ (55) 210864	40		
△ *Prachuap Khiri Khan* Tawee Sea Resort YH, No 46 Moo 9, Tambon Tongchai, Ampur Bang Sapan, Prachuap Khiri Khan 77140: (family-run beach bungalows on Gulf of Thailand).		20		
△ *Rayong* Ban Kon Ao YH, 89/4 Moo 1 Mae Ram Puang Beach Rd, Phae, Rayong 21160.	☎ (38) 653374 ✆ (2) 6287416	40		

Make your credit card bookings at these centres
Réservez par cartes de crédit aux centres suivants
Buchen Sie mit Kreditkarte in folgenden Buchungszentren
Reserve por tarjeta de crédito en los siguientes centros

English

Australia	☎ (2) 9261 1111
Canada	☎ (800) 663 5777
England & Wales	☎ (1629) 581 418
France	☎ (1) 44 89 87 27
Northern Ireland	☎ (1232) 324 733
Republic of Ireland	☎ (1) 830 1766
New Zealand	☎ (9) 303 9524
Scotland	☎ (541) 553 255
Switzerland	☎ (1) 360 1414
USA	☎ (202) 783 6161

Français

Angleterre & Pays de Galles	☎ (1692) 581 41
Australie	☎ (2) 9261 1111
Canada	☎ (800) 663 577
Écosse	☎ (541) 553 255
États-Unis	☎ (202) 783 616
France	☎ (1) 44 89 87 2
Irlande du Nord	☎ (1232) 324 73
Nouvelle-Zélande	☎ (9) 303 9524
République d'Irlande	☎ (1) 830 1766
Suisse	☎ (1) 360 1414

Deutsch

Australien	☎ (2) 9261 1111
England & Wales	☎ (1629) 581 418
Frankreich	☎ (1) 44 89 87 27
Irland	☎ (1) 830 1766
Kanada	☎ (800) 663 5777
Neuseeland	☎ (9) 303 9524
Nordirland	☎ (1232) 324 733
Schottland	☎ (541) 553 255
Schweiz	☎ (1) 360 1414
USA	☎ (202) 783 6161

Español

Australia	☎ (2) 9261 1111
Canadá	☎ (800) 663 577
Escocia	☎ (541) 553 255
Estados Unidos	☎ (202) 783 616
Francia	☎ (1) 44 89 87 2
Inglaterra y Gales	☎ (1629) 581 41
Irlanda del Norte	☎ (1232) 324 73
Nueva Zelanda	☎ (9) 303 9524
República de Irlanda	☎ (1) 830 1766
Suiza	☎ (1) 360 1414

Tunisia

TUNISIA

TUNISIE
TUNESIEN
TUNEZ

Association Tunisienne des Auberges de Jeunesse,
10 rue Ali Bach Hamba,
BP 320-1015 Tunis RP, Tunisia.

☏ (216) (1) 353277
✆ (216) (1) 352172

Office Hours: Monday-Friday, 08.30-18.00hrs and
Saturdays, 08.30-13.00hrs

A copy of the Hostel Directory for this Country can be obtained from:
The National Office.

Capital:	Tunis	Population:	8,780,000
Language:	Arabic	Size:	163,610 sq km
Currency:	D (dinar)		

Tunisia

Bizerte
Rimel
Tunis-
Medina
Tunis
Nabeul
Ain Draham
Sousse
Kairouan
ALGERIA
Gafsa
Jerba
Gabès
TUNISIA
LIBYA
N
100   200   300   KMS
0
50   150   100   MLS

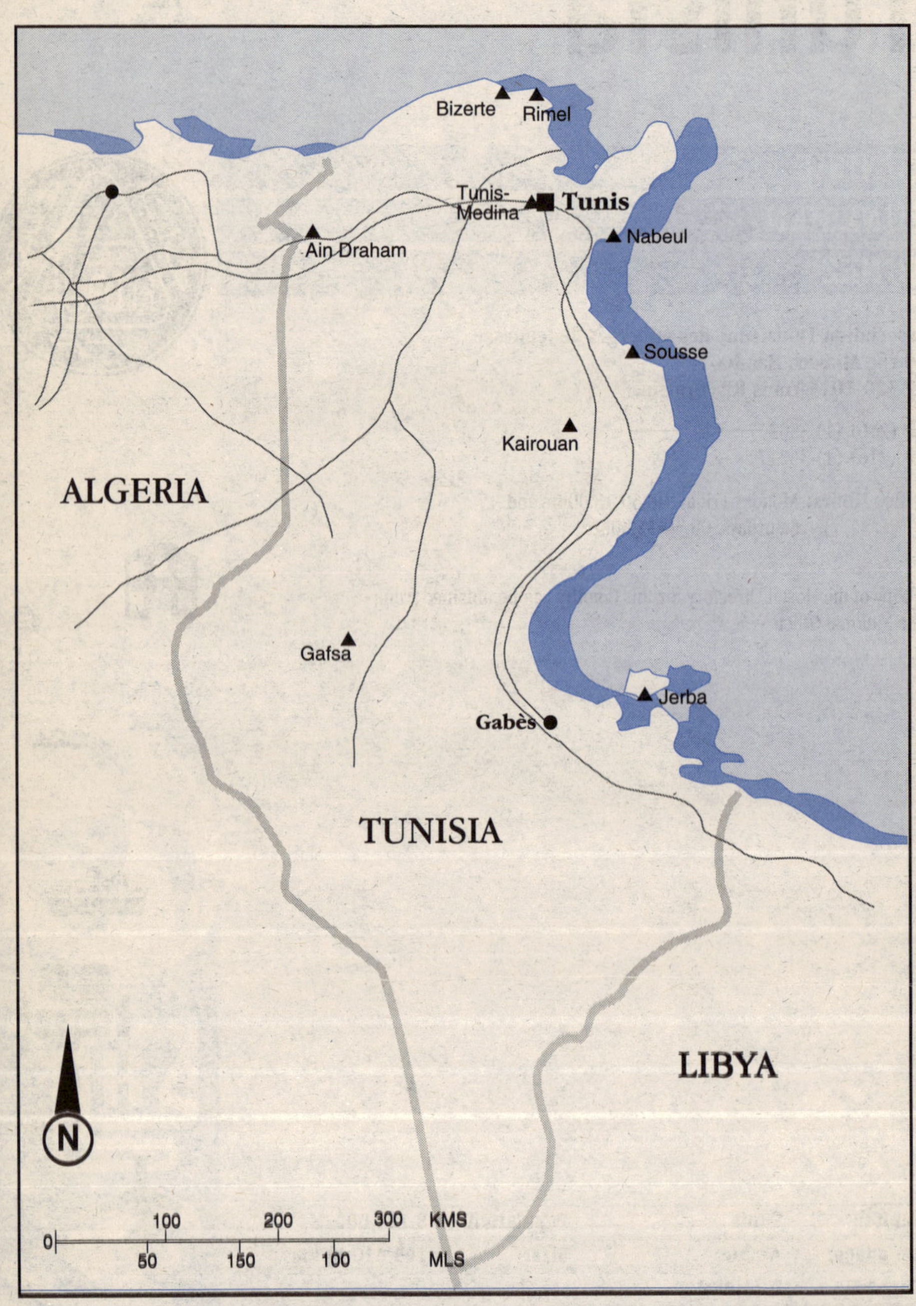

English

TUNISIAN HOSTELS

Accommodation is provided for over 15s and children accompanied by their parents. Although there is no upper age limit, priority is given to younger travellers.

Hostels are open 07.00-23.00hrs. You should expect to pay in the region of 3-4 Dinars per night plus linen hire if needed. A small charge of 300-400 Millimes is made for the use of self-catering facilities when available.

PASSPORTS AND VISAS

Valid passports are required for all visitors to Tunisia, and it is advisable to check visa requirements with the nearest Tunisian embassy or consulate.

BANKING HOURS

Banks are open from 1 January to 30 June and from 1 September to 31 December from 08.00-11.00hrs and from 14.00-17.00hrs, and from 07.30-11.30hrs from 1 July to 31 August. Banks at the Airport are open all day and every day of the week.

POST OFFICES

Post office opening hours are 07.30-13.00hrs and 15.00-17.00hrs.

TRANSPORT

Air
Tunisia is well served by international flights.

Rail
A rail network connects major towns and cities.

TELEPHONE INFORMATION

Country Code	216
Main City Area Codes	
Tunis	1
Sousse	3
Sfax	4
Gabès/Djerba	5
Bizerte/Nabeul	2
Tabarka	8

Français

AUBERGES DE JEUNESSE TUNISIENNES

Les jeunes de plus de 15 ans et les enfants accompagnés de leurs parents sont accueillis dans les auberges. Bien qu'il n'y ait pas d'âge limite supérieur, priorité est donnée aux jeunes voyageurs.

Les auberges sont ouvertes de 7h à 23h. Une nuit vous coûtera entre 3 et 4 dinars, plus location de draps le cas échéant. 300 à 400 millimes vous seront demandés si vous utilisez la cuisine, si cette possibilité existe dans votre auberge.

PASSEPORTS ET VISAS

Tous les visiteurs entrant en Tunisie doivent être munis d'un passeport valide et il est conseillé de vérifier les exigences en matière de visa auprès du consulat ou de l'ambassade de Tunisie le/la plus proche.

HEURES D'OUVERTURE DES BANQUES

Les banques sont ouvertes du 1 Janvier au 30 Juin et du 1 Septembre au 31 Décembre de 8h à 11h et de 14h à 17h et de 7h30 à 11h30 du 1 Juillet et 31 Août. Les banques à l'Aéroport sont ouvertes toute la journée et tous les jours de la semaine.

BUREAUX DE POSTE

Les bureaux de poste sont ouverts de 7h30 à 13h et de 15h à 17h.

DEPLACEMENTS

Avions
La Tunisie est bien desservie par des vols internationaux.

Trains
Un réseau ferroviaire relie les grandes villes.

TELEPHONE

Indicatif du Pays	**216**
Indicatifs régionaux des Villes principales	
Tunis	1
Sousse	3
Sfax	4
Gabès/Djerba	5
Bizerte/Nabeul	2
Tabarka	8

Deutsch

TUNESISCHE JUGENDHERBERGEN

In Jugendherbergen werden Jugendliche und Erwachsene über 15 Jahren und Kinder, die sich in Begleitung ihrer Eltern befinden, aufgenommen. Es gibt zwar keine obere Altersgrenze, aber jüngere Reisende werden bevorzugt aufgenommen.

Die Herbergen sind von 7.00 bis 23.00 Uhr geöffnet. Es ist mit einem Preis von ca. 3 bis 4 Dinar pro Nacht plus, bei Bedarf, einer Gebühr für die Miete von Bettwäsche zu rechnen. Für die Benutzung von Einrichtungen für Selbstversorger wird, sofern vorhanden, eine kleine Gebühr von 300 bis 400 Millimes erhoben.

PÄSSE UND VISA

Für alle Tunesienbesucher wird ein gültiger Reisepaß verlangt, und wir raten Ihnen, sich bei der nächsten tunesischen Botschaft oder beim nächsten Konsulat nach den Visumsbestimmungen zu erkundigen.

GESCHÄFTSSTUNDEN DER BANKEN

Öffnungszeiten der Banken: 1. Januar bis 30. Juni und 1. September bis 31. Dezember von 8.00-11.00 Uhr und von 14.00-17.00 Uhr und vom 1. Juli bis 31. August von 7.30-11.30 Uhr. Die Banken auf den Flughäfen sind an allen Wochentagen ganztägig geöffnet.

POSTÄMTER

Öffnungszeiten der Postämter: von 7.30-13.00 Uhr und von 15.00-17.00 Uhr.

REISEN

Flugverkehr
Aus dem Ausland gibt es gute Flugverbindungen nach Tunesien.

Eisenbahn
Ein Schienennetz verbindet die größeren Städte.

FERNSPRECHINFORMATIONEN

Landes-Kennzahl	**216**
größere Städte - Ortsnetzkennzahlen	
Tunis	1
Sousse	3
Sfax	4
Gabès/Djerba	5
Bizerte/Nabeul	2
Tabarka	8

Español

ALBERGUES DE JUVENTUD TUNECINOS

Se ofrece alojamiento a mayores de 15 años y a menores acompañados por sus padres. Aunque no hay límite máximo de edad, se da prioridad a los más jóvenes.

Los albergues abren de 07.00 a 23.00 horas. El precio es de alrededor de 3-4 dinares por noche más alquiler de sábanas, de ser necesario. Se cobra la reducida tarifa de 300-400 millimes por el uso de la cocina para huéspedes, de haberla.

PASAPORTES Y VISADOS

Todos los visitantes que entren en Túnez deben estar provistos de un pasaporte válido y se recomienda verificar si es necesario un visado en la embajada o consulado tunecino más próximo.

HORARIO DE BANCOS

Los bancos están abiertos del 1° de enero al 30 de junio y del 1° de septiembre al 31 de diciembre de 08.00 a 11.00 horas y de 14.00 a 17.00 horas y de 07.30 a 11.30 horas del 1° de julio al 31 de agosto. Los bancos del aeropuerto están abiertos todo el día y toda la semana.

OFICINAS DE CORREOS

Las oficinas de correos abren de 07.30 a 13.00 horas y de 15.00 a 17.00 horas.

DESPLAZAMIENTOS

Avión

Túnez tiene un buen servicio de vuelos internacionales.

Tren

Una red ferroviaria conecta las principales poblaciones y ciudades.

INFORMACION TELEFONICA

Código Nacional	216
Prefijos de las Ciudades Principales	
Túnez	1
Sousse	3
Sfax	4
Gabes/Djerba	5
Bizerte/Nabeul	2
Tabarka	8

Assured Standards – visited by our Liaison team and by you the guest – tell us when we don't measure up (reply slips at the end of this Guide) ▲

des Normes Garanties, par les visites de notre Equipe de Liaison et par vous, les usagers – faites-le nous savoir quand nous ne sommes pas à la hauteur (Fiches-commentaires à la fin du Guide) ▲

Zugesicherte Standards – beurteilt von unserem Liaison Team und von Ihnen, unserem Gast – sagen Sie es uns, wenn wir Sie enttäuschen (Antwortkarten hinten im Führer) ▲

Normas Garantizadas – comprobadas por nuestro Equipo de Enlace y por Ud., el usuario – si fallamos en algo, díganoslo (al final de esta Guía encontrará nuestras hojas de comentarios ▲

Location/Address	Telephone No. Fax No.	Beds	Opening Dates	Facilities

SUPPLEMENTARY ACCOMMODATION OUTSIDE THE ASSURED STANDARDS SCHEME

Location/Address	Telephone No. / Fax No.	Beds	Opening Dates	Facilities
Ain Draham Ain Draham: Tunis 200km.	☎ (8) 647087	150		⑪ ☞
Bizerte Route de la Corniche, Bizerte.	☎ (2) 431608	100		⑪ 1N ☞
Gafsa Gafsa.	☎ (6) 220268	60		⑪ ☞
Jerba 11 rue Moncef Bey, Houmt, Souk Jerba.	☎ (5) 650619 🖷 (5) 650619	120		
Kairouan Kairouan.	☎ (7) 220309	70		⑪ ☞
Nabeul Town centre 2km: Tunis 70km	☎ (2) 285547	56		
Rimel Rimel: Bizerte 3km.	☎ (2) 440804	50		
Sousse plage Boujaafar.	☎ (3) 227548	90		⑪ ☞
Tunis AJ Tunis, Medina, 25 rue saida Ajoula, Tunis: located in the old city of Medina, 500m from La Place du Gouvernement la kasbah.	☎ (1) 567850 🖷 (1) 567850	70		

The Tunisian Youth Hostel Association offers a network of student accommodation 'Maison des Jeunes' which is supplementary accommodation outside the 'Assured Standards Scheme'. Please contact the National Office for details.

not just a cheap bed, but a cheaper ticket, meal, insurance package (see your national Association for details...)

pas simplement un lit bon marché, mais aussi un billet, un repas, un forfait assurance moins chers (contactez votre Association nationale pour plus de renseignements...)

nicht nur ein preiswertes Bett, sondern auch preisgünstigere Eintrittskarten, Mahlzeiten und Reiseversicherungen (mehr darüber von den nationalen Mitgliedsverbänden...).

no sólo alojamiento a precios asequibles, sino también billetes, comidas y seguros más económicos (para más información, diríjase a su Asociación nacional...)

United Arab Emirates

EMIRATS UNIS D'ARABIE

VEREINIGTE ARAB. EMIRATE

EMIRATOS ÁRABES UNIDOS

United Arab Emirates Youth Hostel Association,
PO Box 19536, Al Qusaiss Road,
Near Al Ahli Club, Dubai,
United Arab Emirates.

☎ (971) (4) 665078
🖷 (971) (4) 667989

A copy of the Hostel Directory for this Country can be obtained from:
The National Office.

Capital:	Abu Dhabi	Population:	2,200,000
Language:	Arabic	Size:	83,600 sq km
Currency:	Dh (dirham)		

United Arab Emirates

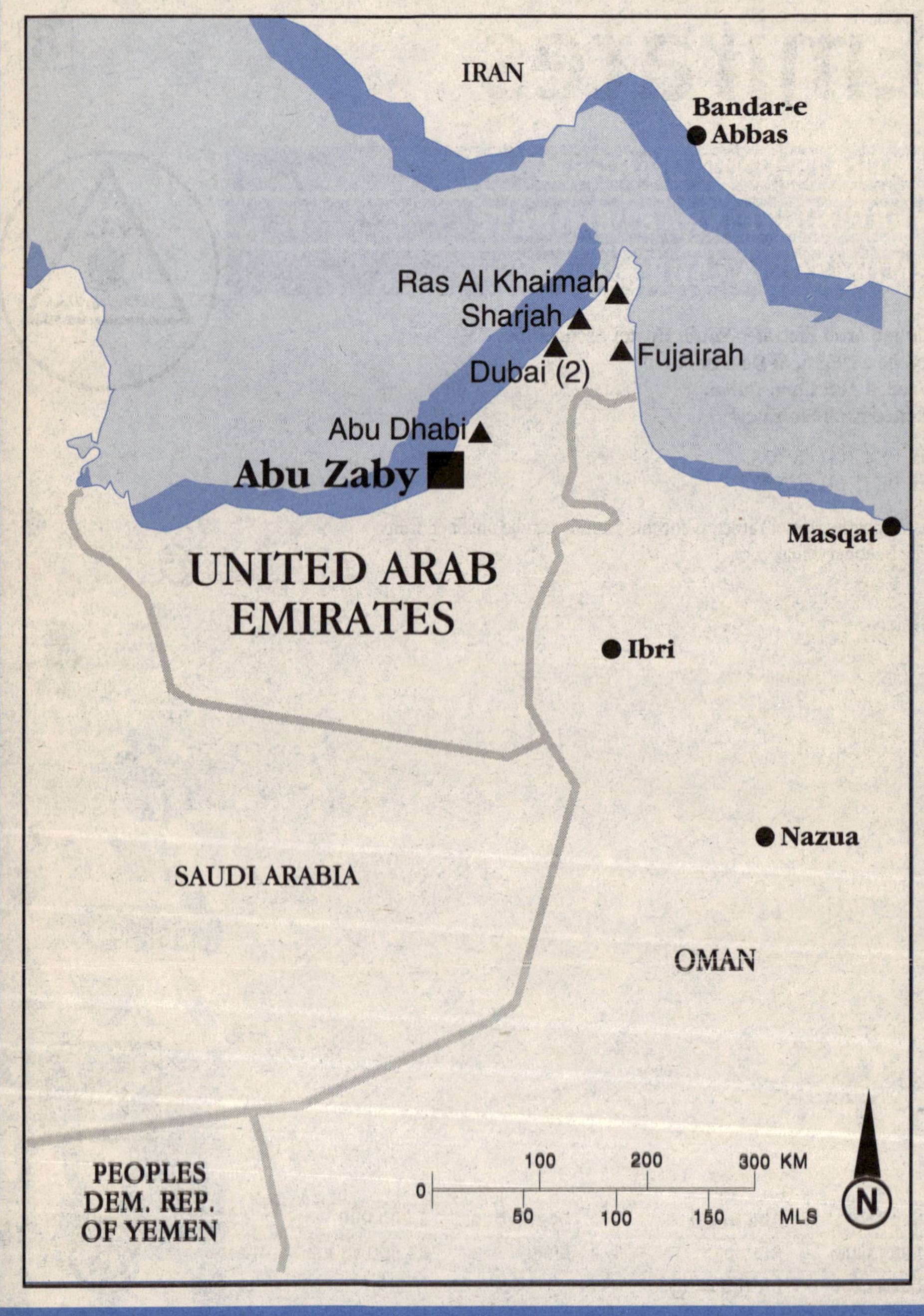

English

UNITED ARAB EMIRATES HOSTELS

All the Youth Hostels are open daily between 08.00 and 24.00hrs. Expect to pay in the region of Dhs 15-35 per night. All hostels have a self-catering kitchen.

PASSPORTS AND VISAS

Visas are required except by citizens of the Gulf Corporation Council States.

HEALTH

Vaccinations are not required.

TELEPHONE INFORMATION

Country Code	971
Main City Area Codes	
Abu Dhabi	2
Dubai	4
Sharjah	6
Al-Ain	3

Français

AUBERGES DE JEUNESSE DANS LES EMIRATS UNIS D'ARABIE

Toutes les auberges sont ouvertes de 8h à 24h tous les jours. Une nuit vous coûtera environ 15-35 dirhams. Il est toujours possible de cuisiner soi-même.

PASSEPORTS ET VISAS

Seuls les citoyens des Etats du Golfe appartenant à la fédération peuvent entrer sans visa.

SOINS MEDICAUX

Aucune vaccination n'est requise.

TELEPHONE

Indicatif du Pays	971
Indicatifs régionaux des Villes principales	
Abu Dhabi	2
Dubaï	4
Chardja	6
Al-Ain	3

Deutsch

JUGENDHERBERGEN IN DEN VEREINIGTEN ARABISCHEN EMIRATEN

Alle Jugendherbergen sind täglich zwischen 08.00 und 24.00 Uhr geöffnet. Es ist mit einem Preis von ca. Dhs 15-35 pro Nacht zu rechnen. Alle Herbergen haben Einrichtungen für Selbstversorger.

PÄSSE UND VISA

Außer Staatsbürgern der Staaten des Golfrats brauchen alle Reisenden ein Visum.

GESUNDHEIT

Impfungen sind nicht erforderlich.

FERNSPRECHINFORMATIONEN

Landes-Kennzahl	971
größere Städte - Ortsnetzkennzahlen	
Abu Dhabi	2
Dubai	4
Sharjah	6
Al-Ain	3

Español

ALBERGUES DE JUVENTUD DE LOS EMIRATOS ARABES UNIDOS

Todos los albergues están abiertos a diario entre las 08.00 y las 24.00 horas. Los precios oscilan entre 15-35 dirhams por noche. Todos los albergues tienen cocina para huéspedes.

PASAPORTES Y VISADOS

Todos los turistas necesitan visado, excepto los ciudadanos de los Estados del Golfo miembros de la Federación.

SANIDAD

No se necesita ninguna vacuna.

INFORMACION TELEFONICA

Código Nacional	971
Prefijos de las Ciudades Principales	
Abu Dhabi	2
Dubai	4
Sharjah	6
Al-Ain	3

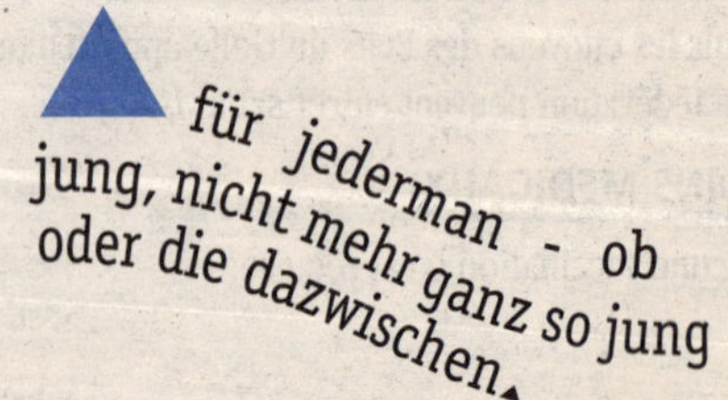

Dubai

**Al Qusais Rd,
Dubai. (near Al Ahli Club)**
☎ (4) 625578
✆ (4) 667989

Open Dates:	
Open Hours:	
Reservations:	**R**
Price Range:	DHS 35
Beds:	91 - 8x² 17x³ 6x⁴
Facilities:	11x ... TV 1x ...

Directions:

✈	Dubai International 5km
A🚌	#3 250m
⛴	Rashed 10km
🚌	3, 13, 17, 2 50m ap Dura Bus Station
Attractions:	5km 500m 2km

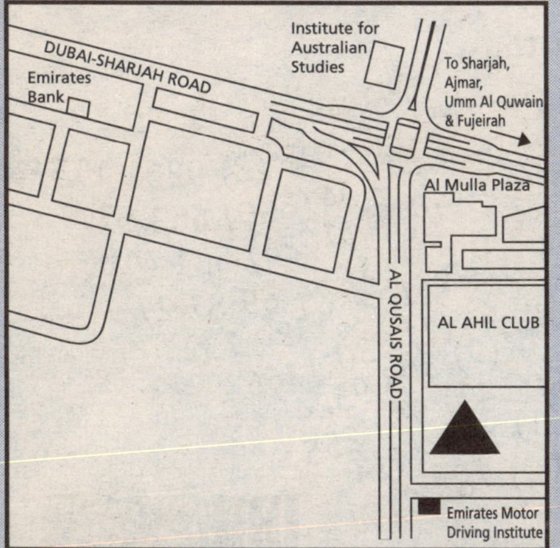

Assured Standards – visited by our Liaison team and by you the guest – tell us when we don't measure up (reply slips at the end of this Guide)▶

des Normes Garanties, par les visites de notre Equipe de Liaison et par vous, les usagers – faites-le nous savoir quand nous ne sommes pas à la hauteur (Fiches-commentaires à la fin du Guide)▶

Zugesicherte Standards – beurteilt von unserem Liaison Team und von Ihnen, unserem Gast – sagen Sie es uns, wenn wir Sie enttäuschen (Antwortkarten hinten im Führer)▶

Normas Garantizadas – comprobadas por nuestro Equipo de Enlace y por Ud., el usuario – si fallamos en algo, díganoslo (al final de esta Guía encontrará nuestras hojas de comentarios)▶

Location/Address	Telephone No. Fax No.	Beds	Opening Dates	Facilities
▲ **Abu Dhabi** Abu Dhabi.	☎ (2) 378400	50	Temporarily closed for reconstruction	
▲ **Al Fujairah** - Youth Hostel Fujairah. (near the Supreme Council of Youth and Sports Office)	☎ (9) 222347 📠 00971 4 667989	42		
▲ **Dubai** **Al Qusais Rd, Dubai. (near Al Ahli Club)**	☎ (4) 625578 📠 (4) 667989	91		
▲ **Dubai** Dubai Hostel of Al Shabab Club, Al Waheda Rd, P.O. Box 19536 Dubai.	☎ 00971 4 651451 📠 00971 4 667989	41		
▲ **Ras Al Khaimah** Ras Al Khaimah. (near the Supreme Council of Youth and Sports Office)	☎ (7) 663711	45		
▲ **Sharjah** Traffic Square, Sharkan, Sharjah. (near Sharjah Sports Club)	☎ (6) 225070	49		

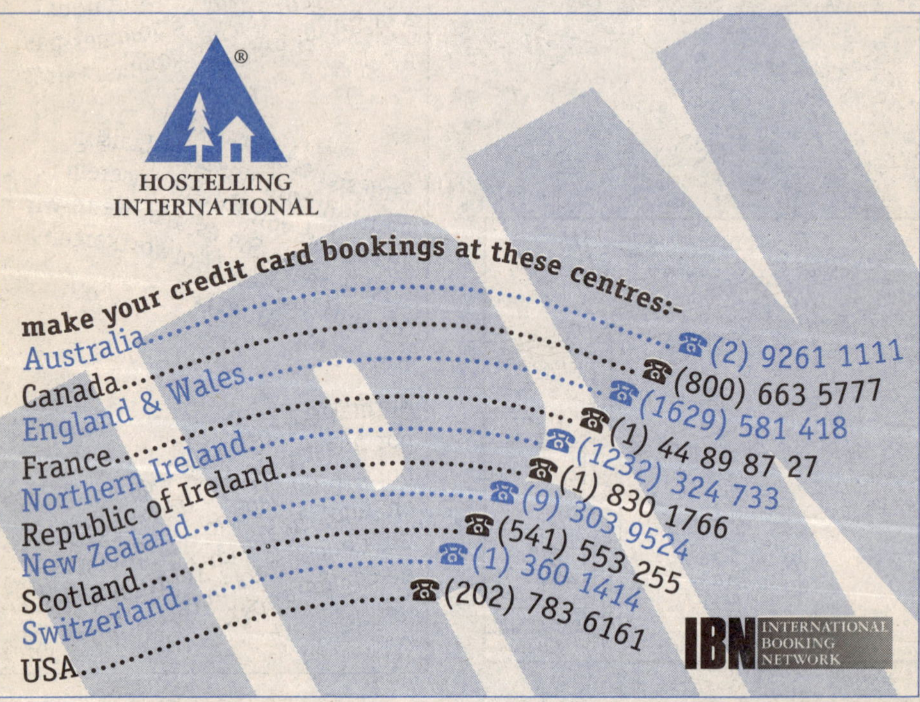

United States

ETATS UNIS

VEREINIGTE STAATEN

ESTADOS UNIDOS

HOSTELLING INTERNATIONAL

American Youth Hostels, Inc
733 15th Street NW, Suite 840, Washington, DC 20005,
United States of America.

☎ (1) (202) 783-6161
📠 (1) (202) 783-6171
E-mail: General enquiries & information: hiayhserv@hiayh.org
WWW address: http://www.hiayh.org

A copy of the Hostel Directory for this Country can be obtained from:
The National Office.

IBN Booking Centres for outward bookings

- **Boulder** - Rocky Mountain Council, Travel Center, 1310 College Avenue, Suite 310, Boulder, CO 80302
  - **☎** (1) (303) 442-1166
  - **📠** (1) (303) 442-4453
- **Boston** - Boston Travel Center, 1105 Commonwealth Ave, Boston, MA 02215.
  - **☎** (1) (617) 731-8096
  - **📠** (1) (617) 734-7614
- **Chicago** - Chicago Metro Council Travel Center, 2232 West Roscoe Street, Chicago, IL 60618.
  - **☎** (1) (773) 327-8327
  - **📠** (1) (773) 327-4287
- **Los Angeles** - Los Angeles Travel Center,1434 Second Street, Santa Monica, CA 90401
  - **☎** (1) (310) 393-3413
  - **📠** (1) (310) 393-1769
- **Philadelphia** - Delaware Valley Council Travel Center, 624 South 3rd Street, Philadelphia, PA 19147
  - **☎** (1) (215) 925-6004
  - **📠** (1) (215) 925-4874
- **San Francisco** - Golden Gate Council Travel Center, 308 Mason St, San Francisco CA 94102.
  - **☎** (1) (415) 788-2525
  - **📠** (1) (415) 788-2558
- **St. Louis** - Gateway Council Travel Center, 7187 Manchester Road, St. Louis, MO 63143-2450
  - **☎** (1) (314) 664-4660
  - **📠** (1) (314) 664-6192
- **Washington** - *via HI-AYH National Office above*
  - **☎** (1) (202) 783-6161
  - **📠** (1) (202) 783-6171

Capital:	Washington, DC	Population:	234,000,000
Language:	English	Size:	9,363,123 sq km
Currency:	US$		

United States

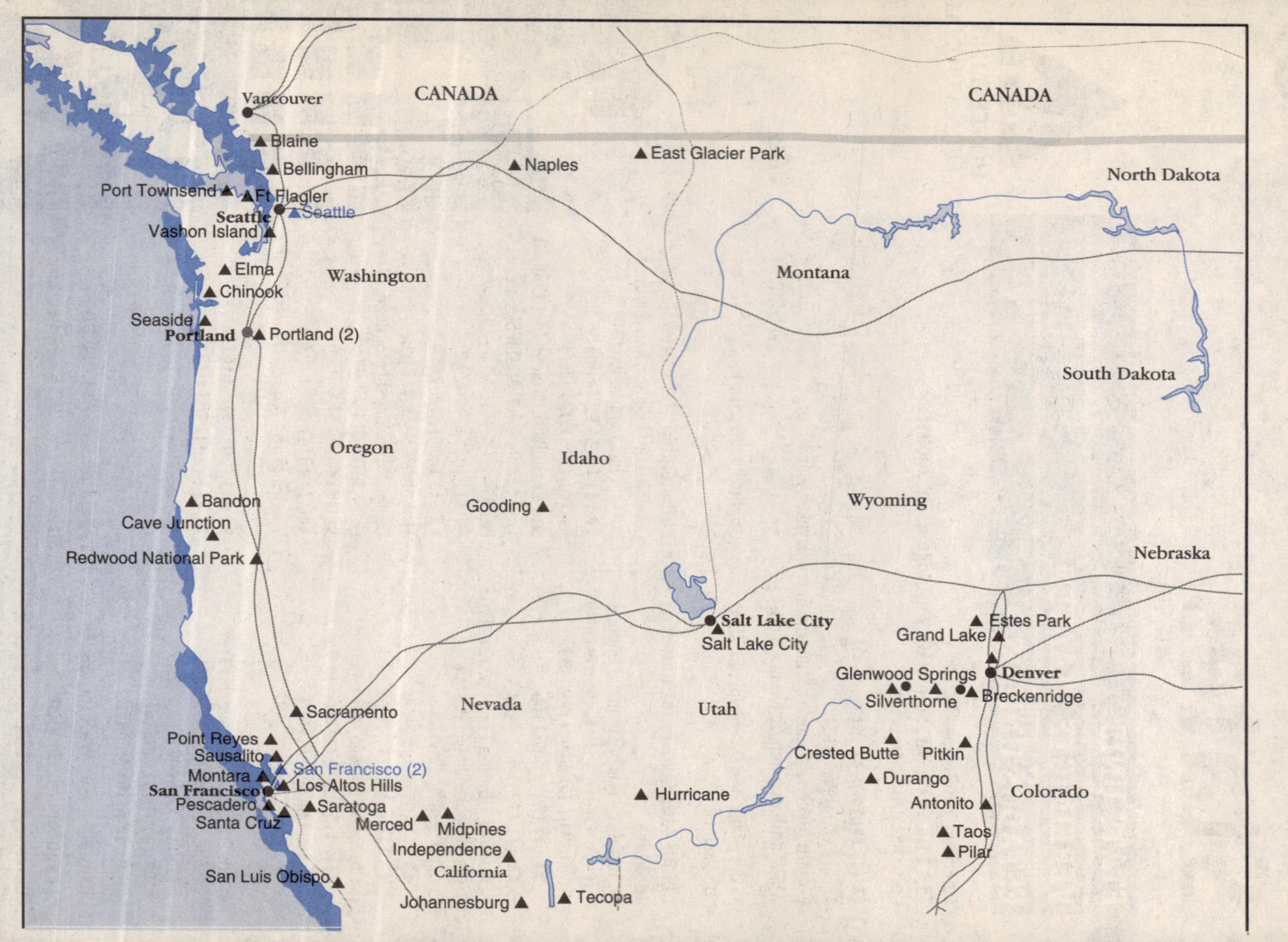

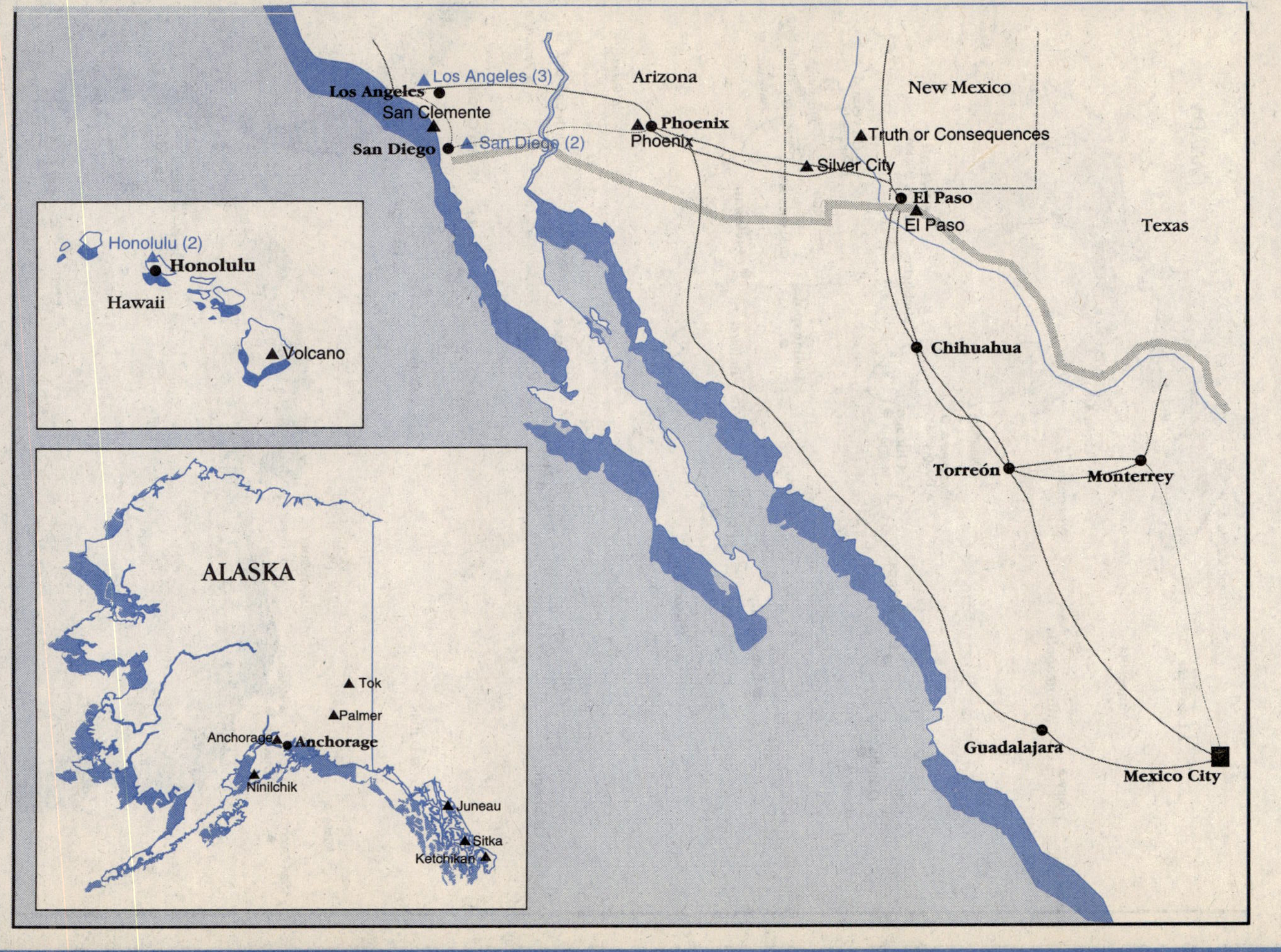
Los Angeles (3)
Los Angeles
San Clemente
San Diego
San Diego (2)
Arizona
Phoenix
Phoenix
New Mexico
Truth or Consequences
Silver City
El Paso
El Paso
Texas
Chihuahua
Torreón
Monterrey
Guadalajara
Mexico City
Honolulu (2)
Honolulu
Hawaii
Volcano
ALASKA
Tok
Palmer
Anchorage
Anchorage
Ninilchik
Juneau
Sitka
Ketchikan
UNITED STATES

United States

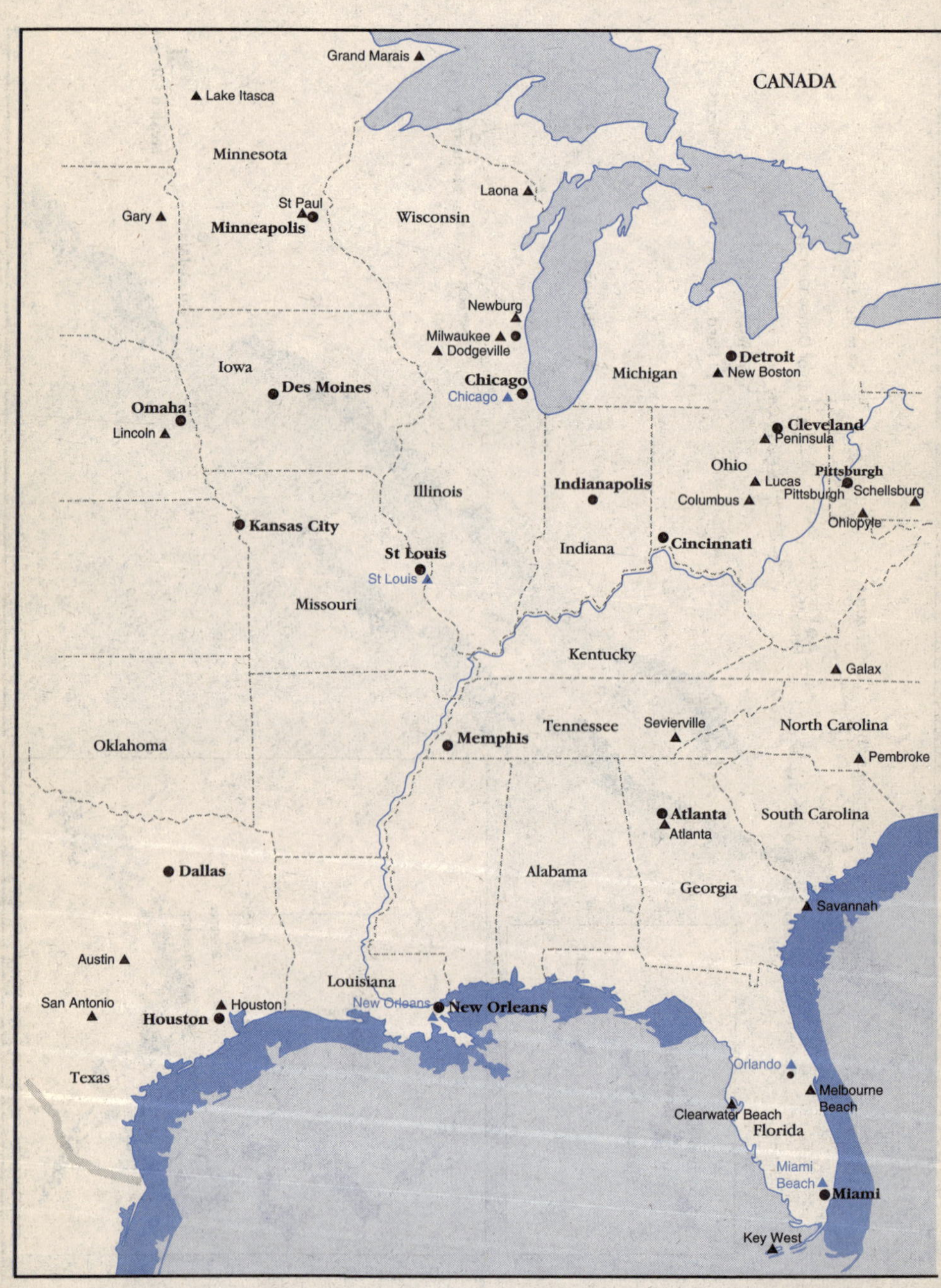

UNITED STATES

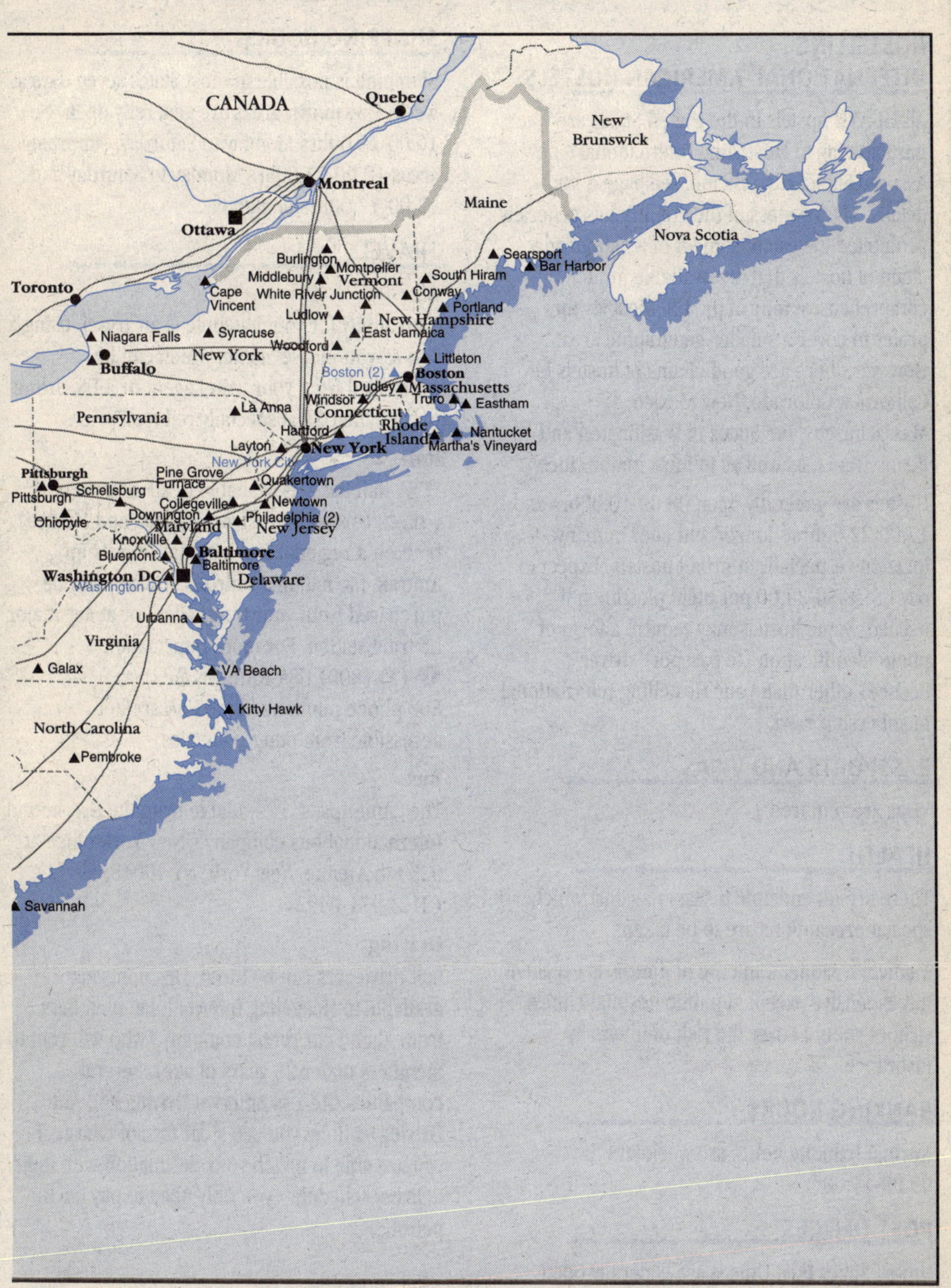
CANADA
Quebec
New Brunswick
Montreal
Maine
Ottawa
Nova Scotia
Toronto
Burlington
Montpelier
Searsport
Middlebury
Vermont
South Hiram
Bar Harbor
Cape Vincent
White River Junction
Conway
Ludlow
Portland
Niagara Falls
Syracuse
New Hampshire
Woodford
East Jamaica
New York
Littleton
Buffalo
Boston (2)
Boston
Dudley
Massachusetts
Windsor
Truro
Eastham
Pennsylvania
La Anna
Connecticut
Rhode Island
Nantucket
Hartford
Layton
Martha's Vineyard
New York
Pittsburgh
New York City
Pine Grove Furnace
Quakertown
Pittsburgh
Schellsburg
Collegeville
Newtown
Ohiopyle
Downington
Philadelphia (2)
Maryland
New Jersey
Knoxville
Bluemont
Baltimore
Washington DC
Baltimore
Delaware
Washington DC
Urbanna
Virginia
Galax
VA Beach
Kitty Hawk
North Carolina
Pembroke
Savannah

English

HOSTELLING INTERNATIONAL-AMERICAN HOSTELS

All HI-AYH hostels in the United States are participating in Hostelling International's new Assured Standards Scheme, see page 4 for details. The vastness of the country has generally prohibited the establishment of a nationwide chain of hostels that are available for a comprehensive tour of the US. Most visitors prefer to cover a smaller geographic area. However, there are good chains of hostels in California, Colorado, New Mexico, Massachusetts, the States of Washington and Pennsylvania, as well as in most major cities.

Hostels are generally open 08.00-10.00hrs and 17.00-22.00hrs - longer and later in many locations especially at urban hostels. Expect to pay US$ 8.50-24.00 per night plus linen if needed. Some hostels may require a form of photo identification (ie passport, driver's licence) other than your Hostelling International membership card.

PASSPORTS AND VISAS

Visas are required.

HEALTH

There are no endemic diseases against which special precautions are to be taken.

Medical treatment, in case of illness, is excellent but expensive except at public hospital clinics; visitors should cover the risk of illness by insurance.

BANKING HOURS

Normal banking hours are weekdays 09.00-15.00hrs.

POST OFFICES

United States Post Offices are generally open Monday to Friday 09.00-17.00hrs. Many are open until midday on Saturdays - exact times of opening are displayed at each post office.

SHOPPING HOURS

Shopping is possible in most States seven days a week. Downtown areas are generally open 10.00-18.00hrs Monday to Saturday, suburban areas 10.00-21.00hrs Monday to Saturday and 12.00-17.00hrs on Sunday.

TRAVEL

Air

A great buy for young people is air travel, using a "go-as-you-please" ticket which can be purchased from your travel agent or a US airline outside the USA at specially reduced prices.

Rail

"USA Rail Pass" is available to all international visitors (except those from Canada and Mexico) both on a regional and national basis from Amtrak, the national railroad. Tickets may be purchased from your travel agent or at any major US train station. For more information ☎ (1) (800) USA-RAIL. (in the USA). 800 phone numbers in the USA are not accessible from other countries.

Bus

The "Ameripass" is available from the Greyhound International bus company's New York office at 625 8th Avenue, New York, NY 10018; ☎ (1) (212) 971-0492.

Driving

Self-drive cars can be hired. Discounts are available to Hostelling International members from Alamo car rental company (who will rent to members under 25 years of age). Several companies (Across America Driving and Auto Driving) will let you use a car free of charge if you are able to match your destination with their delivery schedule - you only need to pay for the petrol.

TELEPHONE INFORMATION

Country Code	**1**
Main City Area Codes	
Boston	617
Los Angeles	310
Miami	305
New York	212
San Francisco	415
Washington DC	202

Français

AUBERGES DE JEUNESSE AMERICAINES HOSTELLING INTERNATIONAL

Il y a 140+ auberges de jeunesse (HI-AYH) en Amérique. Toutes participent au Plan Hostelling International pour la Garantie des Normes (Voir page 12 pour plus de renseignements). L'immensité du pays s'est révélée être, dans l'ensemble, un obstacle à l'établissement d'une chaîne nationale d'auberges pour les voyageurs souhaitant visiter tout le pays. La plupart des touristes préfèrent explorer un secteur géographique plus petit. Cependant, il y a de bonnes chaînes d'auberges en Californie, au Colorado, au Nouveau Mexique, dans le Massachusetts, dans les états de Washington et de Pennsylvanie, ainsi que dans la plupart des grandes villes.

Les auberges sont en général ouvertes de 8h00 à 10h00 et de 17h à 22h - plus longtemps et plus tard dans de nombreuses régions, surtout lorsqu'il s'agit d'auberges urbaines. Une nuit vous coûtera entre 8.50 et 24 $US, plus les draps, si nécessaire. Certaines auberges pourront vous demander de présenter une preuve d'identité photographique quelconque (passeport, permis de conduire) en plus de votre carte d'adhérent Hostelling International.

PASSEPORTS ET VISAS

Les visas sont nécessaires.

SOINS MEDICAUX

Il n'y a pas de maladies endémiques contre lesquelles il est nécessaire de se protéger.

Les traitements médicaux, en cas de maladie, sont excellents mais chers, sauf dans les services hospitaliers publics; il est conseillé aux personnes se rendant dans ce pays de souscrire à une police d'assurance maladie.

HEURES D'OUVERTURE DES BANQUES

Les banques sont normalement ouvertes en semaine de 9h à 15h.

BUREAUX DE POSTE

Aux Etats-Unis, les bureaux de poste sont en principe ouverts du lundi au vendredi de 9h à 17h. De nombreux bureaux sont ouverts jusqu'à midi le samedi - les heures d'ouverture exactes sont affichées à chaque bureau.

HEURES D'OUVERTURE DES MAGASINS

Dans la plupart des états, il est possible de faire des achats sept jours sur sept. Dans les villes et quartiers commerçants, les magasins sont en général ouverts entre 10h et 18h, du lundi au samedi, et en banlieue, ils sont en général ouverts entre 10h et 21h du lundi au samedi et de 12h à 17h le dimanche.

DEPLACEMENTS

Avions

Les transports aériens sont très avantageux pour les jeunes munis d'un billet "go-as-you-please", en vente dans votre agence de voyages ou auprès d'une compagnie aérienne américaine en dehors des Etats-Unis, à des prix spéciaux.

Trains

La carte "USA Rail Pass" est disponible pour tous les visiteurs étrangers (sauf ressortissants canadiens ou mexicains) au niveau régional ou national et peut être obtenue auprès d'Amtrak, les chemins de fer nationaux. Vous pouvez acheter ces billets dans votre agence de voyages ou aux Etats-Unis, dans les gares principales. Pour de plus amples renseignements

 (1) (800) USA-RAIL.

Les numéros de téléphone 800 aux USA ne sont pas accessibles depuis l'étranger.

Autobus

La carte "Ameripass" est en vente dans les bureaux de la compagnie d'autobus Greyhound International à New York, 625 8th Avenue, New York, NY 10018; (1) (212) 971-0492.

Automobiles

Il est possible de louer des voitures. L'agence de location de voitures Alamo (qui loue aux membres de moins de 25 ans) offrent des remises aux membres d'Hostelling International. Plusieurs agences (Across America Driving et Auto Driving) vous laisseront utiliser une voiture gratuitement si votre destination correspond à leur programme de livraison - il ne vous en coûtera que l'essence.

TELEPHONE

Indicatif du Pays	**1**
Indicatifs régionaux des Villes principales	
Boston	**617**
Los Angeles	**310**
Miami	**305**
New York	**212**
San Francisco	**415**
Washington DC	**202**

Deutsch

HOSTELLING INTERNATIONAL-AMERIKANISCHE JUGENDHERBERGEN

Alle HI-AYH Herbergen in den Vereinigten Staaten sind am 'Assured-Standards-Plan' des Hostelling International beteiligt (siehe Seite 20 für weitere Einzelheiten). Die Größe des Landes hat die Gründung eines nationalen Netzes von Herbergen verhindert. Die meisten Reisenden beschränken sich auf einen kleineren geographischen Bereich. Es gibt ein gutes Herbergsnetz in Kalifornien, Colorado, New Mexico, Massachusetts, den Staaten Washington und Pennsylvania sowie in den meisten größeren Städten.

Die Herbergen sind im allgemeinen von 8.00-10.00 Uhr und von 17.00-22.00 Uhr geöffnet. An vielen Orten, und besonders in Städten, sind sie jedoch länger geöffnet. Sie werden dann auch abends später geschlossen. Es ist mit einem Preis von US$ 8,50-24,00 pro Nacht plus, bei Bedarf, einer Gebühr für die Miete von Bettwäsche zu rechnen. Bei einigen Jugendherbergen ist ein Ausweis mit Foto (Paß, Führerschein) sowie ein Mitgliedsausweis Hostelling Internationals erforderlich.

PÄSSE UND VISA

Es wird ein Visum benötigt.

GESUNDHEIT

Es gibt hier keine Krankheiten, gegen die besondere Vorsichtsmaßnahmen ergriffen werden müssen.

Im Krankheitsfalle wird hervorragende ärztliche Betreuung geboten, die aber - außer in öffentlichen Krankenhäusern - teuer ist. Reisende sollten deshalb eine Krankenversicherung abschließen.

GESCHÄFTSSTUNDEN DER BANKEN

Banken sind gewöhnlich werktags von 9.00-15.00 Uhr geöffnet.

POSTÄMTER

In den Vereinigten Staaten sind die Postämter im allgemeinen montags bis freitags von 09.00-17.00 Uhr geöffnet. Viele sind auch samstags bis zur Mittagszeit geöffnet. Die genauen Öffnungszeiten hängen in jedem Postamt aus.

LADENÖFFNUNGSZEITEN

In den meisten Staaten kann an allen sieben Wochentagen eingekauft werden. In der Innenstadt sind die Geschäfte im allgemeinen montags bis samstags von 10.00-18.00 Uhr geöffnet, während sie in den Vororten montags bis samstags von 10.00-21.00 Uhr und sonntags von 12.00-17.00 Uhr geöffnet sind.

REISEN

Flugverkehr

Mit einem "go-as-you-please"-Ticket, das Sie in Ihrem Reisebüro oder von einer US-Fluggesellschaft außerhalb der USA mit Sonderermäßigung kaufen können, sind Flugreisen für junge Leute sehr preiswert.

Eisenbahn

Der "USA Rail Pass" ist für alle internationalen Reisenden (außer denen, die aus Kanada und Mexiko kommen) auf regionaler und nationaler Basis vom nationalen Eisenbahnunternehmen Amtrak erhältlich. Fahrkarten können Sie in Ihrem Reisebüro oder auf jedem größeren Bahnhof in den USA kaufen. Nähere Auskunft über

✆ (800) USA-RAIL. (in den USA). Telefonnummern in den USA, die mit 800 beginnen, sind vom Ausland nicht erreichbar.

Busse

Der "Ameripass" ist von der New Yorker Geschäftsstelle des Busunternehmens von Greyhound International erhältlich: 625 8th Avenue, New York, NY 10018; ✆ (1) (212) 971-0492.

Autofahren

Fahrzeuge können gemietet werden. Mitglieder von Hostelling International erhalten bei der Firma Alamo (die an Mitglieder unter 25 Jahren vermietet) einen Nachlaß. Die Firmen 'Across America Driving' und 'Auto Driving' stellen kostenlos Überführungswagen zur Verfügung; die Reiseroute muß allerdings mit den Firmen abgestimmt werden. Sie brauchen in diesem Fall nur für das Benzin zu bezahlen.

FERNSPRECHINFORMATIONEN

Landes-Kennzahl	**1**
größere Städte - Ortsnetzkennzahlen	
Boston	**617**
Los Angeles	**310**
Miami	**305**
New York	**212**
San Francisco	**415**
Washington DC	**202**

Español

ALBERGUES DE JUVENTUD AMERICANOS HOSTELLING INTERNATIONAL

Todos los albergues juveniles de la HI-AYH en los Estados Unidos participan en el nuevo Plan Hostelling International de Normas Garantizadas (ver la página 28 para más información). Las dimensiones del país han impedido en gran medida el establecimiento de una red nacional de albergues que permita realizar una visita completa de los EE.UU. La mayoría de los visitantes prefieren cubrir un área geográfica más pequeña. No obstante, existen buenas cadenas de albergues en California, Colorado, Nuevo México, Massachusetts, en los estados de Washington y Pennsylvania, así como en las principales ciudades del país.

Los albergues suelen abrir de 08.00 a 10.00 horas y de 17.00 a 22 horas, si bien algunos, sobre todo en zonas urbanas, abren más horas y hasta más tarde. El precio oscila entre US$ 8,50 y 24,00 por noche, más sábanas, de ser necesarias. Algunos albergues pueden exigir un documento de identidad con fotografía (p.ej. pasaporte, permiso de conducir) aparte de la tarjeta de socio de Hostelling International.

PASAPORTES Y VISADOS

Se requiere visado.

SANIDAD

No existen enfermedades endémicas contra las que haya que tomar precauciones especiales.

La asistencia médica, en caso de enfermedad, es excelente pero cara excepto en hospitales públicos. Se recomienda a los visitantes cubrir con un seguro el riesgo de enfermedad.

HORARIO DE BANCOS

Normalmente los bancos abren los días laborables de 09.00 a 15.00 horas.

OFICINAS DE CORREOS

Las oficinas de correos de los Estados Unidos suelen abrir de lunes a viernes de 09.00 a 17.00 horas. Muchas abren hasta el mediodía los sábados. En cada una de ellas se indica el horario exacto de atención al público.

HORARIO COMERCIAL

En la mayoría de los estados se pueden hacer compras los siete días de la semana. En las áreas céntricas, las tiendas suelen abrir de 10.00 a 18.00 horas de lunes a sábado. En las afueras abren de 10.00 a 21.00 de lunes a sábado y de 12.00 a 17.00 los domingos.

DESPLAZAMIENTOS

Avión

Viajar en avión resulta ideal para los jóvenes si compran un billete "go-as-you-please" (ve por donde quieras) que pueden conseguir en su agencia de viajes o aerolínea estadounidense fuera de los EE.UU. a precios especialmente reducidos.

Tren

El abono "USA Rail Pass" de Amtrak, la compañía ferroviaria nacional, puede ser adquirido por todos los visitantes internacionales, excepto los turistas canadienses y mejicanos, para viajar tanto a nivel regional como nacional. Los billetes se pueden comprar en las agencias de viajes o en cualquier estación importante de los EE.UU. Para más información llame al

☎ (1) (800) USA-RAIL (en los EE.UU.).
Los números telefónicos que empiezan por 800 no se pueden marcar desde otros países.

Autobús

El "Ameripass" se puede comprar en la oficina de Nueva York de la compañía de autobuses Greyhound International, 625 8th. Avenue, Nueva York, NY 10018; ☎ (1) (212) 971-0492.

Coche

Se pueden alquilar coches sin conductor. Los socios de Hostelling International pueden conseguir descuentos en Alamo (que alquila coches a socios menores de 25 años). Varias compañías (Across America Driving y Auto Driving) le permitirán utilizar su coche de forma gratuita si el itinerario que piensa seguir coincide con su programa de entregas, en cuyo caso sólo hay que pagar la gasolina.

INFORMACION TELEFONICA

Código Nacional	**1**
Prefijos de las Ciudades Principales	
Boston	**617**
Los Angeles	**310**
Miami	**305**
Nueva York	**212**
San Francisco	**415**
Washington DC	**202**

Discounts And Concessions

Your Hostelling International membership card entitles you to a very wide range of discounts at or near hostels, including admission to popular attractions, museum entrance fees, cinemas, day trips and excursions, sporting equipment and rentals, cameras and film, grocery stores, restaurants, gift and clothing stores.

In addition, several national discounts are available, including:

Alamo Rent A Car: 10-15% off daily and weekly rentals with unlimited mileage in the USA and Europe. No charge for additional drivers.

A complete listing of all the area discounts is posted at each hostel. All discounts and hostels are included in "Hostelling North America: The Official Guide to Hostels in the United States and Canada", available free at all HI-AYH offices and hostels.

There for everyone - young, not so young and those in the middle.

c'est pour tout le monde -les jeunes, les moins jeunes et tous les autres.

albergues para todos - los jóvenes, los menos jóvenes y los jóvenes de espíritu.

für jederman - ob jung, nicht mehr ganz so jung oder die dazwischen.

Anchorage

**700 'H' St,
Anchorage AK 99501.**
☎ (907) 2763635
🖷 (907) 2767772

Open Dates:	🗐
Open Hours:	08.00-23.00hrs
Reservations:	R CC
Price Range:	$16.00
Beds:	95 - 4x^3 7x^4 11x^5
Facilities:	5x ... 1x ...

Directions:

✈	Anchorage International 10km
A🚌	Rt 6, 4 times daily to Transit Centre
🚂	Alaska RR 500m
Attractions:	1800 250m

Atlanta

**223 Ponce de Leon Ave,
Atlanta GA 30308.**
☎ (404) 8721042
🖷 (404) 8700042

Open Dates:	🗐
Open Hours:	08.00-12.00; 17.00-24.00hrs
Reservations:	R CC
Price Range:	$15.00 BB inc
Beds:	80 - 2x^1 4x^2 13x^4 2x^5 1x^6
Facilities:	2x ...

Directions: 2N from city centre

✈	Hartsfield International 15km
🚂	Amtrak 3km
🚌	Greyhound 1.5km
🚋	350m
U	From ✈, to N Avenue, #2 to Myrtle (Request). From 🚂, #23 South to Arts Center, then U to N Avenue. 300m

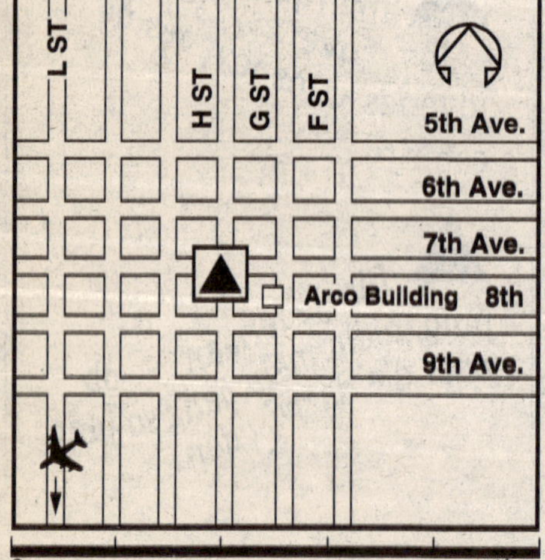

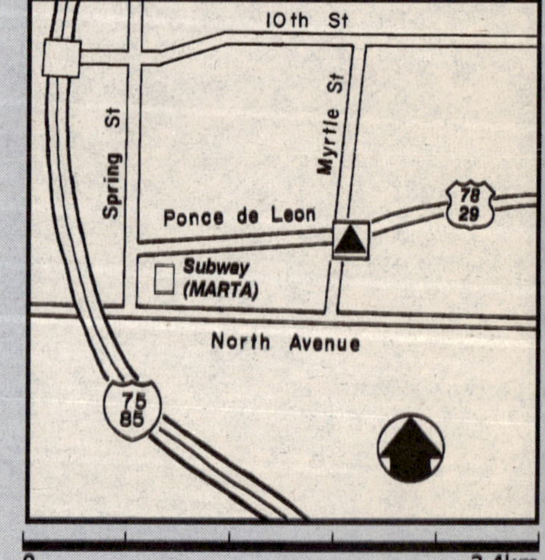

Austin

2200 S Lakeshore Blvd,
Austin TX 78741.
☎ **(512) 4442294**
🖷 **(512) 4442309**

Open Dates:	🗓
Open Hours:	08.00-11.00; 17.00-22.00hrs
Reservations:	⌐CC⌐
Price Range:	$14.00 🗍
Beds:	40 - 1x³🛏 3x⁶🛏
Facilities:	♿ 🏃🏃🏃 🍴🏠 📺 🧺 1x🔭 🔒 💼 🏢 🔲 🧃 🅿 ℹ 🛝 🌿 🏢 🏠

Directions:

✈	Robert Mueller 5km
A🚌	20 to Capitol Bldg then 26 or 27 to Burton or Riverside 100m
🚂	Amtrak 5km
🚌	Greyhound #7 to Butron and Riverside 100m

Attractions: 🌳⛰ 🚴 🚶 ⚲3.5km 🏊2.5km

Boston

12 Hemenway St,
Boston MA 02115.
☎ **(617) 5369455**
🖷 **(617) 4246558**

Open Dates:	🗓
Open Hours:	🕐
Reservations:	Ⓡ ⌐IBN⌐ ⌐CC⌐
Price Range:	$19.00-20.00 🗍
Beds:	205 - 4x¹🛏 5x²🛏 1x³🛏 8x⁴🛏 26x⁶🛏
Facilities:	♿ 🏃🏃 9x🍴🏃 🏠 🧺 1x🔭 🔒 💼 🏢 🔲 ℹ 🛝 🏠

Directions: 3SW from city centre

✈	Logan International 6km
A🚌	Blue/Green "T" bus to Hynes 600m
🚂	South Station to Red/Green "T" 200m
Ⓤ	Green Line "T" Hynes - Convention Center 200m

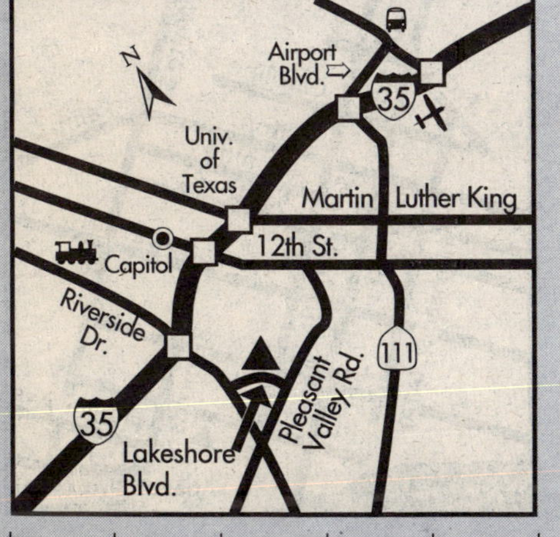

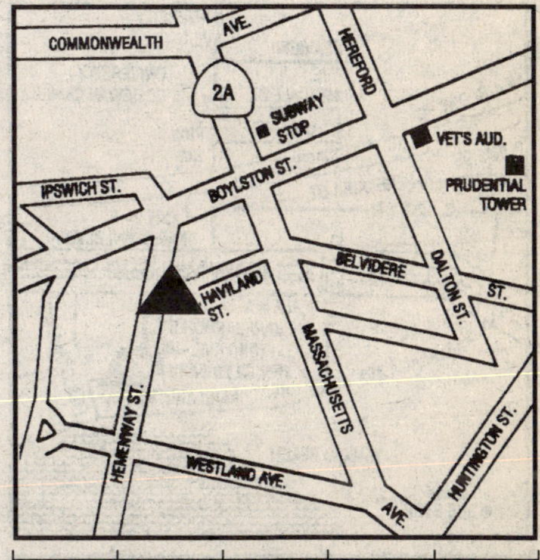

Honolulu

**Waikiki,
2417 Prince Edward St,
Honolulu HI 96815.**
☎ (808) 9268313
✆ (808) 9223798

Open Dates:	🗓
Open Hours:	07.00-03.00hrs
Reservations:	Ⓡ IBN CC
Price Range:	$16.00 📖
Beds:	64 - 4x² 8x³ 4x⁴ 1x⁶
Facilities:	††† 2x††† ✋ 🛏 📺 📓 🔲 💼 8 P ℹ 👥 ⚘

Directions:

✈	Honolulu International 10km
A🚌	#20 to Kings Village 100m
Attractions:	⚲ ≈500m ⚊150m

Key West

**718 South St,
Key West,
FL 33040.**
☎ (305) 2965719
✆ (305) 2960672

Open Dates:	🗓
Open Hours:	🕐
Reservations:	Ⓡ CC
Price Range:	$15.00-17.00 📖
Beds:	92 - 2x⁴ 2x⁵ 5x⁶ 4x⁶
Facilities:	††† ††† 🍴 (BD) ✋ 🛏 📺 📓 ☒ 🔲 💼 ⊜ P ℹ 👥 ⚘

Directions:

✈	Key West International 4.8km
⛴	Ft Myers, Naples, Tampa 36km
🚌	Greyhound 4.8km
Attractions:	⚲ ⚵ ≈20m ⚊20m

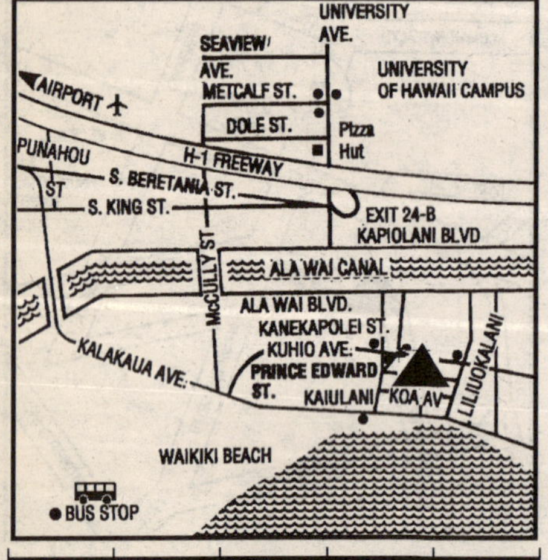

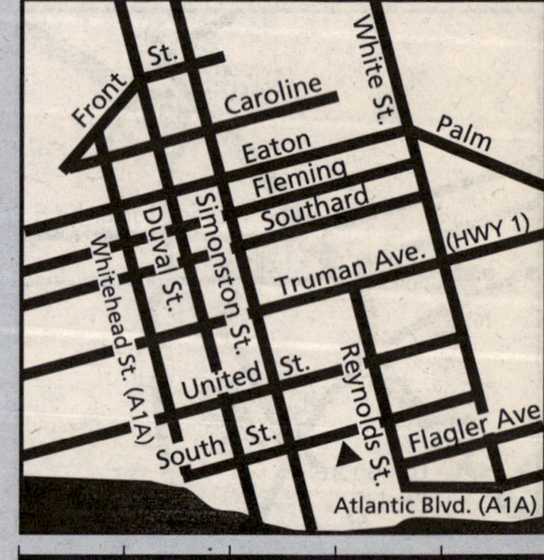

Los Angeles

1436 2nd St,
Santa Monica CA 90401.
☎ (310) 3939913
🖷 (310) 3931769

Open Dates:	🗓
Open Hours:	🕐
Reservations:	**R** IBN CC
Price Range:	$18.00-20.00
Beds:	200 - 7x¹ 4x⁴ 9x⁶ 14x⁶⁺
Facilities:	♿ ♜ 4x♜ 🍽 (B) 🔒 💺 📺 📖 1x 🍸 🔲 💼 ♿ 8 ⬇ 🅿 ✏ ♫ ❀ 🏛

Directions:

✈	Los Angeles International (LAX) 1.2km
🚂	Union (Amtrak) 2.4km
🚌	Greyhound Depot 2.1km
Attractions:	🔍 ⚲1km 🏊1km

Los Angeles

South Bay,
3601 South Gaffey St,
Building 613,
San Pedro CA 90731-6969.
☎ (310) 8318109
🖷 (310) 8314635

Open Dates:	🗓
Open Hours:	07.00-24.00hrs
Reservations:	**R** CC
Price Range:	$11.00-13.00
Beds:	60 - 5x¹ 5x² 4x³ 3x⁵ 1x⁶⁺
Facilities:	♜ 4x♜ 🍽 🔒 💺 📺 🧺 1x 🍸 🔲 💼 8 🅿 ✏ ♫ ⛺ 🏛

Directions: 32S from city centre

✈	LAX 24km
A🚌	Super Shuttle ($14) to Hostel
⛴	LA Harbour 3km
🚂	Amtrak; Metrolink 40km
🚌	446 ap Korean Bell
U	Long Beach Transit Centre 16km
Attractions:	🔍 🚴 🚶 🏊 1km

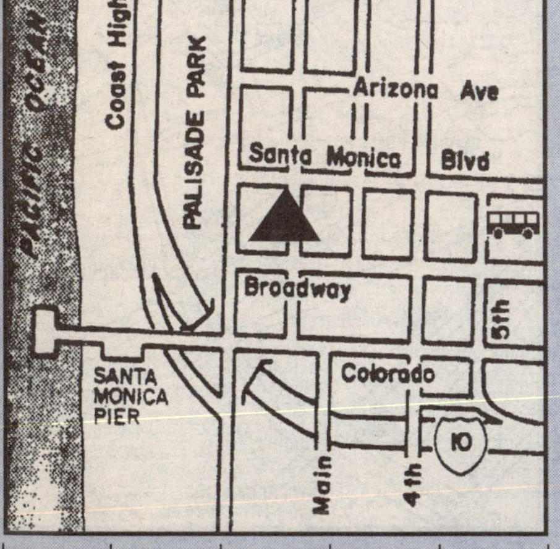

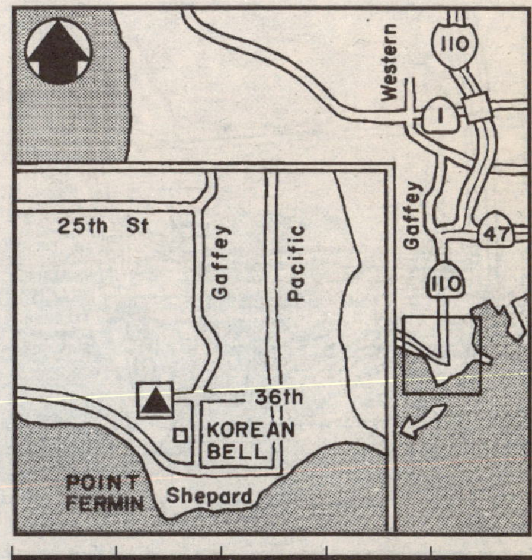

0	100m
0	2km

Miami Beach

**Miami Beach International,
1438 Washington Ave,
Miami Beach FL 33139.**
- ☏ (305) 5342988;
- ☏ (800) 3592529 (R only)
- 🖷 (305) 6730346

Open Dates:	🗓
Open Hours:	🕓
Reservations:	R IBN CC
Price Range:	$14.00 💳
Beds:	200 - 10x² 30x⁴ 10x⁶
Facilities:	10x 1x

Directions:

✈	Miami International 16km
A🚌	Super Shuttle to YH; "J" bus to 41st Street, then "C" bus to alighting point 200m
⛴	Port of Miami 4km
🚆	Amtrak 10km
🚌	Greyhound bus to "C" bus 8km ap Washington and 15th Street 200m

Attractions: 🔍 ⚲50m ⚲50m

New Orleans

**New Orleans-Marquette House,
2253 Carondelet St,
New Orleans LA 70130.**
- ☏ (504) 5233014
- 🖷 (504) 5295933

Open Dates:	🗓
Open Hours:	07.00-24.00hrs (Later by arrangement)
Reservations:	R IBN CC
Price Range:	$13.97 (01.01-02.01; 23.04-02.05; $20.00; 12.02-16.02; $25.00) 💳
Beds:	176 - 8x⁴ 12x⁶⁺
Facilities:	8x (B)

Directions:

✈	New Orleans 18km
A🚌	Elk Place and Tulane Avenue 3km
⛴	New Orleans 4km
🚆	Amtrak/Greyhound 2.5km
🚌	Greyhound 2.5km
🚋	ap Jackson Ave stop #13; St. Charles Avenue 100m

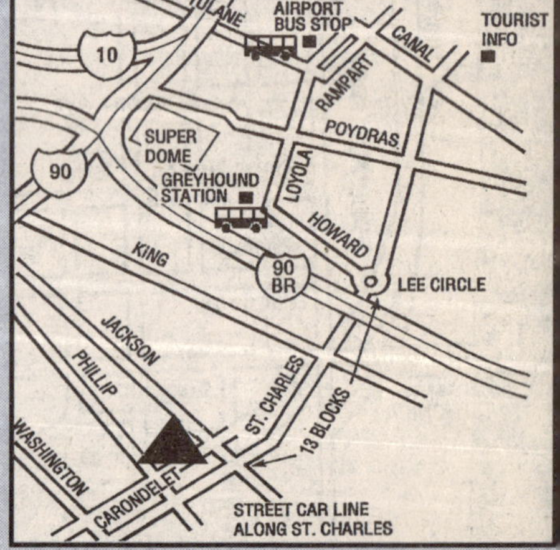

New York

**891 Amsterdam Ave at West 103rd St,
New York NY 10025.**
☎ (212) 9322300
🖷 (212) 9322574
ICN kiosk at hostel,
Kiosque ICN à l'auberge
ICN-Kiosk in der Herberge,
Quisco ICN en el albergue

Open Dates:	🗓
Open Hours:	🕐
Reservations:	® IBN CC
Price Range:	$22.00 (01.11-30.04); $24.00 (01.05-31.10) 🗨
Beds:	624 - 16x⁴ 22x⁶ 38x⁶
Facilities:	♿ ♦♦♦ 6x♦♦♦ 🍴 ☕ ☕ 🏨 📺 📓 🎨 4x🍷 🔌 💼 🚿 8 ⊜ ⇕ ℹ 🛒 ♻ 🏧 🏠🏪 🏠

Directions:

✈	Kennedy 20km; LaGuardia 8km; Newark 25km
A🚌	Grayline to YH
🚆	Penn 4.5km
🚌	Port Authority 3.5km
Ⓤ	#1 or #9 to 103rd St Station 200m

Attractions: ↻1.5km ⚲1.5km 🏊1km

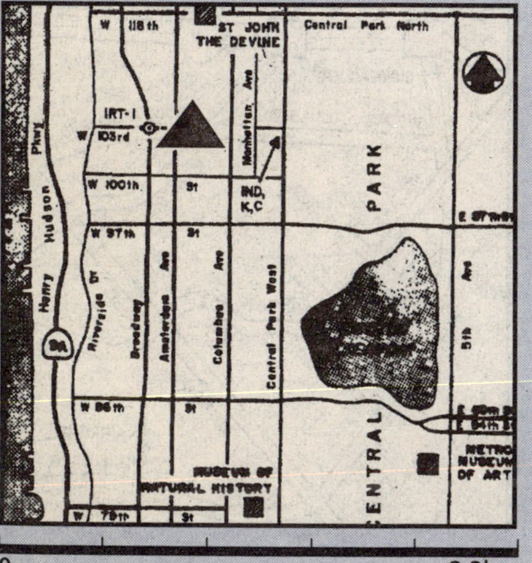

0   2.3km

Orlando

**Orlando/Kissimmee Resort,
4840 W Irlo Bronson Hwy,
Kissimmee FL 34746.
(Route 192 at Route 535)**
☎ (407) 3968282
🖷 (407) 3969311

Open Dates:	🗓
Open Hours:	🕐
Reservations:	IBN CC
Price Range:	$16.00 (+Tax) 🗨
Beds:	192 - 7x¹ 10x² 3x³ 21x⁶
Facilities:	♿ ♦♦♦ 13x♦♦♦ ☕ 🏨 📺 📓 🎨 💼 8 ⊜ 🅿 ℹ 🛒 ♻ 🏧

Directions:

✈	Orlando International 27km
A🚌	Mears to Hostel
🚆	Amtrak - Kissimmee 16km
🚌	Lynx #56 4km ap Bamboo Lane

Attractions: 🏊

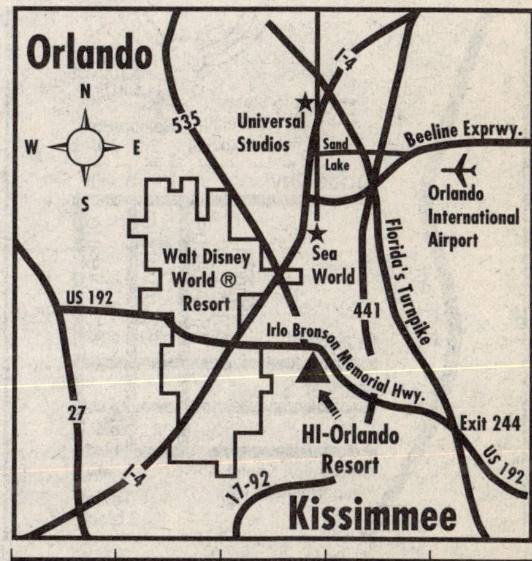

0   5km

San Diego - Downtown

The Metropolitan,
521 Market St,
San Diego,
CA 92101.
☎ (619) 5251531
🖷 (619) 3380129

Open Dates:	🗓
Open Hours:	07.00-24.00hrs
Reservations:	R IBN CC
Price Range:	$16.00-18.00
Beds:	150 - 15x² 20x⁴ 2x⁶ 3x⁶⁺
Facilities:	♿ ♀♂ 2x ♀♂ 🍳 🛋 TV 🧺 1x 🍸 🔒 💼 🔒 🛗 ℹ

Directions:

✈	San Diego International 5km
A🚌	#992 to 5th & Broadway 500m
🚆	Santa Fe Depot (Amtrak) 1km
🚌	Greyhound 500m
🚋	Blue Line ap 5th Avenue 500m

Attractions: 🚴

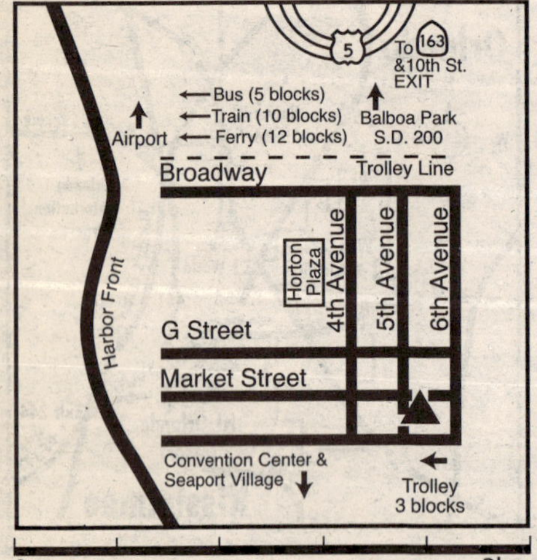

San Diego - Point Loma

Elliott Hostel,
3790 Udall St,
San Diego CA 92107-2414.
☎ (619) 2234778
🖷 (619) 2231883

Open Dates:	🗓
Open Hours:	08.00-22.00hrs
Reservations:	R IBN CC
Price Range:	$13.00-15.00
Beds:	61 - 3x¹ 1x² 2x³ 4x⁴ 1x⁶ 2x⁶⁺
Facilities:	♀♂ 2x ♀♂ 🍳 🛋 TV 📷 🧺 🔒 8 P ℹ 🌺

Directions:

	10W from city centre
✈	Lindbergh Field 5km
A🚌	#992 - #35 - Voltaire & Poinsettia 5km
⛴	Broadway Pier/Embarcadero 9km
🚆	Santa Fe Depot/Amtrak 9km
🚌	#35 ap Voltaire and Poinsetta 500m
🚋	Oldtown Transit Center 5km ap to 🚌 #35

Attractions: 🏛 🚴 ⛷3km ⚓4km

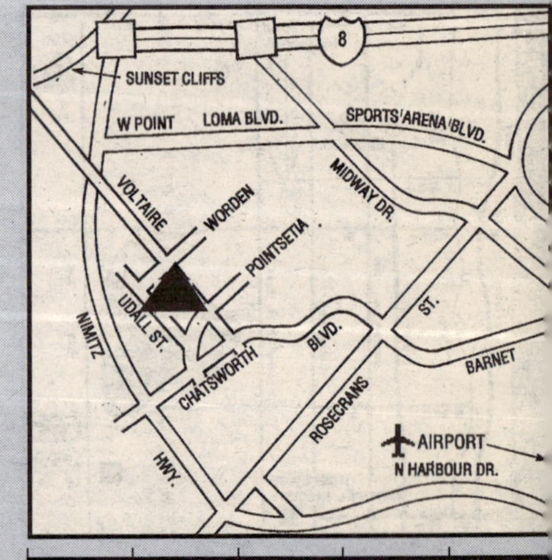

San Francisco -
Downtown

**Union Square,
Downtown, 312 Mason St,
Union Sq,
San Francisco CA 94102.**
(415) 7885604

Open Dates:	
Open Hours:	
Reservations:	**R** IBN CC
Price Range:	$17.00-$19.00
Beds:	230 - 36x^2 20x^3 28x^4 2x^5 1x^6
Facilities:	87x 1x

Directions:

✈	San Francisco International 8.7km
A	#7F to Mission and 5th 200m
	Amtrak 5km
	Greyhound - Transbay Terminal to #38 ap Mason and Geary St Station 100m
	100m
U	Muni/Bart to Powell St Station 100m

Attractions: 50m 50m 10m

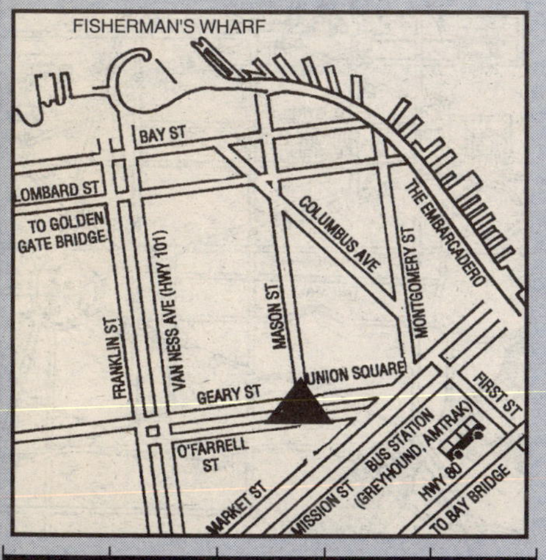

San Francisco -
Fisherman's Wharf

**San Francisco International,
Fisherman's Wharf, Fort Mason,
Building 240, San Francisco, CA 94123.**
(415) 7717277
ICN kiosk at hostel,
Kiosque ICN à l'auberge
ICN-Kiosk in der Herberge,
Quisco ICN en el albergue

Open Dates:	
Open Hours:	
Reservations:	**R** IBN CC
Price Range:	$17.00-$19.00 BB inc
Beds:	150 - 2x^3 7x^4 1x^6 10x^6
Facilities:	4x (B)

Directions:

✈	San Francisco International 22km
A	Lorrie's to Hostel
	San Francisco Ferry Building 4km
	Amtrak/Ferry Building to #32 4km
	30, 32, 42, 47, 49 ap North Point 200m

Attractions:

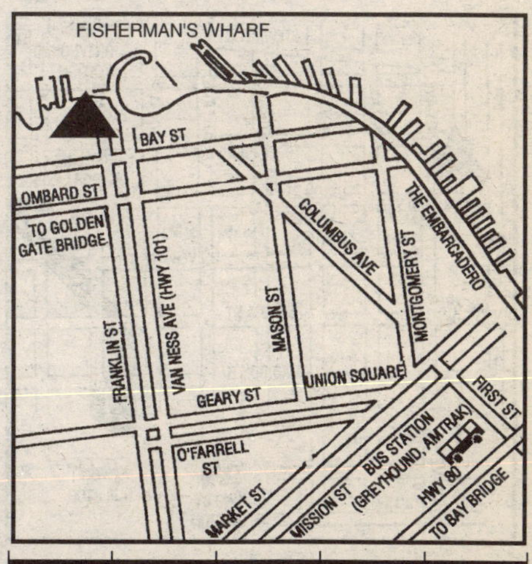

Seattle

**Seattle International,
84 Union,
Seattle WA 98101.**
☎ (206) 6225443
✆ (206) 6822179

Open Dates:	🗓
Open Hours:	🕐
Reservations:	Ⓡ ⒾⒷⓃ ⒸⒸ
Price Range:	$16.00-18.00 (+Tax)
Beds:	199 - 3x³ 10x⁴ 5x⁶ 13x⁶
Facilities:	♿ ††† 4x††† ⧠ (B) ⛱ ⛺ 📺 📓 ⧠ 💼 ⧠ 🛂 ℹ ⧠ ⛺ ⧠

Directions:

✈	Seattle - Tacoma 24km
A🚌	#194 to University or #174 to 4th and Union 200m
⛴	Victoria Clipper 1km
🚂	Amtrak 1.5km
🚌	#15 or #18 ap 1st and Union 100m

Washington, DC

**1009 11th St NW,
Washington DC 20001.**
☎ (202) 7372333
✆ (202) 7371508

Open Dates:	🗓
Open Hours:	🕐
Reservations:	Ⓡ ⒾⒷⓃ ⒸⒸ
Price Range:	$19.00-$20.00
Beds:	250 - 24x⁶
Facilities:	♿ ††† ††† ⛱ ⛺ 📺 ⧠ 💼 ⧠ 🛂 ⧠ ⧠ ℹ

Directions:

✈	Washington National 8.1km; Dulles International 43.4km
A🚌	Orange or Blue line to Ⓤ 200m
🚂	Union to Ⓤ 3km
🚌	2km
Ⓤ	Metro Center 200m

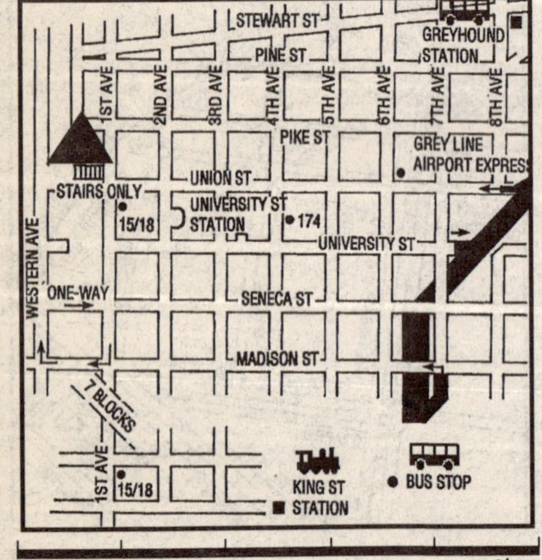

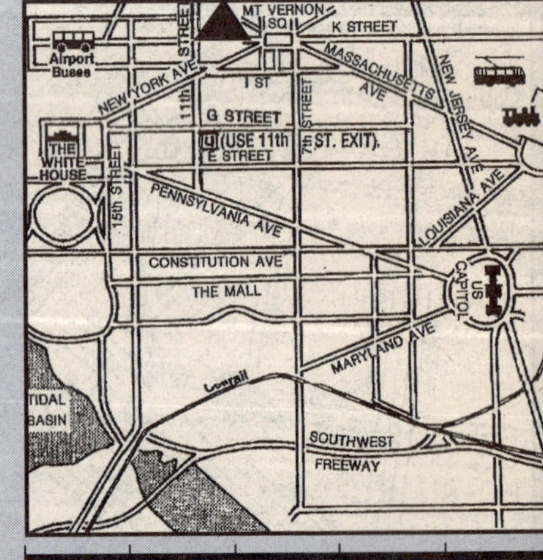

Location/Address	Telephone No. / Fax No.	Beds	Opening Dates	Facilities
Akron ☞ **Peninsula**				
▲ **Anchorage** **700 'H' St, Anchorage AK 99501.**	☎ (907) 2763635 ✆ (907) 2767772	95	🗓	♟ R ♿ CC ♂ ▣
△ *Antonito* *Conejos River Hostel, 3038 County Rd D.5, Antonito CO 81120.*	☎ *(719) 3762518*	10	20.05–20.10	♂ P
▲ **Atlanta** **223 Ponce de Leon Ave, Atlanta GA 30308.**	☎ (404) 8721042 ✆ (404) 8700042	80	🗓	♟ R 2N CC ♂ P
▲ **Austin** **2200 S Lakeshore Blvd, Austin TX 78741.**	☎ (512) 4442294 ✆ (512) 4442309	40	🗓	♟ ♿ CC ♂ P ▣
▲ **Baltimore** 17 West Mulberry St, Baltimore, MD 21201.	☎ (410) 5768880 ✆ (410) 6853574	40	03.01–23.12	R CC ♂ ▣
△ *Bandon* *Sea Star, 375 2nd St, Bandon OR 97411.*	☎ *(541) 3479632* ✆ *(541) 3479533*	38	🗓	♟ CC ♂ ▣
△ *Bar Harbor* *Mount Desert Island-Hostel, 27 Kennebec St, PO Box 32, Bar Harbor ME 04609.*	☎ *ahead (207) 2885587*	20	16.06–06.12	⑃ R CC ♂ P
△ *Bellingham* *107 Chuckanut Drive, Bellingham WA 98225.*	☎ (360) 6711750	10	01.02–30.11	R CC ♂ P ▣
△ *Blaine* *Birch Bay, Bay Horizon Park, 4639 Alderson Rd, Blaine WA 98230.*	☎ (360) 3712180	45	01.05–30.09	CC ♂ P ▣
△ *Bluemont* *Bear's Den, Rt 1, Box 288, Bluemont VA 20135.*	☎ (540) 5548708	20	01.02–24.12; 26–31.12	♟ CC ♂ P ▣
▲ **Boston** IBN **12 Hemenway St, Boston MA 02115.**	☎ (617) 5369455 ✆ (617) 4246558	205	🗓	♟ R 3SW ♿ CC ♂ ▣
△ *Boston* - *Back Bay Summer Hostel* *512 Beacon St, Boston MA 02215.* *(When shut: ENEC Reservations, 12 Hemenway St, Boston, MA 02115)*	☎ *(617) 3533294;* *(617) 5361027* *(When shut)* ✆ *(617) 3534298*	100	07.06–15.08	♟ R CC ▣
△ *Buffalo* - *Buffalo Hostel* *667 Main St, Buffalo, NY 14203.*	☎ *(716) 8525222* ✆ *(716) 8521642*	48	🗓	♟ ♿ CC ♂ ▣
△ *Burlington* *Mrs Farrell's Home Hostel, Vermont.*	☎ *(802) 8653730 for information*	6	🗓	♟ R ♂ P
△ *Breckenridge* *Fireside Inn, Box 2252, 114 N French St, Breckenridge CO 80424.*	☎ (970) 4536456 ✆ (970) 4539577	12	01.01–03.05; 21.05–31.12	⑃ R CC ♂ P
△ *Cape Vincent* *Tibbetts Point Lighthouse Hostel, 33439 County Route 6, Cape Vincent NY 13618. (When shut: 535 Oak St., Syracuse, NY 13203)*	☎ *(315) 6543450;* *(315) 4725788* *(When shut)*	25	15.05–24.10	♟ R ♂ P
△ *Cave Junction* *Fordson Home Hostel, Oregon.*	☎ *(541) 5923203 for information*	3	🗓	♟ R ♂ P
▲ **Chicago** IBN Summer Hostel, 731 S. Plymouth Ct., Chicago, IL 60605. (Mail to: HI-AYH, 2232 W. Roscoe St., Chicago, IL, 60618)	☎ (773) 3275350; (773) 3278114 (When shut) ✆ (773) 3274287	226	05.06–05.09 (☎ for exact dates)	♟ R ♿ CC ♂ ▣

Location/Address	Telephone No. Fax No.	Beds	Opening Dates	Facilities
△ *Chinook* *Fort Columbia, Box 224, Chinook WA 98614.*	☎ *(360) 7778755*	*22*	*01.04–29.09*	♿ R ⌐CC⌐ ✉ P ⊡
▲ **Clearwater Beach** 606 Bay Esplanade, Clearwater Beach, FL 33767.	☎ (727) 4431211 ✉ (727) 4431211	33	▣	♿ ⌐CC⌐ ✉ P ⊡
Cleveland ☞ **Peninsula**				
△ *Collegeville* *Evansburg State Park, 837 Mayhall Rd, Collegeville, PA 19426.*	☎ *(610) 4090113*	*18*	▣	♿ R ♿ ✉ P
△ *Columbus* *95 East 12th Ave, Columbus OH 43201.*	☎ *(614) 2947157*	*22*	*26–23.12*	♿ R ✉ P ⊡
△ *Conway* *Albert B. Lester Memorial Hostel, White Mountains, 36 Washington St, Conway NH 03818.*	☎ *(603) 4471001* ✉ *(603) 4473346*	*43*	*01.12–31.10*	♿ R ♿ ⌐CC⌐ ✉ P ⊡
▲ **Crested Butte** - International Hostel 615 Teocalli Avenue, P.O. Box 1332, Crested Butte, CO 81224	☎ (970) 3490588, (888) 3890588	52	▣	♿ ⌐◎⌐ R ♿ ⌐CC⌐ ✉ P ⊡ ☕
▲ **Denver** 1530 Downing St, Denver, Co 80218.	☎ (303) 861 7777	36	▣	♿ ⌐CC⌐ ✉ P ⊡
△ *Dodgeville* *Folklore Village Farm, 3210 Co Hwy BB, Dodgeville, WI 53533.*	☎ *(608) 9242107*	*25*	*01.04–30.11*	R ⌐CC⌐ P
△ *Downingtown (Lyndell)* *Marsh Creek State Park, East Reeds Rd, PO Box 376, Lyndell, PA 19354.*	☎ *(610) 4585881*	*12*	▣	♿ R 10 NW ✉ P
△ *Dudley* *Dudley Home Hostel, 75 Marsh Rd, Dudley, MA 01571.*	☎ *(508) 9436520* *for information.*	*6*	*01.04–30.11*	R ✉ P ⊡
△ *Durango* *543 E 2nd Ave, Durango, CO 81301.*	☎ *(970) 2479905* ✉ *(970) 3829150*	*18*	▣	♿ ⌐CC⌐ ✉ P
▲ **East Glacier Park** Brownie's Grocery & Hostel, 1020 Montana Hwy 49, PO Box 229, East Glacier Park MT 59434.	☎ (406) 2264426	30	01.05–14.10 (☎ for exact dates)	♿ R ⌐CC⌐ ✉ P ⊡
▲ **East Jamaica** Vagabond Hostel, Rt 30, Box 224, East Jamaica VT 05343.	☎ (802) 8744096	20	01.06–14.10	♿ R 104 N ⌐CC⌐ ✉ P
△ *Eastham/Orleans* *Mid-Cape, 75 Goody Hallet Drive, Eastham MA 02642. (When shut: ENEC Reservations, 12 Hemenway St, Boston, MA 02115)*	☎ *(508) 2552785;* *(617) 5361027* *(When shut)*	*50*	*07.05–12.09*	R ⌐CC⌐ ✉ P
▲ **El Paso** 311 East Franklin Ave, El Paso TX 79901.	☎ (915) 5323661 ✉ (915) 5320302	32	▣	♿ R ⌐CC⌐ ✉ ⊡
△ *Elma* - Grays Harbor Hostel *6 Ginny Lane, Elma, WA 98541*	☎ *(360) 4823119*	*14*	▣	♿ R ✉ P

Location/Address	Telephone No. Fax No.	Beds	Opening Dates	Facilities
▲ **Estes Park** H-Bar-G Ranch Hostel, 3500 H Bar G Rd, Box 1260, Estes Park CO 80517.	☏ (970) 5863688 (in season) ✆ (970) 5865004, (303) 4427296 (When shut) (off season)	100	22.05–14.09	⋔ Ⓡ 10NE ⊏CC⊐ P
Fullerton ☞ **Los Angeles**				
△ *Galax* *Blue Ridge Country Hostel, Blue Ridge Pkwy at milepost 214.5, Eastern Side MAIL, 214507 Blue Ridge Pkwy, Galax VA 24333.*	☏ *(540) 2364962*	20	*01.03–31.12*	P
△ *Gardners* *Pine Grove Furnace State Park, 1212 Pine Grove Rd, Gardners PA 17324.*	☏ *(717) 4867575* ✆ *(717) 4865115*	46		⋔ ♿ ⊏CC⊐ P
△ *Gary* *Pleasant Valley Hostel, South Dakota Hwy 22, Box 256, Gary SD 57237.*	☏ *(605) 2725614*	18		⋔ ⊏CC⊐ P
△ *Glenwood Springs* *1021 Grand Ave, Glenwood Springs CO 81601.*	☏ *(970) 9458545* *(1) (800) 9467835*	42		⋔ Ⓡ P
△ *Gooding* *112 Main St, Gooding ID 83330.*	☏ *(208) 9344374*	8		⋔ Ⓡ ⊏CC⊐ P
▲ **Grand Lake** Shadowcliff, 405 Summerland Park Rd, PO Box 658, Grand Lake CO 80447.	☏ (970) 6279220 ✆ (970) 6279220	14	01.06–25.09	⋔ ⊖ Ⓡ P
△ *Grand Marais* *Spirit of the Land Island Hostel, Wilderness Canoe Base, 12477 Gunflint Trail, Grand Marias MN 55604.*	☏ *(218) 3882241* ✆ *(218) 3382241*	12	*01.01–31.03; 01.05–31.10; 29–31.12*	⊖ Ⓡ ⊏CC⊐ P
▲ **Hartford** The Mark Twain Hostel, 131 Tremont St, Hartford, CT 06105.	☏ (860) 5237255 ✆ (860) 2331767	42		⋔ Ⓡ ⊏CC⊐ P
△ *Hiram* *Wadsworth Blanchard Farm Hostel RR2, Box 5992, Tripp Town Road, Hiram, ME 04041.*	☏ *(207) 6257509*	10	*15.05–20.10*	⋔ Ⓡ P
▲ **Honolulu** - University IBN 2323A Seaview Ave, Honolulu HI 96822.	☏ (808) 9460591 ✆ (808) 9465904	43		Ⓡ ⊏CC⊐ P
▲ **Honolulu** IBN **Waikiki, 2417 Prince Edward St, Honolulu HI 96815.**	☏ (808) 9268313 ✆ (808) 9223798	64		⋔ Ⓡ ⊏CC⊐ P
▲ **Houston** 5302 Crawford, Houston TX 77004.	☏ (713) 5231009 ✆ (713) 5268618	30		⋔ Ⓡ 5S P
▲ **Hurricane** The Dixie Hostel, 73 S.Main St, Hurricane, UT 84737.	☏ (435) 6358202	30		⋔ P
▲ **Independence** The Winnedumah Hotel, 211 N. Edwards St, PO Box 147, Independence, CA 93526.	☏ (760) 8782040 ✆ (760) 8782833	12	13.10–09.10	⋔ ⊖ Ⓡ ⊏CC⊐ P
△ *Johannesburg* *301 Hwy 395, PO Box 277, Johannesburg, CA 93528.*	☏ *(760) 3742323*	12		⋔ ♿ P

Location/Address	Telephone No. Fax No.	Beds	Opening Dates	Facilities
△ *Juneau* 614 Harris St, Juneau AK 99801.	(907) 5869559	46		
△ *Ketchikan* Grant and Main St, PO Box 8515, Ketchikan AK 99901.	(907) 2253319	23	01.06–31.08	
▲ **Key West** **718 South St, Key West, FL 33040.**	(305) 2965719 (305) 2960672	92		CC
▲ **Kitty Hawk** Outer Banks, 1004 Kitty Hawk Rd, Kitty Hawk, NC 27949.	(252) 2612294 (252) 2612294	40		CC
△ *Knoxville* Harpers Ferry, 19123 Sandy Hook Rd, Knoxville MD 21758.	(301) 8347652 (301) 8347652	39	16.03–14.11	
△ *La Anna* Poconos, La Anna Rd, RR 2-Box 1026, Cresco, PA 18326.	(717) 6769076 (717) 6769076	40		12.8N
△ *Lake Itasca* Mississippi Headwaters, Itasca State Park MN 56470.	(218) 2663415 (218) 2663451	34	01.01–13.03; 23.04–13.11; 17–31.12 (☎ for exact dates)	CC
△ *Laona* 5397 Beech St, P.O. Box 7, Laona, WI 54541.	(715) 6742615 (715) 4873400	10		
△ *Layton* Old Mine Rd Hostel, Delaware Water Gap National Recreation Area, Old Mine Rd Box 172, Layton, NJ 07851.	(201) 9486750	12	01.01–25.11; 27.11–23.12; 26–31.12	
△ *Lincoln* Cornerstone, 640 North 16th St, Lincoln NE 68508.	(402) 4760926	7	08.01–17.12	
△ *Littleton* Friendly Crossways, 247 Littleton County Road. PO Box 2266, Littleton MA 01460.	(508) 4563649 (508) 4569757	50		
Los Altos Hills ☞ Palo Alto				
▲ **Los Angeles** [IBN] **1436 2nd St, Santa Monica CA 90401.**	(310) 3939913 (310) 3931769	200		CC
▲ **Los Angeles** **South Bay, 3601 South Gaffey St, Building 613, San Pedro CA 90731-6969.**	(310) 8318109 (310) 8314635	60		32S CC
△ *Los Angeles* 1700 N Harbor Blvd, Fullerton CA 92835. (Disneyland area)	(714) 7383721 (714) 7380925	20		CC
△ *Lucas* Malabar Farm, 3954 Bromfield Rd, Lucas OH 44843.	(419) 8922055	26	15.01–15.12	
△ *Ludlow* Trojan Horse Hostel, 44 Andover St, Ludlow VT 05149.	(802) 2285244, (800) 5477475	18	01.01–31.03; 01.05–20.10; 08.11–31.12	CC

Location/Address	Telephone No. Fax No.	Beds	Opening Dates	Facilities
△ *Martha's Vineyard* *Edgartown Rd, PO Box 3158, West Tisbury MA 02575.* *(When shut: ENEC Reservations, 12 Hemenway St,* *Boston, MA 02115)*	☎ *(508) 6932665;* *(617) 5361027* *(When shut)* ✆ *(508) 6932699*	78	*01.04–06.11*	
▲ **Melbourne Beach** *1135 N. A1A, Indialantic, FL 32903.*	☎ *(407) 9510004*	12		
△ *Merced* *PO Box 3755, Merced CA 95344.*	☎ *(209) 7250407* *for information*	8		
▲ **Miami Beach** [IBN] **Miami Beach International,** **1438 Washington Ave, Miami Beach FL 33139.**	☎ *(305) 5342988;* *(800) 3592529* (Ⓡ only) ✆ *(305) 6730346*	200		
△ *Middlebury* - *Covered Bridge Home Hostel* *Middlebury, VT*	☎ *(802) 3880401* *(for information)*	6		
▲ **Midpines** *6979 Highway 140, PO Box 81, Midpines, CA 95345.*	☎ *(209) 9666666* ✆ *(209) 9666667*	52		
△ *Milwaukee* *Red Barn, 6750 W Loomis Rd, Greendale WI 53129.*	☎ *(414) 5293299*	20	*01.05–31.10*	
△ *Montara* *Point Montara Lighthouse, PO Box 737,* *16th St at California Hwy 1, Montara CA 94037.*	☎ *(415) 7287177*	45		
△ *Montpelier* *Capitol Home Hostel, RD1, Box 2750, Montpelier,* *VT 05602.*	☎ *(802) 2232104* *for information*	3		
△ *Nantucket* *Surfside, 31 Western Avenue, Nantucket MA 02554.* *(When shut: ENEC Reservations, 12 Hemenway St,* *Boston, MA 02115)*	☎ *(508) 2280433;* *(617) 5361027* *(When shut)* ✆ *(508) 2285672*	49	*23.04–16.10*	
△ *Naples* *Hwy 2, Naples ID 83847.*	☎ *(208) 2672947* ✆ *(208) 2674118*	18	*02.01–06.04;* *08.04–24.12;* *26–31.12*	
△ *New Boston* *Country Grandma's Home Hostel, RR3, New Boston,* *MI 48164.*	☎ *(734) 7534901* *for information*	6	*16.03–14.11*	
▲ **New Orleans** [IBN] **New Orleans-Marquette House,** **2253 Carondelet St, New Orleans LA 70130.**	☎ *(504) 5233014* ✆ *(504) 5295933*	176		
▲ **New York** [IBN] **891 Amsterdam Ave at West 103rd St,** **New York NY 10025.**	☎ *(212) 9322300* ✆ *(212) 9322574*	624		
△ *Newburg* *Wellspring, 4382 Hickory Rd, PO Box 72,* *Newburg WI 53060-0072.*	☎ *(414) 6756755*	12	*01.01–02.04;* *04.04–24.11;* *26.11–24.12;* *26–31.12*	
△ *Newtown* *Tyler Hostel, PO Box 94, Newtown, PA 18940.*	☎ *(215) 9680927* ✆ *(215) 5572100*	25	*01.01–24.11;* *29.11–23.12;* *27–31.12*	

Location/Address	Telephone No. Fax No.	Beds	Opening Dates	Facilities
△ **Niagara Falls** *1101 Ferry Ave, Niagara Falls NY 14301.*	☎ (716) 2823700	46	21.01–19.12	R ⚲ P ▣
△ **Ninilchik** *The Eagle Watch, Mile 3, Oil Well Rd, Box 39083, Ninilchik, AK 99639.*	☎ (907) 5673905	8	16.05–14.09	R ⚲ P
△ **Nordland** *Fort Flagler, Fort Flagler State Park, 10621 Flagler Rd, Nordland WA 98358. (Marrowstone Island)*	☎ (360) 3851288	14	16.03–30.09	††† R ⅭⅭ ⚲ P
△ **Ohiopyle State Park** *Ferncliff Rd, PO Box 99, Ohiopyle PA 15470.*	☎ (412) 3294476 ✆ (412) 3294476	24	01.01–22.12; 30–31.12	††† R ⚲ P ▣
▲ Orlando [IBN] **Orlando/Kissimmee Resort,** **4840 W Irlo Bronson Hwy, Kissimmee FL 34746.** **(Route 192 at Route 535)**	☎ (407) 3968282 ✆ (407) 3969311	192	▣	††† ♿ ⅭⅭ ⚲ P ▣
△ **Palo Alto** *Hidden Villa, 26870 Moody Rd, Los Altos Hills CA 94022.*	☎ (650) 9498648 ✆ (650) 9484159	35	01.01–31.05; 01.09–31.12	††† R ⚲ P
△ **Pembroke** *Baptist Student Union House, Odom St, UNC Pembroke, Pembroke NC 28372.*	☎ (910) 5218777, (800) 4844037, code 2274 ✆ (910) 5217166	8	▣	††† R ♿ ⚲ P ▣
△ **Peninsula** *Stanford House, 6093 Stanford Rd, Peninsula OH 44264.*	☎ (330) 4678711 ✆ (330) 4678711	30	▣	††† R ⚲ P ▣
△ **Pescadero** *210 Pigeon Point Rd, Pescadero CA 94060.*	☎ (650) 8790633	52	▣	††† R ♿ ⅭⅭ ⚲ P
△ **Philadelphia** *Bank Street Hostel, 32 S.Bank St, Philadelphia, PA 19106.*	☎ (215) 9220222 ✆ (215) 9224082	70	▣	R ⚲ ▣
△ **Philadelphia** *Chamounix Mansion, Chamounix Drive, W Fairmount Park, Philadelphia PA 19131.*	☎ (215) 8783676 ✆ (215) 8714313	80	16.01–14.12	††† ⅭⅭ ⚲ P ▣
△ **Phoenix** *The Metcalf House, 1026 N 9th St, Phoenix AZ 85006.*	☎ (602) 2549803	36	▣	⚲ ▣
△ **Pitkin** *Pitkin Hotel, 4th & Main Sts, PO Box 164, Pitkin CO 81241.*	☎ (970) 6412757	6	▣	††† R ⚲ P ▣
△ **Pittsburgh** *830 E. Warrington Ave, Pittsburgh, PA 15210.*	☎ (412) 4311267 ✆ (412) 4312625	56	01.01–22.12; 27–31.12	††† R ♿ ⅭⅭ ⚲ P ▣
△ **Point Reyes National Seashore** *Point Reyes (off Limantour Rd), Box 247, Point Reyes Station CA 94956.*	☎ (415) 6638811	44	▣	R ♿ ⅭⅭ ⚲ P
△ **Port Townsend** *The Olympic Hostel, Fort Worden State Park, #272 Battery Way, Port Townsend WA 98368.*	☎ (360) 3850655	24	02.01–24.12	††† R ⅭⅭ ⚲

Location/Address	Telephone No. / Fax No.	Beds	Opening Dates	Facilities
△ *Portland (Maine)* *Summer Hostel, 645 Congress St (in Portland Hall), Portland ME 04101. (When shut: ENEC Reservations, 12 Hemenway St, Boston, MA 02115)*	☎ *(207) 8743281; (617) 5361027 (When shut)* 📠 *(207) 8743399*	*36*	*01.06–23.08 (Call for exact dates)*	
▲ **Portland (Northwest Portland)** 1818 NW Glisan, Portland, OR 97209	☎ *(503) 2412783* 📠 *(503) 5255910*	*33*		
△ *Portland (Oregon)* *3031 Hawthorne Blvd SE, Portland OR 97214.*	☎ *(503) 2363380* 📠 *(503) 2367940*	*33*		
△ *Quakertown* *Weisel, 7347 Richlandtown Rd, Quakertown PA 18951.*	☎ *(215) 5368749*	*20*	*01.01–24.12; 26–31.12*	
△ *Redwood National Park* *14480 Hwy 101 at Wilson Creek Rd, Klamath CA 95548.*	☎ *(707) 4828265*	*30*		
△ *Sacramento* *900 H St, Sacramento CA 95814.*	☎ *(916) 4431691* 📠 *(916) 4434763*	*70*		
▲ **Salt Lake City** The Avenues, 107 F St, Salt Lake City, UT 84103.	☎ *(801) 3593855, (888) 8844752* 📠 *(801) 5320182*	*56*		
▲ **San Antonio** 621 Pierce St, PO Box 8059, San Antonio TX 78208.	☎ *(210) 2239426* 📠 *(210) 2991479*	*42*		
△ *San Clemente* *San Clemente Beach, 233 Avenida Granada, San Clemente CA 92672-4029.*	☎ *(949) 4922848*	*40*	*01.05–31.10*	
▲ **San Diego** - Downtown IBN **The Metropolitan, 521 Market St, San Diego, CA 92101.**	☎ *(619) 5251531* 📠 *(619) 3380129*	*150*		
▲ **San Diego** - Point Loma IBN **Elliott Hostel, 3790 Udall St, San Diego CA 92107-2414.**	☎ *(619) 2234778* 📠 *(619) 2231883*	*61*		10W
▲ **San Francisco** - Downtown IBN **Union Square, Downtown, 312 Mason St, Union Sq, San Francisco CA 94102.**	☎ *(415) 7885604*	*230*		
▲ **San Francisco** - Fisherman's Wharf IBN **San Francisco International, Fisherman's Wharf, Fort Mason, Building 240, San Francisco, CA 94123.**	☎ *(415) 7717277*	*150*		
△ *San Jose (Saratoga)* *Sanborn Park Hostel, 15808 Sanborn Rd, Saratoga CA 95070.*	☎ *(408) 7410166*	*39*		
△ *San Luis Obispo* *1617 Santa Rosa St., San Luis Obispo, CA 93401*	☎ *(805) 5444678* 📠 *(805) 5443142*	*22*		
△ *Santa Cruz* *321 Main St, PO Box 1241, Santa Cruz CA 95061.*	☎ *(408) 4238304* 📠 *(408) 4298541*	*40*		

Saratoga ☞ **San Jose (Saratoga)**

UNITED STATES • ETATS UNIS

Location/Address	Telephone No. Fax No.	Beds	Opening Dates	Facilities
△ **Sausalito** Marin Headlands, 941 Fort Barry, Sausalito CA 94965.	☎ (415) 3312777	103		
△ **Savannah** 304 E Hall St, Savannah GA 31401.	☎ (912) 2367744 ℻ (912) 2367744	18	01.03–09.12	
△ **Schellsburg** Living Waters Hostel, RR # 1, PO Box 206, Schellsburg PA 15559.	☎ (814) 7332162, 7334212 ℻ (814) 7334909	24		
△ **Searsport** - Penobscot Bay Hostel 132 W. Main St (Rt 1), P.O. Box 306, Searsport, ME 04974	☎ (207) 5482506; (978) 2870306 (When shut)	10	01.07–31.08	
▲ **Seaside** 930 N Holladay, Seaside, OR 97138.	☎ (503) 7387911 ℻ (503) 7170163	48		
▲ **Seattle** IBN Seattle International, 84 Union, Seattle WA 98101.	☎ (206) 6225443 ℻ (206) 6822179	199		
▲ **Seattle** Vashon Island Ranch, 12119 Cove Rd SW, Vashon Island WA 98070.	☎ (206) 4632592 ℻ (206) 4636157	36	01.05–31.10	
△ **Sevierville** Great Smoky Mountains, 3248 Manis Rd, Sevierville, TN 37862-8224.	☎ (423) 4298563, (800) 3571857 (800) 8516715	18	16.03–14.12	
▲ **Sheep Mountain (Palmer)** Sheep Mountain Lodge, Alaska Hwy 1, milepost 113, HCO3 Box 8490, Palmer AK 99645. (42km outside Palmer)	☎ (907) 7455121 ℻ (907) 7455120	12	01.05–30.09	
▲ **Silver City** The Carter House (Silver City), 101 North Cooper St, Silver City NM 88061.	☎ (505) 3885485	22		
▲ **Silverthorne** Alpen Hütte, 471 Rainbow Drive, Silverthorne CO 80498.	☎ (970) 4686336 ℻ (970) 4680936	15		
△ **Sitka** 303 Kimsham St, PO Box 2645, Sitka AK 99835.	☎ (907) 7478661	20	01.06–31.08	
▲ **St Louis** Huckleberry Finn Hostel, 1904-1908 S 12th St, Tucker Blvd, St Louis MO 63104.	☎ (314) 2410076	44	21.01–19.12	1 SW
▲ **St Paul** The College of St Catherine, Caecilian Hall, 2004 Randolph Ave, St Paul MN 55105.	☎ (612) 6906604 ℻ (612) 6906768	80	01.06–15.08	
△ **Syracuse** Downing International Hostel, 535 Oak St, Syracuse NY 13203-1609.	☎ (315) 4725788 ℻ (315) 4260662	31		2 NE
△ **Taos (Arroyo Seco)** Taos Ski Valley Rd, PO Box 3271, Taos NM 87571.	☎ (505) 7768298 ℻ (505) 7762107	36		

Location/Address	Telephone No. Fax No.	Beds	Opening Dates	Facilities
△ *Tecopa/Death Valley* *Desertaire Hostel, 2000 Old Spanish Trail Hwy,* *PO Box 306, Tecopa CA 92389.*	☎ *(760) 8524580*	*10*		
△ *Tok* *PO Box 532, Tok AK 99780.*	☎ *(907) 8833745*	*10*	15.05–15.09	
△ *Truro* *North Pamet Road, PO Box 402, Truro, MA 02666.* *(When shut: ENEC Reservations, 12 Hemenway St,* *Boston, MA 02115)*	☎ *(508) 3493889;* *(617) 5361027* *(When shut)*	*42*	18.06–07.09	
▲ Truth or Consequences Riverbend Hot Springs, 100 Austin, Truth or Consequences NM 87901.	☎ (505) 8946183	16		
△ *Urbanna* *Sangraal by-the-Sea, Carlton Rd, Rt 626, Wake,* *VA 23175.*	☎ *(804) 7766500*	*20*		
Vashon Island ☞ **Seattle**				
▲ Virginia Beach Angie's Guest Cottage, 302 24th St, Virginia Beach VA 23451.	☎ (757) 4284690	36	01.04–30.09	
△ *Volcano - Holo Holo In* *19-4036 Kalani Honua Road, P.O. Box 784,* *Volcano, HI 96785*	☎ *(808) 9677950* ☎ *(808) 9678025*	*10*		
▲ Washington, DC **IBN** **1009 11th St NW, Washington DC 20001.**	☎ (202) 7372333 ☎ (202) 7371508	250		
▲ White River Junction The Hotel Coolidge, PO Box 515, 17 S. Main St, White River Junction, VT 05001.	☎ (802) 2953118 ☎ (802) 2955100	26		
△ *Windsor* *Windsor Home Hostel, Connecticut.*	☎ *(860) 6834155* *for information* *07.00-09.30hrs,* *17.00-22.00hrs*	*4*		
▲ Woodford Greenwood Lodge, Prospect Ski Mountain, RT 9, Woodford, PO Box 246, Bennington VT 05201.	☎ (802) 4422547 ☎ (802) 4422547	20	20.05–24.10	

There are some things you can't afford to leave behind

Lonely Planet has all the guide books you need for hostelling around Europe.

Titles include: Austria • Britain • Central Europe
• Czech & Slovak Republics • Denmark • Eastern Europe
• Estonia, Latvia & Lithuania • Finland • France • Germany
• Greece • Hungary • Iceland, Greenland & the Faroe Islands
• Ireland • Israel & the Palestinian Territories • Italy
• Mediterranean Europe • Poland • Portugal
• Russia, Ukraine & Belarus • Scandinavian & Baltic Europe
• Slovenia • Spain • Switzerland • Western Europe

Phrasebooks also available: Baltic States • Central Europe
• French • German • Greek • Italian • Mediterranean Europe
• Russian • Scandinavian Europe • Spanish • Western Europe

Stocked in all good bookshops or buy direct on +44 171 428 4800

Uruguay

URUGUAY
URUGUAY
URUGUAY

Asociación de Alberguistas del Uruguay,
Pablo de Maria 1583/008,
PC 11200 PO Box 10680, Montevideo, Uruguay.

 (598) (2) 4004245, 4000581
 (598) (2) 4001326

E-mail: aau@adinet.com.uy
WWW address: http://www.internet.com.uy/aau

A copy of the Hostel Directory for this country can be obtained from:
The National Office.

IBN Booking Centre for outward bookings
- **Montevideo** - *via National Office above.*

Capital:	Montevideo	Population:	3,061,000
Language:	Spanish	Size:	176,215 sq km
Currency:	$ (Peso Uruguayo)		

Uruguay

Uruguay
BRAZIL
Artigas
Salto Grande Dam
Salto
Rivera
Paysandú
URUGUAY
Durazno (2)
Flores
El Nazareno
La Coronilla
Villa Serrana
Martin Garcia Island 'A'
Colonia Suiza
Barra de Valizas
Montevideo
La Paloma
Montevideo
Piriapolis
Manantiales
Buenos Aires
ATLANTIC OCEAN
100
200 KM
0
50
100
MLS
N

English

URUGUAY HOSTELS

Hostels are open 07.00-13.00hrs and 16.00-24.00hrs. Check in by 22.00hrs in winter and 23.00hrs in summer. Expect to pay in the region of $5.00-11.00 per night plus bed linen if needed. You may need to bring extra blankets in winter!

Self-catering facilities are only available in Barra Valizas, Durazno (El Nazareno), Flores, La Coronilla, La Paloma, Manantiales, Montevideo, Piriápolis (Anton Grassl) and Villa Serrana.

PASSPORTS AND VISAS

Citizens of America, Western Europe, Israel, Japan and Latin American countries do not require a visa to enter Uruguay. Citizens from Argentina, Brazil, Chile and Paraguay are permitted to enter if holding passport or "Cédula de Identidad". Visitors from other countries require a passport, visa and ticket to leave the country.

HEALTH

No vaccinations are required to enter Uruguay.

BANKING HOURS

Banks are open Monday to Friday between 13.00-17.00hrs.

POST OFFICES

Post offices are open Monday to Friday 08.00-18.00hrs and Saturdays 08.00-12.00hrs

SHOPPING HOURS

Most department stores are generally open Monday to Friday 09.00-12.00 and 14.00-19.00hrs and on Saturdays 09.00-12.30hrs.

TRAVEL

Bus

Within Uruguay there is a good bus service to most towns. There are daily services to Buenos Aires and several cities of Brazil as well as twice weekly services to Asunción, Paraguay and Santiago.

Ferry

There is a night ferry service to Buenos Aires via Colonia.

Driving

There are 45,000km of roads in Uruguay, 80% of which are either paved or all weather. The road system is among the best in South America.

TELEPHONE INFORMATION

Country Code	**598**
Main City Area Codes	
La Paloma	47
Montevideo	2
Paysandu	72
Punta del Este	42
Salto	73

Français

AUBERGES DE JEUNESSE URUGUAYENNES

Les auberges sont ouvertes de 7h à 13h et de 16h à 24h. Présentez-vous à l'auberge à 22h au plus tard en hiver et à 23h au plus tard en été. Une nuit vous coûtera entre 5 et 11 $, plus location de draps le cas échéant. Nous vous conseillons d'apporter des couvertures en hiver!

Seules les auberges de Barra Valizas, Durazno (El Nazareno), Flores, La Coronilla, La Paloma, Manantiales, Montevideo, Piriápolis (Anton Grassl) et Villa Serrana sont équipées de cuisines pour les voyageurs.

PASSEPORTS ET VISAS

Les citoyens d'Amérique, d'Europe occidentale, d'Israël, du Japon et des pays d'Amérique latine peuvent entrer en Uruguay sans visa. Les citoyens d'Argentine, du Brésil, du Chili et du Paraguay peuvent entrer s'ils sont munis d'un passeport ou d'une "Cédula de Identidad". Les citoyens d'autres pays doivent être munis d'un passeport, d'un visa et d'un billet indiquant qu'ils comptent quitter le pays.

SOINS MEDICAUX

Les vaccinations ne sont pas nécessaires pour entrer en Uruguay.

HEURES D'OUVERTURE DES BANQUES

Les banques sont ouvertes du lundi au vendredi de 13h à 17h.

BUREAUX DE POSTE

Les bureaux de poste sont ouverts du lundi au vendredi de 8h à 18h et le samedi de 8h à 12h.

HEURES D'OUVERTURE DES MAGASINS

La plupart des grands magasins sont en général ouverts du lundi au vendredi de 9h à 12h et de 14h à 19h, et le samedi de 9h à 12h30.

DEPLACEMENTS

Autobus

Un bon service d'autobus dessert la plupart des villes en Uruguay. Il y a des services journaliers à destination de Buenos Aires et de plusieurs villes brésiliennes; deux fois par semaine, des autobus vont à Asunción, au Paraguay et à Santiago.

Ferry-boats

Il y a un service de nuit pour Buenos Aires, en passant par Colonia.

Automobiles

Il y a 45 000 km de routes en Uruguay, dont 80% sont soit pavées soit goudronnées. Le réseau routier est l'un des meilleurs d'Amérique du Sud.

TELEPHONE

Indicatif du Pays	**598**
Indicatifs régionaux des Villes principales	
La Paloma	47
Montevideo	2
Paysandu	72
Punta del Este	42
Salto	73

Deutsch

URUGUAYISCHE JUGENDHERBERGEN

Die Herbergen sind von 07.00-13.00 Uhr und von 16.00-24.00 Uhr geöffnet. Im Winter muß man sich bis spätestens 22.00 Uhr und im Sommer bis spätestens 23.00 Uhr einschreiben. Es ist mit einem Preis von ca $5,00-11,00 pro Nacht plus, bei Bedarf, einer Gebühr für Bettwäsche zu rechnen. Im Winter sollte man zusätzliche Decken mitbringen.

Einrichtungen für Selbstversorger gibt es nur in Barra Valizas, Durazno (El Nazareno), Flores, La Coronilla, La Paloma, Manantiales, Montevideo, Piriápolis (Anton Grassl) und Villa Serrana.

PÄSSE UND VISA

Staatsbürger der Vereinigten Staaten, Westeuropas, Israels, Japans und lateinamerikanischer Länder brauchen für die Einreise nach Uruguay kein Visum. Staatsbürger Argentiniens, Brasilien, Chiles und Paraguays dürfen einreisen, wenn sie im Besitz eines Reisepasses oder einer "Cédula de Identidad" sind. Besucher aus anderen Ländern brauchen einen Reisepaß, ein Visum und ein Ticket für die Ausreise aus dem Land.

GESUNDHEIT

Für die Einreise nach Uruguay braucht man keine Impfungen.

GESCHÄFTSSTUNDEN DER BANKEN

Banken sind montags bis freitags von 13.00-17.00 Uhr geöffnet.

POSTÄMTER

Postämter sind montags bis freitags von 8.00-18.00 Uhr und samstags von 8.00-12.00 Uhr geöffnet.

LADENÖFFNUNGSZEITEN

Die meisten Warenhäuser sind im allgemeinen montags bis freitags von 9.00-12.00 und von 14.00-19.00 Uhr und samstags von 9.00-12.30 Uhr geöffnet.

REISEN

Busse

Innerhalb Uruguays gibt es einen guten Busverkehr in die meisten Städte. Busse verkehren täglich nach Buenos Aires und in mehrere Städte Brasiliens und zweimal wöchentlich nach Asunción, Paraguay und Santiago.

Fähren

Es gibt eine Nachtfähre nach Buenos Aires über Colonia.

Autofahren

In Uruguay gibt es Straßen von einer Gesamtlänge von 45.000 km, wovon 80% entweder gepflastert oder Allwetterstraßen sind. Das Straßensystem gehört zu den besten in Südamerika.

FERNSPRECHINFORMATIONEN

Landes-Kennzahl	598

größere Städte - Ortsnetzkennzahlen

La Paloma	47
Montevideo	2
Paysandu	72
Punte del Este	42
Salto	73

Español

ALBERGUES DE JUVENTUD URUGUAYOS

Los albergues están abiertos de 07.00 a 13.00 horas y de 16.00 a 24.00 horas. Cierran a las 22.00 horas en invierno y a las 23.00 horas en verano. Pagará entre 5 y 11 dólares por noche, más alquiler de sábanas si las necesita. ¡En invierno, recomendamos se traiga un par de mantas más!

Sólo podrá cocinar usted mismo en Barra Balizas, Durazno (El Nazareno), Flores, La Cornilla, La Paloma, Manantiales, Montevideo, Piriápolis (Anton Grassl) y Villa Serrana.

PASAPORTES Y VISADOS

Los ciudadanos de Norteamérica, Europa Occidental, Israel, Japón y los países latinoamericanos no necesitan visado para entrar en Uruguay. Los ciudadanos de Argentina, Brasil, Chile y Paraguay pueden entrar en el país con pasaporte o "cédula de identidad". Los visitantes de otros países deberán tener pasaporte, visado y billete de vuelta.

SANIDAD

No hace falta ninguna vacuna para entrar en Uruguay.

HORARIO DE BANCOS

Los bancos están abiertos de lunes a viernes de 13.00 a 17.00 horas.

OFICINAS DE CORREOS

Las oficinas de correos abren de lunes a viernes de 08.00 a 18.00 horas y los sábados de 08.00 a 12.00 horas.

HORARIO COMERCIAL

La mayoría de los grandes almacenes suelen abrir de lunes a viernes de 09.00 a 12.00 horas y de 14.00 a 19.00 horas. Los sábados, de 09.00 a 12.30 horas.

DESPLAZAMIENTOS

Autobús

En Uruguay hay un buen servicio de autocares que va a la mayoría de las ciudades. Hay servicios diarios a Buenos Aires y a varias ciudades de Brasil. Salen también dos veces por semana autocares a Asunción, Paraguay y Santiago.

Ferry

Hay servicio nocturno a Buenos Aires vía Colonia.

Coche

Hay 45.000 kilómetros de carretera en Uruguay, con un 80% de rutas pavimentadas o asfaltadas. La red de carreteras uruguayas es de las mejores de Sudamérica.

INFORMACION TELEFONICA

Código Nacional	**598**
Prefijos de las Ciudades Principales	
La Paloma	47
Montevideo	2
Paysandu	72
Punta del Este	42
Salto	73

Discounts And Concessions

The following discounts on sea travel are available.

Luncarti Service: 15% off Carmelo to Tigre (Argentina) service.

Ferryturismo Service: 10% off Montevideo to Buenos Aires (Rio Branco 1368, Montevideo).

There are also discounts available on some bus services, information available from the hostel.

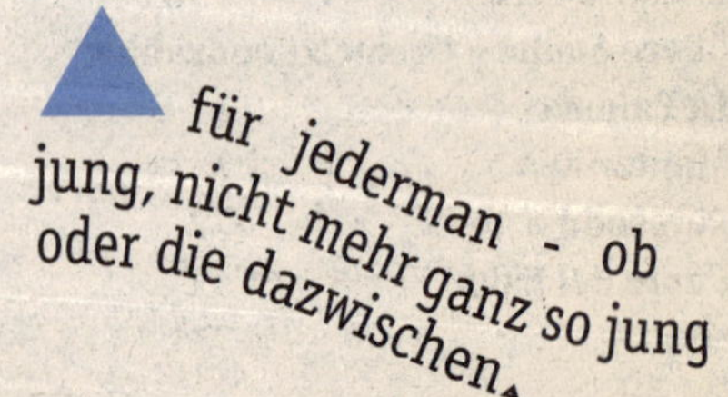

Montevideo

'Schirrmann-Münker' YH,
Canelones 935,
Montevideo.
❶ (2) 9081324

Open Dates:	🗓
Open Hours:	07.30-00.30hrs
Reservations:	Ⓡ IBN
Price Range:	US$ 11.00 BB inc 🛏
Beds:	50 - 1x² 1x⁴ 6x⁶ 1x⁶
Facilities:	👪 🍽 🛄 🏠 📺 📖 🅾 🖼 ℹ

Directions:

✈	Montevideo 16km
A🚌	209, 214 + Copsa Lines 700m
⛴	Montevideo 2km
🚌	116, 117, 118, 164, 165, 409, 411 100m

Attractions: 🚲

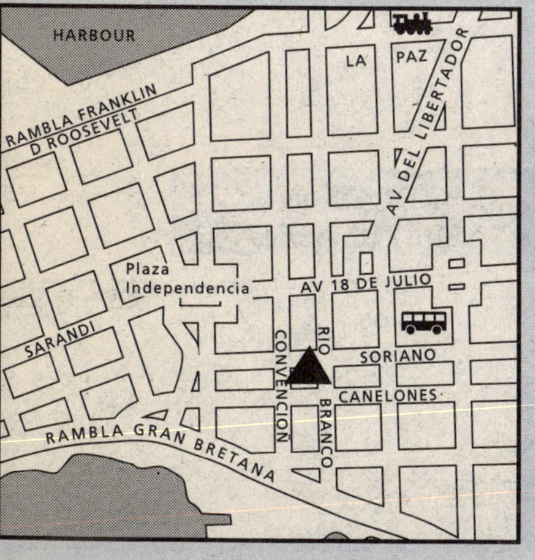

Assured Standards – visited by our Liaison team and by you the guest – tell us when we don't measure up (reply slips at the end of this Guide) ▸

des Normes Garanties, par les visites de notre Equipe de Liaison et par vous, les usagers – faites-le nous savoir quand nous ne sommes pas à la hauteur (Fiches-commentaires à la fin du Guide) ▸

Zugesicherte Standards – beurteilt von unserem Liaison Team und von Ihnen, unserem Gast – sagen Sie es uns, wenn wir Sie enttäuschen (Antwortkarten hinten im Führer) ▸

Normas Garantizadas – comprobadas por nuestro Equipo de Enlace y por Ud., el usuario – si fallamos en algo, díganoslo (al final de esta Guía encontrará nuestras hojas de comentarios) ▸

Location/Address	Telephone No. Fax No.	Beds	Opening Dates	Facilities
△ **Artigas** *Club Deportivo Artigas, Pte Berreta s/n.* *(Montevideo 627km)*	☎ *(772) 3015*	*24*		⑂ Ⓡ
△ **Colonia Suiza** *Hotel del Prado YH, Ruta 1,* *Colonia Suiza. (Montevideo 129km, Colonia 58km)*	☎ *(552) 4169* *Colonia Suiza*	*15*		⑂ Ⓡ
△ **Flores** *Albergue Estancia "El Silencio", Ruta 14-km166,* *Departmento de Flores. (Rural Farm)*	☎ *(598) 3622014*	*15*		⑂ Ⓡ
△ **La Coronilla** *Posada de Las Palmeras, Los Delfines S/N,* *La Coronilla Rocha Province*	☎ *(477) 2021* ✆ *(477) 2021*	*60*		⑂ Ⓟ
△ **La Paloma** *'Altena 5000' YH, Parque Municipal 'Andresito',* *Parada 12, La Paloma, Rocha.* *(Montevideo 240km, Rocha 28km)*	☎ *(473) 6396*	*50*	*01.11–30.04*	⑂ Ⓡ
△ **Manantiales** *Puebla Nueva YH, Km 164, Hwy 10, Manantiales,* *Maldonado.*	☎ *(42) 71427*	*30*	*01.11–30.04*	⑂ Ⓡ
▲ **Montevideo** IBN **'Schirrmann-Münker' YH, Canelones 935,** **Montevideo.**	☎ *(2) 9081324*	*50*		⑂ Ⓡ
▲ **Paysandu** *'La Posada', JP Varela Y Solis, CP 60000 Paysandu*	☎ *(72) 27879* ✆ *(72) 27879·*	*35*		⑂ CC Ⓟ
▲ **Piriápolis** - Anton Grassl IBN *Simón del Pino 1106-36, Piriápolis,* *Maldonado. (Montevideo 100km)*	☎ *(43) 20394* ✆ *(2) 4001326*	*322*		⑂ Ⓡ
▲ **Rivera** *Hotel Nuevo - Ituzaingo 411*	☎ *(622) 3039-3056* ✆ *(622) 3147*	*40*		⑂
△ **Salto** *Club Remeros, Rbla César Mayo Gutierrez y Belén.* *(Montevideo 498km)*	☎ *(73) 23418*	*40*		⑂ Ⓡ
△ **Villa Serrana** *Los Chafas YH, Hwy 8, 145km, Minas, Lavalleja.* *(key from Mrs Yaya)*		*15*		Ⓡ

SUPPLEMENTARY ACCOMMODATION
OUTSIDE THE ASSURED STANDARDS SCHEME

Location/Address	Telephone No. Fax No.	Beds	Opening Dates	Facilities
Barra Valizas Artigas YH, Barra Valizas, Rocha. (Montevideo 265km, Rocha 60km)		56	01.11.99–30.03. 00	Ⓡ
Durazno Campus Municipal de Durazno, Saravia y Dr Pensa, Durazno. (Montevideo 182km)	☎ *(362) 2835*	56		Ⓡ
Durazno - "Hostal El Nazareno" Ruta 5, Km 180 (Rural)	☎ *(362) 3564*	16		03S

AFFILIATED ORGANIZATIONS

The International Youth Hostel Federation also has Affiliated Organizations in a number of countries. These are not listed in the main body of the Guide, as they do not fulfil the minimum requirements for full membership, and hostel standards may be outside the assured standards scheme. In some instances, approval has been given for the inclusion of details on their hostel network and/or other relevant information.

Those organizations which are in the African, American, Asian and the Pacific regions are as follows:-

ORGANISATIONS AFFILIEES

La Fédération Internationale des Auberges de Jeunesse a également des organisations affiliées dans un certain nombre d'autres pays. Celles-ci ne figurent pas sur la liste des pays dans la partie principale du Guide, car elles ne répondent pas aux exigences minimales régissant l'adhésion de membre à part entière et la conformité de leurs établissements aux Normes Minimales n'est pas garantie. Dans certains cas, la publication de renseignementsconcernant leurs auberges de jeunesse et/ou d'autres informations utiles a été approuvée.

Les organisations en question en Afrique, Amérique, Asie et dans le Pacifique sont les suivantes:-

ANGESCHLOSSENE ORGANISATIONEN

Der Internationale Jugendherbergsverband steht ebenso in Verbindung mit angeschlossenen Organisationen in verschiedenen anderen Ländern. Diese sind jedoch nicht im Hauptverzeichnis angegeben, weil sie zum einen keine vollberechtigten Mitgliedsverbände sind und zum anderen der Standard dieser Herbergen nicht den zugesicherten Normen entspricht. In einigen Fällen konnten jedoch Angaben über JH solcher Verbände sowie andere wesentliche Angaben ins Verzeichnis aufgenommen werden.

Es handelt sich dabei um folgende Organisationen in Afrika, Amerika, Asien, und dem Pazifik:-

ORGANIZACIONES AFILIADAS

La Federación Internacional de Albergues Juveniles (IYHF) también posee Organizaciones Afiliadas en otros países. Estas no han sido incluidas en la parte principal de la Guía, ya que no cumplen con los requisitos mínimos necesarios para ser miembros de pleno derecho y es posible que el nivel de calidad de sus albergues no corresponda al garantizado por nuestras normas. En algunos casos, se ha aprobado la publicación de información sobre su red dealbergues y/u otros datos pertinentes.

En Africa, América, Asia y en el Pacífico, estas origanizaciones son las siguientes:

ARGENTINA:

Red Argentina de Alojamiento para Jóvenes (RAAJ), Florida 835 3rd Floor, Of 319, 1005 Buenos Aires
- (t) (54) (1) 511 8712 (f) (54) (1) 312 0089
- **E-mail:** raaj@hostels.org.ar

BANGLADESH:

Bangladesh Youth Hostel Association, 18 Elephant Rd, Dhaka 1205.
- (t) (880) (2) 508505, 506218
- (f) (880) (2) 866915
- **E-mail:** afeef@bdonline.com

COLOMBIA:

Federación Colombiana de Albergues Juveniles, Carrera 7, N.6-10, PO Box 240167, Santafe de Bogotá DC.
- (t) (57) (1) 2803318/3202/3041
- (f) (57) (1) 2803460

ECUADOR:

Idiomas s.a., Junin 203 y Panamá 2do piso - Of. 4, Guayaquil, Mexico.
- (t) (593) (4) 564488 (f) (593) (4) 566939
- **E-mail:** idiomas1@idiomas.com.ec

GHANA:

Student & Youth Travel Organisation, Opp. UNDP Offices Ring Road East, PO Box 9732, KIA, Accra.
- (t) / (f) (233) (21) 776081

GUATEMALA:

Intercambios Culturales Y Academicos, 2 calle 5-28 zona 01, Guatemala C.A.
- (t) (502) 2328919 (f) (502) 2210944
- **E-mail:** intercas@uvg.edu.gr

INDONESIA:

Indonesian Youth Hostels Association, Gdg PKON Kantor Menpora RI, Jalan Gerbang Pemuda No 3, Senayan, Jakarta 10270.
- (t) (62) (21) 5738152, 5720665
- (f) (62) (21) 5738313

MEXICO:

Red Mexicana de Alojamiento para Jóvenes, Insurgentes Sur 1510-D, Mexico D F 03920.
- (t) (52) (5) 6613233
- (f) (52) (5) 6631556
- **E-mail:** info@mundojoven.com.mx
- **WWW address:** http://www.mundojoven.com.mx

L T G Viajes Educativos S A C V, Insurgentes Sur No 1694-5th Floor, Colonia Florida, CP 01030 Mexico DF
- (t) (52) (5) 6614235 (f) (52) (5) 6618733
- **E-mail:** tourjoven@infosel.net.mx

NEW CALEDONIA:

Association des Auberges de Jeunesse de Nouvelle Calédonie, BP 767, 51 Bis Rue Olry, Nouméa
- (t) (687) 275879 (f) (687) 254817

SINGAPORE:

Youth Hostels Association (Singapore), 20 Kramat Lane, #04-12, United House, Singapore 228773
- (t) (65) 7336753 (f) (65) 7336754

STA Travel Pte Ltd, #02-17 Orchard Parade Hotel, 1 Tanglin Rd, Singapore 247905
- (t) (65) 7377188 (f) (65) 7372591
- **E-mail:** sales@sta-travel.com.sg

CIEE Travel Pte Ltd, 220 Orchard Rd, #03-04 Midpoint Orchard, Singapore 238852
- (t) (65) 7340001 (f) (65) 7337421
- **E-mail:** cieetrvl@mbox2.singnet.com.sg

TAIWAN:

Chinese Taipei Youth Hostel Association, 12F-10-50 Chung Hsiao West Rd, Sec 1, Taipei
- (t) (886) (2) 23318366
- (f) (886) (2) 23316427

Federal Vacation Co Ltd, 2F, 329 Chung Hsiao E Road, Sec 4, Taipei.
- (t) (886) (2) 27785812
- (f) (886) (2) 27765414
- **E-mail:** tci@tptsl.seed.net.tw

Kang Wen Culture & Education Foundation,
Suite 1208, No 142 Chung Hsiao East Rd, Sec 4,
Taipei
- ☎ (886) (2) 27751138
- 🖷 (886) (2) 27212784

E-mail: gftours@tptsl.seed.net.tw

Kaohsiung International Youth Hostel, 120 Wen
wu First St, Kaohsiung City.
- ☎ (886) (7) 2012477
- 🖷 (886) (7) 2156322

E-mail: jumper@flash.net.tw

VENEZUELA:

IVI Idiomas Vivos s.r.l. Vivos, Res. La Hacienda,
Local 1-4-T Final Av., Ppal de Las Mercedes, Aptdo
80160, Caracas 1080, Venezuela
- ☎ (58) (2) 9933930
- 🖷 (58) (2) 929626

E-mail: ivi@etheron.net

HI - Venezuela, Av Lecuna, Parque Central, Edif
Tajamar, Nivel Oficinas 1, Of 107, Caracas.
- ☎ (58) (2) 5764493
- 🖷 (58) (2) 5774915

HOSTELLING
INTERNATIONAL

ARGENTINA

Red Argentina de Alojamiento para Jóvenes,
Florida 835 Piso 3 Of 319, 1005 Buenos Aires.
☏ (1) 5118712 📠 (1) 3120089 **E-mail:** raaj@hostels.org.ar

IBN Booking Centre - for outward bookings
● Buenos Aires - RAAJ

SUPPLEMENTARY ACCOMMODATION OUTSIDE THE ASSURED STANDARDS SCHEME

Location/Address	Telephone No. Fax No.	Beds	Opening Dates	Facilities
Bariloche - Alaska Hostel Lilinquen 328 on Llao-Llao Rd. km 7.5	☏ (944) 61564 📠 (944) 61564	48		7W
Buenos Aires Moreno 1273, Ciudad de Buenos Aires	☏ (1) 3819760 📠 (1) 3819760	110	Opening April 1999	
Calafate - Del Glaciar Hostel Los Pioneros s/n El Calafate, Provincia de Santa Cruz.	☏ (902) 91243 📠 (902) 91243	110	01.10–31.03	
El Bolson - El Pueblito Hostel Barrio Lujan el Bolson, Provincia de Rio Negro.	☏ (944) 93560	40		3N
El Chalten - Patagonia Hostel Av. San Martin, No 820 Frente a La Terminal Caltur el Chalten - Provincia de Santa Cruz.	☏ (962) 93019	30		
El Chalten - Rancho Grande Av. San Martin, s/n El Chalten, Provincia de Santa Cruz	☏ (962) 93005 📠 (962) 93005	44		
Esquel - Lago Verde Hostel Volta 1081 (9200) Esquel, Provincia de Chubut.	☏ (945) 52251 📠 (945) 53901	17		0.5N
Mendoza - Campo Base Hostel Lavalle 2028, San Jose Guaymallen, Mendoza.	☏ (61) 457661 📠 (61) 457661	40		0.8NE
Mendoza - Hostel Internacional España 343, Provincia de Mendoza	☏ (61) 240018 📠 (61) 240018	79		
Puerto Iguazu - La Cabaña Hostel Av. Tres Fronteras 434 Pto Iguazu, Provincia de Misiones.	☏ (757) 20564	36		
Puerto Madryn - Madryn Backpackers 25 de Mayo, 1136 Puerto Madryn, Provincia de Chubut	☏ (965) 74426 📠 (965) 74426	25	01.09–31.03	
Salta - Backpacker's Hostel Buenos Aires 930, Salta City, Provincia de Salta.	☏ (87) 235910	30		
San Rafael - Puesta del Sol Hostel Dean Funes 998, San Rafael, Provincia de Mendoza.	☏ (627) 34881 📠 (627) 34881, 30187	200		
Tilcara - Malka Hostel Calle San Martin s/n Tilcara, Provincia de Jujuy.	☏ (88) 955197 📠 (88) 955200	13		
Ushuaia - Torre al Sur Gobernador paz 1437, Ushuaia, Provincia de Tierra del Fuego	☏ (901) 30745, 37291 📠 (901) 30745, 37291	40		

Location/Address	Telephone No. / Fax No.	Beds	Opening Dates	Facilities
Villa Gral Belgrano - El Rincon Valle de Calamuchita, Villa Gral Belgrano, Provincia de Cordoba	☎ (546) 61323 🖷 (546) 61761	56	🔟	⛹ 🍽 ® ☞ P ⊡
Villa Paranacito - Top Malo Hostel Acceso a Villa Paranacito km18, Villa Parancito, Provincia de Entre Rios.	☎ (446) 95255 🖷 (446) 95255, 95125	32	🔟	⛹ ® 2W ☞ P ⊡

COLOMBIA

Federación Colombiana de Albergues Juveniles, Carrera 7 No.6-10, PO BOX 240167,
Santafe de Bogotá DC.
☎ (57) (1) 2803318/3202/3041 🖷 (57) (1) 2803460

SUPPLEMENTARY ACCOMMODATION
OUTSIDE THE ASSURED STANDARDS SCHEME

Location/Address	Telephone No. / Fax No.	Beds	Opening Dates	Facilities
Bogotá D.C. Carrera 7 No.6-10, Bogotá D.C. HI - Bogotá	☎ (91) 2803318, 2803202, 2803041 🖷 (91) 2803460	105	🔟	⛹ 🍽 ® 2S P ⊡ ☕
Cartagena - H.Costa del sol Avenida la. calle 9, Esquina- Bocagrande- Cartagena	☎ (95) 6650844; 6653776 🖷 (95) 6653755	280	🔟	⛹ 🍽 ® 1N ⊂⊂ P ⊡ ☕
Leticia - Albergue Turístico Amazonas Calle 11 # 9-60, Leticia, Amazonas	☎ (9859) 27704 🖷 (9859) 27069	50	🔟	⛹ 🍽 ® 1NE ⊂⊂ P ⊡
Medellin - Hotel Casa Dorada Calle 50, No 47-25, Medellín, Antioquia	☎ (94) 5125300 🖷 (94) 3815400	155	🔟	⛹ 🍽 ® 1NE ⊂⊂ P ⊡
Pasto - Hotel Concorde Calle 19, No. 29A-09, Pasto, Nariño	☎ (927) 221464 🖷 (927) 233232;222357	33	🔟	⛹ ® 0.5N P ⊡
Piapa - H.Cabañas El Portón Avenida Piscinas termales, Paipa, Boyacá	☎ (987) 320282; 320822 🖷 (987) 850864	95	🔟	⛹ 🍽 ® 1SE ⊂⊂ P ⊡ ☕
San Agustin - Alberge Juverni; Sindayo Carrera 12 # 5-23, San Agustín, Huila	☎ (988) 373209 🖷 (988) 373588	50	🔟	🍽 ® 0.5NW P ⊡ ☕
Santa Marta Hostel Tima-Uraka, Calle 18 No.2-59 El Rodadero.	☎ (954) 228433 🖷 (954) 228433	25	🔟	⛹ 🍽 1SW P ⊡
Santa Marta - H. Medellín Calle 22 No. 2A-62, Santa Marta	☎ (954) 213380 🖷 (954) 212654	37	🔟	⛹ 🍽 ® 0.5N ⊂⊂ P ⊡ ☕
Santa Marta - H. Medellín Calle 19 No.1c-30, El Rodadero	☎ (954) 220220; 220202 🖷 (954) 212654	110	🔟	⛹ 🍽 ® 13S ⊂⊂ P ⊡ ☕

Location/Address	Telephone No. Fax No.	Beds	Opening Dates	Facilities
Villa de Leyva - Hostel Los Aceitunos Transversal 10 # 9-41 (Salida al Fósil), Villa de leyva, Boyacá.	☎ (987) 320282; 320822 📠 (91) 2859854	150		⋯
Villavicencio Los Girasoles - Granja Turistica Vacacional A continuación Barrios la Campiña y Chapinerito, Villavicencio, Meta.	☎ (986) 2211191; 2226568	160		⋯

INDONESIA

Indonesian Youth Hostels Association, Ggd PKON Kantor Menpora RI, Jl Gerbang Pemuda No 3, Senayan, Jakarta 10270, Indonesia
☎ (21) 5738152, 5720665 📠 (21) 5738152, 5202506

Due to the current situation in Indonesia, no information has been received about the network of hostels. Please contact the Bali International Hostel for and current information.

SUPPLEMENTARY ACCOMMODATION
OUTSIDE THE ASSURED STANDARDS SCHEME

Location/Address	Telephone No. Fax No.	Beds	Opening Dates	Facilities
Bali - Bali International Hostel ⃞IBN Jalan Mertasari 19, Banjar Suwung Kangin, Sidakarya, Denpasar Selatin, Bali.	☎ (361) 720812 📠 (361) 720812	120		⋯

MEXICO

Red Mexicana de Alojamiento para Jóvenes, Insurgentes Sur 1510-D, Col. Credito Constructor, Mexico D F 03920. ☎ (5) 6613233 📠 (5) 6631556.

E-mail: info@mundojoven.com.mx **WWW address:** http://mundojoven.com.mx

IBN Booking Centres - for outward bookings
● **Mexico** - Mundo Joven *via National Office above*
● **Guadalajara** - Av. Patria 600, local 13-E, Plaza Amistad, Guadalajara, Jalisco 45110.
☎ (52) (36) 730936 📠 (52) (36) 733656

SUPPLEMENTARY ACCOMMODATION
OUTSIDE THE ASSURED STANDARDS SCHEME

Location/Address	Telephone No. Fax No.	Beds	Opening Dates	Facilities
Cuernavaca - Villa Calmecac Zacatecas #114, Col. Buenavista, Cuernavaca, Morelos C.P. 62130	☎ (52) (73) 132146 📠 (52) (73) 132146	32		⋯
Tepoztlan - Casa Iccemanyan Calle del Olivio 26, Barrio San Miguel Tepoztlan, Morelos	☎ (52) (739) 50899, (52) (739) 50096 📠 (52) (739) 52159	11		⋯

NEW CALEDONIA

Fédération Unie des Auberges de Jeunesse (France),
Association des Auberges de Jeunesse de Nouvelle Calédonie, rue Olry, BP 767, Nouméa, Nouvelle Calédonie t (687) 275879 f (687) 254817

Expect to pay in the region of 1200-3000 CFP per night. Sheet sleeping bags are available, free of charge.

SUPPLEMENTARY ACCOMMODATION OUTSIDE THE ASSURED STANDARDS SCHEME

Location/Address	Telephone No. Fax No.	Beds	Opening Dates	Facilities
Nouméa City Hostel 51 bis rue Olry, BP 767, 98845 Nouméa Cedex, New Caledonia, South Pacific.	t (687) 275879 f (687) 254817	94	9	R 0.3NE CC P

SINGAPORE

STA Travel Pte Ltd, #02-17 Orchard Parade Hotel, 1 Tanglin Rd, Singapore 247905
t (65) 7377188 f (65) 7372591 **E-mail:** sales@sta-travel.com.org

IBN Booking Centre - for outward bookings

- **Singapore** - STA Travel, *via National Office above*

TAIWAN

Chinese Taipei Youth Hostel Association, 12F-10, 50 Chung Hsiao West Rd, Sec 1, Taipei
t (2) 23318366, f (2) 23316427

Expect to pay in the region of US$15.00-US$20.00 per night. Travelling information office. It is essential to book in advance during peak periods.

N.B. For Chinese address in detail, please contact head office in Taipei.

IBN Booking Centre - for outward bookings

- **Taipei** - Chinese Taipei YHA, *via National Office above*

SUPPLEMENTARY ACCOMMODATION OUTSIDE THE ASSURED STANDARDS SCHEME

Location/Address	Telephone No. Fax No.	Beds	Opening Dates	Facilities
Kaohsiung Modern Plaza Hotel, 332 Chiuju 2nd Rd, Kaohsiung City.	t (7) 3122151 f (7) 3218282	40	9	R 0.2S CC P
Kenting Wu Fong YH, 12 Foukuang Lane, Kenting Li, Hengchun, Pintong County.	t (8) 8861061, 8861661 f (8) 8861661	26	9	CC P
Tainan Guang Haw Hotel, No. 155 Beimen Rd, Section 1, Tainan.	t (6) 2263171 f (6) 2263175	63	9	P
Taipei Asiaworld YH, 12F-14 No 50 Chunghsiao W Rd, Sec 1 Taipei.	t (2) 23756625, 23318366 f (2) 23316427	25	9	

Federal Vacation Co. Ltd
2F, 329 Chung Hsiao East Rd, Sec 4, Taipei.
☎ (886) (2) 27785812 **📠** (886) (2) 27765414

IBN Booking Centre - for outward bookings
● **Taipei** - Federal Vacation, *via National Office above*

Kang Wen Culture & Education Foundation,
1208A/12F, No 142 Chung Shiao East Rd, Sec 4, Taipei.
☎ (886) (2) 27751138 **📠** (886) (2) 27212784
E-mail: gftours@tptsl.seed.net.tw

IBN Booking Centre - for outward bookings
● **Taipei** - Kang Wen, *via National Office above*

Kaohsiung International Youth Hostel,
120 Wen wu First Street, Kaohsiung City.
☎ (886) (7) 2012477 **📠** (886) (7) 2156322
E-mail: jumper@flash.net.tw

IBN Booking Centre - for outward bookings
● **Kaohsiung** - Kaohsiung International Youth Hostel

SUPPLEMENTARY ACCOMMODATION OUTSIDE THE ASSURED STANDARDS SCHEME

Location/Address	Telephone No. Fax No.	Beds	Opening Dates	Facilities
Kaohsiung - International Wen Wu YH #120 Wen wu First St, Kaohsiung.	☎ 886 (7) 2012477 📠 886 (7) 2156322	28		� ⛀ 🅿 ▤
Kaohsiung - International Lingya YH 2nd Floor, 42 Lingya Second Rd, Kaohsiung.	☎ (7) 3391533	50		♥0 ⛀ 🅿

WHAT IS FIYTO ?

Ever since its inception in 1951, the aim of FIYTO has been to promote educational, cultural and social travel among young people.

In its forty-eight year history, FIYTO has become the largest and most influential organisation in the youth travel industry. Towards the mainstream travel and tourism community, international, governmental and non-governmental organisations, FIYTO advocates the special identity of young travellers and their right to affordable travel and travel-related services.

FIYTO is today the premier trade association for youth travel and tourism, a rapidly growing segment of the travel industry. Today we represent the unique interests of an estimated 20% of the tourism population. Almost 300 members account for a turnover of more than 6 billion US Dollars, serve some 14 million young travellers annually and sell over 6 million air and surface tickets. FIYTO members can be found in over 60 countries on all continents.

FIYTO is an open, worldwide, non-political and non-sectarian organisation. Non-profit and for-profit companies, public and private, retailers, wholesalers, buyers, sellers and suppliers are all represented in the FIYTO membership.

FIYTO is an affiliate member of the World Tourism Organisation (WTO) and a member of the Pacific Asia Travel Association (PATA) and the European Travel & Tourism Action Group (ETAG). FIYTO enjoys operational relations with UNESCO, the United Nations Educational, Scientific and Cultural Organisation.

For qualified companies, actively engaged in incoming or outgoing youth travel, FIYTO provides the pre-eminent professional forum to trade, exchange information and advance the interests of the young traveller.

For more information on FIYTO please contact:

**FIYTO, Bredgade 25H,
1260 Copenhagen K, Denmark
E-mail:** mailbox@fiyto.org
WWW Address: http://www.fiyto.org

International Student Travel Confederation (ISTC)

The International Student Travel Confederation is a not-for-profit confederation of student travel organisations whose focus is to develop, promote and facilitate travel among young people and students.

The ISTC is made up of 5 distinct member Associations, each specialising in aspects of travel-related services: air travel, surface travel, travel insurance, work and educational exchange programmes and the International Student Identity Card (ISIC).

Since 1967, the ISTC has maintained a relationship with UNESCO, the United Nations Educational, Scientific and Cultural Organisation, to promote student travel and international understanding. UNESCO officially endorses and supports the ISIC and recognises it as the unique document for student mobility.

The ISIC Association administers the development and distribution of the International Student Identity Card (ISIC) in over 90 countries. The ISIC is the **only** internationally recognised proof of full-time student status providing worldwide, photo identity documentation for student travellers. It provides travel and other benefits including thousands of discounts and special prices on a variety of goods and services around the world. All cardholders have access to the ISIC Help Line - a free, 24 hour international emergency assistance service and a worldwide telecommunications package.

The objectives of the International Student Surface Travel Association (ISSA) are to support and consult in the development of special surface travel products for travelling students and youth, and to facilitate practical co-operation among members.

The Student Air Travel Association (SATA) is an association of member organisations that negotiate special fares for students with more than 70 major airlines. SATA airline tickets, issued only by SATA members, are generally flexible with very few restrictions and are valid on both scheduled and charter airlines.

The main activities of IASIS, the International Association of Student Insurance Services, are to provide and promote insurance services for the travelling student and young person. IASIS is the world's leading low cost insurance for young people and provides direct refund in case of accidents in many countries.

The International Association for Educational and Work Exchange Programmes (IAEWEP) is a group of organisations that facilitate work exchange programmes between youth, student and educational institutions worldwide. The member organisations of IAEWEP offer "Work Abroad" programmes that make possible the international movement of up to 50,000 students and youth annually.

For more information about the ISTC and it's member Associations, please contact: ISTC, PO Box 15857, 1001 NJ Amsterdam, The Netherlands or check out their web-site at **http://www.istc.org**

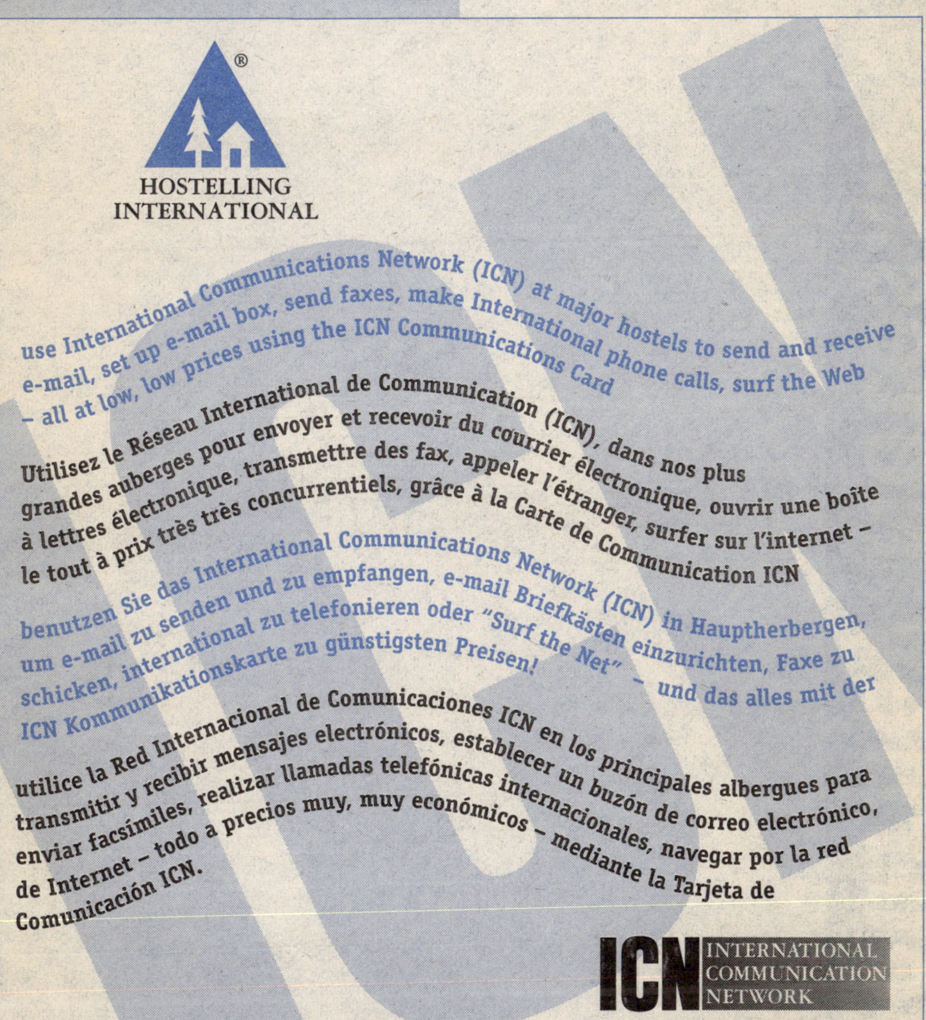

Journey Notes....

Journey Notes....

Journey Notes....

Journey Notes....

Journey Notes....

Journey Notes....

Journey Notes....

... help us to implement our assurance of standards at hostels by writing to us or by using the reply slip in this Guide to tell us what you think of our hostels.

Just tick the boxes to indicate how well the hostel did in the five areas, and remember to let us have your comments on how you found your stay.

Simply put your reply in an envelope and post to us at the address shown on the slip.

NOUS AIMERIONS CONNAITRE VOTRE OPINION...

... aidez-nous à mettre en place les normes garanties dans nos auberges en nous faisant part de ce que vous pensez d'elles, soit en nous écrivant, soit en remplissant la fiche prévue à cet effet que vous trouverez dans ce guide.

Il vous suffira de cocher les cases pour évaluer la performance de l'auberge dans les cinq domaines indiqués, sans oublier d'ajouter vos observations sur votre séjour.

Envoyez-nous votre fiche sous enveloppe, à l'adresse indiquée dessus.

WIR MÖCHTEN IHRE MEINUNG HÖREN...

... helfen Sie uns, unsere zugesicherten Standards zu gewährleisten, indem Sie uns wissen lassen, was Sie von unseren Herbergen halten. Bitte schreiben Sie uns oder benutzen Sie dazu die am Ende dieses Führers beigefügte Antwortkarte.

Kreuzen Sie bitte Ihre Beurteilung für die jeweilige Kategorie in dem entsprechenden Kästchen an und vergessen Sie nicht, uns Ihren Kommentar über Ihren Aufenthalt mitzuteilen.

Ihre Antwort ganz einfach in einen Umschlag stecken und an die auf der Antwortkarte angegebene Adresse schicken.

QUEREMOS SABER LO QUE USTED OPINA...

... ayúdenos a implementar nuestras normas garantizadas en los albergues. Escríbanos, o haga uso de las hojas provistas en la Guía, para comunicarnos lo que piensa de nuestros albergues.

Sólo tiene que marcar las casillas según la opinión que le merezca el albergue en lo que respecta a los cinco apartados de consulta. No olvide añadir comentarios sobre su estancia en el recuadro de las observaciones.

Envíe su comunicación en un sobre dirigido a la dirección indicada.

TELL US WHAT YOU THINK!

DITES-NOUS CE QUE VOUS EN PENSEZ!
SAGEN SIE UNS IHRE MEINUNG!
¡DIGANOS LO QUE OPINA!

Hostel Name-Address/
Auberge Nom-Adresse/
Jugendherberge
Name-Anschrift/
Albergue Nombre-Dirección

City/Ville/Stadt/Ciudad

Country/*Pays***/Land/***País*

Date(s) stayed/*Dates du séjour/*
Daten des Aufenthaltes/
Fechas de la Estancia

Please return to:
INTERNATIONAL YOUTH HOSTEL FEDERATION,
9 Guessens Road, Welwyn Garden City,
Hertfordshire AL8 6QW. ENGLAND

Welcome/*Accueil/*
Aufnahme/*Recibimiento*

Comfort/*Confort/*
Komfort/*Comodidad*

Cleanliness/*Propreté/*
Sauberkeit/*Limpieza*

Security/*Sécurité/*
Sicherheit/*Seguridad*

Privacy/*Intimité, Vie Privée/*
Privatsphäre/*Intimidad, Vida Privada*

COMMENTS/*COMMENTAIRES***/BEMERKUNGEN/***OBSERVACIONES*

Name/*Nom/*
Name/*Nombre*

Address/*Adresse/*
Anschrift/*Dirección*

... help us to implement our assurance of standards at hostels by writing to us or by using the reply slip in this Guide to tell us what you think of our hostels.

Just tick the boxes to indicate how well the hostel did in the five areas, and remember to let us have your comments on how you found your stay.

Simply put your reply in an envelope and post to us at the address shown on the slip.

NOUS AIMERIONS CONNAITRE VOTRE OPINION...

... aidez-nous à mettre en place les normes garanties dans nos auberges en nous faisant part de ce que vous pensez d'elles, soit en nous écrivant, soit en remplissant la fiche prévue à cet effet que vous trouverez dans ce guide.

Il vous suffira de cocher les cases pour évaluer la performance de l'auberge dans les cinq domaines indiqués, sans oublier d'ajouter vos observations sur votre séjour.

Envoyez-nous votre fiche sous enveloppe, à l'adresse indiquée dessus.

WIR MÖCHTEN IHRE MEINUNG HÖREN...

... helfen Sie uns, unsere zugesicherten Standards zu gewährleisten, indem Sie uns wissen lassen, was Sie von unseren Herbergen halten. Bitte schreiben Sie uns oder benutzen Sie dazu die am Ende dieses Führers beigefügte Antwortkarte.

Kreuzen Sie bitte Ihre Beurteilung für die jeweilige Kategorie in dem entsprechenden Kästchen an und vergessen Sie nicht, uns Ihren Kommentar über Ihren Aufenthalt mitzuteilen.

Ihre Antwort ganz einfach in einen Umschlag stecken und an die auf der Antwortkarte angegebene Adresse schicken.

QUEREMOS SABER LO QUE USTED OPINA...

... ayúdenos a implementar nuestras normas garantizadas en los albergues. Escríbanos, o haga uso de las hojas provistas en la Guía, para comunicarnos lo que piensa de nuestros albergues.

Sólo tiene que marcar las casillas según la opinión que le merezca el albergue en lo que respecta a los cinco apartados de consulta. No olvide añadir comentarios sobre su estancia en el recuadro de las observaciones.

Envíe su comunicación en un sobre dirigido a la dirección indicada.

Hostel Name-Address/
Auberge Nom-Adresse/
**Jugendherberge
Name-Anschrift/**
Albergue Nombre-Dirección

City/Ville/Stadt/Ciudad

Country/*Pays*/Land/*País*

Date(s) stayed/*Dates du séjour/*
Daten des Aufenthaltes/
Fechas de la Estancia

Please return to:
INTERNATIONAL YOUTH HOSTEL FEDERATION,
9 Guessens Road, Welwyn Garden City,
Hertfordshire AL8 6QW. ENGLAND

Welcome/*Accueil/*
Aufnahme/*Recibimiento*

Comfort/*Confort/*
Komfort/*Comodidad*

Cleanliness/*Propreté/*
Sauberkeit/*Limpieza*

Security/*Sécurité/*
Sicherheit/*Seguridad*

Privacy/*Intimité, Vie Privée/*
Privatsphäre/*Intimidad, Vida Privada*

COMMENTS/*COMMENTAIRES*/BEMERKUNGEN/*OBSERVACIONES*

Name/*Nom/*
Name/*Nombre*

Address/*Adresse/*
Anschrift/*Dirección*

... help us to implement our assurance of standards at hostels by writing to us or by using the reply slip in this Guide to tell us what you think of our hostels.

Just tick the boxes to indicate how well the hostel did in the five areas, and remember to let us have your comments on how you found your stay.

Simply put your reply in an envelope and post to us at the address shown on the slip.

NOUS AIMERIONS CONNAITRE VOTRE OPINION...

... aidez-nous à mettre en place les normes garanties dans nos auberges en nous faisant part de ce que vous pensez d'elles, soit en nous écrivant, soit en remplissant la fiche prévue à cet effet que vous trouverez dans ce guide.

Il vous suffira de cocher les cases pour évaluer la performance de l'auberge dans les cinq domaines indiqués, sans oublier d'ajouter vos observations sur votre séjour.

Envoyez-nous votre fiche sous enveloppe, à l'adresse indiquée dessus.

WIR MÖCHTEN IHRE MEINUNG HÖREN...

... helfen Sie uns, unsere zugesicherten Standards zu gewährleisten, indem Sie uns wissen lassen, was Sie von unseren Herbergen halten. Bitte schreiben Sie uns oder benutzen Sie dazu die am Ende dieses Führers beigefügte Antwortkarte.

Kreuzen Sie bitte Ihre Beurteilung für die jeweilige Kategorie in dem entsprechenden Kästchen an und vergessen Sie nicht, uns Ihren Kommentar über Ihren Aufenthalt mitzuteilen.

Ihre Antwort ganz einfach in einen Umschlag stecken und an die auf der Antwortkarte angegebene Adresse schicken.

QUEREMOS SABER LO QUE USTED OPINA...

... ayúdenos a implementar nuestras normas garantizadas en los albergues. Escríbanos, o haga uso de las hojas provistas en la Guía, para comunicarnos lo que piensa de nuestros albergues.

Sólo tiene que marcar las casillas según la opinión que le merezca el albergue en lo que respecta a los cinco apartados de consulta. No olvide añadir comentarios sobre su estancia en el recuadro de las observaciones.

Envíe su comunicación en un sobre dirigido a la dirección indicada.

TELL US WHAT YOU THINK!

DITES-NOUS CE QUE VOUS EN PENSEZ!
SAGEN SIE UNS IHRE MEINUNG!
¡DIGANOS LO QUE OPINA!

Hostel Name-Address/
Auberge Nom-Adresse/
Jugendherberge Name-Anschrift/
Albergue Nombre-Dirección

City/Ville/Stadt/Ciudad

Country/*Pays*/Land/*País*

Date(s) stayed/*Dates du séjour/*
Daten des Aufenthaltes/
Fechas de la Estancia

Please return to:
INTERNATIONAL YOUTH HOSTEL FEDERATION,
9 Guessens Road, Welwyn Garden City,
Hertfordshire AL8 6QW. ENGLAND

Welcome/*Accueil/*
Aufnahme/*Recibimiento*

Comfort/*Confort/*
Komfort/*Comodidad*

Cleanliness/*Propreté/*
Sauberkeit/*Limpieza*

Security/*Sécurité/*
Sicherheit/*Seguridad*

Privacy/*Intimité, Vie Privée/*
Privatsphäre/*Intimidad, Vida Privada*

COMMENTS/*COMMENTAIRES/***BEMERKUNGEN/***OBSERVACIONES*

Name/*Nom/*
Name/*Nombre*

Address/*Adresse/*
Anschrift/*Dirección*

... help us to implement our assurance of standards at hostels by writing to us or by using the reply slip in this Guide to tell us what you think of our hostels.

Just tick the boxes to indicate how well the hostel did in the five areas, and remember to let us have your comments on how you found your stay.

Simply put your reply in an envelope and post to us at the address shown on the slip.

NOUS AIMERIONS CONNAITRE VOTRE OPINION...

... aidez-nous à mettre en place les normes garanties dans nos auberges en nous faisant part de ce que vous pensez d'elles, soit en nous écrivant, soit en remplissant la fiche prévue à cet effet que vous trouverez dans ce guide.

Il vous suffira de cocher les cases pour évaluer la performance de l'auberge dans les cinq domaines indiqués, sans oublier d'ajouter vos observations sur votre séjour.

Envoyez-nous votre fiche sous enveloppe, à l'adresse indiquée dessus.

WIR MÖCHTEN IHRE MEINUNG HÖREN...

... helfen Sie uns, unsere zugesicherten Standards zu gewährleisten, indem Sie uns wissen lassen, was Sie von unseren Herbergen halten. Bitte schreiben Sie uns oder benutzen Sie dazu die am Ende dieses Führers beigefügte Antwortkarte.

Kreuzen Sie bitte Ihre Beurteilung für die jeweilige Kategorie in dem entsprechenden Kästchen an und vergessen Sie nicht, uns Ihren Kommentar über Ihren Aufenthalt mitzuteilen.

Ihre Antwort ganz einfach in einen Umschlag stecken und an die auf der Antwortkarte angegebene Adresse schicken.

QUEREMOS SABER LO QUE USTED OPINA...

... ayúdenos a implementar nuestras normas garantizadas en los albergues. Escríbanos, o haga uso de las hojas provistas en la Guía, para comunicarnos lo que piensa de nuestros albergues.

Sólo tiene que marcar las casillas según la opinión que le merezca el albergue en lo que respecta a los cinco apartados de consulta. No olvide añadir comentarios sobre su estancia en el recuadro de las observaciones.

Envíe su comunicación en un sobre dirigido a la dirección indicada.

TELL US WHAT YOU THINK!

DITES-NOUS CE QUE VOUS EN PENSEZ!
SAGEN SIE UNS IHRE MEINUNG!
¡DIGANOS LO QUE OPINA!

Hostel Name-Address/
Auberge Nom-Adresse/
Jugendherberge Name-Anschrift/
Albergue Nombre-Dirección

City/Ville/Stadt/Ciudad

Country/*Pays***/Land/***País*

Date(s) stayed/*Dates du séjour/*
Daten des Aufenthaltes/
Fechas de la-Estancia

Please return to:
INTERNATIONAL YOUTH HOSTEL FEDERATION,
9 Guessens Road, Welwyn Garden City,
Hertfordshire AL8 6QW. ENGLAND

Welcome/*Accueil/*
Aufnahme/*Recibimiento*

Comfort/*Confort/*
Komfort/*Comodidad*

Cleanliness/*Propreté/*
Sauberkeit/*Limpieza*

Security/*Sécurité/*
Sicherheit/*Seguridad*

Privacy/*Intimité, Vie Privée/*
Privatsphäre/*Intimidad, Vida Privada*

COMMENTS/*COMMENTAIRES***/BEMERKUNGEN/***OBSERVACIONES*

Name/*Nom/*
Name/*Nombre*

Address/*Adresse/*
Anschrift/*Dirección*

EXPLICACION DE LOS SIMBOLOS	ZEICHENERKLÄRUNG	EXPLICATION DES SYMBOLES

EXPLICACION DE LOS SIMBOLOS

Albergues que participan en el Plan de Normas Garantizadas

- Categoría Normal
- Categoría Sencilla
- Número de teléfono
- Número de fax
- Open Dates: Fechas de apertura
- Albergue abierto todo el año
- Open Hours: Horas de apertura
- Albergue abierto las 24 horas del día
- Reservations: Información sobre reservas
- R Se aceptan reservas
- IBN Se pueden hacer reservas a través de IBN (véase la introducción general para más información)
- CC Se aceptan tarjetas de crédito
- Beds: Número total de camas
- 1-6 Número de habitaciones con número de camas indicado
- Price (range): Precio por noche
- BBinc Desayuno incluido en el precio por noche
- Sábanas incluidas en el precio por noche
- Alquiler de sábanas
- Facilities: Instalaciones y prestaciones que ofrece el albergue
- Preparado para uso de disminuidos físicos
- Se aceptan grupos
- Habitaciones familiares
- Sólo para mujeres
- Sólo para hombres
- Se sirven todas las comidas (a menos que se indique lo contrario):
- B Desayuno
- L Comida
- D Cena
- Cocina para huéspedes
- Bar-Cafetería
- Salas comunes en el albergue
- Salón de TV en el albergue
- Biblioteca para socios
- Acceso a Internet en el albergue
- Sala(s) de conferencias
- Posibilidad de lavar la ropa/Lavandería en el albergue o cerca de él
- Lugar donde guardar el equipaje/consigna para socios
- Pequeña tienda en el albergue o cerca de él
- Casillas/armarios con cerradura en el albergue
- Aire acondicionado
- Ascensor en el albergue
- P Aparcamiento en el albergue o cerca de él
- Información turística
- Cambio de divisas en el albergue o cerca de él
- Jardín en el albergue
- Parque infantil en el albergue
- Discoteca en el albergue
- Sauna en el albergue
- Ping-pong en el albergue
- Vóleibol en el albergue
- Albergue ecológico
- Albergue en edificio histórico
- Directions: Cómo llegar al albergue: Medios de transporte
- 2NE Dirección y distancia aproximada en km. en línea recta desde el centro de la ciudad hasta el albergue.
- Aeropuerto más cercano
- Autobús al aeropuerto
- Puerto: Nombre y distancia desde el centro de la ciudad
- Tren: Estación más cercana y distancia hasta el albergue
- Autobús (desde el centro de la ciudad) Nº, parada y distancia hasta el albergue
- Tranvía o trolebús (desde el centro de la ciudad) Nº, parada y distancia hasta el albergue
- U Metro: Nombre de la línea, nombre de la estación y distancia hasta el albergue
- Parada de autobús
- Parada de tranvía
- ap Apeadero
- Attractions: Actividades que ofrecen el albergue y sus alrededores
- Zona forestal/bosques
- Zona montañosa/montes
- Playa en el albergue o cerca de él
- Alquiler de bicicletas en el albergue o cerca de él
- Zona de esquí alpino
- Zona de esquí de fondo
- Zona de marcha/senderismo
- Equitación en el albergue o cerca de él
- Tenis en el albergue o cerca de él
- Natación en el albergue o cerca de él
- Mon Tues — Lunes Martes
- Wed Thurs — Miércoles Jueves
- Fri Sat — Viernes Sábado
- Sun — Domingo
- Ave Hwy — Avenida Autopista
- Rd St — Carretera Calle
- Su Wi — Verano Invierno

ZEICHENERKLÄRUNG

Herbergen im Rahmen des zugesicherten Standardprogrammes

- Normaler Standard
- Einfacher Standard
- Telefonnummer
- Telefaxnummer
- Open Dates: Herberge geöffnet (Tage)
- Herberge ganzjährlich geöffnet
- Herberge geöffnet freilassen
- Open Hours: Herberge geöffnet (Zeiten)
- Herberge geöffnet 24 stunden
- Reservations: Reservierungsinformationen
- R Reservierung erforderlich/empfohlen
- IBN IBN Reservierungen verfügbar (siehe: Einleitung für Einzelheiten)
- CC Kreditkarten werden akzeptiert
- Beds: Bettenzahl
- 1-6 Anzahl der Räume mit entsprechender Bettenausstattung
- Price (range): Übernachtungspreis
- BBinc Frühstück ist im Übernachtungspreis enthalten
- Bettwäsche im Preis enthalten
- Bettwäsche kann ausgeliehen werden
- Facilities: Ausstattung in oder in der Nähe der Herberge
- Für Rollstuhlbenutzer geeignet
- Aufnahme von Gruppen
- Familienräume vorhanden
- Nur für Frauen
- Nur für Männer
- Mahlzeiten erhältlich (sofern nicht anders angegeben):
- B Frühstück
- L Mittagessen
- D Abendessen
- Küche für Mitglieder
- Café/Bar vorhanden
- Gemeinschaftsraum vorhanden
- Fernsehraum in der Herberge
- ruhiger Leseraum vorhanden
- Internet-Zugang in der Herberge
- Tagungsräume
- Einrichtungen zur Wäschepflege in (oder in der Nähe) der Herberge
- Gepäckaufbewahrung für Mitglieder
- Kleines Geschäft in (oder in der Nähe) der Herberge
- Schliessfächer vorhanden
- Klimaanlage
- Personenaufzug in der Herberge
- P Parkmöglichkeiten in (oder in der Nähe) der Herberge
- Touristeninformation
- Geldwechsel in der Herberge möglich
- Garten vorhanden
- Spielplatz vorhanden
- Disco in der Herberge
- Sauna in der Herberge
- Tischtennis in der Herberge
- Volleyball in der Herberge
- "Grüne Herberge"
- Herberge in einem historischem Gebäude
- Directions: Verkehrsanbindung zu und von der Herberge
- 2NE Richtung und ungefähre Entfernung in km vom Stadtzentrum bis zur Herberge (Luftlinie)
- Nächster größerer Flughafen
- Flughafenbus
- Hafen: Name und Entfernung vom Stadtzentrum
- Eisenbahn: nächster Bahnhof und Entfernung bis zur Herberge
- Bus (vom Stadtzentrum): Nummer(n), günstigste Haltestelle und Entfernung bis zur Herberge
- Straßenbahn oder O-Bus (vom Stadtzentrum): Nummer(n), günstigste Haltestelle und Entfernung bis zur Herberge
- U U-Bahn: Name der Linie, Name der Haltestelle und Entfernung bis zur Herberge
- Bus-Haltestelle
- Straßenbahn-Haltestelle
- ap günstigste Haltestelle
- Attractions: Attraktionen in der Herberge oder in der Umgebund
- Waldgebiet vorhanden
- Gebirge vorhanden
- Strand in der Nähe der Herberge
- Fahrradverleih in (oder in der Nähe) der Herberge
- Ski-Aplin-Gebiet
- Skilanglaufgebiet
- Gebiet zum Wandern
- Reiten in oder in der Nähe der Herberge
- Tennis in oder in der Nähe der Herberge
- Schwimmbad in oder der Nähe der Herberge
- Mon Tues — Montag Dienstag
- Wed Thurs — Mittwoch Donnerstag
- Fri Sat — Freitag Samstag
- Sun — Sonntag
- Ave Hwy — Allee Landstraße
- Rd St — Straße
- Su Wi — Sommer Winter

EXPLICATION DES SYMBOLES

Auberges participant au Plan pour la Garantie des Normes en Auberge

- Catégorie Normale
- Catégorie Simple
- Numéro de téléphone
- Numéro de facsimilé
- Open Dates: Dates d'ouverture de l'auberge
- Auberge ouverte toute l'année
- Open Hours: Heures d'ouverture de l'auberge
- Auberge ouverte 24 heures
- Reservations: Renseignements sur les réservations
- R Réservation obligatoire/ conseillée
- IBN Réservations IBN disponibles (voir introduction principale à ce sujet)
- CC Les cartes de crédit sont acceptées
- Beds: Nombre de lits
- 1-6 Nombre de chambres au nombre indiqué de lits
- Price (range): Tarif pour une nuitée
- BBinc Petit déjeuner compris dans le prix de la nuitée
- Draps compris
- Location de draps
- Facilities: Prestations offertes par l'auberge
- Convient aux ajistes en fauteuil roulant
- Accueil des Groupes
- Chambres familiales disponibles
- Réservé aux femmes
- Réservé aux hommes
- Tous les repas sont disponibles (sauf indication contraire):
- B Petit déjeuner
- L Déjeuner
- D Dîner (repas du soir)
- Cuisine à la disposition des membres/ contribution requise
- Café/Bar disponibles
- Salles communes à l'auberge
- Salle de télévision à l'auberge
- Bibliothèque pour adhérents
- Accès à l'Internet à l'auberge
- Salles de réunion
- Il est possible de laver son linge à ou près de l'auberge
- Dépôt de Bagages pour adhérents
- Petit magasin à votre service à ou près de l'auberge
- Casiers individuels à l'auberge
- Climatisation
- Ascenseur à l'auberge
- P Possibilités de parking à ou près de l'auberge
- Informations touristiques
- Bureau de Change à ou près de l'auberge
- Jardin à l'auberge
- Terrain de jeu à l'auberge
- Disco à l'auberge
- Sauna à l'auberge
- Tennis de Table à l'auberge
- Volley-Ball à l'auberge
- Auberge écologique
- L'auberge est située dans un bâtiment historique
- Directions: Moyens de transport et indications pour se rendre à l'auberge
- 2NE Direction et distance approximative en km en ligne droite du centre-ville
- Aéroport principal le plus proche
- Autobus pour l'aéroport
- Port: Nom et distance à partir du centre-ville
- Train: gare la plus proche et distance jusqu'à l'auberge
- Bus (à partir du centre-ville): No/Nos, point d'arrivée et distance jusqu'à l'auberge
- Trams ou trolleys (à partir du centre-ville): No/Nos, point d'arrivée et distance jusqu'à l'auberge
- U Métro: Nom de la ligne, nom de la station et distance jusqu'à l'auberge
- Arrêt de bus
- Arrêt de tram
- ap point d'arrivée
- Attractions: Attraits touristiques de l'auberge et de la région
- Région boisée ou forestière
- Région de montagnes ou de collines
- Plage à ou près de l'auberge
- Location de vélos à l'auberge
- Région de ski alpin
- Région de ski de fond
- Région de randonnée pédestre
- Equitation à ou près de l'auberge
- Tennis à ou près de l'auberge
- Natation à ou près de l'auberge
- Mon Tues — Lundi Mardi
- Wed Thurs — Mercredi Jeudi
- Fri Sat — Vendredi Samedi
- Sun — Dimanche
- Ave Hwy — Avenue Autoroute
- Rd St — Route Rue
- Su Wi — Eté Hiver

ENGLISH

HOW TO USE THE SIGNS

❶ OPEN THIS FLAP

❷ TURN TO THE COUNTRY IN WHICH YOU ARE INTERESTED

❸ COMPARE THE SIGNS FOR EXPLANATION

FRANÇAIS

COMMENT INTERPRETER LES SYMBOLES

① OUVRIR CE VOLET

② REPORTEZ-VOUS AU PAYS QUI VOUS INTERESSE

③ COMPAREZ LES SIGNES POUR EN AVOIR L'EXPLICATION

DEUTSCH

ANLEITUNG ZUR BENUTZUNG DER ZEICHEN

❶ ÖFFNEN SIE DIESES FALTBLATT

❷ SUCHEN SIE DAS LAND ÜBER WELCHES SIE AUSKÜNFTE HABEN MÖCHTEN

❸ VERGLEICHEN SIE DIE ZEICHEN AUF DER KLAPPE MIT DENEN DES LANDES

ESPAÑOL

COMO UTILIZAR LOS SIMBOLOS

① ABRA ESTA SOLAPA

② BUSQUE EL PAIS QUE LE INTERESA

③ COMPARE LOS SIMBOLOS PARA OBTENER SU EXPLICACION

Copyright © 1998 International Youth Hostel Federation.

All rights reserved. Typeset in England by Elanders (UK) Limited. Printed in Sweden by Elanders Tryckeri. No part of this book may be used or reproduced in any manner whatsoever without written permission.

Cover Design and pages 1-32 by OXYGEN Creative Solutions Ltd, London.
Design pages 33-385 & "We want to hear from you" pages by Elanders (UK) Limited.

Front cover photograph: Michael Smallcombe

IYHF acknowledges the help of Lonely Planet in providing the following photographs:

Page - 1 Top   Richard I'Anson
   Kryzystof Dydynski
Bottom right-left   Richard I'Anson
   F L Gordon
   Kryzystof Dydynski
   Richard I'Anson

In pursuance of the Environmental Charter adopted by IYHF's 39th International Conference, this book has been produced using only paper from environment-friendly sources. The Nordic Council of Ministers decided in November 1989 to introduce common Nordic environmental labelling of products. Today, the 'Swan' is the only existing environmental label for printed matter in Europe. The criteria is set with this main target area:

The effect on the environment is minimised withing the production process.
The product itself:

The product is 100% recyclable
The ink, varnish and glue does not contain chemicals classified as environmentally hazardous according to EU directives.
The paper used is produced with low environmental impact (emissions) not with chemicals classified as environmentally hazardous according to EU directives.

Published in 1998 by
International Youth Hostel Federation
9 Guessens Road, Welwyn Garden City,
Hertfordshire, AL8 6QW, England

Registered under the Charity Act in England.

Distributed in the United Kingdom by World Leisure Marketing
… and through Hostelling International outlets worldwide.
"Hostelling International" is the brand name of Youth Hostelling Worldwide